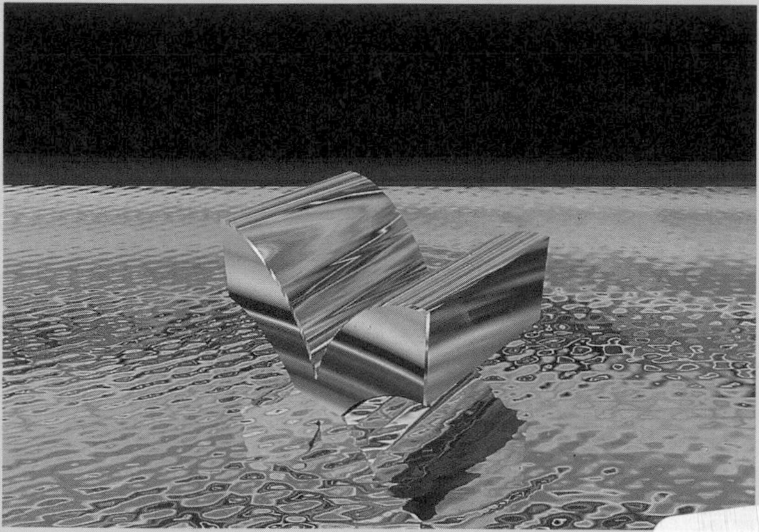

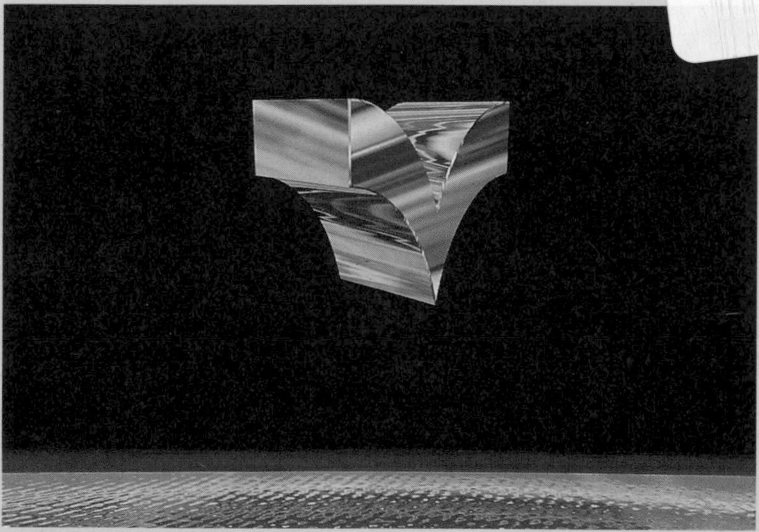

COMPUTER GRAPHICS

Systems & Concepts

COMPUTER GRAPHICS
Systems & Concepts

Rod Salmon
Computer Scientist Consultant

Mel Slater
Queen Mary College, University of London

ADDISON-WESLEY PUBLISHING COMPANY
Wokingham, England · Reading, Massachusetts · Menlo Park, California
New York · Don Mills, Ontario · Amsterdam · Bonn · Sydney
Singapore · Tokyo · Madrid · Bogota · Santiago · San Juan

The programs presented in this book have been included for their instructional value. They have been tested with care but are not guaranteed for any particular purpose. The publisher does not offer any warranties or representations, nor does it accept any liabilities with respect to the programs.

Cover graphic by kind permission of Dicomed.
Illustrations by Chartwell Illustrators.
Typeset by Columns, Reading, Berks.
Printed in Great Britain by The Bath Press, Avon.

First printed 1987.

British Library Cataloguing in Publication Data
Salmon, Rod
Computer graphics : systems and concepts.
1. Computer graphics
I. Title II. Slater, Mel
006.6 T385

ISBN 0-201-14656-8

Library of Congress Cataloguing in Publication Data
Salmon, Rod, 1947-
Computer graphics.

Bibliography: p.
Includes index.
1. Computer graphics. I. Slater, Mel. II. Title.
T385.S24 1987 006.6 86-32073
ISBN 0-201-14656-8

To Judith
and Lynette and Simon

To Freda and Michael

PREFACE

"I have told you, you have to have an unbending intent in order to become a man of knowledge."

Carlos Casteneda, *A Separate Reality*, Penguin, 1973, p. 132.

Computer graphics is a major force in a revolution that is changing the way people perceive and use computers. Moreover, its impact is far beyond the confines of computer science, reaching out to touch many aspects of everyday life, as illustrated by a glance through the colour plates in this book. Computer graphics not only plays an important role in applications such as advertising and entertainment but also in engineering design, medicine, architecture and aerospace. The power of modern computing equipment to generate realistic 3D pictures has also been exploited in the generation of images of often unreal entities. The synthetic production of hitherto only imagined scenarios has found a major application in science fiction films, as well as in medicine and real-time simulation and control.

Aims and Objectives

This book offers a practical guide to the construction and implementation of computer graphics systems. It does this by:

- demonstrating the power and range of applications of computer graphics,
- presenting the basic principles involved in constructing a computer graphics system capable of these applications, and
- introducing the reader to existing computer graphics systems, in particular the international standard Graphical Kernel System (GKS).

A detailed description, evaluation and critique of GKS as an example of a graphics system and its comparison with other graphics systems, including PostScript, is a major theme throughout the book.

The book aims to provide the reader with a detailed knowledge of the *fundamental programming tools* of computer graphics, making it suitable as a basic tutorial text on computer graphics for computing, mathematics and science undergraduates. It also provides a complete tutorial text on GKS, and the reader should become something of an expert in the understanding of the *design* and *use* of the GKS standard. This will suit students in a range of disciplines, as well as commercial and industrial professionals. Attention is also paid to 'state-of-the-art' approaches such as PostScript, and the application of graphics in the *design* and *implementation* of *modern user interfaces*. As well as becoming proficient in graphics programming systems, the reader should gain insight into the *design* and *organization* of *graphics hardware*. Here, 'hardware' not only means the computer equipment used to display and interact with images, but also the human visual system that perceives and interprets them.

An Overview

The *graphics algorithms* discussed in this book are initially developed in an abstract programming notation based on a *functional language*, which can be understood independently of any actual programming language. The proposed *Pascal language binding* for GKS is also used. It is assumed throughout that the reader has some familiarity with basic geometry and computing terminology.

Chapter 1 introduces computer graphics by reviewing some important applications, thus setting the scene for the rest of the book. Part One really begins with Chapter 2, which attempts to extract the basic features of a graphics library system by considering a paradigm based on the printed page. Chapter 3 discusses the architecture of device-independent software systems. Chapter 4 then discusses the fundamental algorithms needed to generate computer graphics. Chapter 5 considers the heart of any graphics system – its functions for graphical output and interaction. In this chapter, graphical output of geometric pure entities (for example, infinitesimally thin lines) is discussed, whereas Chapter 6 introduces methods for specifying style – such as line thickness and colour. Chapter 7 introduces the basic modelling tool of picture segments. Chapter 8 considers some special features of GKS which an applications programmer or systems implementor needs to understand to be aware of GKS in actual operation. Chapter 9 presents an abstract view of the GKS event input model.

Chapter 10 goes beyond GKS by discussing the essential ideas of graphics modelling. This is done by first considering functional graphics, and then widening this to a more traditional approach. In this chapter, the basics of perhaps the most far reaching, recent development in computer graphics is considered, the PostScript system. Many PostScript examples and programs are given in this chapter. There is also a brief discussion of some of the ideas of modelling as embodied in the proposed PHIGS standard.

The revolution in computing mentioned at the beginning of this Preface has at its base the introduction of bitmapped display technology and the concomitant development of powerful personal workstations with bitmapped graphics. The basic concepts of bitmapped graphics are discussed in Chapter 11, based on the Smalltalk-80 model.

Having considered alternative systems in Chapters 10 and 11, Chapter 12 compares these with GKS, as part of a critical assessment of the standard. The chapter concludes with a strategy for the use of GKS in large-scale projects.

Part One concludes with an introduction to the basic features of 3D graphics. Sufficient information is given in this chapter to enable the reader to construct quite a powerful 3D system.

Another major aspect of the computer revolution has been the growing desire of systems designers to provide interfaces to their products which people can easily learn to use, and which people like to use. Some of the main concerns of human–computer interaction research, and user interface design, are discussed in the opening chapter of Part Two. Chapter 14 concludes with a detailed discussion of the human response to colour.

Chapter 15 moves into the area of graphics hardware, discussing the different types of display technology. Chapter 16 supplements Chapter 15 with a discussion of graphics hardware architecture and organization. Chapter 17 surveys various types of input devices – the physical basis of interactive graphics. Chapter 18 discusses hardcopy devices, including the latest laser printer technology.

Chapter 19 concludes Part Two with an integrating discussion on general ideas of building a graphics system from the first approach of a client to the delivery of the finished product.

Finally, there are two appendices. The first reviews the main ideas of the abstract programming language used in Part One, and the second presents a complete PostScript program for 3D graphics.

Using the Book in Teaching or Training

Teaching and learning computer graphics is hard work, requiring organization and planning. To do either effectively, those new to computer graphics need to gain considerable practical experience. This requires a laboratory with modern bitmapped (ideally colour) display workstations, which can be used for several hours per week.

An excellent way of re-inforcing the major concepts of computer graphics is to design and implement a complete (although simple) graphics library for interactive graphics, based on a few primitive machine-dependent functions. The student will find the exercise of providing full documentation for the system particularly useful. Further insights can be achieved by tackling the problem of re-implementing the library on a different machine – this re-inforces at an early stage the important issues of device independence. Finally, the student should attempt to write a non-trivial applications program using only the functions of the library. Here, a choice in the type of project can be given: some students are attracted by interactive graphics, with the desire to invent good user interfaces, while others are interested in non-interactive 3D graphics.

This book provides support for a course based on practical work such as that just outlined. It is not a book with lots of programs to generate 'pretty' pictures, but it is one that gives sufficient information to enable a hard-working student to construct a respectable graphics system. It is an introductory book in the sense that many fundamental algorithms and methods are discussed; however, more advanced issues can be followed up by tracing the references.

The book also encourages self-study. A synopsis at the beginning of each chapter outlines the major topics, and links the material with previous and subsequent chapters, putting it into a meaningful context. In addition, each chapter concludes with a summary, pointing to later chapters that build on this material, and exercises to test the reader's understanding and provide relevant project work.

This book represents an integration of the authors' combined experience, and originated from a joint venture to implement and install a large graphics system (GKS). Rod Salmon has had considerable experience in the industrial sector, which has been invaluable in preparing the sections on graphics systems and hardware of Part Two. Mel Slater's experience in computer graphics teaching and research is represented mainly in the chapters forming Part One, on graphics concepts and programming systems.

Writing this book has proved to be a long, sometimes painful, but often enjoyable experience for the authors. The task of producing written material in a form that readers will find enjoyable and understandable is a humbling experience. Computer graphics is not an easy or trivial subject and readers will sometimes have to work hard to understand and apply the ideas presented. The experience of the authors suggests that the effort will be worthwhile.

Rod Salmon
Mel Slater
June 1987

Acknowledgements

We are grateful to many people who have contributed directly or indirectly to making this book possible. The following people in the Department of Computer Science, Queen Mary College (QMC) have contributed through sharing of ideas about graphics, user-interface design, or programming, or materially in the form of help with equipment: Alan Ball, Don Beal, Richard Bornat, Hilary Buxton, Mike Clarke, Steve Cook, George Coulouris, Allan Davison, Kieron Drake, Ian Page (now with the Programming Research Group, University of Oxford), William Roberts, Antony Simmins, and to all the staff of the Departmental Office. In addition, the following people have critically read one or more chapters: Edwin Blake, Keith Clarke, Peter Hemmingway, Peter Johnson, Siamak Masvani and Steve Reeves.

We further thank Jacques A. C. Halè of Coopers & Lybrand Associates (London), Rob Gale of Sigmex Ltd., and Julian Gallop of the Informatics Division at Rutherford Appleton Laboratories, for critically reading many of the chapters. We are grateful to Mike Milne of Electric Image and Howard Rippiner of Tektronix UK for their invaluable cooperation.

We thank the Addison-Wesley staff, especially the editor-in-chief Sarah Mallen for her patience and encouragement, and the production editor Debra Myson-Etherington for her editorial expertise, enthusiasm and hard work.

We are grateful to all staff and students of the Department of Computer Science at QMC for making it an exciting place in which to teach and research, and to Yvonne Slater for being a patient model. We are indebted to Judith Salmon, for patience beyond the call of duty.

Finally, the help of others has been invaluable, but we alone bear the responsibility for the opinions stated, the technical details and any faults of this book.

The authors and publishers would like to thank the following for providing kind permission to reproduce figures and supplying photographs:

Rendel, Palmer and Tritton, Consulting and Designing Engineers, London (Fig. 1.1); Prime Computer, Inc. (Fig. 1.2); Mullard Ltd. (Fig. 15.2); Tektronix UK (Figs. 15.9, 18.4 and 18.8); Sinclair Research Ltd. (Figs. 15.10 and 15.11); Philips Research Laboratories (Figs. 15.12(b), 15.13 and 15.14); Barco Industries, Belgium (Fig. 15.19); Barco Electronic, N.V. (Fig. 15.20); Interstate Electronic Corporation (Fig. 15.22); GRiD Systems Corporation (Fig. 15.23); Sony UK Ltd. (Fig. 15.25); Westwood Technology Ltd. (Figs. 16.2, 17.1 and 17.5); Sun Microsystems (Figs. 16.14, 19.1 and 19.3); Summagraphics Corporation (Figs. 17.3, 17.6, 17.7 and 17.12);

Marconi Electronic Devices (Fig. 17.8); Evans & Sutherland (Fig. 17.11); Wild Heerbrugg (UK) Ltd. (Figs. 17.13(a) and (b) and 17.14); Hewlett Packard Ltd. (Figs. 18.2 and 18.3); Canon (UK) Ltd. (Fig. 18.5); Facit Ltd. (Fig. 18.6); Versatec (Fig. 18.7).

Production of the Figures

About half of the figures in Part One, especially those illustrating the output of programs, were produced by an unusual method. Those relating to GKS were produced using a GKS implementation written at Queen Mary College (QMC), Department of Computer Science and Statistics. Initially, the images were 'screen dumped' and the output sent to an Apple LaserWriter. However, pictures that look acceptable on a screen often do not transfer well to paper by screen dumping, because all of the inadequacies of low resolution (for example, jagged lines, poor quality text) are caste in permanent form and easily noticeable (our expectations are higher for the printed page than for computer screens). Thus, an alternative strategy was adopted: a new GKS abstract workstation that delivered PostScript programs in a file was developed. Hence, the GKS program was executed and the result, as well as appearing on the screen, was also represented by a file of PostScript commands. This file was then interpreted on the LaserWriter, with much better results than before.

Other figures were produced by writing PostScript programs directly, or PostScript programs produced by ML. Still others were produced by traditional means, by an illustrator.

The authors would like to thank Siamak Masvani, a postgraduate student at QMC, for writing the GKS programs, in addition to the Department of Computer Science and Statistics, QMC, for use of the equipment – a Sun 3, a Whitechapel Workstations MG1 and the Apple LaserWriter.

TRADEMARKS

CONTENTS

PART TWO GRAPHICS SYSTEMS AND INTERFACE

PART ONE

GRAPHICS PROGRAMMING

CHAPTER 1

INTRODUCING COMPUTER GRAPHICS AND ITS APPLICATIONS

The aim of this chapter is to introduce the reader to the world of computer graphics. Following a brief outline of the history of computer graphics and some examples of its applications and uses, the chapter goes on to describe the basic features of computer graphics needed to follow the rest of this book. The chapter concludes with an outline of the programming notation used to describe the basic concepts and algorithms.

1.1 A Brief History

When the very earliest computers emerged in the late 1950s and early 1960s it soon became apparent that these machines were going to be prolific in their generation of results, and that a means of displaying the data *graphically* would clearly be necessary. As the **cathode ray tube** had been in use for some time for displaying the internal behaviour of electrical and electronic equipment, it became a natural candidate for the display of the required graphics.

In the spring of 1963 Ivan Sutherland, a research student, first demonstrated an interactive computer graphics system known as **Sketchpad** (Sutherland, 1963). This system uses a light pen (see Section 17.4) to point to positions on the display to define elements of the picture, such as lines, arcs and polygons. Once drawn, these elements can then be moved, made larger or smaller, copied and/or otherwise modified using what has become known as a **vector refresh** graphics architecture. This revolutionary and historic system set the standard for future interactive graphics systems. Subsequently, Sutherland, in conjunction with Dave Evans, founded the pioneering company Evans & Sutherland (E&S), whose work is illustrated throughout this book.

Unfortunately, the high cost of the hardware needed to support systems such as Sketchpad inhibited their widespread adoption and they were usually found only in research organizations and some universities. In the mid 1960s, commercial vector refresh systems began to appear, but they were still costing several hundred thousand dollars each, way beyond the budget of all but the most advantaged organizations. Mechanical pen plotters were available to produce vector drawn hardcopy, but they were slow and, of course, had no *interactive* facilities.

The development of time-sharing systems and the almost simultaneous introduction of the mini-computer increased the need for the development of a cost-effective interactive display system, and eventually this arrived in the form of the storage tube CRT produced by Tektronix Inc. This device opened the door to interactive graphics systems for most medium-sized companies and universities, and also meant that the development of the computer programs and graphics systems could seriously begin. The storage tube CRT is not, however, a truly dynamic display system, a requirement that could still only be filled by the relatively expensive vector refresh device.

In the mid 1960s, some work had been done on the development of pixel-based raster display systems, which had been envisaged as being able to provide high quality black and white and multi-shade displays, but had a requirement for large amounts of computer memory. The development in the early 1970s of semiconductor and integrated memory hardware began to lower the size and costs of pixel image storage systems, and raster devices began to appear on the commercial market. The introduction of these memory systems was paralleled by the development of the microprocessor, and the control logic for graphics generators for both raster and vector refresh systems began to shrink rapidly in both size and cost. This trend continues to the present day with colour graphics display systems now commonplace and inexpensive.

The development of the software for computer graphics had in the mean time reflected the development of the hardware. Although the new hardware usually required new software algorithms, little had changed in the basic concepts and interaction techniques since Sutherland's Sketchpad system. However, in the early 1970s, researchers at Xerox's Palo Alto Research Centre (PARC) had begun to consider the use of a graphical interface with the computer system using *images* instead of text to communicate with the user. This work eventually led to the development of the Smalltalk-8O system (Goldberg *et al.*, 1983), which is a complete computational environment that assumes graphics to be a natural interface between the computer and the user, and not just a display medium. It undoubtedly represented the next conceptual step forward in computing and a massive leap in the human–computer interface (HCI).

The history of the applications of computer graphics has been a case of human ingenuity constrained by current technology and cost. Because human beings live in a world of ever-changing images, it is not difficult to imagine the boundless uses for graphics. Even now, there are severe limits to what are realistic applications. Initially, graphics systems were employed in computer-aided design and command and control systems where the data could be displayed using the early vector refresh systems. The computer-generated systems for flight simulators led to the development of many new techniques, which are now to be found in commercially available personal display devices. With every new development in graphics technology there is always a queue of applications engineers ready to use it.

1.2 The Applications and Uses of Computer Graphics

The applications of computer-generated graphics seem to grow more numerous by the day. None of the applications will be described in detail here because, unfortunately, there simply is not the space. Furthermore, some applications represent complete subjects in their own right and require complex algorithms and techniques. Some, however, are remarkably simple and can be achieved on very inexpensive equipment, while others require systems costing millions of dollars. Wherever possible the applications will be illustrated, but again space limits the number of examples that can be shown. It should be noted that the examples given here are by no means exhaustive as new applications are being developed all the time. However, it is hoped that these examples will show what computer graphics is currently being used for and, perhaps, sow the seeds for a few ideas for new applications. Some of the terminology in this section may be new to the reader but with a little patience their meanings will become clear through the course of the book.

The perceptive reader will notice that the same basic process tends to recur; that is, the use of graphics to display the results of computer calculations, a process known as **data visualization**. The massive amounts of data that computers generate when they have been programmed to calculate the behaviour of physical systems are often beyond comprehension when displayed simply as a stream of numbers. If, however, the data can be shown as a graphical image, then their meaning can often be gleaned immediately.

1.2.1 Computer-Aided Engineering

Engineering is a vast, multidisciplined subject and graphics has been extensively employed within its many branches. The various disciplines of mechanical, electrical and civil engineering have all used computers in **computer-aided engineering** (**CAE**) systems. In particular, computer graphics has been employed in **computer-aided design** (**CAD**) systems, this being a general term used to describe the application of computers to the design process in any engineering field (Machover, 1980).

The most common use of graphics display systems in engineering is in **computer-aided draughting**. (Note the rather confusing identity of mnemonics with computer-aided design – CAD.) These systems have been designed to replace or improve on the use of draughting boards and associated equipment that traditionally have been used for the detailed design of mechanical, electrical, electronic and civil systems. Initially, CAD systems employed high-resolution vector refresh displays, but the recent increase in the performance and resolution of raster graphics displays has led to their use in CAD systems. In addition, rapid decreases in the cost of medium-resolution raster graphics displays has brought about the use of CAD systems in engineering environments in which they previously would not have been cost effective. Before these low-cost systems became available, high resolution was a prerequisite for the graphics display of a CAD system. But the need to reduce engineering design costs and the advent of low-cost systems prompted the system designers to think again about how CAD systems could be used. High-speed redraw and windowing techniques allowed small areas of the design to be shown quickly and the need to view the whole design in detail became less important. CAD systems are now becoming available on personal computers using medium-resolution raster graphics displays.

Computer-aided draughting systems are capable of drawing all the traditional lines and shapes of manual drawing systems. They usually operate under prompting and menu control with a screen cursor being used to designate coordinate data points and to interact with the drawing. Most systems have 'intelligence' that partially automates the drawing process, such as the generation of circles, arcs, tangents, fillets and so on. CAD systems can, by generating and storing *standard* shapes, also considerably reduce the work load of the draughtsman. For example, when a set of standard nuts and bolts are used in the assembly of an object, they need to be shown on the engineering drawings. These are very time consuming to draw by hand, so are often left out altogether. However, the CAD system can keep the *shape* of the nuts and bolts in a library (as a segment or procedure), reproducing it quickly and accurately with little effort on behalf of the operator.

The use of colour also adds a new dimension to the drawings. The final drawings are stored on a computer backing store for later use or for transmission to other systems that require the drawings. Plotters and printers are used to generate hardcopy displays when required.

The job of skilled draughtsmen is not only to draw lines and curves – they play a far more significant role in the design process. It is part of their job to check the correctness and integrity of the design being drawn, and when carried out by hand this is a very time-consuming process as well as being approximate. Sophisticated and specialized CAD systems often have the ability to check the design using preprogrammed knowledge of the subject and high accuracy calculations. Figure 1.1 shows a CAD drawing of a dredger ship. It was produced on a high-quality pen plotter and shows the quality that these systems can achieve.

Both two- and three-dimensional CAD systems are available. Two-dimensional (2D) systems simply store the data that describes the drawing in terms of the cartesian coordinates for the various projections required, and tend to have little or no knowledge of the overall shape of the objects being drawn. Three-dimensional systems (3D), on the other hand, store and work with a full 3D description of the design and can display perspective views as well as the usual 3D projections. Perspective views showing just the edges or edge contours of the objects are known as **wire-frame views** or **wire-frame models**. Views of this type allow visualization of the object using more familiar projections. Plate 1 is an example of this type of 3D wire-frame display. It shows a perspective view of the representation of a McDonnell Douglas F-15 fighter aircraft with each of the major components drawn in a different colour. Notice that in this particular view all edges are drawn even though some, when viewing the *real* object, would be hidden from view by parts of the object closer to the viewer. In other words, no attempt has been made to remove **hidden lines**.

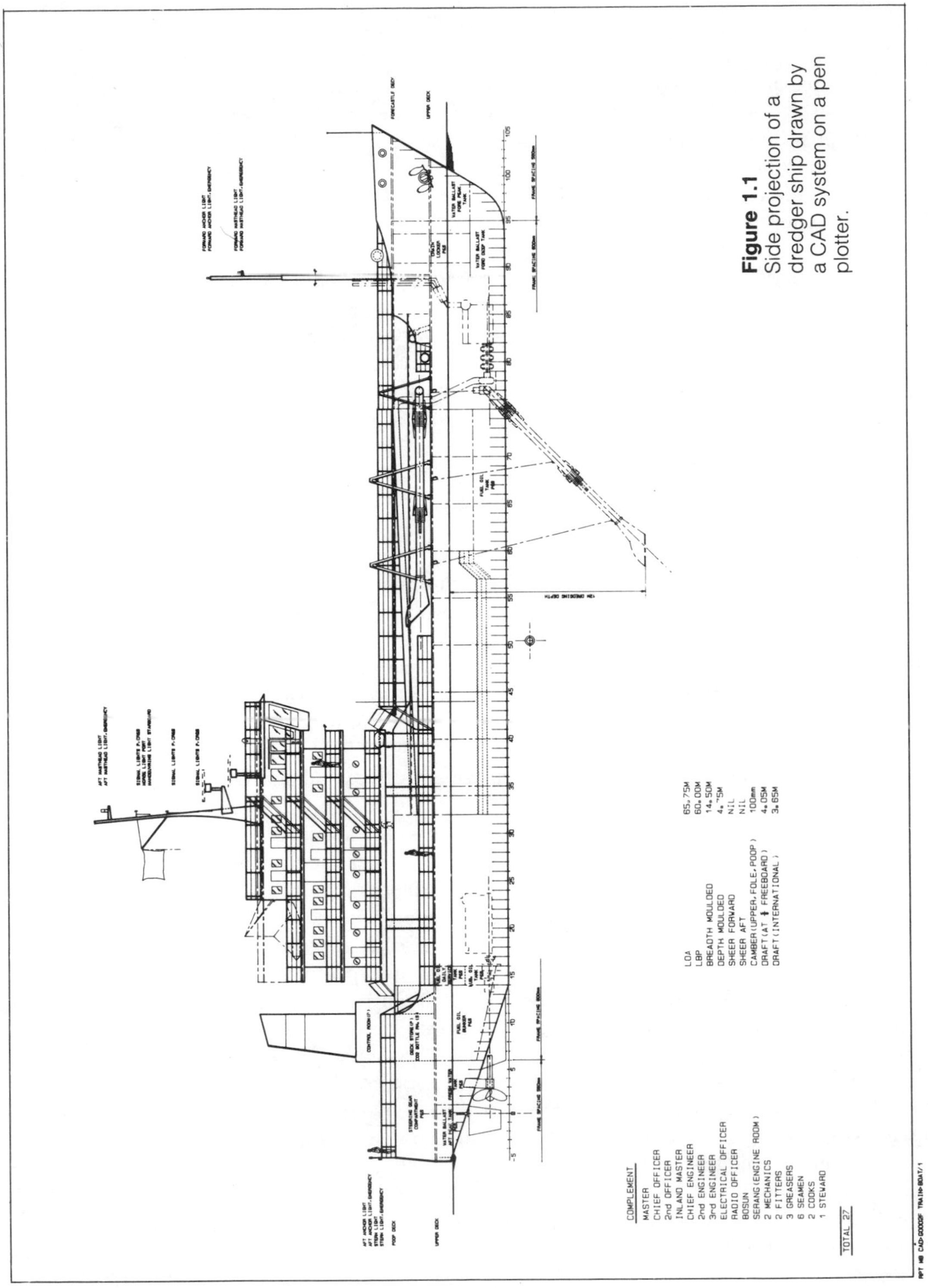

Figure 1.1 Side projection of a dredger ship drawn by a CAD system on a pen plotter.

Some 3D systems of this type also contain data describing the relationships between the edges and surfaces of the object, thus enabling the object to be displayed in solid 3D view. Such systems are known as **solid modelling systems** and provide a complete representation of the object. They will also support other aspects of the design and manufacturing process as well as visualization of the object under design or study. These systems require a raster scan display system and a powerful CPU to calculate the view parameters. An important and time-consuming part of these calculations is the identification of the **hidden surfaces** of the object. An introduction to the mathematics of solid modelling is given in Woodwark (1986) and an example of a solid model display is illustrated in Plate 2, which shows a perspective view of a British standard 13-amp domestic mains plug with the top cover removed.

Expansion of the data base in CAD systems allows information on the materials and manufacturing processes to be used. Partial automation of the design process is then possible in **computer-aided manufacture (CAM)** systems. CAM systems, because of the wealth of data that they contain, are capable of designing and specifying much of the manufacturing process required to produce an object.

An interesting example of a special-purpose CAD system is illustrated in Figures 1.2(a) and (b). These are wire-frame illustrations generated by a **human factors CAD** system known as SAMMIE. Figure 1.2(a), which shows a pilot in an aircraft cockpit, allows evaluation of the ease, or otherwise, with which the controls can be reached and used. Figure 1.2(b), in contrast, displays the pilot's view of the aircraft's instruments when seated in a particular position. This system enables new cockpit layouts to be quickly entered into the CAD system and their suitability assessed without the manufacturers having to resort to building an expensive prototype cockpit. This type of system is not just limited to aircraft, but can be used to assess almost any HCI configuration.

1.2.2 Visualization for Engineering Design

Computer graphics has allowed the design engineer to *visualize* processes and system behaviour that previously have had to be left to the imagination. Designers often use the technique of computational simulation to predict the behaviour of their design. This technique can be used to model the behaviour of almost any system – be it mechanical, electrical or chemical – that can be described in terms of mathematical equations and programmed into a computer. Without graphics, such results would have to be presented to the designer usually as pages of numbers or possibly graphs. However, using graphics displays, a 2D or 3D representation of the design can be drawn using the results of the simulation.

As an example, consider the behaviour of an automobile as it moves

(a)

(b)

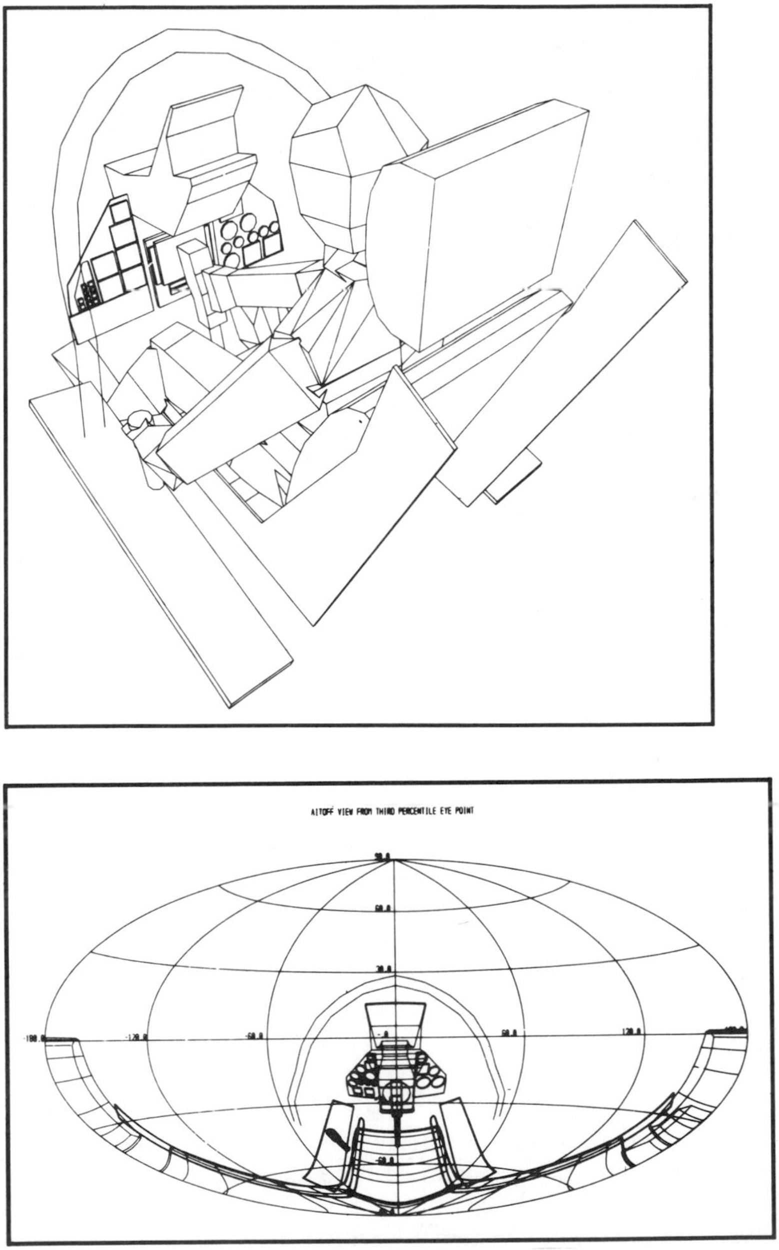

Figure 1.2
(a) Evaluating the position of the controls in an aircraft cockpit.
(b) View of the controls and instruments as seen by the pilot.

over the ground. If the characteristics of the suspension, steering, bearings and tyres, as well as the road surface, are programmed into a computer as a mathematical model, the position of all of the parts of the automobile can be calculated at any point in time. Further calculation of these positions over a period of *simulated* time allows the movement of all the suspension parts and the vehicle as a whole to be calculated. Then, if the data from these simulations is used to define a series of graphics images of the automobile, running these images together shows the movement of the vehicle pictorially. Higher performance graphics systems may be capable of generating the new images fast enough to show the movements themselves, but the images from other systems may have to be recorded on film or video to generate the appearance of smooth real-time movement. A sequence of such images is shown in Plate 3. In this case, a 3D analysis program has been used to simulate the changing of lanes by a Ford Bronco II, a four-wheel drive compact automobile. The images are drawn as wire-frame views with the vehicle body and major suspension parts displayed in different colours for clarity.

It is not just dynamic movement that can be simulated and displayed in this way: the stress and strain within rigid structures such as bridges and buildings can also be shown where, typically, the different levels of stress or strain are shown using different colours; heat dissipation by objects that are subject to changing levels of heating can be shown either as static or dynamic images; and the flow of air over an aircraft may be similarly shown.

1.2.3 Civil Engineering

The world of civil engineering has readily adopted graphics displays for its design work. As already described, graphics can be used to display the results of mathematical simulations of buildings, bridges and so on. However, the civil engineer has other uses for graphics.

The job of the civil engineer often involves measuring the shape and constituents of the earth's surface and then adapting the results for a specific use. This may be to build a road, a bridge or a building. Consequently, the ability to visualize the environment and the way in which changes will affect it is very useful. Plate 4 shows a perspective view of a ground model, constructed from real land contour data, on to which has been superimposed a standard design of an airport. The final image therefore shows what effect the construction of such an airport would have on that area.

Architects also use graphics systems for the display of both the interior and exterior of building designs. The layout of the interior of a building is particularly important for factory and office planners where space and lighting has to be carefully planned. The visualization of a new building and how it will fit into the surrounding environment is a major task for designers and city planners. An application of this aspect of computer graphics is illustrated in Plate 5. The plate shows a solid model perspective display of buildings whose dimensions have been obtained from an archaeological survey. In this case, the graphics system has generated a view of the Roman buildings in Bath, England circa AD 200. By moving the viewpoint it is easy to visualize what it would have been like to have walked around the town, with its baths, temples and altars, all those centuries ago. This image was created using a solid model display technique known as **ray casting** or **ray tracing**, which allows the detailed aspects of scene lighting to be reproduced on the image. The technique involves tracing each light *ray* contributing towards each pixel on the display. Although it is very time consuming, ray tracing will automatically generate shading, complete or partial shadows and mirroring (Woodwark, 1986).

The art of map making, better known as **cartography**, also makes use of graphics systems, in addition to digital storage techniques. The task of digitizing the various types of maps in everyday use is enormous. Although automatic digitizing systems can do a lot of the work, it is usually necessary for the map data detail to be completed by human operators. Street maps, contour maps and maps showing the positions of public services, such as the distribution of water, gas and electricity, are also suitable for digitizing and display on graphics systems. Once digitized, the maps can be easily updated and reproduced on hardcopy devices for distribution. In the future, it will be possible to display this type of data on small portable devices that could, for example, be mounted in an automobile.

1.2.4 Automation and Robot Systems

The development of automated factories, robot assembly and production systems has generated a requirement for the use of graphics in the planning of robotic work areas or cells. The layout of these cells has a considerable effect on the robots' productivity, especially when there is more than one robot working per cell. Plate 6 shows a 3D wire-frame view of a work cell with a robot at work. The system is used to design and verify the robot sequences and cell programs with the whole process displayed as an animation.

1.2.5 Electrical and Electronic System Design

The design of printed circuit boards and microprocessor chips has benefited from the use of graphics. For example, the design of a microprocessor chip can be entered into a computer system either directly or interactively with the overall design shown on the display. It is possible to show not only the electronic schematic diagram but also the layout of the various layers of semiconductor and metal oxide used to create the circuit. Mathematical simulations of the behaviour of the chip can also be carried out in the CPU.

1.2.6 Fine Arts, Graphics Design and Product Design

As soon as a new display medium ...

world adopts
fascinating
lso have the
ents.
er-generated
ierated on a
ie book that
vays present
colours and
ment, trying
period and
ely satisfied
ve quite the
ty image is
medium for
has, in fact,

l. Any one
ng another
ossible for
ftware that
ules on the
ldition, the
ssibility of
new trends
s, who see
becoming
edium that

ter design
8 shows a
This shape,

which is known as the *last*, is entirely dependent on such things as heel height, style and foot shape. Notice particularly the smooth surface and the lighting effects on the image. The shoe designer, using free-form interaction with the 3D image display, describes the shapes and the patterning of the material of the shoe as shown in Plate 9. The shoe's colours are then selected from a palette facility and the computer adds the sole and creates a visualization of the shoe, without the last in place, as shown in Plate 10. Finally, if the shoe is selected for production, the computer calculates the

3D to 2D *flattening* as shown in Plate 11. These 2D patterns represent the shape of the material required to construct the shoe. The data for these patterns is then used to drive computer-controlled machines to produce the special knives that will cut the material. Using this system the designer can quickly create the image of a new shoe and show it to prospective marketing and sales persons saving time, manpower and money.

The product design system just described is one of the first of many such systems, and the use of computers and graphics displays will find its way into many varied fields of design and development.

1.2.7 Entertainment and Advertising

It should be evident by now that computer graphics systems are capable of generating exciting and stunning displays, a feature that makes them highly suited for producing images for entertainment and advertising purposes, especially since the use of such systems has become cost effective. The use of computer graphics in interactive computer games has played a large part in generating public awareness of graphics. Few people in the western world can have failed to encounter the arcade and home computer games that have become such a major aspect of people's leisure time. Computers have also become film stars in their own right and the use of graphics can make their *acting* more effective.

Computer systems are now being increasingly used to assist in the production of cartoon films. Not only can they be used to create the figures and objects, but these systems can be programmed to calculate the step-by-step animation sequences, a process known as **in betweening**. Such animation has not found use so much in the creation of traditional cartoon films of the cinema but more in the production of title and introduction sequences for films and TV programmes. Much use is made of the techniques of solid modelling to generate these images. The world of advertising is also using computer graphics techniques and some of the most interesting sequences generated have been in this field. Plate 12 shows a single computer-generated frame from a TV advertisement for Michelin tyres. This advertisement consists of several smoothly animated sequences of solid modelled images. For further information on this application readers should refer to Hayward (1984), Magnenat–Thalmann and Thalmann (1985), and Fox *et al.* (1983). Plates 18 and 27 also show single frames from computer-generated animations.

1.2.8 Education and Training

Human beings usually learn faster and better when presented with an image of the items about which they are learning. Although not all subjects lend themselves to the use of images, or would necessarily benefit from them if thcy could, some disciplines, such as science and engineering, make great use of illustrations for learning purposes. This type of learning has come to be known as **computer-aided learning** (**CAL**) or **computer-aided instruction** (**CAI**). The computer can be programmed to progress through a sequence of learning steps and generate images relevant to those steps as required. Some systems are capable of displaying dynamic images that show the behaviour of the subject over a period of time or under the effect of certain changes in condition. In some cases, the computer may ask the student to interact with the display to modify the behaviour of the system shown in the image. Sophisticated systems are capable of sensing the student's response to questions and modifying the teaching sequence accordingly. For example, if the CAI system detects that the student is responding incorrectly to a significant number of questions, then it can re-organize the learning sequence so that the subject is repeated or approached more slowly and carefully.

This type of learning system has been of great use in the areas of modern electrical and mechanical technology. Service engineers or technicians often find it difficult to maintain their knowledge base on new pieces of equipment, especially when time for attending courses is at a premium. Plate 13 shows a dynamic schematic graphic of the electrical system of a Boeing B727 jet airliner. The display's dynamics are driven by a mathematical simulation of the aircraft's electrical system, and the effects of cockpit inputs by the pilot and flight engineer are accurately modelled and displayed. Using this type of system and display the student can, using an interactive device, open and close switches and so on to see clearly the effects of the actions. Such an interaction would not be possible on a real aircraft without considerable cost and the possibility of damaging the aircraft. An interesting introduction to computer-based instruction is given in Alessi and Trollip (1985).

Graphics images are also used in sophisticated flight-training simulators for the display of *out-of-window* scenes viewed by the crew under training. Plate 14 shows a photograph of a modern flight simulator with its hydraulic motion system, cockpit and computer-generated image display system. In the case of this particular flight simulator, the image is projected on to a wide angle display surface so as to offer the most realistic scene to the crew. The systems providing the image for the simulators are special-purpose, high-performance graphics generators capable of generating 3D perspective images at rates of 30 frames per second. The displays are sophisticated systems, some of which combine raster scan and vector refresh display techniques to generate the high-speed dynamic images. These systems have large data bases containing the information necessary to produce images of runways, buildings, airport vehicles, other aircraft and obstacles. Although the cost of such systems is measured in millions of dollars, they are capable of saving the airlines many times this in training expenses.

As an example of the images that these systems can generate, Plate 15 shows an air-to-air view of a pair of McDonnell Douglas F-15 fighter aircraft, as seen from the cockpit of a third F-15 flying in formation. The aircraft images are shown in considerable detail including a true transparent cockpit canopy, their underwing armaments and accurately modelled incident lighting effects against realistic ground and sky effects. The system used to generate this image is a pure raster system. Plate 16 shows an image generated by the very latest computer-generated image techniques, which also employs 2D texturing carried out by special hardware in the system. Now the ground and sky is given a far more realistic *feel* compared with the flat surfaces of Plate 15. This texturing has been found to give much better depth cues for low-level *nap-of-the-earth* flying, especially in emergency situations where the pilot may be required to eject from the aircraft. In the case of the helicopter shown in the plate, the rotor effect is remarkable with its dynamic translucent obscuring of the aircraft and the background.

1.2.9 Business Graphics

Computer graphics is used in the commercial business world to assist with visualization of data during the decision-making process. The large amount of data defining the current state of the market or a company can be condensed on to graphs and charts. With business graphics systems it is normal to generate a hardcopy of the graphic. If the graphic is to be used in a business report, then the hardcopy would be produced on a pen plotter or matrix printer dump from the display. However, one of the main uses for business graphics is in group presentations, and for this purpose it would be normal to generate the hardcopy on to a projection slide. There are now specialist systems for the production of such display images.

The illustration in Plate 17 shows an example of the type of image that computer graphics systems are constructing for business graphics use. Computer graphics has been used here, to good effect, by using the product – lipsticks in this case – to represent the histogram values of cosmetic sales over a period of time. It would have taken a traditional artist some considerable time to create this graph with the careful use of shading to give a 3D effect. However, once the picture of the lipstick has been created, with the help of the computer system, it can be transformed and positioned to the required ordinate. The result is a display with much more life and interest than a normal histogram would give but created in a cost-effective manner. Images of this type can be created directly using business data already available in the computer, again saving time and cost to create the display.

1.2.10 Command and Control

Many aspects of modern life require the collection of large quantities of data, its interpretation and, in some cases, the issue of control instructions based on the collected data. Systems such as electricity, water and gas distribution, the monitoring and control of railway systems, and the scheduling of aircraft into and out of an airport require this type of data collection, display and control. All of these systems fall under the same general heading of **command**, **control**, **communication and intelligence (C^3I) systems** or simply **command and control systems**. For operators to understand and interpret the large quantities of data often generated by the monitoring of these systems the only viable way of displaying it is to use dynamic computer schematic or tabular images.

Systems of various sizes and complexity, ranging from small systems for the control of a factory to huge systems controlling the nationwide distribution of electricity, can be managed in this way. Command and control systems used to monitor and control the processes running in a factory are usually known as **process control** systems. Sensor devices measure the state and performance of the system and send the data to the central computer, which interprets and stores it in a data base. The information in this data base is regularly updated with new data from the sensors and the display system extracts the data it requires to generate the current image. Most command and control systems have many different images which display the various parts of the system being monitored; for example, there will probably be a set of images showing the system at different levels of detail in the form of a hierarchy of images. In addition, the display system has the capability to modify the information shown on the current image at regular intervals as new data updates the data base.

The use of graphics displays in command and control systems helps the operators visualize the current state of the system. The more complex the system or the more data that needs to be monitored, the more the requirement for graphics displays. Plate 19 shows an interesting use of graphics for command and control in a system where there is a requirement to monitor the positions of the thousands of satellites in the earth's orbit. This plate shows a 3D representation of several satellites in orbit clearly illustrating the position and altitude of each. Different colours are used to differentiate between the satellites.

The image shown in Plate 13, illustrating a dynamic schematic of the electrical system of a Boeing B727 jet airliner, is typical of some command and control display systems. Although this particular image was generated on a training system, the image could just as well have been generated on a command and control system for the electrical system. Sensors throughout the system measure the state of the system and pass the data to the data base in the aircraft's onboard computer system. The display system then uses this data to generate the schematic image of the electrical system.

The control of an aircraft requires the use of instruments to give the pilot information on the attitude and position of the aircraft. The traditional electromechanical instruments are now being replaced by graphics displays fed by information from the aircraft's inertial, airspeed and radar sensors, and its navigation system. These systems are known as **electronic flight instrumentation systems (EFIS)**. In modern jet airliners, the first and second officers (the pilot and co-pilot) each have two CRT displays driven by mixed raster and vector refresh mode display generators. The CRTs are capable of displaying graphics representations of the standard primary flight display, the navigation display and map displays. EFIS systems are also capable of displaying various aircraft system displays, such as engine performance instrumentation and system schematic displays as described above, although these type of displays usually require CRTs additional to those of the pilots primary display for redundancy purposes.

Plate 20 shows an **electronic attitude direction indicator (EADI)** as used on the Fokker 100 commercial airliner. This type of instrument, in its previous mechanical form, was represented by a suspended sphere with one hemisphere coloured sky blue and the other brown, and the aircraft's pitch angles were marked on the surface to show the aircraft's 3D attitude. This 6″ by 7″ EFIS display emulates the mechanical display system with additional primary flight information displayed, including the flight modes engaged by the pilots and the aircraft's speed and altitude. Electronic displays of this type allow considerably more information to be presented to the flight crew on a single instrument, thus saving valuable time in the pilots' search for information on the state of the aircraft.

Plate 21 shows the cockpit of the Airbus Industrie A320 aircraft which employs EFIS instrument displays for primary, navigational and aircraft systems information. Such a cockpit employs considerably less instrumentation than those that, in the past, have used all mechanical instruments. The first and second officers both have a set of the primary flight displays, consisting of an EADI and a navigation display. This latter display is able to combine a graphics display of data from external sensors, such as the aircraft's radar, and computer-generated data, such as the aircraft's flight path. Note also the two central screens showing aircraft systems information, in this case engine status data on the upper display and systems configuration on the lower. New generation aircraft cockpits of this type are changing the role of the crew from *seat-of-the-pants pilots* to *system managers* with the aircraft cab beginning to look more like an office than the traditional cockpit. Systems of this type are now beginning to be implemented in both civil and military aircraft, and similar systems will soon be found in ships and land-based vehicles.

More advanced systems now in development will be capable of showing superimposed TV images from visible light and infra-red cameras and radar systems on the aircraft. Perhaps the time of the *windowless* or virtual cockpit with all sensor and computer information combined into a single artificial view of the outside world is not that far away.

1.2.11 Scientific Research

To try to describe all the uses of computer graphics in scientific research would almost be like trying to describe all of the fields of scientific research itself. All the other applications described here could also be used in a research environment. However, there is perhaps one which is unique to the research field; that is, the visualization of entities that cannot be seen, either with the naked eye or with the aid of an optical or electron microscope. Typical of these entities are molecules, and the computer graphics display system is proving a valuable tool in the field of molecular biology and molecular modelling. Plate 22 shows the display created by a molecular modelling package of B-DNA showing ten base pairs with highlighting and shading. Such displays allow the visualization of entities that otherwise can only be imagined.

1.2.12 Medical Systems

The medical world has benefited considerably from the introduction of computer graphics and image display systems. Again, it is its use as a visualization aid that graphics is of most use. Data taken from X-ray and other through-body sensors can be used to specify the size and shape of the internal construction and contents of the body and its organs. In this way, any damage to the body or, more often, the position of any growths or lesions can be accurately and clearly displayed to the medical staff. Such images can then be used to assist in the operating theatre and treatment room in helping the medical staff locate and remove or destroy the material.

Medical training can also benefit from computer graphics in that visualizations of the organs, together with details of the associated diseases when necessary, can be displayed to staff. Unusual ailments and behaviour can be modelled and displayed so that medical staff can recognize them when they occur in real life.

Plates 23 and 24 show images from a TV educational series about the human body. Here, 3D solid modelled images of the body's organs have been created and can be *examined* either separately or together. Plate 23 shows the human body outline as a vector pattern with the brain, heart, lungs, liver, stomach and small and large intestine in place. Plate 24 shows the human heart with the venous and arterial sides indicated. Although these images were created for training and educational purposes, this type of reconstruction can be used to help with diagnosis and treatment.

1.3 Picture Definition – The Graphics Pipeline

The production of a graphics image for display on a computer graphics device is carried out in a number of stages (see Figure 1.3). The production process starts with a **model** of the scene, which describes in high-level terms what is to be displayed. For example, if the display is the scene as shown in Figure 1.3, then it would consist of a list of the contents and their interrelationships – a house, a tree and an automobile – and the dimensions required for sizing, positioning and scaling, as well as information on colour and shading. Not all graphics will be of such real-world or well-structured scenes, but the general principle of defining a model to be displayed remains the same.

The description of the model to the computer graphics system must be in terms that the computer can understand while, at the same time, preserving the original model structure. For example, the structure of the house consists of a set of related walls, roof, windows and doors. This is analogous to the drawing of a **picture**. At the picture stage, the definition of

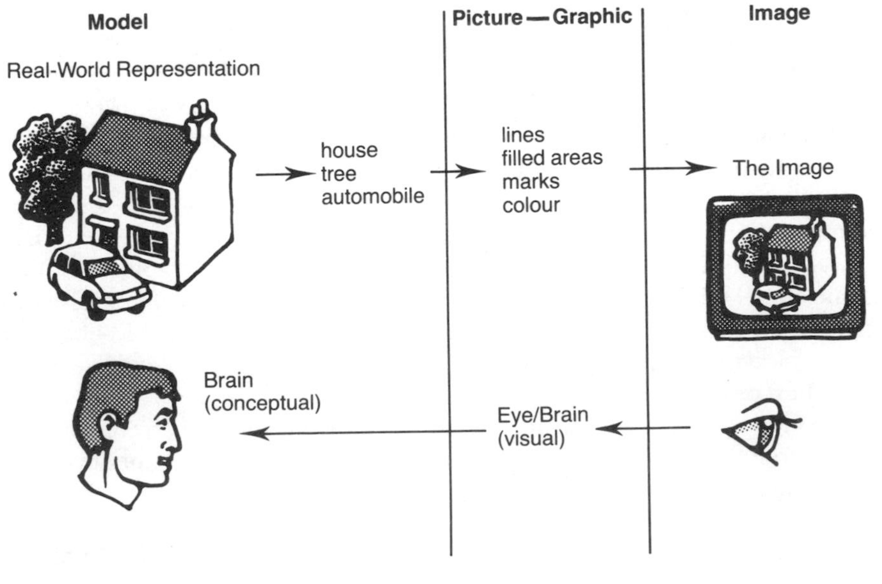

Figure 1.3
Image-production sequence.

the scene consists of the set of the smallest individual objects that constitute the scene, in addition to their positional and logical relationships, their dimensions and their colour. The description of the picture is still recognizable as the original scene but is in terms that can be represented in a computer.

The final stage of the process is the creation of the **image**. This is the graphic representation that can be viewed by the human being. Now the original model structure disappears and is replaced by the image **primitives** – lines, filled areas, marks, for example – and their **attributes** – line width, colour and so on. (Generation of the image will be discussed in more detail in the following section.)

Figure 1.3 also illustrates the reverse process carried out by the human eye/brain system. This system takes the image and, it is assumed, decomposes it into its picture features and then into the model again, although this is now in the human consciousness.

Although a more detailed scheme of the image-creation process could be developed, the crude breakdown given here will provide a useful basis for discussion in this book.

1.4 The Image-Generating Process

The image, as introduced in the previous section, represents the final stage of the graphics-generating process, but its actual form depends on the type of display hardware being used in addition to the primitives and attributes used in the picture description.

An image does not retain any of the structure of the original picture. It consists entirely of elements of varying intensity which, when viewed by a human, convey *information* to the conscious mind via the eye/brain system. The image will resemble, unless it is abstract in nature, what the human would see of a physical or *real* scene. It is a *simulation* of a real-world scene.

The varying intensity of the image elements can take several forms. In the simplest form, an image element can be *black* or *white*; that is, the image is true **monochrome** consisting of white elements on a black background or black elements on a white background. Such an image can be produced by using a pen with black ink on white paper. Monochrome images are not, however, restricted to generating pure black and white effects. Subtlety in the range of intensities can be obtained by **shading**. If, for example, an area of white is partially covered with black dots, then the effect of a shade of grey will be obtained. The closer together the black dots, the *darker* the shade of grey perceived by the viewer. This is the technique used to produce pictures on newsprint (see Figures 2.1 and 2.2). Monochrome images of this type do not have to be black and white, but can be of any two suitable colours.

1.4.1 Vectors

Images can be generated by using either straight lines or dots although a dot is, of course, simply a degenerate line. Straight lines must have a position, a length and a direction and such lines are known as **vectors**. Simple vector images can convey a great deal of information, as can be seen from some of the plates and figures displayed and described in the previous sections. Closely spaced vectors will produce shading: the closer the lines the more intense the effect. Certain types of graphics display devices generate their images entirely using vectors.

1.4.2 Pixels

The elements of images of varying intensity can also be produced by a type of shading that uses dots. These are often known as **picture elements**, **pels** or, most commonly, **pixels**. As pixels are regularly spaced across the image in both the horizontal and vertical directions, the shading intensity is generated by the *absence* or the *brightness* of the pixels, and not by their relative position. When a pixel is present it is said to be *on*; when it is absent it is *off*. Each pixel has a defined horizontal and vertical position in the image and is the smallest addressable unit on the display. The horizontal separations of the pixels are equal, as are the vertical separations. However, these two separation distances can be different. Pixels may be square or rectangular depending on the type of display. Sets of pixels can be used to generate the effect of various shapes. In particular, the effect of a straight line can be generated by a roughly linear set of pixels (see Figures 2.1 and 2.2).

A rectangular array of pixels, some black and some white, can therefore constitute acceptable images. This is indeed fortunate as such an arrangement is analogous to a 2D array of memory locations in a computer's memory with, in the case of pure monochrome images, a single memory *bit* representing a single pixel. This particular arrangement, known as a **pixel memory** or **frame buffer**, is used in several different types of graphics display.

1.4.3 Grey Levels

So far, only vectors and pixels of pure monochrome intensity have been considered and, although perfectly acceptable images can be generated using them, a greater range is generally required. Therefore, the concept of levels of intensity, or **grey levels**, is used where the basic image elements can have a range of intensity values. Instead of using shading to generate the image effects, the local intensity of each pixel or vector can be used. Far more subtle shading can thus be generated producing higher quality images.

Vectors and pixels now have an extra attribute, known as the **grey scale**, and a value must be assigned to represent the grey level. For example, 0 may represent black, 10 white and the other values 1 through 9 the shades of grey in between.

1.4.4 Colour

One further attribute that primitives such as vectors and pixels can have is colour. This is effectively an extension of the grey level as more information on the image, at any point, is being conveyed to the viewer. The display and perception of colour by the human brain is examined in detail in Chapter 14 and will not be discussed further here.

1.5 Computers, Computer Systems and Software

Figure 1.4 illustrates schematically the basic layout of a computer. It consists of a processor unit and a memory unit, possibly divided into program memory and data memory. There is also a need for the computer to be able to communicate with external devices or other computers or systems. The processor is controlled by the programs (or **software**), which are usually loaded into the program memory before the processor can operate on the data in memory. This memory is known as **random access memory** (**RAM**). In some systems, this is permanently loaded or *burnt* into the program memory so that reloading is unnecessary. Special types of memory can also be used; for example, **programmable read only memory** (**PROM**) or **erasable programmable read only memory** (**EPROM**). The latter type of memory can be erased using special devices that bombard the memory devices with ultra-violet radiation, wiping the memory so that it can be subsequently loaded with new programs. When the software is stored in this way it is known as **firmware**.

Where a computer is required to carry out an applications task, usually in conjunction with humans, it forms part of a **computer system**. Other parts of the system may include program and data storage devices (such as magnetic disk and tape units), devices for printing results (such as line printers) and interactive devices (such as visual display units).

A computer graphics system is simply a particular type of computer system. As such, it consists of a computer and a set of additional (or

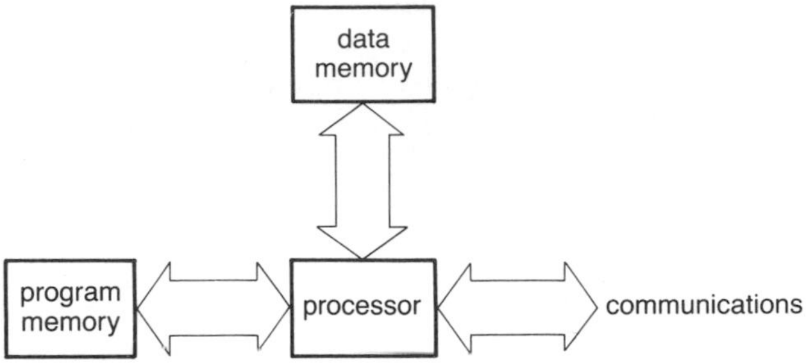

Figure 1.4
Schematic of a computer.

peripheral) equipment that tailor it to its role in computer graphics. Modern single-user **workstations** are computers with a highly integrated design with the graphics system closely coupled to the central processing unit (CPU).

1.6 Graphics Standards

In the mid 1970s, several national and international standards bodies began the search for a standard computer graphics system. At that time (and also currently), the methods and functions used to draw pictures on various graphics systems were very different. This work was, and still is, coordinated by the International Standards Organization (ISO) in cooperation with the national standardization bodies of the member countries, which include the West German Deutsches Institute fur Normung (DIN), the British Standards Institute (BSI) and the American National Standards Institute (ANSI). Several of the national standards organizations submitted systems for adoption. One of these was the 3D graphics system known as **CORE** (ACM, 1978), which was submitted on behalf of the American Association of Computing Machinery's (ACM) SIGGRAPH (Special Interest Group in Graphics). Eventually, however, ISO decided to concentrate on the **Graphical Kernel System (GKS)**, put forward by DIN, and subjected it to an international technical review. GKS then went through several stages of modification before it reached its current status as an international standard.

As a graphics system, GKS is not perfect. It is now over a decade since its basic design and four years since its last significant change. In that time computer graphics has come a long way. This is especially true in the case of raster and pixel-based graphics systems, and a proposal with a more recent design would need to contain additional elements to handle these systems and their functionality. GKS is, however, a good starting base.

1.6.1 The GKS Specification

The GKS standard (ISO 7942 and BS6390) consists of a set of 209 graphics functions arranged into a structure with three levels of output (0 through 2) and three levels of input (*a* through *c*). A GKS implementation can conform to any input level and any output level, and the combination of functions defines a valid level of GKS. A GKS implementation of level 2*c* has all of the defined functions.

The functions include those for graphical display and interaction in addition to those for managing the overall computation and hardware environment, such as controlling graphics workstations and for storing data in standard form for later use. Each function definition exactly specifies the actions and the final state of the system after its use.

1.6.2 Language Independence

Perhaps one of the most important aspects of GKS as a computer graphics standard is that it is not defined in terms of any particular computer software language. The specification of GKS consists of a set of functions that are defined in English (translations into other languages will be available where required). Each function is defined in terms of its name and detailed action, the parameters it uses, any secondary effects and the state of the system upon successful completion. Each function's definition contains enough information for its full implementation in any computer language.

The advantages of computer language independence for such a computer-related standard is very important for the following reason. If the standard were bound to any particular language, then the standard would only be a standard for that language. Furthermore, if the language did not happen to be available on a particular type of computer, then neither would the standard.

However, for the standard to be usable it must be made available to the system builders in terms of one or more of the common computer languages. The GKS standard is defined in each computer language by means of a **language binding**. For each function in the standard there is a function, subroutine or procedure, depending on the type of language, defined in the language syntax that implements fully the functionality described in the standard. Therefore, for each language, there will be software that represents and implements GKS and this will be available as a software package.

1.6.3 Device Independence

GKS does not assume that any of the devices used for display or input have any particular features or restrictions. There are functions defined in the standard that allow the applications programmer to customize the display image to the features of particular devices. For example, an application using GKS can inquire whether an output device is capable of displaying colour and, if not, can substitute another form of display feature, such as a particular line style, to convey the information that would normally be carried by colour. This allows applications written using the standard to be easily transferred from one computer system to another where the various display and input hardware devices are quite different in capability.

1.6.4 Display Management

GKS also provides the applications programmer with a suite of functions for the management of graphics images. It is important that a standard of this type should not only have functions for the definition and manipulation of pictures, but it should also provide functions for the overall control of the graphics devices and other related peripherals. Therefore, GKS provides an environment for controlling display and input devices as well as for storing graphics data and recording the progress of a particular graphics processing session.

1.6.5 Two-Dimensional Standard

The specification of GKS defines a two-dimensional (2D) graphics system; that is, only a flat, 2D world model can be used to define the picture. Work is currently in hand to develop a three-dimensional standard, **GKS-3D**, which will extend the current standard. GKS, however, does not prevent the use of 3D image definition and manipulation at the applications level with the 2D projections being passed to a system implementation of the current standard.

1.6.6 Future Standards

A more comprehensive system known as the **Programmer's Hierarchical Interactive Graphics System** (**PHIGS**), supported by ANSI, is currently under review by ISO. It is felt that there is a requirement for a standard that has more powerful functions for structuring the picture definitions (see Chapter 10).

Also under present development is a standard device communications protocol known as the **Computer Graphics Interface** (**CGI**). This standard will exactly specify the codes sent from the CPU to the computer graphics hardware to define each of the functions the devices can perform. Flexibility is provided through the availability of option sets of functions. The consequences of this standard are two-fold and will have, if universally adopted, a considerable effect on graphics hardware. Computer graphics displays and input devices will be interchangeable without the need for modification to the software, and device-dependent software could become a thing of the past.

Complete standardization of graphics devices is, in reality, impossible and probably undesirable. Features such as cost, device intelligence and resolution are conflicting ones, and the requirement for inexpensive graphics devices means that there will always be a considerable range of device performance available.

A related standard is the **Computer Graphics Metafile** (**CGM**). This defines the way in which graphics images are stored on peripheral storage devices for transfer to other systems and for later use. It defines the codes, in the same way as the proposed CGI, to command each graphics function on a device and the encoding format of the data used to specify the picture.

1.7 Image Processing and Image Analysis

A subject closely related to computer graphics, and sometimes confused with it, is that of **image processing**. Although the two, in fact, do share some of the same techniques, they can be regarded as being logical opposites. In Section 1.4, the end product of the picture definition process was described as being the image itself, appearing as either a vector or pixel representation. Under certain circumstances, however, the image may already exist, and in such cases the requirement is to discover what the scene contains. The image may have been obtained from a variety of sources, including video cameras, space satellites or medical scanner systems to name but a few. But images do not have to be those that would normally be viewed in the visible light spectrum. For example, X-rays, gamma rays and ultrasound can also be captured and displayed as 2D grey scale or false colour images.

Image processing can only be carried out on pixel images when the scene has been captured, for example, by a camera and digitized into a frame buffer. As with images produced by computer graphics systems in this pixel form, the picture in the image is now a completely random set of data points containing no logical structure. Images that have been captured from

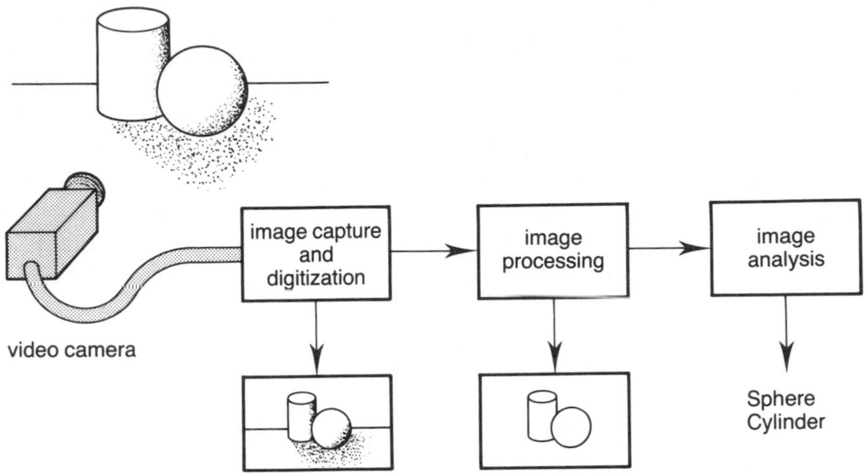

Figure 1.5
Image-analysis system.

a real-life scene will almost certainly contain *noise*, which means that each pixel is not an exact value, as in the case of the computer-generated image, but is an *estimate* of its value. The task of analyzing the image is, therefore, very complex.

Figure 1.5 shows a schematic of the processes required to analyze an image. The image is first captured by the camera system, digitized and then stored in a frame buffer. The accuracy of the representation of the scene in the frame buffer depends on the camera as well as the horizontal and vertical resolution of the frame buffer and the maximum pixel value of each pixel that can be stored. If colour information is required, then more frame buffer range will be required. Once stored in a frame buffer, the image undergoes processing (to remove noise, to restrict the pixel value range and so on) until the basic image information content is reduced to a level at which **image analysis** can be carried out. For example, the result of the image processing may reduce the image so that only the *edges* of the objects contained in the image are visible. The image may then be analyzed and broken down into its constituent objects. Alternatively, a knowledge of what the image contains may already exist; in this case, the task is to find the position and orientation of any objects in the image.

This simple description of the tasks of image processing and image analysis belittles their true complexity. The ease with which the human eye/brain system can view and understand the world about it gives little clue to the difficulty of these tasks. Considerable research has been, and is being, invested in computer vision, and progress has been slow. Only now are simple computer vision inspection and gauging systems beginning to become available, although their ability is still limited. It is hoped that, in the relatively near future, the combination of knowledge-based systems and cheap and powerful microprocessor systems will produce the advance in these systems that industry badly needs.

1.8 The Geometry of Computer Graphics

The mathematical basis of computer graphics is that of coordinate geometry and in particular cartesian coordinate geometry. The requirement of any geometry system used in graphics is that it should be capable of describing both 2D and 3D objects in a form that can be understood by computer programmers and that can be stored and manipulated by the computers themselves. Alternative geometries could be used, but the cartesian system lends itself to computer graphics most logically, economically and conveniently.

1.9 Programming Notation

Two programming notations are used in this book; namely, an abstract programming language based on Standard ML (Milner, 1985) and Pascal. An informal description of the abstract notation is given in Appendix A.

The abstract programming notation is used because it allows a transparent and concise way of expressing many of the programming concepts and algorithms involved in computer graphics. For example, consider the representation of a sequence of points outlining a unit square. In the ML language, this could be expressed as:

```
val square = [(0.0, 0.0), (1.0, 0.0), (1.0, 1.0), (0.0, 1.0)];
```

In Pascal, this might be rendered as:

```
type Point = record
                 x, y: real
             end;
type PointArray = array[1..4] of Point;

var square : PointArray;
.
.
.
with square[1] do begin x := 0.0; y := 0.0 end;
with square[2] do begin x := 1.0; y := 0.0 end;
with square[3] do begin x := 1.0; y := 1.0 end;
with square[4] do begin x := 0.0; y := 1.0 end;
```

If the sequence were to be dynamically allocated, then the Pascal representation would be even more clumsy, requiring the definition of a recursive-linked list data structure.

Pascal has been used in the text wherever it was thought appropriate to illustrate the use of GKS functions in a familiar programming notation, supported by widely available compilers. In other words, Pascal is treated here as an implementation language. Throughout, the Pascal binding to GKS submitted to ISO as a Draft International Standard (ISO, 1986c) has been used. Since this has not yet been ratified as a full standard at the time of writing, it is likely that some of the GKS Pascal notation used in this book may not be present in the final standard, although the standard is unlikely to change significantly from its present state. For an introduction to the early thinking behind the Pascal interface to GKS see Slater (1984).

The programming notation based on ML is used most heavily in Chapters 3 to 13, and the reader is advised to consult Appendix A before studying these chapters. However, because the notation is remarkably clear, the reader should not experience any difficulty by this choice of language for expressing programs. For an introduction to the ideas of functional programming see *BYTE* (1985).

Summary

This chapter has set the scene for the subject of computer graphics. It has looked at its origins, applications and standards, and some of the ideas, concepts and terminology that will be encountered by the reader later in this book. It has shown that the applications of computer graphics cover a very wide range and encompass most of the scientific, business, engineering and technical worlds. Anyone involved in any of these disciplines is most likely to encounter computer graphics sooner or later.

Exercises

1.1 Give five features that would be useful on an interactive computer graphics system for use by a fine artist. For example, one such feature might be the ability to select the width of the brushes. Describe how each feature would be used.

1.2 Project yourself into the future and imagine that your house or apartment is equipped with a system that allows the current state of every electronic device to be monitored. For example, the system will know whether each light switch is ON or OFF, or whether the freezer is on and to what temperature it is set. Design a set of displays that will show the electronic state of your home. You should be able, when using the displays, to quickly see which systems are operating, which are not, which are faulty and need repair, and so on.

CHAPTER 2

A FRAMEWORK FOR COMPUTER GRAPHICS

The objective of computer graphics is to produce pictures. This objective is far from unique to computer graphics since the production of pictures has been a concern of art for thousands of years, and today's mass media, cinema and television use pictures as a normal means of communicating information, persuasion and entertainment. The viewing of static and animated pictures forms an enormous part of the everyday lives of people in the modern world.

For every subject, it is important that there is a suitable *paradigm*; that is, an overall model providing a reference point for the development of ideas and a framework in which to think about the subject. This chapter considers a *printed page* paradigm for computer graphics, where graphics is seen as a means of producing pictures.

2.1 Introduction

Figure 2.1 shows a page such as might appear in a magazine displaying a series of advertisements. Study this page, as it illustrates many of the elements of computer graphics.

For the purposes of exposition, it is assumed that the final responsibility for the appearance and production of the printed page lies with an art director. While the art director may design the initial layout and composition, the detailed artwork is subcontracted out to different studios, each being responsible for the design and production of its own advertisement. This artwork (or *copy*) is ultimately returned to the art director, who must then integrate the individual components into the overall product. In reality, the magazine would sell space on such a page as this, and the different advertisers would employ studios to produce finished copy, according to the standards specified by the magazine, and would send this copy in a reproducible form to the magazine.

Historically, the art director and the studios accomplished their tasks using the traditional tools of the art and media world – photography, the tools of the artist and illustrator, and of the compositing and printing trades. Nowadays, these are supplemented by an ever-increasing application of computing, especially in regard to the preparation and layout of visual material. Clearly, computer graphics plays an essential role.

The remainder of this chapter is devoted to outlining the components of a graphics software system suitable for the production of pictures like those displayed in Figures 2.1 and 2.2. Such a software system, which is termed a **graphics library**, is an integrated set of functions providing the graphics programmer with tools suitable for the construction of pictures, in much the same way as an artist relies on paper and pencil. A programmer who constructs pictures by the application of functions in the graphics library is referred to as an **applications programmer**. On the other hand, the programmer who designs and constructs the graphics library from more primitive components is termed the **graphics systems programmer**. (In reality, these 'programmers' may be a team, rather than single individuals.)

2.2 Picture Layout

The most noticeable feature of Figure 2.1 is that the subpictures, corresponding to individual advertisements, are each located in rectangular areas. Although the art director has to decide where to place each subpicture and how much space each is allowed to occupy, this decision is constrained by the overall page size of the magazine and how many advertisements are to be displayed. Moreover, questions of good design must be considered: it would not be a good idea to have too many advertisements on one page because this would result in an unattractive cluttered effect, making individual advertisements difficult to read.

The different studios responsible for producing the individual subpictures do not necessarily prepare the *copy* to the size of the final advertisement to be displayed. Instead, the illustrators and typographers use a paper size appropriate to the needs of the initial design and production process. For example, it is highly unlikely that the illustration for AIKIDO in Figure 2.1 was drawn by the artist to the scale shown. It was probably drawn on much larger sheets of paper and then reduced to the required size. Hence, there is a problem of *transforming* the copy produced by each studio to the size necessary to fit the allotted space on the page.

Figure 2.2 shows another example of an advertising page with a similar layout, except that there are only two rectangular areas displayed. In addition, the one occupying the lower part of the page displays another interesting feature – there is a photograph of a person that has been *clipped* to a circular boundary so that only the face remains. When planning an advertisement of this kind, it is easier for the photographer to shoot a full photograph and then cut away everything outside of the clipping region.

Similar considerations also apply to the generation of computer graphics. In this case, the applications programmer (playing a role similar to the art director) is constrained by the overall size of the **display space** on the graphics device (just as the art director is constrained by the paper size). The display space can be divided into a number of rectangular regions called **viewports**, into which the different subpictures are mapped. Moreover, a particular subpicture requires the use of a suitable application coordinate system. Such a coordinate system is the **world coordinate (WC)** system, in which the application chooses a rectangular **window**. This system is, in this instance, the whole of the 2D plane, stretching to infinity in all directions. Any finite rectangular region of this infinite space, where the sides of the rectangle are parallel to the x and y axes, is a window in the WC system. Just as different paper sizes are preferred for different pictures, so different windows are appropriate in the graphics realm: the pictures are drawn in WC space relative to a particular window and are then clipped to the window. A method of transforming these windows to their allotted viewports on the screen must then be applied – just as the finished advertising copy from a studio has to be scaled to the required size to fit on the magazine page. Windows, then, correspond to the illustrators' preferred paper size, whereas viewports correspond to the rectangular regions on the final page in which each subpicture is to appear.

It is clear from the foregoing that procedures must exist in the graphics library for specifying windows, viewports and appropriate coordinate systems. Although there are a number of alternative procedure and parameter definitions that could be employed for this purpose, only one will be described here. (Such definitions are discussed in more detail in

Cut Price Records
all major labels stocked
huge discounts
11 Empire Lane SW12
AIKIDO
The ultimate in self defence
Mon-Fri 6-9pm
14 Wash Street,
London E1
She looks happy!
She learned to program
Learn to Program
in 10 minutes!
Our REVOLUTIONARY
technique
will make you
a fully qualified
PROGRAMMER
effortlessly!
Simple Brain Ltd
22 Nutter Lane
East Cheam, NW 17

Figure 2.1

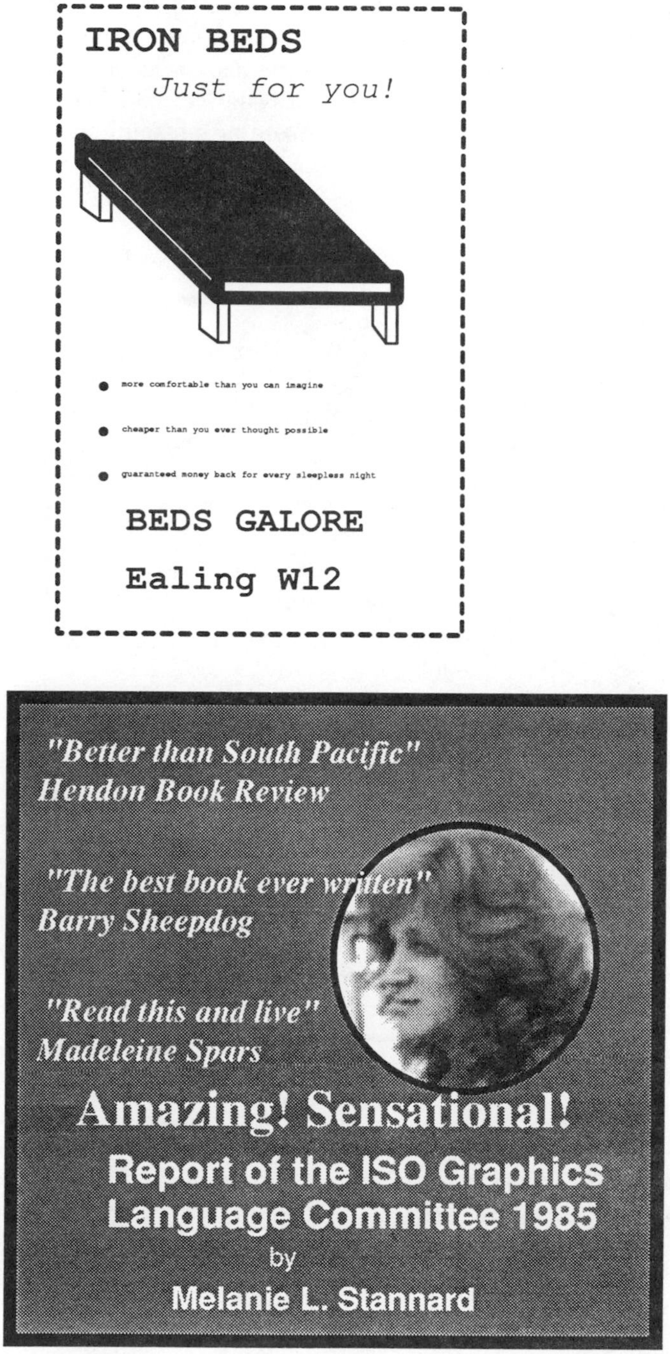
IRON BEDS
Just for you!
more comfortable than you can imagine
cheaper than you ever thought possible
guaranteed money back for every sleepless night
BEDS GALORE
Ealing W12
"Better than South Pacific"
Hendon Book Review
"The best book ever written"
Barry Sheepdog
"Read this and live"
Madeleine Spars
Amazing! Sensational!
Report of the ISO Graphics
Language Committee 1985
by
Melanie L. Stannard

Figure 2.2

Chapter 4.) The *SetWindow* procedure must take a rectangular boundary as its parameter in WC, where the edges of the rectangle are parallel to the x and y WC axes. The *SetViewport* procedure also takes a rectangular boundary as its parameter. The most obvious choice for the coordinate system in which this boundary is expressed is **device coordinates (DC)**, which is the coordinate system used for representing absolute positions on the graphics display space. For example, the following program describes the picture shown in Figure 2.3(a).

Assume a screen resolution of 768 by 512.
SetWindow(−10.0, 10.0, −10.0, 10.0);
SetViewport(256, 511, 100, 355);
A circle of radius 10 drawn with 20 line segments per quadrant.
Circle(10.0, 20)

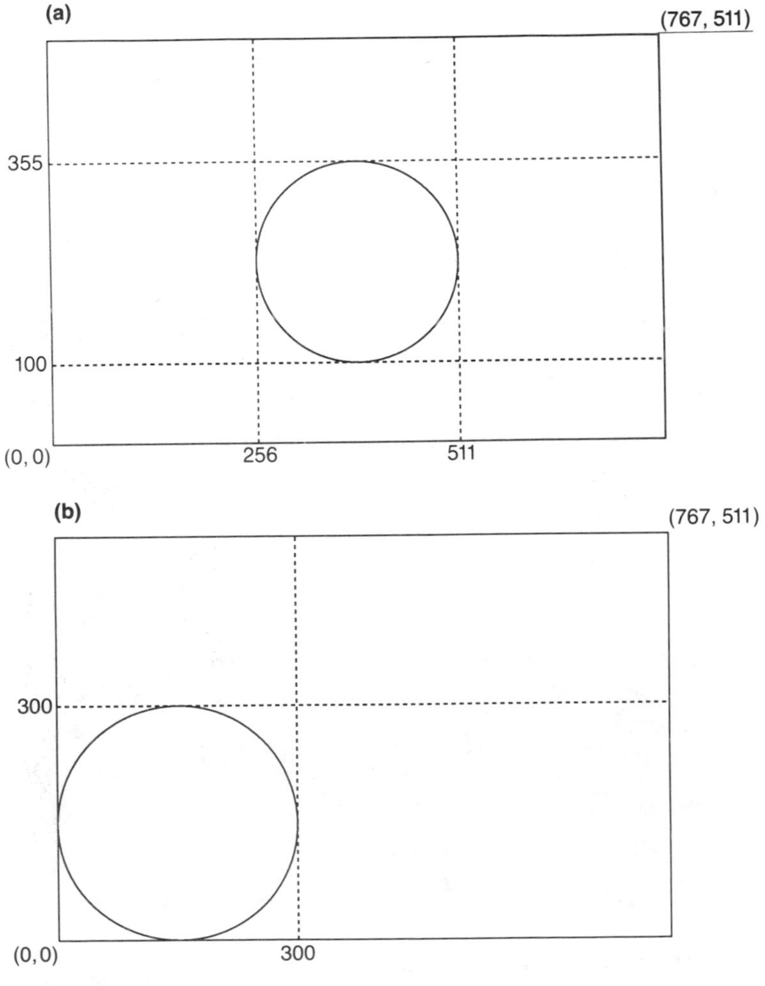

Figure 2.3
Relationship between window and viewport.

A window is specified with both x and y bounds ranging from -10 to $+10$. A rectangular boundary will always be given in the form of the horizontal range (minimum x to maximum x and then the vertical range minimum y to maximum y). Hence, the general version of a *SetWindow* procedure is of the form:

SetWindow: real*real*real*real → Void;

SetWindow(Xmin, Xmax, Ymin, Ymax)
sets the current window to be the given x and y ranges.

The first line here describes the type of the *SetWindow* function as one which takes as its parameter four reals and returns a *Void* result – meaning that the application of the function is useful for its *side effect* of setting the current window (that is, it returns the 'nothing' value).

The device coordinate system for this imaginary device ranges from (0, 0) at the bottom left-hand corner of the display to (767, 511) at the top right-hand corner. Such a device is sometimes said to have a **display resolution** of 768 by 512.

The *SetViewport* function in this case defines a viewport on the display space to be the middle third of the screen horizontally and approximately one-fifth to three-fifths vertically. A circle is described in the current window and appears on the screen in the position shown in Figure 2.3(a).

It is important to note from this example that the window and viewport form logically independent coordinate systems. If the window and circle were unchanged, but the viewport defined to be from (0, 0) to (300, 300), then the display changes as shown in Figure 2.3(b). The circle still appears, but its *position* on the display space has moved since this is determined by the viewport, not the window. An analogy can be drawn here to the printed page paradigm: each studio produces its final copy, but the art director can place the copy at any position on the page, and even change its size (compatible with the overall page size and with other items to appear on the page).

Often, a graphics system supports many different devices, and the graphics library must provide a means of controlling these in as uniform a manner as possible. It would be very undesirable for a different set of procedures to be needed for each particular device, as the applications programmer may wish to use two or more devices when executing one program. For example, one device may be used to display a picture in full colour, another to produce a hardcopy of the picture, and a third to display a magnification of a subregion. The programmer would expect the graphics library to support all of these different devices in exactly the same manner. The library would soon fall into disuse if every different device required a modified set of procedures. Furthermore, chaos would ensue on introduction of a brand new device – perhaps a whole new version of the graphics library would have to be prepared. Similarly, no magazine would survive for

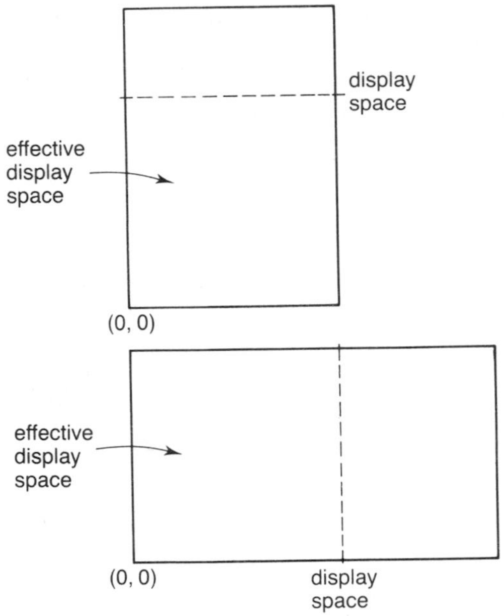

Figure 2.4
The effective display space is the largest square.

very long if it had to send out entirely different instructions to cater for the different operating conditions and personnel in the organizations with which it cooperates.

Determination of the viewport by using DC is acceptable if only one graphics device is ever used, or if all graphics devices have exactly the same coordinate systems to represent their display spaces. However, neither of these provisos holds true. It is better to adopt a uniform method of addressing different display spaces to overcome the problem of device disparity. The standard solution is to introduce an intermediate coordinate system called **normalized device coordinates** (**NDC**). Conventionally, this coordinate system is the unit square, where (0, 0) is at the bottom left-hand corner and (1, 1) is at the top right. The origin of NDC usually corresponds to the bottom left-hand corner of the display space. For reasons to do with the scaling of pictures, which is fully discussed later, the point (1, 1) in NDC represents not the top right-hand corner of each display space, but the top right-hand corner of the *largest square* on the display space (see Figure 2.4). This largest square is termed here the **effective display space**. The *SetViewport* procedure then becomes defined as follows:

SetViewport: real∗real∗real∗real → Void;

SetViewport(*Xmin*, *Xmax*, *Ymin*, *Ymax*)
Xmin, Xmax, Ymin, Ymax are reals between 0.0 and 1.0, with Xmin ≤ Xmax and Ymin ≤ Ymax, and determine the current viewport.

For example:

> *SetViewport*(0.25, 0.75, 0.25, 0.75)
> All graphical output would now appear in the middle portion of the effective display space on every device.

To summarize, windows allow the user of the graphics library to choose a coordinate system appropriate to the current application. In the printed page paradigm, windows correspond to the actual paper sizes used by the studios when preparing the pictures for the magazine art director. Viewports, on the other hand, allow the user of the graphics library to determine where a particular window is to be represented on the physical display space of a graphics device. This corresponds to the reduction or enlargement of the pictures produced by the studios and their positioning on the magazine page. The overall image finally produced consists of a number of windows, each displayed in a viewport somewhere on the effective display space of each graphical device in use.

2.3 The Basic Elements of an Image

Chapter 1 outlined the three stages of the image-generation process: model, picture and image. In addition, the most basic elements, or primitives, of the image were discussed, these being the straight line or vector or, more basic still, the picture element or pixel. All images can be constructed from these basic elements. Some display devices, such as vector refresh devices or pen plotters, have vectors as their most basic element while others, such as raster scan devices, have pixels as their most basic element. Naturally, vector systems have to be able to display dots, whereas pixel systems have to be able to display lines.

Devices that have pixels as their basic display element usually store a representation of the image in a special area of computer memory, known as the pixel memory, the refresh buffer or, most commonly, the frame buffer. Even when the display device does not actually use one of these memories, it is still convenient to consider one as being present in order to define the image. The hardware implementation of these memories is discussed extensively in Chapter 16.

The 'She looks happy!' advertisement in Figure 2.2 may be considered as a 2D array of 0s and 1s, such as might be stored in a frame buffer. If a graphics display were generating this picture, it would start from the top left-hand corner of the array and scan through it row after row. On finding a pixel with a value '1' it would put a black dot on the corresponding position of the display space (assuming that the background colour of the display space is white). Our minds do the rest of the work, and organize this pattern of dots into an image of a woman.

The relationship of the image to the real world was discussed in Chapter 1, and it should be stressed that the tones and shading patterns generate an illusion of being *something else*. Look once again at Figure 2.2, in particular at the drawing of the woman in the 'She looks happy!' advertisement. Although obvious, it is worth saying 'There isn't really a woman there!', it is just an illusion. All that is really there is a set of tiny black dots on a white background.

The pixel is a very elementary component of an image and from the point of view of a set of procedures forming a graphics library, it is often at too primitive a level to be of direct use. There are, however, some important image-generation techniques that compute the value of each pixel individually. This is the case with **halftoning** techniques which are used to generate the illusion of shades of grey on bilevel displays. The results of such techniques are seen everyday in newspaper photographs, the 'She looks happy!' advertisement being a prime example. In 3D graphics, the creation of realistic images in full colour, which emulate the shading and reflective properties of objects in the real world, involves computing the (colour) value of each pixel individually. However, in less esoteric applications, programmers prefer to work with a functional interface to graphics which is at a higher level than the pixel. A suitable set of higher level functions for the generation of graphical output can be derived from a further consideration of Figure 2.1.

The most obvious feature of Figures 2.1 and 2.2 is the sequences of connected straight lines. Every one of the 'viewports' on the page is demarcated by a border – a sequence of four straight lines. The drawings within each viewport are also made up in part of lines, such as the illustration of a bed. Lines are so fundamental in graphics that it is perfectly conceivable for a graphics library to cater *only* for the drawing of lines. Even single pixels could be defined in this way since a dot is but a degenerate line (a line with identical endpoints) and, of course, must be so on vector-generating devices. However, it would not be viable for a graphics library to support only the setting of pixels as the process of converting from higher level output, such as lines, to their constituent pixels is not trivial. The purpose of a graphics library is to make life relatively easy for the applications programmer, to abstract away from the basics of how images are produced on the display space, and provide tools the programmer can use directly and easily.

While it is true that a pixel can be considered as a degenerate line, to generate a line out of pixels requires a relatively complex algorithm (which in any case is best handled by the hardware or firmware of the graphics device itself). While pixels are fundamental to the manner in which an image is *formed* in the frame buffer, lines are fundamental to the way in which the graphics applications programmer *thinks*. The graphics library's set of functions should correspond to the programmer's conceptual view of how to create a picture, and not to the underlying device hardware or the architecture of the display system. Nevertheless, the graphics systems programmer, the person responsible for *implementing* the graphics library, has to know how to build fundamental primitives directly out of pixels. Algorithms for generating pixels in the frame buffer – that is, for determining which pixels best represent a given line – are discussed in Chapter 4.

A procedure for the generation of lines must be included in the graphics library. The following type of procedure would be useful for this purpose:

```
type Point = real*real;

Polyline: Point sequence → Void;
Polyline(p) draws the sequence of connected straight lines, joining p[0] to p[1] to p[2]
through to p[n − 1], where n = Length p ⩾ 2. Each point is of the form (x, y).
```

For example:

```
Drawing a triangle
Polyline[(0.0, 0.0), (1.0, 0.0), (0.5, 1.0), (0.0, 0.0)]
Polyline is applied to a sequence of four points defining a triangle in the unit square.
```

The following more complex example shows how the *Polyline* procedure may be used to describe a quadrant of a circle of radius *r* with centre at the origin. The quadrant is divided into *segs* (line segments).

```
fun CircleQuad(r, segs) =
  let val t = store 0.0 and u = store r and v = store 0.0
     and inc = π/(2.0*segs)
  in
    let val p = store [(u, v)]
    in
      for 1 ⩽ i ⩽ segs do
        t     := t + inc;
        u, v := r*cos t, r*sin t;
        p     := (u, v) :: p
      od;
      Polyline ?p
    ni
  ni
nuf
```

In this procedure definition, a point sequence store variable *p* is constructed

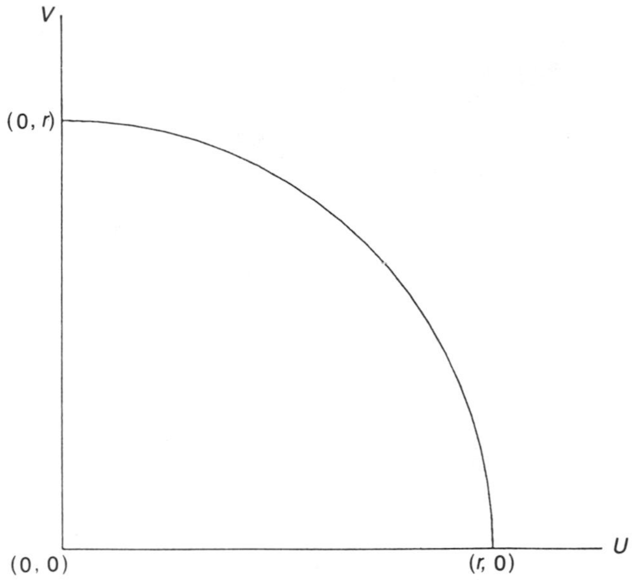

Figure 2.5
Quadrant of a circle as described by the *Polyline* procedure.

by placing a new point (u, v) at the head of the sequence, where (u, v) is a point on the circle quadrant. At the completion of the **for**...**do**...**od** iteration, the content of the store variable t is $segs*inc$, which is $\pi/2$ (90°). Note that from the way the point sequence is constructed, the polyline is described in a clockwise direction from the point $(0.0, r)$ through to $(r, 0.0)$. These ideas are illustrated in Figure 2.5.

This procedure can be extended to draw a complete circle, by taking symmetry into account. If the point (u, v) lies on the circle, then so do $(-u, v)$, $(-u, -v)$ and $(u, -v)$, each occurring in a different quadrant. Hence:

```
fun Circle(r, segs) =
  let val t = store 0.0 and u = store r and v = store 0.0
      and inc = π/(2.0*segs)
  in
    let val p = store [[(u, v)], [(−u, v)] [(−u, −v)], [(u, −v)]]
    in
      for 1 ≤ i ≤ segs do
        t                        := t + inc;
        u, v                     := r*cos t, r*sin t;
        p[0], p[1], p[2], p[3]   := (u, v)      :: p[0],
                                    (−u, v)     :: p[1],
                                    (−u, − v)   :: p[2],
                                    (u, −v)     :: p[3]
      od;
```

```
        for 0 ≤ i ≤ 3 do Polyline ?p[i] od
      ni
    ni
  nuf
```

The second important feature of Figures 2.1 and 2.2 is the presence of shaded areas. Ignoring for the moment the different styles of shading, a shaded area is demarcated by a boundary consisting of (sometimes very many) connected straight line edges. A typical example of this type of primitive is in the 'Cut Price Records' advertisement of Figure 2.1, as well as the AIKIDO advertisement. This type of primitive is called a **fill area**, and can be generated by the following procedure:

> FillArea: Point sequence → Void;
> FillArea(p) the interior of the polygon defined by edges joining vertices p[0] to p[1] to p[2] to ... to p[n − 1] to p[0], where n = Length p ≥ 3. Each p[i] is of the form (x, y).

Note that the actual border itself is not drawn (unless the shading rule is *hollow*). The closed polygon defines a boundary and the space inside the boundary is to be shaded. This is a very general definition since it places no real restrictions on the shape of the boundary. The polygon might be concave or convex, and edges might intersect. The only restriction is that the polygon is defined by at least three points. Some examples of shaded polygons are shown in Figure 2.6.

Just as lines can be constructed out of pixels, so a (solid) fill area can be constructed out of horizontal lines. The algorithm for generating these lines for a fill area involves computing the intersections of each line with the edges of the polygon boundary, and displaying the line segments corresponding to the polygon interior. This is discussed in detail in Chapter 4.

Finally, the most evident type of graphics primitive in Figures 2.1 and 2.2, in terms of frequency of appearance, is **text**. Text is of fundamental importance in many applications of computer graphics. Even where graphics is used simply for the display of scientific charts and graphs, text is important for *annotation*. Of course, in advertising, the text is crucial – very few products are so well known that they can be advertised without any written (or spoken) mention of the name of the product. Ignoring for the time being the many different styles in which text can appear, the creation of text requires a procedure specifying its location and the actual string of characters to be displayed. A text procedure could be defined as follows:

> Text: Point∗string → Void;
> Text(p, s) draws the string of characters s, positioning the lower left-hand corner of the first character at the point p.

Text may be generated in one of two ways. Firstly, a character can be

Figure 2.6
Examples of polygons as defined by *FillArea*.

considered as a 2D array of pixels. For example, Figure 15.9 shows the letter *S* represented in this way. Hence, an efficient method for generating characters on a pixel-based display device is to store such representations of character sets in local memory. When text is generated, the arrays corresponding to the required characters are copied into the frame buffer. This is a fast method of text generation, since the only computation required is that of correctly placing the arrays in the frame buffer to which the characters are to be copied.

An alternative and more complex method of text generation is called **vector** or **stroke precision**. Here, the characters are decomposed into curves and a vector procedure is used to generate each character. This is often a less efficient method in terms of time of execution, but is more flexible since it allows easy manipulation, such as expanding or shrinking the characters, drawing them at an angle (in *italics*) or rotating the text string in relation to the horizontal axis. Moreover, characters generated in this way are aesthetically more pleasing. Text is a very complex area of computer graphics and is discussed further in Chapters 6 and 15.

2.4 Style in Graphics

The graphical output procedures discussed in the previous section to draw lines (*Polyline*), to shade areas (*FillArea*) and draw text (*Text*) specify a picture in purely geometric terms. The output functions determine *what* is to be drawn, not *how* it is to be drawn. Consider, for example, the following:

```
fun Triangle(p0, p1, p2) =
  let val p = [p0, p1, p2, p0]
  in
    Polyline(p); FillArea(tail p);
    Text(p[2], "This is a triangle")
  ni
nuf
```

Figure 2.7 shows a number of different triangles, all produced by invoking this one procedure *Triangle*. Although all the triangles have the same geometrical structure, they differ from each other because the lines, shading and text are drawn using differing attributes. The one geometrical construct in the mind of the applications programmer can be rendered in an infinite variety of different styles, depending on the attributes used by the graphical output primitives. Of course, within the same picture, many different styles of line and shading can appear.

This latter feature is also well illustrated in Figures 2.1 and 2.2. The IRON BEDS advertisement, for example, has a border drawn with a dashed line. The bed itself is drawn with thin and thick lines, and some of these lines have rounded ends. Areas are sometimes shaded in solid black and sometimes with a pattern. Text is drawn using multifarious fonts and sizes, and not always horizontally.

Generally, the attributes associated with a line will include its **type** (whether, for example, *solid* or *dashed*), its **thickness** and its **colour**. A fill area can be displayed using many possible **patterns** and colours for shading, or there can be no shading at all, with only the border of the polygon displayed using straight lines.

Text is a rather complex primitive in terms of its attributes. Attributes include its **font**: for a given font the spacing between the characters and the width of the characters. Of course, text can also be displayed in different colours. Irrespective of font, the **character height** can also be varied, together with the **direction** of the text (which might be *up* or *down* or *left* as well as the usual *right*). To complicate matters further, the text can be drawn at various angles, irrespective of direction, and even the **alignment** of the text relative to the string position, given as a parameter to the *Text* procedure, does not have to be at the bottom left-hand corner of the text extent rectangle. These various possibilities are illustrated in Figure 6.7.

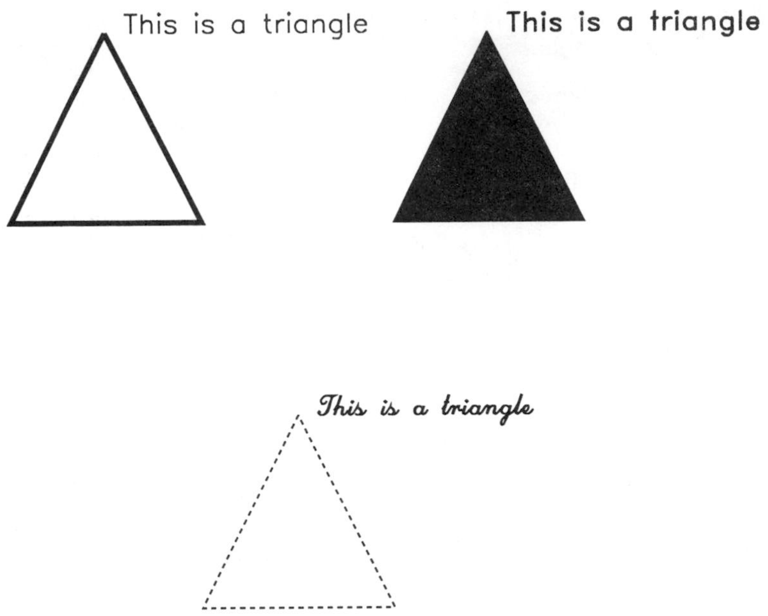

Figure 2.7
Triangles with different attributes, as invoked by the procedure *Triangle*.

To summarize, the appearance of a picture depends on more than the purely geometric properties addressed by graphical output procedures. There clearly has to be a good procedural interface to the output attributes available in any graphics library. Various possible choices are discussed in Chapter 6.

2.5 Interacting with the Picture

Perhaps the most important aspect of computer graphics, as far as potential users are concerned, has been left until last. This is the idea of **interactive** graphics. If the pictures on the magazine pages were to be created using computer graphics, the last thing the illustrators would wish to do would be to write computer programs. Rather, the illustrators would be happiest using a computer in a manner not too dissimilar from the traditional methods of creating their pictures.

Many users of computer equipment know nothing about programming, and do not have to know anything. The user of a word processor, for example, cares in the main about the *ease of use* of the equipment, not about how it works. Ease of use includes a sense of familiarity, in the sense that the word processor allows a method of working that is similar to that of using an old-fashioned typewriter but with none of the problems, and many advantages. For example, word processors usually give the user the ability to selectively modify part of a text, without having to retype the whole page. With an ordinary typewriter, however, deletion and replacement of a passage of text usually requires a complete retyping job, or at best a messy use of scissors and paste. Moreover, the word processor provides the advantage of taking care of layout of the text, within parameters determined by the typist.

An analogy to the difference between output-only graphics programming compared to interactive graphics is provided by comparing two different ways of making a picture – by taking a photograph or by sketching or painting. When a photograph is to be taken, the essentially creative stage occurs when the scene is being composed in the viewfinder. Once the photographer has squeezed the shutter button the image on the film is fixed, and the picture is more or less determined. Of course, there are processes that can be used at the developing stage to further influence the final appearance of the picture, but the geometric components of the image are fixed, and the attributes relatively fixed. If the photographer changes his or her mind about some important component of the picture, then the only realistic course of action is to retake the photograph (if it is not too late). If the subsequent picture is still not good enough, then once again the process has to be repeated.

Consider now the artist painting or sketching a picture. At any moment in the process of creation, the artist can change his or her mind. Parts of the picture can be overpainted with ease. Erasers can be used to delete unwanted sections, and these can be redrawn. Of course, as with the photographer, the artist begins the picture with a mind's eye view of the final product. But unlike the photographer, the artist has the luxury of being able to change his or her mind at any stage.

The artist works *interactively*, whereas the photographer works in *batch* mode. The photographer creates pictures in much the same way as the user of a graphics library would if restricted to the graphics output and attribute functions. The programmer writes a program using these functions; this is the creative part of the process, equivalent to the photographer composing a scene in the viewfinder. The programmer composes the program according to the scene in his or her mind. Once the program is compiled and the command given for its execution, the image appears on the display space. If a change is desired at this stage, then the program has to be edited, recompiled and executed once again. This process continues until a satisfactory picture has been generated.

A camera captures an image in its totality. For example, consider the still from the feature film 'The Draughtsman's Contract' on page 614. The image portrays the draughtsman taking a drink, presumably contemplating work on the forthcoming illustration. Everything is in readiness: the picture shows the equipment, a group of people framed in the easel, the mansion beyond the trees. The movie camera captured this image in its entirety. However, the draughtsman will create his illustration in a totally different manner to the camera, sketching structured components one after the other, components that exist as a synthesis of what is in the scene and in the draughtsman's mind as he sips his drink.

Given the still photograph and the draughtsman's illustration, which is easier to modify? For example, suppose the film director decided that the artist's tressle on the right of the picture should not be there after all. It might be possible to do some sophisticated post-processing on the film negative to produce a final print without the tressle. Far more likely, the director would have to re-assemble the caste and equipment, wait for the right weather and lighting conditions, and retake the film sequence.

The draughtsman, however, can modify his illustration with greater ease and at rather less time and expense, and employing the very methods used to sketch the picture in the first place – simply by erasing any unwanted part of the scene and drawing over it.

Interactive graphics allows the creator of a picture to act in much the same way as the painter. An **input device** attached to the graphics display allows the user to point to areas of the screen and effect changes. One popular input device is called a **mouse** (see Figure 16.7). When the user moves a mouse around on a desk top, a **cursor**, or symbol that responds to the movements of the mouse, moves around on the screen. This can be used to effect changes to the current picture and to the underlying data structure representing the screen image. For example, while this very paragraph was being typed, the author decided that a comma needed to be placed after the phrase 'movements of the mouse'. The author then moved the mouse upwards on the desk, and the cursor moved up the screen in response. When the cursor reached the desired position, after the word 'mouse', a comma was typed, inserting it into the text at that point. Then the mouse was moved again to the bottom of the text, ready to continue typing this passage. The change was effected to the text as it appeared on the screen, and also to the representation of the piece of text in the computer memory.

The artist or illustrator would also like to create images in this interactive manner. To do so, an input device would be used to position a cursor at various points on the display and so generate changes at that point. Ideally, to the illustrator, this would, after practise, seem like using a pencil, paper and paint. However, he or she would feel at home with such a system only if it embodied the same sort of concepts employed when the normal tools of the trade were used. A good graphics system for an illustrator is designed not only to model these old tools of the trade, but to provide all the advantages of speed and ease of use of a computer. For example, computer graphics is now used for creating animation frames in the film industry. The animators create the main frames using interactive programs and output-only batch programs are used to provide the in-between frames (see, for example, Hayward, 1984 and Magnenat–Thalmann *et al.*, 1985).

A basis for the kind of interaction described is a set of **graphical input** procedures to be included in the graphics library. Interactive programs are then written employing a combination of these. One simple example of this is an input procedure, which can be used to find the coordinate of a position on the display space. Its definition might be:

RequestLocator: state → Point;
RequestLocator(..) evaluates to a WC point. The value depends on the state of the system – including, obviously, the position of the input device.

When this procedure is executed, during the running of a program, the system would wait until some event occurs, such as the pressing of one of the buttons on the mouse, before proceeding. Meanwhile, the user would have positioned the mouse so that its reflected cursor was at the desired position on the display. When the button is depressed, the position of the cursor is evaluated in WC, and this point is the value of the function. For example, a very simple interactive program to draw a triangle would be as follows:

let val *p* = **store** [*RequestLocator*(..)]
in
  for $1 \leqslant i \leqslant 2$ **do** *p* := *RequestLocator*(..) :: *p* **od**
  FillArea ?*p*
ni

Interactive graphics is a very difficult, but also rewarding, component of computer graphics. It has two major aspects. The first is concerned with the design of a set of library procedures for graphical input that are sufficiently general and flexible to cater for a range of possible interactive applications. Requesting the coordinate of a point is only a basic example of the kind of procedure required.

The second aspect is concerned with using the interactive procedures to design programs that users find helpful and easy to use. This raises a large number of problems, which go beyond the purely computing aspects of graphics. When designing an interactive system, an analysis must be undertaken of the working methods of people in the field and how computer graphics could help, if at all.

Designing interactive systems that people like using is by no means an easy matter. Such exercises sometimes result in the computer graphics expert *insisting* to the user of an animation system, for example, that the graphics system *is* wonderful, if only he or she would stop moaning and realize it. Management, in order to be modern, may be tempted to 'ram' such new systems down their employees' throats – irrespective of their real merits. Such an experience is likely to put people off computers for life. Further discussion on the subject of human–computer interaction can be found in Chapters 6, 7 and 14.

Summary

This chapter has used the printed page as a model for computer graphics and has generated some ideas about the objectives of graphics and a set of procedures, called a graphics library, needed to effect graphics. These procedures are concerned with graphical output, such as the drawing of lines and text; with coordinate systems, layout and viewing; with the need for a class of attribute procedures to provide styling information when the output procedures are activated; and, finally, with input procedures needed for the creation of interactive systems.

Subsequent chapters consider each of these procedures in detail, in addition to a number of related problems. In the next chapter, the architecture of a graphics library is discussed, while Chapters 4 to 13 concentrate on the design of the system, implementation of the library functions, data structures for the representation of pictures and interactive graphics. Chapters 14 to 19 are concerned mainly with graphics device hardware, systems and systems design.

Exercises

2.1 This chapter has used the example of a magazine page to infer the functions that would be necessary for a computer graphics system to be able to reproduce such a page. Suppose the example had been of *movies* rather than pages. Design a set of graphics functions that you think might be suitable for generating animated cartoons.

2.2 Write a general-purpose bar chart function. This takes as arguments an array of strings representing the bar chart labels, and a corresponding array of frequencies or percentages. For example, [“Conservative”, “Labour”, “Alliance”] with percentages [22, 55, 23]; or [“Republican”, “Democrat”, “Independent”, “Socialist”, “No Hoper”] with percentages [45, 40, 5, 2, 8]. Your function must display an appropriate graphical representation.

2.3 Define any graphical object you wish (called P), made up of $n + 1$ line segments based on points p_0, p_1, ..., p_n (as a simple example, a square). Now define another object, Q, based on exactly the same number of points and lines (for example, a rectangle). Suppose the points are $q_0, q_1, \ldots, q_n$. Choose a mapping so that each point p_i corresponds to a unique point q_j, and so that all of the points in the two sets are used up. For example, in the simplest case $p_i \rightarrow q_i$. Let α be any number between 0 and 1, and define:

$$r_i = \alpha p_i + (1 - \alpha)\, q_i$$

For any $0 \leq \alpha \leq 1$, the set of points defined by r_i will define an object, R, which is intermediate between P and Q. *Note*: These ideas can be used as a basis for animation, where P and Q represent *key frames* and each possible R is an *in-between* frame. Implement this method, which is called in betweening.

CHAPTER 3

DESIGN PRINCIPLES FOR DEVICE-INDEPENDENT GRAPHICS

This chapter considers some of the problems associated with the implementation of a computer graphics library. The name 'library' in this context refers to an integrated set of functions providing programming tools for computer graphics. Chapter 2 used the printed page analogy to suggest the range of possible tasks that such a library might be required to perform, and therefore the functions needed. This chapter concentrates on the problems of designing the library implementation in such a way as to be relatively *device independent*.

3.1 Introduction

Device independence is of major importance to graphics software. It would be pointless considering the features of a library for computer graphics if its design and nature were always heavily dependent on the particular graphics hardware available. Graphics display devices are rather more varied in their design and capabilities than, for example, different makes and models of motor cars. Ultimately, cars all do the same thing and all are driven in almost exactly the same way (otherwise the driving proficiency test would be unworkable). The differences between models of car are essentially marginal – some are bigger than others, some go faster or consume less gasolene than others. The only relatively major functional difference is that some have automatic transmission – the fact that this is a major difference is reflected by the attitude driving test authorities in the UK take to those who pass their test in an 'automatic' vehicle.

The differences between computer graphics devices, on the other hand, are often major. If such differences were reflected in the world of motor cars, then some cars would have steering wheels and others not, or some would only go forwards or only backwards. The cars would differ in their basic design and construction, in their capabilities and in their method of use.

3.2 Graphics Devices

For the purposes of this chapter, it is worth considering a simple classification of graphics devices. The most popular type of device today is often called a **raster device**. The essential feature of such a device is that the display image is refreshed from a special area of computer memory called the frame buffer. Conceptually, this is a 2D array of pixels. The name 'raster' occurs because the process of image generation involves scanning through the frame buffer in horizontal raster scan lines, in much the same way as a broadcast television picture is constructed. Other types of graphics device (such as plasma panel and laser) also represent the image as a 2D array of pixels. The name 'pixel-based devices' is reserved here for the class of all such devices.

An older although still important alternative technology is called **vector refresh display devices**. In this system, the image is stored as a **display list** which contains the instructions to a 'pen' about how the image should be drawn. For example, move to ($x1$, $y1$), draw a line to ($x2$, $y2$), draw another line to ($x3$, $y3$) and another to ($x1$, $y1$) is a sequence of display instructions for generating the image of a triangle. There are many variations on this theme: the 'pen' might actually be a pen in the normal sense of the word attached to a mechanical arm that moves across a flat surface on which there is a piece of paper. When such **pen plotters** receive a *PenDown* instruction followed by a *WriteLine* instruction, a line is drawn on the piece of paper. Alternatively, the 'pen' might be an electron beam that writes on a display screen. In such a system, the instructions in the display list must be executed many times a second to maintain the image. (See Chapters 15 and 16 for further discussion of these devices.)

The terms 'pixel based' and 'vector based' are used to emphasize the differences between the most primitive instructions that can be obeyed by such graphics devices. In the case of pixel-based devices, the most primitive instruction is:

WritePixel(x, y, *colour*)

where (x, y) is the coordinate offset from the origin of the frame buffer array: usually with y *increasing* from top to bottom as in an upside-down coordinate system, mimicking the path of the raster scan process. The effect of this instruction is to set the specified *colour* for the (x, y)th element of the frame buffer. All other graphics output must eventually be constructed from this most primitive of instructions. Pictures are formed by the illusion generated from the mosaic of colours on the display at any given time.

In the case of vector refresh devices, images are constructed out of straight lines – these devices are modelled on the movements of a hypothetical (or sometimes real) pen. The usual basic instructions are of the form:

PenUp
PenDown
MoveTo
LineTo

with obvious meaning. These can be encapsulated in a single instruction:

WriteLine($p1$, $p2$)

where $p1$ and $p2$ are the coordinates of the endpoints of a line.

This brief discussion of graphics devices should not lull the reader into the belief that there is uniformity within these two major classes of devices. Amongst pixel-based devices, for example, there are major differences both with respect to limitations imposed by the hardware and with respect to their functional capabilities. The dimensions of the frame buffer (that is, the number of pixels per row, the number of rows) determine the **spatial resolution** of the device. This is related to the **pixel density**, which is the number of pixels per centimetre on the display. Geometric objects such as lines are defined in an abstract continuous coordinate system. However, in the process of displaying such objects they are *sampled*, in the sense that the infinite continuity of the object is represented as a finite number of points on a discrete grid. Therefore, the greater the display resolution and density, the more representative the sample can be. Unfortunately, greater resolution not only means greater smoothness in the picture, but also greater cost because a larger capacity frame buffer is needed to store the image.

Sampling also occurs in another sense when the graphical objects are endowed with colour. Colour variations in the real world are continuous. However, only a finite number of colours can ever be displayed on a graphics device. When there are only two colours (black and white), pixel-based devices are referred to as **bitmapped**; the frame buffer is in this case a 2D array of 1s and 0s with 1 representing black and 0 white. Devices that support a large number of colours may be used to depict realistic scenes, as shown in many of the colour plates. Once again, high colour resolution requires greater memory and therefore financial cost.

Spatial and colour resolution are two of the most important hardware parameters that determine the characteristics of graphics devices. However, graphics devices are designed with different levels of functional capability. For example, as seen earlier, the most basic primitive of pixel-based devices is *WritePixel*. But this is so basic that manufacturers of display hardware provide a number of extra features. A graphics display device is after all a special type of computer, and can have built-in programs to provide functionality of greater or lesser sophistication. Algorithms have been devised (see Chapter 4) to determine the 'best' set of pixels for representing graphics objects, such as lines, circles and area fills. Pixel-based devices are usually equipped with at least some variety of these functions in addition to the *WritePixel* primitive.

Some graphics devices go far beyond these fundamental requirements and provide built-in implementations of sophisticated graphics libraries, such as GKS. Most, however, are more modest, but may provide additional basic facilities such as *clipping* to rectangular windows.

3.3 Virtual Graphics Devices

A solution to the problems involved in designing device-independent graphics software is provided by the concept of a **virtual graphics device (VGD)**. The graphics library is constructed to drive an *imaginary* display device, rather than any particular set of real devices. This VGD is endowed with a set of properties according to the needs of the library. Obviously, the characteristics of the VGD must bear some resemblance to the real world of graphics devices, because the key to device independence is that *only* the implementation of the VGD is device dependent, and not the rest of the library. However, the VGD still does have to be implemented for real devices.

This apparent abandonment of reality has an extremely useful consequence. It is important to remember that graphics libraries are designed for people to use. As will be shown later in this chapter, the VGD idea ensures relatively easy incorporation of new devices into the system; the library software does not have to deal with all the special cases necessary if it were targeted for real devices rather than a VGD. In addition, if the core of the library is based on a VGD, then library users do not have to understand the peculiarities of many different display terminals, since all actual displays can be treated as mere instances of the VGD. For example, if the VGD incorporates the idea of clipping, then whether or not clipping is directly supported on any given piece of hardware is irrelevant to the applications programmer.

The VGD, therefore, performs a number of roles crucial to the understanding of graphics systems supporting a range of physical devices controlled by a central software library of functions. These roles can be summarized as follows.

(1) The VGD is the sum total of assumptions about the physical characteristics and performance capabilities of devices that can be driven by the software. The display space is assumed to be flat and rectangular. Instructions are obeyed more or less immediately; for example, when a device receives a *WriteLine* instruction the line is displayed *now*, and not at some time in the future. These physical parameters of devices are often only implicit in a description of a VGD – as they are obvious. Nevertheless, they are important. For example, it is perfectly admissible to build a VGD model based on the assumption that 3D holograms could be generated. However, with today's technology such a VGD, and therefore the library itself, could not be implemented because real graphics devices supporting these features do not yet exist.

(2) The VGD includes a specification of a set of attributes and operations. For example, it may be specified that the display space is addressed by a rectangular coordinate system with (0, 0) at the bottom left-hand corner and only integer coordinates being possible. In addition, the device may be required to support a minimal set of colours. The operations include the types of graphical output that can be generated and also the possible styles of such output (for example, lines of varying degrees of thickness, text in different fonts). Higher order operations such as clipping may also be included in the model.

It should be realized in this context that a VGD may be parameterized in the sense that variations on the basic model are permitted. It would be sensible to parameterize the VGD on at least spatial and colour resolution. For example, it would be pointless to specify that the VGD support, say, 256 colours, for this would immediately rule out a large number of real devices used as a realization of the VGD. The number of colours supported would be a VGD parameter.

(3) The VGD provides an interface between the applications programmers who use the graphics system and the real graphics display devices supported. The programmers only have to understand that *any* graphics device used will behave according to the model provided by the VGD. But this is not quite the whole story. In principle, the true capabilities of any piece of hardware are hidden from the library user. However, if a particular device does happen to directly support the operations specified by the VGD, then the user will notice this in performance terms. For example, if the VGD requires that solid fill areas may be generated, then a device that has the solid fill capability available internally will (usually) fill areas faster than a device not having this immediate capability.

(4) The VGD provides an interface between the demands of the graphics system and the true functionality of the real devices to be used by the system. The system implementation is designed as if all the real devices were spawned from the VGD model. How this ideal state of affairs is to be matched against reality is, in a sense, not the concern of the graphics library.

3.4 Specification of a Simple Graphics Library

The ideas just expressed will now be illustrated by outlining the construction of a simple graphics library suitable for the generation of wire-frame displays – that is, pictures made up entirely of straight lines. A rather sophisticated wire-frame drawing is shown in Plate 1. Although Chapter 2 suggested a number of functions suitable for the description of such pictures, the attention here is restricted to the following set of function headings.

3.4.1 Data Types

type Boundary = real*real*real*real;
type Point = real*real;

Two data types are introduced by the library. The *Boundary* type is used to represent the boundaries for windows and viewports. The convention adopted is that the four real values are in the order (*xmin*, *xmax*, *ymin*, *ymax*).

3.4.2 Viewing

SetWindow: int*Boundary → Void;

SetWindow(*i*, *w*)
sets the *i*th window to the boundary values in *w*, where *w* consists of (*xmin*, *xmax*, *ymin*, *ymax*).

SetViewport: int*Boundary → Void;

SetViewport(*i*, *v*)
sets the *i*th viewport to the boundary values in *v*, where *v* consists of (*xmin*, *xmax*, *ymin*, *ymax*).

SelectNtran: int → Void;

SelectNtran i
selects the *i*th window and viewport pair to be the current window and viewport. Together, the window and viewport form the **normalization transformation**.

InqWindow: int → Boundary;

InqWindow i
returns the boundary associated with the *i*th window.

InqViewport: int → Boundary;

InqViewport i
returns the boundary associated with the *i*th viewport.

InqNtranNum: Void → int;

InqNtranNum ( )
returns the current normalization transformation number.

The meanings of window and viewport used here are the same as discussed in Chapter 2: a window represents an applications coordinate space and a viewport is a place on the display to which a window is mapped. The viewport is expressed in NDC, the unit square, where (0, 0) represents the bottom left-hand corner of the display space and (1, 1) the top right-hand corner of the largest square. However, in contrast to Chapter 2, the application is here allowed to define a number of windows and viewports, each associated with an integer value. When the *SelectNtran* (select a normalization transformation) function is executed, its argument (i) selects the ith window/viewport pair to be the current window and viewport. The convention adopted is that these normalization transformations are numbered by non-negative values ($i \geq 0$) and that the default, initial value for all windows and viewports is the unit square, and the initial transformation number is 0. The **inquiry functions**, *InqWindow*, *InqViewport* and *InqNtranNum* allow an applications program to inquire the window and viewport boundaries for a particular index.

The window also acts as a clipping region, and all graphical output is therefore always clipped to the window. The viewing model specifies that graphical output is transformed from WC to NDC and then, for each graphics device in use, transformed to DC and displayed. There are three places in which clipping might occur: the WC lines may be clipped to the window; the transformed NDC lines may be clipped to the viewport; or, finally, the DC transformed lines may be clipped to the viewport as expressed in DC. The viewport transformed to DC is termed the **DC clipping region**. Mathematically, the final result is the same irrespective of the stage at which the clipping takes place. The reader is invited to consider the various advantages and disadvantages of the three options (see Exercise 3.1). In this chapter, the last of the three options is used.

3.4.3 Graphical Output

Polyline: Point sequence → Void;

Polyline p
describes the line sequence $p[0]$ to $p[1]$ to ... to $p[n - 1]$, where $n = Length(p)$ ($n \geq 2$).

3.4.4 Device Control

OpenDevice: int → Void;

OpenDevice i
initialises the graphics device associated with type number i, where i is a non-negative integer. The device is put into the 'open' state.

ActivateDevice: int → Void;

ActivateDevice i
activates the graphics device associated with type number i. Activation means that graphical output (i.e., polylines) may henceforth appear on this

device. A device can only be activated if it has already been opened by the application of *OpenDevice* to this type. The device is then put into the 'active' state.

DeactivateDevice: int → Void;

DeactivateDevice i
deactivates a graphics device previously put into the active state by a call to *ActivateDevice*. Subsequent graphical output (i.e., polylines) will not appear on this device. The device is put into the 'open' state.

CloseDevice: int → Void;

CloseDevice i
closes a device in the 'open' state, putting it into the 'closed' state.

These functions are required in the event that the library supports several graphics devices. Each graphics device is associated with a unique **type number**, which identifies its type to the overall system. Initially, all devices are in a 'closed' state, but they may be put into the 'open' state by application of the *OpenDevice* function to the appropriate type number. In the simple system described in this chapter, little can be done with a device in the 'open' state – except close it or activate it. The latter means that the device is prepared to accept graphical output instructions – in this case *Polyline*.

3.4.5 System Control

OpenSystem: Void → Void;

OpenSystem ()
This initialises the overall graphics system. In particular, the windows and viewports are all initialised to the unit square. No other functions in the library may be applied before this function is used.

CloseSystem: Void → Void;

CloseSystem ()
The whole graphics system is closed down. This function cannot be legally applied while any device is in the 'open' or 'active' state.

The *OpenSystem* function is needed to ensure that all the system variables, in particular the windows and viewports, are initialised to the unit square, and the normalization transformation number to 0.

3.5 A Virtual Graphics Device for the Library

The suite of functions documented in Section 3.4 is intended to be implementable with any graphics device. However, to avoid the complications of differing device features, a VGD is defined. This is an abstract machine designed specifically so that it can meet the demands of the overall graphics system, while also bearing in mind that ultimately it has to be implementable in terms of real devices. The problem of device dependence is, however, deferred to the last instance.

The VGD has the following features:

(1) A flat rectangular display space addressed in integer device coordinates, with (0, 0) at the bottom left-hand corner.

(2) The VGD accepts the instruction to draw a line as clipped by a clipping region. The line endpoints and clipping region are expressed in integer coordinates.

(3) Lines displayed are visible against a background of different and contrasting colour. For example, the background may be white and the foreground (or graphical output) black.

Suppose *Ntran* is a function that maps a WC point to NDC according to the current window and viewport, and that *dtran* maps an NDC point into the DC appropriate for a particular device. The composition:

val *dntran* = *dtran* ∘ *Ntran*

thus provides the function *dntran* which maps a WC point directly to DC. Furthermore, if *p* is a sequence of WC points, then:

val *dcp* = *map dntran p*

is the sequence of points expressed in DC (the *map* function applies *dntran* to each point in the sequence *p*).

Now, if *clipregion* is the current viewport expressed in DC (in other words, the *dtran* function applied to a suitable representation of the viewport), then the way that the VGD works with respect to *Polyline* can be summarized as follows:

```
for 0 < i < Length p do
  let val line = [dcp[i − 1], dcp[i]]
  in
    DrawLine(clipregion, line)
  ni
od
```

The function *DrawLine* takes a line expressed as a sequence of two points, together with a clip region, and displays the clipped line on the display space of the graphics device. (Of course, if the line is entirely outside the clipping region, then nothing is displayed.)

3.6 The Library Implementation

The foregoing discussion has covered the intentions of the library in addition to the underlying VGD. Attention must now be focused on the implementation, which can be divided into five major components.

(1) *Global data* Variables are defined that are global to all functions in the implementation. This data is normally hidden from the applications program – that is, it is private to the implementation.

(2) *Utilities* A number of utility functions are defined that may be used by any of the functions in the implementation. These utilities are also private to the implementation.

(3) *Top-level functions* These are the only functions visible to the applications programmer – that is, those functions introduced in Section 3.4. To the applications programmer, these are the functions that may be applied and which are listed in the library documentation.

(4) *VGD driver functions* These functions are determined by and effectively define the VGD.

(5) *Installation and device-dependent (code generator) functions* These functions are used to install the system in an environment that includes a particular configuration of graphics devices. The functions include the **code generator**, so named because historically it served the purpose of sending instruction codes from a CPU to the graphics terminals.

These components will now be discussed in detail for the simple library constructed in this chapter.

3.6.1 Global Data

There are six global variables in the implementation.

- *window* is a store containing a sequence of window values each initialised to the unit square.
- *viewport* is a store containing a sequence of viewport values similarly initialised.

- *NtranNum* is a store containing the current normalization transformation number, initialised to 0.
- *Ntran* is a store containing a function that maps a WC point to an NDC point according to the current window and viewport. Initially, it is the identity function, since the initial window and viewport are the same.
- *OpenDeviceSet* is a store containing the set of type numbers corresponding to the currently open devices, initialised to be empty.
- *ActiveDeviceSet* is a store containing the set of type numbers corresponding to the currently active devices. (This will always be a subset of *OpenDeviceSet*.) It is initialised to be empty.

These variables are defined and initialised by the *OpenSystem* function:

```
fun OpenSystem () =
  val window = store (0.0, 1.0, 0.0, 1.0)~∞
  and viewport = store (0.0, 1.0, 0.0, 1.0)~∞
  and NtranNum = store 0
  and OpenDeviceSet = store ∅
  and ActiveDeviceSet = store ∅
  and Ntran = store (fn p : Point ⇒ p);
  InitialiseDeviceFunctions ()
nuf
```

Here, *window* and *viewport* contain unbounded sequences with each element equal to the 4-tuple (0.0, 1.0, 0.0, 1.0). As already mentioned, such 4-tuples (with type name *Boundary*) represent the (*xmin*, *xmax*, *ymin*, *ymax*) values of a window or viewport. The sets in *OpenDeviceSet* and *ActiveDeviceSet* are each initialised to be empty. *Ntran* is a store containing a function which given a *Point p* delivers *p* (that is, the identity function for the *Point* type). This function is defined using the lambda notation briefly discussed in Appendix A. After initialising the global variables, the *InitialiseDeviceFunctions* is invoked to initialise the device-dependent functions used by the system.

3.6.2 Utility Functions

The utility functions used are only listed here as their details are, for the most part, the subject of Chapter 4. The convention adopted is that these functions begin with the characters *u_*.

New data types are introduced for the representation of points, lines and boundaries in DC in the following way:

```
type DC_Point = int*int;
type DC_Line = [DC_Point,  DC_Point];
type DC_ClipRegion = int*int*int*int;
```

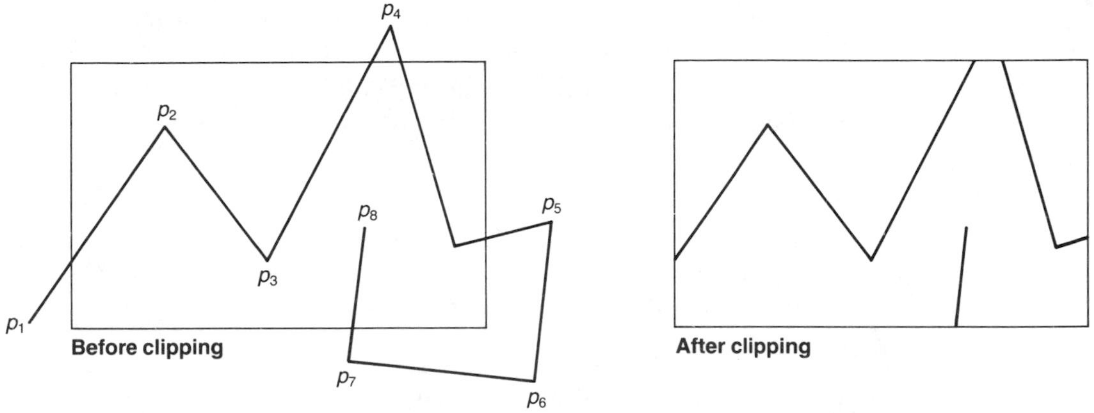

Figure 3.1
The *clip* function.
Note that [*p*5, *p*6] and [*p*6, *p*7] become nil on clipping.

The first two utility functions are for composing the normalization transformation and the device transformation from NDC to DC.

Consider:

u_ntran: Boundary*Boundary → (Point → Point);

u_ntran when applied to a window and viewport (w, v) results in a function that maps a WC point to the corresponding NDC point. For example, suppose that w = (−3.0, 3.0, 0.0, 10.0) and v = (0.0, 0.5, 0.5, 1.0), then *u_ntran*(w, v) is a function that maps a point from WC to NDC assuming the window w and viewpoint v. Therefore:

u_ntran(w, v) (−3.0, 0.0) = (0.0, 0.5)

Next, consider:

u_dtran: int*int → (Point → DC_Point);

u_dtran when applied to the width and height of the display space for a particular device results in a function that maps an NDC point to the corresponding DC point for this device. For example, if the display space is 1000*1000, then:

u_dtran(1000, 1000) (0.5, 0.5) = (500, 500)

The function used for clipping lines is as follows (see Figure 3.1):

u_clip: DC_ClipRegion*DC_Line → DC_Line;

u_clip(*clipregion*, [*p*1, *p*2]) clips the DC line [*p*1, *p*2] to the given *clipregion*. A general version of this function would actually take a point sequence of any length and deliver the clipped polyline. However, in this chapter it is assumed that only single lines are catered for at a time.

Finally, the function that converts a DC line into a sequence of pixel positions is as follows:

```
u_LineToPixels: DC_Line → DC_Point sequence;
```

u_LineToPixels [*p*1, *p*2] results in a sequence of DC pixel positions representing the line [*p*1, *p*2]. It is required for pixel-based devices that do not directly support the generation of lines.

3.6.3 Top-Level Functions

The first function belonging in this category is *OpenSystem*, which was defined in Section 3.6.1 along with the global variables to be initialised.

The device control functions are very simple:

```
OpenDevice: int → Void;
fun OpenDevice d =
  if d ∉ ?OpenDeviceSet ⇒
    InitialiseDevice d;
    OpenDeviceSet := OpenDeviceSet ∪ {d}
  fi
nuf

fun ActivateDevice d =
  if (d ∈ ?OpenDeviceSet) ∧ (d ∉ ?ActiveDeviceSet) ⇒
    ActiveDeviceSet := ActiveDeviceSet ∪ {d}
  fi
nuf
```

The *OpenDevice* function initialises the device and records the device type number in the set of open devices, provided that the device is not already open. *ActivateDevice* simply records the device as active, provided it is currently open, but not active. The reader is invited to complete the definition of the remaining device control functions as an exercise (see Exercise 3.2).

The next set of functions are concerned with the normalization transformations. The *SetWindow* function:

```
SetWindow: int*Boundary → Void;
fun SetWindow(i, w) =
  window[i] := w
nuf
```

replaces the global data *window* by a sequence that has the new boundary *w* in the *i*th place. For simplicity, no error checking is specified in these rule definitions; that is, *i* must be a non-negative integer and the boundary *w* must be such that if (*xmin*, *xmax*, *ymin*, *ymax*) = *w*, then *xmin* < *xmax* and *ymin* < *ymax* (see Exercise 3.3). The only difference between this function and the following *SetViewport* function is that the error checking on *v* in the latter must be more extensive, since the viewport must be within the unit square:

```
SetViewport: int*Boundary → Void;
fun SetViewport(i, v) =
  viewport[i] := v
nuf
```

SetWindow and *SetViewport* therefore simply update the global data maintaining the window and viewport records.

SelectNtran, the next function, is needed to enable an application to select a current window and viewport combination:

```
SelectNtran: int → Void;
fun SelectNtran i =
  NtranNum := i;
  Ntran := u_ntran(window[i], viewport[i])
nuf
```

This function redefines the global variable *NtranNum*, which records the current normalization transformation number. In addition, the utility function *u_ntran* is used to redefine the global variable *Ntran* to contain a function that maps a WC point to the corresponding NDC point according to the newly selected window and viewport.

The remaining functions concerned with the normalization transformation are the inquiry functions. The reader is invited to complete the definition of these functions as an exercise (see Exercise 3.4).

The *Polyline* function is, in a sense, the centre piece of the entire library, for without it nothing can be displayed. Its rule can be given as follows:

```
Polyline: Point sequence → Void;
fun Polyline p =
  forall d ∈ ?ActiveDeviceSet do
    DriverPolyline(d, p)
  od
nuf
```

This is a surprisingly simple definition. The top-level *Polyline* function merely sends the point sequence to all the VGDs in the active state. The function *DriverPolyline* belongs to the VGD driver component of the library which is discussed next.

3.6.4 VGD Driver Functions

The VGD, as already stated, is an abstract machine. Like any machine it must be operated or 'driven' in some manner, a term usually used in graphics (and in other similar contexts in computing) in connection with the operation of peripheral devices such as printers. All machines have an engine powered by some kind of fuel. The VGD is no exception: its 'engine' consists of the functions that implement it, while its 'fuel' consists of the code generator functions used to send instructions to the real graphics devices underlying the VGDs.

To represent such an arrangement, a new data structure has to be introduced, which is used to describe any particular real device in terms of its corresponding VGD driver. The required data structure is called *DeviceFunctions* and is a sequence of 3-tuples, where each element in the tuple is a certain function. Although this seems complicated, it is actually quite straightforward.

Device type *i* occupies the *i*th place in the *DeviceFunctions* sequence. Each element of the sequence consists of a tuple of three functions, say *f*1, *f*2 and *f*3. These functions have types as follows:

f1: Point → DC_Point;
f1 is used to map an NDC point into the corresponding DC point according to the display resolution (width and height) of the real graphics device.

f2: DC_Line → Void;
f2 is used to send the instructions to display a line on the real graphics device.

f3: DC_ClipRegion → Void;
f3 is used to send the instructions to set the current clipping region on the real graphics device.

Hence, *DeviceFunctions* is a sequence with elements of the type:

(Point → DC_Point)*(DC_Line → Void)*(DC_ClipRegion → Void)

For example:

val *DeviceFunctions* = [(*f*01, *f*02, *f*03), (*f*11, *f*12, *f*13), (*f*21, *f*22, *f*23)]

in the case of three graphics devices, where the functions *f*01, *f*02 and so on have been suitably defined for these devices.

Assuming a definition for *DeviceFunctions*, the VGD driver function for *Polyline* may now be given in full:

```
DriverPolyline: int*(Point sequence) → Void;
fun DriverPolyline(d, p) =
  let val (dtran, displayLine, clip) = DeviceFunctions[d]
     and (x1, x2, y1, y2) = ?viewport[?NtranNum]
  in
    let val [(cx1, cy1), (cx2, cy2)] = map dtran [(x1, y1), (x2, y2)]
       and DrawLine = displayLine ○ clip
       and dcp = map (dtran ○ ?Ntran) p
    in
      let val clipregion = (cx1, cx2, cy1, cy2)
      in
        for 0 < i < Length dcp do
          let val line = [dcp[i − 1], dcp[i]]
          in
            DrawLine(clipregion, line)
          ni
        od
      ni
    ni
  ni
nuf
```

Pattern matching is used to unscramble the device functions for the *d*th device type, and also for the current viewport. These values are used in expressions for mapping the viewport into DC, obtaining a *DrawLine* function as the composition of the *clip* and *displayLine* device functions. In addition, the WC points in sequence *p* are transformed to the DC point sequence *dcp*. The *clipregion* is expressed in the appropriate format and finally the values obtained are used in an iteration through the edges of the polyline.

This driver function for *Polyline* is quite device independent. The features of the real graphics devices used in the library are communicated to the function via the *DeviceFunctions* data. The considerations that go into constructing the *DeviceFunctions* are discussed in the next section.

3.6.5 Installation

As mentioned earlier, the device-dependent aspects of the library system are introduced in the last instance. To make this discussion more concrete, a detailed example is given here. The example chosen has three different graphics devices called device type 0, device type 1 and device type 2. Table 3.1 summarizes their capabilities.

Table 3.1 Three graphics devices.

Device Type	Resolution	Line Drawing	Line Clipping	Description
0	320 × 256	not supported	not supported	pixel based
1	768 × 512	supported	not supported	vector
2	800 × 1000	supported	supported	vector

DEVICE TYPE 0

This is a very simple graphics device, whose only facility is to set a pixel – not even line drawing is directly supported. The single code generator function for this device is:

D0_WritePixel: DC_Point → Void;

D0_WritePixel p
sets the pixel corresponding to the DC point p.

DEVICE TYPE 1

This device, assumed here to be vector based (not that this makes any particular difference), also has a single code generator function, but in this case to draw a line:

D1_DrawLine: DC_Line → Void;

D1_DrawLine line
generates the line on the display space.

DEVICE TYPE 2

This device is also assumed to be vector based, and has capabilities very similar to those of the VGD. It supports line drawing and clipping with two code generator functions:

D2_SetClip: DC_ClipRegion → Void;

D2_SetClip clipregion
sets the device into a mode where subsequent lines are clipped to the given clipping region.

D2_DrawLine: DC_Line → Void;

D2_DrawLine line
generates the line as clipped by the current clipping region.

To define the *InitialiseDevice* installation function, the case analysis form of the function definition is used. This approach allows a function rule to be specified for each of a number of different cases of argument values. In this situation, the values are integers representing the device types. In the ML language, on which the abstract language used here is based, it is possible to define functions in this way. However, in the present application the ML interpreter would accept the function definition, but warn that not all cases of the argument have been catered for. This is not surprising since only the integers 0, 1 and 2 are considered – for the example assumes that there are only three real devices in use in this installation of the library.

```
fun InitialiseDeviceFunctions () =
  val DeviceFunctions =
  let val f1 = u_dtran(400, 400)
      and f2 = fn l : DC_Line ⇒ ()
      and f3 = fn (c : DC_ClipRegion, l : DC_Line) ⇒ ()
  in
    (f1, f2, f3)~∞
  ni
nuf

fun InitialiseDevice 0 =
  val DeviceFunctions =
  let val funcs = (
                   u_dtran(320, 256),
                   (map D0_WritePixel) ○ u_LineToPixels,
                   u_clip
                  )
  in
    (DeviceFunctions[0] = funcs)
  ni
|
   InitialiseDevice 1 =
  val DeviceFunctions =
  let val funcs = (
                   u_dtran(768, 512),
                   D1_DrawLine,
                   u_clip
                  )
  in
    (DeviceFunctions[1] = funcs)
  ni
|
   InitialiseDevice 2 =
  val DeviceFunctions =
  let val funcs = (
                   u_dtran(800, 1000),
                   fn x : DC_Line ⇒ (),
                   fn (clip : DC_ClipRegion, line : DC_Line) ⇒
```

```
                    (D2_SetClip clip; D2_DrawLine line)
                )
    in
      (DeviceFunctions[2] = funcs)
    ni
  nuf
```

InitialiseDeviceFunctions has the task of setting up *DeviceFunctions* as an unbounded sequence of the appropriate type. The *InitialiseDevice* function is then defined, case by case, for the three types of device assumed. In each case, the *u_dtran* utility is used to obtain the correct function for mapping NDC points to DC points, according to the display resolution.

For device type 0, the *u_LineToPixels* utility is used to convert lines to a sequence of points, and then the code generator function for writing pixels is applied to each point in the sequence. Since device type 0 cannot clip lines, the utility *u_clip* is used for this purpose.

Device type 1, on the other hand, can draw lines, but not clip. Therefore, the code generator function is used for the line drawing, and the utility for clipping.

In the case of the more sophisticated device type 3, the line drawing component of the tuple is set to a function that results in the void result () when given a *DC_Line*. The reason for this is that the clipping component first sends out the clip region to the device by using the code generator, and then sends out the required line. Checking back to see how this is used in *DriverPolyline*, it can be seen that the correct result is achieved: for in the driver, the line drawing and clipping components are combined to produce a single function that clips and draws the clipped line. (The inefficiency introduced by sending out a clipping region with every line is addressed in Exercise 3.5.)

The *InitialiseDevice* function clearly has the role of bringing the device dependencies into the system. The device-dependent component is only attached to the system (by affecting the appropriate entry into *DeviceFunctions*) at the time a device is opened. For example, if device type 2 is never used by a particular applications program, then the corresponding *DeviceFunctions* entry will never be constructed.

To summarize, *DeviceFunctions* is initialised to a sequence of 3-tuples of functions of the correct type. When a device is opened, the appropriate 3-tuple of functions for driving this device is copied into the place in the sequence corresponding to its type number. When graphical output (polylines) is generated, the driver function obtains these functions from the sequence and uses them in a way so as to meet the operational requirements of the VGD underlying the library. Of course, this is a very simple library, but the principles of its implementation can be extended to more realistic and complex systems. The changes would be in terms of quantity rather than method.

3.7 Device Independence

Section 3.6 was concerned with the implementation of a simple graphics library. It was seen that a library has a number of interrelated components, starting with the specification and documentation of the top-level functions. A VGD is designed as an abstract machine capable of supporting the tasks required by the library, as well as realistic implementation on real devices. The implementation of the library involves global data, driver functions and installation functions. Many details, especially those relating to functions that implement special algorithms, represented in the utilities component of the implementation, have been deferred until Chapter 4.

The *DeviceFunctions* data structure provides an interface between the demands of the VGD driver and the true capabilities of the devices to be used by the library. Each element of *DeviceFunctions* consists of a series of function definitions, special to the corresponding device. These functions are ultimately responsible for generating graphical output on the display. In most cases, this will mean sending special codes and data to the device defining the operations to be carried out on the data supplied.

The purpose of this chapter is to show how it is possible to design a graphics library that is device independent. Of course, this is not truly possible, because computer graphics ultimately depends on displaying pictures on devices. Device independence means that device-dependent features are incorporated in the library in such a way that they can, so to speak, be factored out and treated independently of the rest of the system. The library is built on an abstract model. Device-dependent features are used in such a way so as to make real devices behave according to the requirements of the abstract model.

A good test of the extent to which the attempt at device independence has been successful is to examine the upheaval caused to the library by the addition of a new device into the system. Suppose then that a device type 4 is to be added. The only change necessary is the addition of a new case in the *InitialiseDevice* function.

The reader may have noted that a major dimension of computer graphics is not catered for in the library – namely, graphical input. This is discussed in Exercise 3.6, where the reader is invited to use the principles discussed in this chapter to provide an interactive capability.

3.8 The GKS Workstation Concept

The Graphical Kernel System (GKS) is itself a library of functions for computer graphics. At its core is an explicit VGD model, in GKS terminology a *workstation*. A workstation is a VGD with a certain minimal set of capabilities. The capabilities of a GKS workstation depend on the *level* of GKS implemented and on the **workstation category**. The level of the GKS refers to one of nine possible conformance configurations, as discussed in Chapter 8.

The workstation category is one of *output*, *input*, *outin*, *workstation-independent segment storage*, *metafile output* and *metafile input*. The last three of these are special, non-graphical workstations, which are discussed in Chapters 7 and 8. An output workstation is one that supports graphical output, but not interactive graphics. An example of a graphics device that might be presented to GKS as an output workstation is a pen plotter. An input workstation is one that is capable of interaction, but cannot be used for displaying graphical output. An example of such a device is a digitizer (see Section 17.2.2), which can be used to input coordinates, but which cannot be used, say, as the destination of a call to *Polyline*. An outin workstation is one that can be used for both graphical output and input. Most graphics devices fall into this category.

A GKS workstation has one connected rectangular display space and, if it is an input or outin workstation, at least one associated graphical input device capable of supporting a number of logical interactions (see Chapter 5). The functional capabilities of the workstation are covered in this book as the occasion arises.

Generally (taking the highest level of GKS), the workstation can display a number of graphical output primitives (for drawing lines, filling areas, text and so on); the output primitives can be drawn using various attributes; the geometric parameters to the output primitives are expressed in WC that are passed through a viewing pipeline, which includes clipping, before being displayed on the device; and output primitives can be grouped and treated together in segments.

On the input side, each workstation supports at least one logical input device for each of six classes of input, using one of three modes of interaction. An example of an input class is a locator, an input device that can return a WC position. Discussion of modes of interaction is left to Chapter 5.

In the library system discussed earlier in this chapter, global variables were used as a means of maintaining information about the state of the system. For example, the normalization transformation function, window and viewport definitions, as well as the current normalization transformation number, were stored. *DeviceFunctions* stores definitions of the functions to be used by the different devices.

GKS maintains the system status by a set of **state lists**. These are data structures that store information about the states of the overall system, the various workstations and other devices. The **GKS state list** consists of those global system variables that are device independent. For example, the window and viewport definitions and the current normalization transformation number are stored in the GKS state list. It also stores the set of currently open and active workstations as well as maintaining information about a large number of other system variables.

For each workstation, GKS maintains a **workstation description table**. This is like the *DeviceFunctions* sequence in the sense that this data structure holds information on fixed properties of the workstation, such as the display space resolution. However, it does not, strictly speaking, hold information about the actual properties of the underlying device of which the workstation is a virtual image. The workstation description table gives information about the workstation (which is an abstract thing), not about the real device. The other data structures used by GKS are discussed in their appropriate context.

The GKS data structures, such as the workstation description table, are not directly accessible to the applications programmer. An entry can only be changed on successful execution of a GKS function. For example, the entry giving the value of a viewport can only be affected by a call to the GKS *SetViewport* function. GKS provides a large number of functions to allow the programmer to obtain information about the values stored in these data structures. These functions, as already mentioned, are called inquiry functions. For example, there is a function to find out the current normalization transformation number from the GKS state list. In Pascal, this is represented as:

```
{Inquire Current Normalization Transformation Number}
procedure GInqCurNormtranNum(var errorind : integer;
                             var number : GTint0);
```

The *errorind* parameter is provided in every inquiry function (except for one) and returns an error code depending on whether the information required is available. If this procedure is successfully used, then *number* holds the value of the current normalization transformation number (which is a non-negative integer, hence the *GTint*0 type).

GKS provides functions for opening and activating workstations. In Pascal, these are defined by the following procedures:

```
{Open Workstation}
procedure GOpenWs(
                  wsid       : GTWsId;     {workstation identifier}
                  connection : GAConnId;   {workstation connection
                                            identifier}
                  wstype     : GTWsType    {workstation type}
                 );

{Activate Workstation}
procedure GActivateWs(
                      wsid : GTWsId
                     );
```

The types *GTWsId* and *GTWsType* are defined as integer in the Pascal interface to GKS. The type *GAConnId* is a fixed length string type.

The **workstation type** parameter identifies to GKS the type of workstation being opened and informs the system as to which workstation description table to use. In effect, this has exactly the same meaning as the device type number used in the library implementation defined earlier in this chapter. Its crucial effect is that it informs the system as to which device functions to use for this workstation driver.

The workstation type numbers are implementation defined. A user of GKS has to consult the implementation documentation to find out what are the valid workstation type numbers. From the point of view of the user of the system, the workstation type identifies a particular class of graphics display equipment installed at the local site. From the point of view of the GKS system, the workstation type is only a way of informing the system which particular device functions are to be used.

The **workstation connection identifier** is another parameter with possible values that are implementation defined. The connection identifier informs the system as to the route by which information is to be sent to the graphics device. For example, the connection identifier might be the name by which an interface channel is known to the computer's operating system environment.

The **workstation identifier** is a user-chosen identifier (in Pascal an integer) for the particular workstation identified by the connection identifier and type. All subsequent references to the workstation are by means of this identifier. When a workstation is opened, by a call to the *GOpenWs* procedure, the workstation is, so to speak, 'brought to life'. The properties of the workstation are made known to GKS from the information in the workstation description table. Deep down in the system a device driver is allocated, and the device driver functions are used whenever any action is taken with reference to this workstation. As far as a programmer watching the unfolding of a program execution, the most noticeable event on execution of the open workstation function would be the clearing of the display space of the device corresponding to the workstation. The activate workstation function, on the other hand, puts the workstation in the active state, so that it is ready to receive graphical output. As in the case of the library discussed earlier, graphical output is routed to all active workstations.

Corresponding to *GOpenWs* and *GActivateWs* there are *GDeactivateWs* and *GCloseWs*. These each take the workstation identifier as their single parameter.

GKS itself is put into various possible states depending in part on the state of the workstations. Before any GKS functions can be properly used GKS must be opened. For this there is an 'Open GKS' function (*GOpenGKS* in Pascal). The system is then in the state 'GKS open'. When a workstation is opened, the system is put in the state 'At least one workstation open'. When a workstation is activated, then the system is put into the state 'At least one workstation active'. As workstations are deactivated and closed, the system drops back into earlier states, until finally, when the 'Close GKS' (*GCloseGKS*) function is called, GKS is put into its initial 'GKS closed' state. (There is another state, but this will be discussed in Chapter 7.)

To complete this section, the remaining functions defined in the library are shown in GKS Pascal:

```
type GTint0 = 0..MAXINT;
     GTint1 = 1..MAXINT;
     GTint2 = 2..MAXINT;
     GRBound = record
                 LeftBound, RightBound,
                 LowerBound, TopBound : real
               end;
     GRPoint  = record
                 x, y : real
               end;
{Set Window}
procedure GSetWindow(ntrannum : GTint1; window : GRBound);
{Set Viewport}
procedure GSetViewport(ntrannum : GTint1; viewport : GRBound);
{Select Normalization Transformation}
procedure GSelectNormtran(ntrannum : GTint0);
{Polyline}
procedure GPolyline(numpoints : GTint2;
                    var points : array[min..max : integer] of GRPoint);
```

One different feature in the case of GKS is that the normalization transformation number 0 cannot be redefined by an applications program, so that it always refers to the unit square window and viewport. This is for a reason connected with graphical input, and is discussed in Chapter 5.

□□ EXAMPLE

This example illustrates the use of the library functions to carry out the simple task of drawing a border around the currently selected window. The example is shown first of all using the abstract notation and then in GKS Pascal.

It is important to realize that the data structures underpinning a library are not directly accessible to the applications program. As mentioned earlier, the GKS data structures can be changed only by successful application of GKS functions, and can be examined only by the use of the inquiry functions. To draw a border around the current window, whatever that may be, it is necessary to find out what the window coordinates are. One way of doing this is to make the applications program responsible for 'remembering' the state of the system, in particular the list of all the windows and viewports. This is inconvenient (a library is supposed to be helpful) and wasteful, since the library implementation itself maintains this information. The applications program is refused direct access to the library environments (why should this be the case? – see Exercise 3.11), so the library itself must provide access functions. The following defines an additional function based on those provided by the library to return the current window setting. (There is no directly corresponding GKS inquiry function, but see Exercise 3.12.)

```
fun CurrentWindow () =
  let val i = InqNtranNum ()
  in
    InqWindow i
  ni
nuf
```

Now a *DrawBorder* function may be easily defined:

```
fun DrawBorder () =
  let val (x1, x2, y1, y2) = CurrentWindow ()
  in
    Polyline[(x1, y1), (x2, y1), (x2, y2), (x1, y2), (x1, y1)]
  ni
nuf
```

The following Pascal program defines a procedure *DrawBorder* which is to draw a border around the current window. It illustrates the GKS functions discussed in this chapter. The line *include 'gksdefs'* is included to highlight the fact that every GKS Pascal implementation must provide some way of importing the GKS procedure and data type declarations into an applications program. The *include* directive will be assumed throughout this book.

```
program DrawBorderExample(input, output);
include 'gksdefs';
procedure DrawBorder(var error : integer);
var
  ntran             : GTint0;
  window, viewport  : GRBound;
  p                 : array[1..5] of GRPoint;
```

```
begin
  {find out the current normalization transformation number}
  GInqCurNormtranNum(error, ntran);
  if error = 0 then
  {find corresponding window}
  GInqNormtran(ntran, error, window, viewport);
  if error = 0 then
  begin
    with window do
    begin
      p[1].x := LeftBound;  p[1].y := LowerBound;
      p[2].x := RightBound; p[2].y := LowerBound;
      p[3].x := RightBound; p[3].y := UpperBound;
      p[4].x := LeftBound;  p[4].y := UpperBound;
    end;
    p[5] := p[1];
    GPolyline(5, p);
  end;
end;

procedure example;
const
  display    = 1;        {any integer will do}
  connection = 'port1';  {implementation defined}
  wstype     = 500;      {implementation defined}
  errorfile  = 1;

var
  window, viewport  : GRBound;
  p, q              : array[1..2] of GRPoint;
  error             : integer;

begin
  GOpenGKS(errorfile, GCdefmemory);
  GOpenWs(display, connection, wstype);
  GActivateWs(display);
  with window do
  begin
    LeftBound   := -10.0; RightBound  := 10.0;
    LowerBound  := 0.0;   UpperBound  := 100.0;
  end;
  with viewport do
  begin
    LeftBound   := 0.2; RightBound  := 0.8;
    LowerBound  := 0.4; UpperBound  := 0.9;
  end;

  GSetWindow(1, window);
  GSetViewport(1, viewport);
  GSelectNormtran(1);
  DrawBorder(error);

  if error = 0 then
```

```
  begin
    {draw diagonals}
    with window do
    begin
      p[1].x := LeftBound;  p[1].y := LowerBound;
      p[2].x := RightBound; p[2].y := UpperBound;
      q[1].x := LeftBound;  q[1].y := UpperBound;
      q[2].x := RightBound; q[2].y := LowerBound;
    end;
    GPolyline(2, p);
    GPolyline(2, q);
  end;

  {deactivate and close workstations and GKS}
  GDeactivateWs(display);
  GCloseWs(display);
  GCloseGKS;
end;
{*******************************************************************}

{main}
begin
  example
end.
```

Summary

This chapter has considered some of the ideas used in the construction of an integrated and device-independent set of functions for computer graphics – a graphics library. The idea of a VGD plays a key role in this process. The library is defined so as to support this imaginary device, rather than any particular real device – and then only the implementation of the VGD is device dependent. These ideas were considered in an abstract way in the first part of the chapter, and then their embodiment in the GKS workstation concept was discussed as a particular example. Details of the library implementation were generally avoided, as these are discussed in the next chapter.

Exercises

3.1 Section 3.4.2 noted that there are three places where clipping might be applied: WC lines are clipped to the window before transformation to NDC; NDC lines are clipped to the viewport; or DC lines are clipped to the DC clipping region. Give some arguments for and against these various options.

3.2 Give the implementation of the complete set of device control functions and the *CloseSystem* function.

3.3 The function definitions of this chapter have ignored the possibility of invalid arguments to functions. Redefine the functions so that, for example, the possibility of incorrect window and viewport parameters is catered for.

3.4 Give the implementation of the complete set of inquiry functions.

3.5 The functions defined in this chapter suggest that for device type 2 the clipping region is reset on the device when each line is generated. This is highly inefficient. Suggest some ways in which this problem could be overcome.

3.6 The library only supports graphical output. Suppose that the following top-level function is introduced:

Locator: int*state → Point;

Locator(*d*, ..)
delivers a WC point, according to the position of a cursor on device d.

(The .. is the value associated with type *state*; in this case the position of the input device – a mouse, for example – which is reflected in the position of the cursor on the display.)

Now suppose that there is a code generator function for the locator. This behaves in such a way that when the appropriate instruction is received by the device, then the current cursor position is returned to the host computer. The point returned by this code generator function is in DC. Discuss the problems involved in implementing this locator function. Introduce a *level* concept into the library, so that it supports both output-only devices or alternatively only input/output devices. Discuss the implications for the VGD.

3.7 Consider the following addition to the library:

FillArea: Point sequence → Void;

Execution of this function generates a solid area fill demarcated by the closed polygon defined by the array of points *p*, as illustrated in Figure 2.6. Suppose that device type 2 can generate such a solid fill, but cannot perform the required clipping of the polygon, and device type 3 can clip and generate the solid fill (device type 1 being basic).

Show in detail how the abstract library implementation would be changed with the addition of this function.

3.8 This chapter has used an abstract programming notation to describe the principles involved in device-independent graphics systems. This programming notation was chosen to make this task easy. It would have been more difficult to explain the ideas if, for example, FORTRAN or Pascal had been used. Nevertheless, the unfortunate reality is that an imperative computer language would have to be used to achieve real results. The reader is invited to transcribe the ideas presented by means of the abstract programming notation into Pascal.

3.9 Use the GKS procedures introduced so far to write a program that generates a picture of a bicycle wheel.

3.10 Definition and selection of the normalization transformation has been treated here as device independent. This is certainly correct in the sense that the normalization transformation applies globally – it is the same for all devices. (This is not the case, for example, with the clipping region, which in GKS may be different across devices, even though the WC window is global.) However, it is possible for the normalization transformation functions to be provided as extra features built into devices. How would this change the structure of the library implementation?

3.11 What are the arguments for and against allowing an applications program direct access to library data structures? For example, in a Pascal implementation of GKS there will be an internal variable used to store the value of the current normalization transformation number. Why does GKS insist that the name of this variable be kept private, and that the only method for setting and inquiring the transformation number is by means of the GKS functions?

3.12 Using the two GKS inquiry functions given in Section 3.8, write a procedure that returns the value of the currently set window.

CHAPTER 4

SOME FUNDAMENTAL ALGORITHMS

Chapter 3 was concerned with the structure of device-independent graphics systems. Many of the component functions were defined, but their rules were not given – this was the case with the utilities. The purpose of this chapter is to give detailed definitions of these basic building block functions. These are concerned with implementing the normalization transformations and clipping, and converting lines and fill areas to pixel sequences.

4.1 Mapping Windows to Viewports: Normalization Transformations

The function *u_ntran* was introduced in Section 3.6.2 as one that takes as its argument a window and viewport pair, and results in a function that maps a WC point into a corresponding NDC point. To simplify the notation here, the resulting function is denoted by *Ntran*. This function therefore maps WC points to NDC for a given window and viewport. (In fact, the argument below does not rely on the viewport being in NDC.) For example:

```
val Ntran =
let val w = a window and v = a viewport
in
  u_ntran(w, v)
ni
```

Such a function must have the following properties if it is to be sensible.

(1) Any point that is on the boundary of the window must be mapped to the boundary of the viewport. Let:

$$(wx_1, wx_2, wy_1, wy_2)$$

represent the window limits and:

$$(vx_1, vx_2, vy_1, vy_2)$$

the viewport. Let (x, y) be a point in the window and (xv, yv) the corresponding point in the viewport. Then:

$$Ntran(wx_i, y) = (vx_i, yv) \qquad (i = 1, 2)$$

and:

$$Ntran(x, wy_i) = (xv, vy_i) \qquad (i = 1, 2)$$

This is illustrated in Figure 4.1.

(2) A straight line in the window is mapped to a straight line in the viewport. Let p_1, p_2 be two WC points, then it is required that any point on the line $[p_1, p_2]$ is mapped to a point on the line $[Ntran(p_1), Ntran(p_2)]$ in the viewport. This is shown in Figure 4.2.

(3) The viewport coordinate system is not rotated with respect to the window coordinate system. For example, a line that is horizontal in the window must be horizontal in the viewport, and obviously a similar relationship must hold for vertical lines. In particular, the two x axes and the two y axes must be parallel.

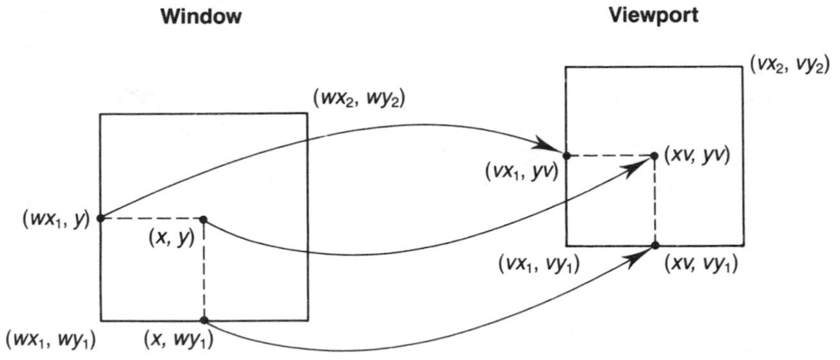

Figure 4.1
Window boundaries map to viewport boundaries.

Condition (2) implies that the window to viewport transformation must be linear, and together with condition (3) it follows that the relationship between (x, y) and (xv, yv) is of the form:

$$(xv, yv, 1) = (x, y, 1) \begin{pmatrix} a & 0 & 0 \\ 0 & c & 0 \\ b & d & 1 \end{pmatrix}$$

The boundary conditions given in (1) lead to linear simultaneous equations which can be solved for the constants (a, b, c, d). The solution leads to the result:

$$Ntran(x, y) = \left(vx_1 + \left(\frac{dvx}{dwx}\right)(x - wx_1),\ vy_1 + \left(\frac{dvy}{dwy}\right)(y - wy_1) \right)$$

where $dvx = vx_2 - vx_1$, $dwx = wx_2 - wx_1$, and similarly for dvy and dwy. The original function *u_ntran* can therefore be defined as follows:

```
u_ntran: Boundary*Boundary → (Point → Point);
fun u_ntran(w, v) p =
  let val (wx1, wx2, wy1, wy2) = w
      and (vx1, vx2, vy1, vy2)  = v
      and (x, y)                = p
  in
    let val dwx = wx2 − wx1 and dwy = wy2 − wy1
        and dvx = vx2 − vx1 and dvy = vy2 − vy1
    in
      (vx1 + (dvx/dwx)*(x − wx1), vy1 + (dvy/dwy)*(y − wy1))
    ni
  ni
nuf
```

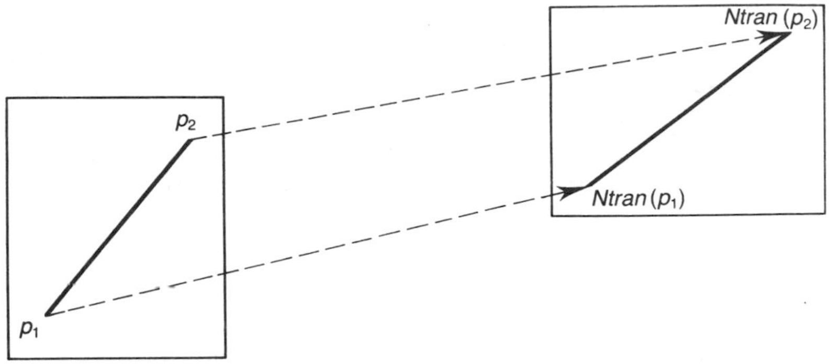

Figure 4.2
A straight line in the window maps to a straight line in the viewport.

(Note that error handling is not taken into account in this definition.) The reader should at this point verify that the function definition does satisfy requirements (1) to (3). (See Exercises 4.1 and 4.2.)

4.2 The Device Transformation

Figure 4.3 illustrates a use of the *Ntran* function. A circle is drawn in a window, which has a different aspect ratio to the viewport. (The **aspect ratio** is the ratio of height to width.) *Ntran* is a non-uniform transformation, which means that the *x* and *y* multipliers – that is, (dvx/dwx) and (dvy/dwy) in the function definition – may differ. This situation is acceptable for the normalization transformation, as it is fully under the control of the applications programmer. If a uniform transformation is required at this level, this can be ensured by the choice of corresponding windows and viewports which have the same aspect ratios (see Exercise 4.3).

However, if the same strategy is adopted for the device transformation, *Dtran*, this could lead to unacceptable results, beyond the control of the programmer. Suppose, for example, that *Dtran* is defined in an obvious way, returning the DC point:

$$(XMAX*x,\ YMAX*y)$$

where $(XMAX,\ YMAX)$ is the coordinate of the top right-hand corner of the display space, and $(x,\ y)$ is an NDC point. This choice for *Dtran* is simple and obvious because:

$$Dtran(0,\ 0) = (0,\ 0)$$

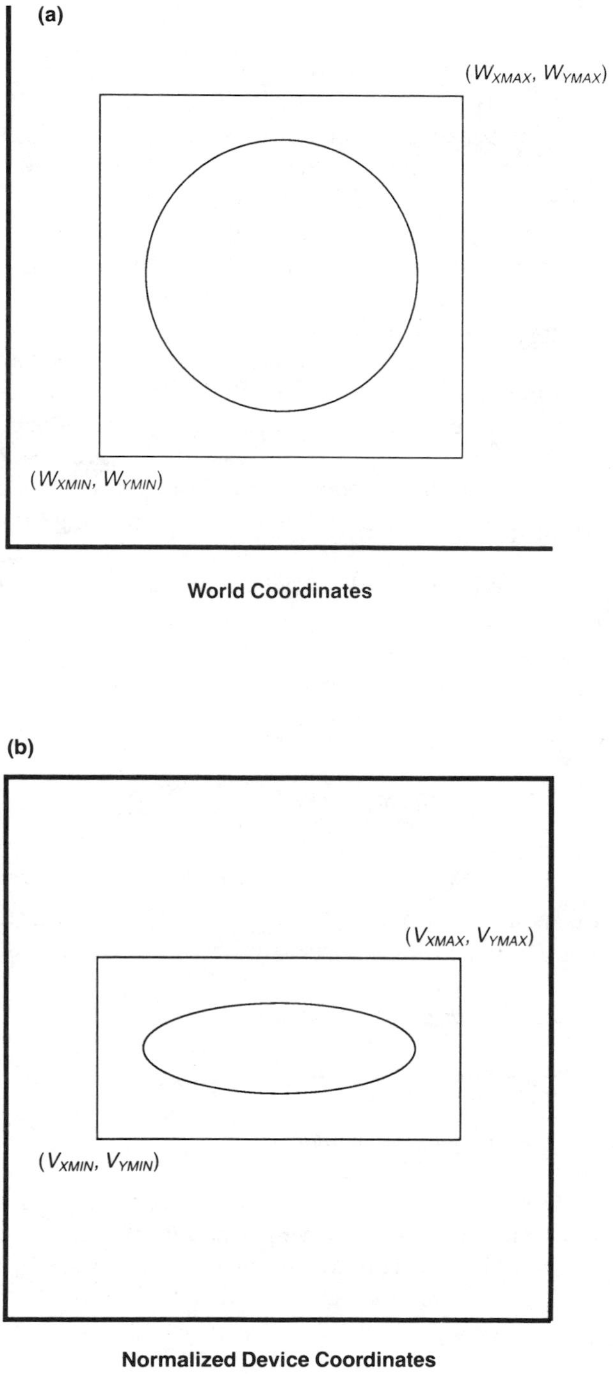

Figure 4.3
A circle appears as an ellipse in a non-uniform transformation.
(a) A circle in WC.
(b) The same circle represented in NDC.

and:

$$Dtran(1, 1) = (XMAX, YMAX)$$

However, as a consequence, the final appearance of the graphical output would be, in a sense, accidental, depending on the display resolution of the devices in use. For example, suppose the programmer has chosen corresponding windows and viewports to have the same aspect ratios, then even though in NDC space a circle would be represented as a circle, its actual appearance in DC space would depend on the aspect ratio of the display space. Hence, if a circle is sent to each of the three devices discussed in Chapter 3, it would appear as a *different* ellipse on each device.

To overcome this problem, the image, as it exists in the conceptual NDC space, must have the same appearance (with respect to x and y scaling) on all devices. An NDC circle must be displayed as a circle on *all* devices, irrespective of the display space dimensions. This requires that *Dtran* be a uniform transformation, where the multiplying factors for x and y are the same.

The generic definition of the device transformation, recalling *u_dtran* from Section 3.6.2, is therefore:

```
u_dtran: int*int → (Point → DC_Point);
fun u_dtran(width, height) p =
  let val (x, y) = p and scale = min (width − 1, height − 1)
  in
    (round(scale*x), round(scale*y))
  ni
nuf
```

(Note that it is assumed throughout that DC may be addressed as integers.) For example, for a particular device with *width* = 1024 and *height* = 800:

```
let val Dtran = u_dtran(1024, 800)
```

so that:

$$Dtran(x, y) = (round(x*799), round(y*799))$$

The effect of this approach is that NDC space is mapped to the largest square on the device display space which has its origin at the lowest left-hand corner of the display. This was discussed in Chapter 2 and illustrated in Figure 2.4, and, as mentioned there, this largest square is called the effective display space.

4.3 Clipping Lines

The function *u_clip* introduced in Section 3.6.2 requires the clipping of a line to a rectangular clip region, each specified in DC. In this chapter, for notational convenience, the function is referred to as *ClipLine*. The function *ClipLine* has three cases to consider (see Figure 4.4):

(1) The line may be completely outside the clipping region, in which case the function results in *nil*.

(2) The line may be entirely inside the clipping region, in which case the *ClipLine* function results in the original line. Note, however, that points exactly on the border of the clip region are counted as being inside.

(3) The line may be undecidable, in the sense that neither (1) nor (2) occur. In this case, the intersection of the line with one of the clipping edges is computed, and the *resulting* line is clipped.

The classical algorithm for clipping a line is known as the Cohen–Sutherland algorithm (Newman and Sproull, 1979). The importance of this approach is that it provides a simple method for quick determination of cases (1) and (2) – that is, there is a quick method for trivially rejecting or accepting a line. The function derived in this section is based on a form of the Cohen–Sutherland algorithm.

Any point can be classified as either lying inside the clipping region (including its border) or outside the region. If it is outside the region, then the set of edges it is outside may be determined as shown in Figure 4.5.

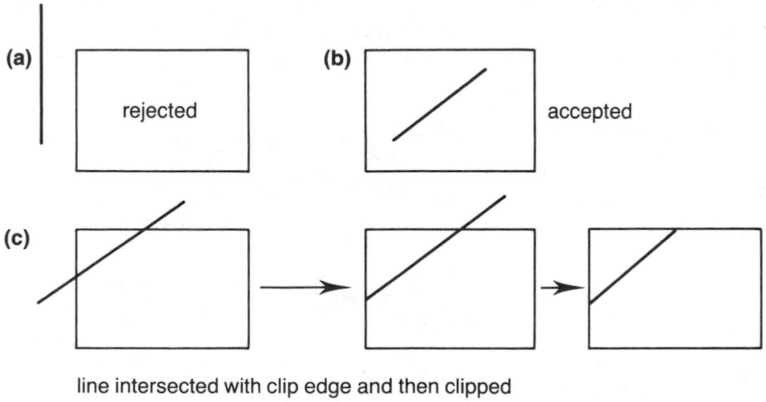

Figure 4.4
Clipping lines.

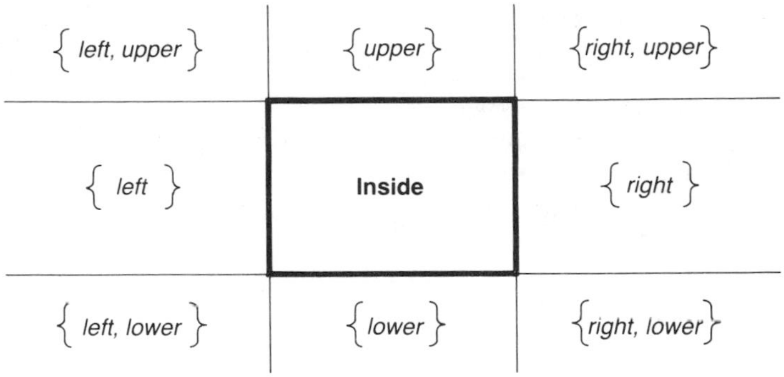

Figure 4.5
Classification of points in relation to the clip region.

Let *EdgeSet* be a function returning the set of edges that a point is outside. This function may be defined as:

```
type DC_ClipRegion = int*int*int*int;
type DC_Point  = int*int;

EdgeSet: DC_Point*DC_ClipRegion → int set;
fun EdgeSet(p, clipregion) =
  let val (x, y) = p and (left, right, lower, upper) = clipregion
  in
    let val isoutside = [x < left, x > right, y < lower, y > upper]
    in
      {edge | isoutside[edge]}
    ni
  ni
nuf
```

isoutside is an array of Boolean values, true or false. Hence the function results in the set of *edge* (an integer value 0, 1, 2, 3) such that *isoutside*[*edge*] is true. (Clearly, the function is making the identification 0 for left edge, 1 for right, and so on.)

Now consider a line [*p*1, *p*2] and suppose:

```
val out1 = EdgeSet(p1, clipregion)
```

and:

```
val out2 = EdgeSet(p2, clipregion)
```

Now, if *out*1 ∩ *out*2 (the intersection of the sets) is *not* empty, then the line must be outside of the clipping region. But if *out*1 ∪ *out*2 (the union of the sets) is empty, then the line lies entirely within the clipping region.

Otherwise, the union consists of the set of edges that the line crosses. First the intersection function is defined so that, given a line, the edge (i.e., 0 for left, 1 for right, and so on) and the clip region, the function delivers the point of intersection of the line with the edge:

```
Intersection: DC_Line*int*DC_ClipRegion → DC_Point;
fun Intersection(line, edge, clipregion)
  let val [(x1, y1), (x2, y2)] = line
      and (left, right, lower, upper) = clipregion
  in
    let val dx = x2 − x1 and dy = y2 − y1
        and c = [left, right, lower, upper]
    in
      if
           edge ∈ {0, 1} ⇒ (c[edge], y1 + (dy/dx)*(c[edge] − x1))
         □ edge ∈ {2, 3} ⇒ (x1 + (dx/dy)*(c[edge] − y1), c[edge])
      fi
    ni
  ni
nuf
```

Now, given a clip region and a line, the function *ClipLine* results in the clipped line:

```
ClipLine: DC_ClipRegion*DC_Line → DC_Line;
fun ClipLine(clipregion, line) =
  let val [p1, p2] = line
  in
    let val out1 = EdgeSet(p1, clipregion)
        and out2 = EdgeSet(p2, clipregion)
    in
      if
           out1 ∩ out2 ≠ ∅ ⇒
             nil
         □ out1 ∪ out2 = ∅ ⇒
             line
         □ out1 ∪ out2 ≠ ∅ ⇒
         let val edge ∈ out1 ∪ out2
         in
           let val pd = Intersection(line, edge, clipregion)
           in
             let val nl = if
                                    edge ∈ out1 ⇒ [p2, pd]
                                  □ edge ∈ out2 ⇒ [p1, pd]
                          fi
             in
```

```
                    ClipLine(clipregion, nl)
                  ni
                ni
              ni
            fi
          ni
        ni
      nuf
```

4.4 The GKS Viewing Pipeline

The **viewing pipeline** is the term used in GKS to denote the journey of a coordinate through the system: it starts out as a WC point generated by a call to an output primitive procedure, on through the normalization transformation stage, until finally passing through the device transformation when it is expressed in DC.

In GKS, the *Dtran* transformation has an extra level of complexity to that discussed so far. The **GKS workstation transformation** is a uniform transformation that maps a window on NDC to a viewport expressed in DC. This is a richer transformation than the *Dtran* function of Section 4.2, which mapped the whole of NDC on to the effective display space There are two advantages to this extra layer in the viewing pipeline:

(1) The applications program gains control of where the image is to appear on the display space.

(2) Different subregions of NDC can be simultaneously displayed on different devices, as the workstation transformation can be set up to be different on each of the workstations used by an application. For example, one device might be used to display a weather map of the whole of Europe, corresponding to the whole of NDC, while another display can be used simultaneously to display only that part of NDC that is a rectangle enclosing Great Britain.

The GKS Pascal procedures for the workstation transformation are as follows; Program 4.1 and Figure 4.6 illustrate their use.

```
{Set Workstation Window}
procedure GSetWsWindow(wsid : GTWsId; WsWindow : GRBound);

{Set Workstation Viewport}
procedure GSetWsViewport(wsid : GTWsId; WsViewport : GRBound);
```

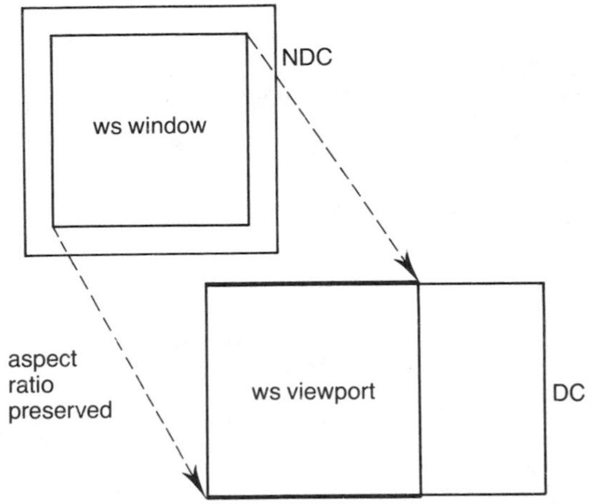

Figure 4.6
The workstation transformation.

Program 4.1 illustrates some important ideas in computer graphics. The effect of procedure *Star* is to generate a star-like shape consisting of four triangles attached to the sides of a square. The particular manner in which the star shape is constructed is instructive. It can be argued that there is one primitive object in the shape, which is a triangle. This primitive triangle is generated by the procedure *Triangle*, which draws it with the centre of its base at the origin, and in a vertical orientation. The displayed star shape is put together by transforming it into four different positions. First, the triangle is shifted from the origin vertically by an amount equal to half the base. The second triangle (looking anti-clockwise round the star) is obtained from the primitive triangle by first rotating it anti-clockwise by one right-angle, and then shifting it horizontally by the half-base distance. Similarly, the third (upside-down) triangle is obtained by rotating the primitive triangle through 180° and then shifting it vertically downwards. And similarly for the last triangle. The method used here is, for illustrative purposes, more complex than it needs to be.

This method is a simple illustration of the use of a transformation matrix to accomplish **graphics modelling**. It is implemented here using the *SetTran* and *Display* procedures: *SetTran* maintains a transformation for rotating and then shifting coordinates, relative to the origin; *Display* takes as input an array of points representing a primitive shape, applies the current modelling transformation to the points and then displays the transformed points using *Polyline*. These ideas of graphics modelling that use object descriptions as functions with points expressed in **master coordinates** and with the operation of **instances** via a **current transformation matrix** are discussed in Chapter 10.

```
Program wstran(input, output);
include 'gksdefs';
type Transformation = record
                        cosine, sine, dx, dy : real;
                      end;
var model : Transformation;
{*************************************************************************************}
procedure SetTran(xshift, yshift, rotation : real);
begin
  with model do
  begin
    cosine = cos(rotation);
    sine   = sin(rotation);
    dx     = xshift;
    dy     = yshift;
  end;
end;
{*************************************************************************************}
procedure Display(n : integer;
             var p : array[min..max : integer] of GRPoint);
var
  i : integer;
  xn, yn : real;
begin
  {rotate and shift points}
  for i := 1 to n do
  with p[i] do
  begin
    with model do
    begin
      xn := x*cosine - y*sine + dx;
      yn := x*sine + y*cosine + dy;
    end;
    x := xn;
    y := yn;
  end;
  GPolyline(n, p);
end;
{*************************************************************************************}
procedure Triangle(base, height : real);
var
  p : array[1..4] of GRPoint;
  halfbase : real;
begin
  halfbase := 0.5*base;
```

Program 4.1 Workstation transformation.

```
  with p[1] do begin x := -halfbase; y := 0.0    end;
  with p[2] do begin x :=  halfbase; y := 0.0    end;
  with p[3] do begin x :=  0.0;      y := heightend;
  p[4] := p[1];
  Display(4, p);
end;
{****************************************************************************************}

procedure Star(base, height : real);
const
  piover2 = 1.570796;
  pi      = 3.141593;
var
  halfbase : real;
  xshift, yshift, rotation : array[1..4] of real;
  i : integer;
begin
  halfbase := 0.5*base;
  xshift[1] := 0.0;       yshift[1] := halfbase;  rotation[1] := 0.0;
  xshift[2] := -halfbase; yshift[2] := 0.0;       rotation[2] := piover2;
  xshift[3] := 0.0;       yshift[3] := -halfbase; rotation[3] := pi;
  xshift[4] := halfbase;  yshift[4] := 0.0;       rotation[4] := -piover2;
  for i := 1 to 4 do
  begin
    SetTran(xshift[i], yshift[i], rotation[i]);
    Triangle(base, height);
  end;
end;
{****************************************************************************************}

procedure Show;
const
  ws1 = 1;
  ws2 = 2;
  wstype1  = 1;          {implementation-dependent values}
  wstype2  = 2;
  wsconn1 = 'wsconn1';
  wsconn2 = 'wsconn2';
  errorfile  = 1;
var
  height, base, dim : real;
  wcwindow, ws1window, ws2window : GRBound;
begin
  GOpenGKS(errorfile, GCdefmemunits);
  GOpenWs(ws1, conn1, wstype1);
  GOpenWs(ws2, conn2, wstype2);
  GActivateWs(ws1);
  GActivateWs(ws2);
```

Program 4.1 (cont.)

```
  height := 20.0; base := 15.0; {any values ok}
  dim := (height*base)/4;
  with wcwindow do
  begin
    LeftBound := -dim; RightBound := dim;
    LowerBound := -dim; UpperBound := dim;
  end;
  GSetWindow(1, wcwindow);
  GSelectNormTran(1);

  {Initialise the modelling transformation system}
  SetTran(0.0, 0.0, 0.0);

  {Set up the workstation transformations}
  with ws1window do
  begin
    LeftBound := 0.0; RightBound := 0.5;
    LowerBound := 0.0; UpperBound := 1.0;
  end;
  with ws2window do
  begin
    LeftBound := 0.0; RightBound := 0.5;
    LowerBound := 0.0; UpperBound := 0.5;
  end;
  GSetWsWindow(ws1, ws1window);
  GSetWsWindow(ws2, ws2window);
  {Update both workstations so that the windows take effect}
  GUpdateWs(ws1, GVperform);
  GUpdateWs(ws2, GVperform);

  Star(base, height);

  {Deactivate and Close}
  GDeactivateWs(ws1);
  GDeactivateWs(ws2);
  GCloseWs(ws1);
  GCloseWs(ws2);
  GCloseGKS;
end;

{main program}
begin
  Show
end;
```

Program 4.1 (cont.)

Procedure *Show* opens and activates two workstations. It sets up normalization transformations to hold a window suitable for the picture to be displayed. As the corresponding viewport is not set, it is by default the unit square.

The workstation window for workstation 1 is the left half of NDC. For workstation 2 it is the bottom left-hand quadrant. Notice that the program calls the GKS update workstation procedure (*GUpdateWs*). This is because of the curious way that the workstation transformations operate. When the set workstation window (or viewport) function is called the system usually responds by only accepting the *request* to change the workstation transformation; that is, the current transformation remains in force. The reason for this is that a call to change the workstation transformation values is an implicit instruction to possibly change the image already displayed – by redrawing it using the new workstation transformation. In other words, GKS gives the programmer the option to determine *when* this update to the display image is to be put into effect. The use of *GUpdateWs* in this context forces the current transformation to be changed to the requested one – that is, to be enforced immediately. The general problem of dynamic changes to the display is discussed in Chapter 8. The workstation transformation is a particular example.

When both workstations have had their workstation windows set, the procedure *Star* is invoked, giving the results shown in Figure 4.7. Note that this particular example illustrates that the relation of the workstation window with respect to NDC space is the same as that of the normalization transformation window to WC space. Similarly, the viewport determines a rectangular area in NDC space, as the workstation viewport determines such an area in DC space. The only way in which the two transformations are different is that the normalization transformation is not uniform (does not preserve aspect ratios), whereas the workstation transformation is uniform. If the aspect ratio of the workstation window does not equal the aspect ratio of the workstation viewport, then the window is mapped to the viewport in such a way that the ratio is maintained. Unfortunately, this leads to a wastage of space on the display, as can be seen in both Figures 4.6 and 4.7 (see also Exercises 4.5 and 4.8).

4.5 The Role of Clipping in GKS

Conceptually, there are two places in the viewing pipeline where clipping takes place: WC points are clipped to the window; NDC points are clipped to the workstation window. From the point of view of efficiency, it would seem that clipping should take place *before* coordinates are transformed; that is, points should be clipped to the WC window and then transformed. This also avoids the inefficiency of transforming points that may lie outside the clipping region. In a graphics system where there is only one level of clipping, this argument would be a strong one. However, there are several reasons why clipping, in GKS, is deferred until the last possible moment.

(a)

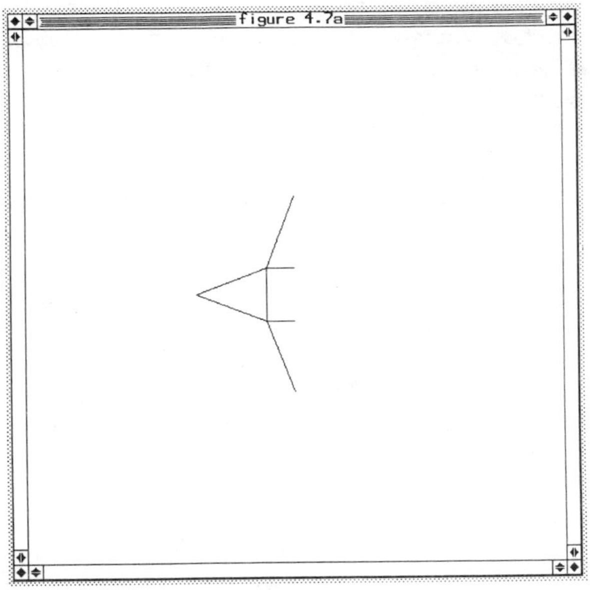

(b)

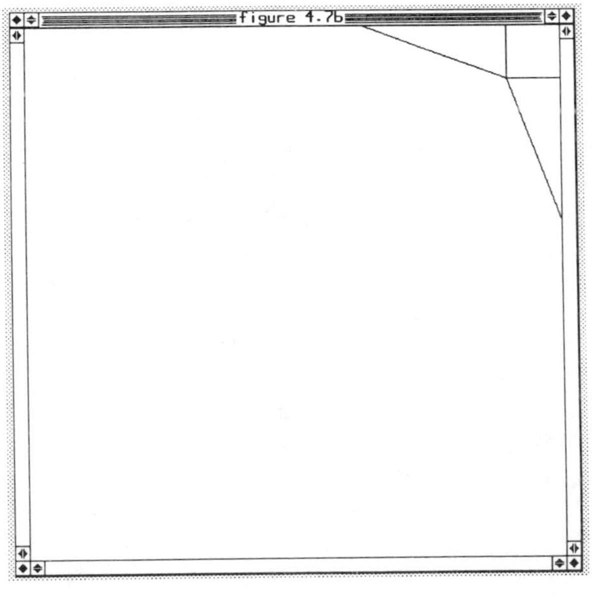

Figure 4.7
Output of Program 4.1.

(1) Since clipping to the workstation window must always occur to ensure that no attempt is made to draw outside the display space, a further clip to the WC window would mean that two separate clips are

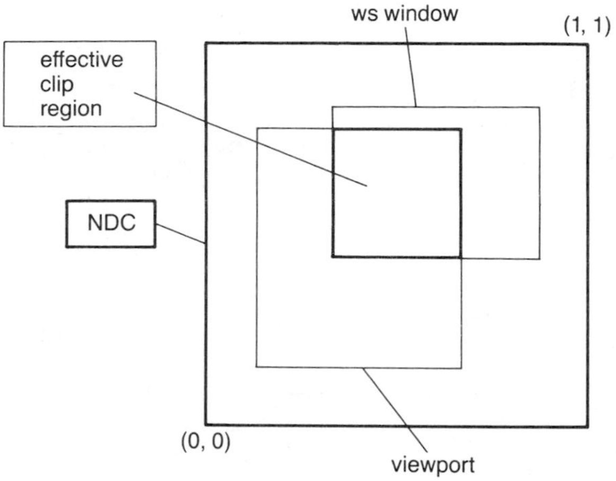

Figure 4.8
The effective clipping region.

necessary. But the clipping operation is computationally expensive, so a design requiring two clips should be avoided.

(2) It is possible to combine the two conceptual clips into one actual clip. Clipping WC points to the WC window is equivalent to clipping the transformed NDC points to the viewport. Hence, the effective clipping region is the intersection of the viewport and the NDC window. This is shown in Figure 4.8.

(3) In practice, the effective clipping region is transformed into DC for two reasons:

    (a) DC units are often expressed in integers, and the clipping operation on most machines is faster if carried out in integer rather than real arithmetic. Also, the clipping algorithm involves comparisons (in the function *EdgeSet*). Integer comparisons are unambiguous, whereas real comparisons depend on the floating-point representation and word length of the computer.

    (b) Many graphics devices actually have a built-in clipping operation, so that the clip region can be transmitted to the device and subsequent graphical output is clipped to this region.

Finally, it should be noted that GKS allows the programmer to switch off the conceptual clip to the WC window. The procedure:

type *GTclip* = (*GVclip*, *GVnoclip*);
GSetClip(*clipindicator* : *GTclip*)

enables or disables clipping to the window. In the default situation clipping is enabled. The overall clipping structure is shown in Figure 4.9.

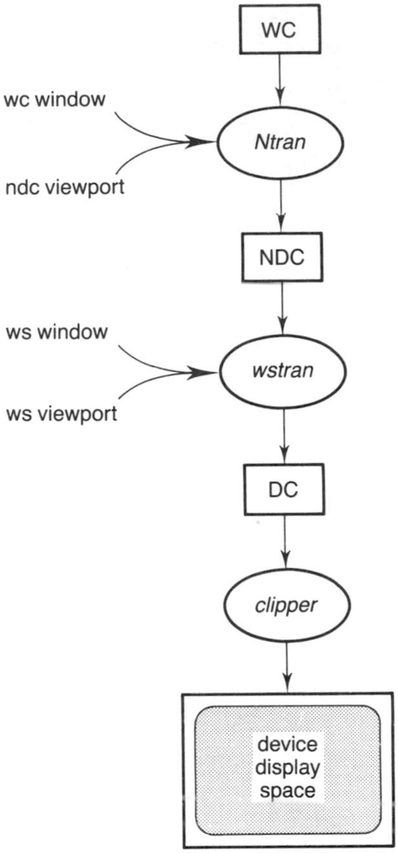

Figure 4.9
A partial view of the GKS viewing pipeline.

4.6 Generating Lines

A line whose two endpoints are $(x1, y1)$ and $(x2, y2)$ can be represented by $[(x1, y1), (x2, y2)]$. To display such a line many graphical devices have the following two procedures, which are programmed in at the firmware level:

MoveTo(x, y)
LineTo(x, y)

MoveTo positions a virtual pen at position (x, y), usually known as the **current position**, on the display space. *LineTo* draws a line from the current position to the new position given as the argument. This new position then becomes the current position. As the *Polyline* function applies to a sequence of n points describing $(n - 1)$ connected edges, it can be decomposed into a call to *MoveTo* followed by $(n - 1)$ calls to *LineTo*.

For pixel-based devices, the most primitive instruction is *WritePixel*. Therefore, for such devices the receipt of a *LineTo* instruction requires the device to compute a sequence of pixel positions to best represent the line, given the constraints imposed by the physical display resolution. If, however, the device does not have a built-in program to convert a line, the graphics system software implementation must provide a function to compute the pixel positions for use by the *WritePixel* function. In Chapter 3, the utility function *u_LineToPixels* was introduced for this purpose.

In the case of raster graphics devices, the process of converting higher level graphics primitives, such as lines or fill areas, to pixel positions is sometimes referred to as **scan conversion**. Whether this process takes place in the graphics system software or in the device firmware, a suitable algorithm must be employed. It is easy to develop such an algorithm from the equation of the straight line $[(x1, y1), (x2, y2)]$.

$$y = y1 + \left(\frac{dy}{dx}\right)(x - x1) \qquad \text{where } dy = y2 - y1 \text{ and } dx = x2 - x1 \tag{4.1}$$

When $x = i$:

$$y_i = y1 + \left(\frac{dy}{dx}\right)(i - x1) \tag{4.2}$$

and when $x = i - 1$:

$$y_{i-1} = y1 + \left(\frac{dy}{dx}\right)(i - 1 - x1) \tag{4.3}$$

and subtracting Equation (4.3) from (4.2):

$$y_i = y_{i-1} + \left(\frac{dy}{dx}\right) \qquad \text{where } i = 1, 2 \ldots, dx \text{ and } y_0 = y1 \tag{4.4}$$

This leads to the following algorithm:

```
LineToPixels: DC_Line → DC_Point sequence;
fun LineToPixels line =
  let val [(x1, y1), (x2, y2)] = line
  in
    let val dx = x2 − x1 and dy = y2 − y1
    in
      let val slope = dy/dx and p = store [(x1, y1)]
         and ry = store real(y1)
      in
        for 1 ≤ i ≤ dx do
          ry := ry + slope;
          p := p @ [(x1 + i, round(ry))]
```

```
                        od;
                        ?p
                      ni
                    ni
                  ni
                nuf
```

This function returns a sequence of points (x_i, y_i) according to Equation (4.4). There are, however, some problems.

(1) The function assumes that $x2 > x1$ and that $dx > dy$. However, this is not an important problem, since the function rule can easily be generalized to cover all cases (see Exercise 4.11).

(2) Generating lines is fundamental to graphics systems, hence it must execute as fast as possible. Consequently, the algorithm ought to be one that is easily represented in assembly language or machine code, since it is most likely to be implemented at that level. Hence, the floating-point calculations involved in computing the slope (dy/dx) and successive y values $(y_{i-1} + (dy/dx))$ are unfortunate. Moreover, since the frame buffer addressing is by integer, a *round* function would also have to be used to $round(y_{i-1} + (dy/dx))$. (Once again, it is assumed that DC are expressed as integers. If they are not, then fixed-point arithmetic could be used instead.)

The algorithm given in *LineToPixels* is an example of a **digital differential analyzer (DDA)**. It is based on the simple observation that a unit increment in x results in a change in y, which is given by the amount of the slope, or derivative, dy/dx. However, the literal application here of this idea has led to an algorithm that is open to improvement, as shown by Bresenham (1965).

It should be realized that in practice a sequence would not be used to store the pixel positions before passing them to a *WritePixel* function. In reality, each pixel would be set as soon as it was generated. However, it is the method of scan conversion that is important in this discussion, not the actual implementation in a real language (where, of course, storing the pixel positions in an array might not be sensible).

To understand Bresenham's algorithm it is worth considering the question: What does it *mean* to generate a line? An answer might be: Find all the pixel positions that best represent the line. What is meant by *best* in this context? This question can be answered by considering Figure 4.10, which assumes that $dx > dy$ and $dx > 0$.

Suppose that at $x = i - 1$ the point $(i - 1, y_{i-1})$ best represents the true position of the line. Then, at $x = i$, the pixel position chosen should be that which is closest to the true line. From Figure 4.10, it can be seen that

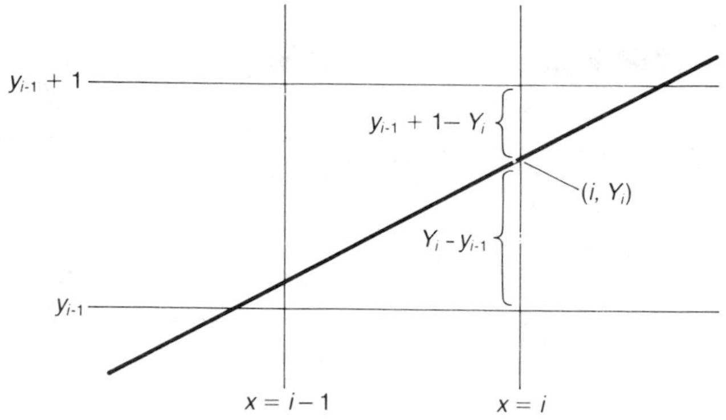

Figure 4.10
Line through pixels.

the rule for selecting the pixel position at $x = i$ should be:

if $(y_{i-1} + 1 - Y_i) < (Y_i - y_{i-1})$ **then choose** $(i, y_{i-1} + 1)$
else choose (i, y_{i-1}) **(4.5)**

where Y_i is the true height of the line at $x =$ i. This rule can be decomposed as follows:

choose $(i, y_{i-1} + 1)$ **if** $2\mathrm{y}_{i-1} + 1 - 2Y_i < 0$

That is, if:

$$c_{i-1} < 0 \quad \textbf{(4.6)}$$

where $c_{i-1} = 2y_{i-1} + 1 - 2\,(dy/dx)\,i$. Since $dx > 0$, Equation (4.6) is equivalent to:

choose $(i, y_{i-1} + 1)$ **if** $e_{i-1} < 0$ **(4.7)**

where $e_{i-1} = 2dx\,y_{i-1} + dx - 2dy\,i$. Now, from Equation (4.7):

$$e_i = 2dx\,y_i + dx - 2dy\,(i + 1)$$

so that by subtraction:

$$e_i = e_{i-1} + 2dx(y_i - y_{i-1}) - 2dy \quad \textbf{(4.8)}$$

However, from Equation (4.7):

if $e_{i-1} < 0$ **then** $y_i - y_{i-1} = 1$
else $y_i - y_{i-1} = 0$

Therefore, Equation (4.8) can now be expressed as follows. Suppose (i, y_i) is the best pixel position at $x = i$, then at $x = i + 1$:

$$\textbf{choose } (i + 1, y_i + 1) \textbf{ if } e_i < 0 \qquad \text{where } e_i = \begin{cases} e_{i-1} + 2(dx - dy) \text{ if } e_{i-1} < 0 \\ e_{i-1} - 2dy \text{ otherwise} \end{cases}$$

$$\textbf{else choose } (i + 1, y_i) \qquad (i = 1, 2, \ldots, dx) \tag{4.9}$$

It only remains to determine the initial situation; that is, the value of e_0. From Equation (4.7), when $i = 1$, $e_0 = dx - 2dy$. Bresenham's algorithm (in the case $dx > 0$ and $dx > dy$) can now be expressed as follows:

```
LinetoPixels: DC_Line → DC_Point sequence;
fun LineToPixels(line) =
  let val [(x1, y1), (x2, y2)] = line
  in
    let val dx = x2 − x1 and dy = y2 − y1
    in
      let val Decision = fn e ⇒ if
                                    e < 0 ⇒ e + 2*(dx − dy)
                                  □ e ⩾ 0 ⇒ e − 2*dy
                                fi
        and NextPoint = fn (p, e) ⇒ let val (x, y) = p
                                        and newe = Decision(e)
                                    in
                                      if
                                          newe < 0 ⇒ ((x + 1, y + 1),
                                                       newe)
                                        □ newe ⩾ 0 ⇒ ((x + 1, y), newe)
                                      fi
                                    ni
        and e = store (dx − 2*dy)
        and p = store [(x1, y1)]
      in
        for 1 ⩽ i ⩽ dx do
          let val (newp, newe) = NextPoint(?p[i − 1], ?e)
          in
            p, e := p @ [newp], newe
          ni
        od;
        ?p
      ni
    ni
  ni
nuf
```

4.7 Polygon Fill

There are several ways of specifying a region to be shaded. The **seed fill** methods, for example, determine the shaded area by relying on what is already on the display. (These methods are discussed in Exercises 4.14 and 4.15 and in Section 16.4.6.) Polygon fill, on the other hand, is a method of specifying shading that relies only on coordinate data, and has the same effect irrespective of what is on the current display.

The argument to a polygon fill function is a sequence of points representing the polygon's vertices. The lines connecting successive vertices are termed **edges**. A polygon is said to be **closed** if it is possible to trace round its edges and always end up at the starting point (see Figure 4.11). Some of the polygons in Figure 4.11 have edges that intersect one another. This raises the question of how to determine which points are **inside** the polygon. The solution adopted by GKS is as follows. A point can be determined to be inside a polygon according to the **inside test**:

> Given a polygon P = $[p_0, p_1, \ldots, p_{n-1}, p_n]$ $(p_n = p_0)$, a point p is inside P if the following condition is satisfied. Draw a line from p in any direction to infinity and count the number of edges intersected by the line. If the number of edges intersected is *odd*, then p is *inside* the polygon, otherwise it is *outside*. If p lies exactly on an edge then it is *inside*. This is shown in Figure 4.12.

The problem of shading such a polygon is equivalent to finding the set of pixels that lie inside the polygon and setting these to *on*, or whatever colour is desired, and obviously has a solution. For example, for every pixel in the frame buffer, the inside test can be used to determine whether or not the pixel is within the polygon, and if so set it to the desired colour. On a computer with parallel architecture this method could be attractive, although its speed would depend on the size of the parallel processor array. Unfortunately, since most available machines are sequential, this algorithm is impractical. It will certainly work, but could take several hours of computation (depending on the size of the frame buffer), irrespective of the complexity of the polygon.

A second and preferred solution to this problem is to take account of the fact that each horizontal scan line will either intersect the polygon on an *even* number of edges or not at all. Thus, drawing horizontal lines between pairs of intersections will result in the polygon being filled if repeated for every scan line. Although this method will work at reasonable speed, it does not take into account the fact that if scan line i intersects a certain set of edges, then scan line $(i + 1)$ is very likely to intersect the same, or almost

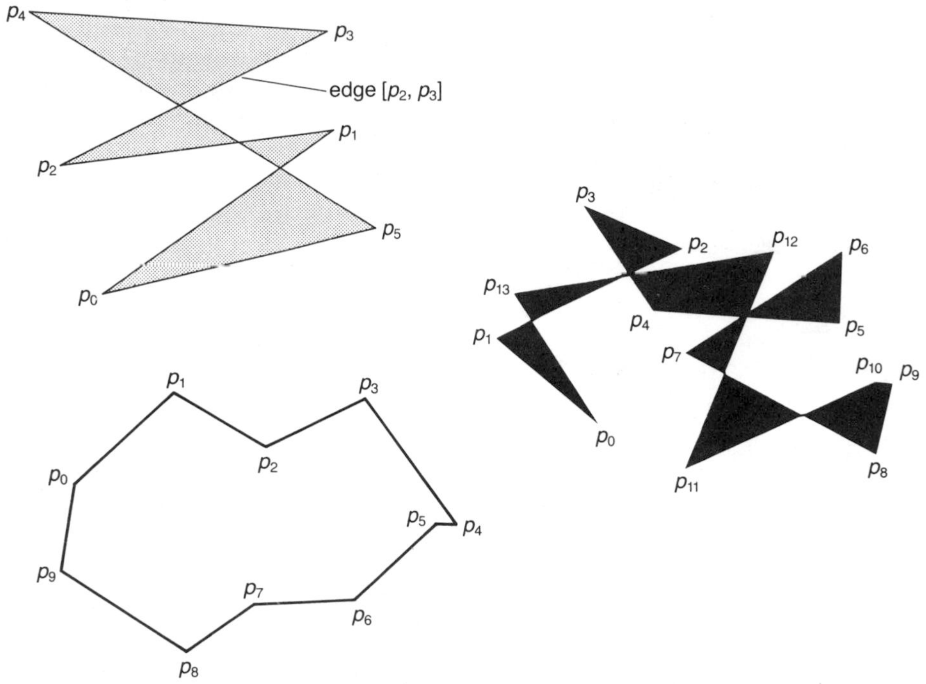

Figure 4.11
Polygons.

the same, set of edges. This property, known as **edge coherence**, is the basis of an algorithm (Baeker, 1979; Foley and Van Dam, 1982), which will now be described.

The algorithm relies on constructing a (so-called) **edge table (ET)**. The edge table has an entry for every scan line; that is, if the vertical resolution of the display is *YMAX*, then the edge table will be the sequence $ET[0]$, $ET[1]$, ..., $ET[YMAX - 1]$, where 0 is the scan line at the bottom of the screen and $YMAX - 1$ is the top. Now the entry for $ET[i]$ will consist of a sequence of information concerning all of those polygon edges with lowest point at $y = i$ (horizontal lines are ignored). If $edge = [(x1, y1), (x2, y2)]$ $(y1 < y2)$ is a particular edge, then the information about *edge* will be stored in sequence $ET[y1]$ and will consist of the record:

$$(y2, x1, Dx) \qquad \text{where } Dx = \frac{(x2 - x1)}{(y2 - y1)}$$

(there is no danger that $y2 = y1$, since horizontal lines are ignored). To summarize, the information about the edge consists of:

(1) the maximum *y* vertex of the edge ($y2$);

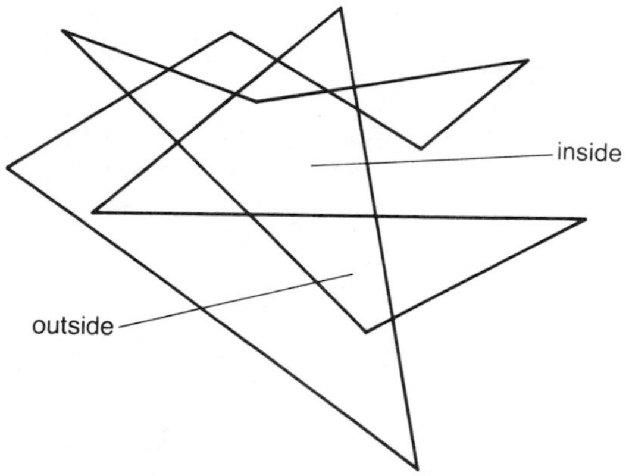

Figure 4.12
The inside test for polygons.

(2) the x coordinate of the other vertex ($x1$); and
(3) the inverse of the slope of the edge (Dx).

The reason for storing the information Dx is discussed next.

The equation of the edge is:

$$y = y1 + \left(\frac{dy}{dx}\right)(x - x1)$$

Let x_i be the x intersection of this edge with the ith scan line (that is, with the line $y = i$). Hence:

$$i = y1 + \left(\frac{dy}{dx}\right)(x_i - x1)$$

and:

$$i + 1 = y1 + \left(\frac{dy}{dx}\right)(x_{i+1} - x1)$$

By subtraction:

$$\left(\frac{dy}{dx}\right)(x_{i+1} - x_i) = 1$$

which results in:

$$x_{i+1} = x_i + Dx$$

Thus, Dx is the amount to be added to x_i, the intersection of the edge with the ith scan line, to obtain the intersection of the edge with the next scan line up ($y = i+1$).

To derive the rule for a fill area function, it is necessary to introduce some new data types to represent the edge table:

```
type ETValue  = int*real*real;
type ETEntry  = ETValue sequence;
type ETable   = ETEntry sequence;
```

Hence, an edge table consists of a sequence with each element itself a sequence of 3-tuples. An edge table is a special representation of the edges of the polygon to be filled and may be constructed by use of the following function:

```
MakeET: DC_Point sequence → int*int*ETable;
fun MakeET p =
  let val q = p @ [p[0]]                        Close the polygon.
    and ET = store (nil ~∞) : ETable            Initialise the table.
    and ymin = store ScreenYmax                 Maximum y coordinate of screen.
    and ymax = store 0
  in
    for 1 ≤ i < Length q do
      DrawLine([q[i − 1], q[i]]);               Draw this edge, and then... .
      let val (u1, v1) = q[i − 1] and (u2, v2) = q[i]
      in
        let val (x1, y1, x2, y2) = if
                                     v1 ≤ v2 ⇒ (u1, v1, u2, v2)
                                   □ v1 > v2 ⇒ (u2, v2, u1, v1)
                                   fi
        in
          if
            y1 < y2 ⇒ let val Dx = (x2 − x1)/(y2 − y1)
                       in
                         ET[y1] := (y2, x1, Dx) :: ET[y1]
                       ni;
                       ymin, ymax := min(ymin, y1), max(ymax, y2)
          fi
        ni
      ni
    od;
    (?ymin, ?ymax, ?ET)
  ni
nuf
```

This function *MakeET* puts the information for each polygon edge at the head of the sequence at a location corresponding to the lower y coordinate of the edge. As each edge is traversed it is drawn and, in addition, the minimum and maximum y vertex values are computed during the iteration.

Now, the entries to the edge table contain sufficient information to compute the horizontal lines corresponding to the polygon interior. Consider, for example, any particular entry, say $ET[i]$. This contains information about every polygon edge that has its lower vertex at $y = i$. This can now be used to process an **active edge table (AET)** as follows:

```
ProcessET: DC_Point sequence → Void;
fun ProcessET p =
  let val (ymin, ymax, ET) = MakeET p
  in
    let val AET = store (nil : ETEntry)
    in
      for ymin ≤ i ≤ ymax do
        AET := sort (UpdateAET(i, AET) @ ET[i]);
        JoinLines(i, AET)
      od
    ni
  ni
nuf
```

Here, the function *UpdateAET* applied to (i, *AET*) results in a new *AET* sequence with every entry having $y2$ equal to i deleted, and with the remaining entries changed by replacing $x1$ by $x1 + Dx$. If *AET* is *nil*, then *UpdateAET* delivers *nil*. The resulting sequence is concatenated with the sequence at the ith entry of the edge table, and this new sequence is then given as the argument to the *sort* function that sorts the sequence in increasing order of the x entries. The function *JoinLines* draws the horizontal lines between successive pairs of x values at height $y = i$. As this process is repeated from the lowest to highest y vertex in the polygon, the polygon is filled by horizontal scan lines.

For the algorithm to work, it is crucial for there to be an *even* number of elements in the *AET* sequence supplied to *JoinLines*. If this is the case, then the inside test ensures that the algorithm indeed generates the required area fill. An informal proof that this requirement is true can quite easily be constructed. Just prior to the **for**...**do**...**od** iteration in *ProcessET* the sequence *AET* is set to *nil* and therefore has zero elements. The number of elements in *AET* at the end of the first iteration (when $i = ymin$) is equal to the number of elements in $ET[ymin]$. This must be an even number, since this is the number of edges that start at the lower bound of the polygon. (Remember that horizontal edges are ignored in the construction of the edge table.) Now at each subsequent iteration there are four possibilities depending on i:

(1) If $ET[i] = nil$, then no polygon edges have their lower y vertex at i.

Since the polygon is closed (that is, every edge is always joined to two other edges) it follows that there can be no entries in *AET* with $y2 = i$. *UpdateAET* will not return an *AET* with deleted entries. Hence, the number of elements in *AET* remains unchanged.

(2) For every local minimum at $y = i$ *two* new edges join *AET* via concatenation of the *ET*[*i*] entry.

(3) For every local maximum at $y = i$ *two* edges are deleted from *AET* through thc operation of *UpdateAET*.

(4) If there is a vertex at *i* that is neither a local minimuim nor a maximum, then one edge is *deleted* (the one with its *y*2 value equal to *i*) and another *joins* (since it must have its *y*1 value equal to *i*).

It follows therefore that the number of elements in *AET* must always be even when given to *JoinLines*, since the number starts out as zero and multiples of two entries are added or deleted, and for each single entry that is deleted (or joins) another joins (or is deleted). It is important to note that this discussion also shows that pixels corresponding to vertices that are local maxima will not be set (see Exercise 4.18). This is the reason why each edge is drawn as it is encountered during the construction of the edge table – the polygon boundary is therefore drawn before the interior. (This does not conform to GKS, which requires that only *hollow* polygons should have their boundary drawn.)

Readers interested in further proof and implementation of this function should see Exercise 4.16 which discusses the definitions of *UpdateAET*, *sort* and *JoinLines*. The following example illustrates the algorithm.

□□ EXAMPLE

Figure 4.13 shows a polygon with vertices (1, 1), (2, 4), (4, 4), (4, 2), (3, 2) and (3, 0), with the last edge being [(3, 0), (1, 1)]. The edge table is therefore:

ET[0] = [(1, 3, −2), (2, 3, 0)]
ET[1] = [(4, 1, 1/3)]
ET[2] = [(4, 4, 0)]
ET[3] = *nil*
ET[4] = *nil*

The *ymin* and *ymax* rules are:

$$ymin = 0 \quad \text{and} \quad ymax = 4$$

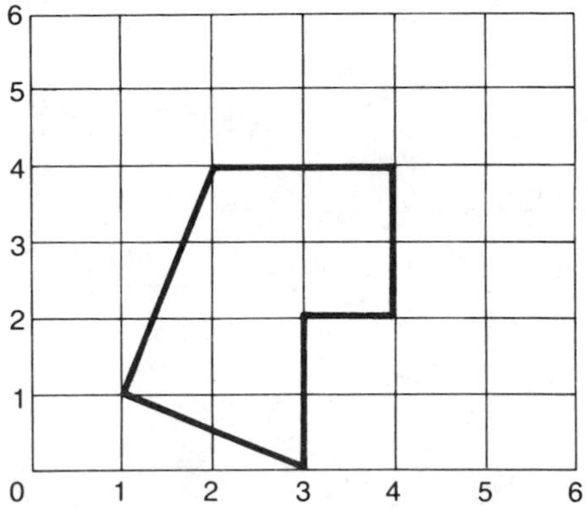

Figure 4.13
Polygon fill example.

The successive values for the active edge table are therefore:

$AET = nil$

(1) When $i = 0$
$AET = [(1, 3, -2), (2, 3, 0)]$
which results in the scan line [(3, 0), (3, 0)] (the single vertex).

(2) When $i = 1$
$UpdateAET(1, AET) = [(2, 3, 0)]$, therefore
$AET = [(4, 1, 1/3), (2, 3, 0)]$
which results in the scan line [(1, 1), (3, 1)].

(3) When $i = 2$
$UpdateAET(2, AET) = [(4, 4/3, 1/3)]$, therefore
$AET = [(4, 4/3, 1/3), (4, 4, 0)]$
which results in the scan line [(4/3, 2) (4, 2)].

(4) When $i = 3$
$UpdateAET(3, AET) = [(4, 5/3, 1/3), (4, 4, 0)]$, therefore
$AET = [(4, 5/3, 1/3), (4, 4, 0)]$
which results in the scan line [(5/3, 3), (4, 3)].

(5) When $i = 4$
$UpdateAET(4, AET) = nil$ and the process terminates.

4.8 Clipping Polygons

Clipping a polygon is inherently more complex than clipping a line because of the stipulation that the result of the clipping process is itself a closed polygon (see Figure 4.14). Furthermore, a polygon can be divided into several polygons in the process of clipping.

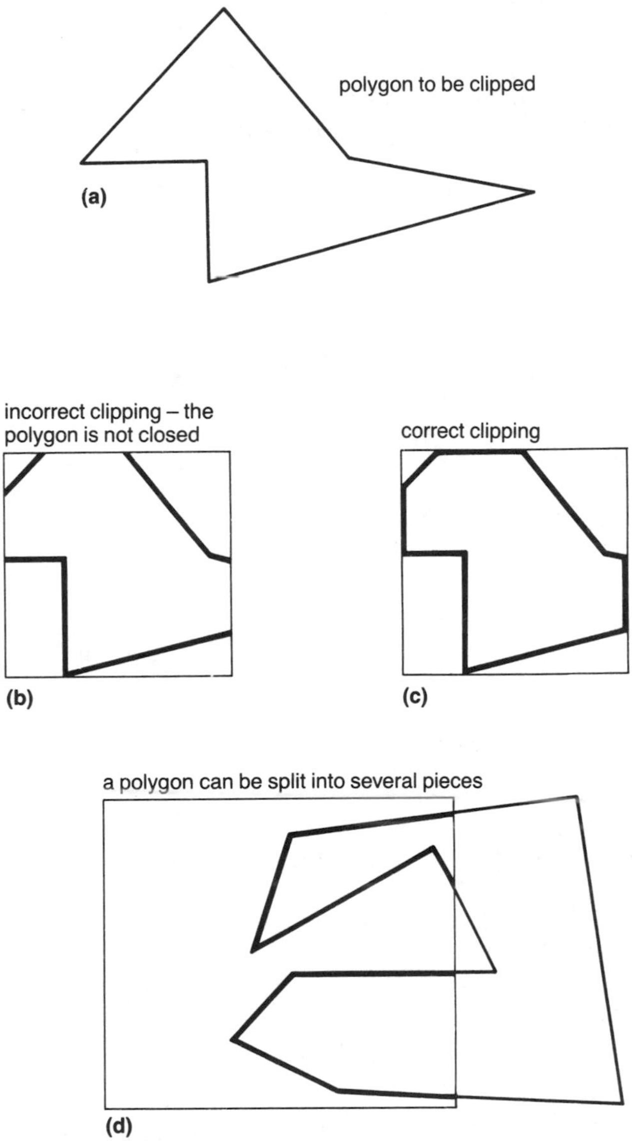

Figure 4.14
Clipping polygons.

Surprisingly, it is a simple matter to clip a polygon that is to be solid filled. The discussion in Section 4.7 showed that a solid-filled polygon is actually generated from horizontal scan lines. Therefore, the solid polygon will be correctly clipped if the horizontal lines are clipped, and it is a very simple process to clip horizontal lines to a rectangular clipping region. Nothing more needs to be said about this case. The real difficulty involved is in clipping a hollow polygon – that is, where only the edges are to be drawn.

Note from Figure 4.14 that the clipping process will generally add *new* edges to the polygon.

This section describes two algorithms for polygon clipping. The first is a combination of ordinary line clipping and ideas from Section 4.3. The second is the classical Sutherland–Hodgman algorithm (Sutherland and Hodgman, 1974), which adopts a different approach. There is also a more general polygon clipping algorithm known as the Weiler–Atherton algorithm (Weiler and Atherton, 1977), which shows how to clip a polygon to non-rectangular clipping regions, and which takes care of the problem seen in Figure 4.14(d) where one polygon may be split into several polygons on clipping. However, this is beyond the scope of this book. (In GKS, clipping regions are always rectangular.)

The function *ClipPolygon* has two parameters: an array of points, which are the polygon vertices, and a clip region. The simplest form of clipping would be achieved by the following definition:

Definition 4.1 Clipping a polygon.

```
ClipPolygon: DC_ClipRegion*(DC_Point sequence) → Void;
fun ClipPolygon(clipregion, p) =
  let val q = p @ [p[0]]
  in
    for 1 ≤ i < Length q do
      let val line = ClipLine(clipregion, [q[i − 1], q[i]])
      in
        DrawLine(line)
      ni
    od
  ni
nuf
```

The idea of the first definition is that the polygon edges are traversed and each one is subjected to the line clipping function defined in Section 4.3. This is unsatisfactory because the result is no longer a closed polygon, as shown in Figure 4.14(b). However, the correct result can be achieved by making a modification to *ClipLine* and introducing a closure procedure.

At the moment, *ClipLine* results in the line as clipped by the clip region. The following modification can be introduced that results in *ClipLine* also storing information about the intersection points. Let *LeftEdgeList*, *RightEdgeList*, *LowerEdgeList* and *UpperEdgeList* be four sequences of reals initialised to be empty. Whenever *ClipLine* encounters a line that intersects an edge, an intersection value is inserted into the relevant sequence. This value is inserted in such a way as to maintain the sequence in ascending order of the coordinate values inserted. For example, if the line crosses the left edge, then the y value of the intersection point is inserted in order into the *LeftEdgeList*. Similarly, if the line crosses the upper edge, then the x value of the intersection point is inserted into the *UpperEdgeList*.

When all the polygon edges have been dealt with as shown in Definition 4.1, the polygon can be closed by processing each of the four lists. This processing is simple enough. First, note that the number of entries in each list will always be *even* (including zero). (Why?) Now consider, for example, the *TopEdgeList* and successive *pairs* of intersection values (these will, of course, be x intersection values). For any such pair of values, $x1 \leqslant x2$, adopt the following rule:

> Let $X1 = max(x1, Clip[left])$ and $X2 = min(x2, Clip[right])$. Then draw the horizontal line between $X1$ and $X2$ at y = *clipregion*[UPPER] only if $X1 \leqslant X2$.

By processing each of the four lists in a manner similar to this, the displayed polygon will be closed (see Exercise 4.20).

There is a lack of symmetry between the definition of *ClipLine* as discussed in Section 4.3 and the *ClipPolygon* function based on Definition 4.1 and modified according to the subsequent discussion. This is because the *ClipLine* function is given a line as its argument and returns a line as its result – no drawing is involved. However, the *ClipPolygon* function does not return a polygon at all – in fact, it returns nothing (the *Void* result). It is a function useful only for its side effect of actually displaying a closed polygon as clipped by a clipping region. In contrast, the Sutherland–Hodgman algorithm is given a polygon as its argument and returns a clipped (closed) polygon as its result. No drawing is involved, although obviously the resulting clipped polygon can be given as an argument to a *Polyline* or *FillArea* drawing function.

The main idea of the Sutherland–Hodgman algorithm is to clip the whole polygon against one clip edge at a time, for each of the four clip region edges (see Figure 4.15). Given a sequence of points p, *ClipByEdge*(p, *edge*, *clipregion*) is a new sequence of points which are the vertices of the polygon p clipped against the given *edge* of the *clipregion*. Hence, the algorithm may be defined as follows:

Definition 4.2 Sutherland-Hodgman polygon clipping.

```
ClipPolygon: DC_ClipRegion*(DC_Point sequence) → DC_Point sequence;
fun ClipPolygon(clipregion, p) =
  let val p1 = ClipByEdge(p, LEFT, clipregion)
  in
    let val p2 = ClipByEdge(p1, RIGHT, clipregion)
    in
      let val p3 = ClipByEdge(p2, LOWER, clipregion)
      in
        ClipByEdge(p3, UPPER, clip)
      ni
    ni
  ni
nuf
```

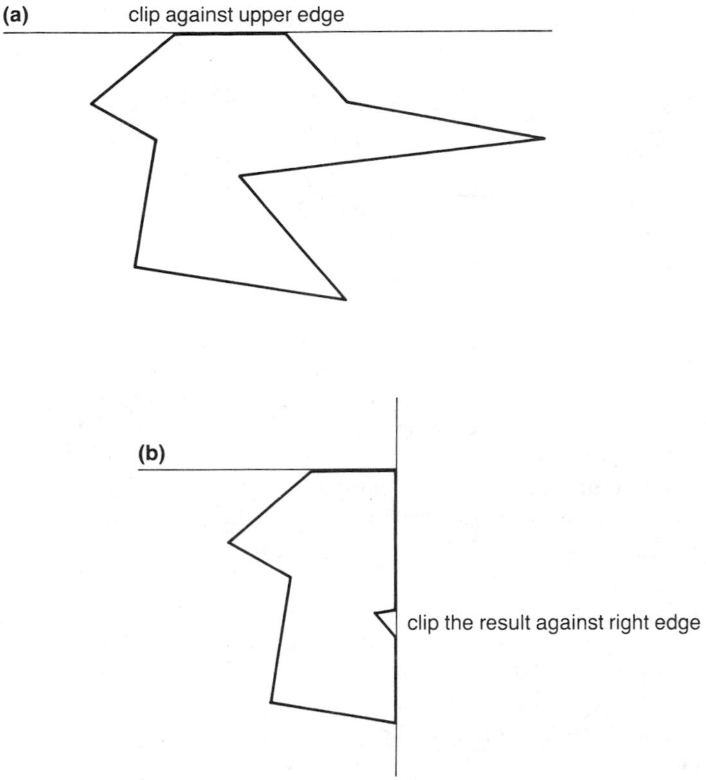

Figure 4.15
Clipping a polygon against one clip edge at a time.

Thus the polygon is first clipped against the left edge, the result is clipped against the right edge, and so on. Of course, the clip region edges can be considered in any order.

The function *ClipByEdge* is based on the considerations shown in Figure 4.16. Consider clipping the polygon against any edge. This may be achieved by the following:

Definition 4.3 Clipping against an edge.

```
ClipByEdge: (DC_Point sequence)*int*DC_ClipRegion → DC_Point
            sequence;
fun ClipByEdge(p, edge, clipregion) =
  let val qs = store nil : (DC_Point sequence)
    and q = p @ [p[0]]
  in
    for 1 ≤ i < Length q do
      qs := qs @ output(q[i − 1], q[i], edge, clipregion)
    od;
    ?qs
  ni
nuf
```

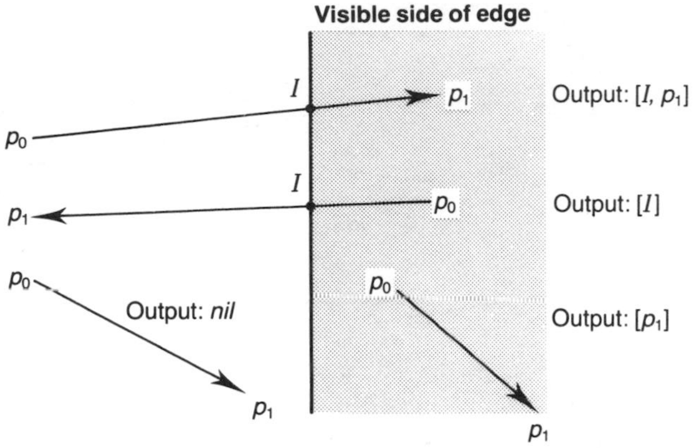

Figure 4.16
Clipping a polygon against a clipping edge.

qs is initially an empty sequence of points and it is successively concatenated with the sequence resulting from the *output* function. This may be defined as follows:

Definition 4.4 Clipping a line against an edge.

output: DC_Point∗DC_Point∗int∗DC_ClipRegion → DC_Point sequence;
fun *output*(*p*0, *p*1, *edge*, *clip*) =
  let val *out*0 = *EdgeSet*(*p*0, *clip*)
    and *out*1 = *EdgeSet*(*p*1, *clip*)
  in
    if
      Case a – line is wholly invisible.
        $edge \in out0 \cap out1 \Rightarrow nil$

      Case b – line is entering into visible side of clip region.
      $\square\ edge \in out0 - out1 \Rightarrow$ **let val** *Ip* =
              Intersection([*p*0, *p*1], *edge*, *clipregion*)
            in
              [*Ip*, *p*1]
            ni

      Case c – line is leaving visible side of clip region.
      $\square\ edge \in out1 - out0 \Rightarrow$ **let val** *Ip* =
              Intersection([*p*0, *p*1], *edge*, *clipregion*)
            in
              [*Ip*]
            ni

      Case d – line is wholly within the visible side.
      $edge \notin out0 \cup out1 \Rightarrow [p1]$
    fi
  ni
nuf

The functions *Intersection* and *EdgeSet* here are those defined in Section 4.3. It should be recalled that *EdgeSet* is a function that returns the set of edges a point is 'outside'. Therefore, if (as in case a) *edge* is a member of the intersection $out0 \cap out1$, then the line is wholly invisible. If (as in case b) *edge* is a member of $(out0 - out1)$, then this means that the first point $p0$ is outside the edge and the second point $p1$ is inside the edge, so that the line must be entering into the visible side of the clipping edge. Similar considerations apply to $(out1 - out0)$, the set of edges in *out*1 but not in *out*0, and to $out0 \cup out1$, the union of the two sets. The reader is advised to consider Exercises 4.21 and 4.22 for further discussion of this clipping algorithm.

Summary

This chapter has looked at some basic issues at the algorithmic core of 2D computer graphics, especially as applied to pixel-based devices. In addition, some points concerning the structuring and sequencing of the GKS viewing pipeline have been covered. It should be noted that only issues relating to *graphical output* have been discussed, and a number of important areas have been avoided – especially in relation to the attributes of graphical output, such as the style of lines or area fills, and the importance and use of colour.

Only a small fraction of the important algorithms in use in computer graphics have been considered in this chapter. An excellent text devoted almost entirely to algorithms is by Rogers (1985). This gives a large number of further references. Readers who intend to take up computer graphics seriously will eventually have to become acquainted with the literature of computational geometry. This discipline was invented in the 1970s by M.I. Shamos (Shamos, 1978) and is concerned with algorithms for the solution of problems in geometry. One of the inspirations for computational geometry was computer graphics. Two recent texts are Melhorn (1984), and Preparata and Shamos (1985).

Exercises

4.1 Derive the *Ntran* function given in Section 4.2 and prove that the definition satisfies conditions (1), (2) and (3) of that section.

4.2 Incorporate the workstation transformation into your Pascal version of the simple graphics library.

4.3 Show that *Ntran* is not in general a uniform transformation. Show that *Ntran* results in a uniform transformation if the window and viewport have the same aspect ratios.

4.4 What will the effective display space be in each of the following cases of display resolution (assuming the default workstation transformation)?

(a) 500 by 800
(b) 900 by 800
(c) 400 by 400
(d) 100 by 700

4.5 Suppose that the display space is A4 size with a pixel resolution 768 by 1024. Would it be possible to draw a diagonal line across the whole display space (from (0, 0) to (767, 1023)) if the viewing pipeline included the *Dtran* function?

4.6 Given the definition of *EdgeSet* in Section 4.3 and supposing that:

$$out0 = EdgeSet(p0, clip) \quad \text{and} \quad out1 = EdgeSet(p1, clip)$$

prove that if $out0 \cap out1$ is not empty, then the line $[p0, p1]$ is entirely outside the clipping region. Prove that if $out0 \cup out1$ is empty, then the line is entirely inside the clipping region.

4.7 Show that the *Intersection* function defined in Section 4.3 correctly finds the point of intersection between a line and a clipping edge. In the context of the clipping algorithm, is it necessary to test for $dx = 0$ or $dy = 0$ in the *Intersection* function?

4.8 Show how the additional workstation transformation layer overcomes the problem encountered in Exercise 4.5 concerning the use of the entire display space. Give the actual parameters that would allow use of the whole display space for Exercise 4.5. Give the general solution to this problem – that is, for any display space size show how to set a window, viewport, workstation window and workstation viewport to ensure that the whole display space is usable.

4.9 Write a program to generate a (probably crude!) map of Northern Europe. Show how the workstation transformation can be used to display different subregions of the total map.

4.10 Consider Program 4.1. Extend the transformation to include scaling. Use the idea of the transformational approach to show how to generate graphical text – that is, write a number of procedures similar to *Triangle*, where each procedure defines an alphabetical character. Use the *Display* procedure to display these characters at different places and orientations on the screen.

4.11 The *LineToPixels* functions defined in Section 4.6 required $dx > 0$ and $dx > dy$. Why is this the case? Show how the DDA algorithm can be generalized to cover all cases. Why are the incremental y values stored as reals?

4.12 Fully implement Bresenham's line drawing algorithm in Pascal. Do not store the generated pixels in an array, but provide an incremental algorithm where each pixel is set as it is generated.

4.13 Consider how Bresenham's approach might be used for the generation of circles and ellipses.

4.14 A seed fill algorithm will set all pixels flooding outwards from a given seed point until boundaries are hit – that is, from the seed point set all pixels adjacent to the seed point (which are not already set). Treat each newly set pixel as a seed point and continue while pixels are encountered which are still not set. Define and attempt to implement this idea in as efficient a manner as possible. Your first attempt will probably be recursive, recursing on the pixels. Later attempts might recurse on scan lines, starting with the scan line at the original seed point. Still later attempts might not be recursive.

4.15 Under what conditions would it be more appropriate to use a seed fill rather than a polygon fill method of filling?

4.16 To implement the polygon fill algorithm it is necessary to define the *Update* function of Section 4.7:

```
fun Update(i, nil)              = nil                              |
    Update(i, (i, _, _) :: t)   = Update(i, t)                     |
    Update(i, (y, x, Dx) :: t) = (y, x + Dx, Dx) :: Update(i, t)
nuf
```

(a) Prove that this definition of the *Update* function is correct.

(b) Define a *sort*(*sequence*) function, which sorts the sequence in ascending order of x components.

(c) Define the *JoinLines* function.

(d) Implement the entire polygon fill procedure in Pascal.

4.17 Show how the polygon fill algorithm can be amended to produce hatch instead of solid fills. First, tackle the case where the hatch lines are horizontal. Next, consider the case where the hatch lines are vertical. Next, consider the case where the hatch lines can be at any angle.

4.18 The version of the polygon fill algorithm given in this chapter avoids the problem usually encountered in definitions of this algorithm concerning scan lines that exactly cross the polygon vertices (see Newman and Sproull, 1979, pp. 234–236). However, the algorithm given in this chapter does have the drawback that pixels corresponding to vertices that are local maxima will not be set – hence, the necessity of drawing the polygon boundary first (which is done in the *MakeET* function). Prove that the algorithm defined by *ProcessET* does successfully fill the polygon, except for vertices that are local maxima.

4.19 If the horizontal scan lines generated by the polygon fill algorithm are to be clipped, is there any way of preventing scan lines that are above or below the clipping region from being generated at all?

4.20 Define a Pascal linked-list data structure where each node of the list contains a single real value. Write a procedure to insert a value into such a linked list such that the list is maintained in ascending order. Implement in Pascal a line-clipping algorithm, but one which not only returns the clipped line but which stores the clip value according to the discussion of Section 4.8. Hence, implement the first polygon clip algorithm discussed in Section 4.8. Is it necessary for the intersection values to be stored as reals?

4.21 If the Sutherland–Hodgman algorithm were implemented in Pascal, then internal storage would be needed to store the four successive vertex arrays. Try to find an alternative (recursive) formulation of the algorithm that does not require such intermediate storage.

4.22 If the Sutherland–Hodgman algorithm is used on a polygon that is split into several polygons by the clipping region, what kind of polygon is returned? What would happen if such a returned polygon were given as input to the polygon fill algorithm?

CHAPTER 5

GKS FOR INTERACTIVE GRAPHICS

Chapters 3 and 4 concentrated on issues relating to the design and implementation of a graphics library. Moreover, attention was paid exclusively to graphical output. In this chapter, there is a change of emphasis. The focus is on achieving results using the GKS graphical output and interactive functions. The graphical output functions are discussed in Section 5.1, and then graphical input is introduced and discussed in Sections 5.2 to 5.5. The chapter concludes with a consolidating example program.

5.1 Graphical Output Primitives

GKS was designed with the aim of being a **kernel** system; that is, a system providing a core set of functions useful for 2D interactive graphics. The designers of GKS wanted to provide a minimal and orthogonal set of functions suitable for creating a wide range of possible effects. The idea of *minimality* was to make the system as small as possible while still being flexible and powerful. *Orthogonality* in this context means that in principle there should be no two ways of producing the same effect; that is, the functions provided should be logically independent. In Chapter 3, it was shown that only *one* function – *WritePixel* – is needed to produce graphical output (on pixel-based devices), everything else being based on this. A standard that provided only one function for graphical output would truly be minimal, and by definition orthogonal. However, it would be a very difficult standard to use, and graphics programmers would soon start to build more friendly and extensive library software on top of such a standard. Hence, the set of graphical output functions provided by GKS extends to the following five distinct capabilities:

(1) Drawing straight lines.
(2) Marking positions.
(3) Drawing text.
(4) Filling polygonal areas.
(5) Drawing a rectangular array of colours.

The corresponding functions are as follows.

(1) *Polyline*(*p*) where *p* is a sequence of WC points, *Length*(*p*) $\geqslant$ 2. In Pascal, this is bound to:

```
procedure GPolyline(
                    n : GTint2;
                    var p : array[min..max : integer] of GRPoint
                   );
```

(2) *Polymarker*(*p*) where *p* is a sequence of points, *Length*(*p*) $\geqslant$ 1. In Pascal:

```
procedure GPolymarker(
                      n : GTint1;
                      var p : array[min..max : integer] of GRPoint
                     );
```

(3) *Text*(*p*, *string*) where *p* is a point and *string* is a character string. In Pascal:

```
procedure GText(
                p : GRPoint;
                charstring : packed array[min..max : integer] of char
                );
```

(4) *FillArea*(p) where p is a sequence of points, *Length*(p) $\geqslant$ 3. In Pascal:

```
procedure GFill(
              n : GTint3;
              var p : array[min..max : integer] of GRPoint
              );
```

(5) *CellArray*($p1$, $p2$, dx, dy, *colour*) where $p1$ and $p2$ are points specifying opposite corners of a rectangle; dx, $dy > 0$ are integers specifying the number of divisions of the rectangle along the x and y axes, respectively, thus forming a two-way array of rectangular cells; and *colour* is a 2D array of colour indices, where the colours are mapped on to the array of cells. In Pascal, this becomes:

```
procedure GCellArray(
                    p1, p2 : GRPoint;
                    dx, dy : GTint1;
                    var colour : array[min1..max1 : integer;
                                       min2..max2 : integer]
                    of GTint0
                    );
```

It is assumed here that colours are specified by integers where the association between each number and the actual colour it represents is determined by a coding, which is discussed in Chapter 6. This chapter assumes that only two colours are available, 0 for white and 1 for black, and that the display is a white screen (that is, 0 is the colour of the background).

It should be remembered that for graphical output to occur in GKS, the system must be in the state where at least one workstation is active. In other words, GKS must be 'open'; that is, a workstation must be open and the open workstation must be activated. An attempt to use the graphical output primitives when the system is not in the correct state will result in error messages. If the system is in the correct state, then graphical output is routed to all active workstations.

Furthermore, it is important to remember that by default the normalization transformation number 0 is in effect, having window and viewport as the unit square. Also, by default, all of the other normalization transformation numbers have this default window and viewport. To change this state of affairs the *SetWindow* and *SetViewport* functions must be used, and then the desired transformation selected with *SelectNtran*. And then

Figure 5.1
The clock example, which uses each GKS output primitive.

there are the workstation windows and viewports lurking in the background with their defaults – the workstation window being the whole of NDC and the viewport the largest square on the display. Thus, there are clearly many things that need to be taken into account when generating graphical output.

□□ EXAMPLE

Figure 5.1 shows a clock displaying a time of 3:00 in the afternoon. Each one of the graphical output primitives has been used in the creation of this picture.

- *CellArray* has been used to draw the chequered background and the inner white square.
- *FillArea* has been used to draw the circular border of the clock.

- *Polymarker* has been used to draw the asterisk shapes denoting the time positions.
- *Polyline* has been used to draw the clock hands.
- *Text* has been used to draw the digital readout.

Note that the *Text*, *Polyline*, *Polymarker* and *FillArea* primitives are each drawn using their default styles. The default line style is a solid line; *Polymarker* by default marks a position with the * symbol; the default *FillArea* is, strangely enough, hollow. *CellArray* is the odd one out because it has no separate style – its style is determined by the contents of the array of colours given as the input parameter.

The following program shows how this picture can be constructed (see also Exercise 5.1):

Example 5.1 A clock.

fun *Clock*(n, D, V, d, r, g) =

n = number of x and y divisions in cell array.
D = half the width and height of the window WC for the analogue clock.
V = the lower left-hand corner of a viewport which is to be symmetrical about (0.5, 0.5).
d = half the width and height of the inner rectangle.
r = radius at which time division markers are drawn.
g = height of the digital readout box.

```
  Set up the normalization transformations.
  SetWindow(1, [−D, D, −D, D]);
  SetViewport(1, [V, 1.0 − V, V, 1.0 − V]);
  SelectNtran(1);
  SetViewport(2, [V, 1.0 − V, V − g, V]);
  SetWindow(2, [V, 1.0 − V, V − g, V]);

  Draw the chequered cell array.
  let val p1 = (−D, D) and p2 = (D, −D) and colour = store 0~(∞, ∞)
  in
    for 0 ≤ i < n do
    for 0 ≤ j < n do
      colour[i, j] := if odd(i + j) ⇒ 0 □ even(i + j) ⇒ 1
    od
    od;
    CellArray(p1, p2, n, n, ?colour)
  ni;

  Define the inner cell array as all white.
  let val p1 = (−d, d) and p2 = (d, −d) and colour = 0~(1, 1)
  in
    CellArray(p1, p2, 1, 1, colour)
  ni;

  Draw the circle of radius d.
  let val NINC = 20   Number of divisions on the circle.
```

```
in
  let val p = store (0.0, 0.0)~NINC and c = 2.0*π/NINC
  in
    for 0 ≤ i < NINC do
      let val t = i*c
      in
        p[i] := (d*cos t, d*sin t)
      ni
    od;
    FillArea(p)
  ni
ni;

Draw the markers.
let val p = store (0.0, 0.0)~12 and c = 2*π/12
in
  for 0 ≤ i < 11 do
    let val t = c*i
    in
      p[i] := (r*cos t, r*sin t)
    ni
  od;
  Polymarker(p)
ni;

Draw the hands at 3:00.
Polyline [(0.0, 0.9*r), (0.0, 0.0), (0.7*r, 0.0)];

Draw the border.
Polyline [(-D, -D), (D, -D), (D, D), (-D, D), (-D, -D)]

Draw the digital readout box and draw text.
SelectNtran(2);
Polyline [(V, V), (V, V - g), (1.0 - V, V - g), (1.0 - V, V)];

Set the character height to 1/20 of height of digital readout box.
SetCharacterHeight(g/20.0);

Set text position to be 1/4 in from left and bottom.
let val p = ((2.0*V + 1.0)/4.0, V - 3.0*g/4.0);
in
  Text(p, "15:00 hours")
ni;

Return to the default normalization transformation.
SelectNtran(0)
nuf
```

This program would be used, for example, by the call:

```
Clock(40, 100.0, 0.2, 60.0, 55.0, 0.1)
```

5.2 A Model for Graphical Input

Once the clock program of Example 5.1 is translated into Pascal and compiled, and the execution command given to the computer system, no further human intervention is required. This was also the case for the photograph analogy described in Chapter 2 – it is a batch graphical programming mode. If the program is correctly specified, then the clock picture will appear on the screen.

Graphical input, however, is fundamentally different, as it requires the intervention of a human operator. Graphical input involves a *human action*, using an *input device* that is bound to a *workstation*. The actions involved in using the input device are translated by the graphical system into meaningful **events** depending on the **class** of the input device used. These ideas are illustrated in Figure 5.2.

For the purposes of exposition, only two input classes are considered in this section: **locator input** and **valuator input**. It is important to understand that the input class determines how the graphics system interprets operator actions on physical input devices (see Chapter 17). In the case of a locator input, the operator action translates into an event that generates the **measure** of a locator, which is a WC position and a normalization transformation number. With a valuator input, the measure generated is a **value**. Generally, the measure of an input class refers to the data type generated by an event of that class.

For the moment, it is best to think of the locator and valuator input interactions as being carried out on two physically distinct input devices. For the locator, a mouse might be used. The human operator moves the mouse across a desk top, and relative movements of the mouse are translated into movements of a cursor on the screen. (This is fully discussed in Section 17.3.4.) For the valuator, imagine a dial on which a numerical scale is marked. The operator can turn the dial and select any number on the scale.

Now the human actions required to generate an event depend on the class of input and the input **mode**. The mode may be **request**, **sample** or **event**. The request and sample modes are explained here in the context of an example (event mode is discussed extensively in Chapter 9).

5.2.1 Request Input Mode

Consider adding some interactive features to the clock program. Instead of merely executing the program and passively watching the display unfold according to the preset parameters, an operator is allowed to intervene to determine two features of the display. First, the operator is able to select the

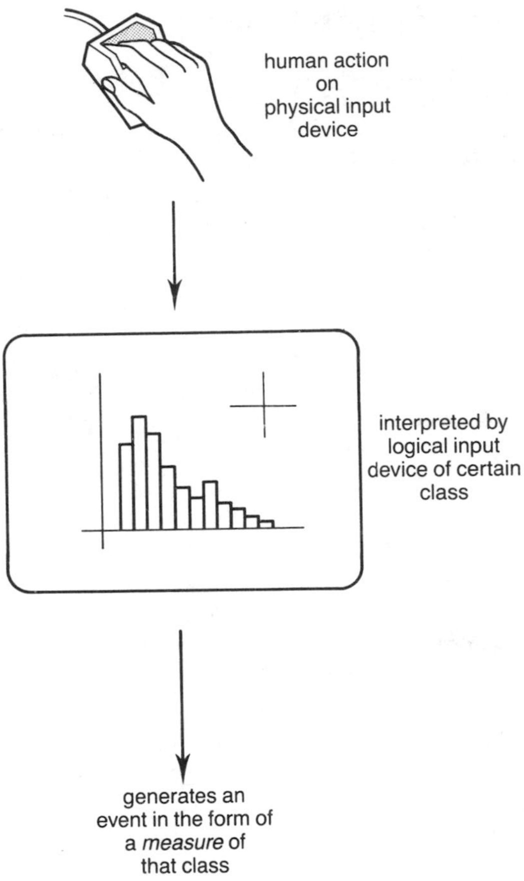
human action on physical input device
interpreted by logical input device of certain class
generates an event in the form of a *measure* of that class

Figure 5.2
Generating events.

size of the clock by determining the value *V* used in the *SetViewport* function. Second, the operator can select the time displayed by choosing the position of the hands of the clock. The first operator action is to be accomplished using the valuator input class and the second by the locator input class.

□□ EXAMPLE

Example 5.2 Valuator input class.

let val (*V*, *status*) = *RequestInput*(VALUATOR, ..)
in
  if *status* = OK ⇒ *SetViewport*(1, [*V*, 1.0 − *V*, *V*, 1.0 − *V*]) **fi**
ni

This example sets the viewport bounds as before, but now the value *V* is obtained as a result of the *RequestInput* function using the valuator input class. This function is evaluated as follows:

(1) The human operator is made aware of the fact that an interaction of valuator class has been initiated. The method by which this is accomplished depends on the nature and implementation of the input device in use. For example, in the case of a valuator dial, a light might start to flash. This warning to the operator that some action is expected is part of what is known in GKS as the **prompt and echo**. It is the prompt part of the prompt and echo.

(2) The program execution is suspended allowing the operator to, in this example, use the dial to select the value desired.

(3) Once the operator has turned the dial to the desired position, he or she must **trigger** the event by taking the required, specified action. In the case of a valuator dial, this action might involve pressing a button. There are two other aspects of the prompt and echo type of importance here. First, the operator should at any time know the value that would be generated if the trigger action is taken at that time. For example, the values on the dial should be clearly labelled, and the value that would be currently selected should be obvious. Second, when the operator has triggered the event, the system should respond and indicate that the input has been accepted. For example, the light that started flashing at the beginning of the interaction might now stop flashing. This provides **acknowledgement** to the operator that the interaction has terminated.

    The prompt and echo, together with the acknowledgement, provide crucial **feedback** to the operator, so that there is a level of predictability at every stage of the interaction.

(4) If the interaction has been successfully completed, then the *RequestInput* function will, in the case of valuator input, result in the selected value *V* together with a **status** value, which should be OK. If the interaction was unsuccessful, then the status value will be NONE, and the returned value *V* undefined.

To summarize:

(1) The system *prompts* the operator (for example, by flashing a light).

(2) The operator selects the value (for example, turns the dial) and the system provides a suitable *echo* so that the operator can see the value that would be selected at any time.

(3) The operator *triggers* the event (for example, by pressing a button), and the system provides an *acknowledgement* (for example, the light stops flashing).

(4) The *RequestInput* function returns the input event – in this case the value selected – together with the status. If everything is successful, the status is OK otherwise it is NONE.

Generally, there are various ways in which a NONE status can be generated. With every *RequestInput* interaction there must be a **break action** that the operator is able to take which forces a NONE return status. The point of this is that there must be a way in which a program can allow an operator to end a sequence of interactions, or change his or her mind about whether to start an interaction at all. Program code such as:

repeat...*interaction*...**until** *status* = NONE

is catered for by this break facility. In the case of the valuator dial, the break action might involve the operator pressing a special button marked *BREAK*.

The same ideas can be applied in the context of the locator input class. In this case, the operator positions the cursor on the display by moving a mouse on the desk top. First, the cursor is positioned to set the hour hand of the clock, and then again to set the minute hand. Ignore the complication that not all hour hand/minute hand combinations are possible in reality (see Exercise 5.4).

□□ EXAMPLE

Example 5.3 A clock (locator input class).

```
let val ntran = 1 and reftran = 0
in
  Set priority of ntran higher than reftran.
  SetViewportInputPriority(ntran, reftran, HIGHER)
ni;

Initialise two store variables of appropriate type for locator measure.
let val hour = store ((0.0, 0.0), 1, NONE)
   and min = store ((0.0, 0.0), 1, NONE)
in
  Request first the hour hand and then the minute hand.
  hour := RequestInput(LOCATOR, ..);
  min  := RequestInput(LOCATOR, ..);
  let val ((xH, yH), ntranH, statusH) = ?hour
     and ((xM, hM), ntranM, statusM) = ?min
  in
    let val D1 = sqrt(xH*xH + yH*yH) and D2 = sqrt(xM*xM + yM*yM)
    in
```

r is as defined in Example 5.2.

```
        let val p1 = (0.7*r/D1)*(xH, yH) and p2 = (0.9*r/D2)*(xM, yM)
        in
          Polyline [p1, (0, 0), p2]
        ni
      ni
    ni
  ni
```

Note that c*(x, y) is used to represent (c*x, c*y).

The *RequestInput*(LOCATOR) function is evaluated in the same manner as in the valuator case:

(1) There is a prompt to warn the operator of the impending interaction. In the case of locator input this might be announced, for example, by the cursor appearing on the display.

(2) The operator positions the cursor in the desired place on the display. The echo here is very simple: the cursor moves in response to the hand movements of the operator moving the mouse. The operator can easily see the position to be returned, since it corresponds to the position of the cursor.

(3) The trigger action in this case would normally be the operator pressing a button on the mouse. If the mouse has several buttons, then one button may be reserved exclusively for the break action.

(4) The acknowledgement of termination of the interaction may be a short sound, or the cursor briefly flashing or changing to another shape, or any one of a number of other methods.

Now the locator input class returns the located position in WC. However, the clock example shows that such a returned value in isolation would be ambiguous because there are concurrently *two* windows actually defined in the program and, of course, all the other windows exist as the unit square. So if the locator input class returns a WC point, it must also return which normalization transformation this point belongs to. Hence, the locator input class returns a WC point and the appropriate normalization transformation number. In addition, the *RequestInput* function returns the status, which may be OK or NONE as before.

Figure 5.3 shows a situation where there are several normalization transformations with different and overlapping viewports. Suppose the operator pointed to position *A* and triggered the locator event. This position is in normalization transformation numbers 0, 1, 2 and 3. Which should be returned? Normalization transformations are priority ordered and the one returned would be the one with the highest priority. The initial ordering is that the higher the number, the lower the priority. So by default,

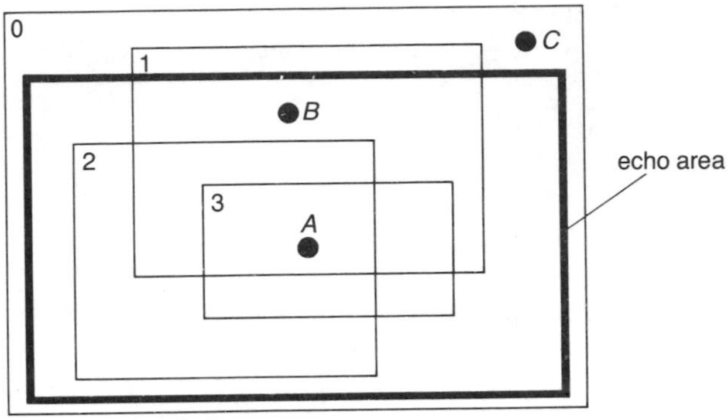

Figure 5.3
Priority ordering of transformations.

A is inside 0, 1, 2, 3
B is inside 0 and 1
C is inside 0 but outside the echo area

transformation 0 has the highest priority, 1 the next highest and so on. The *SetViewportInputPriority* function allows this ordering to be changed by the applications program. This is used in Example 5.3 to ensure that 1 has a higher priority than 0, and provided that this was the first change from the default ordering, 1 would have the highest priority of all. Hence, the locator input class returns a value that is the selected position transformed to a WC point in the window of highest priority containing that point.

5.2.2 Sample Input Mode

The *SampleInput* function results in values similar to the *RequestInput* function except that the sample mode of input does not require operator-triggered action, and does not return a status. Rather, the current values of the input devices are returned and the system does not suspend while waiting for an operator action. In the case of the valuator dial, the value of the current setting is returned, and in the case of the locator the WC point and relevant transformation number is returned, as discussed earlier, corresponding to the current locator position.

The request input mode means that the system suspends until the operator explicitly *requests* the input event by taking the appropriate trigger action. The sample input mode means that the input device is sampled and the current value is returned. There is a GKS function *SetInputMode* that can be used to set a given input device into one of the request, sample (or event) modes, and also the same function can be used to set the echo to ON or OFF. For example:

SetInputMode(LOCATOR, *wsid*, *devicenumber*, OFF, SAMPLE) would set the locator device numbered *devicenumber* on the workstation with identifier *wsid* to be in sample input mode, with the echo switch OFF. If the echo switch is OFF, the current position of the LOCATOR would not be shown – that is, the cursor would be invisible.

5.2.3 Logical Input Devices

Up to now, it has been assumed that the valuator and locator input classes are bound to physically different devices. In practice, however, this is not generally the case (see Chapter 17). Usually, one physical input device, such as a mouse, is used to implement several **logical input devices**. (This is akin to the discussion of the virtual graphics device and the GKS abstract workstation concept of Chapter 3.) A logical input device is an abstract input device that behaves according to a certain model. For example, in the case of locator input in request mode it behaves according to the description given earlier. The physical input device used as the basis of the interaction is not as such important. For example, in the case of request valuator input an ordinary keyboard could be used as the physical basis of the device. The operator would type the value using the keyboard in the normal way, and the event would be triggered by pressing the RETURN key. The break action might involve pressing the ESCAPE key. Similarly, a locator input can be implemented very crudely by the use of a keyboard. One logical device type can be implemented using many different types of physical device; one physical device can be used to implement many different logical devices.

It is important to realize that even though the physical input device used for a particular operation has no logical implications, the choice made can have far reaching ergonomic effects. An obvious example is that it is usually much easier and meaningful for an operator to input a point (that is, locator interaction) using a pointing device than by using a keyboard. There are also arguments for and against the various pointing devices such as the desk-top mouse, light pen, tablet and puck. Issues relating to such human–computer interaction are discussed in Chapter 14.

A common method for implementing a valuator using a mouse as the selection tool is for the system to display a scale on the screen, representing the range of values available for selection. The scale may look like a ruler or thermometer, or even a circular dial. This representation pops up on the screen – usually near the current cursor position – when a request valuator interaction is invoked. This acts as the prompt and echo. Now the operator moves the mouse so that the cursor points to a position on the valuator scale. Feedback serves to tell the operator what value would be selected should the event be triggered. This feedback is usually in two forms: in the same way that the current temperature reading on a thermometer is shown by the height of the mercury, so the current valuator reading is shown by the

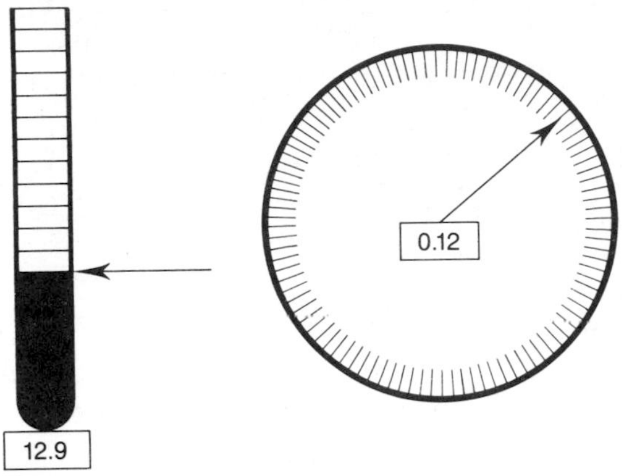

Figure 5.4
Pop-up valuator.

height of a simulated mercury level that rises and falls corresponding to cursor movements; in addition, a digital readout may be displayed to show the operator *exactly* what value would currently be returned. Finally, when the operator clicks the mouse button (the trigger action) the scale representation disappears from the display and the interaction is complete. This is shown in Figure 5.4. The one physical device, the mouse, is used as the physical embodiment of both the valuator and locator logical input devices.

5.3 Initialisation of Input Devices

The situation as discussed so far is that there are input classes (for example, locator and valuator) and input modes (for example, request and sample). But this is far from the complete picture.

Consider again the clock example. Suppose there was a (sensible) requirement to restrict the area of valid locator input to the inner square. For example, if the operator chose point *C* in Figure 5.3, then this should return a NONE status. The so-called **echo area** allows this restriction to be enforced. The echo area serves two roles:

(1) it specifies the area in which the prompt and echo occurs, and
(2) it determines the area from which valid input can be returned.

In the case of locator input the meaning is clear: an attempt to return a position that is outside the echo area will result in a NONE status. Also, strictly speaking, the locator cursor should disappear outside the locator echo area. In the case of valuator input, any prompt and echo appearing on the display should appear within the required valuator echo area. For example, a digital readout associated with a separate physical dial should appear on the screen in the echo area. Or, a valuator implemented in the pop-up style described in Section 5.2 should be displayed within the echo area.

In addition to determining the echo area of an input device, the applications program should also have the freedom to choose a style for the prompt and echo type. The prompt and echo is a very important part of the interaction because it helps to inform the operator of the meaning of his or her actions. For example, when a valuator is used to select a measurement (for example, the size of the clock), then echoing the valuator as a scale on a ruler helps to inform the operator that a measurement is being selected. On the other hand, suppose that a valuator is used to select an angle, then echoing the valuator as a circular dial (like a clock in fact) with a hand that can be moved around the circumference helps to inform the operator that an angle is to be selected. These representations of the valuator are shown in Figure 5.4.

In the case of locator input, there are several possible choices for the prompt and echo.

(1) The echo is simply a cursor (for example, an arrow) on the display, with the current locator represented by the position of the cursor.

(2) A **rubber band line** echo may be required. This is where a straight line is drawn from some initial position to the current position of the cursor. As the mouse (and therefore the cursor) moves, so the line stretches or shrinks giving the appearance of an elastic rubber band stretched between two points (the initial point and the current point). When the interaction ends, the line disappears. This echo would be ideal for allowing the operator to interactively set the hour and minute hands in the clock example. The initial point would be at the centre of the clock, and the rubber band line would stretch out in accordance with cursor movements.

(3) A **rubber band rectangle** echo may be required. This is the same as (2) except that the representation is now a rectangle with one corner anchored to an initial point and the other to a cursor position.

(4) The cursor itself may be represented in many different ways. The usual form is a small arrow, with the significant point of the cursor at the tip of the arrow head. The *significant point* is the true position of the cursor; that is, the position returned as an input. Another common cursor shape is a **tracking cross**, a small cross + with the significant position at the intersection point. (Some cursor shapes are shown in Figure 17.4.)

(5) A **cross hair** or **spanning cross** is another locator prompt and echo type. This is where a vertical and a horizontal line are drawn across

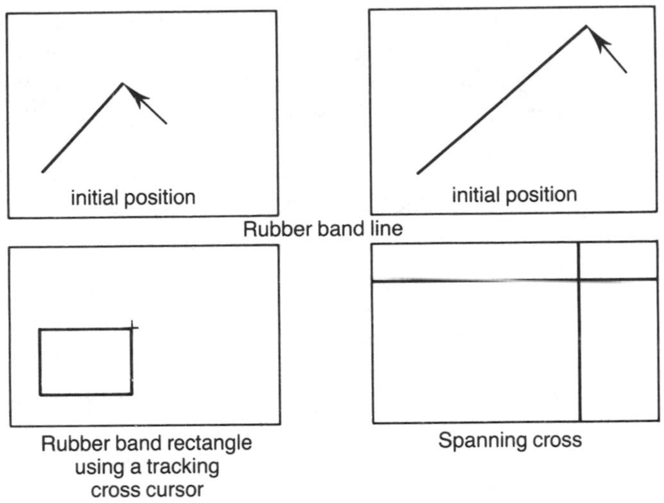

Figure 5.5
Styles of prompt and echo types.

the entire display area (or perhaps restricted to the workstation viewport); the intersection of the two lines then represents the current locator position. As the mouse is moved, so the cross changes its position on the display.

These ideas about styles of prompt and echo types are illustrated in Figure 5.5 (see also Exercise 5.7) and are further discussed in Chapter 17.

A third factor affecting the interaction, which should be under the control of the applications program, is the ability to make use of any special features of the input device not specified by GKS, but nevertheless possible on a certain implementation. The most obvious example is that it might be possible to provide data to an input device that determines the shape of a cursor. Such extra device-specific information is known in GKS as a **data record**.

Now the capability of setting these three features – echo areas, prompt and echo types, and data records – is catered for in GKS by *Initialise Input* functions. GKS requires that for every workstation capable of graphical input there must be a least *one* logical input device for each of *six* classes of input (of which only locator and valuator have been mentioned so far in this chapter). In other words, a workstation that is categorized as outin (output and input) or input has an input device for each of the required classes of input. There may be several input devices for each class; for example, there may be five logical input devices of class locator.

Each logical input device can be initialised according to the following features.

(1) An initial value – this determines the initial value, for example, as

used by the rubber band locator echo, for the initial position of locator input.

(2) A prompt and echo type number.

(3) A rectangular echo area given in DC.

(4) A data record.

The generic form of the function is as follows:

InitialiseInput(input class,
workstation identifier,
input device number,
initial value,
prompt and echo type number,
echo area,
data record)

Luckily (for the programmer), this function does not have to be used before graphical input is possible, for sensible defaults are provided. In the abstract programming notation, the strategy adopted is that *key words* are used to specify which parameters are to be changed in any use of this function. For example:

InitialiseInput(LOCATOR, wsid = 1, device = 1, EchoArea = [0, 500, 0, 500])

means that locator device number 1, on workstation with identifier 1, has its echo area set as shown, and all other values are left as they were previously. GKS maintains this information in the state list data structures, so that at any moment during program execution each input device has a state as given in this data structure. The state of any input device can be inquired, and hence the effect of changing only some of the parameters needed in the *InitialiseInput* function can be achieved by first inquiring the current setting of these values, and then calling the *InitialiseInput* function with the required arguments changed.

5.4 The Six GKS Input Classes

The six input classes are locator, stroke, valuator, string, choice and pick. Discussion of pick is deferred until Chapter 7.

In the following discussion of prompt and echo types, the term **implementation defined** is used to mean that the particular technique may be chosen by a GKS implementation. In other words, the effects that result when an implementation-defined technique is employed may vary across different GKS implementations. In addition, prompt and echo types with *negative* numbers may be supported for particular logical input devices in some GKS implementations. Where data records are discussed, it is assumed that they are represented as appropriate tuples. In the standard, the particular type representation of data records is not specified. An empty data record will therefore be represented by the void value ().

5.4.1 Locator Input

The major features of this class have been discussed in detail in the earlier sections of this chapter. Thus it only remains to mention the prompt and echo types available through the initialise input function.

- echo type 1 is implementation defined.
- echo type 2 is a cross hair (spanning cross).
- echo type 3 is a tracking cross.
- echo type 4 is a rubber band line.
- echo type 5 is a rubber band rectangle.
- echo type 6 is a digital representation of the current locator position.

□□ EXAMPLE

Example 5.4 Locator input.

```
InitialiseInput(LOCATOR, wsid = 1, device = 1,
                InitialValue     = (0, (0.5, 0.5)),
                PromptEcho       = 4,
                EchoArea         = [0.0, 500.0, 0.0, 500.0],
                DataRecord       = ());

val (p, ntran, status) = RequestInput(LOCATOR, wsid = 1, device = 1, ..);
```

This initialises locator input device 1 on workstation 1 to have the initial value of normalization transformation number 0, with the initial position at (0.5, 0.5). The echo area is as given and the data record is empty. The *RequestInput* function is then used, returning the WC point, the normalization transformation number and states. (Recall that .. indicates that this is not a true function in the sense that the value returned depends on the system state.)

The request (and sample) input functions must, of course, be supplied with the name of the workstation and input device on which the interaction is to take place.

5.4.2 Stroke Input

The stroke input class is similar to the locator class, except that a *sequence* of points is returned rather than a single point. The prompt echo types available are:

- echo type 1 is implementation defined.
- echo type 2 displays a digital representation.
- echo type 3 displays a marker at each stroke point.
- echo type 4 displays a line joining successive points of the stroke. This would normally be implemented using a rubber band line between each successive point.

□□ EXAMPLE

Example 5.5 Stroke input.

InitialiseInput(STROKE, wsid = 1, device = 1,
    InitialValue = (0, [(0.0, 0.0), (0.5, 0.5)]),
    EchoArea = [0.0, 500.0, 0.0, 500.0],
    DataRecord = (100));

let val (*n*, *p*, *ntran*, *status*) = *RequestInput*(STROKE, wsid = 1,
    device = 1, ..)
in
  if $n \geqslant 2 \wedge status$ = OK ⇒ *Polyline*(*p*) **fi**
ni

The *InitialiseInput* function is used to initialise stroke device number 1 on workstation 1 to have the initial value, echo area and data record as shown. The initial value consists of a normalization transformation number (here 0) and the sequence of points for the initial stroke. The first entry of the data record *must* contain the size of a buffer to be used to store the returned points from a stroke input. Here the required buffer size is 100. If the device cannot support a buffer size as large as this, then an error will be reported.

In the *RequestStroke*, *ntran* is the normalization transformation number of the window containing *all n* returned points in the array *p*. In the example, the polyline would only be drawn if the number of points returned in the stroke interaction is greater than 1 and if the status is OK.

5.4.3 Valuator Input

This has been discussed extensively in the earlier sections of this chapter. The prompt and echo types available are as follows:

- echo type 1 is implementation dependent.
- echo type 2 displays a graphical representation (e.g., the pop-up valuator).
- echo type 3 displays a digital representation.

□□ EXAMPLE

Example 5.6 Valuator input.

```
InitialiseInput(VALUATOR, wsid = 1, device = 1,
                InitialValue        = 0.5,
                PromptEcho          = 1,
                EchoArea            = [0.0, 500.0, 0.0, 500.0],
                DataRecord          = (0.0, 1.0));

let val (value, status) = RequestInput(VALUATOR, wsid = 1, device = 1, ..)
in
  if status = OK ⇒ SetViewport(1, value, 1.0 – value, value, 1.0 – value) fi
ni
```

The data record for a valuator input must contain as the first two items the range of permissible values. This function would initialise valuator device number 1 on workstation 1 to have an initial value of 0.5 with a range of 0.0 to 1.0. The initial value must, of course, be within the range. In the example, the value returned is used to set the viewport for normalization transformation number 1.

5.4.4 String Input

The string input class allows input of a character string. The most common physical device used to input the string is a keyboard. A good choice for the prompt and echo type for this class is a *query box* (also called a *dialogue box*) that is displayed on the screen, with the initial string (as set by the *InitialiseInput* function) shown. For the request mode of input, the operaor

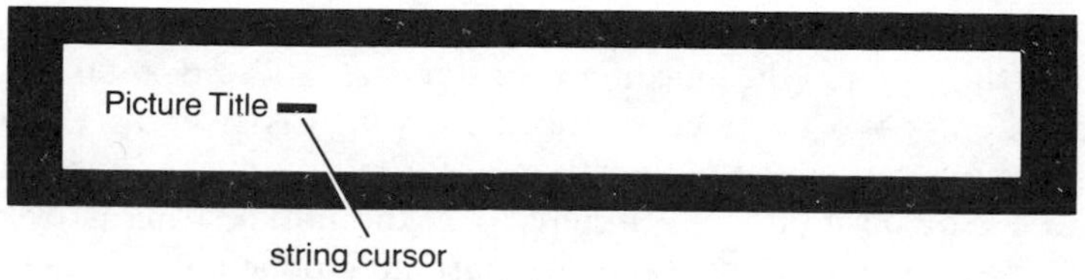

Figure 5.6
A string input query box.

would type in a string on a keyboard and the characters would be echoed in the query box as they were typed. The RETURN key would be used as the trigger and perhaps the ESCAPE key as the break. The idea of a query box is shown in Figure 5.6.

The prompt and echo types for string input are:

- echo type 1 displays the current string value (in the echo area of course). In practice, this could mean many different things.

□□ EXAMPLE

Example 5.7 String input.

```
InitialiseInput(STRING, wsid = 1, device = 1,
                InitialValue  = "Picture Title",
                PromptEcho    = 1,
                EchoArea      = [20, 400, 300, 400],
                DataRecord    = (80, 1));

let val (p, ntran, status) = RequestInput(LOCATOR, wsid = 1, device = 1, ..)
in
  if status = OK ⇒
    SelectNtran(ntran);
    let val (title, status) = RequestInput(STRING, wsid = 1, device = 1, ..)
    in
      if status = OK ⇒ Text(p, title) fi
    ni
  fi
ni
```

In this example, first the string input device number 1 on workstation 1 is initialised, then a point is obtained using *RequestLocator*. Finally, a string is described at that point where the character string is obtained using *Request String*. This example illustrates how an operator might interactively choose a title for a picture and place the title string at some position on the screen.

The initial value supplied to the *InitialiseInput* function is a string that is displayed in the query box. The data record must contain at least two entries. The first entry is taken as the size of a buffer used for storing the returned string. Here, the maximum buffer size allowed is 80 characters. The second entry is a string cursor position, which is given as 1. The string that is input overwrites the initial string at the position given by this cursor. Since the cursor position is given here as 1, the initial string is overwritten from the start of the string (at least partially, depending on how many characters are returned by the *RequestString*). For example, if the operator types *GKS slide number 1*, then the returned string is exactly the same as this. However, if the data record had been (80, 15), then the returned string would be:

"*Picture Title GKS slide number 1*"

Finally, if the data record had been (80, 9), then the string would be:

"*Picture GKS slide number 1*"

5.4.5 Choice Input

The choice input class allows input of a positive integer representing a selection amongst alternatives. This is usually used as the basis of a **menu selection** tool. It is in this class of input where the use of the data record is crucial, as the record is normally packed with a sequence of character strings that give meaningful names for the choices open to selection by the operator. In the clock program, for example, it would be useful to allow the operator to interactively select between a number of different styles of time representation around the circumference of the clock. These choices might be any one of the following:

(1) Use asterisks (as in the original program).
(2) Use small circles.
(3) Use numerals.
(4) Use Roman numbers.
(5) Use nothing.
(6) Use whatever the default is.

Some of the echo types available are:

- echo type 1 is implementation dependent.
- echo type 2 envisages a physical choice device such as an array of buttons each associated with some means of prompting an operator – such as a light. In this case, the data record has two mandatory

entries, the first being the number of choice alternatives and the second an array of values each set to ON or OFF. If the value for the *i*th entry is ON, then prompting for the corresponding button is allowed.

- echo type 3 allows the operator to choose between a number of choice strings displayed in the echo area. How the selection is made is not specified – a pop-up menu might be one implementation of this prompt and echo type. The data record in this case contains the number of choice alternatives followed by the strings.
- echo type 4 is similar to echo type 3 except that it is stated in GKS that the choice is made using the alphanumeric keyboard. Exactly *how* this is to be used is not specified. For example, the operator might be expected to type one of the strings displayed in the echo area, and then the implementation would match the type string against the strings displayed. Alternatively, each string might be displayed alongside a number, and then keyboard function keys would be used to select the desired choice.
- echo type 5 associates menu items with segments, which are discussed in Chapter 7.

□□ EXAMPLE

Example 5.8 Choice input.

```
InitialiseInput(CHOICE, wsid = 1, device = 1,
                InitialChoice   = (OK, 1),
                PromptEcho      = 3,
                EchoArea        = [0, 500, 0, 500],
                DataRecord      = (6, ["Asterisk", "Circle", "Numeral",
                                       "Roman", "Nothing", "Default"]));

let val (choice, status) = RequestInput(CHOICE, wsid = 1, device = 1, ..)
in
  if status = OK ⇒
    if
        choice = 1 ⇒ DrawAsterisks ()
      □ choice = 2 ⇒ DrawCircles ()
      □ choice = 3 ⇒ DrawNumerals ()
      □ choice = 4 ⇒ DrawRoman ()
      □ choice = 5 ⇒ DoNothing
      □ choice = 6 ⇒ DrawAsterisks ()
    fi
  fi
ni
```

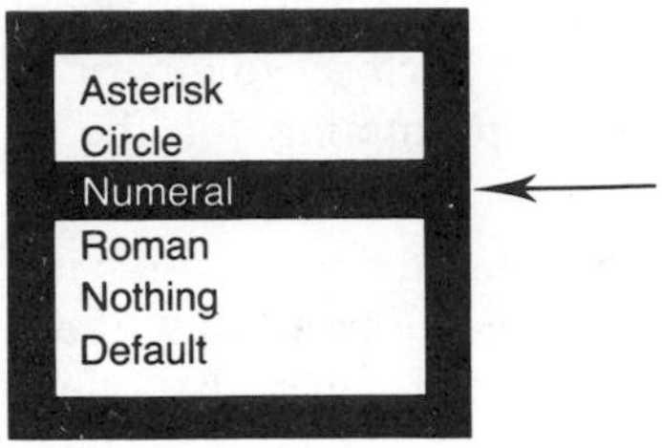

Figure 5.7
A pop-up menu.

In this example, the initial choice contains two fields, an initial choice number (given as 1 in the example) and an initial status, which can be OK or NOCHOICE. The point is that a choice measure is either a positive integer and the choice status returned as OK, or the choice is returned as NOCHOICE. Hence, to initialise the choice input device the choice status and the initial choice must be provided. If the initial choice is given, for example, as (NOCHOICE, 1), then this is contradictory, for the choice device has as its value NOCHOICE – in which case 1 is not a valid choice number. Similarly, (OK, 0) is also invalid. Now the complication arises because on *RequestChoice* a status is, of course, returned. This status can have the value NONE if the break is used or NOCHOICE if no choice is selected, otherwise OK. In other words, the return status from a *Request Choice* is a confusion of the status that is part of the choice value and the status that is by definition returned from a *RequestInput*.

A popular way of implementing the choice prompt and echo type is by a pop-up menu. Then, a *RequestChoice* function application would result in a menu popping up on the display within the echo area. This menu might look as shown in Figure 5.7. Now, as the operator moves the cursor across the menu box, the items are highlighted – for example, by inverting the video effect so that black becomes white and vice versa. The trigger action could be generated, for example, by the operator clicking a mouse button, after which the menu box disappears from the display and the interaction ends. The break action could be a specially reserved mouse button and the NOCHOICE value could be generated by the operator clicking the mouse button while the cursor was outside the menu box.

5.4.6 Concluding Remark

A final remark in this section concerns the situation where the prompt and echo types used in an interaction appear on the workstation display. This is, of course, the usual state of affairs. It is important that the interaction results in no permanent change to the display. For example, the cursor used as an echo for locator input must not leave any marks on the screen. A cursor is *not* part of the output generated by GKS and must not alter any part of the picture it passes over. Similarly, rubber band echoes have an ephemeral existence – at the end of the interaction they must vanish and leave the display exactly as it was before the input function was used. Similarly, pop-up echoes, such as might be used for string, valuator and choice input, may temporarily obscure part of the picture, but when they disappear what was 'underneath' them must once again become immediately visible and be unchanged. Methods for implementing such techniques are discussed in Chapter 11.

5.5 GKS Graphical Input in Pascal

There are 24 GKS functions dealing with request and sample input alone (and another eight for event input), and this is ignoring inquiry functions. This figure arises because each of the six input classes can be initialised, set into the required mode, requested and sampled. The proposed GKS Pascal, as defined in the Draft International Standard, provides a uniform and concise method of invoking these functions – in fact, it cuts down the number of procedures required from 24 to 4. This is achieved by making use of the rich data structuring available in Pascal. Some of the salient features are given here.

First, there is an enumerated type which is at the basis of the Pascal representation:

```
type GEInputClass = (GVLocator, GVStroke, GVValuator, GVChoice,
                     GVPick, GVString);
```

Second, there is a variant record containing the values returned by each input class:

```
type GRInput = record
                 case InputClass : GEInputClass of
                   GVLocator  : (NormTranLocator : GTint0;
                                 Position        : GRPoint);
                   GVStroke   : (NormTranStroke  : GTint0;
                                 Num             : GTint0;
                                 Points          : GAPointArray);
                   GVValuator : (Value           : real);
                   GVChoice   : (ChoiceStatus    : GEInputStatus;
                                 ChoiceNum       : GTint1);
                   GVPick     : (PickStatus      : GEInputStatus;
                                 Seg             : GTSeg;
                                 Pickid          : GTPickId);
                   GVString   : (Stringlength    : GTint0;
                                 Charstring      : GAString);
                 end;
```

Then, for example, in the case of request input, there is *one* function covering all six cases:

```
procedure GReqInput(class  : GEInputClass;
                    wsid   : GTWsID;
                    device : GTint1;
                var status : GEReqStatus;
                var value  : GRInput);
```

A curious result of the process of international negotiations resulting in a standard is that although this scheme was agreed for Pascal, it was decided that a more conventional binding, where each of the 24 GKS functions is represented by a separate Pascal procedure, would also be available. Hence, there are also functions called *GReqLocator*, *GReqValuator*, etc. available to the applications programmer. However, provision is made in the standard to encourage programmers to adopt one or other of the two interfaces in their programs.

This is also a convenient point to mention problems about the input data records. The structures of the data records are hardly defined in GKS, except in certain contexts where GKS insists that they must contain certain minimal information (such as the range in the case of valuator input). In the Pascal binding to GKS, data records are represented as Pascal records, where the detailed structure of these is (inevitably) implementation defined. However, where GKS specifies certain minimal information, then this is explicitly given in the Pascal data structures.

□□ EXAMPLE

The example outlined here consolidates the ideas introduced in this chapter. The purpose of the program is to allow an operator to interactively use each one of the GKS output primitives.

Example 5.9 An interactive drawing program.
Assume that an outin workstation has been opened and activated and that it has workstation identifier 1. In the initialise input functions, the echo area is taken as default, as is the prompt and echo where not explicitly given. (For notational convenience, the .. system state parameter is not shown.)

```
InitialiseInput(CHOICE, wsid = 1, device = 1, PromptEcho = 3,
          DataRecord     = (6, ["Polyline",
                                "Polymarker",
                                "Text",
                                "FillArea",
```

```
                                        "CellArray",
                                        "QUIT"]));

InitialiseInput(STRING, wsid = 1, device = 1,
            InitialValue      = "Type in a string",
            DataRecord        = (80, 1));

InitialiseInput(STROKE, wsid = 1, device = 1,
            PromptEcho        = 4);

InitialiseInput(LOCATOR, wsid = 1, device = 1,
            PromptEcho          = 2);

InitialiseInput(VALUATOR, wsid = 1, device = 1,
            PromptEcho            = 2,
            DataRecord            = (0.0, 1.0));

val LINE     = 1
and MARKER  = 2
and TEXT    = 3
and FILL    = 4
and CELL    = 5
and QUIT    = 6;

fun Interpret(selection) =
  if
      selection = LINE ⇒
        let val (n, p, ntran, status) = RequestInput(STROKE, 1, 1)
        in
          if status = OK ∧ n > 1 ⇒ Polyline(p) fi
        ni

    □ selection = MARKER ⇒
        let val (n, p, ntran, status) = RequestInput(STROKE, 1, 1)
        in
          if status = OK ∧ n > 0 ⇒ Polymarker(p) fi
        ni

    □ selection = TEXT ⇒
        let val (p, ntran, status) = RequestInput(LOCATOR, 1, 1)
        in
          if status = OK ⇒
            let val (string, status) = RequestInput(STRING, 1, 1)
            in
              if status = OK ⇒ Text(p, string) fi
            ni
          fi
        ni

    □ selection = FILL ⇒
        let val (n, p, ntran, status) = RequestInput(STROKE, 1, 1)
        in
```

```
                if status = OK ∧ n > 2 ⇒ FillArea(p) fi
              ni

           □ selection = CELL ⇒
              let val (p1, status) = RequestInput(LOCATOR, 1, 1)
              in
                if status = OK ⇒
                   Choose rubber band rectangle.
                   InitialiseInput(LOCATOR, 1, 1, PromptEcho = 5);
                   let val (p2, status) = RequestInput(LOCATOR, 1, 1)
                   in
                     if status = OK ⇒
                        Choose cell array increment.
                        let val (d, status) = RequestInput(VALUATOR, 1, 1)
                        in
                          if status = OK ⇒
                             let val n = round(d)
                             in
                               let val colour = store 1~(n, n)
                               in
                                 for 0 ≤ i < n do
                                 for 0 ≤ j < n do
                                    colour[i, j] := if odd(i + j) ⇒ 0
                                                    □ even(i + j) ⇒ 1
                                                    fi
                                 od
                                 od;
                                 CellArray(p1, p2, n, n, ?colour)
                               ni
                             ni
                          fi
                        ni
                     fi
                   ni
                fi
              ni;
              InitialiseInput(LOCATOR, 1, 1, PromptEcho = 2)
        fi
      nuf;

      fun Interaction ()
        let val result = store true
        do
          ?result ⇒ let val (selection, status) = RequestInput(CHOICE, 1, 1)
                     in
                       if status = OK ⇒
                         if
                           □ selection ≠ QUIT ⇒ Interpret(selection);
                                                 result := true
                           □ selection = QUIT ⇒ result := false
```

```
                fi
              fi
            ni
    od
  nuf;
```

A call to the function *Interaction* will initiate the main iteration of the program. This continues until the *QUIT* selection is made.

This same example is now represented in GKS Pascal:

```
program Draw(input, output);
include 'gksdefs'
const
  wsid        = 1;
  connection  = 'port1'
  wstype      = 500;
  device      = 1;
  errorfile   = 1;
  CLINE       = 1;
  CMARKER     = 2;
  CTEXT       = 3;
  CFILL       = 4;
  CCELL       = 5;
procedure InitialiseALL;
var
  class : GEInputClass;
  initialvalue : GRInput;
  typereturn : GEreturn;
  error : integer;
  mode : GEmode;
  echoswitch : GEecho;
  promptecho : integer;
  area : GRBound;
  datarecord : GRInputData;
begin
  GOpenGKS(errorfile, GCDefMemory);
  GOpenWs(wsid, connection, wstype);
  GActivateWs(wsid);
  for class := GVLocator to GVString do
  begin
    {inquire input device state}
    GInqInputDeviceSt(class, wsid, device, typereturn, error,
                      mode, echoswitch, initialvalue, promptecho, area,
                      datarecord);
    case class of
      GVLocator  : promptecho := 2;
      GVStroke   : promptecho := 4;
```

```
GVValuator : begin
               promptecho := 2;
               with datarecord do
               begin
                  LowValue := 0.0;
                  HighValue := 1.0;
               end;
             end;
GVChoice   : begin
               promptecho := 3;
               with datarecord do
               with ChoiceData do  {assumes a structure for
                                    implementation-defined
                                    data record}
               begin
                  Empty := false;
                  NumChoices := 6;
                  Choice[1]    := 'Polyline     ';
                  Choice[2]    := 'Polymaker    ';
                  Choice[3]    := 'Text         ';
                  Choice[4]    := 'FillArea     ';
                  Choice[5]    := 'CellArray    ';
                  Choice[6]    := 'QUIT         ';
               end;
             end;
GVPick     : {do nothing};
GVString   :   begin
                 with initialvalue do
                 begin
                    StringLength := 17;
                    CharString := 'Type in a string';
                    {depends on max string size allowed in
                     implementation}
                 end;
                 with datarecord do
                 begin
                    StringBufSize := 80;
                    InitialPosition := 1;
                 end;
               end;
end; {case}
GInitialiseInput(class, wsid, device, initialvalue,
                 promptecho, area, datarecord);
end; {for loop}
end;
{**************************************************************}
```

```
procedure DrawPoints(var status : GEReqStatus;
                     validnum : integer;
                     procedure proc(n : integer; p : GAPointArray));
var stroke : GRInput;
begin
  GReqInput(GVStroke, wsid, device, status, stroke);
  if status = GVStatusOK then
  with stroke do if num >= validnum then proc(num, points);
end;
{*************************************************************}
procedure DrawText(var status : GEReqStatus);
var pos, str : GRInput;
begin
  GReqInput(GVLocator, wsid, device, status, pos);
  if status = GVStatusOK then
  begin
    GReqInput(InputString, wsid, device, status, str);
    if status = GVStatusOK then
    with pos do with str do GText(position, charstring)
  end
  else
  status := GVStatusNONE
end;
{*************************************************************}
procedure DrawCell(var status : GEReqStatus);
begin
  {see Exercise 5.8}
end;
{*************************************************************}
procedure Interpret(selection : integer; var status : GEReqStatus);
begin
  case selection of
    CLINE    : DrawPoints(status, 2, GPolyline);
    CMARKER  : DrawPoints(status, 1, GPolymarker);
    CTEXT    : DrawText(status);
    CFILL    : DrawPoints(status, 3, GFill);
    CCELL    : DrawCell(status);
    QUIT     : status := StatusNONE;
  end; {case}
end;
{*************************************************************}
procedure Interaction;
var
  status    : GEReqStatus;
  selection : GRInput;
begin
  InitialiseALL;
```

```
    status := GVStatusOK;
    while status = GVStatusOK do
    begin
      GReqInput(GVChoice, wsid, device, status, selection);
      if status = GVStatusOK then
      with selection do Interpret(choicenum, status)
    end;
    GDeactivateWs(wsid);
    GCloseWs(wsid);
    GCloseGKS;
  end;
  {*****************************************************************}

  {main}
  begin
    Interaction;
  end.
```


Summary

The GKS output primitives *Polyline*, *Polymarker*, *Text*, *FillArea* and *CellArray* have been defined and illustrated in this chapter. (A further output primitive called the generalized drawing primitive is discussed in Section 8.4.4.) The input classes locator, stroke, valuator, choice and string have been defined, with discussion of pick deferred until Chapter 6. The modes of input – request and sample – have been defined (event input is discussed in Chapter 9).

The style of graphical input is determined by the prompt and echo types; for example, rubber band lines for the case of locator or stroke. The styles of graphical output are discussed in detail in Chapter 6.

Exercises

5.1 Translate the clock program into Pascal.

5.2 In the clock program, the circle is drawn in a very inefficient way. It is possible to reduce the amount of calculation by taking into account the symmetry of the circle. For a circle centred at the origin, if (x, y) is on the circumference, then so is $(x, -y)$, $(-x, y)$ and $(-x, -y)$. Using this information, write a more efficient circle-generating procedure. By extending this idea further, an even more efficient circle procedure can be written.

5.3 Alter the clock program so that the hands are drawn more realistically, at the very least with arrows at the tips.

5.4 In the interactive version of the clock program in which the operator can position the hands, find a way to overcome the problem that almost certainly the hands will be positioned at 'impossible' times.

5.5 To compute the WC point corresponding to a DC point the inverse of the *Dtran* and *Ntran* functions must be used – or, in GKS, the inverse of the workstation transformation and normalization transformation. Give a detailed specification of functions to realize these inversions.

5.6 Given that the normalization transformations are ordered in an input priority order, show that for any point on the effective display space there is a unique normalization transformation corresponding to that point. Consider the problems involved in implementing the locator and stroke inputs given that the normalization transformation numbers have to be computed.

5.7 Give examples where different prompt and echo types might be appropriate in the case of locator input; for example, when would a rubber band rectangle be preferred to a spanning cross, and vice versa?

5.8 Fully implement the interactive drawing program, smartening it up in any way that you think appropriate; for example, at the very least draw a border around the drawing area.

5.9 Add options to the drawing program to allow the operator to draw circles, ellipses and rectangles.

5.10 Experiment with your drawing program implementation and decide how easy or difficult it is to draw the pictures you require. Ask other people to similarly test your program. Taking into account your experience with the program, design and implement a completely new program in an attempt to overcome the difficulties. Repeat the process. Does the new program solve earlier problems but introduce new ones? Be honest – is the new program easy to use? How long does it take for a new user to learn it? Analyze the errors that new and experienced users make.

CHAPTER 6

GKS FOR STYLE

Chapter 5 was concerned with the core of GKS – generating graphical output and interactive graphics. Although the style of graphical input was discussed (the prompt and echo types), the style of graphical output was ignored, except to say that defaults would be assumed. But style can radically affect the nature of a picture and is a crucial component of computer graphics.

Up to now, lines have always been solid, filled areas hollow, markers asterisks, with only one text font. The only luxury allowed in Chapter 5 was a change in character height. In this chapter, horizons are broadened: GKS, in fact, provides two different methods, each complete in itself, for determining the attributes of the output primitives.

6.1 Choosing Colours

A picture with colour is often more interesting than the same picture in black and white. Colour is an extremely important mechanism for conveying information in an aesthetically pleasing manner. It can also be a source of beauty, as many of the plates in this book illustrate, and, of course, this is essential when producing 'realistic' pictures by computer graphics. The field of colour display and perception is quite extensive and difficult. Methods for realizing and generating colour effects on graphics systems are discussed extensively in Part Two of this book, while the human response to colour is discussed specifically in Chapter 14. In this chapter, the concern is with the method of representing colours in GKS.

GKS uses the so-called **RGB colour model**. This is an **additive** method of generating colours from three primaries red, green and blue: every colour can be represented by a certain combination of red, green and blue intensities. The intensity levels are measured on a 0 to 1 scale, where 0 represents no intensity (an absence of light) and 1 represents the maximum intensity possible. Every combination (red, green, blue), where each of red, green and blue are numbers between 0 and 1, results in a colour. The primary and secondary colours are represented as follows (see also Plate 25):

(0.0, 0.0, 0.0) = black
(1.0, 1.0, 1.0) = white
(1.0, 0.0, 0.0) = red
(0.0, 1.0, 0.0) = green
(0.0, 0.0, 1.0) = blue
(1.0, 1.0, 0.0) = yellow
(1.0, 0.0, 1.0) = magenta
(0.0, 1.0, 1.0) = cyan

Percentage values of maximum intensity for each of the additive primary colours can also be used as in Chapter 14. Other colours may be produced by using fractional intensities. For example, (0.55, 0.35, 0.1) can be used to produce the colour normally described as pink. Deep blue is approximately (0.15, 0.2, 0.65), and so on. Additional colour models are discussed in Chapter 14.

This colour model is not particularly suitable for human understanding, but corresponds closely to how colours are generated on graphics display RGB equipment. However, although in the model, colour intensities are a continuum on a 0 to 1 scale, in practice graphics devices must represent intensities as discrete quantities; for example, intensities for each primary colour may range between 0 and 15. Issues relating to hardware colour representations are discussed in Chapter 15.

In GKS, each workstation maintains a table of colour definitions. The entries in the tables represent RGB colour mixes. The table entries are referred to as **colour representations**, and are referenced by means of index numbers. These colour definitions can be set within the applications program. So, for example, colour index 1 can be set to mean cyan, colour index 2 red, colour index 3 deep purple, and so on. Colour index 0 always refers to the background colour on the display. If, for example, a line is drawn using colour index 0, then it will be indistinguishable from the background.

The function *SetColourRepresentation* is used to define the colour mix for a particular index on a workstation. For example:

SetColourRepresentation(*wsid*, *i*, (*red*, *green*, *blue*))

sets the *i*th entry in the colour table to be the particular (*red*, *green*, *blue*) mix for the workstation with identifier *wsid*. For example:

SetColourRepresentation(*wsid*, 0, (0.0, 0.0, 1.0));
SetColourRepresentation(*wsid*, 1, (1.0, 0.0, 0.0));
SetColourRepresentation(*wsid*, 2, (1.0, 1.0, 0.0));
SetColourRepresentation(*wsid*, 3, (0.55, 0.35, 0.1));

sets the first four colour entries to the table on the workstation with identifier *wsid* to be blue for the background colour, red for colour index 1, yellow for colour index 2 and pink for colour index 3.

Each workstation also has a default colour table, so that if the applications program does not define the representations for a certain colour index, then a valid colour representation still exists.

It should be noted, if it is not obvious, that this scheme allows the indices to be defined *differently* on different workstations. For example, on workstation 1 the representation for colour index 5 may be red, while on workstation 2 colour index 5 may be blue. Workstations whose underlying physical devices do not support colour cannot, of course, provide this workstation capability. Some devices support grey scale rather than colour, and some simulation is possible here.

6.2 Bundles

Just as a colour table is maintained on each workstation, so tables are defined for the attributes of lines, markers, text and fill areas. However, unlike the models used to define colour, which are based on concepts drawn from physics and perceptual psychology, there are no corresponding theories that can be used to define the output primitives. But in analogy with colour, the idea of a table of representations for polyline, polymarker, text and fill area styles can be used. In this case, the entry to each table is called a **bundle**, which is an apt name, for it conjures up the idea of a collection of disparate things wrapped together in one parcel.

The functions for setting the representations of each of the primitives are: *SetPolylineRepresentation*, *SetPolymarkerRepresentation*, *SetText Representation* and *SetFillAreaRepresentation*. However, the following generic function is used here:

SetPrimitiveRepresentation(*Primitive*, *wsid*, *i*, *bundle*)

which sets the *i*th entry on workstation *wsid* to be the specified *bundle*. In addition:

SetPrimitiveIndex(*Primitive*, *i*)

selects the *i*th bundle in the given primitive table to be the current one in force across all workstations.

6.2.1 Polyline Bundles

The polyline bundle has three components:

- the line style,
- the line width scale factor, and
- the colour index.

The line style denotes the type of line to be drawn. Every workstation has the capability of, at least, drawing lines in the solid style (which is chosen by default), a dashed style, a dotted style or a dash–dot pattern.

A workstation normally draws lines in some 'normal' (or usual) thickness; in other words, the thickness obtained if nothing different is requested. This thickness is called the *nominal* thickness in GKS. The line width scale factor provides a way of producing lines that are multiples of this nominal thickness. For example, if the line width scale factor is 2.6, then ideally lines are rendered using a width of 2.6 times the nominal thickness. In practice, workstations interpret this scale factor as best they can – for example, by rounding 2.6 to 3 and producing lines of three times the usual thickness. It is legal for a GKS workstation to support *only* the nominal thickness and ignore the line width scale factor.

The polyline colour index acts as a pointer to the workstation's colour table, which defines the colour mix to be used by a particular polyline representation. For example, if polyline index number 3 refers to colour index 15, which happens to be, say, (1.0, 1.0, 1.0) on a particular workstation, then polylines drawn using polyline index 3 are white, when drawn on this workstation. It all sounds very complicated, but this state of affairs can easily be brought into being, as shown by the function calls in the following example.

□□ EXAMPLE

Example 6.1 Polyline bundles.
SetColourRepresentation(*wsid*, 15, (1.0, 1.0, 1.0));
SetColourRepresentation(*wsid*, 21, (1.0, 0.0, 0.0));
SetPrimitiveRepresentation(POLYLINE, *wsid*, 3, (SOLID, 1.0, 15));
SetPrimitiveRepresentation(POLYLINE, *wsid*, 1, (DASHED, 2.0, 21));

SetPrimitiveIndex(POLYLINE, 3);
Polyline(*p*); This polyline would be drawn in white on wsid.

SetPrimitiveIndex(POLYLINE, 1);
Polyline(*q*); This polyline would be drawn in red on wsid.

Note that this example does *not* specify the style of polylines drawn on any other workstations that might happen to be active at the time. It is possible that on some other workstation, say *wsid*2, the first polyline might be drawn in red and the second in white. Polyline bundles are illustrated in Figure 6.1.

6.2.2 Polymarker Bundles

There are three components to the polymarker bundles:

- the marker type,
- the marker size scale factor, and
- the polymarker colour index.

The scale factor and colour index have the same meaning as in the case of the polyline bundle. The marker types that must be available on every workstation are dot, plus (+), asterisk (*), circle (○) and cross (X).

□□ EXAMPLE

Example 6.2 Polymarker bundles.
SetPrimitiveRepresentation(POLYMARKER, *wsid*, 1, (ASTERISK, 1.0, 1));
SetPrimitiveRepresentation(POLYMARKER, *wsid*, 2, (PLUS, 2.0, 3));

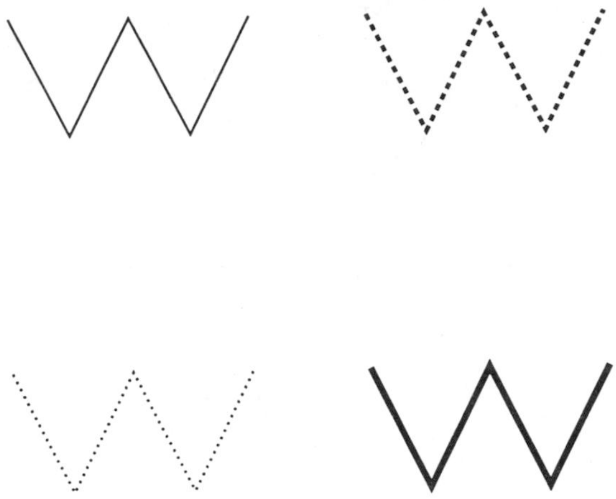

Figure 6.1
Varying the polyline bundles.

SetPrimitiveRepresentation(POLYMARKER, *wsid*, 3, (CROSS, 4.0, 5));

SetPrimitiveIndex(POLYMARKER, 1);
Polymarker(*p*1);

SetPrimitiveIndex(POLYMARKER, 2);
Polymarker(*p*2);

SetPrimitiveIndex(POLYMARKER, 3);
Polymarker(*p*3);

In this example, the sequence of points *p*1 are marked by asterisks using the colour representation defined as index 1 on *wsid*; the sequence *p*2 by plus signs; and the sequence *p*3 by diagonal crosses. This is shown in Figure 6.2.

6.2.3 Text Bundles

The text bundle has four components:

- the font and precision,
- the expansion factor,
- the spacing, and
- the text colour index.

The range of fonts available on a workstation is workstation dependent. Fonts are represented by numbers, and font number 1 must cater for all the printable characters found on a normal keyboard. The precision can have one of three values: STRING, CHAR or STROKE. Stroke precision means that text output conforms exactly to all the requirements of the applications

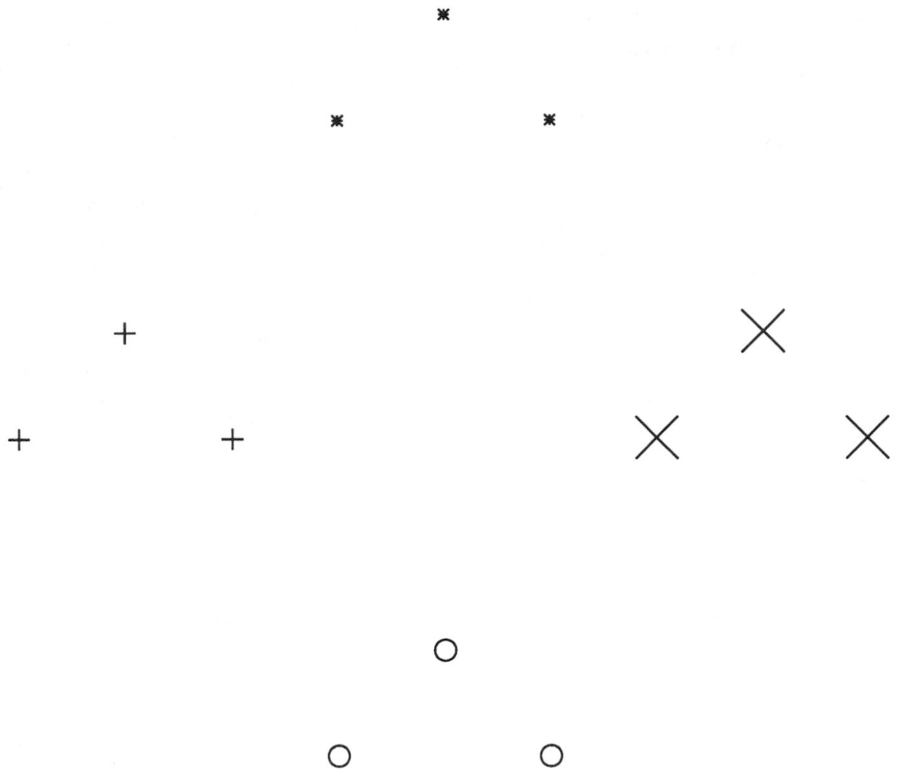

Figure 6.2
Varying the polymarker bundles.

program. It is in the exact position, orientation and size specified. It is also fully subject to clipping, so that a character that is partly outside the clipping region is correctly clipped. (The full meaning of this will become clear in Section 6.4.) Char precision text is a lower precision – that is, individual characters in a text string are positioned, sized and oriented in the best way possible on the workstation. For example, suppose the text is to be drawn at 45° to the horizontal. Then, even if it is not possible to rotate the individual characters, at least each character is in the correct position spaced along the 45° line. If a character is partially outside the clipping region, then the whole character may be clipped according to the capabilities of the workstation. Finally, string precision text is the lowest precision; that is, the only guarantee is that the starting point of the entire string is in the correct place on the display. The characters may not be of the correct size or orientation, and if the string is partly outside the clipping region, the whole string may or may not be clipped, depending on the capabilities of the workstation.

The advantage of string precision is that it is usually very fast, being based on character generators built into the underlying hardware or firmware of the graphics device. The advantage of stroke precision is that it produces geometrically correct and therefore predictable output. However, it is likely to be noticeably slower in execution than string or char precision.

GKS recognizes that not all fonts are available at all precisions, hence the notion of font and precision pairs.

Expansion has a similar meaning to the polyline and polymarker scale factors. Every font has its characters defined with a 'normal' aspect ratio corresponding to expansion factor 1.0. Hence, if the expansion factor is greater than 1.0, the text is expanded, and if it is less than 1.0 this has the effect of shrinking the displayed text. Of course, this effect is guaranteed to happen only with stroke precision.

Spacing refers to the spacing between characters. The spacing can have a value that is positive or negative. It determines the *extra* spacing between characters compared to the norm and is measured as a fraction of the character height. (Normal spacing is defined to be 0.0.) If spacing is negative, then characters are closer together than normal; if positive, then characters are wider apart.

□□ EXAMPLE

Example 6.3 Text bundles.

```
let val textrep = [((1, STROKE), 1.0, 0.0, 1)),
                   ((1, STROKE), 2.0, 0.0, 1)),
                   ((2, STROKE), 1.0, 0.5, 1)),
                   ((2, STROKE), 1.0, −0.5, 1)),
                   ((1, STROKE), 2.0, 0.5, 1)),
                   ((3, STROKE), 1.0, 0.0, 1))]
    and     p = [(0.1, 0.8), (0.1, 0.7), (0.1, 0.6), (0.1, 0.5), (0.1, 0.4), (0.1,
                   0.3)]
in
  for 1 ≤ i ≤ 6 do
    SetPrimitiveRepresentation(TEXT, wsid, i, textrep[i − 1]);
    SetPrimitiveIndex(TEXT, i);
    Text(p[i], "This is an example");
  od
ni
```

Figure 6.3 shows an example.

6.2.4 Fill Area Bundles

The fill area bundle has three components:

- the fill area interior style,

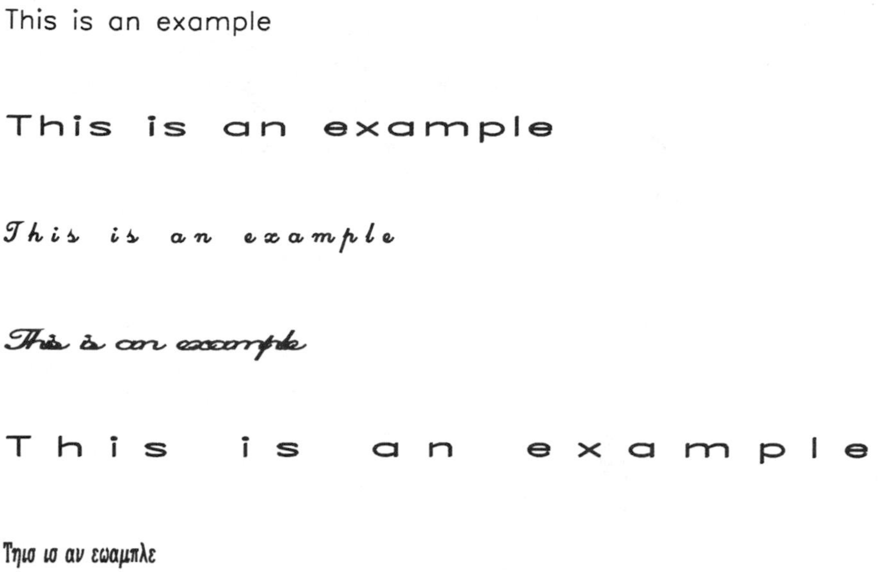
This is an example
This is an example
This is an example
This is an example
This is an example
Τηισ ισ αν εωαμπλε

Figure 6.3 Varying the text bundles.

- the style index, and
- the colour index.

The interior style may be HOLLOW, SOLID, PATTERN or HATCH. A hollow fill area is the polygon boundary. The solid fill area style generates a solid fill, where the colour used is determined by the colour index. The hatch style results in a workstation-dependent hatching pattern. A workstation may support a number of different methods of hatching. The one used is determined by the style index, which in this context is a pointer to a workstation-defined table of hatching methods. For example, on a certain graphics workstation, hatch style 1 might produce horizontal hatch lines, 2 vertical lines, 3 lines at 45°, and so on. Hence:

> *SetPrimitiveRepresentation*(FILLAREA, *wsid*, *i*, HATCH, 3, 2);
> *SetPrimitiveIndex*(FILLAREA, *i*);
> *FillArea*(*p*)

results in the fill area rendered using hatch style number 3 and colour index 2 on workstation with identifier *wsid*.

The pattern interior style allows the polygon to be filled with a pattern defined in the applications program. First, the program may define a pattern in the form of a rectangular array of colours akin to a cell array, using the following function:

> *SetPatternRepresentation*(*wsid*, *index*, *dx*, *dy*, *colour*)

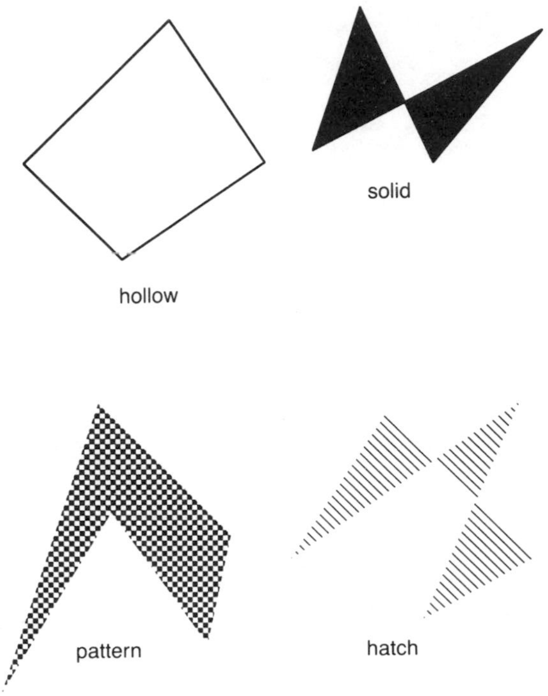

Figure 6.4
Varying the fill area bundles.

which can be used to define a table of pattern representations on a workstation. In other words, the table entry corresponding to *index* is the 2D array of *colour* indices. *dx* and *dy* are the bounds of the array.

The following additional points should be noted:

(1) When the pattern style of filling is used, the colour index of the fill area bundle is not relevant, because colours are determined by the colour indices in the pattern array.

(2) The interior style, the style index and the colour index are *workstation-bound* attributes of the fill area primitive; that is, the fill area bundles are bound to workstations, and so the table entries generally differ from workstation to workstation. However, the pattern size and pattern reference point are workstation-independent *global* attributes of graphical output. Once the pattern size or reference point has been set it is global to all workstations; that is, it is the same for all workstations.

(3) The distinction between attributes bound to workstations (which are the components of the primitive bundles) and those that are global reflects the need to distinguish between the **geometric** aspects of a

primitive and aspects concerned only with style. It is argued that the interior style, the pattern and the colour are concerned purely with the visual appearance of the primitive, which is independent of its geometry. However, the size of the pattern and the reference point are geometric entities and hence are independent of the workstation. This distinction between the workstation-bound attributes and the geometric attributes also manifests itself with respect to the text primitive.

□□ EXAMPLE

Example 6.4 Fill area bundles.

let val *colour* = [1, 1, 0, 0,
1, 1, 0, 0,
0, 0, 1, 1,
0, 0, 1, 1,
1, 1, 0, 0,
1, 1, 0, 0,
0, 0, 1, 1,
0, 0, 1, 1]
in
SetPatternRepresentation(*wsid*, 3, 8, 4, *colour*);
SetPrimitiveRepresentation(FILLAREA, *wsid*, 1, PATTERN, 3, 1)
ni

In this example, fill area index 1 is defined on the given workstation to have interior style PATTERN. The style index is 3, and on the given workstation the corresponding entry in the pattern table is shown. Now, when a fill area primitive is generated with the fill area index number 1 in force, the pattern is replicated over the interior of the polygon, as shown in Figure 6.4. The remaining questions concern the actual size of the pattern defined by *SetPatternRepresentation* and the point from which replication is to be started. Note that the pattern representation function really only defines the pattern, not its size; and for a pattern to be tiled into a polygon it has to have a starting point. These two necessities are covered by the functions:

SetPatternSize(*Xsize*, *Ysize*)

which determines the size of the pattern in WC, and:

SetPatternReferencePoint(*p*)

which gives the WC position of the starting point of the pattern replication.

6.3 The Geometric Attributes of Text

One of the workstation-independent geometric attributes of text has already been used in examples, this is the character height:

SetCharacterHeight(height)

which sets the WC height of text on all workstations. Of course, not only the *height* of characters is affected, but also their general size. This is because every character in a stroke precision font has a conceptual character box enclosing it. The aspect ratio of this box is maintained with changes to the character height, hence the width also changes. Of course, the aspect ratio is also changed by the character expansion factor, which is one of the components of the text bundle. Presumably, the character height is counted as a geometric attribute because it is set in WC, wheres the expansion factor is workstation dependent because it is a dimensionless factor.

The text path may be RIGHT, LEFT, UP or DOWN as set by the function:

SetTextPath(path)

The effect of these four paths is shown in Figure 6.5.

The text path works in conjunction with the character-up vector, which is set by:

SetCharacterUpVector(x, y)

The *direction* of the vector (x, y) (that is, the direction of the line from the origin to (x, y)) determines the vertical orientation of the characters. Imagine writing on lined paper, where the lines of the paper are the character base line. Further imagine that the bottom edge of the sheet of paper is parallel to the edge of the desk. Thus, when writing on the paper in a normal orientation the character base line is horizontal. This corresponds to the character-up vector (0, 1) (that is, a vertical direction). Suppose the sheet of paper is now turned so that its lower left-hand corner stays where it is while the lower right-hand corner is rotated upwards (anti-clockwise) so that the bottom edge of the sheet makes a 45° angle to the horizontal. In this case, the character-up vector is $(-1, 1)$ – that is, the upward direction of the text points to the North–West.

Whatever the character-up vector, when the text path is *right* the actual path of the text is at 90° to the character-up vector in a clockwise direction. When the text path is *left*, the actual text path is at 90° in an

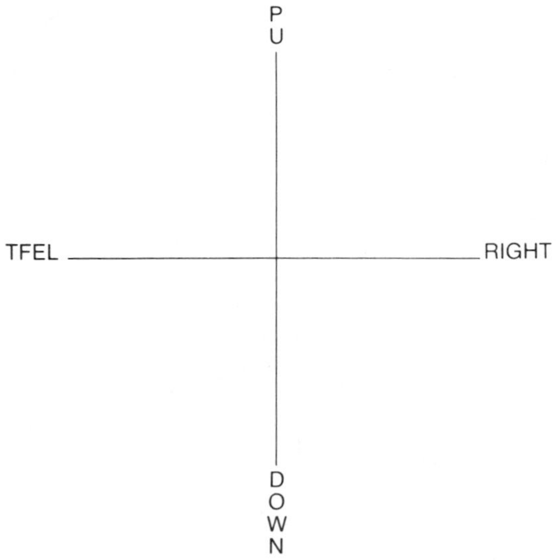

Figure 6.5
The text paths.

anti-clockwise direction to the character-up vector. When the text path is *down*, the direction of text is in the opposite direction to the character-up vector, and when the text path is *up* the direction is the same as the character-up vector. These interrelationships are easy to visualize and are shown in Figure 6.6.

The final geometric attribute of text is the character alignment. Imagine a box enclosing a text string. This box is called the **text extent**. When the function *Text*(*p*, *string*) is executed, the point *p* in relation to the text extent is determined by the character alignment. The normal alignment position depends on the path of the text. The normal alignment position is shown as a small circle in Figure 6.7. For text in its usual orientation, with path right and character-up vector (0, 1), the normal alignment is at the lower left-hand corner of the imaginary box enclosing the text string. The alignment is determined generally by the function:

SetTextAlignment(*alignment*)

where the value of *alignment* = (*Horizontal*, *Vertical*) with the following possible values:

Horizontal = NORMAL, LEFT, CENTRE, RIGHT
Vertical = NORMAL, TOP, CAP, HALF, BASE, BOTTOM

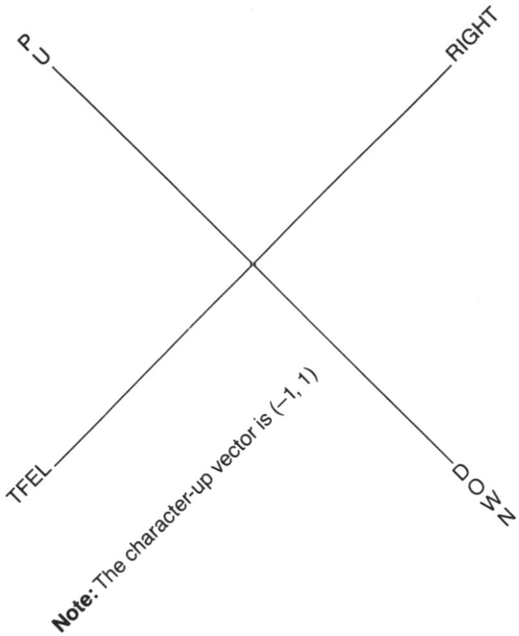

Figure 6.6
The character-up vector and text paths.

Again, it is easy to visualize the effects of these settings; Figure 6.7 shows some text alignment positions.

The geometric and workstation attributes of text provide a flexible means for controlling text output in GKS. However, two important aspects have not been mentioned yet, both of which make text different from the other output primitives. One concerns the ability to join sequences of text together in an easy manner, while the other makes it possible to predict the precise location in WC of any piece of text generated by a call to the text primitive. These two requirements are made possible by the *InquireTextExtent* function, which returns the text extent rectangle and a concatenation point given a potential input to the text primitive function.

GKS has many inquiry functions, all of which are useful for finding out the state of the system and the workstations. The text extent inquiry is particularly important as it provides useful geometric information for the text primitive. All GKS inquiry functions return error number codes – however, these are sometimes not used in the programming examples employing the abstract notation. If the error code is zero, then no error has occurred, otherwise an error has occurred and it can be interpreted according to a list of error numbers specified in GKS.

Figure 6.7
Examples of text alignment.

□□ EXAMPLE

Example 6.5 The InquireTextExtent function.

let val (*catpoint*, *extent*) = *InquireTextExtent*(*wsid*, (0.3, 0.7), "*Hello* ")
in
  Fill the text extent box in yellow.
  SetColourRepresentation(*wsid*, 1, (1.0, 1.0, 0.0));
  SetPrimitiveRepresentation(FILLAREA, *wsid*, (1, SOLID, 1, 1));
  SetPrimitiveIndex(FILLAREA, 1);
  FillArea(*extent*);

  Now draw the text in blue.
  SetColourRepresentation(*wsid*, 2, (0.0, 0.0, 1.0));
  SetPrimitiveRepresentation(TEXT, *wsid*, 1, ((1, STROKE), 1.0, 0.0, 2));
  SetPrimitiveIndex(TEXT, 1);
  Text((0.3, 0.7), "*Hello* ");

  Now join on some more text, using a different font and expansion.
  SetPrimitiveRepresentation(TEXT, *wsid*, 2, ((2, STROKE), 1.5, 0.0, 2));
  SetPrimitiveIndex(TEXT, 2);
  Text(*catpoint*, "*how are you*?")
ni

In this example, the *InquireTextExtent* function is used to return the concatenation point (*catpoint*) and the text extent rectangle. The concatenation point is the position from which a new text string should start if it is to continue from the given text string; that is, it is the point at which

Figure 6.8
An example of the *InquireTextExtent* function.

concatenation of the two strings takes place. The text extent rectangle is a sequence of four points describing the extent starting from its bottom left-hand corner, and then from there anti-clockwise around the rectangle corners. If the inquiry function call succeeds in this example, then the area of the text extent box is filled with yellow, the text is drawn in blue, and additional text is concatenated to it, but using a different font and expansion (see Figure 6.8).

6.4 Dynamic and Static Binding of Attributes

The primitive bundles offer a dynamic method of binding attributes to the output primitives. For example, when a polyline is generated, an intrinsic component of the polyline output is the current polyline index. For each of the polyline, polymarker, text and fill area bundles, the current setting of the corresponding primitive index should be considered as part of the output.

Now consider the following:

SetColourRepresentation(*wsid*, 7, (1.0, 0.0, 0.0));
SetPrimitiveRepresentation(POLYLINE, *wsid*, 1, (SOLID, 1.0, 7));
SetPrimitiveRepresentation(FILLAREA, *wsid*, 1, (SOLID, 1, 7));

SetPrimitiveIndex(POLYLINE, 1);
Polyline(*p*1);

SetPrimitiveIndex(POLYLINE, 2);
Polyline(*p*2);

FillArea(*p*3);

SetPrimitiveRepresentation(POLYLINE, *wsid*, 1, (DASHED, 1.0, 7));
SetColourRepresentation(*wsid*, 7, (0.0, 0.0, 1.0));

First, the colour representation 7 on workstation *wsid* is set to be red. The polyline representation 1 on this workstation is set to be solid with normal thickness using colour index 7. Fill area representation 1 is also set to use colour index 7. Polyline index 1 is set and a polyline of the sequence of points *p*1 is drawn. The polyline index is reset to 2 and another polyline is drawn. A fill area is displayed. Now the representation of polyline index 1 is changed to a dashed line of normal thickness. What should occur on the display? In principle, the first polyline should immediately change its appearance to conform to the new representation for the polyline representation index 1. The same applies to all other polylines drawn while the current polyline index was 1. However, the appearance of the second polyline is unchanged. Finally, the colour representation for index 7 is changed to blue. Now all primitives on the display using colour index 7 change to blue. In particular, the first polyline changes to blue and so does the fill area.

Hence, the primitive attributes provide a *dynamic* method of determining the style of graphical output. When the representation corresponding to an index is changed, then current (and, of course, future) graphical output tied to that index is correspondingly and immediately changed. (With most GKS implementations, immediate changes do not occur, except in the case of colour representation. This problem is discussed in Chapter 8.)

GKS also provides a *static* method for binding attributes to primitives, known as the **individual attributes**. For each aspect of each of the primitive bundles there is a corresponding function to set the value of that aspect individually. Therefore, there are 13 such individual attribute functions, each providing a static binding of an attribute to an output primitive. Moreover, it is important to realize that these static bindings are *global* – that is, the same value applies to all workstations. The 13 functions are:

SetLineType(*Linetype*)
SetLinewidthScaleFactor(*width*)
SetPolylineColourIndex(*index*)

SetMarkerType(*markertype*)
SetMarkersizeScaleFactor(*size*)
SetPolymarkerColourIndex(*index*)

SetTextFontAndPrecision(*font*, *precision*)
SetCharacterExpansionFactor(*expansion*)
SetCharacterSpacing(*spacing*)
SetTextColourIndex(*index*)

SetFillAreaInteriorStyle(*style*)
SetFillAreaStyleIndex(*styleindex*)
SetFillAreaColourIndex(*index*)

The parameters have the same type and meaning as the components of the corresponding bundles.

The problem now is that there are two methods for setting the attributes of a primitive. Firstly, the workstation primitive attributes determine the style by means of a table of representations for each workstation, and the current primitive index number determines which table entry should be used. Alternatively, each individual aspect of the style can be set to be in force globally – to apply to all workstations. Left as it is, this situation would lead to contradictions, as shown in the following example.

□□ EXAMPLE

Example 6.6 Fill area interior style.

SetPrimitiveRepresentation(FILLAREA, *wsid*, 1, (SOLID, 1, 1));
SetPrimitiveIndex(FILLAREA, 1);
SetFillAreaInteriorStyle(HOLLOW);
FillArea(*p*);

Here the fill area interior style is solid on workstation *wsid*, but hollow across all workstations. Which should be used – solid or hollow?

6.4.1 Aspect Source Flags

For each of the 13 individual aspects of the primitive attributes, GKS maintains a so-called **aspect source flag** (**ASF**). If the ASF for the fill area interior style is set to the value INDIVIDUAL, then the fill area of Example 6.6 is drawn hollow. However, if the ASF is set to BUNDLED, then the fill area is solid.

The following function is used to set the aspect source flags:

SetAspectSourceFlags(*asf*)

where *asf* is an array of 13 entries, each of which has the value BUNDLED or INDIVIDUAL. The array entries are in the order of the functions given earlier.

At any moment during the execution of a program the ASF for each component of the primitive bundle independently determines the source of the setting for that attribute. If the ASF is individually determined, then the source is the current individual value. If the ASF is BUNDLED, then the source is the setting of the component in the relevant table entry on each workstation. Styles set individually are statically bound to the graphical output – that is, once the output has been generated the style cannot be changed. Styles set in the bundle mode are dynamically bound. Changing the representation referenced by the index in force when the output occurred, changes the appearance of the output. It should be clear from this discussion that for a given primitive, some aspects of its style might be set statically and some dynamically. However, to avoid complications, applications programs will often set all of the ASF settings to INDIVIDUAL or all to BUNDLED, depending on preference and on the needs of the application.

Finally, it should be noted that all of the settings for the global and individual attributes are stored in a GKS state list (along with all the other global settings, such as those concerned with the normalization transformations). Defaults exist, and may be inquired. So it is possible for applications programmers never to have to worry much about the various settings, and just use the defaults as provided by the GKS implementation.

□□ EXAMPLE

Example 6.7 Aspect source flags.

```
let val asf =
  [BUNDLED, BUNDLED, BUNDLED,                    ASFs for polyline.
   BUNDLED, BUNDLED, BUNDLED,                    AFSs for polymarker.
   BUNDLED, BUNDLED, BUNDLED, BUNDLED,           ASF for text.
   INDIVIDUAL, BUNDLED, BUNDLED]                 ASF for fill area.
in
  SetAspectSourceFlags(asf)
ni;

SetPrimitiveRepresentation(FILLAREA, wsid, 1, (SOLID, 1, 1));
SetPrimitiveIndex(FILLAREA, 1);
SetFillAreaInteriorStyle(HOLLOW);
FillArea(p);
SetPrimitiveRepresentation(FILLAREA, wsid, 1, (HATCH, 200, 4))
```

This example has every ASF set to BUNDLED except for the fill area interior style. The fill area is therefore drawn using the hollow interior style. The representation for fill area index 1 is changed on the workstation to have the hatch interior style, and colour 4 instead of 1. Since the interior style has been determined statically for this fill area, the interior style remains hollow. However, the colour is set dynamically (the ASF for the fill area colour is bundled when this fill area is drawn), so the appearance of the fill area reflects the colour representation 4 rather than 1 on this workstation.

6.5 The Pascal Representation

The Pascal interface to the attribute functions is similar to the abstract language used here. The key features are the following data types and procedures.

```
type
  {the primitive attributes}
  GEPrimAttr = (GVLineType, GVLineWidth, GVLineCol,
                GVMarkerType, GVMarkerSize, GVMarkerCol,
                GVFontPrec, GVExpan, GVSpacing, GVTextCol,
                GVFillInterior, GVFillStyleInd, GVFillCol);

  {the primitives}
  GEPrim     = (GVPolyline, GVPolymarker, GVText, GVFill);

  {the aspect source flags}
  GEasf      = (GVBundled, GVIndividual)
  GAasf      = array[GEPrimAttr] of GEasf;

  {the primitive representations}
  GRPrimRep = record
                case Prim : GEPrim of
                  GVPolyline : (LType : integer;
                                Width : real;
                                LCol  : GTint0);
                  GVPolymarker : (MType : integer;
                                  Size  : real;
                                  MCol  : GTint0);
                  GVText : (FontPrec : GRFontPrec;
                            Expan, Spacing : real;
                            TCol  : GTint0);
                  GVFill : (GEInterior : GTinterior;
                            StyleInd  : integer;
                            FCol : GTint0);
              end;

{a generic Set...Representation procedure}
procedure GSetPrimRep(prim  : GEPrim;
                      wsid  : GTWsId;
                      index : GTint1;
                      rep   : GRPrimRep);

{a generic Set...Index procedure}
procedure GSetPrimIndex(prim : GEPrim; index : GTint1);
```

There are, of course, similar data types and procedures for setting the pattern and colour representations and the pattern reference point. There are 13 more procedures for setting the individual attributes, such as *GSetMarkerType* for setting the marker type individually.

The Pascal interface provides both the generic approach to setting the primitive representations and the indices, but it also provides a series of procedures to set each of the polyline, polymarker, text and fill area representations and indices separately. For example:

```
type GRLineRep =  record
                    LType: integer;
                    Width : real;
                    LCol  : GTint0;
                  end;

procedure GSetPolylineRep(wsid  : GTWsId;
                          index : GTint1;
                          rep   : GRLineRep);

procedure GSetPolylineIndex(index : GTint1);
```

provides an alternative method for setting the polyline representation and index.

□□ EXAMPLE

```
{Example 6.8   To set the polyline representation.}
var rep : GRPrimRep;
begin
  with rep do
  begin
    Prim := GVPolyline;
    LType := GCSolidLine;
    Width := 2.0;
    LCCol := 1
  end;
  GSetPrimitiveRepresentation(GVPolyline, wsid, 1, rep);
end;
```

□□ EXAMPLE

```
{Example 6.9   To set the ASFs to individual, except for the fill area interior
style.}
var
  asf : GAasf;
  attr : GEPrimAttr;
begin
  for attr := GVLineType to GVFillCol do asf[attr] := GVIndividual;
  asf[GVFillInterior] := GVBundled;
  GSetASF(asf);
end;
```

6.6 A Simple User Model for the Drawing Program

The drawing program of Chapter 5 allowed an operator to interactively select and use any of the GKS output primitives. The styles used for each of the primitives were those provided as default by GKS. This section looks at some of the issues involved in extending the drawing program to allow the operator to choose the styles to be used for the output primitives.

It is a well-known saying amongst sales personnel that 'the customer knows best'. Computer scientists who construct interactive systems for use by other people have slowly come to realize that in this field 'the user knows best'. From the outset of the design of an interactive program, the comfort of potential users must be the prime consideration. Here, comfort is taken in its broadest sense (literally) for the physical aspects of the system are vital to its use for possibly many hours at a time, and more generally in the sense of the ease of use of the system. Further issues relating to the human–computer interface are discussed in Chapter 14. However, the importance of these issues must be noted here because they affect the way in which new features might be added to the drawing program.

It would be easy enough to add a series of menus to the drawing program allowing the selection of style options. However, thinking about the range of possible options, and exactly how the operator is to use the program, shows that the interaction between the program and the user can become complicated. For example, the operator might have to first select from a main menu whether drawing or setting a style option is required. If the drawing option is selected, then another menu appears, which is the one given in the program in Chapter 5. If the style option is selected, then a different menu is shown giving the user the option to select a line, marker, text or fill area style menu. If the line menu is selected, then another menu appears giving the option to select the line style, the line thickness or the line colour. If the line thickness is selected, then a valuator pops up allowing the selection of a line width scale factor, and so on. While using such a system composed of a series of *hierarchically* ordered menus is a novelty at first, it can quickly become extremely tedious for the user.

The interaction between user and program is clearly a dialogue. The program initiates the dialogue by presenting the user with a number of alternatives. The user makes a selection and the system responds. The dialogue should be explicitly constructed, and designed to be as simple and as consistent as possible. Moreover, the user should be provided with a familiar *frame of reference*, so that the actions he or she is required to take are related to a context that provides an analogy to something known about from some other life experience. Such a frame of reference is usually called a **user model**. (There is a vast amount of literature on this subject. A good starting point is Newman and Sproull, 1979, pp. 443–478; and Foley and Van Dam, 1982, pp. 218–243.) For a more recent work see Clowse *et al.* (1985).

For the purposes of exposition, the example here is limited to line drawing, filling and drawing text, with only some of the possible GKS styles allowed for each. A simple frame of reference is that of providing the user with three tool boxes, one for each of line drawing, filling and text. The user 'opens a box' and the tools become available. The user continues to choose tools within the box until he or she decides to 'close the box' and either choose another box or start drawing. When an open box is closed, the user is currently holding the 'pen' from that box. For example, the user opens the line tool box and selects a dashed thick drawing style. If the user then closes the box and starts drawing, then lines can be drawn. At any time the user can 'choose another pen' or 'open another box', and so the interaction continues. A closed box, other than the one corresponding to the currently held pen, may be thought of as having its current pen sitting 'on top' of it.

The possibilities can be summarized as follows:

- *Initial State*
  All three boxes are closed and the line pen is currently held.
- *User Opens Box*
  Selection of tools (styles) possible within that box.
- *User Closes Box*
  The pen of this box is currently held.
- *User Chooses Pen*
  The current pen becomes the pen selected by the user from amongst the pens on top of the closed boxes.

The next step in the design is to decide how to lay out the display to *represent* these possible situations, and how to allow the user to take the various actions. The following simple ideas could be used in this example.

- A 'closed box' is represented by a small rectangle with the label of the box shown. The border of the box is drawn with relatively thick lines. If the box is not that of the current pen, then a symbol is drawn above the rectangle indicating the style of pen currently available for selection. The closed box corresponding to the current pen only displays its label.
- An 'open box' is represented by a menu of items, where each menu item is a possible style selection.
- The 'screen layout' shows a rectangular drawing pad and another area where the tool boxes are displayed.
- The user 'selects a pen' by moving the cursor inside a tool box and

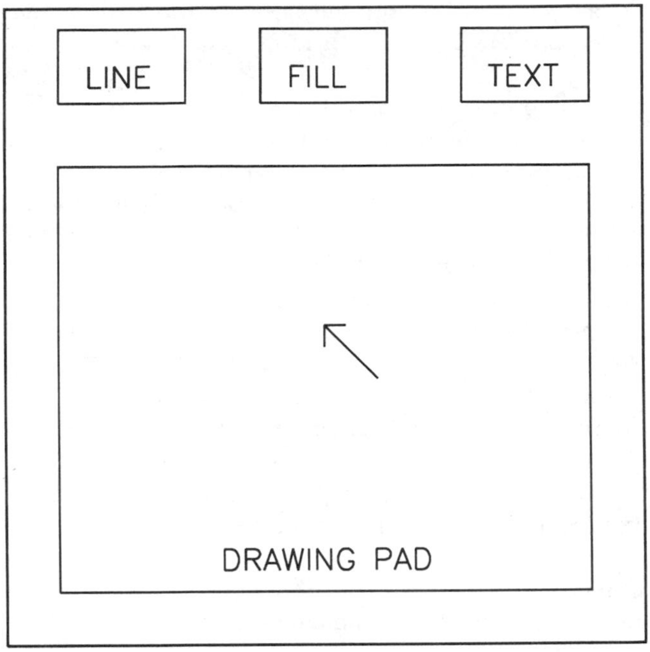

Figure 6.9
A simple screen layout for the drawing program.

clicking the appropriate mouse button once. This can only occur when all boxes are closed.

- The user 'opens a box' by moving the cursor inside the rectangle corresponding to the currently held pen and clicking the appropriate mouse button once. In other words, to open the tool box of the current pen, click once inside the corresponding rectangle. To open the tool box of a pen that is not the current one, click twice inside the rectangle for that box (once to select the pen and once to open the box).
- The user 'closes a box' by clicking over the close box option in the menu, or by clicking outside the menu box, or by clicking the break button on the mouse.

A possible screen layout is shown in Figure 6.9.

After having defined a potential user model and the methods of representation, the next step is to consider problems relating to implementation. There are three interactive subsystems that need to be implemented.

(1) The interpreter is concerned with the recognition and interpretation of the top-level stream of inputs generated by user actions. 'Top level' is in contrast to (2) and (3), which are concerned with specific subsystems.

(2) The menu subsystem is concerned with the selection of items within an open box – that is, menu selection.

(3) The drawing subsystems are concerned with the methods of generating lines, fills and text when the pens have been selected and are in use.

The menu subsystem is catered for directly by GKS using the choice input class. The drawing subsystems have already been implemented in Chapter 5. The interpreter can be easily implemented using request locator input together with the normalization transformations – each tool box can correspond to a different normalization transformation. When the request locator function is used, a normalization transformation is returned together with the WC point. The normalization transformation number corresponds directly to the tool box selected.

Let the normalization transformation numbers for the three tool box rectangles be 1 for line, 2 for fill and 3 for text. The drawing pad area is transformation number 4 and, of course, the effective display space remains transformation number 0.

To generate the function to interpret the input stream for the main subsystem, consider the system to be in any one of three possible states.

- state 1: corresponding to the line tool currently selected;
- state 2: corresponding to the fill tool currently selected;
- state 3: corresponding to the text tool currently selected.

The interaction generates a stream of inputs to the system. Each input is categorized as 0, 1, 2, 3 or 4 depending on which of the normalization transformation numbers is returned by the request locator function – that is, which of the viewports is selected.

Now for every possible input in each of the three states, an action is generated. For example, if the system is in state 1 and the input 1 is selected, then the line tool box menu is opened. If input 2 or 3 is selected, then the corresponding pen is selected; whereas if input 4 is selected, then drawing takes place. If 0 is selected, then nothing happens.

These transitions may be summarized as follows, which in fact describes the interpretation of the input stream as a finite-state machine (see, for example, Wulf *et al.*, 1981).

Set of possible states {1, 2, 3}
Initial state = 1
Set of possible inputs {0, 1, 2, 3, 4}
Set of possible actions {*nothing*, *SelectPen*, *OpenToolBox*, *Draw*}

The function *NextState* determines the next state from the current state and input symbol:

```
NextState: int*int → int;
fun NextState(input, state) =
  if
        input ∈ {1, 2, 3} ∧ input ≠ state ⇒ input
      □ input ∈ {0, state, 4}              ⇒ state
  fi
nuf
```

The function *Action* determines the action depending on the state and the input (including the point returned by the request locator function):

```
Action: Point*int*int → Void;
fun Action(p, input, state) =
  if
        input = 0                          ⇒ ()  Do nothing.
      □ input = state                      ⇒ OpenToolBox(input)
      □ input = 4                          ⇒ Draw(p, state)
      □ input ∈ {1, 2, 3} ∧ input ≠ state  ⇒ SelectPen(input, state)
  fi
nuf
```

This analysis leads to the following function for the interpretation of the input stream of the main subsystem:

```
Interaction: Void → Void;
fun Interaction () =
  let val state = store 1
  in
    do
      true : let val ((p, input), status) = RequestInput(LOCATOR, _, ..)
             in
               if status = OK ⇒ Action(p, input, ?state);
                                 state := NextState(input, state);
               fi
             ni
    od
  ni
nuf
```

The reader should notice that this interaction never terminates. This and other issues are discussed in detail in Exercises 6.3 to 6.9.

The important point to note is that the interaction involves a dialogue between the user and the computer. This dialogue occurs according to a well-defined grammar, which can be rigorously described and analyzed (in fact, as a finite-state machine). The rigorous description translates into a program for interpreting 'sentences' of the dialogue. Having started with a user model, through the various stages of design, representation and analysis, an interactive program is achieved. Even in this relatively simple example the emphasis is on constructing the interactive system in a manner that allows *reasoning* about the system according to some known mathematical framework. A finite-state machine is chosen here because of its simplicity. However, realistic systems usually require more sophisticated representations. (Some examples are Jacob, 1986; Sufrin, 1986b; Moran, 1981; and Reisner, 1981.)

Finally, the *SelectPen* function plays the role of providing important feedback to the user of the interactive system. This function is applied when the current pen is changed by the user clicking inside a rectangle corresponding to one of the other two boxes. What should happen is that the symbol representing the current pen (corresponding to the *state* parameter) is redrawn above the closed box rectangle for this pen. The symbol representing the newly selected pen (the *input* parameter) should be erased from above its box and, in addition, the cursor shape should be changed to embody this newly selected pen. Ideally, whenever the user is about to start drawing, the style of drawing that occurs should be clear from the shape of the cursor. The *SelectPen* function mimics the action of the user putting down one pen and picking up another – except that the 'putting down' happens by default in the action of 'picking up'. This is illustrated in Figure 6.9 (see also Exercise 6.5). Some further details of the drawing program are now given in the following example.

□□ EXAMPLE

Example 6.10 An interactive drawing program – revised version.

```
fun SetGlobal () =
  val wsid = 1

  Define some names.
  and DRAW_PAD = 4
  and LINE_TOOL = 1
  and FILL_TOOL = 2
  and TEXT_TOOL = 3

  Define a sequence of choice data records for menu items.
  and menu = [(5, ["Solid Line", "Dashed Line", "Double Width",
                   "Triple Width", "CLOSE BOX"]),
              (5, ["Hollow Fill", "Solid Fill", "Pattern Fill",
                   "Hatch Fill", "CLOSE BOX"]),
              (9, ["Font 1", "Font 2", "Double Expansion",
                   "Half Expansion", "Normal Expansion",
                   "Double Spacing", "Half Spacing", "Normal Spacing",
                   "CLOSE BOX"])]
nuf;
```

```
fun Initialise () =
  SetGlobal ();

  OpenGKS(_, _);
  OpenWorkstation(wsid, _, _);
  ActivateWorkstation(wsid);

  Set up viewports for the drawing area and tool boxes.
  SetViewport(DRAW_PAD, [0.2, 0.8, 0.1, 0.7]);
  SetViewport(LINE_TOOL, [0.1, 0.3, 0.75, 0.95]);
  SetViewport(FILL_TOOL, [0.4, 0.6, 0.75, 0.95]);
  SetViewport(TEXT_TOOL, [0.7, 0.9, 0.75, 0.95]);

  Set viewport input priorities.
  for 1 ≤ i ≤ 4 do
    SetViewportInputPriority(i, 0, HIGHER)
  od;

  Set aspect source flags to individual.
  let val asf = INDIVIDUAL~13
  in
    SetAspectSourceFlags(asf)
  ni;

  Draw borders.
  SetLineWidthScaleFactor(3.0);
  let val p = [(0, 0), (1, 0), (1, 1), (0, 1), (0, 0)]
  in
   for 1 ≤ i ≤ 4 do
     SelectNTran(i);
     Polyline(p)
   od;
  ni
  SetLineWidthScaleFactor(1.0);

  Draw text in tool boxes.
  SetTextFontPrecision(1, STROKE);

  SetCharacterHeight(0.2);

  let val p = (0.01, 0.4) and expansion = store 1.0 and t = "Text Tools"
  in
    do
      true ⇒
        let val (_, extent) = InquireTextExtent(wsid, p, t)
        in
          let val (x, y) = extent[1]  Rightmost position of text extent.
          in
            if
                x ≥ 1.0 ⇒ expansion := expansion*0.95;
                          SetCharacterExpansion(expansion)
              □ x < 1.0 ⇒ breakdo      Break out of do...od.
            fi
```

```
          ni
        ni
    od
  ni;

  let val label = ["Line Tools", "Fill Tools", "Text Tools"]
  in
    for 0 ≤ i ≤ 2 do
      SelectNtran(i + 1);
      Text((0.01, 0.4), label[i]);
    od
  ni
nuf;

fun OpenToolBox(input) =

  InitialiseInput(CHOICE, wsid, device = 1, InitialValue = (1, OK),
                  PromptEcho = 3, area = _, DataRecord = menu[input − 1]);

  do
    true ⇒
    let val (item, status) = RequestInput(CHOICE, wsid, 1, ..)
    in
      if status = OK ⇒

      if
          input = LINE_TOOL ⇒
          if    item = 1 ⇒ SetLineType(1) Solid
            □ item = 2 ⇒ SetLineType(2) Dashed
            □ item = 3 ⇒ SetLineWidthScaleFactor(2.0)
            □ item = 4 ⇒ SetLineWidthScaleFactor(3.0)
            □ item = 5 ⇒ breakdo

          fi
        □ input = FILL_TOOL ⇒
          if    item = 1 ⇒ SetFillAreaInteriorStyle(HOLLOW);
            □ item = 2 ⇒ SetFillAreaInteriorStyle(SOLID);
            □ item = 3 ⇒ SetFillAreaInteriorStyle(PATTERN);
            □ item = 4 ⇒ SetFillAreaInteriorStyle(HATCH);
            □ item = 5 ⇒ breakdo;

          fi
        □ input = TEXT_TOOL ⇒
          if    item = 1 ⇒ SetTextFontPrecision(1, STROKE)
            □ item = 2 ⇒SetTextFontPrecision(2, STROKE)
            □ item = 3 ⇒ SetCharacterExpansionFactor(2.0)
            □ item = 4 ⇒ SetCharacterExpansionFactor(0.5)
            □ item = 5 ⇒ SetCharacterExpansionFactor(1.0)
            □ item = 6 ⇒ SetCharacterSpacing(2.0)
            □ item = 7 ⇒ SetCharacterSpacing(0.5)
            □ item = 8 ⇒ SetCharacterSpacing(1.0)
            □ item = 9 ⇒ breakdo
          fi
```

```
          fi
            □ status ∈ {NOCHOICE, NONE} ⇒ breakdo
         fi
       ni
     od
   nuf;

   fun Draw(p, state) =
     if
         state = LINE_TOOL ⇒ Initialise stroke to start at p.
           InitialiseInput(STROKE, wsid, 1, InitialValue = (1, [p]));
           let val (n, q, ntran, status) = RequestInput(STROKE, wsid, 1, ..)
           in
             if status = OK ∧ n > 1 ⇒ Polyline(q)
             fi
           ni
       □ state = FILL_TOOL ⇒
           InitialiseInput(STROKE, wsid, 1, InitialValue = (1, [p]));
           let val (n, q, ntran, status) = RequestInput(STROKE, wsid, 1, ..)
           in
             if status = OK ∧ n > 2 ⇒ FillArea(q)
             fi
           ni
       □ state = TEXT_TOOL ⇒
           let val (string, status) = RequestInput(STRING, wsid, 1, ..)
           in
             if status = OK ⇒ Text(p, string)
             fi
           ni
     fi
   nuf

   fun program () =
     Initialise ();
     Interaction ()
   nuf
```

The *Initialise* function opens GKS, opens and activates a workstation, establishes the appropriate normalization transformations and draws the screen layout. It also sets all the aspect source flags to INDIVIDUAL. (The use made of the character expansion factor to fit the tool box labels into the right window size is crude but effective.)

Execution of the function *program* executes *Initialise* and then enters the infinite iteration of the *Interaction* function. Each cycle gets the next input (*RequestInput*(LOCATOR)), takes the appropriate action (*Action*) and determines the next state (*NextState*). The *Action* function either applies the drawing function, opens the tool box menu, changes the pen or does nothing. The *Draw* function is similar to that in the program of Chapter 5.

The *OpenToolBox* function repeatedly applies *RequestChoice* and the attribute-setting function, depending on the option selected from the menu. (The reader should examine the exercises for further discussion of this program.)

Summary

This chapter has introduced the two methods for determining the style of graphical output in GKS. For each of the polyline, polymarker, text and fill area primitives there is a corresponding current global index. The value of this index, for example, in the case of polyline is a pointer into the polyline bundle tables defined on the workstations. Each entry in the bundle table consists of a setting for the line type, line thickness and an index into the workstation colour table. These bundle table representations may be redefined by the applications program using the *SetRepresentation* functions. If for a particular attribute, such as line type, the aspect source flag is BUNDLED, then when a polyline is generated the line type is determined from the appropriate entry in the polyline bundle tables on each of the active workstations. If the aspect source flag is INDIVIDUAL, then the line type is determined from the globally set line type. Finally, some of the ideas of this and previous chapters have been brought together in an example interactive drawing program. The major concept of a user model was used in the design of this simple interactive system.

Exercises

6.1 Use the *SetColourRepresentation* function to write a program to display the colour chart of Plate 25. Implement the program on a colour graphics display to the greatest accuracy permitted by the colour resolution of the display.

6.2 The dynamic property of the colour representation is that a change in definition of the colour represented by an index changes the colour of all output primitives drawn with that index. Use this fact to show how to animate the hands of the clock generated by the clock program of Chapter 5. What are the limitations of animation based on the colour representations?

6.3 Why do you think that the interactive drawing program of

Example 6.10 adopted the strategy of setting all the aspect source flags to INDIVIDUAL?

6.4 Can effects be produced by using mixed aspect source flags (that is, some BUNDLED and some INDIVIDUAL) which could not be produced by setting the flags either all to INDIVIDUAL or all BUNDLED?

6.5 The function *SelectPen* was discussed in Section 6.5 but no rule was given. Give a complete specification of this function. Note that it should be possible in a GKS implementation to change the cursor shape by use of the data record argument of *InitialiseInput*. However, this is not guaranteed, for it is not required by GKS.

6.6 Add a method to allow the user to terminate the program. The method chosen should fit cleanly into the user model.

6.7 Suppose the interactive drawing program is able to support three workstations:

(a) a bitmapped display that is suitable for very fast graphical output and interaction, but which only has black and white colours;

(b) a high-resolution raster-based colour display;

(c) a pen plotter with six different coloured pens.

The aim of the system is to allow users to quickly generate pictures on the bitmapped display and to copy them to the colour display for reproduction of 35 mm slides, or alternatively to copy them to the plotter to produce overhead projector style slides. Design a suitable user model and dialogue to allow the user to set the styles (possibly differently) on these three workstations.

6.8 An important requirement in interactive drawing is to allow the user's drawing to be guided by a rectangular grid (mimicking drawing on squared graph paper). This requires two additional features.

(a) It must be possible to draw a grid on the display, and also to delete it without ruining the picture. Is this possible using the features of GKS discussed so far?

(b) During the drawing interaction (for lines, fill and text), when the user inputs a point (as delivered by *RequestInput* LOCATOR or STROKE), the actual point used by the program should be at the nearest grid intersection if the grid is displayed. In other words, the vertices of polylines and fill areas should always be at the grid intersections. How is this form of interaction achieved?

6.9 Complete the interactive drawing program by adding colour selection and the drawing of markers. Implement the program fully in Pascal.

CHAPTER 7

PICTURE SEGMENTS

The graphics system described so far is quite powerful and flexible. A number of output primitives and their attributes have been discussed, and some fundamental interactive tools introduced. Moreover, the drawing program of Chapter 6 is usable as a basic means for constructing pictures, especially with the addition of colour. This chapter examines how the program can be further improved by using segments – to allow modification of the picture.

7.1 Introduction

Although the drawing program of Chapter 6 is interactive, it still does not possess a crucial capability first mentioned in Chapter 2. That is, the user of the program can create and add to a picture, but cannot *modify* anything once it has been displayed. Modification requires at least the following features:

(1) the ability to selectively *delete* part of the picture;

(2) the ability to *transform* part of the picture, in particular by translation, scaling or rotation.

The first of these features can be achieved within the capabilities of GKS as described to date: selective deletion can be catered for by allowing the user to construct a fill area with a solid interior style and using the colour of the background (colour index 0) for shading. This can be useful as a quick method of deleting some unwanted part of the picture. However, difficulties arise if the part to be deleted overlaps something that is not to be deleted. In any case, the problem with this approach is that it is a trick – it makes use

Figure 7.1
A famous face stored in segments.

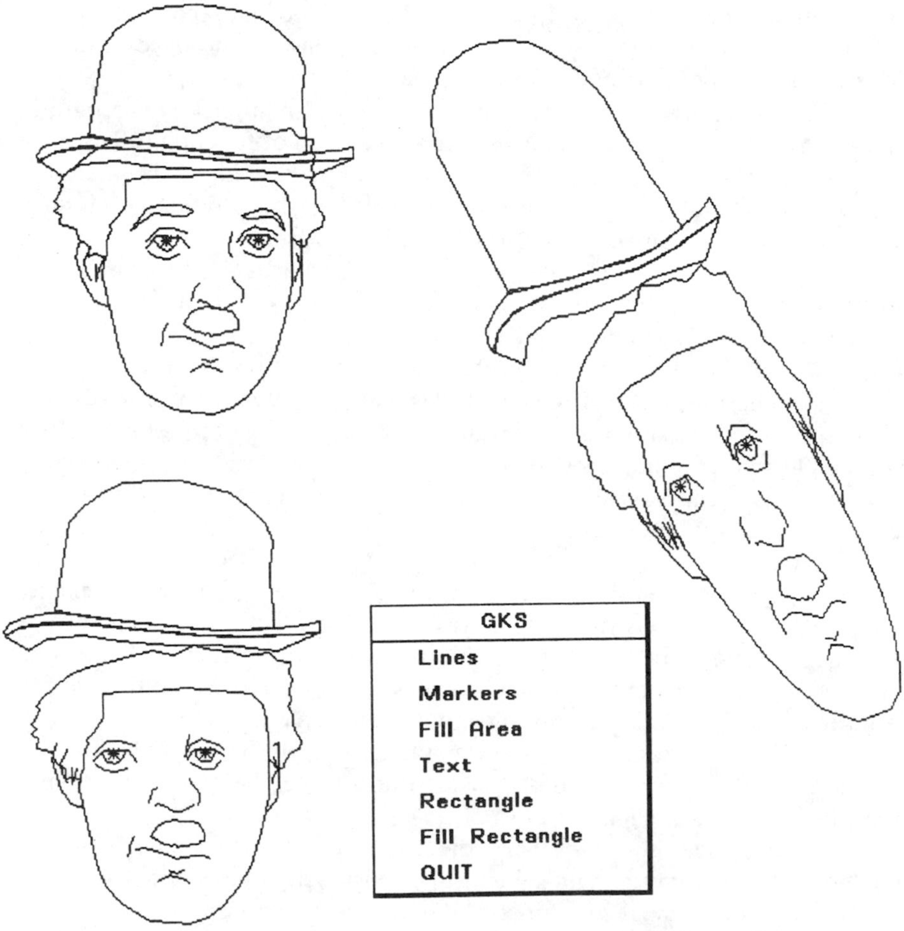

Figure 7.2 Modification of the segments produces new faces. This figure also shows one of the menus used to create the pictures.

of a capability of the system to achieve an effect quite different from its main purpose. It is surely preferable to look for a new concept purposely designed for picture modification.

7.2 Segments

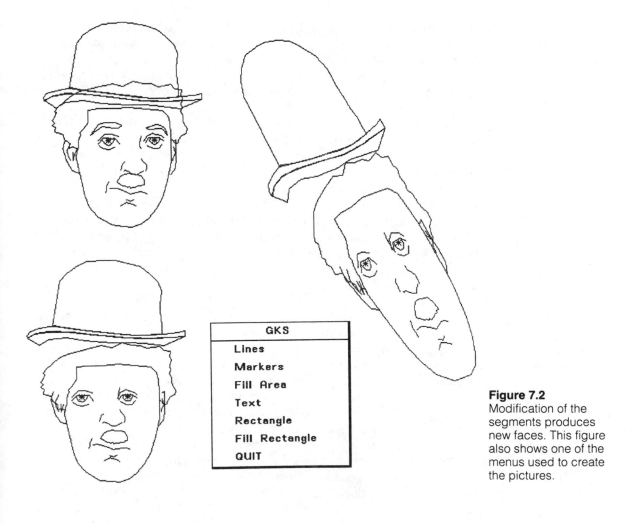

Segments provide a way of creating a picture in a structured manner. Pictures are usually made up of a number of components, which are often only meaningful to the author. Consider Figure 7.1, for example, which shows a picture of a famous face. This face is made up of several separate, major components – eyes, nose, mouth, hair, face outline. Figure 7.2 shows how these components can be independently modified and recombined using different transformations of the original versions to produce different looking faces – perhaps potential relatives.

For such a transformation to be achieved by an applications program, the program must be able to specify that a collection of function calls, which generate graphical output primitives, can be grouped together and treated as a single entity, referred to by a unique identifier. In addition, each such group of output primitives must be *retained* by the graphics system and have associated *attributes* determining its state. Considering again the examples of Figures 7.1 and 7.2, the most obvious attribute is the one that describes the current translation, rotation and scaling for each group in relation to its original rendering. Finally, such a retained group must be *re-executed* – most obviously when its state has changed. Typically, re-execution requires that the display representation of the group is instantly changed to reflect its new state. (On real graphics systems, this requirement is an ideal rather than a reality.) The terms *redraw* or *redisplay* are used interchangeably here to mean the same as re-execute.

Such a group of output primitives is usually called a **segment**. The foregoing has only outlined the basic ideas involved. Graphics packages adopt different detailed views of the structure and functions of segments. A very general model provides for the hierarchical construction of pictures by allowing segments to execute each other as well as their component output primitive functions. Such an arrangement provides a powerful environment for graphics modelling, and has been adopted as the core of the PHIGS standard (ISO, 1986d), which is discussed in Chapter 10. An illustration of the idea is shown in Figure 7.3.

In such hierarchical systems, the data structure defining the picture (called here the **segment data structure**) is an acyclic graph. GKS adopts a relatively simple view of segments. The data structure describing the picture is a sequence of segments (a linear list), where each segment consists of the attributes whose values define its state (for example, its current transformation and its visibility) and the sequence of its constituent output primitives. The details of precisely what is stored in GKS segments is discussed in Section 7.3. Although conceptually the GKS segment data structure is a linear list, implementors may choose a different data representation for the purposes of efficiency (see Exercise 7.1). The remainder of this section considers an example based on a subset of the GKS segment functions.

Creation of a segment by an applications program requires bracketing a group of consecutive output primitive function calls. Therefore, there must be a way of opening and closing the 'brackets'. These are provided by the two functions *CreateSegment* and *CloseSegment*, which are now introduced together with some other basic functions.

(1) *CreateSegment*(*SegmentIdentifier*) When this function is executed, a new entry is added to the segment data structure to hold the segment

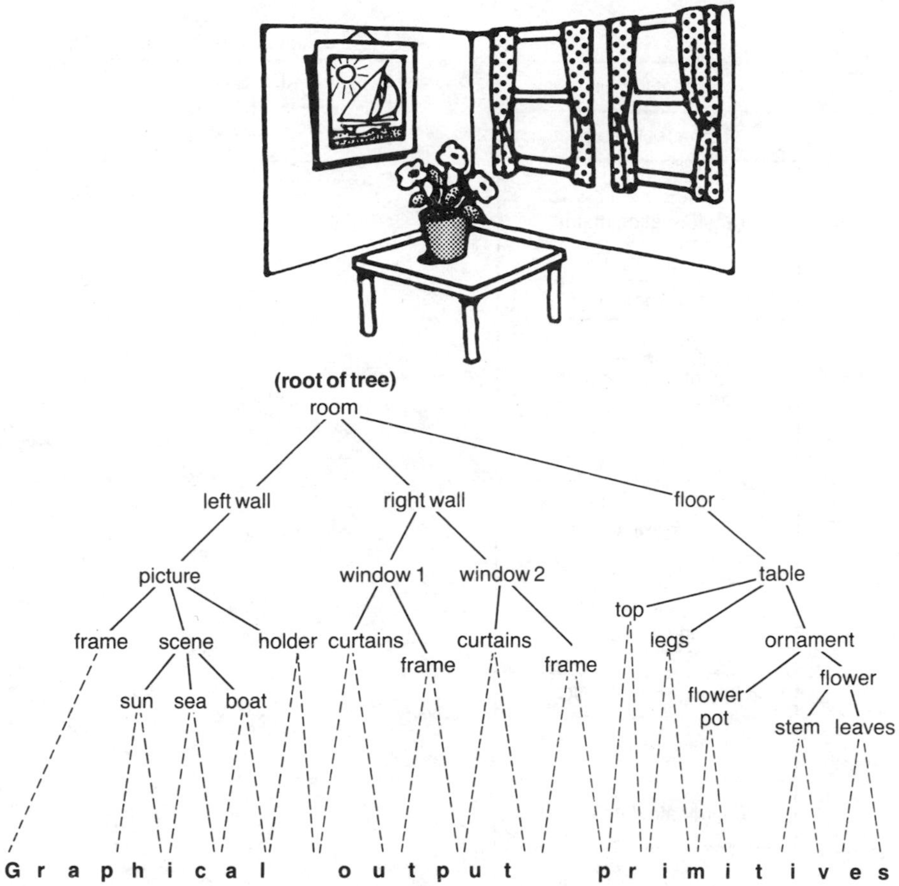

Figure 7.3
Illustration of a segment hierarchy.

definition. The argument to the function is the segment identifier, a name for the segment chosen by the applications programmer. Each entry in the segment data structure represents a segment. The structure of this representation must consist of:

the segment identifier
the segment attributes (initialised to their default values)
the (initially empty) sequence of output primitives

This arrangement is shown in Figure 7.4.

(2) *CloseSegment* () When the *CreateSegment* function is executed, the segment is said to be 'open'. In GKS, only one segment can be open at a time. A segment is closed by the execution of the *CloseSegment* function (which obviously can only be successfully executed when a segment is open). Once a segment has been closed in GKS it can never be re-opened. The only way a segment can be changed is by changing its attributes – three of which are now discussed.

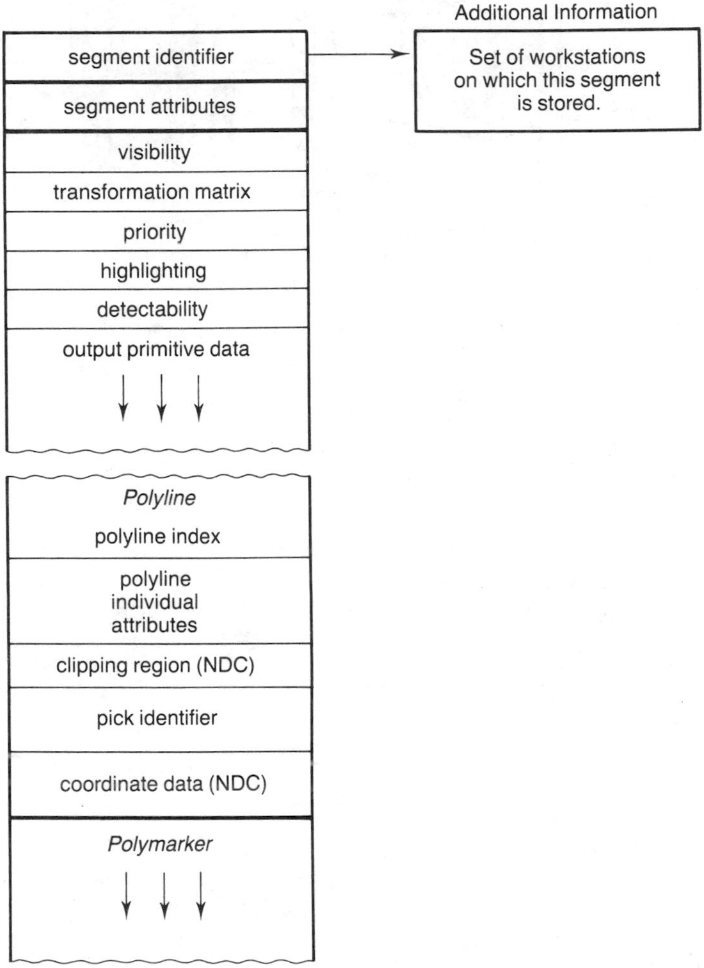

Figure 7.4
Structure of a GKS segment.

(3) *SetVisibility*(*SegmentIdentifier*, *VisibilityState*) When this function is executed, the visibility state of the named segment is set to ON or OFF. If the segment's visibility is set to OFF, then it is no longer displayed on the screen. If an invisible segment is made visible, then it is immediately shown on the display.

(4) *SetSegmentTransformation*(*SegmentIdentifier*, *TransformationMatrix*) In GKS, the transformation is specified by a 2 by 3 transformation matrix. For example, if (x, y) is a point, then:

$$(x', y') = \begin{pmatrix} a & b & c \\ d & e & f \end{pmatrix} \begin{pmatrix} x \\ y \\ 1 \end{pmatrix}$$

is the transformed point for the transformation matrix shown. Such a transformation matrix is used to represent a translation, rotation and scale (relative to some fixed point). At the time a segment is created, the transformation matrix retained in the segment's data structure represents the identity transformation, which has scaling of unity for both x and y, a zero rotation and a zero translation vector. When the *SetSegmentTransformation* function is executed, the matrix given as argument is written into the segment data structure, replacing the previous transformation. When a segment is displayed, the coordinates of its component output primitives are transformed by the segment transformation. Note that the segment transformation in this scheme is not cumulative: when two transformations are applied, the second transformation is not accumulated with the first – but, as stated, *overwrites* it.

For simplicity in the following example, this transformation is represented by separate translation, scaling and rotation parameters, and to distinguish it from the GKS *SetSegmentTransformation* it is called *TransformSegment*.

(5) *SetSegmentPriority(SegmentIdentifier, Priority)* When this function is executed, it sets the priority of the named segment. Priority is a number in the range 0 to 1. Segments with a higher priority overlay those of a lower priority. If segment A intersects segment B, and A has a higher priority than B, then, for example, any solid fill areas in A will obscure parts of B. In practice, this means that priority determines the order in which segments are drawn relative to one another. Thus, a lower priority segment is drawn *before* a relatively higher priority one so that output corresponding to the latter overwrites the former. When a segment is created, its initial priority is 0.

☐☐ EXAMPLE

An envelope, envelope flap and letter are each drawn in a separate segment. The flap is opened and the letter removed. The dimensions of the envelope are $2L$ units long by $2H$ units high (with $L > H$). The letter, which is to go inside the envelope, is $2l$ units long by $2h$ units high where $l < L$ and $h < H$. A window is defined to be $2W$ units by $2W$ units with origin in the centre of the square with $W > 3.5L$.

Example 7.1(a) Taking a letter out of an envelope.

fun *MakeLetter*(W, H, L, h, l) =

SetWindow(1, [$-W$, W, $-W$, W]);
SelectNtran(1);

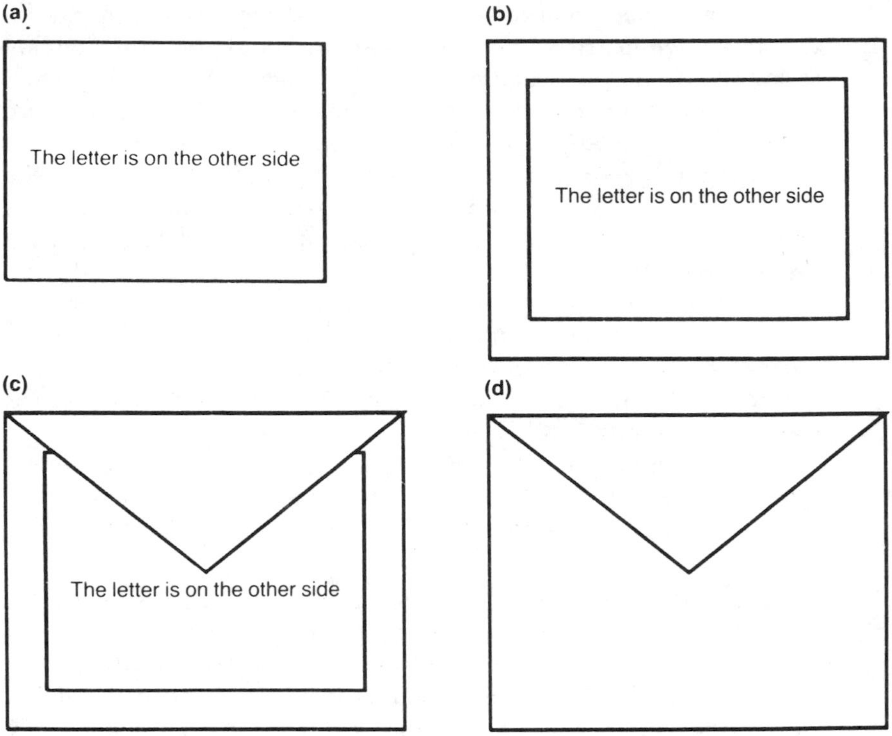
(a)
The letter is on the other side
(b)
The letter is on the other side
(c)
The letter is on the other side
(d)

Figure 7.5
(a) The letter.
(b) The letter in the envelope.
(c) The letter in the envelope showing the flap.
(d) The final picture of the letter in the envelope.

```
    SetTextAlignment(CENTRE, HALF);
    SetCharacterHeight(h/10.0);

    SetASF(INDIVIDUAL~13);
    SetFillAreaInteriorStyle(SOLID);
    SetFillAreaColourIndex(0);

    CreateSegment(LETTER);
      FillArea [(−l, −h), (l, −h), (l, h), (−l, h)];
      Polyline [(−l, −h), (l, −h), (l, h), (−l, h), (−l, −h)];
      Text((0.0, 0.0), "The letter is on the other side");
    CloseSegment ();
    SetSegmentVisibility(LETTER, OFF);

    CreateSegment(ENVELOPE);
      FillArea [(−L, −H), (L, −H), (L, H), (−L, H)];
      Polyline [(−L, −H), (L, −H), (L, H), (−L, H), (−L −H)];
    CloseSegment ();

    CreateSegment(FLAP);
      FillArea [(−L, H), (0.0, 0.0), (L, H)];
      Polyline [(−L, H), (0.0, 0.0), (L, H), (−L, H)];
    CloseSegment ();
nuf
```

This program defines a normalization transformation, the character height and alignment, and sets all the ASFs to INDIVIDUAL – although only the fill area interior style ASF is relevant. All the other attributes may be taken as default. The fill area interior style and colour are set up so that fill areas are drawn in whatever the background colour is. So if the screen is white, fill areas are white. This is because the solid fills are to be used in conjunction with the segment priorities as a means for overlaying. When the fill area interior style is anything but hollow the polygon demarcating the area is not drawn. Hence *Polyline* is used here to draw the borders of the solid fill areas. Figure 7.5 illustrates the process of removing a letter from an envelope.

The example continues by opening the flap and taking out the letter. The effect of opening the flap is achieved by using vertical scaling to scale the flap until it is nearly horizontal, then rotating it about 180° and rescaling it to full size. The letter is taken out by translating it vertically until it is half out of the envelope and then shifting it out completely, and finally rotating it through 45°. Segment priority is used to ensure that the envelope always obscures any part of the letter still inside it, and the letter obscures the open flap as it emerges from the envelope.

Example 7.1(b) Opening the flap.

```
fun OpenFlap () =
  for 0 ≤ i ≤ 7 do
    let val shift = (0.0, 0.0)
        and fixedpoint = (0.0, H)
        and (scale, rotation) =
          if
                i < 4 ⇒ ((1.0, 1.0/2.0^i), 0)
             □ i ≥ 4 ⇒ ((1.0, 1.0/2.0^(7−i)), π)
          fi
    in
      TransformSegment(FLAP, scale, rotation, shift, fixedpoint)
    ni
  od
nuf;

fun RemoveLetter(h) =
  SetSegmentPriority(ENVELOPE, 1.0);  Envelope drawn last.
  SetSegmentPriority(LETTER, 0.5);    Letter drawn second.
  SetSegmentPriority (FLAP, 0.0);     Flap drawn first.

  SetSegmentVisibility(LETTER, ON);

  Move letter half out of envelope .
  let val  scale = (1, 1)
      and rotation = 0
      and shift = (0, h)
      and fixedpoint = (0, 0)
  in
```

```
    TransformSegment(LETTER, scale, rotation, shift, fixedpoint)
  ni;

  Move letter out of envelope.
  let val scale = (1, 1)
      and rotation = 0
      and shift = (0, 2*h)
      and fixedpoint = (0, 0)
  in
    TransformSegment(LETTER, scale, rotation, shift, fixedpoint)
  ni;

  Rotate letter.
  let val scale = (1, 1)
      and rotation = 45
      and shift = (0, 2*h)
      and fixedpoint = (0, 0)
  in
    TransformSegment(LETTER, scale, rotation, shift, fixedpoint)
  ni
nuf;
```

The following program shows an example of the use of these functions:

```
fun Letter () =
Open and activate a workstation etc., then... .

  SetViewport(1, [0.05, 0.95, 0.05, 0.95]);
  let val W = 100 and H = 20 and L = 25 and h = 15 and l = 20
  in
    MakeLetter(W, H, L, h, l);
    OpenFlap ();
    RemoveLetter(h);
  ni;
  Close and deactivate etc.
nuf

Now call the main function.
Letter ()
```

7.3 Segments in GKS

The previous sections have described the idea of segments without going into the fine details of the particular manifestation of the segment concept in GKS. There are a number of important aspects of GKS segments of which the applications programmer must be aware to avoid problems and make full use of the functions available.

7.3.1 Segments Exist on Workstations

A GKS segment always exists on a workstation and has no independent life other than on a workstation. Each segment is created on every workstation that is active at the time of creation. It follows that a segment cannot be created unless GKS is in the state of at least one workstation active. When the *CreateSegment* function is called, GKS is put into the new state 'Segment Open'. It remains in this state until the *CloseSegment* function is executed. All graphical output generated while GKS is in the 'Segment Open' state is saved in the currently open segment. Only one segment can be open at a time. Once a segment is closed, it is closed forever – it cannot be re-opened and appended to.

In GKS Pascal, segment identifiers are integers, although given the special type name *GTseg*:

```
{GKS Pascal data type – segment identifiers are integers}
type GTseg = integer;
```

The following example serves to clarify these ideas.

□□ EXAMPLE

```
{Example 7.2   Segments are bound to workstations.}

{open three workstations}
GOpenWs(display1, conn1, type1);
GOpenWs(display2, conn2, type2);
GOpenWs(display3, conn3, type3);

{activate the first two workstations}
GActivateWs(display1);
GActivateWs(display2);

{create some segments}
GCreateSeg(1);
  GPolyline(n1, p1);
  GFill(n2, p2);
  GText(pos1, 'This is in segment 1');
GCloseSeg;

GCreateSeg(2);
  GPolymarker(n3, p3);
  GText(pos2, 'This is in segment 2');
CloseSeg;

GCreateSeg(3);
  GText(pos3, 'This is in segment 3');
CloseSeg;

{segments 1, 2 and 3 exist on workstations display1 and display2}
```

```
{activate display3 and create segment 4}
GActivateWs(display3);
GCreateSeg(4);
  GText(pos4, 'This is in segment 4');
GCloseSeg;

{delete segment 1}
GDelSeg(1);

{segments 2, 3 and 4 exist on workstations display1 and display2, but
 only segment 4 exists on workstation display3}

{delete segment 2 from workstation display1}
GDelSegWs(display1, 2);

{segments 2 and 3 still exist, but segment 2 only exists on display2
 and only segment 4 on display3}

GDeactivateWs(display2);
GCloseWs(display2);

{now since display2 has been closed, segment 2 no longer exists at all}

GRenameSeg(3, 1);
{segment 3 has been renamed to 1}
```

First, three workstations are opened and two of them are made active. Next, three segments are created on the two active workstations *display*1 and *display*2. Workstation *display*3 is then activated and a new segment (4) is created. This new segment exists on all three workstations. The delete segment function (*GDelSeg*) deletes segment 1 on all workstations. Segment 2 is deleted only from workstation *display*1 by use of the delete segment from workstation function (*GDelSegWs*), but it still exists since it remains on workstation *display*2. When *display*2 is deactivated and closed, segment 2 no longer has any home – and therefore ceases to exist. Finally, segment 3 is renamed to 1.

It follows that there are three ways in which a segment can be deleted: first, if the delete segment function is called; second, if the delete segment from workstation function is called and the segment exists on no other workstations; third, if all the workstations on which a segment exists are closed. In addition, to ensure that a segment is identical on all workstations on which it is created, GKS does not allow a workstation to be activated or deactivated while GKS is in the 'Segment Open' state.

7.3.2 Segments Store Output Primitive Attributes

What exactly gets stored when an output primitive is written into a segment? Obviously, the geometry of the primitive is stored, and in the case of text the actual text string, and in the case of cell array the array of colours.

However, it should be remembered from Chapter 6 that when, for example, a polyline is generated, the current polyline index is intrinsically a part of the polyline. The primitive indices are therefore also stored in segments. However, the indices are not sufficient to determine the attributes of the output primitives, since when the ASFs are INDIVIDUAL rather than BUNDLED, the style is determined by the individual settings of the attributes rather than from the primitive representations. This all seems very confusing, but actually it is quite straightforward. When an output primitive is stored in a segment, the attributes saved together with the primitive may be determined from the following rule:

> If at least one of the ASFs for this primitive is BUNDLED, then the current primitive index is saved. For every relevant ASF that is INDIVIDUAL, the corresponding current setting of the individual attribute is saved.

This rule implies:

(1) If all the ASFs for this primitive are BUNDLED, then only the primitive index is saved.

(2) If all the ASFs for this primitive are INDIVIDUAL, then only the current settings of the individual attributes are saved.

Otherwise:

(3) The primitive index is saved together with some of the individual attributes.

The systems programmer faced with the task of implementing GKS segments must choose a data structure sufficiently flexible to allow the various possible combinations of individual attributes and primitive indices to be saved.

The main ideas relating to the attributes are illustrated with respect to *Polyline* in Example 7.3, with the result shown in Figure 7.6.

□□ EXAMPLE

```
{Example 7.3    Primitive attributes.}
program PrimAttr(input, output);

include 'gksdefs';

const
  display1 = 1;
  conn1    = 'wsconn 1';
  type1    = 'wstype 1';
  errorfile = 1;
```

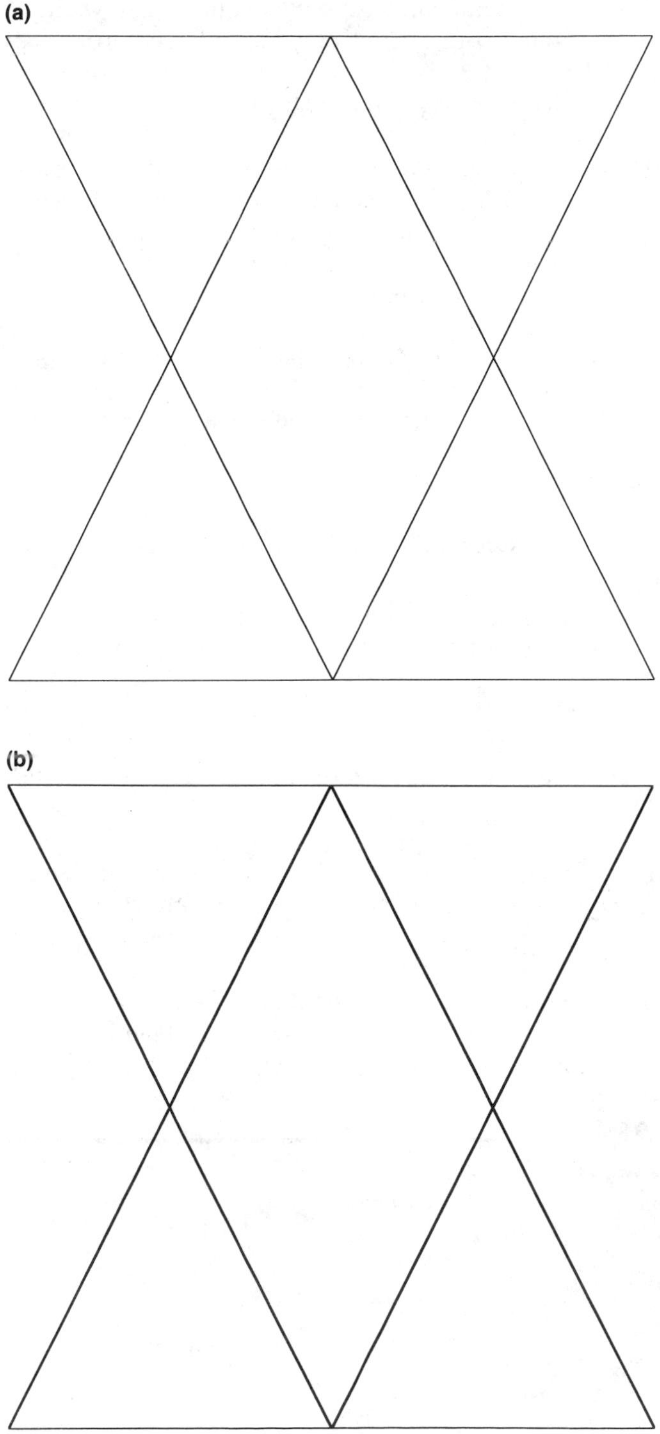

Figure 7.6
Four triangles in segments.
(a) Initial triangles with line width BUNDLED, and type and colour INDIVIDUAL.
(b) Segments redrawn after changed *Polyline* representation.
(c) The ASF for line type and the bundle changed, with a new line added.

(c)

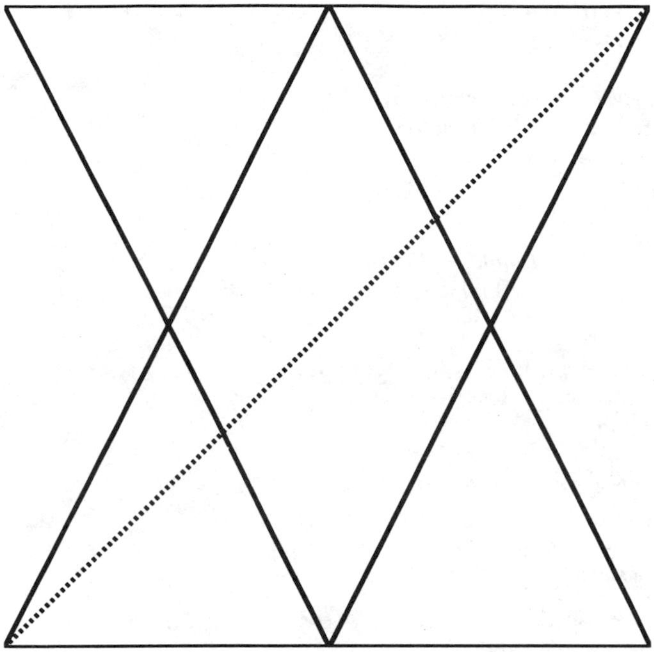

```
procedure Triangle(start : GRPoint; width, height : real);
{draws a triangle with corner at start}
var p : array[1..4] of GRPoint;
begin
  p[1] := start;
  with p[2] do
  begin
    x := p[1].x + width;
    y := p[1].y;
  end;
  with p[3] do
  begin
    x := p[1].x + 0.5*width;
    y := p[1].y + height;
  end;
  p[4] := p[1];
  GPolyline(4, p);
end;

procedure Picture(window, viewport : GRBound);
{creates a picture of four triangles each in a different segment}
```

```
var
  p    : GRPoint;
  w, h : real;
begin
  GSetWindow(1, window);
  GSetViewport(1, viewport);
  GSelectNormTran(1);

  with window do
  begin
    w := (LeftBound + RightBound)/2.0;
    h := (LowerBound + UpperBound)/2.0;
  end;

  GCreateSeg(1);
    with window do
    begin
      p.x := LeftBound;
      p.y := LowerBound;
    end;
    Triangle(p, w, h);
  GCloseSeg;

  GCreateSeg(2);
    with window do
    begin
      p.x := RightBound;
      p.y := LowerBound;
    end;
    Triangle(p, -w, h);
  GCloseSeg;

  GCreateSeg(3);
    with window do
    begin
      p.x := LeftBound;
      p.y := UpperBound;
    end;
    Triangle(p, w, -h);
  GCloseSeg;

  GCreateSeg(4);
    with window do
    begin
      p.x := RightBound;
      p.y := UpperBound;
    end;
    Triangle(p, -w, -h);
  GCloseSeg;

end;
```

```
procedure Draw;
  const index = 1;
var
  error       : integer;
  listindiv   : GAPrimRep;
  asf         : GAasf;
  rep         : GRPrimRep;
  win, view : GRBound;
  p           : array[1..2] of GRPoint;
begin
  GOpenGKS(errorfile, GCdefmemory);
  GOpenWs(display1, conn1, type1);
  GActivateWs(display1);

  {inquire current individual attributes}
  GInqCurIndivAttr(error, indiv, asf);
  {set the Polyline asf}
  asf[GVLineType]  := GVIndividual;
  asf[GVLineWidth] := GVBundled;
  asf[GVLineCol]   := GVIndividual;
  GSetASF(asf);

  {set the polyline representation and individual attributes}
  GSetLineType(GCSolidLine);
  GSetLineColInd(1);
  GSetPrimInd(GVPolyline, index);
  with rep do
  begin
    Prim   := GVPolyline;
    LType  := GCSolidLine;
    Width  := 1.0;
    LCol   := 1;
  end;
  GSetPrimRep(GVPolyline, display1, index, rep);

  {determine the window and viewport}
  with win do
  begin
    LeftBound   := 0.0;
    RightBound  := 100.0;
    LowerBound := 0.0;
    UpperBound := 100.0;
  end;
  with view do
  begin
    LeftBound   := 0.05;
    RightBound  := 0.95;
    LowerBound := 0.05;
    UpperBound := 0.95;
  end;
```

```
    {create the picture}
    Picture(win, view);

    {now change the bundle representation}
    with rep do
    begin
      Prim   := GVPolyline;
      LType  := GCDashedLine;
      Width  := 2.0;
      LCol   := 2;
    end;
    GSetPrimRepresentation(GVPolyline, display1, index, rep);

    {change the bundle again after changing the asf}
    asf[GVLineType] := GVBundled;
    GSetASF(asf);
    with rep do
    begin
      Prim    := GVPolyline;
      LType   := GCDottedLine;
      Width   := 3.0;
      LCol    := 4;
    end;
    GSetPrimRepresentation(GVPolyline, display1, index, rep);

    {draw a line diagonally across the display}
    with p[1] do x :=   0.0; y :=   0.0 end;
    with p[2] do x := 100.0; y := 100.0 end;
    GPolyline(2, p);

    {deactivate and close}
    GDeactivateWS(display1);
    GCloseWs(display1);
    GCloseGKS;
  end;

  {main}
  begin
    Draw;
  end.
```

In this example, four triangles are created using the *Polyline* function, with each in a different segment. The polyline ASFs are set up so that only the line width scale factor is BUNDLED, whereas the line type and the polyline colour index are INDIVIDUAL and set respectively to solid and 1. Now, when the triangles are drawn, the polyline in each segment is saved along with the polyline index (1), the line type (solid) and the line colour index (1). The polyline representation for index 1 has the normal line width scale factor (1.0). Next, the polyline representation is changed so that index 1 is now a dashed line with width 2.0 and colour index 2. The segments are re-executed (or redrawn), but only the width of the triangle lines is changed. Finally, the ASF for the line type is changed to BUNDLED and the polyline representation for index 1 is changed to a dotted line with width 3.0 and colour index 4. Once again, the triangles already on the display are redrawn, now with the width scale factor of 3.0. The displayed line type is still solid and the colour index 1. However, *subsequent* polylines are dotted with a width of 3.0 (though still using the colour index 1).

REMARKS

The discussion of this section complements the ideas about the static and dynamic binding of attributes raised in Chapter 6. Attributes written into segments that are INDIVIDUAL are truly static – they can never be changed once in the segment. Attributes bound dynamically to the primitives in a segment can be changed, by changing the representation corresponding to a primitive index. Notwithstanding the statements of Chapter 6, this full dynamic and static binding can only be expected to operate for primitives inside a segment. On most GKS implementations, primitives drawn outside of segments only have an ephemeral existence on the display – there is no guarantee that they will not disappear altogether when some dynamic modification is made to the picture, such as a change to a primitive representation. This is fully discussed in Chapter 8.

Readers should in no way be under the illusion that the authors are *recommending* the style of GKS programming illustrated in Example 7.3 – far from it in fact. Inbreeding of BUNDLED and INDIVIDUAL attributes from within the same primitive is rather like inbreeding in real life – it might lead to a genius approach to some difficult problem in style, but this is at the risk of producing a monstrous program rather difficult to construct, prove and debug.

7.3.3 Segments Have Attributes

The attributes of the output primitives are stored in segments. But segments also have attributes that are a property of the segments themselves, rather than of the primitive elements in the segments. The attributes include:

- the transformation matrix,
- the visibility,
- the highlighting, and
- the priority.

THE SEGMENT TRANSFORMATION MATRIX

Every segment has an associated 2 by 3 transformation matrix that by default corresponds to the identity transformation. For example, let this matrix for a particular segment be denoted by:

$$\mathbf{M} = \begin{pmatrix} a_{11} & a_{12} & a_{13} \\ a_{21} & a_{22} & a_{23} \end{pmatrix}$$

If $p = (x, y)$, then **M** applied to this point results in the coordinate shown in the following schematic function definition:

type *tranmatrix* = *real*˜*(2, 3);*

S: tranmatrix → *(Point* → *Point);*
fun $S\ M\ p = (a_{11}x + a_{12}y + a_{13}, a_{21}x + a_{22}y + a_{23})$
nuf

In other words, *S M* is a function that maps from point to point according to the matrix *M* and (*S M p*) is the point resulting from the application of this function to *p*.

Let $p = (x, y)$ be a WC point and suppose that a segment is open that has transformation matrix *M*. Then, if *Ntran* and *Wtran* are the normalization and workstation transformation functions, respectively, the following function will compute the corresponding DC point:

fun *ViewFunction*(*p*) =
  let val *f* = *S M*
  in
    (*Wtran* ∘ *f* ∘ *Ntran*) *p*
  ni
nuf

ViewFunction describes the transformational aspect of the viewing pipeline from WC to DC, when a segment is open. First, the WC points are transformed by the normalization transformation determined from the current window and viewport. Next, the NDC point is transformed by the transformation matrix of the open segment. The resulting point is still in NDC (although of course it might actually be outside of the unit square). Finally, the NDC point is mapped to DC on every active workstation according to the current workstation window and viewport as set on each workstation.

The coordinate data belonging to the primitives are stored in segments in normalized form (in NDC). When a segment is *executed* the pipeline followed by the primitive data is similar to that shown in *ViewFunction*, except that, of course, *Ntran* is not applied.

This throws further light on why a GKS implementation does not clip graphical output to the WC window prior to the normalization transformation. The reason is that the whole primitive is stored in the segment, rather than the primitive as clipped by the current window. For although, initially, points might be outside of the window, a segment transformation might bring these points back inside the window. If the primitives inside the segment are clipped to the WC window prior to their entry into the segment, then a segment transformation could result in the display of partially deleted output.

The GKS *SetSegmentTransformation* function is represented in Pascal as:

```
type GAmatrix = array[1..2, 1..3] of real;
{set segment transformation}
procedure GSetSegTran(segid : GTseg; matrix : GAmatrix);
```

The effect of this function is to redefine the *current* transformation matrix for the segment – it overwrites the transformation matrix of the segment with the new matrix. In principle, the result of the function is that the current transformation matrix is applied to the coordinates of all primitives in the segment, which are then redisplayed in their new position. For example, consider Example 7.4, which is the same as Example 7.3 but with procedure *Draw* replaced by *DrawSeg*.

□□ EXAMPLE

```
{Example 7.4   Draw replaced by DrawSeg.}
procedure DrawSeg;
var
  win, view : GRBound;
  matrix    : GAmatrix;
  i, j      : integer;
begin
  GOpenGKS(errorfile, GCdefmemory);
  GOpenWS(display1, conn1, type1);
  GActivateWs(display1);

  {determine the window and viewport}
  with win do
  begin
    LeftBound  := 0.0;
    RightBound := 100.0;
    LowerBound := 0.0;
    UpperBound := 100.0;
  end;
```

```
with view do
begin
  LeftBound  := 0.05;
  RightBound := 0.95;
  LowerBound := 0.05;
  UpperBound := 0.95;
end;

{create the picture}
Picture(win, view);

{define a shift transformation}
for i := 1 to 2 do
for j := 1 to 2 do
begin
  if (i = j) then matrix[i, j] := 1.0
  else matrix[i, j] := 0.0;
end;
matrix[1, 3] := -0.1;
matrix[2, 3] := 0.0;

{transform segment 4}
GSetSegTran(4, matrix);

{deactivate and close}
GDeactivateWs(display1);
GCloseWs(display1);
GCloseGKS;
end;

{main}
begin
  DrawSeg;
end.
```

In this example, first the four segments are created as before and then segment 4 is transformed by the defined matrix. The elements of the matrix are dimensionless, except for the last column which specifies a translation in *normalized* coordinates. Here, the x translation is -0.1 and the y translation is 0. The result of this transformation is shown in Figure 7.7.

REMARKS

When an output primitive is written to the open segment, it is stored in the segment in NDC; that is, immediately after the application of *Ntran*, and when the segment is executed, these coordinates are transformed by its current transformation matrix as discussed earlier. As seen in Section 7.3.2, the attributes of the primitive are also stored in the segment. In addition, the current clipping region is stored with the primitive. This region is identical to the current viewport if clipping is enabled, and if clipping is

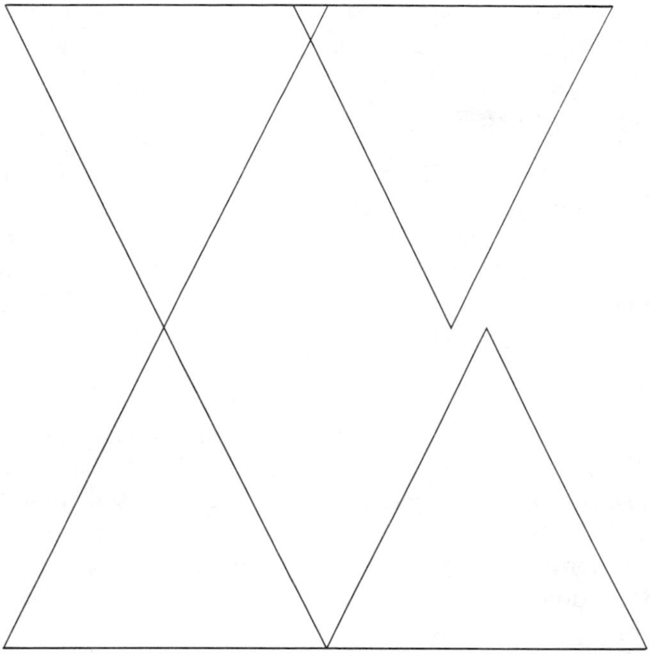

Figure 7.7
One of the segments transformed.

disabled it is the whole NDC unit square. An applications programmer must be aware of this to avoid unexpected results. For the sake of a name, call the clipping region written into a segment along with a primitive the *PrimInSeg* clip region. At the time when a segment is redisplayed, it is obviously possible for it to be transformed in such a way that some or all of the primitives within it move partially or wholly outside of their *PrimInSeg* clip regions. These primitives are clipped to their *PrimInSeg* regions rather than to the clipping region in force at the time of redisplay.

□□ EXAMPLE

Example 7.5 Clipping regions are saved in segments.

Define a normalization transformation with viewport as the centre of NDC.
SetWindow(1, [*wx*1, *wx*2, *wy*1, *wy*2]);
SetViewport(1, [0.25, 0.75, 0.25, 0.75]);
SelectNtran(1);

Create segment 1 consisting of a polyline which draws a border around the current window.
CreateSegment(1);
  Polyline [(*wx*1, *wy*1), (*wx*2, *wy*1), (*wx*2, *wy*2), (*wx*1, *wy*2), (*wx*1, *wy*1)];
CloseSegment ();

Change the clipping region to the whole of NDC.
SelectNtran(0);

Transform the segment by clockwise rotation of 45° about the fixed point (0.5, 0.5).
SetSegmentTransformation(1, *fixed* = (0.5, 0.5), *rotate* = π/4);

Figure 7.8 shows the original polyline and the transformed segment. The effect of the clipping region inside the segment is that when it is redisplayed as a result of, for example, *SetSegmentTransformation*, the transformed polyline is clipped to the clipping region in force at the time that the polyline was generated.

REMARKS

Unfortunately, the applications programmer cannot specify a transformation as easily as in the abstract notation of Example 7.5. As has been seen, the *SetSegmentTransformation* function requires the transformation to be given in the form of a 2 by 3 matrix. A 2 by 3 matrix can be used to represent any combination of rotation, shift and scale, and normally it is in these terms that the applications programmer thinks, rather than in terms of transformation matrices. GKS provides two utility functions which compute a transformation matrix from parameters representing a scale, rotation and shift with respect to a fixed point. These functions are called *Evaluate TransformationMatrix* and *AccumulateTransformationMatrix*, and are defined in Pascal as follows:

```
procedure GEvalTran(fixedp : GRPoint
                     shift : GRVector;
                  rotation : real;
                     scale : GRVector;
                    switch : GECoordSwitch;
                var matrix : GAmatrix);

procedure GAccumTran(inmatrix : GAmatrix;
                       fixedp : GRPoint;
                        shift : GRVector;
                     rotation : real;
                        scale : GRVector;
                       switch : GECoordSwitch;
                var outmatrix : GAmatrix);
```

The *GEvalTran* procedure evaluates a transformation matrix from the given arguments. The scale, rotate and shift are applied (in that order) relative to a fixed point, and the corresponding output matrix returned. *GAccumTran* works in a similar manner, except that the matrix produced by the scale, rotate and shift about the fixed point is then concatenated with the input matrix to produce the output matrix. This procedure is useful for

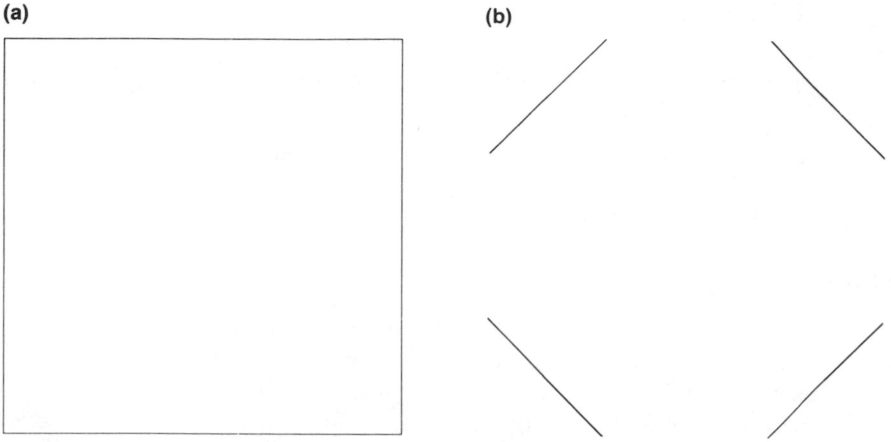

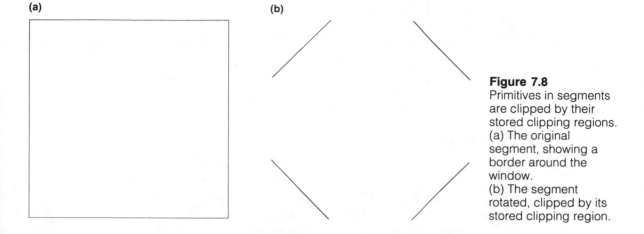

Figure 7.8
Primitives in segments are clipped by their stored clipping regions.
(a) The original segment, showing a border around the window.
(b) The segment rotated, clipped by its stored clipping region.

maintaining a succession of accumulated transformations. The angle is measured in radians and determines a clockwise rotation. The *switch* parameter determines whether the fixed point and shift parameters are given in WC or NDC.

SEGMENT VISIBILITY

The second segment attribute is segment visibility – segments may be visible (the default) or invisible. The *SetVisibility* function is defined in GKS Pascal as:

```
type GEvis = (GVVisible, GVInvisible);

{set visibility}
procedure GSetVis(segname : GTseg; vis : GEvis);
```

SEGMENT HIGHLIGHTING

GKS requires that segments may be highlighted, although how this effect is to be achieved is left as workstation dependent (which, in practice, means that it is determined by the GKS implementor). Some possibilities include highlighting by making the displayed segment primitives blink on and off while the segment highlighting is enabled; alternatively, the segment can be graphically highlighted, for example, by an arrow pointing at some part of it. On colour or grey scale displays, highlighted segments can be turned to a maximum intensity level reserved specifically for this attribute – other possibilities are left to the imagination of the reader.

In GKS Pascal, this attribute is set by:

```
type GEHighlight = (GVNormal, GVHighlighted);

{set highlighting}
procedure GSetHighlight(segname : GTseg; highlight : GEHighlight);
```

SEGMENT PRIORITY

When two fill area primitives shaded with differing patterns or colours overlap one another, which should obscure the other? For fill areas outside of segments, the fill area of higher priority (that is, the one which obscures the other) is determined solely by the order in which the fill areas are drawn – that is, by the calling sequence in the applications program. If the fill areas are in segments, then the answer depends in principle on the relative priority of the two segments.

The segment priority is a number between 0 and 1. The higher the number, the greater the priority of the segment. Primitives within segments of relatively higher priority obscure those of lower priority. Of course, this applies to all primitives, not only filled areas.

On a raster display, the importance of this function becomes evident whenever a workstation is put into a state necessitating the redrawing of all its segments. Situations that might lead to this are discussed in Chapter 8. When all segments are redrawn, those of lower priority are drawn before those of higher priority. This is the simplest way in which the segment priority might be implemented in practice.

In GKS Pascal, the priority may be set by:

```
{set segment priority}
procedure GSetSegPriority(segname : GTseg; priority : real);
```

7.4 Interacting with Segments

Pick input is the last of the GKS input classes, deferred for discussion from Chapter 5. The measure of a pick input device – that is, the type of value returned by a pick interaction – is a segment identifier together with a pick identifier and a pick status. A common implementation requires the operator to use an input device such as a mouse and associated cursor to point at a position on the screen, whereupon the pick measure corresponding to the segment at that position, if any, is returned (see Chapter 17).

The pick identifier is an additional level of naming suitable for providing identifiers for each individual primitive within a segment. The *SetPickIdentifier* function is used to set the current pick identifier. Whenever an output primitive is written into a segment the current pick identifier is stored with it (together with the primitive attributes and the clipping region). In Pascal, the pick identifier is represented as an integer, although given the type name *GTPickId*. Example 7.6 illustrates how the pick identifier is used to provide names for components within a segment.

The only use for the pick identifier is when a pick input interaction occurs – as in some applications it may be useful to be able to determine not only which segment is being 'picked' but also which primitive element within a segment. For example, a displayed segment might represent a typewriter keyboard as part of a typing simulation program. Each individual keyboard character could have its own pick identifier. As the operator points to one of the character keys drawn on the display, so the *RequestPick* function returns the name of the keyboard segment, and within this segment the pick identifier corresponding to the character selected. The resulting action in such a program might be that another segment representing the typing paper has this character written into it using the GKS text primitive.

The *InitialisePick* function follows the same pattern as for the five other input classes:

InitialiseInput(PICK, *wsid*, *device*, InitialValue = (*segment*, *pickid*, *status*),
prompt, *EchoArea*, *DataRecord*)

The *InitialValue* of a pick device consists of a segment name, a pick identifier and a status. The status may be OK or NOPICK. A NOPICK status means that the segment cannot be picked; that is, it is not detectable by a pick input function. For example, the operator points at a segment on the display and the result of the *RequestPick* is NOPICK. A segment can be put into this state by the *SetDetectability* function, which determines the segment's detectability.

The prompt and echo types are:

- echo type 1 is implementation defined, but the actual primitive within the segment should be echoed (or highlighted in some way) at least momentarily.
- echo type 2 echoes all primitives within the detected segment that have the same pick identifier as the picked primitive (and if not all primitives, then at least those closest to the picked primitive).
- echo type 3 echoes all primitives in the detected segment.

□□ EXAMPLE

```
{Example 7.6   Using the pick identifier.}
var
  n1, n2, n3 : integer;
  p1, p2, p3 : GAPointArray;
  pos1, pos2 : GRPoint;
          .
          .
          .

{segment 1 is created}
GSetPickId(1);
GCreateSeg(1);
  GPolyline(n1, p1);
  GSetPickId(2);
  GText(pos, 'string');
  GSetPickId(3);
  GPolymarker(n2, p2);
  GSetPickId(4);
  GFillArea(n3, p3);
  GText(pos2, 'Another String');
GCloseSeg;
```

□□ EXAMPLE

```
Example 7.7   Further use of the pick identifier.
CreateSegment(1);
  SetPickId(1);
  Polyline [(x1, y1), (x2, y1)];
  SetPickId(2);
  Polyline [(x1, y2), (x2, y2)];
  SetPickId(3);
  Polyline [(x1, y3), (x2, y3)];
CloseSegment ();

CreateSegment(2);
  FillArea [(x1, y1), (x1, y3), (x2, y1)];
CloseSegment ();

Initialise Input(PICK, wsid = 1, device = 1, InitialValue = (1, 1, OK),
                 prompt = 2, area = _, DataRecord = _);
do
  true ⇒
    let val (segment, pickid, status) = RequestInput(PICK, wsid = 1,
                                                     device = 1, ..);
    in
```

```
        if status = OK ⇒ SetHighlighting(segment, HIGHLIGHT);
                         SetSegmentTransformation(segment, matrix);
                         breakdo
        fi
    ni
od
```

In this example, segment 1 is created and consists of three horizontal lines. The pick input class is initialised, and the prompt and echo type 2 is used. The operator must then repeatedly perform the pick interaction until a successful hit occurs – that is, the status returns as OK. At this point, whichever of the primitives is pointed at will be highlighted in some way, which provides the necessary feedback to the operator. The picked segment is then transformed according to the value of the transformation matrix. Note that the whole segment is transformed – the pick identifier cannot be used in any manipulative manner, such as partially transforming a segment. The pick identifier is purely a method for naming.

Segment 2 consists of a fill area (which will also have pick identifier 3, since this is the one currently in force). There is an obvious problem here because it is possible for the operator to point to a position that is the coincidence of two or more segments. Which segment should be returned as the 'picked' one? The rule is that the one with the highest segment priority is returned. So segment priority not only resolves overlap ambiguities but also pick priority.

The *status*, which is part of the pick measure, is similar to the choice status. On a *RequestPick*, the returned status is a confusion of the status that is returned with any *RequestInput* (OK, NONE) and the peculiar status of the pick input class (OK, NOPICK). The *RequestPick* combines these two into one overall status with possible values in the set (OK, NOPICK, NONE).

REMARKS

This is an appropriate point to take up prompt and echo type 5 for choice input, a discussion deferred from Chapter 5. If this prompt and echo type is used in the *InitialiseChoice* function, then it allows the choice prompt to be represented by a segment, and the pick identifiers in the segment to form the basis of the return values from a choice interaction. This is achieved by naming the segment as the first item in the choice data record. Then when, for example, a *RequestChoice* interaction is required, the segment is displayed in a position and scaling determined by a transformation of the unit square to the choice echo area. (Recall that the primitives in segments are stored in normalized form.) The pick identifiers of primitives in the segment are mapped to the choice numbers (this mapping being implementation defined). This method can be used to implement an iconic form of interaction, where the type of choice to be made is represented by a symbol, and the choices by the components of the symbol.

7.5 The Workstation-Independent Segment Storage

It was pointed out in Section 7.3.1 that segments live on workstations and cannot exist otherwise – there is no such thing as a homeless segment. However, this restriction causes problems if adhered to rigidly in a multi-workstation environment. Consider the drawing program of earlier chapters. A typical way in which this program might be used is for an operator to create the required picture interactively on a fast display and, assuming that the segment capability has been added to the program, edit the picture until it is acceptable. Having created the final polished image, the operator now requires 'hardcopy'. For example, he or she might wish to copy the image to a laser printer or a colour display. The picture only exists as segments stored in a workstation-dependent manner on the main fast display workstation. It would be unrealistic for GKS to insist that segments on a workstation should be retrievable for copying to other workstations. It must be understood that segments in GKS really are local to workstations, and ideally are stored and manipulated in a workstation-dependent and highly efficient manner in the underlying firmware of the graphics device. Reading back such segments from the device, converting them into some neutral device-independent format and then copying them to another device would place a great burden on graphics device manufacturers and GKS implementors.

To overcome this problem, the GKS designers introduced a new and ingenious concept that borders on being self-contradictory, but which is nevertheless very useful. This is the idea of a 'workstation' that has the sole function of storing segments – yet in a workstation-independent manner. This is called the **workstation-independent segment storage** (**WISS**) workstation. WISS may be opened and activated as any other workstation. However, it differs from other workstations in the sense that output primitives are only written into it when it is 'active' (like any other workstation) *and* when a segment is 'open'.

WISS is an 'abstract' workstation in the sense that it is not tied to any graphical device as such. It can be implemented as a file (although this is rather slow) or, more likely, as a centrally allocated and expandable block of memory available to the GKS system. WISS is unlike other workstations because it has no bundle representations and no display space. To call it a workstation at all is something of a misnomer. However, the name workstation is used to describe it because it is in the same position in the GKS viewing pipeline as every other GKS workstation (although there is no corresponding workstation transformation).

There are three segment functions which can only be carried out on segments that are on the WISS.

7.5.1 Associate Segment to Workstation

This function is represented in Pascal as:

procedure *GAssocSegWs*(*wsid* : *GTWsId*; *segname* : *GTseg*);

It is used to bind a segment to a workstation that was not active at the time the segment was created. The supplied *wsid* parameter cannot, of course, be the WISS workstation identifier, since the segment is assumed to be on the WISS. The function has two effects. First, if the segment is visible, then it is displayed on the workstation with identifier *wsid*. Second, it becomes one of the segments that exists on *wsid* – as if this workstation had been active at the segment's creation time.

7.5.2 Copy Segment to Workstation

This function is represented in Pascal as:

procedure *GCopySegWs*(*wsid* : *GTWsId*; *segname* : *GTseg*);

It only carries out the display action of the *AssociateSegmentToWorkstation* function. The segment in WISS is displayed on the screen of *wsid*, but is not bound to this workstation – it does not become one of the segments that live on *wsid*. If GKS is in the 'Segment Open' state when this function is called the primitives are not stored in the open segment.

7.5.3 Insert Segment

This function is represented in Pascal as:

procedure *GInsertSeg*(*segname* : *GTseg*; *matrix* : *GAmatrix*);

It inserts the primitives, as transformed by the matrix, to all active workstations. The transformation matrix supplied as a parameter is applied to the primitives in the segment after they have been transformed by the transformation matrix belonging to the segment. If the *InsertSegment* function is called while GKS is in the 'Segment Open' state, then the primitives generated are written into the open segment. Hence, this function provides a way of copying primitives from a closed segment into an open segment. This is a very useful function, and is illustrated in the following examples. (It is assumed that there are functions *identity*, *shift* and *scale* which return corresponding matrices.)

The *InsertSegment* function can be used:

(1) To insert primitives in a segment on WISS into the stream of output primitives sent to all active workstations.

(2) To make multiple display copies of the primitives in a segment by repeatedly inserting the segment under a different transformation matrix.

(3) To make a new segment consisting of all the primitives in a number of other segments.

(4) To achieve the effect of appending new primitives to an already existing segment (even though this is not possible directly).

□□ EXAMPLE

Example 7.8 Using the insert segment function.

SetWindow(1, [*wx*1, *wx*2, *wy*1, *wy*2]);
SetViewport(1, [*vx*1, *vx*2, *vy*1, *vy*2]);
SelectNtran(1);
OpenWs(wsid = DISPLAY, connection = _, type = _);
OpenWs(wsid = SEGSTORE, connection = _, type = WISS);
ActivateWs(SEGSTORE);

CreateSegment(1);
  Polyline [(*wx*1, *wy*1), (*wx*2, *wy*1), ((*wx*1 + *wx*2)/2, *wy*2), (*wx*1, *wy*1)];
CloseSegment();

ActivateWs(DISPLAY);
InsertSegment(1, *identity*());

In this example, a triangle is drawn into segment 1, which exists only on the WISS workstation. The display workstation is activated and segment 1 is inserted under the identity transformation. The triangle is displayed, but segment 1 does not exist on the display workstation.

□□ EXAMPLE

Example 7.9 Extension of Example 7.8.

InsertSegment(1, *shift*(0.1, 0.1));

Here, the transformation matrix is equivalent to a shift of 0.1 units for both x and y in NDC. Hence, the triangle is displayed above and to the right of the first triangle. However, the new triangle is partially clipped. (Why?)

☐☐ EXAMPLE

Example 7.10 Extension of Example 7.9.

CreateSegment(2);
  InsertSegment(1, *scale*(0.5, 0.5));
CloseSegment ();

Now the triangle is displayed scaled to one-half in both x and y directions (the first two triangles are still on the display). However, this triangle now exists in segment 2, both on the display workstation and on the WISS (since this is still active).

☐☐ EXAMPLE

Example 7.11 Extension of Example 7.10.

SelectNtran(0);
CreateSegment(3);
  InsertSegment(1, *scale*(2.0, 2.0));
CloseSegment ();

Once again, segment 3 consists of the original triangle, except that it is now scaled up by a factor of two. This segment exists on the display workstation and on the WISS. The difference here is that the clipping region written into the segment as an aspect of the *Polyline* primitive is taken from the *current* clipping region rather than from the region written into segment 1. The current clipping region happens to be the whole of NDC (since this is always the case for transformation 0). This is important, as in Example 7.9 the triangle is clipped by the original clipping region, whereas now it is not clipped (except to the workstation window).

7.6 Structured Interactive Drawing – Without Hidden States

Some of the ideas presented here can be used to improve the drawing program of Chapter 6. Suggestions for improvement are given here, but the details are left as an exercise for the reader.

(1) The use of choice menus to select items from the tool boxes can be abandoned in favour of **icons** – that is, graphical symbols easily identifiable with the choices to be made.

(2) The picture created by the user can be stored in segments to allow modification.

(3) Suitable interactive tools for modification must be provided.

To achieve (1), the *OpenToolBox* function needs to be changed, together with the *Initialise* function. Each tool box, and the drawing pad area, must be stored in a different segment. When a tool box is opened, graphical symbols can be displayed rather than a textual representation of the items available, as displayed by the *RequestChoice* function. In other words, an actual dashed line is displayed, rather than the words 'Dashed Line'. Each such graphical symbol is included in the opened tool box segment and has a unique pick identifier. The pick identifier value returned by the *RequestPick* function identifies which tool option has been selected.

The closed tool boxes are represented by small rectangles containing the tool box name, as before. The open tool boxes are represented by larger rectangles showing small drawings symbolizing the various choices. The closed and open tool boxes belong to different segments. While a tool box is closed, the open tool box segments are invisible. When a tool box is opened, these segments are made visible and have a higher priority than the closed tool box rectangles. Alternatively, when a tool box is opened, the closed tool box rectangle segment can be made invisible.

For interactive picture editing to be possible, the picture must be constructed in segments. One way to achieve this is to provide menu options allowing the user to open, close or otherwise manipulate segments. However, there are strong arguments against this direct method of bringing segments into the drawing program. This idea does not naturally fit with the user model introduced in Chapter 6. This is a very straightforward model – there are tool boxes and a drawing area. The operator can open a tool box and select items within it, and can select a pen and draw with it. This model is mapped in a simple way to operator actions (mouse button clicks and cursor movements) and screen representation (rectangles representing the tool boxes and drawing pad, menus representing the open tool boxes). Now the idea of segments does not fit into this scheme at all. There is no way they can be brought directly into the user model without destroying its simplicity – they would be seen as something arbitrary from the world of computers rather than drawing.

A second reason why the addition of segments in this direct manner is not a good idea is that it would introduce **hidden states** into the system. A state, in this context, is the set of variables governing what is and what is not possible at any moment during the execution of the program. For example, when the *LINE* tool box is open, the system is in a state where drawing cannot take place and where items in, say, the *FILL* tool box cannot be selected. When drawing is taking place, it is always determined by the currently selected pen – so that text cannot be drawn while the *FILL* pen is selected. So the system as it stands clearly does have states. However, these are obvious, visible states, much as the states associated with the actions of the illustrator using real pens, brushes and paint. If the paintbrush was last dipped in the red paint the illustrator cannot paint in blue. While in the process of choosing a pen from the pen box, the illustrator is unlikely to be simultaneously drawing.

However, the addition of segments by allowing the operator to open and close segments by providing these functions as menu selection options would add perilous new states to the system opening up the possibility of all sorts of errors, which correspond to nothing real in the user model. For example, the user may *forget* to open a segment, and so all output created would remain outside of segments and therefore not be amenable to modification. Alternatively, the user may forget to *close* the segment, in which case the whole picture would be in one segment, thus making it impossible to selectively modify parts of the image.

The user may also attempt to open another segment while a segment is open or attempt to close the segment while no segment is open. Special error messages would have to be devised to cater for this eventuality – and such error messages suddenly popping up on the screen are liable to frighten, confuse and alienate users (especially novices), since these errors are outside of the bounds of users' experience. Remember, graphics segments do not form part of the user model, and therefore errors associated with them are difficult to interpret. An error in the second case could be particularly disconcerting if the user had *thought* that a segment had been open and then realized that the items created were lost as a result of the mistaken belief.

In spite of these arguments against the direct use of segments, it is important to find some way of incorporating segments into the drawing program without disrupting the user model. Now, in the program, the operator creates drawings by using the *LINE* (*Polyline*), *FILL*, (*FillArea*) and *TEXT* (*Text*) tools. The user model can be naturally extended by allowing each *primitive* generated by the user to be independently open to modification. In other words, the user can be told that the product of each discrete use of the *LINE*, *FILL* and *TEXT* tool results in something on the screen that can be modified (or erased). Moreover, groups of these items can be selected and similarly modified or erased.

Such an effect can be achieved without too much difficulty by enclosing each individual call to a graphical output primitive function between a *CreateSegment* and *CloseSegment* call. The implementation must maintain a list of segment names that have been used and be careful not to supply names that are not in this 'used' list. GKS also provides inquiry functions for this purpose (*Inquire Set of Segment Names In Use* and *Inquire Set of Segment Names On Workstation*).

In addition to the *LINE*, *FILL* and *TEXT* tool boxes there must also be an *EDITOR* tool box. When the editor pen is selected (in the usual way by clicking once over it), then subsequent mouse button clicks and cursor movements are used to select a group of items to be treated as a single object. The program implements this as repeated calls to the *RequestPick* function until the break action is taken. The set of segments picked is maintained as the currently active segment group (the highlighting function is clearly useful here). When the edit tool box is opened (in the usual way by clicking twice), then the *EDITOR* tool box becomes available. Its options might include *delete*, *copy*, *move*, *rotate* and *scale*. There might also be an additional option, *undo*, which reverses the last segment action performed; for example, if the last action was *delete* the currently active segment group, then these segments are restored. This can be achieved by making deleted segments at first invisible and putting them into a *pending deletion* state maintained by the program. They are only really deleted when a subsequent segment operation occurs. The detailed representation of the other options are left to the imagination of the reader.

Summary

The introduction of segments in GKS provides the system with an extra dimension of flexibility. There are so many ramifications that at first it must be difficult to see the wood from the trees. However, the ideas are straightforward:

- Segments provide a way of creating a high-level representation of the total picture. Each segment consists of attributes determining the state of the segment and a sequence of output primitives.
- All graphical output generated while a segment is open is written into the segment, together with the primitive attributes, the clipping region and the pick identifier.
- The segment exists on every workstation active at creation time.
- Each segment has an associated transformation matrix, can be made visible or invisible, can be highlighted, has a priority, can be deleted, or renamed. A segment may be detectable, in which case it can be picked.
- The WISS workstation exists as a global means of storing segments. Segments in the WISS may be associated with another workstation, copied to another workstation or inserted under a transformation to all active workstations.

GKS provides a simple form of picture segments. Hierarchical structures are discussed in Chapter 11.

Exercises

7.1 In GKS, the segment data structure is a sequence of segments, where segments store their identifier, attribute and sequence of primitives (each primitive with additional attribute, clipping and pick identifier information). Implementing the segment data structure as a simple linked list is not always very efficient. It might be acceptable if the only operation is list traversal (this might be used, for example, when the GKS function *RedrawAllSegmentsOnWorkstation* is invoked). However, even here, segment priority would cause a problem, since the list should be maintained in priority order (since the segments have to be drawn in priority order). Furthermore, to access a single segment (in order to transform it), a linked list is hardly ideal if the segment transformation matrix is actually stored with the segment. Consider in detail suitable data structures and functions allowing efficient implementation of the segment operations, especially:

(a) priority;

(b) deletion;

(c) insertion;

(d) fast access to individual segments;

(e) not all segments exist on all workstations.

Bear in mind that the GKS standard recommends that at least 32 000 different segment names should be available to an applications program (although this does not imply that it should be possible to *create* 32 000 different segments).

7.2 Implement the *EvaluateTransformationMatrix* and *Accumulate TransformationMatrix* functions.

7.3 Implement the typewriter example. Display a keyboard, where each key has a different pick identifier. Another segment represents a sheet of paper which is initially blank. As the operator selects keys (*RequestPick*), so the corresponding characters are 'typed' on to the paper.

7.4 When would it be important, in the interactive drawing program, for the segments representing the closed and open tool boxes and the border of the drawing pad area to be not detectable?

7.5 An alternative design for the drawing program would be to keep all tool boxes open and abandon the idea of closed and open tool boxes. Discuss the merits of this arrangement.

7.6 Design methods that allow the user of the drawing program to scale, rotate or shift (groups of) segments. In other words, what prompts and feedback would be provided, how would the interaction be represented? Remember, users would somehow have to select a fixed point about which the transformation is effected, together with the transformation parameters. Your solution should be a direct one; that is, do not use a VALUATOR to allow users to, for example, input scaling values.

7.7 Fully complete your design for the drawing program including segments and transcribe it to GKS Pascal.

7.8 GKS does not allow the re-opening of a segment once it has been closed, so that it is not possible to append further primitives to a closed segment. Nevertheless, it is possible to achieve the required effect by using the *InsertSegment*, *RenameSegment* and *DeleteSegment* functions. Write a complete *AppendToSegment* function built on top of the GKS functions.

7.9 Use segments to animate the hands of the clock discussed in Chapter 5.

7.10 Following on from your design of a segment data structure in Exercise 7.1, now consider the problems involved in the implementation of *PickInput*. In particular, suppose that (as is usual) the *Request Pick* is triggered by a mouse button click, and the position of the cursor at the moment of the trigger is used to identify which segment (if any) is to be returned. This requires that the point be transformed from DC back to NDC, and then compared with all the primitives in all the segments in the segment data structure which exist on the given workstation. The segment data structure must be searched in priority order. How is the point returned from the mouse interaction to be compared with the primitives in the segments to determine whether or not a 'hit' has occurred? (*Hint*: The clipping functions might prove useful here.)

CHAPTER 8

GKS PERFORMANCE AND ADDITIONAL FEATURES

Chapters 5 to 7 have discussed the major components of GKS – graphical output and interaction, the primitive attributes and segments. The functions defined in these chapters are the core of GKS, and applications programmers must become thoroughly familiar with them. However, to use GKS successfully in practice, an additional class of problems, and an extra set of functions, concerned with the real operation of GKS, must be mastered. These form the topic of this chapter.

8.1 Introduction

Readers who have implemented the drawing program of Chapters 6 and 7 on their GKS systems are likely to be disappointed for several reasons. First, the program does not behave entirely as expected. The most striking example of this is that, in all probability, segment modifications do not take effect: when a segment is transformed nothing happens on the display. No doubt readers have invested time looking for 'bugs' and researching their GKS documentation. At best, a solution may have been found that is still far from satisfactory: segment modifications take effect, but only at the cost of a complete display redraw. Second, there are a number of features missing from the program; for example, the ability to clear the display to start a fresh picture or to save an image produced by using the program, for later display or further editing. Third, there will be complaints of the form: 'My graphics device has a built-in capability for drawing ellipses, but there seems to be no corresponding GKS primitives'. These and a number of other issues relating to the performance and additional features of the system are the concerns of this chapter.

8.2 Dynamic Modification

Consider the following Pascal program for dynamic modification:

```
program modify(input, output);
include 'gksdefs';
const
  display   = 1;
  discon    = 'port 1';
  distype   = 500;
  errorfile = 1;
procedure SegShift(seg : GTseg; shift : GRVector);
{transforms segment by a shift}
var
  error      : GRSegAttr;
  attributes : GRSegAttr;
  fixed      : GRPoint;
  scale      : GRVector;
  matrix     : GAMatrix;
begin
  {inquire segment attributes}
  GInqSegAttr(seg, error, attributes);
  if error = 0 then
```

```
  begin
    {accumulate current segment transformation with shift}
    with fixed do begin x := 0.0; y := 0.0 end;
    with scale do begin xValue := 1,0; yValue := 1.0 end;
    GAccumTran(attributes.segtran, fixed, shift, 0.0, scale, GVwc, matrix);
    GSetSegTran(seg, matrix);
  end;
end;
{**************************************************************}

procedure CreateModify;
var
  p          : array[1..4] of GRPoint;
  shift      : GRVector;
  alignment : GRAlign;
begin
  with p[1] do begin x := 0.0; y := 0.0 end;
  with p[2] do begin x := 1.0; y := 0.0 end;
  with p[3] do begin x := 0.5; y := 1.0 end;
  p[4] := p[1];
  GCreateSeg(1);
    GPolyline(4, p);
  GCloseSeg;
  with shift do begin xValue := 0.0; yValue := 0.5 end;
  SegShift(1, shift);
  with alignment do
  begin
    horizontal := GVHcentre;
    vertical    := GVVbottom;
  end;
  GSetTextAlign(alignment);
  GSetCharHeight(0.05);
  GText(shift, 'Segment now shifted');
end;

{main}
begin
  GOpenGKS(errorfile, GCdefmemory);
    GOpenWs(display, discon, distype);
    GActivateWs(display);
      CreateModify;
    GDeactivateWs(display);
    GCloseWs(display);
  GCloseGKS;
end.
```

The reader is urged to try this program, if possible, even if it means using another language, such as FORTRAN. The results are unexpected and at a first glimpse it seems that there is an error either in the program or in the

GKS implementation. What is almost certainly likely to happen when this program is executed is as follows:

(1) There is a short delay while GKS is opened.

(2) The screen is cleared if it is not already clear (a result of the *OpenWorkstation* call).

(3) A triangle is drawn with its base along the bottom of the display space and its vertex in the middle of the top of the effective display space.

(4) The text *Segment now shifted* appears in the centre half-way up the display.

(5) The screen is cleared again.

(6) The triangle is redrawn, now half-way up the display and partially clipped.

The overall effect seems to be incorrect: the *SetSegmentTransformation* procedure is called *before* the call to draw the text, yet the text is displayed *and then* the segment is shifted. (Some rather more fortunate readers may have access to GKS implementations or graphics devices where the results not only occur in the correct order, but where there is no intermediate clearing of the display between redraws of the triangle.) Yet, in spite of expectations, this sequence of events is what will and should occur with the majority of GKS implementations and graphics devices.

Modern graphics hardware, with bitmapped or raster displays (or any pixel-based displays), cannot easily perform **dynamic modifications** to images in the manner desired by GKS. A dynamic modification should occur whenever there is an execution of a GKS function that requires a change to something that has *already* been displayed. An example of this is an execution of *SetSegmentTransformation*, where the segment is visible. This requires a modification of something already on the screen, for example, by a rotation. In contrast, a call to *Polyline* or any graphical output function while a segment is not being created (when GKS is in the state where at least one workstation is active) does not require a dynamic modification, since whatever is on the screen already remains unchanged. Suppose, however, that a segment with priority 0.5 is open and that a solid fill area is generated which overlaps a segment visible on the display that has a higher priority (for example, priority 1). In this case, a dynamic modification is required since the desired effect is that the new fill area be 'underneath' (obscured by) the segment with the higher priority. The fill area cannot be drawn in its correct place in the segment priority order without requiring a partial redraw of what is on the screen already.

There are a number of GKS actions that can require a dynamic modification:

(1) *SetPrimitiveRepresentation*: Primitives displayed with the redefined

bundle should be redisplayed in the new guise (bearing in mind the influence of the aspect source flags). This is only required of primitives in segments, although ideally those outside of segments should also be affected. The same applies to *SetColourRepresentation* and *SetPatternRepresentation*.

(2) A change to the workstation transformations, *SetWorkstationWindow* and *SetWorkstationViewport*: Here, all primitives should be redrawn to conform to the new transformation. Again, only primitives in segments have to be affected. If dynamic modification to the workstation transformations is carried out immediately, then this would be a basis for a panning and zooming capability.

(3) The generation of graphical output primitives while a segment is open and which overlaps segments of higher priority: This could be caused by an *InsertSegment* call as well as by direct calls to the output functions.

(4) Any segment function that requires a reshuffling of visible segments because of priority considerations: For example, suppose segments 1, 2 and 3 overlap and have corresponding priorities. Now, if segment 2 is deleted, or made invisible, segments 1 and 3 must be redrawn, as shown in Figure 8.1. Obviously, the *SetSegmentPriority* function itself can cause such a change.

(5) *SetSegmentTransformation*: This requires a dynamic modification, unless the transformation matrix is actually unchanged or the segment is invisible or the segment overlaps no other segments both in its original and transformed state.

(6) *SetVisibility*: An invisible segment made visible, or a visible segment made invisible, may lead to a dynamic modification.

In the 1960s and 1970s, the common form of graphics hardware had an architecture quite different to the raster display. Vector refresh devices (see Section 16.3) refresh the image from a **segmented display list**. The display list is a program consisting of a sequence of subroutines each containing primitive graphics instructions – usually for drawing straight lines (vectors) and a jump instruction to the next subroutine to be executed. In the refresh cycle, each subroutine is executed in turn and at a speed fast enough so that the complete cycle takes no longer than 1/30 of a second. This is for reasons to do with the hardware used to display the vectors: the image of each vector decays (disappears from the screen) noticeably in about 1/30 of a second, hence the refresh speed is necessary to maintain an acceptable screen image.

The technology is expensive in comparison to today's raster devices. However, it has the advantage that the screen image is stored and manipulated by the graphics device in geometric form – as a sequence of vectors, each belonging to a segment corresponding to a subroutine. This

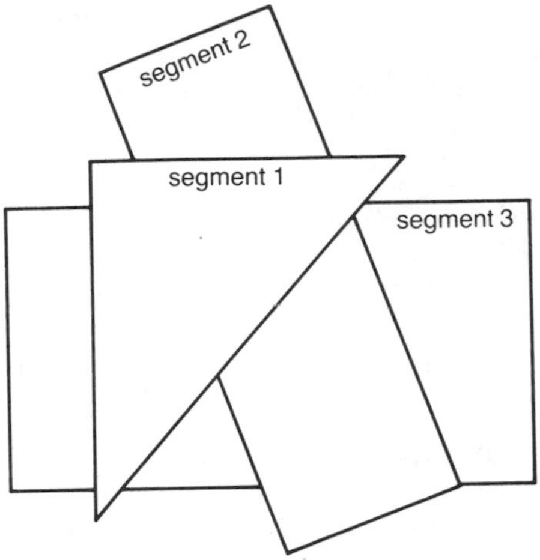

Figure 8.1
Priority considerations require dynamic modification.

method of representing the image corresponds closely to the way in which the picture might be conceived and constructed by the applications programmer. Moreover, segment manipulation functions can be executed at great speed. For example, transforming a particular segment involves making a copy of the corresponding subroutine, but with appropriate changes to the coordinates, and then substituting this new version for the old version. Such a substitution only requires a change in the jump instruction of the segment executed prior to the affected one, so that control now jumps to the new, modified subroutine rather than the old one. Moreover, the space occupied by the old version can be reclaimed for later use. To an onlooker it might seem as if the segment transformed instantaneously on the display.

Vector refresh display architecture corresponds closely to the segment concept. This is in stark contrast to the raster architecture. Here, the image is refreshed from a frame buffer, which conceptually is a 2D array of pixels (in the case of a bitmapped display each being 1 or 0 – black or white); that is, the image is refreshed from this relatively low-level representation. Furthermore, once a vector or any other graphical primitive has been drawn into the frame buffer, its geometry is not recoverable.

In an implementation of any graphics package for use with raster devices, segments may be represented as linked list data structures. There might be a list of pointers, each to the address of a segment where the segment attributes and primitive elements are stored. Also, the device frame buffer will be a pixel matrix representation of all the primitives in all the visible segments (together with any primitives outside of the segments). Ideally, for speed and efficiency reasons, the linked list segment data will actually be implemented on the graphics device. However, it is important to note that the image is *not* refreshed from this segment data list but from the frame buffer. The segment list is concurrent with and orthogonal to the

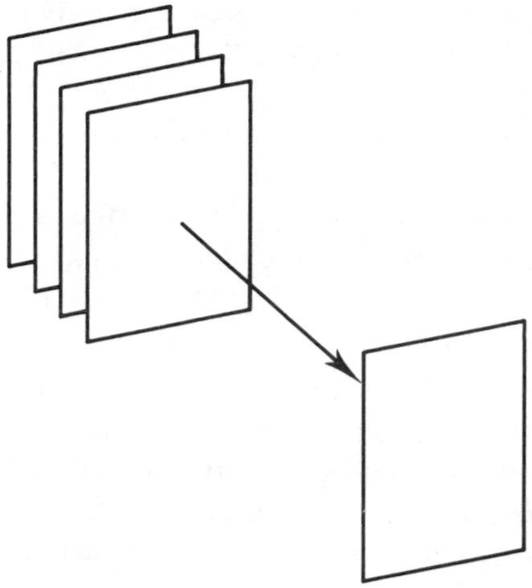
Conceptual pixel matrix for each segment . . .
. . . superimposed to form the real frame buffer.

Figure 8.2
Segment list to frame buffer.

frame buffer. The same is clearly true if the graphics device is not sophisticated enough to store the segment list, in which case it will be implemented on the host computer. The point of the segment list is that whenever an action is taken with respect to segments, such as a transformation or priority change, the change is made first in the segment data structure and then somehow reflected on the screen. This 'somehow' is what disguises the problem.

Figure 8.2 helps to clarify these relationships. The frame buffer can be viewed as the superimposition of conceptual pixel matrices corresponding to each segment. This superimposition is in order of segment priority. In other words, each segment corresponds to a set of pixel positions and associated colour values, and the frame buffer is the composition of all of these. The problem is that it is *not* possible to recover the unique list of segments (that is, sequences of primitives) which led to any given frame buffer.

The task of, for example, making a segment invisible can be stated in terms of this model. From the frame buffer, as it is at any given moment, it is necessary to identify the pixel positions and colours corresponding to the segment to be deleted. A new total display must be formed excluding the pixel matrix of the deleted segment. Since it is impossible to identify this, it is not possible to carry out this operation using only the information in the frame buffer. Similarly, it can be seen that it is impossible to perform a segment transformation given only the frame buffer representation of the display.

Consider two possible solutions to this incompatibility between the segment concept and a frame buffer display representation:

(1) Since the pixel-based technology cannot satisfactorily handle seg-

ments, abandon the concept altogether and invent new models for image modification based on ideas more suited to the 2D frame buffer approach – see, for example, Cook (1983). (Such raster-based methods are discussed in Chapter 11.)

(2) A high-level representation of segments is stored in a data structure. When a segment modification is applied (to delete or transform a segment), then the modification is applied to the segment data structure, which is used to recreate the display pixel matrix in its entirety. Essentially, this means that *all* segments are redrawn. This process can be accomplished in two ways:

   (i) The current frame buffer is erased (all pixels are set to the background colour) and the segment data structure is traversed segment by segment in order of priority. The primitives in each segment are then drawn into the frame buffer. An observer would see the screen cleared and all visible segments redrawn one after the other.

   (ii) On some systems, it is possible for GKS to maintain an 'off-screen' memory buffer which has the same size as the screen display buffer and into which graphical primitives can be drawn. On such a system, there are in effect two frame buffers, called here buffer A and buffer B. At any moment, one of these is the *foreground* and the other the *background*. The video controller always scans the foreground buffer, so that this corresponds to the actual display. Now suppose at some moment buffer A is the foreground and B the background. Output primitives outside of segments, or in the open segment, are destined for buffer A and displayed immediately. Suppose that a target segment is to be made invisible. Then the segment data structure may be traversed but with buffer B as the destination of the segment primitives (and, of course, with the target segment omitted). At the end of this traversal, buffers A and B can switch roles, so that B now becomes the foreground and A the background. This switch must happen at exactly the right instant – during the vertical fly-back in the refresh process. The observer might notice a delay while the segments were redrawn off screen, but then there would be a change to the state of the display reflecting the segment modification and without intermediate screen clearing. The length of the delay depends on the processing speed of the computer and on the number and complexity of segments to be redrawn. This is described in detail in Section 16.4.10.

Neither method (i) nor (ii) provide a satisfactory solution to the problem of achieving real-time segment modifications, at least to the extent that dynamic display changes can be included in an interactive system. In addition, method (i) is not acceptable because it involves intermediate clearing of the display. However fast the redraw takes place it will still not be good enough to allow the simplest of operations – dragging (or letting a segment follow the cursor). (In GKS, this would be theoretically achieved by repeated *SampleLocator* and *TransformSegment* calls.) The obvious reason why this is unacceptable is that the screen clearing would result in a very jerky appearance while a segment was being modified, which would certainly disconcert and probably hurt the eyes of an observer.

Method (ii), however, is workable up to a point – the point where, as would happen in reality, the segment list becomes long enough so that there is a noticeable delay between the instruction to modify a segment and the changed state of the display: a gap of even a second in an interactive setting will probably cause the user of the system to begin wondering what has gone wrong; and a gap of two or more seconds will probably result in the user trying out various actions (mouse clicks, keyboard presses) in an attempt to put things right – and these actions might result in further actions on the part of the system, thus leaving the user in a confused state. In this situation, method (ii) is possibly a worse solution than method (i) because of this inherent lack of feedback; at least in method (i) the clearing of the screen and the redrawing of the whole picture shows the user that something is happening in response to the instruction requiring a dynamic modification. In addition, method (ii) is, of course, relatively expensive because of the memory and processing speed required, and non-portable across devices.

A third possible solution to the problem of segments on raster displays is to construct a high-level segment representation as in (1), and to use this to *partially* alter the frame buffer to achieve the desired effect, but at the cost of possibly leaving the displayed image in a 'messy' state (this was adopted by Bramer and Sutcliffe, 1981). Consider what would happen if a segment is to be transformed. First, the segment with its current transformation matrix is redrawn into the frame buffer, except that the colour used for all primitives in the segment is the background colour. (This is easiest to envisage on a black on white display, so that the first step is to redraw the segment in white.) The segment quickly disappears from the display, more or less – 'more or less' because traces of its former existence will be left wherever it intersected with other segments. Second, with the new transformation applied the segment is again drawn, but this time with the correct colours. The final effect is that the segment is displayed according to the required transformation. In some cases, this can achieve exactly the right result, and at great speed. But if the segment in its original position overlapped the segments, then, as already pointed out, traces will be left: in the best case, small gaps where lines crossed; in the worst case, whole areas will be erased where fill areas in the transformed segment impacted primitives of other segments. These ideas are illustrated in Figure 8.3.

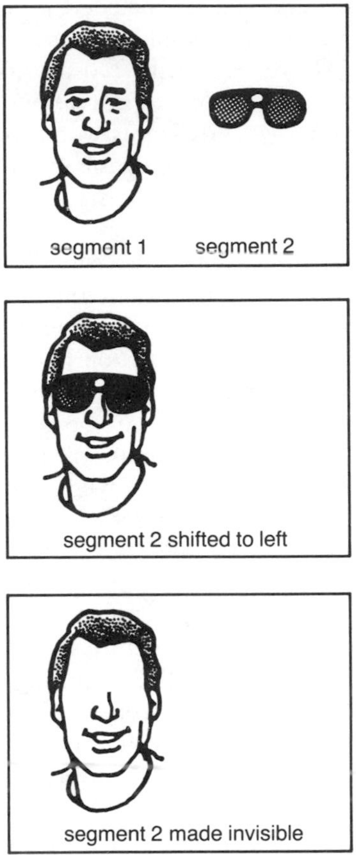

Figure 8.3
Messy segment modifications.

A fourth method uses the **selective erase** facility of raster devices and the idea of a rectangular **segment extent**. This approach attempts to minimize the amount of redrawing performed in order to realize a dynamic modification, while preserving the integrity of the display (Warner and Keifhaber, 1979). As before, a display list data structure is used to maintain the segment information. However, in this case the extent is stored with each segment; that is, the smallest rectangle enclosing all the primitives in the segment. Once again, consider what happens when a segment is to be transformed (see Figure 8.4 where segment 1 is to be transformed). First, the area of the segment extent rectangle is erased (set to the background colour). Next, those segments (2 and 3) that have extents overlapping that of the transformed segment (1) are redrawn, using the extent of segment 1 as a clipping region. At this stage, the effect is that the segment (1) to be transformed has been cleanly deleted from the display. Finally, the segment is redrawn using its new transformation matrix (see Figure 8.4).

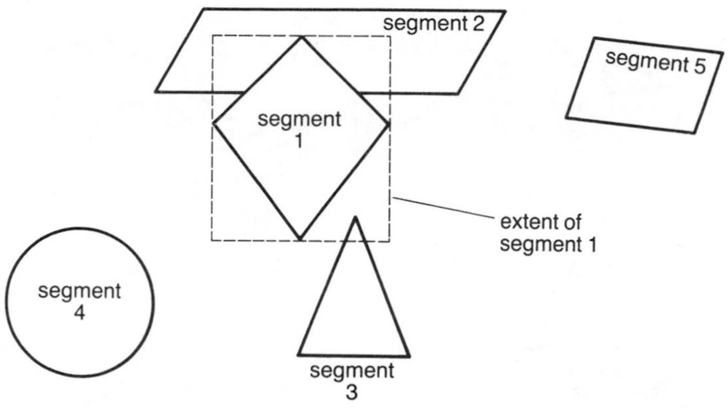

Figure 8.4
Using segment extents.

Although this method minimizes the amount of redrawing by only redrawing those segments that are likely to overlap the original segment, there are some problems associated with it:

- The extent method of capturing segments that overlap with the segment to be modified is in fact very crude. For example, suppose the segment to be changed includes a diagonal line across the screen. Then even if no other segment actually overlaps or is anywhere near this segment, still *all* segments will be redrawn.
- The example outlined should have rang warning bells in the reader's mind. It is not clear how segment priority is to be taken account of in this method. Priority considerations may require more than the segments with overlapping extents to be redrawn (see Exercise 8.6).

A recent approach for the treatment of dynamic modifications on raster displays is called the **tiling method** (Slater, 1987). This involves imposing a rectangular grid on the display space, where each grid cell is called a **tile**. The objective of this method is for each tile to maintain information about which segments pass through it, so that when a segment (S) is to be made invisible the union of all the segment names stored at tiles that S passes through identifies the set of segments that need to be redrawn. (Making S invisible is always the first step in any segment modification.) An outline of how this can be achieved is as follows.

Suppose there are M horizontal and N vertical divisions, then there is an $M*N$ tiling coordinate system, as shown in Figure 8.5, and a corresponding $M*N$ array of sets of segment names. For example, if the segment identifiers are integers, then the type of this array is:

type *TilingArray* = (*int set*) ~(*M*, *N*);

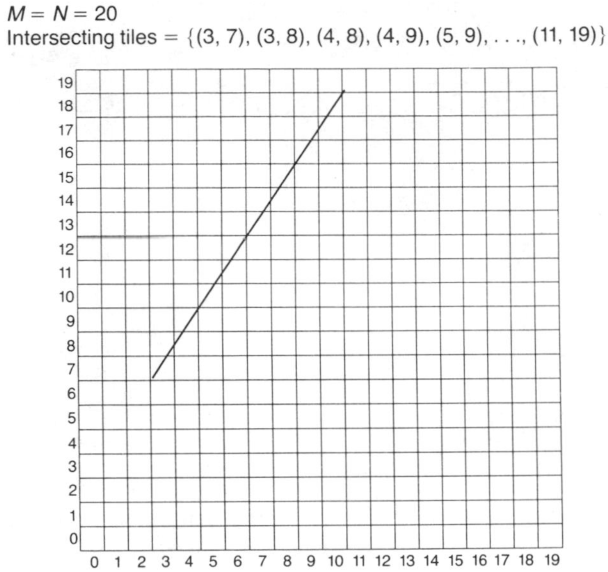

Figure 8.5
The tiling method.

Whenever a primitive belonging to a visible segment (with name S, say) is generated, the set of tiles it passes through is computed, and the segment identifier (S) is appended to the corresponding element in the tiling array. Hence, each tile element maintains the set of segment names that have primitives passing through the tile.

Now suppose a target segment is to be made invisible. A sequence called the **active segment list (ASL)** is initialised to be empty, and each primitive in the target is traversed and redrawn using the background colour. In addition, as each tile it intersects is encountered the set of segment names in the tiling array element corresponding to that tile is appended to the ASL. Hence, by the time all the primitives in the segment have been redrawn, the ASL contains the names of all the segments that the target segment intersects (or is very close to). The final step is to redraw all the segments in the ASL. If the target segment is to be transformed, then it is first made invisible, as described above, and then redrawn in its new position, with the corresponding changes to the entries in the tiling array.

The advantage of this method as compared to the extent method is that the procedure for finding the set of segments to be redrawn when a target segment is modified is rather more sophisticated. In the tiling method, only segments with a high probability of intersecting the target are identified as needing to be redrawn. There are also possible advantages with respect to *PickInput* and segment priority (see Exercises 8.4 and 8.6).

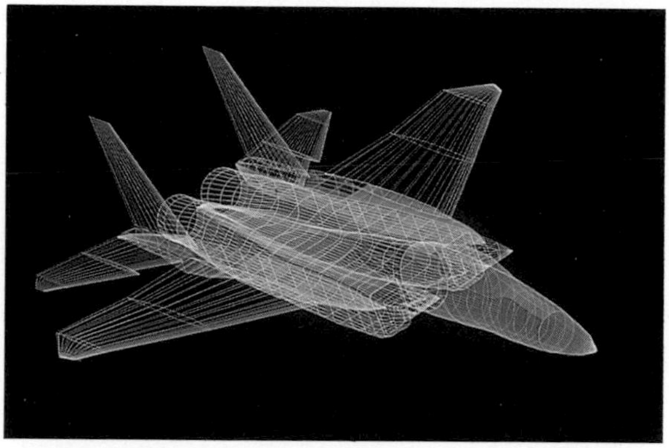

Plate 1 3D wire-frame view of a McDonnell Douglas F-15 fighter aircraft displayed on a colour calligraphic display system. (Courtesy: Evans & Sutherland)

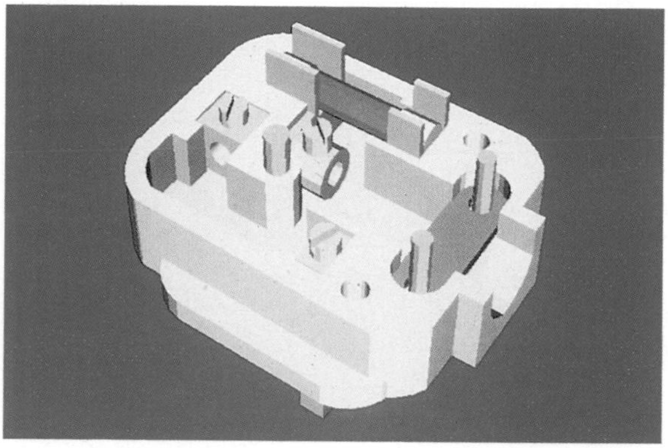

Plate 2 3D solid modelled view of part of a British standard 13-amp domestic mains plug. (Courtesy: Dr J.R. Woodwark © and the School of Engineering, University of Bath)

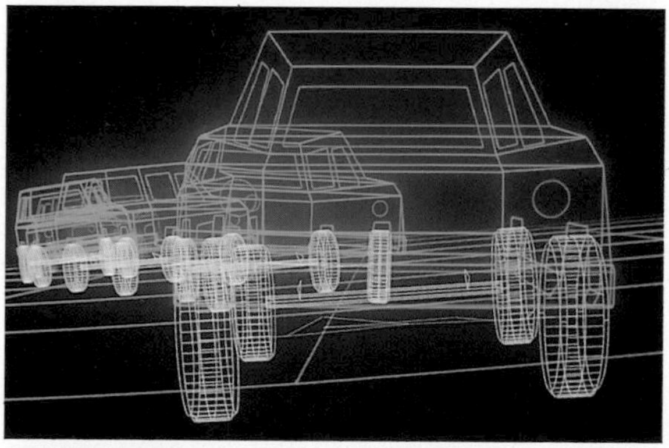

Plate 3 Multiple frame image of the dynamic behaviour of a 4WD automobile while changing lanes. (Courtesy: Evans & Sutherland and Mechanical Dynamics, Inc)

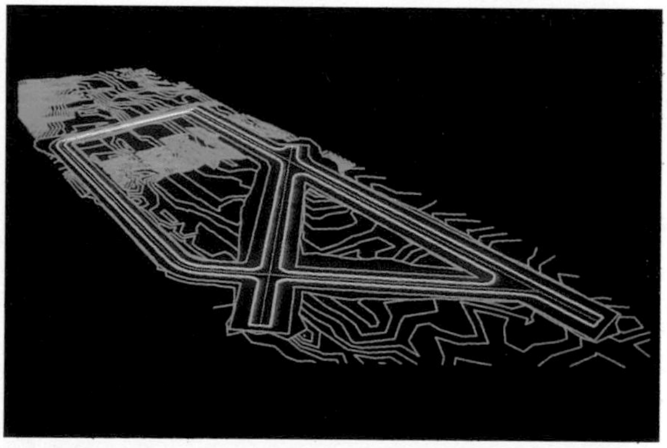

Plate 4 Perspective 3D view of ground model data with a standard airport design superimposed. (Courtesy: Australian Department of Housing and Construction and Moss Systems Limited)

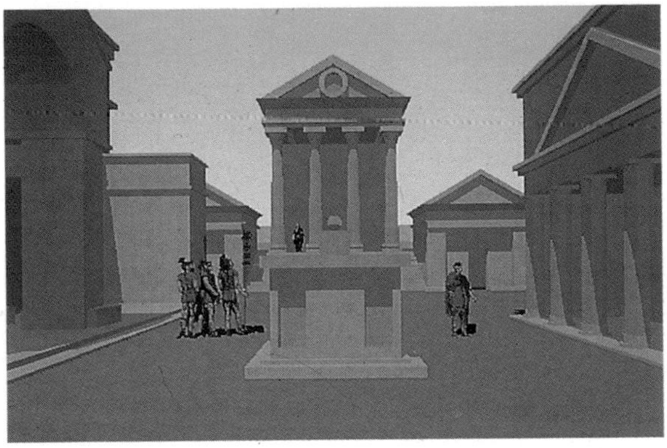

Plate 5 Computer-generated view of the City of Bath during Roman Times. (Courtesy: Dr J.R. Woodwark © and the School of Engineering, University of Bath)

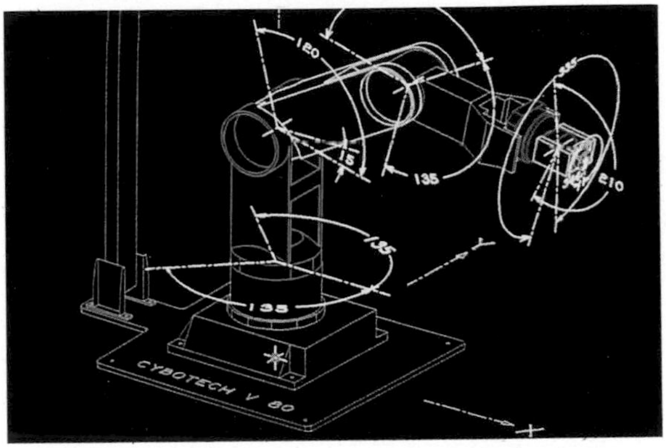

Plate 6 Wire-frame representation of a robot at work. (Courtesy: McAuto (UK) Limited – a McDonnell Douglas Information Systems International Company)

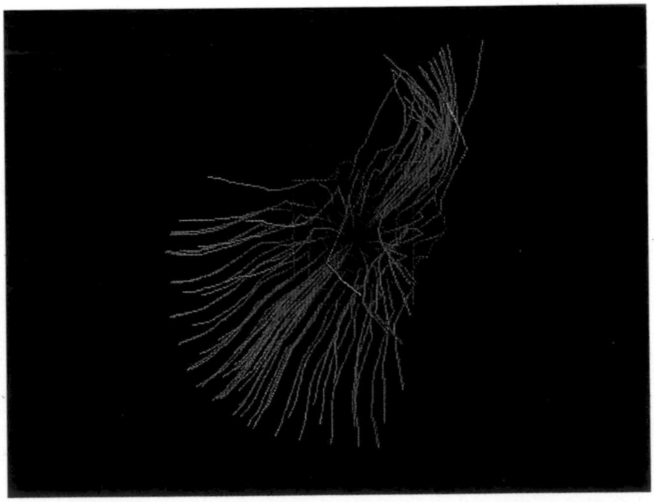

Plate 7 "Grid Explosion #1". (Photo: Rory Coonan; Courtesy of the artist: Stephen Bell)

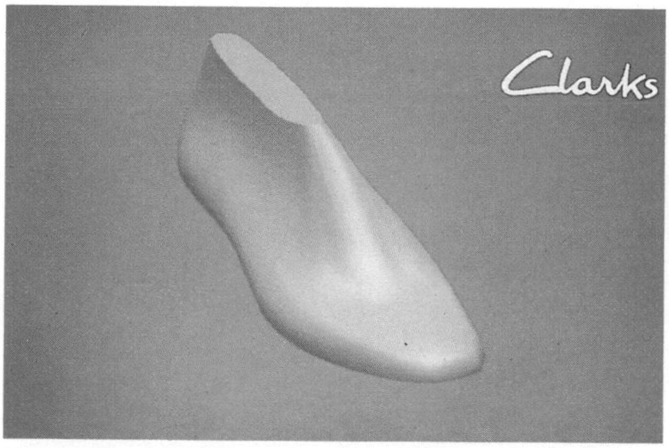

Plate 8 3D solid modelled view of the last of a shoe.

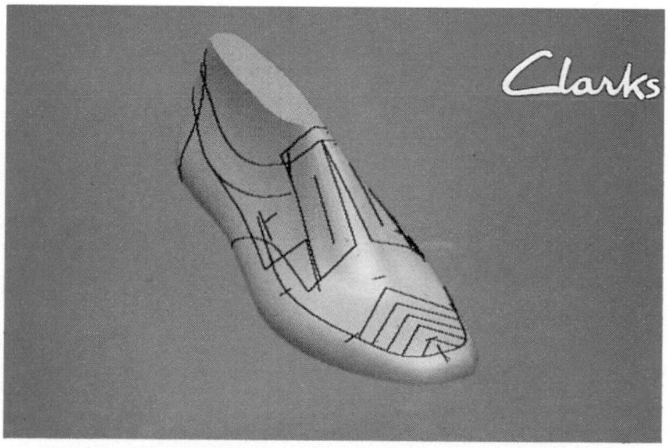

Plate 9 Shoe last with free-form styling superimposed.

Plate 10 Three visualization views of completed shoe design.

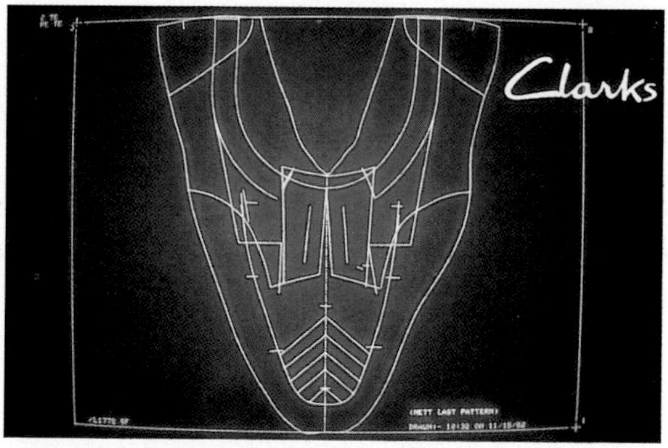

Plate 11 2D flattening of shoe design for pattern cutting. (Plates 8 to 11 all Courtesy: Clarks Limited, Shoemakers of Street, Somerset)

Plate 12 Frame from a computer animation for a TV commercial for Michelin tyres. (Design by Lodge Cheesman; Computer Graphics by Digital Pictures Limited, London)

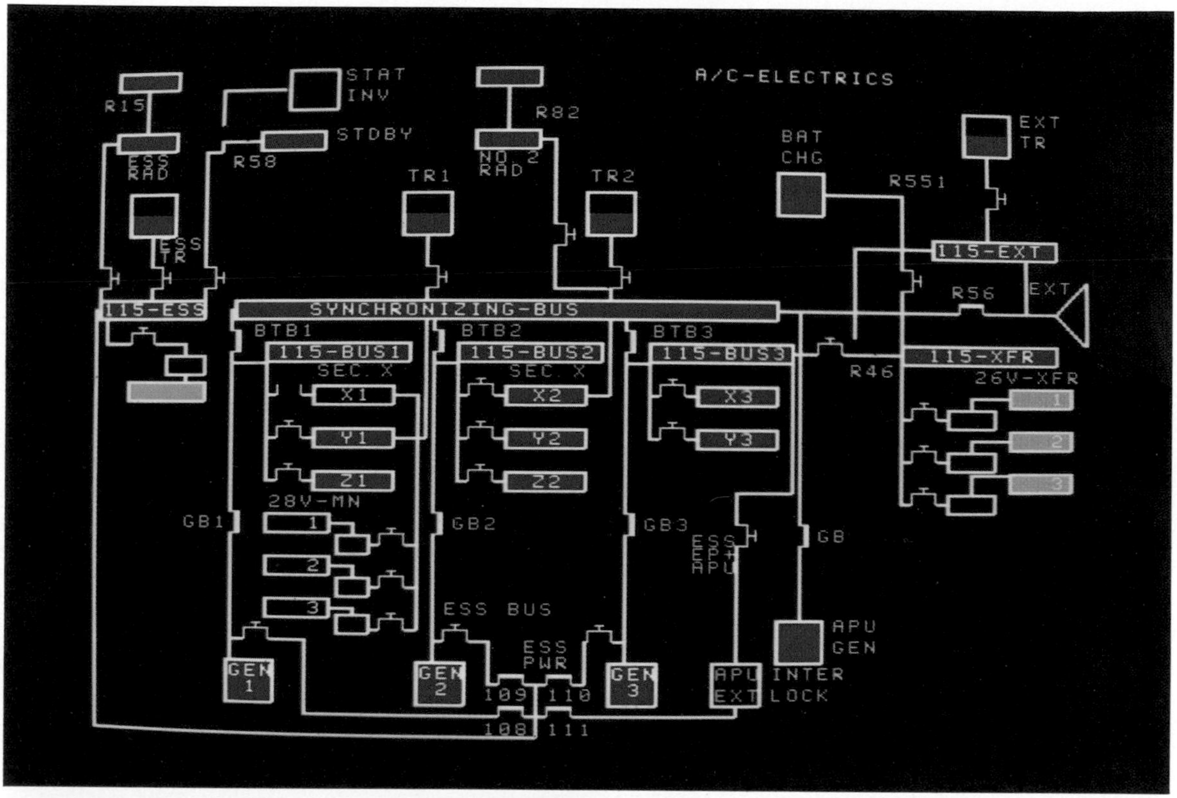

Plate 13 Dynamic schematic image of the A/C (alternating current) electrical distribution system of a Boeing B727 commercial jet aircraft. (Courtesy: Rediffusion Simulation Limited)

Plate 14 Modern flight simulator showing the WIDE CGI display system. (Courtesy: Rediffusion Simulation Limited)

Plate 15 Flight simulator computer-generated image of a pair of McDonnell Douglas F-15 fighter aircraft as seen from the cockpit of a third aircraft in formation. (Courtesy: Evans & Sutherland)

Plate 16 Flight simulator computer-generated image with 2D texturing of surfaces. (Courtesy: Evans & Sutherland)

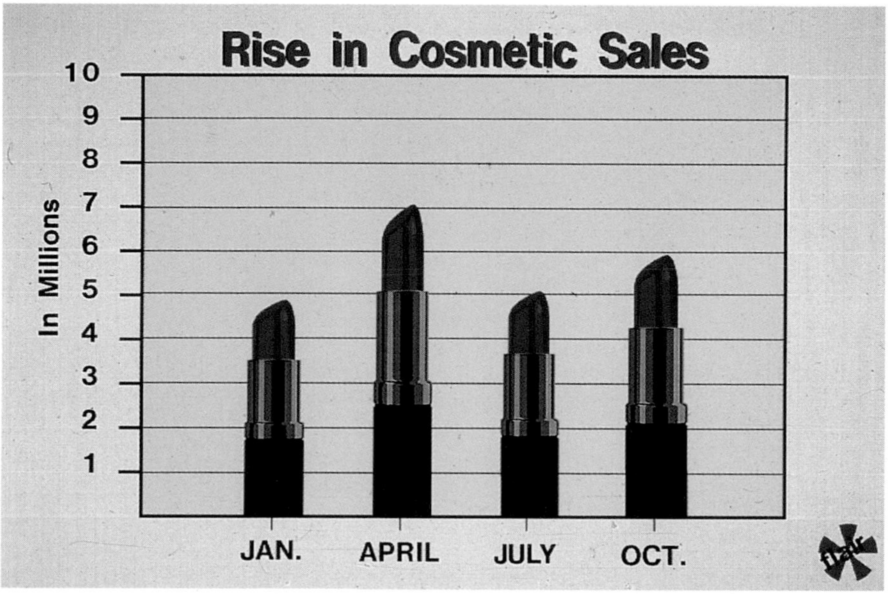

Plate 17 Business graphics display using 3D effects to add life and interest to a histogram display. (Courtesy: DICOMED (UK) Limited)

Plate 18 Frame from a BBC TV news title sequence featuring a computer simulation of a professional video camera. (Computer Animation: Electric Image; Design: Leslie Hope-Stone; © British Broadcasting Corporation)

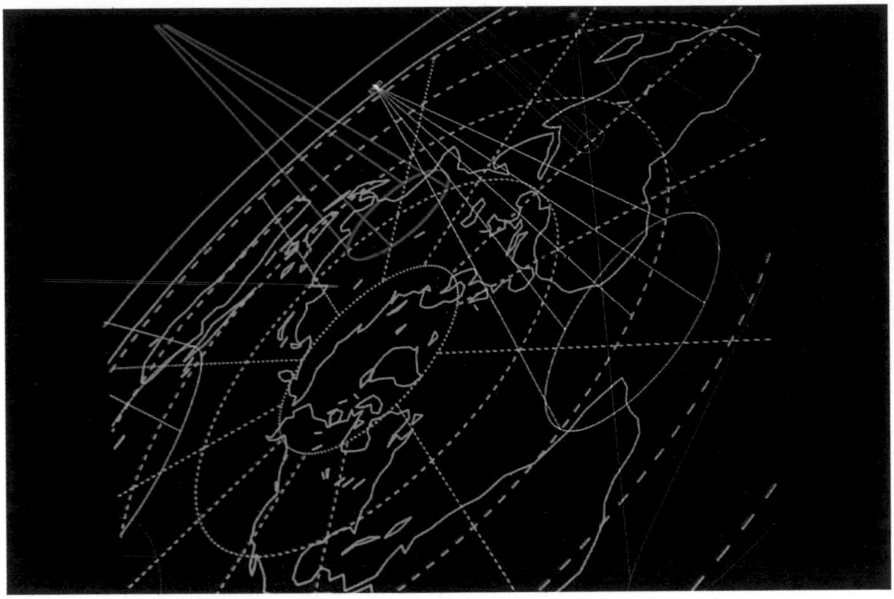

Plate 19 3D representation of satellites in orbit to show their position and altitude. (Courtesy: Evans & Sutherland and Martin Marietta Aerospace)

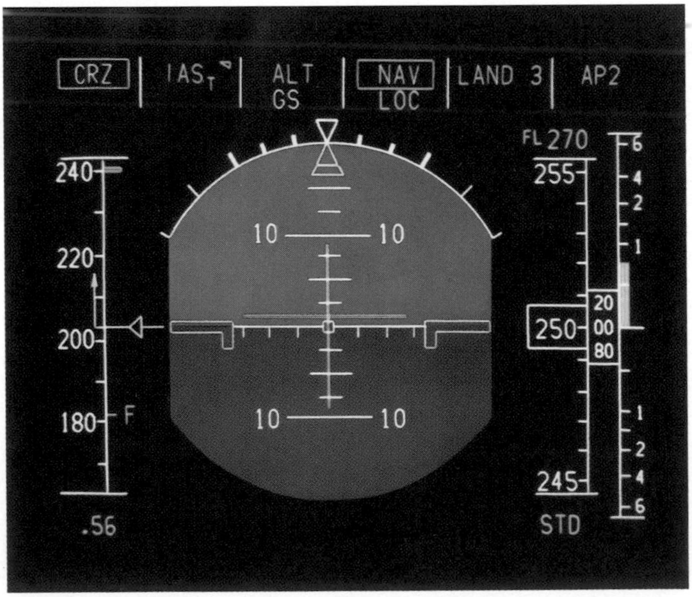

Plate 20 An electronic flight instrumentation system (EFIS) displaying an electronic attitude direction indicator (EADI). (Courtesy: Rockwell International Corporation, Collins Air Transport Division)

Plate 21 Cockpit of the A320 jet airliner with EFIS displays for the primary, navigational and aircraft system instrumentation. (Courtesy: Airbus Industrie)

Plate 22 3D image of part of a DNA molecule created using a molecular modelling system. (Courtesy: Chemical Design Limited)

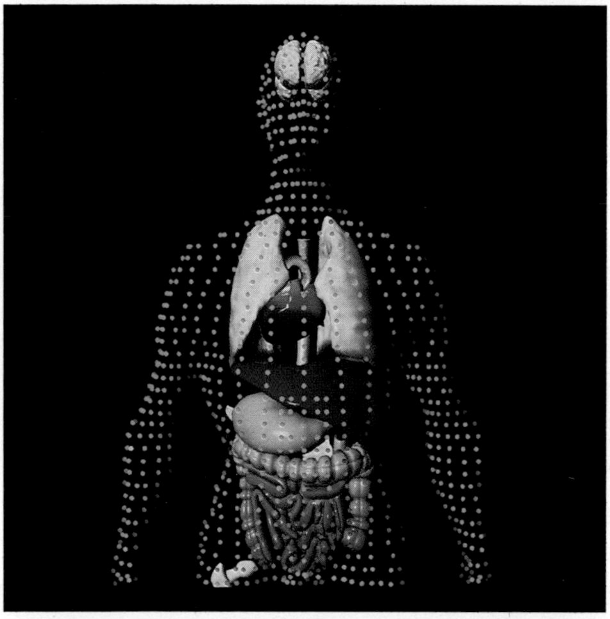

Plate 23 Human body in vector pattern with the major organs in position. (Courtesy: Cranston/Csuri Productions, Columbus, Ohio)

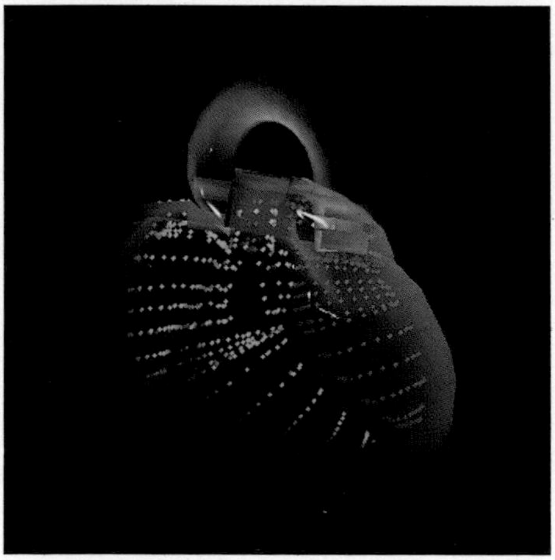

Plate 24 Human heart showing the arterial and venous sides. (Courtesy: Cranston/Csuri Productions, Columbus, Ohio)

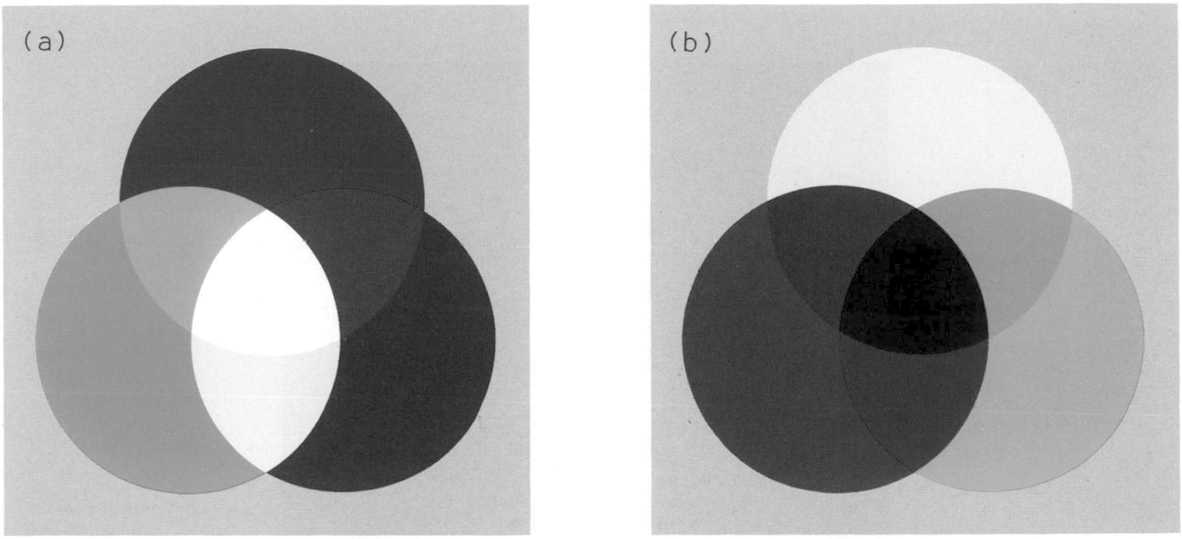

Plate 25 The (a) additive and (b) subtractive primary colours.

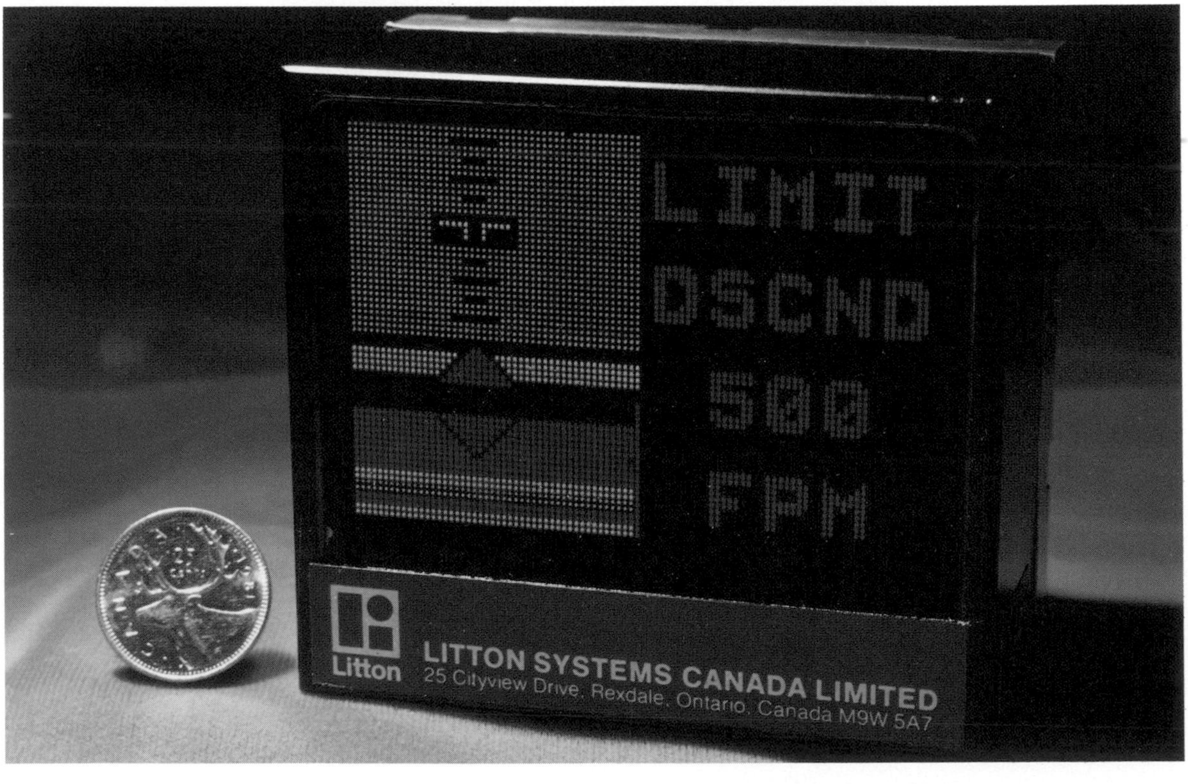

Plate 26 Multi-coloured LED dot matrix display. (Courtesy: Litton Systems, Canada, Limited)

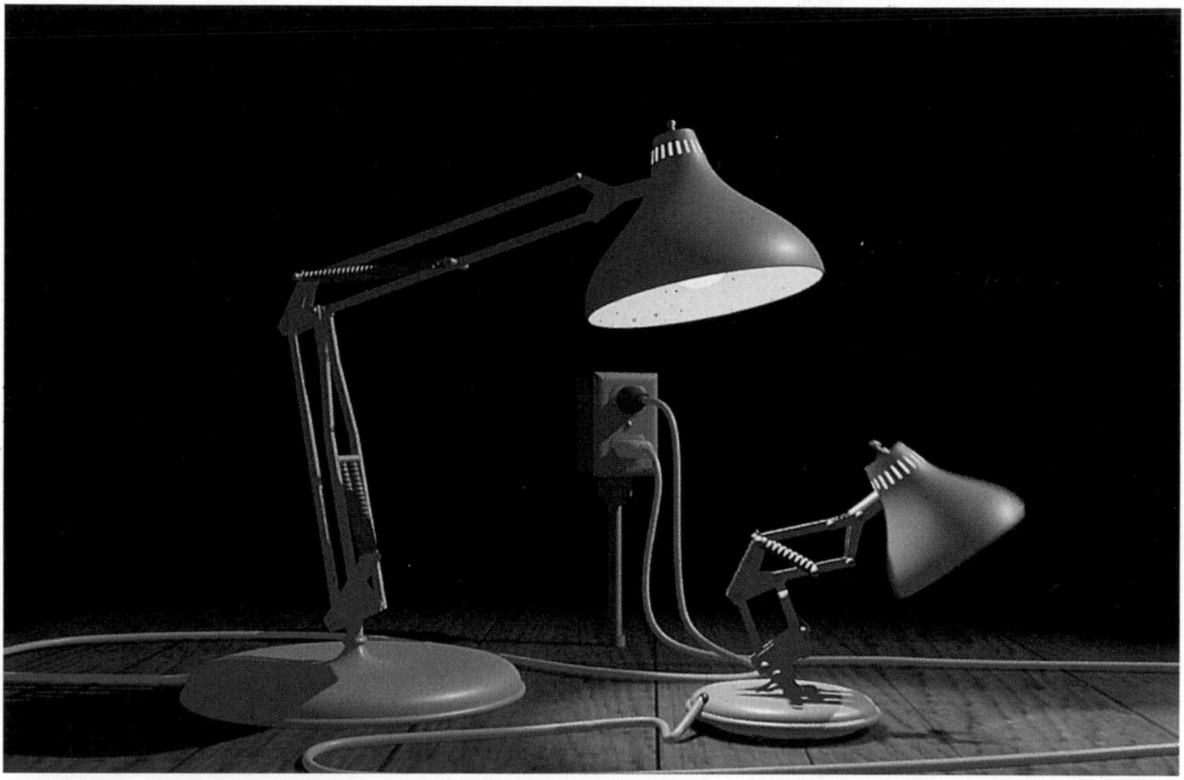

Plate 27 *Luxo Jr.* Frame from a computer animation of an illustrative story of a father and son relationship between two Luxo desk lamps. (Direction, animation, models: John Lasseter; Technical direction, models, rendering: Bill Reeves; Models, procedural animation, rendering: Eben Ostby; Rendering: Sam Leffler; Laser output scanning: Don Conway; © 1986 Pixar; "Luxo" is a Trademark of Jak Jacobson Industries)

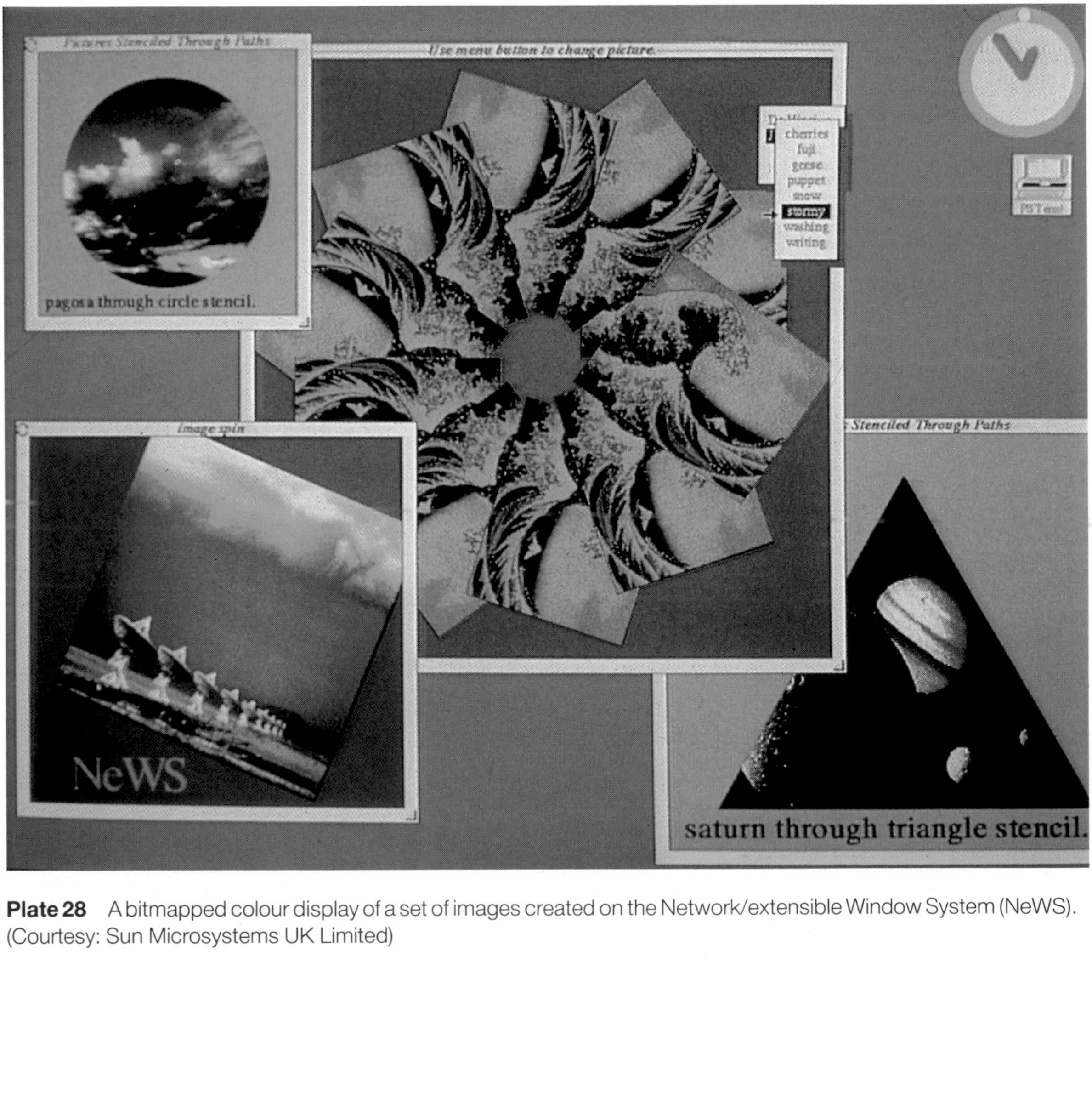

Plate 28 A bitmapped colour display of a set of images created on the Network/extensible Window System (NeWS). (Courtesy: Sun Microsystems UK Limited)

Plate 29 An experimental image of a room, produced for the front cover of Televisual Magazine, demonstrating the use of several different lighting and modelling techniques. (Computer animation: Electric Image; Design: Paul Docherty and Mike Milne; © Electric Image)

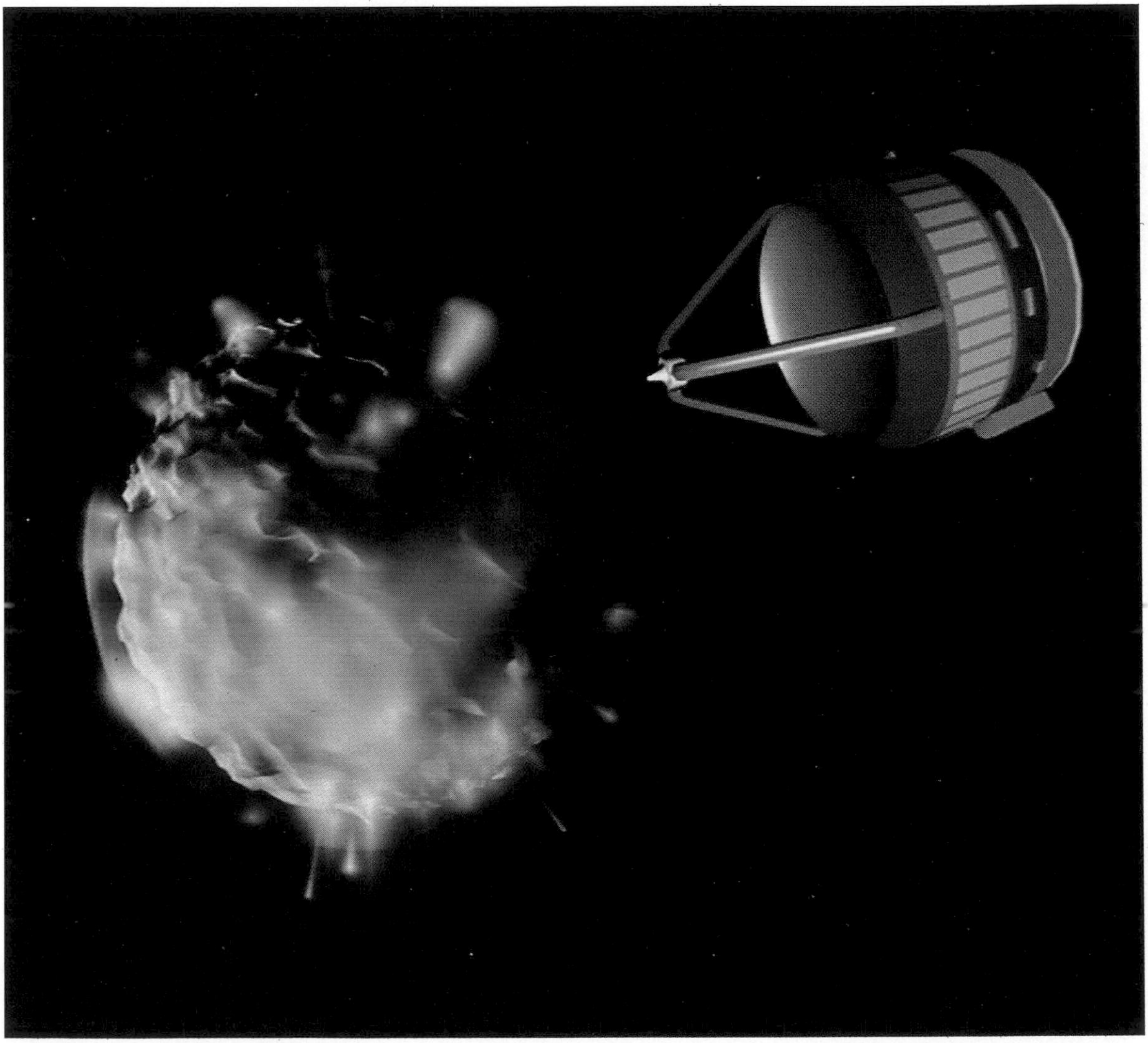

Plate 30 Frame from an animated computer simulation of Europe's Giotto space probe's encounter with Halley's Comet. (Courtesy: CAL Video Graphics Limited)

8.3 Controlling Dynamic Modifications in GKS

GKS started its life in the 1970s as a FORTRAN subroutine package developed (in West Germany) for applications in CAD in engineering. Given these origins, and bearing in mind that vector refresh devices are the traditional equipment used in CAD where segment manipulation plays a prominent part, it is not surprising that GKS provides picture segments as the only means of achieving picture modification. Given that segments are a crucial part of GKS, the system has to have some way of coping with the fact that they are difficult to implement efficiently for raster devices.

Several functions and associated variables are incorporated in GKS to deal with this problem. Recall that GKS maintains a series of data structures that record the states and control the performance of the system. The *GKS state list* stores information global to the system, such as the primitive indices, the set of active workstations, the normalization transformations, the set of segment names used and so on. The *workstation state list* (one for every open workstation) maintains information about the current state of the workstation; for example, the bundle representations, the current and requested workstation window and viewport, the set of segments defined on this workstation, etc. The *workstation description table* (one for every workstation) maintains static information (it can never be changed by a program execution) describing the workstation features; for example, the display size, the number of colours, number of line widths and so on including default bundle representations. When a workstation is opened, the entries in the workstation description table are used to help construct the initial state of the workstation state list. There is also a *segment state list* (one for every segment) which holds information about the current values of segment attributes.

The workstation description table has a number of entries relating directly to the problem of dynamic modification. For each one of the possible actions leading to a modification, there is a corresponding entry that determines whether the action can be performed immediately or whether an **implicit regeneration** is required to execute the action. An implicit regeneration corresponds to method 2(i) of Section 8.2; that is, the action is carried out by clearing the display and redrawing all segments using all the up-to-date information in the various state lists – in particular, using the correct primitive attributes (workstation state list) and segment attributes (segment state list). Hence, immediately after such a regeneration the display accurately reflects the entries of *all* the GKS data structures. (Of course, where individual attributes are used for primitives in segments these are never changed, irrespective of the current settings of individual attributes.)

If the workstation is capable of carrying out the required action immediately, then the entry in the workstation description table will say so. This may be the case, for example, if the underlying device is vector refresh and the action is a segment modification. Similarly, if the underlying graphics device has the functionality of a GKS workstation, then it ought to be able to perform most actions fast enough for the entries in the workstation description table to say 'can be performed immediately'. For each of the primitive representations, pattern and colour representations, workstation transformation functions and segment operations (transformation, visibility, highlighting, priority and deletion), the entry in the workstation description table will be either 'implicit regeneration necessary' (IRG) or 'can be performed immediately' (IMM). Remember that these entries are *fixed* – they describe the properties of the workstation.

The workstation state lists also have two entries that describe the states existing during a program execution and that control modification effects. These are the **workstation transformation update state**, which may be either 'pending' or 'not pending', the **new frame action necessary**, which can be 'yes' or 'no', and the **implicit regeneration mode**, which can be 'suppressed' or 'allowed'.

Consider the simplest case first (yes, there are simple cases!). If the workstation description table entry for a particular action is 'can be performed immediately', then when that action is required it is performed immediately. If the action is to set the workstation window or viewport, then the workstation state list entry for workstation transformation update state would always be 'not pending' for such a workstation. For other actions that can be performed immediately, there will be no effect on the value of the new frame action (NFA). If NFA = 'no' and an action is called for which can be performed immediately, then NFA remains 'no' – since a regeneration is *not* required to make the display match the current state list entries (for example, a change in the segment transformation matrix, or in the representation associated with a primitive index). (NFA will remain 'no' provided that the required action does not lead to other actions that cannot be performed immediately; for example, a segment transformation that a device can perform immediately but which leads to other changes generated as a result of priority considerations that cannot be performed immediately.) If, on the other hand, NFA = 'yes' and an action is called for that can be performed immediately, then NFA remains 'yes', because it must have been some other action that put NFA into the 'yes' state, and that other action is yet to be performed (otherwise NFA would not be 'yes'!).

For example, suppose, not unrealistically, that a workstation can perform segment transformations immediately, but cannot perform changes resulting from effects on the segment priority without redrawing everything. The NFA is initially in the 'no' state. Then an action occurs that leads to a rearrangement of the segments on the display so that the priorities are now incorrect. NFA is set to 'yes'. Suppose now that a segment is transformed, but in such a way that no segment priorities are affected – the segment overlapped no other with higher priority and overlaps no other with higher priority after transformation. Then the transformation is performed immediately and NFA remains 'yes', since there are still priority actions that have been deferred and are awaiting a complete display regeneration in order to be satisfied. It is only by an implicit regeneration (redrawing everything) that the NFA would be set to 'no'.

The program in Section 8.1 showed that an implicit regeneration occurs when the workstation is closed (the triangle appeared in its correct place as a result of the execution of *CloseWorkstation*). However, it would be inconvenient to the applications programmer, to say the least, if closing a workstation were the only way to achieve an implicit regeneration. The functions *SetDeferralState*, *RedrawAllSegmentsOnWorkstation* and *UpdateWorkstation* are designed to give the applications program control over the circumstances leading to an implicit regeneration. These functions are now discussed, using the Pascal binding.

8.3.1 Set Deferral State

For the named (open) workstation, the following function sets the deferral mode and the implicit regeneration mode:

```
type GEDefer = (GVasap, GVbnig, GVbnil, GVasti);
     GEImplicitRegen = (GVSuppressed, GVAllowed);

procedure GSetDeferSt(wsid : GTWsId;
                  deferral : GEDefer;
                     regen : GEImplicitRegen);
```

where:

asap = as soon as possible
bnig = before next interaction globally
bnil = before next interaction locally
asti = at some time

The idea of the deferral mode of a workstation is that when graphical output is sent to a workstation it is not necessarily immediately displayed, but may be stored in a buffer. This is *not* the same kind of deferral as related to an implicit regeneration; rather, it is to do with saving up a sequence of instructions to execute at a moment dictated by efficiency considerations. If the deferral mode is set to *asap*, then it is not stored in the buffer but immediately displayed. If the state is *bnig*, then it is stored in a buffer, but the buffer is guaranteed to be cleared and sent to the display at the start of *any* interaction (for example, *RequestInput*) of *any* workstation. *bnil* has the same meaning except that the buffer is emptied when an interaction is about to start on the specific workstation named in the procedure call. Finally, *asti* means that the buffer is cleared at some time; for example, if it is of fixed size and becomes full, or when some other GKS function is called that requires this. Of course, the buffer will be immediately cleared if the set deferral state function is called with *asap*.

There is a reason behind this function, which at first sight appears rather strange. For interactive graphics, the usual deferral mode is clearly *asap*, since it is hardly suitable to expect the user of an interactive program to be able to successfully carry out interactions when the display is not up to date. At the other extreme, there are situations where large amounts of data need to be sent to a remote device (for example, cell arrays) and for efficiency reasons such data is best sent in one lump, rather than in small pieces at a time. Here, *asti* would be appropriate. The middle settings are compromises between these extremes – where devices are in use that require efficient data flow but where interaction is taking place so that at least some of the displays must be brought up to date at the moment an interaction is initiated.

The *implicit regeneration* mode is an entry in the workstation state list which can be set to *Suppressed* or *Allowed*. If it has the value *Suppressed*, then whenever any function execution requires an implicit regeneration, the regeneration does *not* take place and the NFA entry is set to 'yes'. If the entry is set to *Allowed*, then such implicit regenerations occur when required (and the NFA entry is always 'no'). In particular, a call to:

GSetDeferSt(*wsid*, *x*, *GVAllowed*)

results in an immediate regeneration *if* the NFA entry is 'yes.' After the regeneration, the NFA flag is set to 'no'.

8.3.2 Redraw All Segments on Workstation

The function:

procedure *GRedrawSegWs*(*wsid* : *GTWsId*);

forces a regeneration. All deferred actions for the workstation are taken, resulting in the display being brought up to date. This is achieved by:

- displaying all items remaining in the workstation buffer;
- clearing the display space;

- bringing the workstation transformations up to date (if the transformation update state is 'pending');
- redrawing all visible segments on the workstation;
- setting the new frame action (NFA) variable to 'no' as a result of the execution of this function.

8.3.3 Update Workstation

This is represented in Pascal as:

> **type** *GEUpdRegen* = (*GVPerform*, *GVPostpone*);
>
> **procedure** *GUpdWs*(*wsid* : *GTWsId*; *regen* : *GEUpdRegen*);

If the *regen* parameter is set to *Postpone*, then a call to this procedure merely results in the output of all items in the workstation buffer. If the *regen* parameter is set to *Perform* and if the NFA is currently 'yes', then this results in the same actions as 'redraw all segments on workstation', irrespective of the current setting of the deferral and implicit regeneration modes.

There are perhaps three typical situations leading to appropriate combinations of these functions:

(1) The workstation is so fast that even a complete screen redraw takes such a short amount of time that some interactive picture modification is feasible. The function call here would be:

GSetDeferSt(*wsid*, *GVasap*, *GVAllowed*);

Hence, every action requiring a dynamic modification (which would set NFA to 'yes') would lead to an implicit regeneration. Moreover, there would be no need to ever call *GRedrawSegWs* or *GUpdWs*.

(2) The application is such that a redraw every time a modification is required would be unacceptably slow:

GSetDeferSt(*wsid*, *GVasap*, *GVSuppressed*);
...
GUpdWs(*wsid*, *GVPerform*);
...
GRedrawSegWs(*wsid*);

The implicit regeneration mode is set to *Suppressed*. A regeneration only occurs when a call to update or redraw all the segments is executed.

(3) Here, only the final result of the program execution is of interest,

rather than any intermediate stages:

GSetDeferSt(*wsid*, *GVasti*, *GVSuppressed*)

Output is buffered and regeneration only occurs on the call to close the workstation.

8.4 Additional Workstation Control Functions

There are three further functions useful for workstation control; namely, to clear a workstation, to send a message and to make use of non-standard workstation-dependent functions not otherwise supported in GKS.

8.4.1 Clear Workstation

This function is represented in Pascal as:

type *GEcontrol* = (*GVConditionally*, *GVAlways*);

procedure *GClearWs*(*wsid* : *GTWsId*; *control* : *GEcontrol*);

The most obvious effect of *ClearWorkstation* is that the display space is cleared – that is, all pixels are set to the background colour. Another crucial side effect is that all segments bound to the workstation are deleted from this workstation – that is, the workstation is cleared of segments. (Segments that *only* exist on this workstation are deleted entirely.)

The workstation state list includes a variable called ‘display surface empty’, which can have the value ‘empty’ or ‘not empty’. Typically, the entry is ‘empty’ if the screen is actually clear and ‘not empty’ otherwise. If the *control* parameter is set to ‘conditionally’, then the instruction to clear the display space is transmitted by GKS to the graphics device only if the ‘display surface empty’ variable has the value ‘not empty’. If the *control* parameter is ‘always’, then the clear display instruction is transmitted irrespective of the workstation state list entry. But what is the point of this?

Suppose the graphics device is a pen plotter and that during the execution of an applications program all output is clipped, or that all segments are invisible, so that nothing is drawn on the paper. If, in such an unlikely situation, the *ClearWorkstation* function is called with *control* as ‘always’, then the paper is advanced even though it has nothing drawn on it. It is to cater for situations where clearing a possibly empty display is inefficient or in some manner expensive that the 'display surface empty' controlling mechanism has been devised.

The only really important point here is that an execution of the call:

GClearWs(*wsid*, *GVConditionally*)

guarantees that the display space is clear.

8.4.2 Message

The following function:

```
procedure GMessage(wsid : GTWsId;
                   message : packed array[min..max : integer] of char);
```

outputs a message string on the workstation in an implementation-defined position. This function can also be useful with a pen plotter, as a way of warning a machine room operator that fresh paper is required. Applications of the *message* function are left to the imagination of the reader.

8.4.3 Escape

This function is represented in Pascal as:

```
type GTEscapeId = integer;
     GREscapeData = record
                      empty : boolean;
                      {implementation defined}
                    end;

procedure GEscape(escapeID : GTEscapeId;
                  inputrecord : GREscapeData;
              var outputrecord : GREscapeData);
```

The *Escape* function is a standard way of incorporating non-standard features into GKS. The data records are used to catch all input and output parameters. For example, suppose that a workstation is capable of producing musical notes, then the input data record might be used to supply the notes and chord sequences, while the output record supplies the applications program with timing or other useful control information.

This function is usually used for operations not catered for by GKS (not fitting into the GKS model) but which are nevertheless useful and important. The most obvious example of such an operation is the **screen dump** – that is, to simply save a representation of the frame buffer contents in a file, or send the frame buffer image to a hardcopy device such as a laser printer. Here, the input data record is used to provide a file name or other destination for the dump and maybe other information such as device coordinates corresponding to a rectangular region of the display from which the dump is to be taken. There is no obvious role for the output record in this example.

There are important restrictions on what an *Escape* function is allowed to do. It must not alter anything in any of the GKS data structures and it must not generate geometric output on the workstation: it knows nothing of WC, NDC or DC.

There are proposals in the ISO arena to have a standard set of *Escape* functions, but at the time of writing these are not defined. It is envisaged that common *Escape* functions will be incorporated into GKS as mandatory functions in a future revision.

8.4.4 The Generalized Drawing Primitive

In this context, it is worth noting the *GeneralizedDrawingPrimitive* (GDP) function, which does not belong to the category of workstation control functions, but is similar to the *Escape* function in that it provides a means for incorporating non-standard items into a GKS implementation, depending on device capabilities. The GDP belongs to the class of GKS functions termed output primitives, such as *Polyline*, *Polymarker* and so on. The Pascal definition is:

```
type GTgdpId = integer;
     GRgdpData = record
                    empty : boolean;
                    {implementation defined}
                 end;

procedure Ggdp(numpoints : GTint0;
               var points : array[min..max : integer] of GRPoint;
                   gdpid : GTgdpId;
                 datarec : GRgdpData);
```

Here, the *numpoints* and *points* parameters define a sequence of WC points, which are passed down the viewing pipeline and subject to segment considerations as with any other output primitive. The interpretation given to the points at the workstation destination depends on the GDP identifier (and subject to any additional information given in the data record). The purpose of this function is that where the graphical devices underlying GKS workstations directly support such things as circle and arc drawing, then the GDP function is a means open to implementors to exploit these possibilities.

The GDP functions use the attribute information for the other (mainstream) primitives as appropriate. For example, in the case of circle

GDPs the *Polyline* attributes would be most appropriate; if there is a solid fill circle device capability, then the *FillArea* attributes would be used.

As in the case of the *Escape* function, there are proposals to have a standard set of GDPs, which are likely to become fully incorporated into GKS in future revisions.

8.5 Metafiles: Filing a Picture

There is an important feature missing in the interactive drawing program under design in this book. Once a picture has been created there seems to be no way to save it. The need for saving a picture arises for a number of reasons:

(1) If a picture is created, for example, to be photographed, then it is almost certainly not going to be convenient to take the photograph at the moment the picture is finished. It is more likely for several pictures to be created and photographed at some other time. Generally, a picture save facility is essential whenever a picture is created to be used at some later date.

(2) A user may wish to create a library of pictures or picture components. For example, a cartoonist might create several different stock characters or background scenes so that they do not have to be drawn over and over again.

(3) Someone creating a picture using an interactive drawing program might actually become tired before it is finished. Worse still, the computer might be unreliable and crash, so destroying any work in progress. The need to save the intermediate stages in the construction of an image is clear in such circumstances. It is essential to be able to save a picture for later retrieval and further work.

(4) An image constructed at one site using GKS may need to be transmitted for display or further work at another location. Saving a picture in a file is a means for accomplishing this.

GKS provides two categories of workstation for filing graphical output. These are called the **metafile output (MO)** and **metafile input (MI)** workstations. The general term is GKSM, standing for GKS metafile. The MO workstation is treated as any other output-only workstation. Such a workstation may be opened and activated. When it is active, all graphical output is sent to it. Segments may be stored on it in the usual ways, either by the MO workstation being active at the time of the segment's creation or by the use of *AssociateSegment*. Everything is the same as usual except, of course, that MO has no associated display space.

The destination of output routed to an MO workstation is a file. An Annexe to GKS suggests file formats and identifications for the GKS function names, but these formats and identifiers are not strictly part of the standard. There is, in fact, an independent standardization process called the **CGM** (**Computer Graphics Metafile**) which has some compatibility with GKS (ISO, 1986e).

It is important to understand what gets saved in a metafile, as it is not only the geometric graphical output. It is the environment used to determine the shape of that output as well: the normalization transformation (the NDC clipping region), the primitive and individual attributes, the aspect source flags and so on. Moreover, it is possible to set the representations, the workstation window and viewport, and all the workstation control functions with respect to a metafile output workstation. Geometric output is stored in normalized form (*not* clipped) for easy interfacing to any graphical device on which the metafile might be interpreted. When the metafile is replayed, it is not only the graphical output that is displayed, but also all the attribute and control functions written into the metafile are executed.

An MI workstation is used for the *interpretation* of a metafile that has at some previous time already been created and now needs to be replayed into the system. When a metafile is interpreted it affects *every* active workstation.

There are several special functions defined for metafile interpretation.

{*Get Item Type from GKSM*}
procedure *GGetItemType*(*wsid* : *GTWsId*;
var *itemtype*, *datarecordlength* : **integer**);

This function is used to *inspect* the type and length of the item at the current reading position in the file, identified by the workstation identifier, which must be an MI workstation. The *itemtype* identifies the type of metafile item – for example, it might be a *Polyline*, *FillArea* or *RedrawAllSegments OnWorkstation* item. Each item is represented by an integer number, which generally has to be discovered by reading the implementation documentation, although it is probable that the number given in the GKS Annexe would be the one used. If the application only ever requires interpretation of a complete metafile, then the only important *itemtype* is the end-of-file marker, which is type 0. The data corresponding to the item – for example, the number of points and the points in the case of *Polyline* – is stored as a record in the file, the length of which is returned in the second parameter. The length is in implementation–defined units.

{*Read Item from GKSM*}
procedure *GReadItem*(*wsid* : *GTWsId*;
maxdatalength : *GTint0*;
var *datarecord* : *GRFileData*);

This function reads the data corresponding to the current item into the application supplied variable of type *GRFileData* (which is an implementation-defined record), provided that the current item is not the end-of-file marker. The current reading position is updated to the next item in the file. The *maxdatalength* parameter is used to inform GKS of the maximum amount that can be read into the data record variable. If the actual record is longer than this, then the excess data is lost. If *maxdatalength* = 0, then the item is skipped over.

```
{Interpret Item}
procedure GInterpretItem(itemtype : integer;
                    itemdatalength : GTint0;
                var itemdatarecord : GRFileData);
```

Here, the item is interpreted, causing changes in the various state lists as appropriate. For example, if the item corresponds to the *SetAspectSourceFlags* function, then the ASF entry in the GKS state list is changed just as if this function had been called directly. Graphical output and segments are generated on all active workstations. Items relating to a workstation, such as *UpdateWorkstation* or *ClearWorkstation*, are also executed on all active workstations.

□□ EXAMPLE

Example 8.1 MO workstation.

```
OpenGKS(_, _);
OpenWs(MO, _, MOTYPE);
ActivateWs(MO);
  Polyline(p);
  FillArea(q);
  CreateSegment(1);
    Text(pos, "Hello there");
  CloseSegment ();
DeactivateWs(MO);
CloseWs(MO);
CloseGKS ();
```

□□ EXAMPLE

```
{Example 8.2  Interpreting a metafile.}
function FileInterpret(wsid : GTWsId) : boolean;

{Interprets a complete metafile. Returns true if this workstation is of type MI
else false.}
```

```
const
  ENDRECORD = 0;
  MAXLENGTH = 1000;

var
  item, length, error, conn : integer;
  DataRecord                : GRFileData;
  wstype                    : GTWsType;
  conn                      : GAConnId;
  wscategory                : GEWsCategory;
begin
  {inquire workstation connection and type}
  GInqWsConnType(wsid, error, conn, wstype);

  {inquire workstation category}
  if error = 0 then GInqWsCategory(wstype, error, wscategory);
  if (error = 0) and (wscategory = GVmi) then
  begin
    GGetItemType(wsid, item, length);
    while (item <> ENDRECORD) do
    begin
      if length<= MAXLENGTH then
      begin
        GReadItem(wsid, MAXLENGTH, DataRecord);
        GInterpretItem(item, length, DataRecord);
      end
      else {skip} GReadItem(wsid, 0, DataRecord);
      GGetItemType(wsid, item, length);
    end; {while}
    FileInterpret := true
  end
  else
  FileInterpret := false;
end;
```

8.6 Inquiry Functions

Almost 40% of all the GKS functions (of which there are just over 200) are so-called inquiry functions; that is, they do not actually *do* anything but are used to provide information. This information can be of various sorts:

- Information about the GKS implementation, such as the maximum number of normalization transformations supported.
- Information about the fixed properties of the GKS workstations (on the workstation description tables), such as the display surface sizes.
- Information about the current states of the GKS global variables,

such as the current normalization transformation number.

- Information about the current states of the workstations, such as the current deferral and implicit regeneration mode, or the attributes associated with segments, such as the current transformation matrices.

The inquiry functions are used mainly to provide some generality to a procedure, allowing a program execution to follow different paths depending on the state of the GKS system or one of the subsystems (segment, workstation, normalization transformation, input device and so on). A simple example was given in the program of Example 8.2, where an attempt to read the metafile only succeeded if the provided workstation identifier turned out to be the identifier of an MI workstation. Another related use of the inquiry functions is to establish the current environment, whether of GKS itself, of a particular workstation or whatever. The following example illustrates the use of some of the inquiry functions.

□□ EXAMPLE

```
{Example 8.3(a)   Finding out about the workstation types on a GKS
implementation.}
procedure FindOutWsTypes;
var
  error, numwstypes : integer;
  listwstypes       : GPTWsType;
  wscategory        : GEWsCategory;
begin
  {inquire list of available workstation types}
  GInqListWsTypes(error, numwstypes, listwstypes);
  if error = 0 then
  begin
    writeln('Number of workstation types ', numwstypes);
    while (listwstypes <> nil) do
    with listwstypes↑ do
    begin
      writeln('Workstation type ', WsType);

      {find the workstation category}
      GInqWsCategory(WsType, error, wscategory);
      write('This is');
      case wscategory of
        GVOutput  : writeln(' an output workstation');
        GVInput   : writeln(' an input workstation');
        GVOutin   : writeln(' an output and input workstation');
        GVwiss    : writeln(' the segment storage workstation');
        GVmo      : writeln(' a metafile output workstation');
        GVmi      : writeln(' a metafile input workstation');
      end; {case}
```

```
      listwstypes := NextWsType;
    end
    else writeln('Error ', error,' from GInqListWsTypes.');
  end;
end;
```

Note At the time of writing, the method of representing lists in GKS Pascal remains controversial. A linked-list representation has been adopted here.

```
{Example 8.3(b)  Finding out whether a workstation supports colour.}
procedure ColourInfo(wstype : GTWsType);
{find out the colour information about a workstation}
var
  error, numcol, numindices, i : integer;
  typedisplay                  : GEdisplay;
  colour                       : GRCol;
begin
  {inquire colour facilities}
  GInqColFacil(wstype, error, numcol, typedisplay, numindices);
  if error = 0 then
  begin
    if typedisplay = GVColour then write('Colour Display with ')
    else write('Monochrome display with ');
    writeln(numcol, ' intensity levels.');
    writeln('Number of predefined colour indices is ', numindices);

    {for each predefined colour index write the colour}
    for i := 0 to numindices - 1 do
    begin
      {inquire predefined colour representation}
      GInqPredColRep(wstype, i, error, colour);
      with colour do write('red green blue are ', red, green, blue);
    end;
  end
  else
  writeln('Error ', error);
end;
```

```
{Example 8.3(c)  Drawing a border round the current window using thick
lines.}
procedure DrawBorder;
var
  state, error, ntran, numactivews : GEOpSt;
  activews                         : GPTWsId;
  window, viewport                 : GRBound;
  p                                : array[1..5] of GRPoint;
```

```
    attr                          : GAPrimRep;
    oldasf, newasf                : GAasf;
  begin
    {GKS must be in the state where at least one workstation is active}
    {inquire operating state value}
    GInqOpSt(state);
    if (state = GVwsac) then
    begin
      {inquire current normalization transformation number}
      GInqCurNormTranNum(error, ntran);
      {inquire normalization transformation}
      GInqNormTran(ntran, error, window, viewport);

      {set up the border array}
      with window do
      begin
        with p[1] do begin x := LeftBound;    y := LowerBound end;
        with p[2] do begin x := RightBound;   y := LowerBound end;
        with p[3] do begin x := RightBound;   y := UpperBound end;
        with p[4] do begin x := LeftBound;    y := UpperBound end;
        p[5] := p[1];
      end;

      {inquire current individual attribute values}
      GInqCurIndivAttr(error, attr, oldasf);

      {set the aspect source flag for line width to individual}
      newasf := oldasf;
      newasf[GVLineWidth] := GVIndividual;
      GSetASF(newasf);

      {set the line width scale factor to double nominal width}
      GSetLineWidthScale(2.0);

      {draw the border}
      GPolyline(5, p);

      {reset aspect source flags}
      GSetASF(oldasf);

      {reset line width scale factor}
      GSetLineWidthScale(attr[GVPolyline].width);
    end
    else
    writeln('Incorrect operating state from DrawBorder');
  end;
```

The programs of Examples 8.3(a) and (b) illustrate the use of inquiry functions to find out what is available: in the first case with respect to the workstation types in an implementation, and in the second case with respect to colour facilities on a workstation. The third example, 8.3(c), illustrates a typical technique to implement a procedure that has no hidden side effects. Within the procedure, the aspect source flags and the line width scale factor are changed. However, the inquiry functions are used to find out the values of these quantities on entry to the procedure. The values are then reset to what is required within the procedure and the action taken (here the border is drawn). Finally, the changed entities are restored to their original values.

The *InquireOperatingState* function is the only inquiry function that does not have the *error* parameter. For all the other inquiries, if the *error* parameter value is returned as 0, then the inquired information has been supplied. Otherwise, *error* is a positive integer value representing an error message. The associations between error numbers and error messages are provided within the GKS standard and can be found in the GKS documentation. The general issue of error handling in GKS is the topic of the next section.

8.7 Errors in GKS

In any applications program there are a number of types of error associated especially with the use of GKS:

(1) There may be errors trapped at compile time because of invalid parameters supplied to a GKS function. For example, in Pascal, the procedure call:

GPolyline(1, *p*);

will fail at compile time because the first parameter must be of type *GTint*2 (subrange of integer 2..*MAXINT*).

(2) There may be logical errors because the program compiles and executes successfully, but does not do what the programmer expected. Problems associated with designing correct programs are outside the scope of this book, although it is noted in passing here, and is further discussed in Chapter 12, that GKS is structured in such a way that the construction and development of 'correct' programs is not easy.

(3) There may be errors when using inquiries. These are not genuine GKS errors, but rather report a state of affairs where information required is not available or does not make sense. For example, an attempt to inquire the name of the open segment when no segment is open, or an attempt to inquire a pattern representation on a workstation that does not support interior style pattern.

(4) There may be errors caused by an attempt to execute a (non-inquiry) GKS function, when for a variety of possible reasons the function cannot be successfully executed.

GKS errors are usually of the latter type and some examples are as follows:

- a call to execute a graphical output function (for example, *FillArea*) when there are no workstations active;
- a call to *CloseSegment* when no segment is open;
- a call to set a primitive representation when the index number provided is outside the bounds of what can be supported on the given workstation;
- a call to *RequestInput* on an output-only workstation;
- a call to any (non-inquiry) GKS function when GKS has not been opened;
- a call to *SetViewport* where the viewport parameters are outside the unit square;
- a call to *CreateSegment* when a segment is already open;
- a call to *CloseWorkstation* when the workstation is still active;
- a call to the *GeneralizedDrawingPrimitive* function with a GDP that cannot be generated on at least one of the active workstations;
- a call to *OpenWorkstation* with a connection or type that is invalid for the GKS implementation.

There are over 100 such errors identified (and numbered) in the GKS standard. These errors are of the type: invalid parameters are supplied; a function is called when GKS is in an inappropriate state; a call is made to a function that cannot be executed because of the category or limitations of a particular workstation; and where some maximum number on a workstation (for example, maximum number of polyline representations) or on global GKS (for example, maximum number of normalization transformations) is exceeded.

When an error condition is encountered, the standard GKS action is to cleanly abandon the attempt to execute the function, leaving all entries in the GKS data structures unchanged – only an error indicator flag is set to 'error on'. Next, an error-logging function is called. This function has three parameters: an error number identifying the problem that caused the error, the identification of the GKS procedure in which the error was encountered, and a file name to which an error message might be written. This file name is the one referenced in the call to *OpenGKS*.

The error-logging function immediately calls an error-handling function, with the same parameters. This is defined in Pascal as:

```
procedure GErrorHandling(error : integer;
                          proc : GAprocname;
                     errorfile : GTErrorFileName);
```

The standard reaction of this procedure is to write the error message associated with the error number into the error file, together with the name of the procedure (*proc*) where the error was detected. However, the importance of this function is that it may be *replaced* by any user-defined function to handle the error in any way thought appropriate for the applications program. Of course, the replacement procedure must have exactly the same parameter list. The replacement procedure must not call any other GKS function (apart from inquiry functions). In fact, it will not be possible to call another GKS function while the error indicator is set to 'on'. This indicator will be set to 'off' after the error-handling procedure has been executed and control returned to the error-logging function. The last thing that this function does, therefore, is to set the error indicator to 'off'.

8.8 The Levels of GKS

It is not enough for a user to know that he or she has access to a GKS implementation as there are *nine* possible varieties of systems, all with the property of being potentially valid GKS implementations. GKS comes in nine shapes and sizes conforming to one of the GKS levels.

The levels of GKS arose as a compromise to international arguments about what should or should not be in a graphics standard. The ultimate solution was, in a sense, to provide nine graphics standards, thus satisfying everyone to some extent. (The American National Standards Body (ANSI), however, was still not satisfied and introduced an additional level not recognized in ISO GKS.)

The figure of '9' arose because there are three varieties of GKS on each of the output and input side:

- level 0 output is a minimal GKS implementation on the output side. For example, it supports only one open workstation at a time, and such a workstation need have only one bundle representation for each primitive, which cannot be redefined. There are no segments.
- level 1 output has the full GKS output functionality, except that there is no workstation-independent segment storage (although there may be workstation-dependent segments).
- level 2 output is a full GKS output implementation, including the WISS.
- level *a* input is an implementation that supports no workstations of category input or output/input.
- level *b* input is an implementation that supports at least one workstation capable of input, but only for the request mode.

- level *c* input supports at least one workstation capable of input, including sample and event modes.

GKS levels are combinations of the output level and input level referred to as (*L0a*, *L0b*, *L0c*, *L1a*, *L1b*, *L1c*, *L2a*, *L2b*, *L2c*). At level *b*, the difference between *L0b* and *L1b* is that pick input is not supported at *L0b* but is at *L1b*. Pick input is supported at level *L1c* but not at *L0c*. *Pick* is marked out for special consideration in this way because it is argued that pick input is particularly difficult to implement efficiently, and is therefore not a required facility at the lower levels of GKS.

The majority of GKS implementations available to date are at level 2*b*; that is, with full graphical output including workstation-independent segments and pick input, but with input restricted to the request mode only.

Summary

This chapter has considered in some detail the problems associated with dynamic modifications in GKS, and the various control functions and data structures that play an essentially supportive role to the main task of computer graphics programming using GKS. One set of functions may be used to control regeneration of the display image; a second set to cater for implementation and workstation-specific functionality; a third to allow the intermediate storage of pictures; a fourth to inquire about the GKS system; and finally functions for error handling. The next chapter concludes discussion of GKS functionality by a detailed examination of event input.

Exercises

8.1 If a workstation supported immediate dynamic modification with respect to the workstation transformation functions, show how these could be used to implement panning and zooming. Panning is the facility to interactively look at different rectangular subregions of the picture. Zooming allows the possibility of interactively zooming in on one part of the picture (and of course zooming out). Panning simulates looking through a camera and moving the viewfinder around a scene. Zooming simulates a camera zoom lens.

8.2 Dragging a segment means that the segment is attached to a cursor and follows cursor movements. Show how this could be implemented in GKS assuming that dynamic modifications resulting from segment transformations can be performed immediately.

8.3 The tiling method for dynamic segment modification relies on fast algorithms for computing the intersection of output primitives with the tiles. How can these intersections be computed?

8.4 Discuss the implications for the speed of hit detection in pick input of the extent and tiling methods for segment modification.

8.5 Using your segment data structure of Chapter 7, implement the segment extent idea for achieving dynamic modification for segment visibility and transformation. With each segment, compute the bounding rectangle containing all the primitives. Use the overlapping bounding rectangles to derive the set of segments that need to be redrawn when a modification is made to any particular segment. It may be easier to do this by excluding the *Text* function. In fact, it would be worthwhile doing it if only line drawings were included.

8.6 Consider how segment priority can be taken account of in the extent and tiling methods for segment modification.

8.7 When the segments are redrawn, in Exercise 8.5, they can be drawn using the extent of the modified segment as a clipping box or redrawn in total. Suppose segment S is modified, then the extent of S is cleared, and then all segments with extents overlapping the extent of S are redrawn. When they are redrawn the extent of S can act as a clipping region, because it is only the primitives of these segments which are actually inside the extent of S, which were (partially) deleted when the extent of S was first cleared. Does it improve performance time to clip to this extent or not to clip?

8.8 Using the results of the previous exercises that led to an implementation of the segment extent scheme, find the conditions under which real-time dragging, rotation and scaling of segments can be successfully performed.

8.9 Consider how the metafile capability could be incorporated into your design of the interactive drawing program. Remember that these facilities must not be just tacked on to the program, but be incorporated in such a way that makes sense in terms of the user model. This might lead to a completely new user model and hence a redesign of the program.

8.10 Using the GKS inquiry functions, write a procedure that reports all the default settings of all the bundle tables on a workstation. Be sure to test that the workstation is of the correct category.

8.11 Using the GKS text primitives and attributes, write a procedure that draws a personal letter head. The letter head should contain your address and telephone number, the date, and the name and address of the person to whom the letter is to be sent. The latter information would be parameters to the procedure. The procedure should be such that the GKS attribute settings are the same on exit as on entry to the procedure. You may assume that a hardcopy device, such as a pen plotter or laser printer, is the destination of the output. Your procedure must be such that the real dimensions (in centimetres) of the letter page may be determined by the arguments to the procedure.

CHAPTER 9

THE GKS EVENT INPUT MODEL

A common criticism of GKS concerns the supposed simplicity of its input model – simplicity in terms of what can be achieved rather than with respect to ease of use. The purpose of this chapter is to show that such a claim is unfounded in principle, although it is the case in practice. GKS provides a relatively sophisticated input model, but most GKS implementors choose to ignore this model, perhaps with good reason.

9.1 Introduction

Programmers of real GKS applications make use of GKS implementations rather than the GKS standard itself. It is true that the *de facto* GKS input model – that is, the one most commonly implemented – is often too inflexible in applications. This is because most implementations do not support level *c* input (sample and event mode). At the time of writing, the overwhelming majority of versions of GKS on the market are at level *b* (request mode only). (This mode has been fully discussed, together with the idea of sample input, in Chapter 5 of this book.) Some reasons behind implementors' unwillingness to take on the task of implementing level *c* will be discussed at the end of this chapter. (The GKS input model is discussed in Rosenthal *et al.*, 1982.)

9.2 Sequential Input and Simultaneous Input

The request input mode is strictly sequential. The application requests inputs one after another, in response to which the operator triggers the corresponding events, resulting in the return of the appropriate measures to the applications program. This can be described by the process:

RequestInput → trigger → measure → *RequestInput* → trigger → measure...

Sample mode is similar to the request mode in the sense that it is sequential, the difference being that the trigger action is not required, since the current measure of the logical input device is immediately returned:

SampleInput → measure → *SampleInput* → measure...

Now suppose, for example, that the operator of the interactive drawing program is allowed to pick a segment and rotate it. (Assume for the sake of this example that the rotation can be performed immediately; that is, dynamic modification for segment transformations is possible.) This interaction could be implemented by function calls of the form:

RequestInput(PICK, ...);
RequestInput(LOCATOR, ...);
RequestInput(VALUATOR, ...);

The call to *RequestPick* would identify the segment to *RequestLocator* to obtain a reference point for the rotation and to *RequestValuator* to obtain the angle of rotation. (The messy possibilities of NONE status values being returned is ignored here.) This describes a valid sequence of interactions that can be implemented entirely and simply in GKS level 2*b* (see Exercise 9.1). But this would provide a tedious interface to the operator, especially if several rotations were required.

A simpler, and in some circumstances, more natural method would be for the operator to move the cursor to the display representation of the segment, press the mouse button, and only release the button when the segment has rotated to the required degree. (Note that this would not cover the case where the operator wished to rotate the segment about a fixed point not on the segment. This case is discussed in Exercise 9.2.)

An analysis of this alternative interaction shows that at the moment the mouse button is depressed *two* events are generated: the LOCATOR returns the position and the PICK returns the name of the segment. Both of these events are fired by the *same* trigger action (pressing the button) acting on *different* logical input devices. In this example, the mouse is actually supporting *three* logical input devices, since it is assumed that there is a choice device implemented with respect to the mouse buttons where depressing or releasing the button (only one button is needed here) returns a choice event. Hence, the button release is intercepted and interpreted by this choice logical input device.

In general, the event mode of input allows a *set* of events to be *simultaneously* generated by a single trigger action. Some further examples of this type of interaction are as follows:

- Trigger action = the operator typing a sequence of digits and then striking the RETURN key on the keyboard. This could be interpreted (simultaneously) as a string measure (the sequence of characters typed) and a valuator measure (the number represented by the sequence of digit characters).
- Trigger action = the operator pressing a button on a 3-button mouse. This could be interpreted as giving rise to a locator measure (where the cursor position is in WC), a pick measure (the segment and pick identifier pointed at) and a choice measure (the mouse button used corresponding to a certain integer).
- Trigger action = the operator typing a sequence of characters and then striking the RETURN key. The sequence of characters is interpreted as a string measure and also identifies an item in a choice, thus also returning a choice measure.
- Trigger action = a sequence of mouse (or cursor) moves and button clicks. This could be interpreted as a stroke measure (returning a sequence of points and the normalization transformation number). However, the points form the outline of a symbol that a character recognizer interprets and returns as a string input, and also a choice

input (one of a set of symbols). (This example is a bit farfetched, but possible.)

GKS supports this kind of interaction in a reasonably straightforward manner. There are two important entries in the GKS state list called the **event queue** (denoted here by **Q**) and the **current event report** (denoted by **R**). There is also a **more simultaneous events** (**MSE**) variable which can take the values MORE or NOMORE. The meaning and functions operating on these variables are discussed in the following sections.

First, the question of how events join the event queue is discussed, and then how events can be taken off the queue and transferred to the applications program. Generally, events are added to the queue by operator actions (mouse button clicks, keyboard presses, etc.) and taken off the queue by execution of the appropriate GKS functions. In the following analysis, a convention is adopted whereby the schematic functions defined for the purposes of explanation begin with a lower-case letter and the GKS functions with an upper-case letter. (Readers should also note that for the purposes of this explanation, the ML language is hardly adhered to!)

9.3 How Events Join the Queue

As input events are generated they are written into the event queue (**Q**). Simultaneously triggered events are marked as belonging to the same simultaneity class, but join **Q** in an arbitrary ordering. An event taken off the front of the queue becomes the 'current event report' (**R**). If, after this has happened, there remain in **Q** events with the same simultaneity class as in **R**, then the 'more simultaneous events' variable contains the value MORE, otherwise NOMORE. Figure 9.1 illustrates this process.

Let **A** be a set of symbols denoting the operator actions relevant as triggers for the logical input devices supported in a given GKS implementation. Relevant actions might include, for example, mouse moves and button clicks, presses and releases, and keyboard strokes. Relevant actions do not include such things as the operator blowing his nose or raining blows on the display monitor. For example:

A = {
BUTTON_PRESS, BUTTON_RELEASE, BUTTON_CLICK,
MOUSE_MOVE, KEYSTROKE, NOTHING
}

The NOTHING action needs to be included here for generality. A more realistic set might include, for example, different symbols for different mouse buttons.

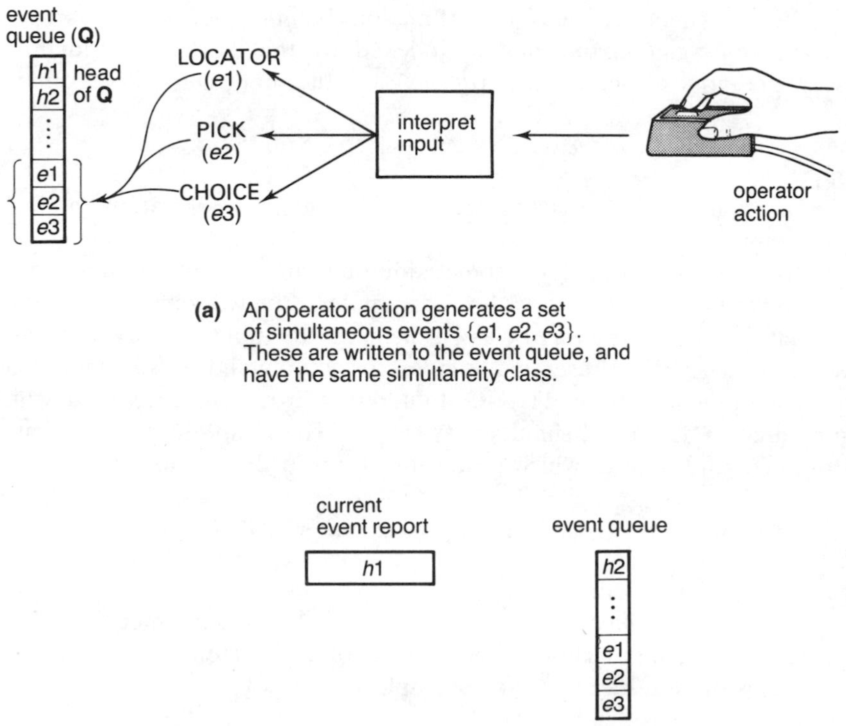

(a) An operator action generates a set of simultaneous events {*e*1, *e*2, *e*3}. These are written to the event queue, and have the same simultaneity class.

(**b**) An event at the front of the queue can be moved to the current event report.

Figure 9.1
The event queue.

In Chapter 5, it was shown that logical input devices on a workstation interpret user actions as meaningful events; that is, as measures corresponding to input classes. So, for example, a button click in the context of a *RequestLocator* interprets as a normalization transformation number and a WC point. In the context of a *RequestChoice*, the same operator action interprets as a choice status and a choice number. This implies that there is a function associated with each logical input device on each workstation that maps operator actions into input class measures. These functions operate by continually sampling the input device. Whenever a valid event occurs with symbol in the set **A**, then, taking into account the current execution state, the appropriate measure is computed. For example, in the case of LOCATOR, where for a particular input device the only valid trigger is a button click, the normalization transformation and viewport input priorities and the echo area are used to compute the measure, if any. If the measure cannot be computed (if the locator cursor is outside of the echo area), then a NONE status is returned.

Let the generic name of these functions be *interpretInput*. An array of such functions can be postulated, indexed by the workstation identifier (*wsid*), the input device number (*device*) and the input class. For example:

interpretInput[*wsid*, *device*, LOCATOR]

is the function for the locator device on the particular workstation and input device named.

To develop this analysis, some additional functions must be assumed. *sampleAction* is a function with three parameters: the workstation identifier, the input device and the input class. It inspects the input device and returns a value in the set **A** representing an operator action valid for this input class on the input device, or NOTHING. In addition, it returns a *signature* which can be used to determine simultaneity classes. The *signature* might be based on the date and time at which the event occurred. For example:

val (*x*, *signature*) = *sampleAction*(*wsid*, *device*, CHOICE)

where *x* is a value in the set **A**.

The function *measure* translates an operator action (member of **A**), together with an input class in the context of the current execution state, into an appropriate *measure*. For example:

val (*point*, *ntran*) = *measure*(LOCATOR, BUTTON_CLICK, ..)

Since the event queue is an item in the GKS state list, it is a global variable available to the functions that implement the input model. It is assumed here to be a sequence store variable, where the elements (events) of the sequence are tuples of the form:

event = (*InputClass*, *measure*, *signature*, *wsid*, *device*)

Using this, a schematic definition of the *interpretInput* functions can now be given as:

```
fun interpretInput[wsid, device, InputClass]() =
  do
    true ⇒
      let val (x, signature) = sampleAction(wsid, device, InputClass)
      in
        if x ≠ NOTHING ⇒
          Q := Q @ [
                      (InputClass,
                       measure(InputClass, x, ..),
                       signature,
                       wsid,
```

```
                    device
                   )
                  ]
      fi
    ni
  od
nuf
```

This function, once executed, forever samples the input device, and whenever it finds a valid operator action, it computes the measure and appends the event to the event queue.

9.4 How Events Leave the Queue

The next step of this analysis requires some further notation and definitions. Let *F* be any function, then:

F() &

stands for the instruction to start up a background execution of *F*; that is, *F* continues execution concurrently with everything else being executed at the time. (No precise definitions are intended here, rather reliance is placed on the intuition of the reader.)

The execution of such a function ends either of its own accord or is stopped by some external agency. Suppose, for example, that *F* and *G* each represent functions that append events to the event **Q**, then *F*() & *G*() & represents the instruction to start executing these functions in the background, so that events are placed at the end of the queue by each. How the scheduling problem is resolved is not important in this discussion.

In contrast, if *F* is a function executing in the background, then:

kill *F*

terminates the execution of *F*.

Finally, *Length*(?**Q**) is the number of events in **Q** at any time, *last* is the last element in ?**Q** (that is, the most recently joined event) and *allButLast* is ?**Q** but with its last element removed. Hence:

allButLast @ [*last*] = ?**Q**

It is now possible to give a schematic definition of the operation of *RequestInput*, which will lead to a definition of *EventInput*.

```
fun waitInput(wsid, device, InputClass) =
  let val n = Length(?Q)
  in
    do
      Length(?Q) < n + 1 ⇒ DoNothing
    od
  ni;
  kill interpretInput[wsid, device, InputClass];
  let val allButLast @ [last] = ?Q
  in
    Q := allButLast;
    ?last
  ni
nuf
```

The *waitInput* function iterates until the event queue (**Q**) has one more entry than at the start of the function execution. At that moment, the *interpretInput* function is killed, **Q** has its last element deleted and that element is returned by the function.

When the *RequestInput* function is invoked, the *interpretInput* function starts up in the background, while *waitInput* executes in the foreground – the first continually sampling the input device and potentially appending events to the queue, and the second in an iteration that only terminates when the queue length increases. However, as soon as a valid operator action occurs, the *waitInput* function kills the execution of *interpretInput* and returns the generated event. The only part of the event of interest to *RequestInput* is the *measure* component.

```
fun RequestInput(InputClass, wsid, device) =
  interpretInput[wsid, device, InputClass]() &
  waitInput(wsid, device, InputClass)
nuf
```

(This begs all sorts of questions about timing of the concurrent executions, which are ignored here. It is assumed that *waitInput* is fast enough so that as soon as one event has been generated, then *interpretInput* is killed. Hence, if **Q** started out as an empty sequence, it would never become more than a single element sequence.)

It is now possible to show that *EventInput* is a straightforward generalization of *RequestInput*. Recall the GKS *SetInputMode* function defined in Chapter 5. For a given input device on a workstation, this function is used to set the input mode of the device (request, sample or event). The execution of this function with the event parameter would, using the notation of this section, result in:

```
interpretInput[wsid, device, InputClass]() &
```

assuming the input device is not already in event mode. In other words, a call to put a given input device into event mode would result in the start up of the appropriate *interpretInput* function. Similarly, if a device is in event mode, then a call to set its input mode to request mode would result in:

kill *interpretInput*[*wsid*, *device*, *InputClass*]

It can be concluded then that while a device is in event mode, the stream of operator actions is translated into a sequence of event reports which are appended to the event queue (**Q**). Another important conclusion is that whenever any *RequestInput* function is executed, its first action must be to suspend the operation of all *interpretInput* functions currently executing, to ensure that only the relevant event is appended to the queue.

This analysis shows that if request mode only is used, then the event queue will only ever have at most one element. Every execution of a *RequestInput* function will temporarily start up an *interpretInput* execution, until one event has been generated, upon which the *interpretInput* is killed, the event report is returned to the applications program and the event queue reduced by one element, so that it again becomes empty.

Now if event mode is used, during the time that at least one input device is in this mode, all relevant operator actions will result in event reports being joined to **Q**. The question remains as to how these events may be interrogated by the applications program.

9.5 Interrogation of the Queue

There are two main GKS functions concerned with the removal of and interrogation of events in **Q**: *AwaitEvent* and *GetInput*. The basic idea is that *AwaitEvent* moves the head of the event queue to the current event report (**R**) while *GetInput* is used to inspect **R**. *AwaitEvent* has a timeout parameter (t) such that if $t > 0$ and $\mathbf{Q} = nil$, then the function waits for a further event for at most t seconds, and if at the end of that time **Q** is still *nil*, then *AwaitEvent* returns NONE. Otherwise, *AwaitEvent* removes the head of **Q** to the current event report (**R**). If the signature of **R** is the same as the (new) head of **Q**, then the more simultaneous events (MSE) flag is set to MORE, otherwise to NOMORE. Finally, *AwaitEvent* returns the workstation identifier (*wsid*), the input device number (*device*) and the input class of the current event report.

For the purposes of exposition, it is necessary to temporarily extend the **do**...**od** instruction so that **do**(t)...**od** means that the iteration continues for at most t seconds. This results in the following definition.

```
fun suspend(t) =
   let val n = Length(?Q)
   in
      do(t)
         Length(?Q) < n + 1 ⇒ DoNothing
      od
   ni
nuf
```

suspend(*t*) waits for *t* seconds or until a new event has joined the input queue. Using this, the following GKS function can be defined:

```
fun AwaitEvent(t) =
   if ?Q = nil ⇒ suspend(t) fi;
   if
         ?Q = nil ⇒ (_, NONE, _)
      □ ?Q ≠ nil ⇒ let val (class, measure, signature, wsid, device)
                             = ?head(?Q)
                   in
                     Q, R := tail(Q), (class, measure, signature);
                     let val s =
                       if
                             ?Q = nil ⇒ 0
                          □ ?Q ≠ nil ⇒ let val (_, _, sig, _, _)
                                                     = ?head(?Q)
                                       in
                                         sig
                                       ni
                       fi
                     in
                       MSE := if
                                      s = signature ⇒ MORE
                                    □ s ≠ signature ⇒ NOMORE
                              fi
                     ni;
                     (wsid, class, device)
                   ni
   fi
nuf
```

AwaitEvent operates as follows. If the event queue is empty, then the function waits for at most *t* seconds for an extra event to join **Q**. If *t* seconds have elapsed and **Q** is still empty, then the return value of the function contains the entry NONE for the input class. Otherwise, the head of the queue is moved to **R**, the current event report. The *signature* of the (new) head of **Q** is compared to that in the current event report. If they are the same, then the more significant events (*MSE*) variable is set to MORE, otherwise to NOMORE. The workstation identifier, input class and input device number form the return value of the function.

The *AwaitEvent* function allows the applications program to move an event from the head of the event queue to the current event report, and suspends GKS for a specified time to force this to take place. The *GetInput* function returns the *measure* of the event in the current event report. For example, *GetInput*(LOCATOR) returns a normalization transformation number and a WC position, if and only if the input class of **R** is LOCATOR (otherwise an error is reported). Generally:

```
fun GetInput(class) =
  let val (InputClass, measure, _) = ?R
  in
    if
        InputClass = class ⇒ measure
      □ InputClass ≠ class ⇒ ERROR
    fi
  ni
nuf
```

There are two other functions useful for manipulating and interrogating the event queue. First:

FlushDeviceEvents(*wsid*, *InputClass*, *device*)

removes all the entries from **Q** corresponding to this combination of workstation, input device and input class. (*CloseWorkstation* will remove all entries corresponding to that workstation.) Second, *InquireMore SimultaneousEvents* is a normal inquiry function that returns the value of the *MSE* flag, or an error status if the information is not available.

GKS also allows for the event queue to overflow, which occurs if there is insufficient room in the queue when an operator action triggers an event. This overflow is reported as an error the next time an attempt is made to remove an event from the queue by *AwaitEvent*, *FlushDeviceEvents* or *CloseWorkstation*.

□□ EXAMPLE

Recall the case outlined in Section 9.2. Suppose that three logical input devices – for LOCATOR, PICK and CHOICE – are implemented using the same mouse as their underlying physical input device. For each, the trigger action would constitute a press or release of a mouse button. The idea is that the operator is expected to move the mouse so that the cursor points at a segment. When the button is pressed, the locator and pick triggers are fired, and when the button is released the choice trigger is fired. Between the press and release, the segment rotates every two seconds about the point. (All issues relating to a no segment hit, the segment being outside of the echo area, etc. are ignored here, but see Exercise 9.4.)

This can be achieved by the following Pascal program, which as usual can be divided into three phases – initialisation, repetition and termination:

```
var
  wsid, ws     : GTWsId;
  device, dev  : GTint1;
  timeout      : real;
  class        : GEEventClass;
  input        : GRInput;
  position     : GRPoint;
  events       : GEevents;

{initialisation}
{assume that the workstation identifier, wsid, and the logical input device
 number to be used for each device are initialised as required}
{ensure an initial state where all input devices on all workstations
 have echoes off, are in request mode and the event queue is empty, then}

{set locator and pick devices to event mode, with echo on}
GSetInputMode(GVLocator, wsid, device, GVEvent, GVEcho);
GSetInputMode(GVPick, wsid, device, GVEvent, GVEcho);

{set the timeout argument to be infinite}
timeout := MAXINT;
GAwaitEvent(timeout, ws, class, dev);

{if no event has occurred, then class.status will be None;
 assume here that an event has occurred within the hour}
{take the events off the event queue}
events := GVMore
while events = GVMore do
begin
  GGetInput(class, input);
  case class of
    GVLocator : position := input.position;
    GVPick    : seg      := input.segment;
  end;
  GInqMoreEvents(error, events);
  GAwaitEvent(0.0, ws. class, dev)
end;

{set locator and pick to request mode with echo off}
GSetInputMode(GVLocator, wsid, device, GVRequest, GVNoEcho);
GSetInputMode(GVPick, wsid, device, GVRequest, GVNoEcho);
```

```
{repetition}
GSetInputMode(GVChoice, wsid, device, GVEvent, GVNoEcho);
GAwaitEvent(2.0, ws, class, dev);
while class.status = GVNone do
begin
  rotateSegment(seg, position, 10.0);
  GAwaitEvent(2.0, ws, class, dev)
end;

{termination}
GSetInputMode(GVChoice, wsid, device, GVRequest, GVNoEcho);
```

Assume here that all input devices are in request mode and that the event queue is empty. First, the input mode for LOCATOR and PICK on the appropriate device is set to *Event* with *Echo* 'on' (the cursor might be a combination of the locator and pick cursors). The *AwaitEvent* function is called with an effectively infinite *timeout* argument – nothing further can happen until the operator initiates the appropriate action. When the operator presses the mouse button, two events are joined to the event queue. The iteration reads the two events (the loop will only be traversed twice) and at the end of this **Q** is empty. Next, the input modes for LOCATOR and PICK are set to *Request* (with *Echo* 'off') and the choice input device is set to *Event* (again with *Echo* 'off', as the echo might be a distraction here). Each cycle of the **while** iteration includes an instruction to wait for two seconds, or until the button is released (whichever happens first). If the full two seconds elapse, then the segment is rotated (by 10°), otherwise the **while** iteration and therefore the interaction terminates (see Exercise 9.4).

9.6 Implementation

These pages on the GKS input model have expanded what is described in approximately one side in the GKS standard document and have demonstrated that the GKS input model is not too simplistic for real applications. In fact, it is quite flexible and not too difficult to use. Its description in the GKS standard is rather terse and at first sight open to interpretation. But on close reading its meaning becomes clear.

The supposed difficulty of the GKS description of event-driven input is not the only or the major reason why implementors have shied away from it. The real reason is that it requires special resources for implementation. It is unlike almost everything else in GKS, since a usable implementation requires genuine special-purpose hardware and software. This is best seen in contrast with request input. Given a keyboard and a pointing device, all six input classes can readily be implemented. Because requests are only ever demanded in sequence, during which time nothing else in the execution of the program can happen, it is easy for the input device events to be interpreted as locator events at one time, at another time as pick events, at another time as valuator events and so on. However, the situation is different for the case of event input. There are six logical input devices, one for each of the input classes. Now, if all are put into event mode, six concurrent and independent processes must be executing, while the output side of GKS might also be functioning – generating an image. In other words, the background *interpretInput* functions must really exist.

Stand-alone workstations generally support the keyboard and mouse by special-purpose hardware running genuinely independent processes. A proper implementation of GKS event-driven input would require similar resources for all six input classes and hardware for interprocess communications. All of these processes must communicate with the process responsible for maintaining the event queue and must share common resources such as the screen.

It is also important to realize that each *interpretInput* function is responsible for generating its own prompts and echoes in addition to appropriate feedback, which usually requires communication with the display. For example, if both LOCATOR and CHOICE are simultaneously in event mode, the locator echo is a rubber band line and the choice echo a pop-up menu, then the interaction with each of these must be simultaneously supported with the appropriate rubber band and menu displays.

GKS had the choice of providing an event input model that was either relatively simple to implement but inflexible or much harder to implement but sophisticated. The GKS levels concept allowed both to be chosen. *De facto* only the inflexible, simple approach actually exists. Whether workstation designers and manufacturers will provide support for the more sophisticated GKS event input model in the future remains to be seen.

Summary

This chapter has considered in detail the GKS event input mode. The event queue was defined, and there was an analysis of methods by which events join and leave the queue. Interrogation of the queue, and definition of the *AwaitEvent* functions were considered, and it was shown that the request input mode can be viewed as a special case of event input. Finally, an example showing the use of some of the functions was given, using GKS Pascal.

Exercises

9.1 Construct a complete implementation of the rotate segment function of Section 9.2 using *RequestInput* only.

9.2 In the version of rotating a segment based on event input, discuss how the rotation of a segment about a fixed point not on the segment could be handled.

9.3 The Pascal program given in the example included a call to a *rotateSegment* procedure which rotates a segment about a fixed point by an angle (in degrees) supplied. Implement this function.

9.4 Complete the program given in the example taking into account tests on the status reports returned by the input procedures. Write the code that ensures the required initial state given in the opening comments to the program.

9.5 Give a specification of the function *FlushDeviceEvents*.

9.6 What does *AwaitEvent*(0) do?

9.7 In the light of the discussion of event input, rethink the design of the interactive drawing program discussed in earlier chapters.

CHAPTER 10

GRAPHICS MODELLING

So far, this book has concentrated almost exclusively on tracing the basic concepts of computer graphics via their representation in GKS. Although GKS is an international standard, it is not the only approach to computer graphics. Moreover, although GKS was only finally ratified as a standard in July 1985, it is not by any means a 'state-of-the-art' system: it does not embody more recent approaches to graphics, nor does it sit easily with modern thoughts about computer programming.

The purpose of this and subsequent chapters in Part One is to take a wider and deeper look at some aspects of computer graphics. The ideas of graphics modelling are introduced in this chapter and their embodiment in an important recent system called **PostScript** is discussed. A proposed ISO standard, PHIGS, has the ideas of graphics modelling at its core, and is discussed in Section 10.5. Chapter 11 is concerned with bitmapped graphics, as introduced by the Smalltalk–80 system. The methods of bitmapped graphics are illustrated by programs for the implementation of some of the GKS input techniques discussed in Chapter 5. This leads to a critical evaluation of GKS in Chapter 12 and an assessment of its role in project development. Finally, Chapter 13 introduces the basic ideas of 3D graphics.

10.1 Introduction

Graphics modelling is the process whereby complex pictures are constructed out of a number of simpler parts, which themselves may be formed out of simpler components, and so on. The idea of transformations plays an essential role in this activity. Picture segments, as discussed in Chapter 7, provide a simple form of modelling.

In this chapter, modelling is introduced in the context of functional programming, since this provides a natural means of expressing the ideas involved. The approach to modelling in the usual imperative programming style, making use of a current transformation matrix, is discussed next. The representation of these ideas in the PostScript and PHIGS systems concludes this chapter.

10.2 Some Ideas on Functional Graphics

10.2.1 Descriptors and Descriptions

A graphical object may be constructed from descriptions of simpler components and other graphics objects. The term **Descriptor** is used here to denote those elements of a description that cannot be further subdivided into yet more primitive elements. The question of what can or cannot be subdivided does not have an absolute answer, but for the purposes of exposition, the following definition is adopted:

> **type** Point = real*real;
> **datatype** *Descriptor* = *moveto* **of** *Point* | *lineto* **of** *Point*;

This definition says that a value of type *Descriptor* can be constructed by applying the 'constructors' *moveto* and *lineto* to values of type real*real. The word 'type' used up to now in this book has been used as a way of introducing a synonym; for example, Point is a synonym for real*real – Point and real*real are the *same* type. A *datatype* is a way of introducing a completely new type, and the definition of *Descriptor* is a simple example of this. For example:

> *moveto*(0.5, 1.8)
> *lineto*(24.0, 25.6)

are *values* of type *Descriptor*.

Clearly, this definition could be extended to include a richer collection of descriptors, such as circle, polygon and so on, but these are not necessary in the context of the present discussion. However, as a further illustration, the constructor for *circle* could be given as:

circle **of** *real*

so that:

circle(4.0)

is a descriptor for a circle with radius 4.

It is important to realize the fundamental difference between the GKS primitive graphics output functions and the descriptors introduced here. The call to, say, *Polyline*[(0.0, 0.0), (1.0, 1.0)] is an instruction to generate graphical output. When this function is encountered during the execution of a program, all sorts of things happen, the final effect being the appearance (possibly) of a line on a screen (see Exercise 10.1). However, the *moveto* and *lineto* constructors, as they are used in this section, provide the means for the formation of **Descriptions**, and do not themselves actually do anything. There is a clear separation between describing or defining a picture and the instruction to generate it on a display device. This separation is analogous to that of representing a computation and the instruction to print the answer on a VDU. For example:

5 + 6 + 7

is different from:

print(5 + 6 + 7)

A *Description* is a sequence of *Descriptors:*

type *Description* = *Descriptor sequence;*

Hence:

val *triangle* = [*moveto*(0.0, 0.0), *lineto*(1.0, 0.0)
lineto(0.5, 1.0), *lineto*(0.0, 0.0)];

val *cross* = [*moveto*(0.0, 0.0), *lineto*(1.0, 1.0),
moveto(1.0, 0.0), *lineto*(0.0, 1.0)];

are *Descriptions* of a triangle and a diagonal cross, respectively.

10.2.2 Graphical Objects

A graphical **Object** is constructed by composing transforms of *Descriptions* and/or *Objects*. The transformations are the identity and the usual shift, scale and rotate. To cope with the transformations, the following definitions are introduced:

```
datatype Transformation = shift of Point | scale of Point | rotate of real;
```

This expresses the idea that the shift and scale transformation functions are each formed by application to two reals, and the rotate transformation function must be supplied with an angle of rotation. Therefore, to transform a *Point*:

```
tranPoint: Transformation → (Point → Point);
fun tranPoint t p =
  let val (x, y) = p
  in
    case t of
        shift(sx, sy)   ⇒ (x + sx, y + sy)
      | scale(sx, sy)   ⇒ (sx*x, sy*y)
      | rotate(a)       ⇒ (x*cos(a) − y*sin(a), x*sin(a) + y*cos(a))
    esac
  ni
nuf
```

Here, a **case** is used for the first time to pattern match the transformation *t*. The value *t* must (by its construction) match one of the three cases shown. The appropriate return value is computed for each case.

tranPoint is a function that when given a transformation as argument delivers a *Point* → *Point* function with the appropriate properties. This can now be used to transform a *Descriptor*:

```
tranDes: Transformation → (Descriptor → Descriptor);
fun tranDes t p =
  case p of
      moveto pt ⇒ moveto((tranPoint t)pt)
    | lineto pt ⇒ lineto((tranPoint t)pt)
  esac
nuf
```

Here, *p* is a *Descriptor* that must match one of the cases. *pt* is the *Point* corresponding to *p*, and in each case *p* is transformed and then the result delivered is a *Descriptor* (by application of the *moveto* or *lineto* constructors).

For example:

(*tranDes shift*(1.0, 10.0)) *moveto*(10.0, 100.0) = *moveto*(11.0, 110.0)

It is now possible to give a concise definition of an object. The method employed is to use the notion of an **abstract data type**. This is an extension of the idea of a datatype, in that it expresses the definition as a set of values and functions defined over the values of the type. The implementation of these functions is entirely hidden from the rest of the program in which the abstract data type is embodied. The notation used matches that of ML (although it is not exactly the same).

```
abstype Object = injectDesc of Description | injectObj of Object
with
  val nilObject = injectDesc nil
  fun object x = injectDesc x nuf
  and
    tranObj t x =
      case x of
         injectDesc xd ⇒ injectDesc((map(tranDes t)xd)
      |  injectObj xo  ⇒ tranObj t xo
      esac
    nuf
  and
    infix ++ (x1, x2) =
      case x1 of
        injectDesc xd1 ⇒ case x2 of
                            injectDesc xd2 ⇒ injectDesc(xd1@xd2)
                         |  injectObj  xo2 ⇒ (injectDesc xd1)++xo2
                         esac
      |  injectObj xo1 ⇒ case x2 of
                            injectDesc xd2 ⇒ xo1 ++ (injectDesc xd2)
                         |  injectObj  xo2 ⇒ xo1 ++ xo2
                         esac
      esac
    nuf
  and
    displayObj x =
      case x of
         injectDesc xd ⇒ displayDescription xd
      |  injectObj  xo ⇒ displayObj xo
      esac
    nuf
end
```

In the case of an abstract data type, the constructors *injectDesc* and *injectObj* are not available outside of the definition, but are used within the values and functions that define the type. The abstract type object is defined by means of one new value belonging to the type and four functions:

- *nilObject* defines the 'empty' object. It is formed by applying the constructor *injectDesc* (which when applied to a *Description* delivers an *Object*) to the *nil* sequence of descriptors.
- *object* is a function that returns an *Object* from a *Description*.
- *tranObj* delivers a function that transforms an *Object* to an *Object* according to the given sort of transformation.
- ++ is the 'compose' function which is declared to be an infix operator. For example, if *A* and *B* are *Objects*, then *A*++*B* is their composition and consists of the union of the elements in the two *Objects*.
- *displayObj* is a function that has the side effect of displaying an *Object* on a screen. It assumes the existence of the function *displayDescription*, which traverses a sequence of *Descriptors* and takes the appropriate drawing action, depending on the *Descriptor* values (see Exercise 10.2).

□□ EXAMPLE

The foregoing discussion has provided a set of modelling tools that can now be used in the discussion of examples. First, to make the notation easier, three transformation functions are defined in terms of the *tranObj* function:

```
shiftObj: Point → (Point → Point);
fun shiftObj p = tranObj (shift p) nuf;

scaleObj: Point → (Point → Point);
fun scaleObj p = tranObj (scale p) nuf;

rotateObj: real → (Point → Point);
fun rotateObj a = tranObj (rotate a) nuf;
```

In Program 4.1, a simple star-like *Object* was built out of triangles. This example is discussed in the present context. First, it is necessary to form a *Description* of a basic triangle, with a unit square extent:

```
val unitTriangle = [moveto(0.0, 0.0), lineto(1.0, 0.0),
                    lineto(0.5, 1.0), lineto(0.0, 0.0)];
```

(**a**) *displayObj* (*shiftObj*(200.0, 200.0) (*scaleObj*(200.0, 200.0)*star*)

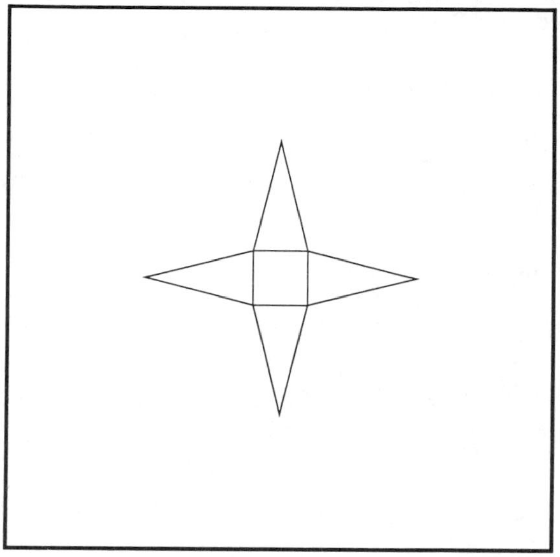

(**c**) *displayObj* (*shiftObj*(200.0, 200.0) (*scaleObj*(200.0, 200.0)*star*16)

(**b**) *displayObj* (*shiftObj*(200.0, 200.0) (*scaleObj*(200.0, 200.0)*star*8)

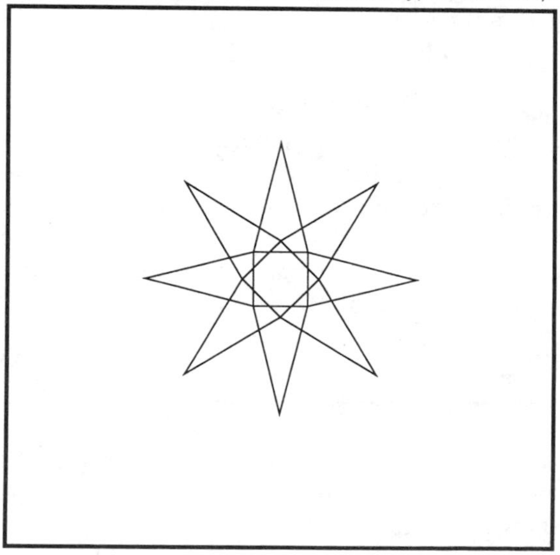

Figure 10.1
Displaying *star*1, *star*8 and *star*16 in a 400 by 400 window.

To achieve the desired star result, a triangle *object* with height equal to twice the base must be defined:

val *triangle* = (*scaleObj*(1.0, 2.0)) *unitTriangle*;

Now the star can be defined as:

Example 10.1 Describing a star.

```
val star1 =
  let val centredT = (shiftObj(−0.5, 0.0)) triangle
  in
    (shiftObj(0.0, 0.5)) centredT
    ++
    (shiftObj(−0.5, 0.0) ∘ rotateObj(π/2.0)) centredT
    ++
    (shiftObj(0.0, −0.5) ∘ rotateObj(π)) centredT
    ++
    (shiftObj(0.5, 0.0) ∘ rotateObj(−π/2.0)) centredT
  ni;
```

*Star*1 is illustrated in Figure 10.1(a) (see also Exercise 10.3). This star exists in the square (−2.5, 2.5, −2.5, 2.5), so to create a star with extent that has sides unity, centred at the origin, the following definition is required:

val *star* = (*scaleObj*(0.2, 0.2)) *star*1;

Having obtained the four-pointed star, more complex shapes can be defined. Consider, for example:

val *star*8 = *star* ++ (*rotateObj* π/4) *star*;
val *star*16 = *star*8 ++ (*rotateObj* π/8) *star*16;

where *star*8 and *star*16 define 8 and 16-pointed stars, respectively. The hierarchical structure of these objects is shown in Figure 10.2.

To generate these *Objects* on any particular display, it is necessary to transform them to the appropriate device coordinate range, and then use the *displayObj* function. In this respect, it is worth noting that it is simple to define a window to viewport function (that is, *Ntran*) from the transformation functions provided here (see Exercise 10.4).

□□ EXAMPLE

As a slightly more complex example, which further illustrates the hierarchical nature of the modelling process, consider the task of describing the simple garden of plants shown in Figure 10.3.

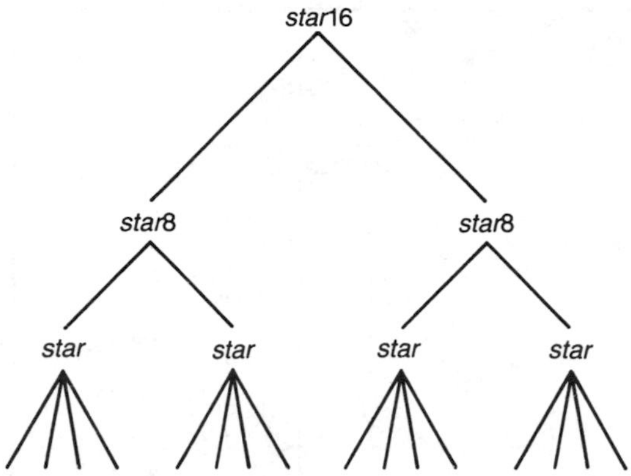

Figure 10.2
Hierarchical structure of stars.

The locii of the point $p(t)$ in:

$$p(t) = (A\ sin(2t)\ cos(t),\ A\ sin(2t)\ sin(t)) \qquad 0 < t < \pi/2$$

describes the shape shown in Figure 10.4. A function for this is:

Example 10.2(a) Describing the petal shape.

```
pet: real*real*real → Description;
fun pet(A, t, dt) =
  if t < π/2.0 then
    let val Asin2t = A*sin(2.0*t)
    in
      lineto(Asin2t*cos(t), Asin2t*sin(t)) :: pet(A, t + dt, dt)
    ni
  else
    [lineto(0.0, 0.0)]
  fi
nuf
```

Hence, a single petal with unit square extent can be defined as:

```
val petal =
  let val A = 0.75*sqrt(3.0)
  in
    object(moveto(0.0, 0.0) :: pet(A, 0.05, 0.05))
  ni
```

(see Exercise 10.5). To define rotated copies of the petal, the following can

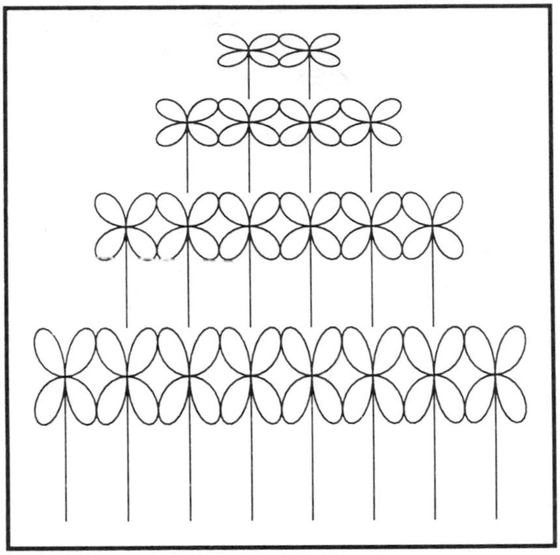

Figure 10.3
A triangle of plants obtained from *trianglePlant*(4, 4, 0.7) in a square window.

be used:

Example 10.2(b) Describing the rotated petal shape.

```
petalR: int*real*Object → Object;
fun petalR(n, t, p) =
  if n = 0 then p
  else
  let val rn = real(n)
  in
    (rotateObj(rn*t)p)++petalR(n − 1, t, p)
  ni
nuf
```

A simple flower can be defined as four rotated copies of the petal:

Example 10.2(c) Describing a simple flower.

```
flower: Object → Object;
fun flowerFunction(p) =
  (scaleObj(0.5, 0.5) ○ shiftObj(1.0, 1.0)) petalR(3, π/2.0, petal)
nuf
```

(The transformations ensure that the flower has unit square extent if the argument *p* has unit square extent.) Hence:

```
val flower = flowerFunction(petal);
```

A plant can be defined as a composition of a stem and a flower. A

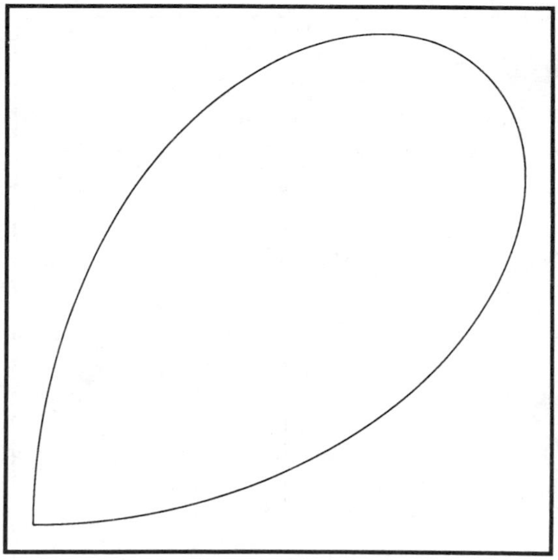

Figure 10.4
The petal shape obtained using *pet*(0.75, 0.01, 0.01).

very simple stem is:

val *stem* = *object*[*moveto*(0.5, 0.0), *lineto*(0.5, 1.5)];

and therefore:

val *plant* = *stem*++(*shiftObj*(0.0, 1.0)*flower*);

These values are displayed in Figure 10.5. The extent of the plant is (0.0, 1.0, 0.0, 2.0).

To build the garden, a row of plants can be defined:

Example 10.2(d) Describing a row of plants.

```
fun row(n) =
  if n = 0 then nilObject
  else
  let val rn = real n
  in
    (shift(−rn, 0.0)plant) ++ row(n − 1) ++ (shift(rn − 1.0, 0.0)plant)
  ni
nuf
```

The value of *row*(*n*) is a row of $2n$ plants with extent $(-n, n, 0, 2)$.

Finally, an m by n triangle of plants can be obtained with the following function. This is defined so that each successive row, from the bottom upwards, is scaled (vertically) by the scale factor f, and has two

Figure 10.5
Display of the plant object.

plants less than the previous row (one disappearing at each end). This is to give the illusion of the rows of plants receding into the distance.

Example 10.2(e) Describing the garden of plants.

```
fun trianglePlant(m, n, f) =
  let fun t(a, b) = shiftObj(0.0, 2.0*a) ∘ scaleObj(1.0, b) nuf
  and tr(k) = if k = 1 then (row(n), 1.0, f)
              else
              let val (a, b, c) = tr(k − 1)
              in
                (a++(t(b, c)row(n − k + 1)), 1.0 + f*b, f*c)
              ni
  nuf
  in
    let val (a, _, _) = tr(m)
    in
      a
    ni
  ni
nuf
```

This function may be somewhat obscure. Its derivation is discussed in Exercise 10.6.

The triangle of plants function may now be used to define and then display gardens, as shown in Figure 10.3. The hierarchical nature of this modelling is shown in Figure 10.6.

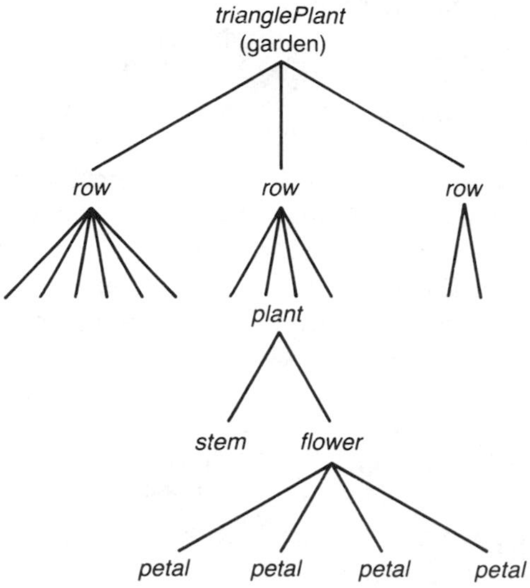

Figure 10.6
Hierarchical structure of the garden.

The generality of this approach should not be overlooked. For example, *flowerFunction* is parameterized with an *Object*. A different sort of flower can be described quite easily by supplying a different *Object* as argument to this and the *petalR* function. Of course, this parameterization on *Object*s (and functions) could be taken further in this example (see Exercise 10.7).

10.2.3 Coordinate Systems

In functional graphics, there is no direct use of windows and viewports. Rather, each *Description* and *Object* is constructed in convenient coordinates. In the examples, care has been taken to keep track of the extent of each *Object* definition, otherwise it becomes difficult to transform and compose *Objects* to achieve the desired effect. When the 'final' *Object* is produced – for example, a particular invocation of compositions and transformations of *trianglePlant* – its extent must be computed and then a function used to carry out the final transformation into a viewport on device space. Suppose a garden *Object*, defined with extent *W*, is to be generated on the screen into viewport *V* (expressed in DC) and *tran*(*W*, *V*) maps an *Object* into an *Object*; then:

displayObject(*tran*(*W*, *V*))*garden*;

would produce the required effect.

It could be argued, therefore, that the extent of the *Object* to be displayed corresponds to WC; that is, in terms of the tree representing the hierarchy, the internal nodes are expressed in 'object coordinates' and the root in WC. Although this is true, the relativity involved should not be forgotten. The *garden* might be framed in a 'picture' to hang on a 'wall' viewed from the opposite corner of the 'room', which contains many other *Objects* besides. In this more complex picture, the final description of the room is in WC, whereas now the garden is described in terms of its own 'object coordinates'. The room itself could be part of a *Description* of a house... and so on. Once this more general view of graphics modelling is introduced, the absolute notion of WC becomes a bit hazy.

10.2.4 Conclusions on Functional Graphics

There are different possible approaches to graphics in the framework of a functional programming language. The style chosen here is deliberately aimed at introducing the ideas of graphics modelling, and does not closely correspond to other examples published to date (to the authors' knowledge).

In Peter Henderson's book on functional programming (Henderson, 1980), a small set of functions for describing the structure of a picture were defined. This work was extended in a fascinating paper (Henderson, 1982) showing how a set of functions could be defined in an attempt to capture the recursive nature of one of Maurits Escher's woodcuts. In addition to basic functions for describing a line, Henderson introduced higher level functions such as *beside*(p, q) and *above*(p, q) so that if p and q are pictures, then *beside*(p, q) is the new picture formed by putting p to the left of q, and *above*(p, q) with p above q. ('beside' and 'above' are judged relative to the extents of the two pictures and have other parameters describing the picture extent.) This original work has been greatly extended by Arya (1984), who embodied graphics functions in the HOPE language. His approach included the possibility of using functional graphics for animation, which has been followed up in Arya (1986).

There are three drawbacks to functional graphics, as it exists at the time of writing. First, to be attractive it must support all of the capabilities of classical graphics. For example, neither the approach of this chapter, nor the work of Henderson or Arya, consider the problem of associating attributes (line style, etc.) with the *Descriptors* (see Exercise 10.7). However, the work on the formal specification of GKS (Duce and Fielding, 1986) represents progress in this area. Second, interactive graphics is not discussed at all, and it is difficult to see how this could be properly treated in a functional framework, although some related work has been carried out (Cook, 1986; Henderson, 1984; Mallegren, 1982). Finally, functional languages running on sequential computers are not efficient, so that the all important execution times of graphics programs are seriously impaired. Perhaps the most realistic use of functional graphics at the time of writing is as a means of program specification, with the functional graphics programs ultimately transcribed for efficiency into imperative languages such as Pascal or C.

10.3 Graphics Modelling in Conventional Languages

Section 10.2 introduced the ideas of graphics modelling in a modern functional programming framework, but the fundamental ideas date back to the origins of computer graphics in Sutherland's Sketchpad system (Sutherland, 1963). The terminology and programming style are obviously different from Section 10.2, although the concepts are similar. (A different terminology was used in Section 10.2 to avoid confusion with concepts that do not match exactly.)

Graphical entities are defined relative to their own **master coordinates** – that is, coordinates that are convenient for their description. **Instance transformations** applied to a graphics entity place *instances* of the entity in the master coordinate definition of a higher level entity – or if this higher entity is the root of the hierarchy (the total picture), then the instance transformation transforms an object to WC. Such transformations are effected by changing a behind-the-scenes global **current transformation matrix** (or **CTM**). In the terminology of Section 10.2, master coordinates are the coordinates used in descriptions, or objects other than the root. Instances correspond to objects.

In such a system, a number of functions are usually defined for manipulation of the CTM, which is stored as a global variable. The first of these functions is:

SetCTM(matrix)

where *matrix* is a 3 by 3 transformation matrix that is used to post-multiply an homogeneous point; that is, $(x', y', 1) = (x, y, 1)\ CTM$. (Note that this is the opposite convention to GKS.)

GetCTM ()

is a function that delivers the CTM.

ShiftCTM(sx, sy)

accumulates the translation (sx, sy) into the CTM; hence, it has the effect of updating the CTM by:

$$CTM := \begin{pmatrix} 1 & 0 & 0 \\ 0 & 1 & 0 \\ sx & sy & 1 \end{pmatrix} CTM$$

Similarly:

ScaleCTM(*sx*, *sy*)

updates the CTM by:

$$CTM := \begin{pmatrix} sx & 0 & 0 \\ 0 & sy & 0 \\ 0 & 0 & 1 \end{pmatrix} CTM$$

Finally:

RotateCTM(θ)

results in:

$$CTM := \begin{pmatrix} \cos\theta & \sin\theta & 0 \\ -\sin\theta & \cos\theta & 0 \\ 0 & 0 & 1 \end{pmatrix} CTM$$

For a full but general discussion of the graphics modelling approach see Foley and Van Dam (1984, Chapter 9). Sections 10.4 and 10.5 consider the use of these concepts in two important systems: PostScript and PHIGS.

□□ EXAMPLE

This example presents another version of the star program given in Example 10.1. Now, it is in a GKS style setting, but with a very important difference with regards to the interpretation of the viewing pipeline.

Example 10.3 Describing a star – alternative version.

```
fun Triangle () =
  let val m = GetCTM ()
  in
```

```
        ShiftCTM(−0.5, 0.5);
        ScaleCTM(1.0, 2.0);
        Polyline [(0.0, 0.0), (1.0, 0.0), (0.5, 1.0), (0.0, 0.0)];
        SetCTM(m)
    ni
nuf

fun Star () =
    let val m = GetCTM ()
    in
        Triangle ();
        for 0 ≤ i ≤ 3 do
            RotateCTM(π/2.0);
            Triangle ()
        od;
        SetCTM(m)
    ni
nuf
```

It is common in this style of programming that on exit from a procedure the CTM is restored to its value prior to the execution of that procedure – hence the use of *GetCTM* and *SetCTM*. This is to isolate the effects of any changes introduced to the CTM during the procedure execution. This example would not be correct without such saving and restoring of the CTM.

Now, *Star* () defines a star in master coordinates with extent (−2.5, 2.5, −2.5, 2.5). Suppose that this is to be inserted into a viewport representing the lower left-hand quadrant of the effective display space. Then, assuming that workstations have been opened and activated, and the default workstation transformation:

```
Set the CTM to the identity matrix.
SetCTM(identity);
SetViewport(1, [0.0, 0.5, 0.0, 0.5]);
SetWindow(1, [−2.5, 2.5, −2.5, 2.5]);
SelectNtran(1);

Display Star ();
```

A *Display* procedure is needed as in the functional approach. The crucial difference compared to the operation of the GKS viewing pipeline is that when a graphical output primitive (*Polyline* in this example) is encountered during the program execution, its coordinate values must first be transformed by the CTM – in effect, into WC. The normal viewing pipeline takes over from then on (see Exercise 10.8).

10.4 PostScript

"The PostScript language is a programming language designed to convey a description of virtually any desired page to a printer."

Adobe Systems Incorporated, 1985a, p. 1. See also 1985b.

There are several points to note about this brief description.

- PostScript is a general-purpose programming language. It has very powerful functions for graphics, but it could be used for many other applications. It was invented by John Warnock and Charles Geschke of Adobe Systems, initially as a system for communicating with printers.
- The concept behind the PostScript graphics model is that a program is a description of a complete page. A page starts off as white and use of the PostScript graphics operators conceptually adds a series of marks to the page in various halftones or colours. When the description is complete, the page is 'shown', or printed (Warnock and Wyatt, 1982).
- Graphics operators alter the current page by painting: the marks produced by each operator overpaint whatever was on the page at these positions, irrespective of colours used – for example, white can be used to overpaint black. However, only the region of the page inside the current clipping region is affected by the graphics operations. The clipping region may be arbitrarily shaped, and hence acts as a stencil through which marks may be added to the page.
- PostScript has seen its first application as a language for controlling laser printers. However, it adopts a raster model of the printed page and within this limitation is device independent. PostScript could be used as a language for controlling any raster-based (output) graphics device. Indeed, it has formed the basis of an implementation of a new window manager system by Sun microsystems (Gosling, 1985; Sun, 1987a).

The following sections amplify these remarks with the limited intention of giving the reader sufficient detail to understand the main ideas.

10.4.1 PostScript Is a Language

PostScript is a stack-based programming language. All operations take place with respect to at least one stack. A **stack** is a 'last in–first out' data structure. Items are *pushed* on to the top of the stack and *popped* off the top

(Wulf, 1981). For example, if a stack is initially empty, *push* 1, *push* 2, *push* 3 would place 1, then 2 and then 3 successively on to the top of the stack resulting in:

top ⇒ 3
        2
        1

Now, the operation *pop* would deliver the result 3, and a second *pop* would deliver 2.

A PostScript program is a sequence of **tokens**. The PostScript interpreter scans this input sequence and as it encounters each token it either pushes it on to the **operand stack**, if it is an operand, or it executes the operation using the required data on the operand stack, if it is an operation. It is a **postfix** language, since operators follow their operands.

For example, a sequence of tokens to add two numbers might be:

```
5 4 add
```

When the interpreter encounters this sequence, it first pushes 5 and then 4 on to the operand stack. It then encounters the operator add and this is executed, which means that it pops the top two elements off the operand stack, forms their sum and pushes this result on to the operand stack. These steps can be illustrated as follows:

top ⇒ ?

top ⇒ 5
        ?

top ⇒ 4
        5
        ?

top ⇒ 9
        ?

Similarly:

```
8 5 mul 3 4 mul add
```

leaves $(8*5) + (3*4) = 52$ on top of the operand stack (where mul is the multiplication operator).

It is possible for the applications program to define associations between literal names and a sequence of operands and operators. For example:

```
/a 5 def
/b 6 def
/c 7 def
/d 8 def

a b mul c d mul add
```

associates a with 5, b with 6 and so on. (The symbol / is used to denote a literal name – a **key** – introduced for the first time.) Then a*b + c*d = 86 is left on top of the operand stack.

When the PostScript interpreter encounters a name such as a or b in the input sequence it searches the **dictionary stack**. This is a stack with system-defined items at the bottom (such as add and mul) and user-defined items above this. A dictionary contains associations between keys and values. Hence:

```
/xyz 100 def
```

pushes the entry 'xyz associated with 100' on to the top of the dictionary stack. When xyz is later encountered, the dictionary stack is searched from the top down looking for the key xyz, and the value 100 is retrieved. This facility is used mainly to allow the definition of user-defined operations. For example:

```
/times10 {10 mul} def
```

associates the procedure body {10 mul} with the (key) name times10. Hence:

```
4 times10
```

is equivalent to:

```
4 10 mul
```

which leaves 40 at the top of the operand stack.

There are always at least two dictionaries present in PostScript: the **system dictionary** and the **user dictionary**. The first of these dictionaries holds the association between keys and values defined by the system (for example, the definition of the procedure mul), while the second holds those defined by the user. At any time, there is a 'current' dictionary, which is the dictionary searched first in the dictionary stack whenever a key is encountered. If the key is not found in the current dictionary, then the next dictionary in the stack is searched. The system dictionary is always at the bottom of the dictionary stack.

The user may define a new dictionary by using the dict operator. The begin operator pushes a new dictionary on to the dictionary stack and the end operator pops the current dictionary off the stack. Consider the following procedure, which illustrates the use of this facility:

```
%procedure to sum squares of two numbers
%x y distance => x² + y²
/distance
{
  2 dict
  begin
    /y exch def
    /x exch def
    x dup mul y dup mul add
  end
} def
```

This procedure expects two values on the operand stack, removes them and leaves their sum of squares at the top of the stack. This is achieved as follows. It creates a new dictionary of size 2 and pushes this on to the dictionary stack. This is now the current dictionary. Two keys /x and /y are defined within this dictionary and with associated values defined from those on the operand stack by using the exch operator, which reverses the order of the top two items on this stack. By the time the end operator has been interpreted, the value of the sum of squares has been left at the top of the operand stack. Note that since /x and /y were defined within the new dictionary, once this has been popped off the dictionary stack, these keys are no longer defined. Hence, dictionaries provide a means of representing the idea of local variables within procedures. An extensive use of this method can be found in the example given in Appendix B.

So far, the PostScript objects mentioned have been numbers, names, dictionaries and procedure bodies. But there are in addition strings, arrays and comments. **Strings** are denoted by a sequence of characters enclosed in round brackets:

```
(this is a string)
```

Arrays are sequences of any type of PostScript object (and not all necessarily of the same type) enclosed in square brackets:

```
[1 3 (this is an element too) {10 mul} [3 4] 42]
```

Comments are introduced by the % symbol:

```
%this is a comment
```

Finally, the PostScript language supports the usual control structures.

For example:

```
n proc repeat
```

(where n is a number) will execute proc *n* times. So:

```
3 times10 repeat
```

will expect a number on the operand stack immediately below 3, and leave 1000 times this number at the top of the stack. Other such operations are for and forall, which are illustrated in Appendix B.

10.4.2 Coordinate Systems and the Current Transformation Matrix

Device space is the PostScript equivalent of GKS device coordinates. This is the coordinate system appropriate to the graphics device in use. In most circumstances, the PostScript user is shielded from the device space and carries out all operations in **user space**. Default user space is a coordinate system with its origin at the bottom left-hand corner of the page (with x and y in their normal mathematical orientation – positive x is East and positive y is North) such that one unit in any direction measures 1/72 inch. (This fraction is chosen because it is almost exactly a point size in printing industry conventions.) This relation between units of measurement and physical dimensions represents a crucial difference between PostScript user space and GKS world coordinates.

The current transformation matrix (CTM) is initialised so that default user space is mapped to device space. In other words, given any point p expressed in user space, $p\ CTM$ is the equivalent point in device space.

The CTM is one of the components of the **graphics state**, and there are a number of graphics state operators for changing the CTM. (The CTM is a 3 by 3 transformation matrix and is used as described in Section 10.3.) The operators translate, scale and rotate are used to accumulate these transformations into the CTM (where translate is used to mean shift). Therefore:

```
tx ty translate
```

results in:

$$\mathrm{CTM} := \begin{pmatrix} 1 & 0 & 0 \\ 0 & 1 & 0 \\ tx & ty & 1 \end{pmatrix} \mathrm{CTM}$$

with corresponding results for:

sx sy scale and θ rotate

By using these (and other) transformation graphics state operators, the user can alter the CTM as required.

The normal way in which a user would describe a picture would be to first define the graphics objects in a master coordinate system and then use the transformation operators to specify instances of these objects on the page. (There is no distinction in PostScript between modelling and viewing. Both are accomplished by means of the CTM.)

Hence, the typical structure of a PostScript program conceptually consists of two components. The **prologue** is a series of procedure definitions, which, in the main, define graphics objects. The **script** makes use of the definitions in the prologue to actually generate the picture on the page. (There is no syntactic distinction between prologue and script, this is just a way of thinking about programming in PostScript.)

10.4.3 Path Constructors and Graphical Output

Graphical output is described by means of graphics output operators applied to the **current path**. This is illustrated by the following example:

```
newpath
    0 0 moveto
    1 0 lineto
    1 1 lineto
    0 1 lineto
    closepath
stroke
```

newpath is an operator to start a new path. Here, the path is described by using the **path constructors** moveto, lineto and closepath. closepath does not end the path, but describes a line joining the current position to the first point of the path. Each path constructor changes the current position of a hypothetical pen, within the current path. stroke is one of the graphics output operators. When applied to the current path, it is as if a pen traced through the path described by the path constructors.

A further example is:

```
newpath
    0.5 0 moveto
    0.5 1 lineto
```

```
    0 0.5 moveto
    1 0.5 lineto
stroke
```

This describes a cross (+). Note that there is no requirement for the lines in a path to be connected end to end as in a polyline.

Figure 10.7 shows a complete, simple PostScript program with its output. First, box is defined as a path describing a unit square. Next, the CTM is accumulated with the scale transformation. Since the original user space coordinate system was 1 unit = 1/72 inch, this scale transformation gives a user space with 1 unit = 1 inch. Next, the current line width in the graphics state is set to 1/10 inch and the box path is stroked. Then the origin of the coordinate system is shifted two inches in from the bottom left-hand corner (the default origin) and the box path is filled (fill being another graphics output operator). The box is filled with a grey scale of 0.5, where 0.0 means black and 1.0 means white.

The findfont operator searches the font dictionary for the font named Times-Roman and pushes this to the top of the stack. scalefont, which operates on the CTM but does not change the CTM, scales the font size to be in this case 0.2 inch. setfont makes the font on the stack the current font. The current position is moved by (1, 8) and the show operator is applied to the string. Finally, showpage is the instruction to print the page (after which the current page is again white).

Figure 10.8 shows another PostScript program where the page is described by constructing more complex images from simpler ones. The gsave and grestore operators are used frequently in this program. gsave saves the current graphics state, which is restored on the next grestore. The CTM is saved and restored in this way. This was seen to be a necessary construct in the modelling transformation discussed earlier.

In this program, a triangle shape is first defined in master coordinates. Second, a star is defined as the rotation of the triangle four times about the centre of its base. Third, an eight-cornered star is similarly defined by rotation. Finally, a four-cornered filled star is described by the application of the fill operator to four rotated copies of the original triangle.

Starline is defined as a column of shapes consisting of triangle, star, twostar and fillstar. Starpage is the page full of shapes defined by translating Starline four times across the page.

The definitions of triangle, star, twostar, fillstar, Starline and Starpage constitute the prologue. The script first uses scale to change user space so that 1 unit = 0.5 inch. The line width is set to 0.1, the line cap is set to rounded caps and the grey scale to 0.5. Starpage is invoked and the scale is reduced by a factor of 0.15, and Starpage is invoked a further 25 times using translate. showpage results in the printing of the page description, as shown in Figure 10.8.

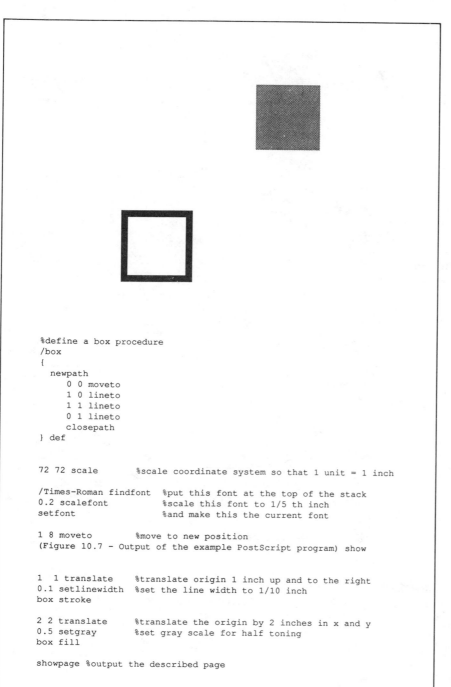

```
%define a box procedure
/box
{
  newpath
     0 0 moveto
     1 0 lineto
     1 1 lineto
     0 1 lineto
     closepath
} def


72 72 scale        %scale coordinate system so that 1 unit = 1 inch

/Times-Roman findfont  %put this font at the top of the stack
0.2 scalefont          %scale this font to 1/5 th inch
setfont                %and make this the current font

1 8 moveto         %move to new position
(Figure 10.7 - Output of the example PostScript program) show


1  1 translate     %translate origin 1 inch up and to the right
0.1 setlinewidth   %set the line width to 1/10 inch
box stroke

2 2 translate      %translate the origin by 2 inches in x and y
0.5 setgray        %set gray scale for half toning
box fill

showpage %output the described page
```

Figure 10.7 PostScript program defining a box and its output. (Note that the figure headers generated by all PostScript programs are not displayed in the figures.)

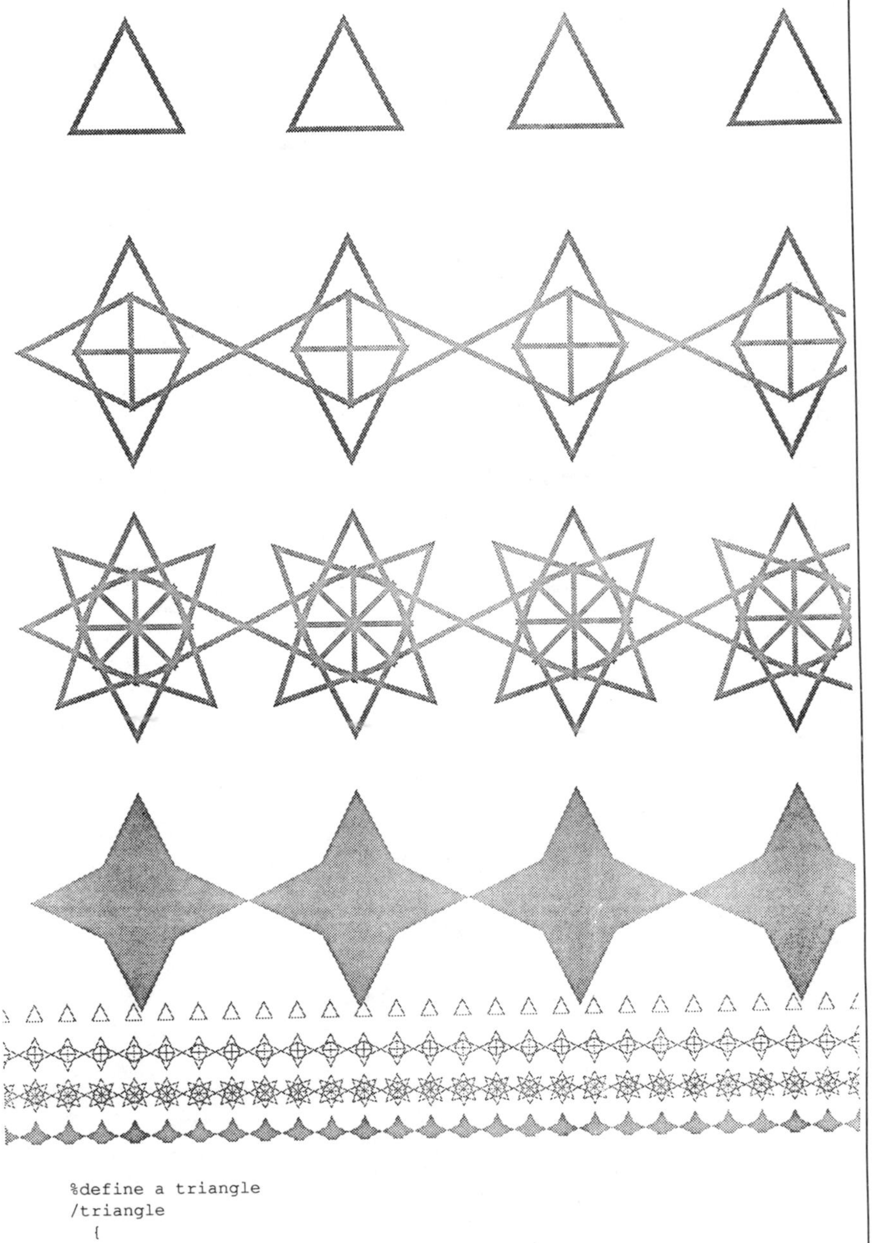

```
%define a triangle
/triangle
  {
   newpath
     -1 0 moveto
      1 0 lineto
      0 2 lineto
   closepath
  } def
```

Figure 10.8
PostScript program describing a star page and its output.

```
%define a star by rotating the triangle by 90 degrees
%and repeating this 4 times
/star
  {
   gsave
     4 {90 rotate triangle stroke} repeat
   grestore
  } def

%define a new star by rotation of star
/twostar
  {
   gsave
     star
     45 rotate star
   grestore
  } def

%define a filled version of two star
/fillstar
  {
   gsave
     4 {90 rotate triangle fill} repeat
   grestore
  } def

%define a line of stars
/StarLine
{
 gsave
  3 19 translate triangle stroke
  0 -4 translate star
  0 -5 translate twostar
  0 -5 translate fillstar
 grestore
} def

%define a page full of lines of stars
/StarPage
{
 gsave
    StarLine
    3 {4 0 translate StarLine } repeat
  grestore
} def

%draw the header
/Times-Roman findfont 12 scalefont setfont
40 800 moveto (Figure 10.8) show
40 765 moveto
(Page of Stars) show

36 36   scale         %one unit is half inch
0.1     setlinewidth
1       setlinecap    %round caps
0.5     setgray

StarPage

0.15 0.15 scale
StarPage
25 {4 0 translate StarPage} repeat

showpage
```

10.4.4 PostScript Power

The PostScript path constructors give a flavour of the expressive power of the language for generating graphics images. As well as the moveto and lineto constructors (and their relative counterparts rmoveto and rlineto), there are operators for describing arcs (arc, arcn and arcto) and curves (curveto and rcurveto) based on the Bezier form (see Section 11.8). In addition, there are operators that take paths as operands and return new paths (such as reversepath) and an image operator useful for rendering digitized images.

Clipping is rather more sophisticated than is possible in GKS. *Any* path description can be used to define a clipping region (the path is automatically closed in the sense of closepath when the clipping operator is applied to it). Quite arbitrary shapes can therefore be defined as clip regions. Moreover, the *inside* of a region is defined by a rule that is different from the inside test used by GKS (see Chapter 4). For example, Figure 10.9 shows a polygon filled using the GKS rule and the PostScript rule. (The inside of a clip region is defined by the same rule as the inside of a region to be filled.) However, PostScript also provides the odd–even inside rule used by GKS as an alternative for clipping and filling. An example of PostScript clipping is shown in Figure 10.10.

Attributes form part of the PostScript graphics state. The setlinewidth operator has obvious interpretation. setlinecap is used to describe the shape of line endings – for example, whether they are round or rectangular. setlinejoin describes the type of join (round or angled) for consecutive lines. setdash allows the user to set a dash pattern for line drawing (which is described in a general way, rather than a fixed set of line types as in GKS). setflat sets the accuracy with which curves are rendered. setgray sets the current grey scale as described earlier. In addition, there is a choice for setting colours according to two different colour models: the RGB (as used by GKS) or the more sophisticated Hue, Saturation and Brightness (HSB) model (see Section 14.6.8).

PostScript can therefore be seen to offer a powerful and compact suite of functions for computer graphics. A number of illustrative examples are shown in Figures 10.11 to 10.16, together with the PostScript program.

10.5 Graphics Modelling with PHIGS

The **Programmer's Hierarchical Interactive Graphics System** (ISO, 1986d) is a working draft for a proposed ISO standard. At the time of writing, it was at least three years away from being adopted as an ISO standard, and many changes may be introduced in that time. The aim of this section is to show how the graphics modelling ideas discussed in this chapter are embodied in PHIGS.

PHIGS is both a 3D and 2D system, and separate 2D and 3D functions are defined, although only the relevant 2D functions are considered here. The system attempts to parallel GKS as far as possible, and its 3D viewing pipeline is similar to the viewing pipeline of the proposd 3D extension to GKS (see Chapter 13). Therefore, PHIGS has workstation and input models similar to those of GKS, and about one-third of its nearly 300 functions have names identical to those of 2D GKS functions.

The reason for the introduction of another graphics standard is due to the absence of graphics modelling in GKS. The working draft gives the reasons for PHIGS as the need to aid applications programmers in understanding 'dynamic hierarchic graphics' and to produce such programs that are easily portable between installations.

10.5.1 The Basic Ideas of PHIGS

The central theme of PHIGS is graphics modelling embodied in a classical graphics GKS-like system. The modelling is data oriented rather than procedural, based on an extension of the segment concept.

PHIGS applications programs create and manipulate a **centralized structure store** (CSS). This consists of a hierarchical arrangement of nodes called **structures**. A structure consists of **elements** which are the functions that generate graphical output primitives and their attributes. These functions are very similar to those of the GKS standard and the proposed 3D extension to GKS. In addition, structure elements can reference other structures by calling for their *execution*, thus allowing the construction of the hierarchical system.

PHIGS ensures the separation between the creation and manipulation of the CSS, and the *display* of structures on workstations. Structures can be **posted** (or displayed) on a workstation or **unposted**. When a structure is posted, all of its child structures are posted as well. The branch of the CSS tree associated with a given structure node is called its **structure network**, so the post and unpost operations always refer to structure networks.

Structures can be edited in various ways: the structure elements are numbered from 0 to n, where 0 is a pointer to the beginning of the structure, 1 to its first element, and so on, with n pointing to its last element. An empty structure only has element 0. To allow structure editing, functions exist for moving the element pointer within the structure and effecting changes at its current position – such as deleting or inserting elements.

When a structure is posted, its elements are traversed and the

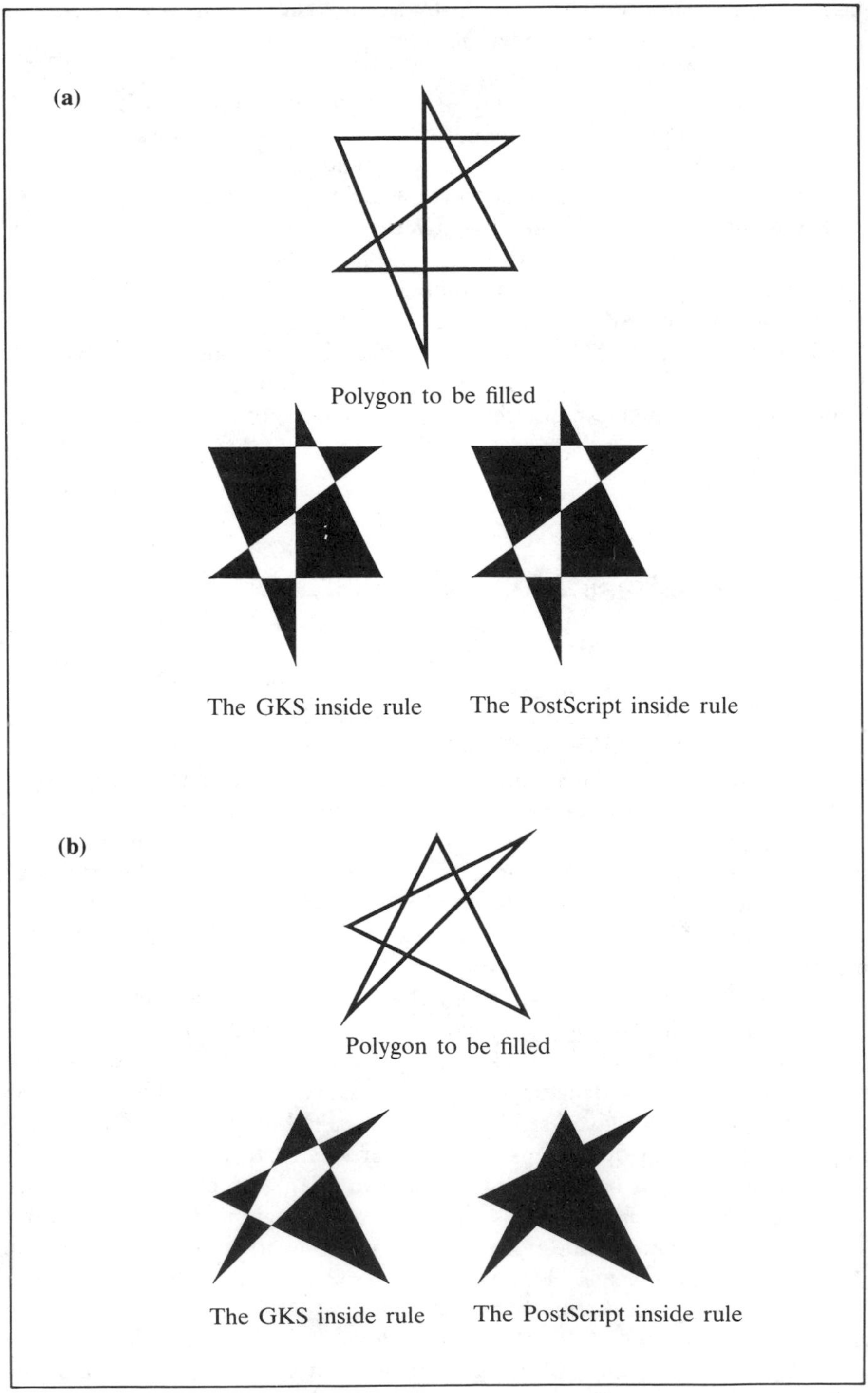

Figure 10.9
Example showing when the GKS and PostScript rules produce (a) the same results and (b) different results.

```
/Times-Roman findfont 12 scalefont setfont
40 800 moveto (Figure 10.9) show
40 765 moveto
(The PostScript and GKS Inside Rules) show


/figure
{
 /title exch def
 newpath
   0 0 moveto
   0.5 1 lineto
   1 0 lineto
   0.0 0.5 lineto
   1 1 lineto
   closepath
   /Times-Roman findfont 0.1 scalefont setfont
   0 -0.5 rmoveto
   title show
} def

72 72 scale
 1 1 translate

gsave
  1.5 7 translate
  2 2 scale
  0.025 setlinewidth
  (Polygon to be filled) figure stroke
grestore

gsave
  0 3 translate
  2 2 scale
  (The GKS inside rule) figure eofill
grestore

gsave
  3 3 translate
  2 2 scale
  (The PostScript inside rule) figure fill
grestore

showpage
```

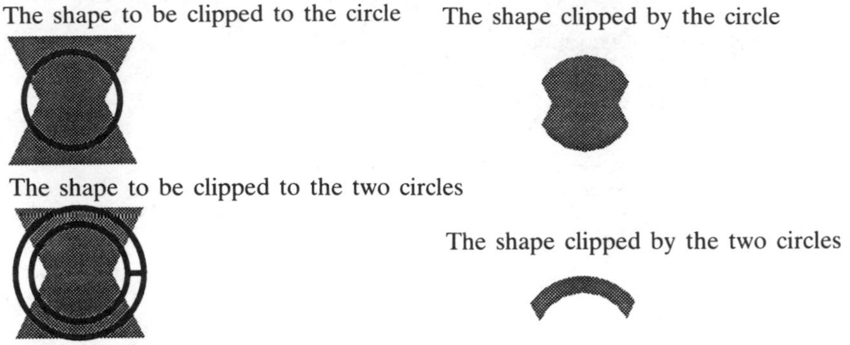

```
/Times-Roman findfont 12 scalefont setfont
40 800 moveto (Figure 10.10) show
40 765 moveto
(An Example of PostScript Clipping) show

/circle
{
 /radius exch def        %reads and defines the radius
  newpath
    0 0 radius 0 360 arc %defines an arc subtending 0 to 360 degrees
                         %in an anti-clockwise direction
                         %centred at (0,0)
} def

/shape
{
 newpath
   -0.5 -0.5 moveto
    0.5 -0.5 lineto
    0.0  0.5 lineto
    closepath
    -0.5 0.5 moveto
     0  -0.5 lineto
     0.5 0.5 lineto
     closepath
} def

/noclipping
{
  %show the drawing with clipping off
  gsave
    0.5 setgray
    shape fill
  grestore
  gsave
    currentlinewidth 2 mul setlinewidth
    0.375 circle stroke
  grestore
  -0.5 0.6 moveto (The shape to be clipped to the circle) show
} def

/circleclip
{
  %now use the circle as clipping region
  gsave
    0.375 circle clip
    0.5 setgray
    shape fill
  grestore
```

Figure 10.10
PostScript program for clipping and its output.

```
  -0.5 0.6 moveto (The shape clipped by the circle) show
} def

/doublecircle
{
  /outerRadius exch def
  /innerRadius exch def
  newpath
    0 0 outerRadius 0 360 arc
    0 0 innerRadius 360 0 arcn  %clockwise (negative) arc
} def


/noclipping2
{
  %show the 2nd drawing with clipping off
  gsave
    0.5 setgray
    shape fill
  grestore
  gsave
    currentlinewidth 2 mul setlinewidth
    0.375 0.5 doublecircle stroke
  grestore
  -0.5 0.6 moveto (The shape to be clipped to the two circles) show
} def


/doublecircleclip
{
  %now use the circle as clipping region
  gsave
    0.375 0.5 doublecircle clip
    0.5 setgray
    shape fill
  grestore
  -0.5 0.6 moveto (The shape clipped by the two circles) show
} def


72 72 scale
0.02 setlinewidth

%set flatness parameter for the arc drawing
4 setflat

/Times-Roman findfont 0.15 scalefont setfont


4.1 8.3 translate
noclipping

0 -2 translate
circleclip

0 -2 translate
noclipping2

0 -2 translate
doublecircleclip

showpage
```

requisite action taken. When, for example, an element that generates an output primitive is encountered, its coordinates are first transformed from the conceptual master coordinates in which the object represented by the structure is defined, into the WC suitable for transmission through the viewing pipeline to the display space of the workstation concerned. The transformation is accomplished by **pre-multiplication** of the master coordinate points (expressed in homogeneous coordinates) by the current **composite modelling transformation** (**CMT**) matrix, which is a 3 by 3 homogeneous transformation matrix. When an element that executes another structure is encountered, the current CMT is saved and passed to the referenced structure as a **global modelling transformation** (**GMT**). During the traversal of this child structure, its GMT is composed with its succession of **local modelling transformations** (**LMT**s) to form suitable CMTs for application to primitive functions which are elements of the structure. When this child structure has been completely traversed (including, of course, the traversal of *its* children), traversal continues in the parent, and with the saved CMT restored.

It is important to note that *all* matrices in PHIGS are, as in GKS, used to pre-multiply coordinate data (represented as a column vector). In addition, the CMT is always formed by pre-multiplying the LMT by the GMT – that is, CMT = GMT*LMT. However, the order in which transformations are multiplied into the LMT to form a new LMT may be specified by the applications program.

10.5.2 Some of the PHIGS Modelling Functions

There are a number of functions for constructing the various transforms and these are now briefly described.

SET LOCAL TRANSFORMATION

SetLocalTransformation(*matrix*, *compositionType*)

where *matrix* is a 3 by 3 homogeneous transformation matrix and *compositionType* has one of the atomic values PRECONCATENATE, POSTCONCATENATE or REPLACE. This determines how the matrix is to be composed with the current LMT – whether by pre- or post-multiplication, or by replacing it with the new matrix. When this function is called, it inserts the corresponding 'set local transformation' element into the currently open structure (one must be open) at its current element pointer.

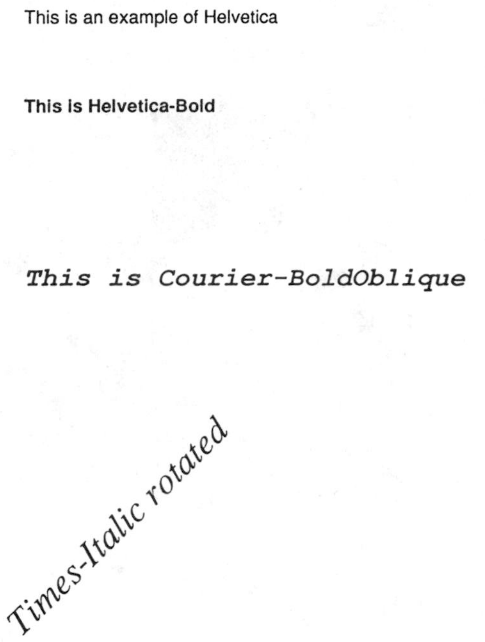


```
/Times-Roman findfont 12 scalefont setfont
40 800 moveto (Figure 10.11) show
40 765 moveto
(Using PostScript Fonts) show


/ChooseFont
{
 /scaling  exch def %exchange two top items of the stack
                    %in order to define scaling
 /fontname exch def %repeat to define fontname

 fontname findfont  %find the font to be used
 scaling  scalefont %scale this font
 setfont            %make this the current font
}
def

72 72 scale  %change scale to inches
1  1  translate %move the origin
/Helvetica 0.2 ChooseFont
1 8 moveto (This is an example of Helvetica) show

/Helvetica-Bold 0.2 ChooseFont
1 7 moveto  (This is Helvetica-Bold) show

/Courier-BoldOblique 0.3 ChooseFont
1 5 moveto  (This is Courier-BoldOblique) show

1 1 translate
45 rotate
/Times-Italic 0.4 ChooseFont
0 0 moveto  (Times-Italic rotated) show

showpage
```

Figure 10.11
Using PostScript fonts.

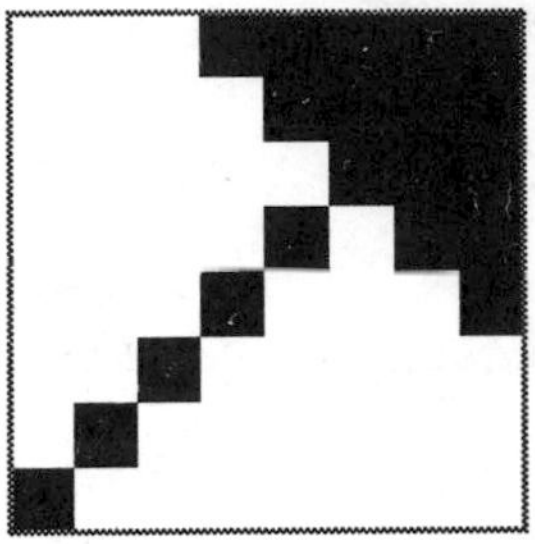

```
/Times-Roman findfont 12 scalefont setfont
40 800 moveto (Figure 10.12) show
40 765 moveto
(Simple Example of the Image Operator) show


%simple example of the image operator

%define a string called buffer of length 8
/buffer 8 string def

/arrow
{
 %number of samples per line = 8
 %number of lines in the image = 8
 %number of bits per sample = 1
 %matrix which determines mapping into a square unit in user space

 8 8 1 [8 0 0 -8 0 8] {currentfile buffer readhexstring pop} image
}
def

0.5 setgray

300 400 translate   %move to centre of page
144 144 scale       %scale to units of 2 inches
arrow
e0f0f8f4eedfbf7f
%the above is a hex string defining the arrow image

%draw a box around the image
0.01 setlinewidth
newpath
  0 0 moveto
  1 0 lineto
  1 1 lineto
  0 1 lineto
  closepath
stroke

showpage
```

Figure 10.12
Simple example of the image operator.

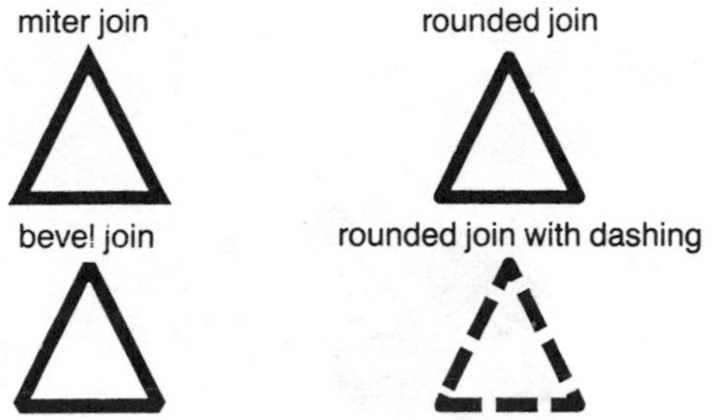


```
/Times-Roman findfont 12 scalefont setfont
40 800 moveto (Figure 10.13) show
40 765 moveto
(Types of Line Join and Dashing) show

/triangle
{
 /label exch def
 newpath
   0 0    moveto
   1 0    lineto
   0.5 1  lineto
   closepath stroke
   0.5 1.1 moveto label show
}
def

72 72 scale
2  1  translate
0.1 setlinewidth
/Helvetica-Oblique findfont 0.2 scalefont setfont

gsave
  0 setlinejoin  %miter joins
  0 7 translate
  (miter join) triangle
grestore

gsave
  1 setlinejoin %rouned join
  3 7 translate
  (rounded join) triangle
grestore

gsave
  2 setlinejoin %bevel join
  0 4 translate
  (bevel join) triangle
grestore

gsave
  1 setlinejoin
  [0.3 0.1] 0 setdash %dash pattern as alternate runs of
                 %0.3 and 0.1 black and white
                 %with 0 offset into the pattern
  3 4 translate
  (rounded join with dashing) triangle
grestore

showpage
```

Figure 10.13
Types of line join and dashing.

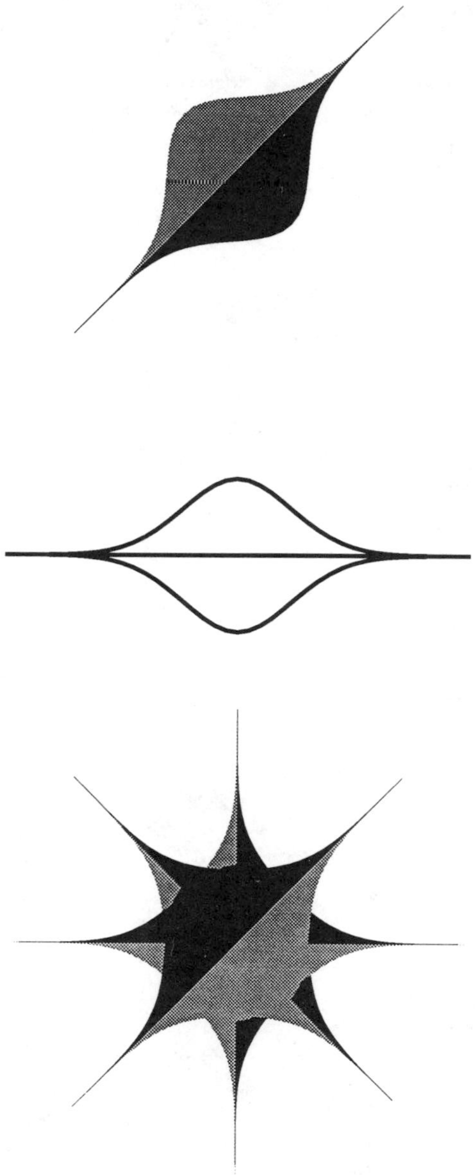

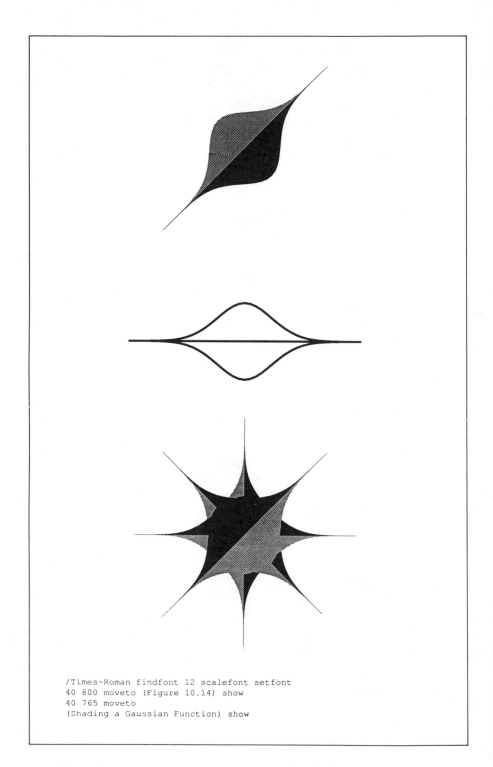

```
/Times-Roman findfont 12 scalefont setfont
40 800 moveto (Figure 10.14) show
40 765 moveto
(Shading a Gaussian Function) show
```

Figure 10.14
Shading a Gaussian function.

```
%define exp(x) ie, x Exp => Exp(x)
%The PostScipt exp operator a b exp delivers a to power b
%and x ln delivers natural log ln(x)

/Exp
{10 ln div 10 exch exp}
def

%defines a path of values exp(-square(x)) for x = -3 to +3
%in steps of 0.15
%dup duplicates the top of the stack
/Gauss
{
 newpath
  -3 -9 Exp moveto
  -3 0.15 3 {dup dup mul neg Exp lineto} for
 closepath
}
def

/StrokedDoubleGauss
{
  gsave
    Gauss stroke
    180   rotate
    Gauss stroke
  grestore
}
def

/FilledDoubleGauss
 {
  gsave
    45   rotate
    0.5  setgray
    Gauss fill
    180   rotate
    0.0  setgray
    Gauss fill
  grestore
 }
def

72 72 scale
0.05 setlinewidth
4.1 5.3 translate %move to centre of page

gsave
  0.6 0.6 scale
  StrokedDoubleGauss
grestore

gsave
  0 3 translate
  0.6 0.6 scale
  FilledDoubleGauss
grestore

gsave
  0 -3 translate
  0.6 0.6 scale
  4 {45 rotate FilledDoubleGauss} repeat
grestore

showpage
```

```
%start of image advert
gsave
72 72 scale    %change to inches
0.5 0.5 translate  %move 0.5 inch in and up the page

gsave %save current graphics state
5 5 scale      %make the image 6 inches by 6 inches


%generate image

/buffer 256 string def

256 256 8
[256 0 0 -256 0 256]
{currentfile buffer readhexstring pop}
image
ffffffffffffffffffffffffffffffffffffffffffffffffffffcac2c7cfcfcdd2d4d4d2d1d3cecfd0cfd1ccc

grestore

/HVB /Helvetica-Bold findfont def
/HVBO /Helvetica-BoldOblique findfont def
HVB 0.5 scalefont setfont
0.25 4.4 moveto (She looks happy!) show
HVB 0.3 scalefont setfont
0.25 3.9 moveto (She learned to program) show

0.5 setgray
newpath
  5 0 moveto 7.5 0 lineto
  7.5 5 lineto 5 5 lineto
  closepath
fill

1 setgray
HVBO 0.2 scalefont setfont
5.1 4.5 moveto (Learn to Program) show
5.1 4.0 moveto (in 10 minutes!) show
5.1 3.5 moveto (Our REVOLUTIONARY) show
5.1 3.0 moveto (technique) show
5.1 2.5 moveto (will make you) show
5.1 2.0 moveto (a fully qualified) show
5.1 1.5 moveto (PROGRAMMER) show
5.1 1.0 moveto (effortlessly!) show

HVB 0.15 scalefont setfont
5.1 0.7 moveto (Simple Brain Ltd) show
5.1 0.5 moveto (22 Nutter Lane) show
5.1 0.3  moveto (East Cheam, NW 17) show

0 setgray
0.1 setlinewidth
1 setlinejoin
newpath
  0 0 moveto 7.5  0 lineto
  7.5 5 lineto 0 5 lineto
  closepath
stroke
```

Figure 10.15
PostScript program used to generate Figure 2.1. (Note that only one line of image data has been shown.)

```
grestore
%end of image definitions advert
%******************************************************************

%start of records advert

/outsidecircletext    %string, pointsize, angle, radius
{circtextdict begin
 /radius exch def
 /centerangle exch def
 /ptsize exch def
 /str exch def
 /xradius radius ptsize 4 div add def

 gsave
   centerangle str findhalfangle add rotate

   str
   {/charcode exch def
    ( ) dup 0 charcode put outsideplacechar
   } forall
 grestore
 end
} def

/insidecircletext
{circtextdict begin
 /radius exch def
 /centerangle exch def
 /ptsize exch def
 /str exch def
 /xradius radius ptsize 3 div sub def
 gsave
   centerangle str findhalfangle sub rotate
   str
   {/charcode exch def
    ( ) dup 0 charcode put insideplacechar
   } forall
 grestore
 end
} def

/circtextdict 16 dict def
circtextdict begin
  /findhalfangle
  {stringwidth pop 2 div
   2 xradius mul pi mul div 360 mul
  } def

  /outsideplacechar
  {/char exch def
   /halfangle char findhalfangle def
   gsave
     halfangle neg rotate
     radius 0 translate
     -90 rotate
     char stringwidth pop 2 div neg 0 moveto
     char show
   grestore
   halfangle 2 mul neg rotate
  } def

 /insideplacechar
 {/char exch def
```

outsidecircletext, insidecircletext, circletextdict, outsideplacechar, insideplacechar and halfangle reproduced from Adobe (1985b, pp. 167–168) by kind permission of Adobe Systems Inc.

```
  /halfangle char findhalfangle def
  gsave
    halfangle rotate
    radius 0 translate
    90 rotate
    char stringwidth pop 2 div neg 0 moveto
    char show
  grestore
  halfangle 2 mul rotate
 } def

 /pi 3.1414923 def
end

/box
{
 newpath
   -150 -200 moveto
    150 -200 lineto
    150  200 lineto
   -150  200 lineto
   closepath
} def

/cutpricerecords
{ %defined in range -150 to 150, -200 to 200
  %draw inside of box
  0.5 setgray
  box fill

  %draw box outline
  0 setgray
  10 setlinewidth
  1 setlinejoin
  box stroke

  %draw circles
  0 setgray
  0 0 100 0 360 arc fill

  20 setlinewidth
  0 0 140 0 360 arc stroke

  %draw text
  1 setgray
  /Times-Bold findfont 22 scalefont setfont
  (Cut Price Records) 22 90 75  outsidecircletext

  /Times-Bold findfont 16 scalefont setfont
  (all major labels stocked) 16 90 50 outsidecircletext

  (huge discounts) 16 270 58 insidecircletext

  /Times-Roman findfont 22 scalefont setfont
  (11 Empire Lane SW12) 22 270 82 insidecircletext
}
def


/ins {72 mul} def

/showrecords
{
 gsave
```

Figure 10.15 (cont.)

```
    2.3 ins 8.5 ins translate
    3.7 4.3 div dup scale
    cutpricerecords
  grestore
} def

showrecords

%end of records advert
%********************************************************
%start of aikido advert

/master
{
  0 setgray
  % black dress
  newpath
    19 15 moveto
    19 14 lineto 20 13 lineto 27  9 lineto 35  7 lineto
    38 17 lineto 37  7 lineto 38  9 lineto 45 10 lineto
    50  8 lineto 49 18 lineto 48 23 lineto 45 24 lineto
    40 26 lineto 37 28 lineto 35 29 lineto 34 30 lineto
    34 32 lineto 33 31 lineto 32 28 lineto 30 25 lineto
    26 20 lineto 21 16 lineto
    closepath
  fill

  1 setgray
  % shaded white part of dress
  newpath
    32 20 moveto 38 24 lineto 38 25 lineto 35 28 lineto
    34 28 lineto 32 25 lineto
    closepath
  fill

  0 setgray
  %top
  newpath
    34 22 moveto 36 37 lineto 37 40 lineto 48 41 lineto
    40 42 lineto 46 42 lineto 49 43 lineto 51 43 lineto
    49 36 lineto 45 35 lineto 41 34 lineto 38 32 lineto
    45 35 moveto 45 33 lineto 41 26 lineto
    45 35 moveto 44 33 lineto 41 28 lineto
    41 32 moveto 28 29 lineto
  %left arm
    45 33 moveto 48 32 lineto 50 31 lineto 47 26 lineto
    46 27 lineto 42 28 lineto
  %left hand
    49.5 29.5 moveto 53 29 lineto 55 30 lineto 56 29 lineto
    55 27 lineto 53 28 lineto 50 27 lineto 48 27 lineto
  %foot 1
    48  9 moveto 47.5 7 lineto 48 6.5 lineto 50 7 lineto
    50  8 lineto
  %head
    39 41 moveto 38 46 lineto 39 47 lineto 40 48 lineto
    43 48 lineto 45 47 lineto 45 46 lineto 43 45 lineto
    44.5 45.5 moveto 44.5 44 lineto 44 42 lineto
  %right arm
    50 42 moveto 55 43 lineto
    49.5 39 moveto 52 40 lineto 56 41 lineto
  %foot 2
    19 13.5 moveto 16 13 lineto 16 8 lineto 17.5 7.5 lineto
    18 8 lineto 18 10 lineto 19 11.5 lineto 20.5 12 lineto
  stroke
```

Figure 10.15 (cont.)

```
}
def

/student
{
 %foot 1
 newpath
   56.5 49 moveto 56 50 lineto  55 51 lineto  51.5 51 lineto
   51.5 52 lineto 53 53 lineto  57 53 lineto  58 54 lineto
   58.5 53 lineto 58 51 lineto 60 49 lineto
 stroke

 %foot 2
 newpath
   76 55 moveto 76 58 lineto 75 61 lineto 78 60 lineto
   78.5 57 lineto 78 55 lineto 75 54 lineto
   closepath
 stroke

 %legs
 newpath
   59 33 moveto 58 36 lineto 55 42 lineto 52 47 lineto
   53 48 lineto 54 49 lineto 55 49 lineto 56.5 48.5 lineto
   58 49 lineto 59 49.5 lineto 60 47 lineto 61 46 lineto
   63 41 lineto 63 37 lineto

   62 43 moveto 65 41.5 lineto 63 38 lineto 68.5 42 lineto
   68.5 44 lineto 69 46 lineto 69 47 lineto 72 55 lineto
   75 53 lineto 78 53.5 lineto 77.5 50 lineto 77 46 lineto
   75.5 44 lineto 73 42 lineto 72 41 lineto

   75.5 44 moveto 75.5 40 lineto

 %arm
   59 33 moveto 60 33 lineto 64 30 lineto 66 30 lineto
   67 29.5 lineto 68 28 lineto 64 29 lineto 63 26 lineto
   62 28 lineto 61 28 lineto 59.5 27.5 lineto 60 29.5 lineto

 %hand
   59 33 moveto 55 32.5 lineto 51 32 lineto 50.5 33 lineto
   52 34.5 lineto 54 34 lineto 56 34.5 lineto 59 33 lineto

 %jacket  (top)
   68 28 moveto 68.5 32 lineto 68 33 lineto 66 36 lineto
   69.5 36 lineto 72 38 lineto 74 39 lineto 78 40 lineto
   78.5 39.5 lineto 77 35 lineto 76.5 33 lineto 76 30 lineto
   76.5 29 lineto 70 22.5 lineto 68 28 lineto 64 29 lineto
   66 26.5 lineto 70 26 lineto 73 26 lineto 75 27 lineto

 %head
   60 16.5 moveto 59 17 lineto 58.5 18 lineto 58 20 lineto
   59 21 lineto 60 21 lineto 60 21.5 lineto 62 23 lineto

 %jacket (bottom)
   64 29 moveto 63 25 lineto 62 23 lineto 62 20 lineto
   61.5 15 lineto 61 13 lineto 60 11 lineto

   62 20 moveto 60 16.5 lineto 58 12 lineto

   60 16.5 moveto 57 14 lineto 56 12 lineto 56.5 10 lineto
   59 9 lineto 62 10 lineto 65 12.5 lineto 68 15 lineto
   71 21 lineto

   70 18 moveto 73 21 lineto 74 24 lineto 75 27 lineto
```

Figure 10.15 (cont.)

```
 %hand
   56 11 moveto 54 12 lineto 53 10 lineto 52 9 lineto
   56.5 9.5 lineto
 stroke
} def

/titlefont {/Helvetica-Bold findfont }def
/sloganfont  {/Helvetica findfont }def


/aikidoframe
{
 gsave
   0.5 setgray
   2 setlinewidth
   newpath
     0 0 moveto
     90 0 lineto
     90 95 lineto
     0  95 lineto
     closepath
   stroke
 grestore
}def

/aikido
{
 gsave
   1 setlinejoin
   4.6 ins 6.1 ins translate
   2.6 2.6 5 3.6 div mul scale
   aikidoframe
   master
   student
   titlefont 8 scalefont setfont
   10 80 moveto (AIKIDO) show
   titlefont 4 scalefont setfont
   10 75 moveto (The ultimate in self defence) show
   sloganfont 4 scalefont setfont
   10 65 moveto (Mon-Fri 6-9pm) show
   10 60 moveto (14 Wash Street,) show
   10 55 moveto (London E1) show

 grestore
} def

aikido

%end of aikido ad
%*********************************************************
showpage
```

Figure 10.15 (cont.)

```
%start of book advert
gsave
72 72 scale    %change to inches
1.5 0.5 translate  %move origin

%draw bordered area
0.5 setgray
newpath
 0 0 moveto 5 0 lineto
 5 5 lineto 0 5 lineto
 closepath
fill

%set clipping region to capture head in the image
0 setgray
0.1 setlinewidth
newpath
  3.5 3 1 0 360 arc stroke
newpath
  3.5 3 1 0 360 arc clip

gsave %save current graphics state
5 5 scale      %make the image 6 inches by 6 inches


%generate image

/buffer 256 string def

256 256 8
[256 0 0 -256 0 256]
{currentfile buffer readhexstring pop}
image
f4ffffffecd7d9ddd8dee0ece7e3d8d0cbd3ffffffffffffffffffddbec0c9caccd2e0fffffffffffffffffff


grestore

%reinitialise clipping
initclip

1 setgray

/Times-BoldItalic findfont 0.25 scalefont setfont
0.25 4.5 moveto ("Better than South Pacific") show
0.2 4.2 moveto (Hendon Book Review) show

0.25 3.5 moveto ("The best book ever written") show
0.2 3.2 moveto (Barry Sheepdog) show

0.25 2.5 moveto ("Read this and live") show
0.2 2.2 moveto (Madeleine Spars) show

/Times-Bold findfont 0.4 scalefont setfont
0.5 1.7 moveto (Amazing! Sensational!) show

/Helvetica-Bold findfont 0.3 scalefont setfont
0.75 1.25 moveto (Report of the ISO Graphics) show
0.75 0.9  moveto (Language Committee 1985) show

/Helvetica findfont 0.2 scalefont setfont
2.0 0.6  moveto (by) show
```

Figure 10.16 PostScript program used to generate Figure 2.2. (Note that only one line of image data has been shown.)

```
/Helvetica-Bold findfont 0.25 scalefont setfont
1.25 0.25 moveto (Melanie L. Stannard) show

0 setgray
newpath
  0 0 moveto 5 0 lineto 5 5 lineto 0 5 lineto
  closepath
stroke

grestore

%end of book advert
%**********************************************************
%beds advert
/bedheader {/Courier-Bold findfont} def
/bedslogan {/Courier-Oblique findfont} def
/bedinformation {/Courier findfont} def


/bed
{
 gsave
   bedheader 9 scalefont setfont
   15 130 moveto (IRON BEDS) show
   bedslogan 7 scalefont setfont
   30 120 moveto (Just for you!) show

   /blob
   {/y exch def
    /x exch def
    newpath x y 1 0 360 arc fill
   } def

   bedinformation 2 scalefont setfont
   20 55  blob
   24 55 moveto (more comfortable than you can imagine) show
   20 45  blob
   24 45 moveto (cheaper than you ever thought possible) show
   20 35  blob
   24 35 moveto (guaranteed money back for every sleepless night) show

   bedheader 8 scalefont setfont
   25 23 moveto (BEDS GALORE) show
   bedheader 5
   25 15 moveto (48 Market St,)
   25 10 moveto (Ealing W12) show

   1 setlinecap  %rounded cap
   1 setlinejoin %rounded joins
   %top
   3 setlinewidth
   0.1 setgray
   newpath
     45 80 moveto 85 80 lineto 55 110 lineto 15 110 lineto
     closepath
   fill
   %frame
   0 setgray
   newpath
     45 80 moveto 45 75 lineto 85 75 lineto 85 80 lineto
     closepath
   stroke
```

Figure 10.16 (cont.)

```
  newpath
    45 80 moveto 15 110 lineto 15 105 lineto 45 75 lineto
    closepath
  stroke
  %legs
  0.5 setlinewidth
  newpath
    45 75 moveto 45 65 lineto 47.5 65 lineto 47.5 75 lineto
    45 65 moveto 41 68 lineto 41 78 lineto
    85 75 moveto 85 65 lineto 82.5 65 lineto 82.5 75 lineto
    82.5 65 moveto 79.5 69 lineto 79.5 75 lineto
    15 105 moveto 15 95 lineto 19 92 lineto 19 102 lineto
    19 92 moveto 21.5 92 lineto 21.5 99 lineto
  stroke

  %border
  newpath
    0.1 setgray
    [2] 1 setdash
    1 setlinewidth
    2 setlinejoin
    10 0 moveto 100 0 lineto 100 140 lineto 10 140 lineto
    closepath
  stroke

 grestore
} def

/ins {72 mul} def

1.5 ins 6.0 ins translate
2.5 2.5 scale
bed

showpage
```

Figure 10.16 (cont.)

SET GLOBAL TRANSFORMATION

SetGlobalTransformation(*matrix*)

allows the current GMT matrix to be replaced by the new *matrix*. This function inserts the corresponding element into the currently open structure.

TRANSLATE

Translate(*dx*, *dy*)

delivers a 3 by 3 transformation matrix corresponding to the specified translation.

SCALE

Scale(*sx*, *sy*)

delivers a 3 by 3 transformation matrix corresponding to the specified scaling.

ROTATE

Rotate(*angle*)

delivers a 3 by 3 transformation matrix corresponding to the rotation in radians, with positive *angle* meaning an anti-clockwise rotation.

The following functions are those used for handling structures.

OPEN STRUCTURE

OpenStructure(*structureID*)

opens the structure with the specified identifier. If this structure already exists, then it is re-opened, otherwise it is created.

CLOSE STRUCTURE

CloseStructure ()

closes the open structure.

EXECUTE STRUCTURE

ExecuteStructure(*structureID*)

inserts an 'execute structure' element into the currently open structure, at the current element pointer.

POST STRUCTURE

PostStructure(*wsid*, *structureID*, *priority*)

posts the structure referenced by *structureID* to the workstation with identifier *wsid*. The *priority* is a real number specifying priority in the same way as the GKS segment priority.

□□ EXAMPLE

Returning to the example of modelling a star out of triangles, the following program would accomplish this task:

Example 10.4 Describing a star – alternative version.

```
fun Triangle () =
  OpenStructure(TRIANGLE);
  let val t1  = Translate(−0.5, 0.0)
     and sc = Scale(1.0, 2.0)
     and t2 = Translate(0.0, 0.5)
```

```
  in
    SetLocalTransformation(t2, POSTCONCATENATE);
    SetLocalTransformation(sc, POSTCONCATENATE);
    SetLocalTransformation(t1, POSTCONCATENATE);
    Polyline[(0.0, 0.0), (1.0, 0.0), (0.5, 1.0), (0.0, 0.0)]
  ni;
  CloseStructure ()
nuf

fun Star () =
  OpenStructure(STAR);
  ExecuteStructure(TRIANGLE);
  let val r = Rotate(π/2.0)
  in
    for 0 ≤ i < 3 do
      SetLocalTransformation(r, PRECONCATENATE);
      ExecuteStructure(TRIANGLE)
    od
  ni;
  CloseStructure ();
nuf;
```

Open workstation with identifier wsid and set up viewing transforms and then.

```
Triangle ();
Star ();
PostStructure(wsid, STAR, 1.0);
```

The function *Triangle* creates a new structure with four elements – three to affect the transformations and one to generate an output primitive. The *Star* function creates a structure with seven elements and the network shown in Figure 10.17. Now, when the star structure is posted, its elements are traversed as follows:

(1) Its GMT is set to the identity matrix.

(2) The triangle structure is executed.

- The triangle structure inherits the identity GMT and has an identity LMT.
- The LMT is post-multiplied by *t*2, then *sc* and then by *t*1, and the result is the current CMT.
- This CMT is applied to the points in the polyline to transform them into the WC sequence [(−0.5, 0.5), (0.5, 0.5), (0.0, 2.5), (−0.5, 0.5)], and the polyline primitive is sent off down the viewing pipeline to the display.

(3) Traversal of the star structure continues with its CMT as the identity matrix.

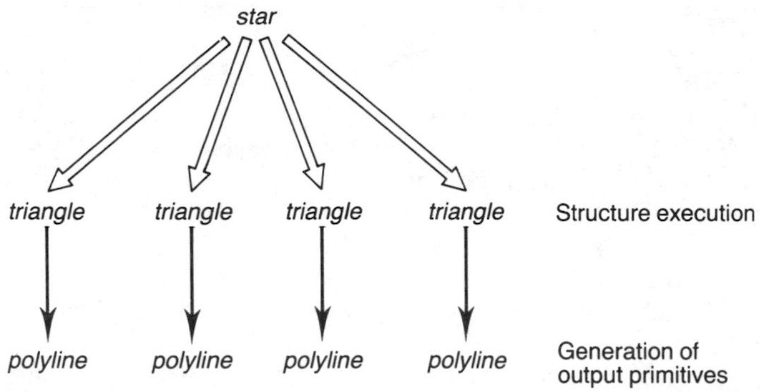

Figure 10.17
PHIGS star structure network.

(4) The LMT becomes the matrix corresponding to a positive rotation by one right-angle (say R).

(5) The CMT is formed (always by post-multiplication of the GMT by the LMT), but since the GMT is currently the identity, its new value becomes R.

(6) The triangle structure is executed.

- The triangle structure inherits the GTM with value R and has an identity LMT.
- The LMT is post-multiplied by $t2$, then sc and then by $t1$ to form the LMT ($t2*sc*t1$).
- The new CMT is then GMT*LMT = $R*t2*sc*t1$, which is then applied to polyline to form the WC sequence [(−0.5, −0.5), (−0.5, 0.5), (−2.5, 0.0), (−0.5, −0.5)]. This is used to generate the polyline output primitive.

(7) Traversal of the star structure continues with its CMT equal to the matrix R.

(8) Another 'set local transformation' element is encountered which now changes the CMT to be the square of matrix R representing a rotation of π radians. The triangle structure is executed again, this time with R^2 as its GMT.

The reader is invited to complete the discussion of this example (see Exercises 10.9 and 10.10).

Summary

This section has examined the ideas of graphics modelling; that is, the process of object description by means of the creation of hierarchies representing the relationships between objects and their components. The relationship is instantiated by transformations.

The functional paradigm was used to define the basic ideas involved with the clarity of expression that is available in applicative programming. The representation of these ideas was shown in two real systems – PostScript and PHIGS.

PostScript represents one of the most important and exciting developments in graphics for several years. It provides a dynamic language for the control of graphical output devices, in addition to very powerful functions for the generation of graphical output. It opens up the possibility of fully integrated interactive graphics systems with fast displays used for creating pictures interactively and hardcopy devices used for generating print quality displays. PostScript and GKS are compared in Chapter 12.

PHIGS is an ambitious proposal that attempts to integrate graphics modelling into large-scale traditional graphics package environments. It is difficult to judge the likely success of the system, or whether there is a real need for another graphics standard for applications programmers in the GKS style.

Exercises

10.1 List all the things that happen when the *Polyline* function in GKS is executed.

10.2 Assume that there is a function *DrawLine*($x1$, $y1$, $x2$, $y2$) which takes two points in DC and draws the line between them on the display. Show in detail how this could be used in an implementation of the *displayObj* function of Section 10.2.2.

10.3 A rather brute force definition of *star*1 was given in Example 10.1. Provide an alternative definition that uses recursion or iteration.

10.4 Show how the transformation functions defined in Section 10.2.2 could be used to define a function, which given a window and device coordinate viewport returns a function for mapping WC points to DC points.

10.5 Prove that the *petal* object and *flowerFunction* of Example 10.2 have unit square extents, as stated in the text.

10.6 (a) The function *trianglePlant* of Example 10.2 shows how to define a triangle of rows of plants starting upwards from a base of $2n$ plants. Each successive row has two plants less than the row below and is scaled vertically by a factor f, compared with the row below. Suppose the function t is defined as in the definition of *trianglePlant* and that $row(n)$ is abbreviated to $r(n)$. Show that the triangle of plants can be expressed as:

$$
\begin{aligned}
&r(n)++\\
&\quad t(1, f)\ r(n-1)++\\
&\quad\quad t(1+f, f^2)\ r(n-2)++\\
&\quad\quad \ldots\\
&\quad\quad t(1+f+f^2+\ldots+f^{m-1}, f^m)\ r(n-m)
\end{aligned}
$$

Hence, use this to derive the definition of the function *trianglePlant* as given in the text.

(b) Many of the functions given in the text, including *trianglePlant*, are not efficient even in functional programming terms (let alone in comparison with equivalent imperative definitions). For example, *trianglePlant* includes an evaluation of *row*, which is itself a recursive function whose evaluation should ideally be computed in the recursion of *trianglePlant* itself. Consider each of the functions defined in Example 10.2 and try to transform them into a more efficient form (although within the functional paradigm).

10.7 Experiment with different definitions of the basic petal shape, and the flower function and the stem with the aim of creating different types of flower and plant.

10.8 The *Star* function in Example 10.3 can also be used to define other pointed stars, as in Example 10.1. Write the functions to do this, as well as functions to draw constellations of stars. From your constellation functions, create a sky full of stars. Use the graphics modelling approach to do this – form a hierarchy with *sky* at the root and the different constellations as internal nodes, and so on. The leaves of the tree will be the basic triangle objects.

10.9 Carry through the complete execution of Example 10.4 and hence show that the correct four-pointed star is described.

10.10 Use the PHIGS functions, as given in the text, to describe the garden of Section 10.2.

10.11 PHIGS introduces the notions of separate local modelling transformations, global modelling transformations and composite modelling transformations. Carefully consider whether there are really three conceptually distinct transformations here, or whether PHIGS is just explaining something quite simple in an over-complex manner.

10.12 PostScript uses a so-called 'non-zero winding number rule' to determine whether a point is inside a closed polygon (or any closed path). This rule can be stated as follows. From any point, draw a line to infinity. Let x be the number of intersections of the line with the edges of the path crossing from left to right, and y with edges crossing the line from the right to left direction. If $x - y$ is 0, the point is outside, otherwise it is inside the path. Construct a fill area algorithm which uses this rule as the inside test.

CHAPTER 11

BITMAPPED GRAPHICS AND ITS APPLICATIONS

This chapter outlines the basic concepts involved in the Smalltalk-80 graphics model, although neither the Smalltalk-80 language nor the corresponding notation are used here. Applications of this approach are discussed in this chapter with implementations of some of the prompt and echo types of the GKS input devices discussed in Chapter 5.

11.1 Introduction

Smalltalk-80 is an object-oriented programming system (OOPS) that was defined over a ten-year period in a research project based at Xerox PARC (Goldberg and Robson, 1983). It is however well beyond the scope of this book to discuss object-oriented programming or the Smalltalk-80 language as such. Instead, the interest is focused on the computer graphics model employed within the language.

It is important to be aware of the impact that the Smalltalk-80 project is having on modern computing. This is not just in respect of the language and object-oriented programming, but also the computational environment it introduced, based on window managers, icons, mice and pop-up menus – sometimes known as WIMPs. This heralded the systems of the 1980s: powerful personal workstations with high-resolution bitmapped displays, running operating systems with a window manager-based user interface, with a mouse as the major interactive tool.

In such a system, the display is partitioned into a series of (possibly overlapping) stacked windows, each running a separate task (Hopgood *et al.*, 1985). For example, in one window an editor program might be executing, in another a program compilation, and another window might represent the display space of a GKS workstation. The user model is that of a desk top covered with sheets of paper and various tools. Perhaps the most popular example of such systems, which can trace their origin to the Smalltalk-80 project, is the Apple Macintosh. An example of a Smalltalk-80 display is shown in Figure 11.1.

11.2 Forms

A **form** is an object that has a *width*, a *height* and a *bitmap*:

type form = int*int*(int sequence store);

A bitmap is a finite sequence of 1s and 0s representing the pixel colours black and white, respectively. In the context of a form, the length of the sequence is width*height, and the width and height values structure the bitmap as a rectangular array. For example:

100010	*width* = 6
010100	*height* = 5
001000	*bitmap* = 100010010100001000010100100010
010100	
100010	

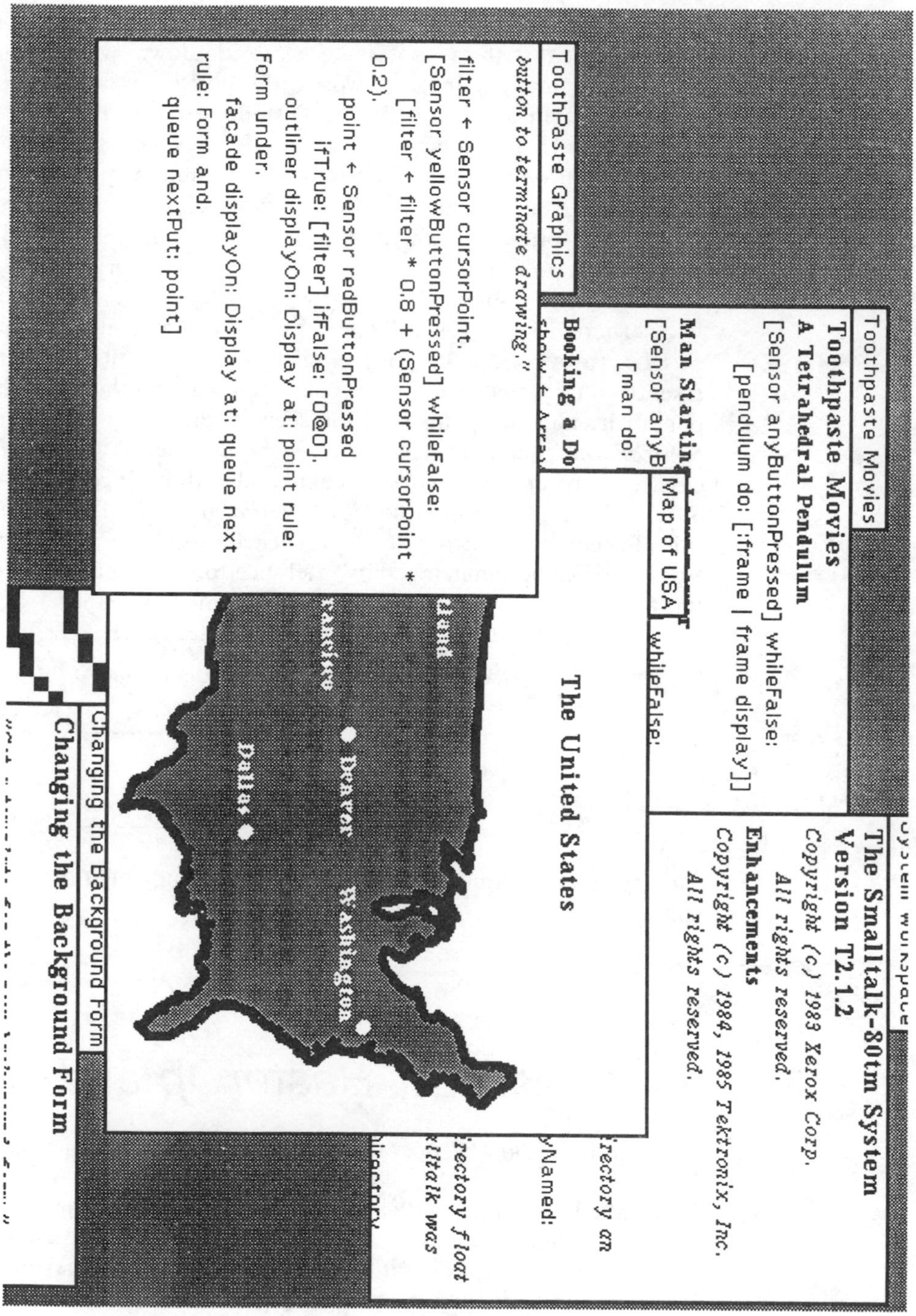

Figure 11.1
Smalltalk-80 display.

The origin of the form is taken as the top left-hand corner (starting at the first element in the bitmap). Positions within the form are denoted by (x, y) pairs, except that the y coordinate is 'upside down' when compared to the usual representation. In other words, the positive y direction is South.

Screen displays are obvious instances of forms, where the bitmap corresponds to the computer memory from which the screen display is refreshed. However, the notion of a form is quite general in the sense that there is no assumption that the form bitmap is in the screen refresh memory. It can and often is located in offscreen memory obtained during the execution of a program, in the same way that memory for any dynamically allocated data is obtained.

There is one general operation for manipulating forms known as *BitBLT* (pronounced bit blit), which stands for **bit block transfer**. The essential idea is that one form is combined with another in such a way as to potentially alter the bitmap of the second form. The two forms are called *SourceForm* (source form) and *DestForm* (destination form). In the simplest case, each pixel of *DestForm* is combined with each corresponding pixel in *SourceForm*, to produce the new *DestForm* pixel. There are 16 possible rules for combining two pixel values (each 0 or 1) to produce a new value. Each rule can be summarized by reference to the bit pattern *abcd* defined in the following table, where each of a, b, c and d is either 1 or 0:

Source	**Destination**	
	0	1
0	*a*	*b*
1	*c*	*d*

The rules are summarized in Table 11.1 and Figure 11.2 gives some examples.

11.3 *BitBLT*, *RasterOp* and Lines

In general, the *BitBLT* operation allows a subrectangle of *SourceForm* to be copied into a subrectangle of the same size in *DestForm*. In addition, a third form called *HalfTone* can be combined with the source in such a way as to produce a replicated pattern over the destination. The region of *DestForm* affected by the whole operation can be limited by a rectangular clip region. Parameters determining the *BitBLT* operation can therefore be defined as

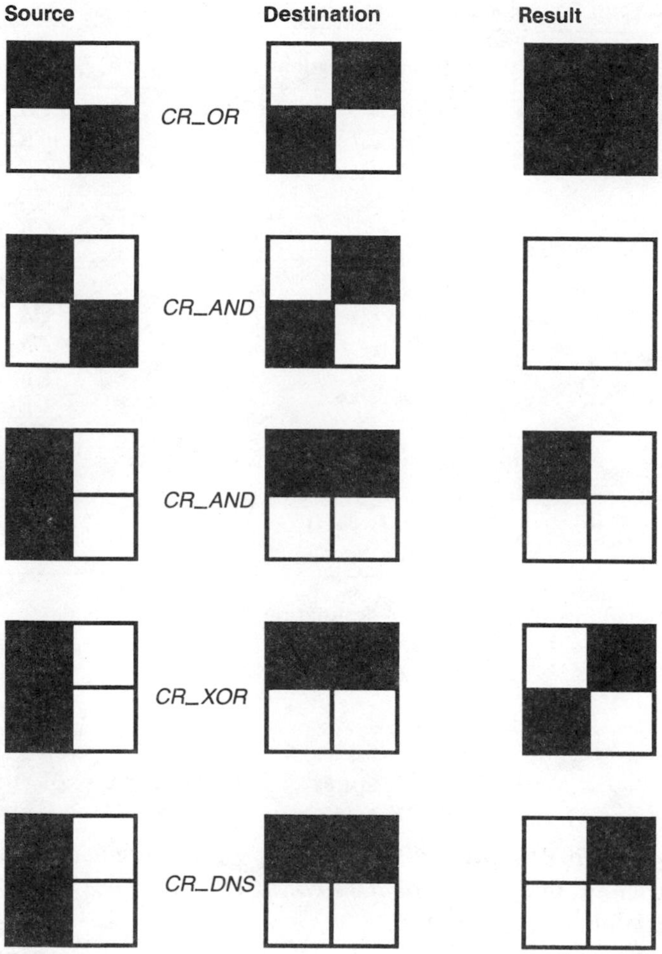

Figure 11.2
Examples of combination rules.

follows:

- Combination rule: one of the 16 Boolean operations defined in Table 11.1
- *SourceForm*: the form from which pixels are copied.
- *DestForm*: the form into which pixels are copied.
- *width*, *height*: the width and height of source and destination subrectangles.
- *DestX*, *DestY*: the upper left-hand corner of the destination subrectangle into which source pixels are copied.

Table 11.1 *BitBLT* combination rules.

Bit Pattern	Boolean Expression	Name of Operation
0000	$d := 0$	*CR_0*
0001	$d := s \wedge d$	*CR_AND*
0010	$d := s \wedge (\tilde{}d)$	*CR_SND*
0011	$d := s$	*CR_S*
0100	$d := (\tilde{}s) \wedge d$	*CR_DNS*
0101	$d := d$	*CR_D*
0110	$d := s \,\hat{}\, d$	*CR_XOR*
0111	$d := s \vee d$	*CR_OR*
1000	$d := \tilde{}\ (s \vee d)$	*CR_NOR*
1001	$d := \tilde{}\ (s \,\hat{}\, d)$	*CR_NXOR*
1010	$d := \tilde{}d$	*CR_ND*
1011	$d := \tilde{}\ ((\tilde{}s) \wedge d)$	*CR_NDNS*
1100	$d := \tilde{}s$	*CR_NS*
1101	$d := \tilde{}\ (s \wedge (\tilde{}d))$	*CR_NSND*
1110	$d := \tilde{}\ (s \wedge d)$	*CR_NAND*
1111	$d := 1$	*CR_1*

Notes: s and d are the source and destination bits. $\wedge$, $\tilde{}$, $\hat{}$ and $\vee$ are Boolean AND, NOT, XOR, OR operators, respectively.

- *SourceX*, *SourceY*: the upper left-hand corner of the source subrectangle from which pixels are copied.
- *ClipX*, *ClipY*, *ClipWidth*, *ClipHeight*: a rectangular clipping region restricting the region of *DestForm* that can be affected by the operation.
- *HalfTone*: a form that is replicated over the destination after combination with the source.

Table 11.2 and Figure 11.3 summarize the effect of these parameters.

A general way of combining the *HalfTone* and the *SourceForm* is to introduce a further combination rule parameter, which determines how the corresponding bitmaps are to be combined. Usually, the size of *HalfTone* (its width and height) is smaller than that of *SourceForm*, and in this case (which is the whole point) the *HalfTone* is replicated horizontally and vertically over the *SourceForm* as in a tiling effect. The resulting form is then combined with the *DestForm* according to the specification of the other parameters. In Smalltalk-80, however, the *HalfTone* combines with the *SourceForm* in a restricted manner. Let *nil* stand for an empty form and *f* for a defined form, then Table 11.3 summarizes the possibilities. (Note that the size of the *HalfTone* is restricted to 16 by 16 in Smalltalk-80.)

Table 11.2 *BitBLT* parameters.

Source Parameters	General Parameters	Destination Parameters
	combination rule	
SourceForm		*DestForm*
	width, *height*	
SourceX, *SourceY*		*DestX*, *DestY*
		ClipX, *ClipY*
		ClipWidth
		ClipHeight
HalfTone		

Another name for implementations of *BitBLT* is *RasterOp*, or raster operation (Newman and Sproull, 1979, pp. 262–266), and forms are called **rasters**. Different personal workstations offer differing versions of this function, and the reader is urged to consult the documentation of as many as possible, although they all embody the concepts just described. For purposes of exposition and simplicity, a *BitBLT* function is defined here which is a simplification of the full *BitBLT*.

11.3.1 Definition

type Position = int*int;

BitBLT: int*form*Position*(int*int)*form*Position*(int*int) → Void;
BitBLT(*Op*, *SourceForm*, *SourcePos*, *SourceSize*,
DestForm, *DestPos*, *DestSize*)

where *Op* is the combination rule, represented as the decimal integer corresponding to the bit pattern. It is assumed that the *CR_* constants are predefined with the appropriate values. *SourceForm* and *DestForm* are the source and destination forms; *SourcePos* and *DestPos* are the (x, y) positions within the respective forms; and *SourceSize* and *DestSize* are (*width*, *height*) values for selecting subrectangles of the forms.

Replication of a source form over the destination, achieving the effect of the Smalltalk *HalfTone*, can be achieved by prepending a 1 at the left-hand (most significant) end of the combination rule bit pattern. For example, the pattern corresponding to *CR_OR* is 0111. Therefore, the combination rule for replicating the source over the destination is 10111. This replication combination rule can be derived by simply ORing the number 16 into the ordinary rule.

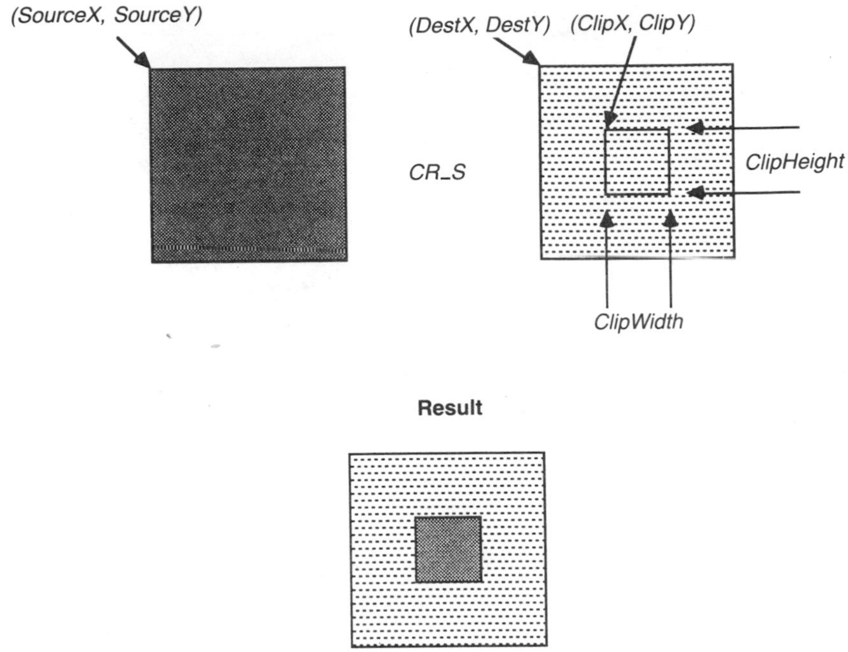

Figure 11.3
An example of *BitBLT/RasterOp*.

The convention adopted here is that if the *Pos* or *Size* arguments are given as _, then these are defaults specifying the whole form. In other words, if *SourcePos* = _, then the position in the source form is the origin, and if *SourceSize* = _, then the width and height are the same as the complete source form. *DestPos* and *DestSize* also act as the clipping region in the destination.

It is assumed that it is possible to mark a form of appropriate size as containing the bitmap from which the screen is to be refreshed. The variable corresponding to the screen form is denoted as *DisplayForm*. The function:

NewForm: int∗int → form;
NewForm(w, h)

delivers a new form with bitmap that is initially all 0s, and with width and height (w, h).

For example:

BitBLT(*CR_0*, *DisplayForm*, (0, 0), (200, 200)
DisplayForm, (0, 0), (200, 200))

will set a 200 by 200 rectangle at the top left-hand corner of the display to black. Here, *DisplayForm* is both the source and destination. Another

Table 11.3 Halftoning in Smalltalk-80.

SourceForm	*HalfTone*	**Result**
nil	*nil*	*DestForm* becomes black
f	*nil*	*HalfTone* ignored
nil	*f*	*HalfTone* tiled over *DestForm*
f	*f*	*HalfTone* is tiled over *SourceForm* using *CR_AND*, and the result is combined with *DestForm*

example shows a possible use of *NewForm*:

```
Obtain a new form called rectangle.
let val (w, h, bitmap) = NewForm(200, 200)
in
  for 0 ≤ i < w*h do
    bitmap[i] := if even(i) ⇒ 1 □ odd(i) ⇒ 0 fi
  od;
  BitBLT(CR_S, (w, h, bitmap), _, _,
                DisplayForm, (0, 0), (200, 200));
ni
```

Here, a new form is obtained; then, the corresponding bitmap is assigned alternate 1s and 0s, thus defining a halftone pattern. The form is then copied to the top left-hand corner of the display.

In real implementations, of course, the bitmap would be stored in a packed manner; for example, as a pointer to an array of bytes where each byte represents eight successive bits. The *BitBLT* is then a block (of bytes) transfer operation as the original name implies. (For discussions on the implementation of *BitBLT* see Newman and Sproull, 1979, and Bennet, 1985). When implemented realistically, the problem of the multiplicity of $w*h$ becomes important (as it might have to be a multiple of 8).

It is clearly tedious to have to always directly address the bitmaps of forms in order to write data into them. For simple patterns such as the halftone (alternative black and white) it is simplest and efficient to do so. But suppose that forms are used to store images created out of the usual graphics functions (lines, fill areas and so on). There is clearly no difference between drawing higher level graphical output primitives into forms or directly into the frame buffer, which in the present context is itself only another form that happens to have the property of being the refresh display buffer. Two parameters, naming the destination form and the combination rule, have to be added to the graphical output functions to achieve the required generalization. For example, the function:

LineToForm(*Op*, *pos*1, *pos*2, *DestForm*)

draws the line [*pos*1, *pos*2] into *DestForm*. (It is assumed that the line end-points are given in coordinates with the positive *y* axis pointing North.) The combination rule *Op* determines how pixels on the line are to be combined with the destination pixels.

In principle, *LineToForm* can be defined as follows:

```
LineToForm: int*Position*Position*form → Void;
fun LineToForm(Op, pos1, pos2, DestForm) =
  let val (w, h, bitmap) = DestForm
  in
    let val rectangle = NewForm(w, h);
    in
      Compute the bits in the bitmap of rectangle corresponding to the line using
      Bresenham's algorithm and set these to 1..., and then... .
      BitBLT(Op, rectangle, _, _,
                  DestForm, _, _);
    ni
  ni
nuf
```

In practice, of course, this is very inefficient, as it involves the time and space overheads of obtaining the new form rectangle, and then *BitBLT*ing this to the required destination. The appropriate bits corresponding to the line could be directly computed and set in *DestForm* without the need of an extra form. However, this example does illustrate the meaning of the combination rule in *LineToForm*.

The ideas presented here have many applications in interactive graphics, especially in regard to the implementation of styles of interaction (prompt and echo types) for the logical input devices. These are considered in later sections.

11.4 Rubber Band Techniques

Rubber band lines and rectangles were introduced as possible prompt and echo types for locator input in Chapter 5. Rubber banding techniques rely on the operation of repeatedly redrawing and deleting an object, and each time the object is redrawn it is modified according to a change in some external agency, such as the screen position of a cursor controlled by a mouse.

In GKS, the locator input device is first initialised (*InitialiseInput*) with an initial position. If a rubber band prompt and echo is selected, then this position is used as the anchor point of the rubber band line. This interaction is implemented in three distinct phases: initialisation, repetition and termination. The initialisation shows the current state of the logical input device – that is, it echoes the current position. Each redraw cycle in the repetition samples the current cursor position and if this is different from the previous position, then the current line is deleted and a new one drawn from the anchor point to the new current position. At the start of each of these redraw cycles, there is a test to see whether an interrupt has occurred. If it has, then the repetition sequence terminates. The termination phase deletes the last line drawn to ensure that at the end of the interaction the rubber band echo has disappeared. It is important to note that the rubber band line is *only* an echo representing the locator interaction, and in a system such as GKS its effect on the display is only transitory. There is a clear distinction between functions that generate graphical output, and those used for input. The rubber band line is, of course, concerned solely with input.

In this section, the following functions are assumed. First, the function:

SamplePos: state → Position;
SamplePos(..)

returns the current (DC) position of a cursor attached to an input device (a mouse is assumed as the most common). The function:

Line: int∗Position∗Position → Void;
Line(*Op*, *p*1, *p*2)

draws the line [*p*1, *p*2] on the display using *Op* as the combination rule. Hence:

fun *Line*(*Op*, *p*1, *p*2) = *LineToForm*(*Op*, *p*1, *p*2, *DisplayForm*) **nuf**

At this point, a definition of:

RubberLine: Position∗(state → boolean) → Position;
RubberLine(*initpos*, *interrupt*)

is required. *initpos* is the anchor point of the rubber band line. The function returns the point selected by the rubber band interaction. *interrupt* is a function argument such that *interrupt*(..) returns true if an interrupt of the required sort has occurred, otherwise false. For example:

fun *interrupt*(..) = *LeftMouseButtonPressed*(..) **nuf**

where *LeftMouseButtonPressed* is a system function that samples the current button state on the mouse, and returns true if and only if the left button is depressed.

The nature of the interrupt depends on the model of the interaction. The rubber band line might be thought of as being picked up by the operator, where the action of 'picking up' is represented by the operator pressing and holding down a mouse button. Correspondingly, the action of 'putting down' the line is represented by a release of the button. Here, the initial point might be selected by a button press requested prior to calling the rubber band function, then the rubber banding continues while the button is pressed, so that the interrupt terminating the process is a button release. Alternative models are possible and in use (see Exercises 11.3 and 11.4). Just as an interactive system must have at its core a consistent and simple user model, so must every representation of each individual interactive tool available within a graphics package.

The form of the rubber band function can be derived from the following argument relating to the repetition phase of the interaction:

At the start of each redraw cycle

- There is a local variable (*pos*) that holds the position of the cursor at the end of the previous redraw cycle.
- There is a visible line [*initpos*, *pos*].

Action within each redraw cycle

- If the interrupt returns true, then the cycle terminates.
- Sample the cursor position (*newpos*).
- If there has been no change in cursor position (*newpos* and *pos* hold the same position), then do nothing; otherwise delete the line [*initpos*, *pos*], draw the line [*initpos*, *newpos*] and set *pos* to hold the same position as *newpos*.

```
RubberBandLine: Position*Position*(state → boolean) → Position;
fun RubberBandLine(initpos, interrupt) =

  Initialisation.
  let val newpos = store initpos and pos = store initpos
  in
    Line(CR_XOR, initpos, pos);

    Repetition.
    do
      ~interrupt(..) ⇒ newpos := SamplePos(..);
                       if ?newpos ≠ ?pos ⇒
                         Line(CR_XOR, initpos, ?pos);
                         Line(CR_XOR, initpos, ?newpos);
                         pos := newpos;
                       fi
    od;
```

Termination.
Line(*CR_XOR*, *initpos*, *newpos*);

Return value.
?*newpos*
ni
nuf

The reader should prove here that:

(1) At the end of each cycle in the iteration there is a line connecting the initial position to the position of the cursor (as returned by *SamplePos*).
(2) The line is only redrawn when the cursor is moved.
(3) On completion of the function the screen is in the same state as immediately prior to the execution of this function.

(See Exercises 11.2 to 11.5 for a discussion of why *CR_XOR* is used as the combination rule and for suggestions for implementing other interactions using this method.)

11.5 Pop-Up Techniques

Possible styles of interaction for choice, valuator and string input involve the appearance on the screen of a rectangular display object on which the interaction is represented and echoed. Choice input can be represented as a pop-up menu as shown in Figure 5.7; valuator as a pop-up dial or scale as shown in Figure 5.4; and string as a pop-up dialogue as shown in Figure 5.6. These pop-up styles follow the same pattern:

(1) An initialisation phase where a rectangular area of the display is replaced by the echo box showing the initial state of the logical input device. This initialisation is heralded by the sudden 'popping up' of the echo box (menu, scale or dialogue box) on the display.
(2) A repetition phase where the physical input device (mouse or keyboard) is used to effect potential state changes. This phase is terminated by an interrupt.
(3) A termination phase where the echo box disappears and the screen is left in its original state. What was 'underneath' the echo box is fully and (ideally) instantaneously restored, as if a piece of paper had been removed from a desk top making visible the part of the desk top formerly obscured.

The following generic pop-up function can be used for this type of interaction.

The implementation of the initialisation phase involves determining the size and position of the echo box on the screen. For a pop-up menu, the size is determined by the number of prompt strings, the length of the longest string, and the character heights and widths. The position of the menu depends on its style. Usually, a pop-up menu 'pops up' near the current cursor position (subject to any restrictions imposed by the echo area). Hence, the part of the function that computes the region of the screen to be affected must sample the current cursor position, as well as determining the size of the menu box. The details of this calculation can have important consequences for the interaction. For example, suppose *pos* is the current cursor position. What relationship should *pos* have to the position of the menu box on the display? (This is discussed in Exercise 11.6.) Here then is the function:

```
PopUpInteraction: α * (state → boolean) → α    α is the relevant type.
fun PopUpInteraction(initvalue, interrupt) =

  Initialisation.
  Compute the region of display to be affected, where (x, y) is the top left-hand
  corner.
  let val (x, y, width, height) =  Depends on the input device.
      and returnvalue = store initvalue
  in
    Save this region in a background form.
    let val Background = NewForm(width, height)
    And obtain an offscreen form for the echo.
       and EchoBox = NewForm(width, height)
    in
      BitBLT(CR_S, DisplayForm, (x, y), (width, height),
                Background, _, _);
      Write a representation of the initial state of the logical input device into the
      echo box.
      Initialise(initvalue, EchoBox);
      Copy to the screen.
      BitBLT(CR_S, EchoBox, _, _, DisplayForm, (x, y), (width, height))

      Repetition.
      do
        ~interrupt(..) ⇒  Depends on the logical input device.
                          Computes return value.
      od;

      Termination.
      Restore the display.
      BitBLT(CR_S, Background, _, _, DisplayForm, (x, y), (width,
                height))
```

```
            Tidy up by deleting obtained forms.
            DisposeForm(Background);
            DisposeForm(EchoBox)
        ni

        Return value.
        ?returnvalue
    ni
nuf
```

After the size and position of the menu, or generally the echo box, has been determined, the function saves the screen image corresponding to that region in a background form. This will be used in the termination phase to restore the screen.

A second offscreen form (*EchoBox*) is then obtained and the representation determined by the initial input data, and the logical input device is drawn into this form. In the case of choice input, at least the actual menu strings are drawn into this offscreen form and the initial choice highlighted. In the case of valuator input, the scale, the minimum and maximum values, and the initial value are drawn while for string input, the initial string and string cursor are drawn. Once complete, this echo box is copied to the screen.

The repetition phase continues until the interrupt occurs. In the case of the pop-up menu, the cursor is moved over the menu strings, highlighting them in turn, with the highlighted string representing the choice that would be made if the interrupt were triggered at that moment. If the cursor is outside of the menu box, then no string should be highlighted indicating that NOCHOICE would be returned in the event of the interrupt occurring at that moment. (Note that when the menu first pops up on the screen, the initial choice should be highlighted, and therefore the echo box should be positioned such that the cursor is correctly pointing at this initial choice – otherwise the model would be inconsistent.)

With valuator input, it is important that the current value be continually displayed, and that there is some clear and obvious way of predicting the NOVALUE state.

String input requires the implementation of a string cursor, to show where the next character would appear if typed. Use of the backspace key should move this string cursor backwards by one character width and rubout the character at that position. This simple line editing facility is crucial to allow the operator to correct typing mistakes. The usual interrupt in the case of string input implemented in this way would be caused by striking the RETURN key (see Exercise 11.9 for a discussion of string input).

At the end of the repetition phase, the original screen state is restored by copying *Background* to the correct position. At this moment, at the completion of the interaction, the screen is in the same state as it was before the interaction commenced (however, see Exercise 11.10 for a further discussion of this point). Finally, the memory corresponding to *Background* and *EchoBox* is released (*DisposeForm*), since these no longer serve any purpose.

The implementation of the repetition phase itself (which is where the interaction actually takes place) involves further use of the *BitBLT* function. For example, highlighting of menu strings is achieved by using the *CR_ND* (1010) combination rule, where the source and destination forms correspond to the rectangle within the menu box enclosing the string. Similar considerations apply to valuator and string input.

11.6 Raster-Generated Text

The implementation of a pop-up menu, valuator or dialogue box clearly requires the ability to write characters into forms – a special case of this being the requirement to write characters to the display. Therefore a function such as:

TextToForm(*Op*, *position*, *string*, *form*)

is needed, which writes the text *string* into the given *form* at the *position* using the *Op* combination rule. The ideas of form and the *BitBLT* function allow a compact way of storing text for writing to any form.

The first and most difficult task in generating text is the design of a font. Each character in the font can itself be represented as a form. For simplicity, suppose that it is a fixed size font, where each character form has the same width and height, say 8 pixels wide by 12 pixels high. Thus, each character in the font must be converted into a bitmap.

But a separate form for each character is not necessary. A more economical representation stores the whole font in a single form. The characters are ordered in some convenient manner, usually as defined in the ASCII character set, which has 96 printable characters. Thus, a form of size $16*w$ by $6*h$, for example, is constructed, where w and h are the width and height of the character boxes, containing all of the characters (see Figure 11.4).

The font form therefore has as its bitmap the representation of all the characters in the font. To obtain any particular character, only the offset (the (x, y) position) of the top left-hand corner of the character box needs to be known. This suggests the following definition of a font data structure:

```
type FontData = int*int*form*(Position sequence);
```

	!	"	£	$	%	&	'	(	)	*	+	,	-	.	/
0	1	2	3	4	5	6	7	8	9	:	;	<	=	>	?
@	A	B	C	D	E	F	G	H	I	J	K	L	M	N	O
P	Q	R	S	T	U	V	W	X	Y	Z	[	\	]	^	—
	a	b	c	d	e	f	g	h	i	j	k	l	m	n	o
p	q	r	s	t	u	v	w	x	y	z	{	|	}	-	

Figure 11.4
Example of a 16*w by 6*h font form stored in ASCII order.

For example:

FontData = (*charwidth*, *charheight*, *FontForm*, *offset*)

charwidth and *charheight* are the width and height of the characters in the font. *offset* is a sequence indexed by the characters, giving the (x, y) position of the corresponding character. For example, suppose *Ord* is a function that delivers the position in the sequence corresponding to any character; then, *offset*[*Ord*(*c*)] is the offset corresponding to character *c*.

Let *CharToForm*(*Op*, *pos*, *ch*, *CurrentFont*, *DestForm*) be a function call that writes the character *ch* at position *pos* into *DestForm* using the *Op* combination rule. Suppose that *CurrentFont* contains the font data to be used. Then, *CharToForm* can be defined as follows:

```
CharToForm: int*Position*char*FontData*form → Void;
fun CharToForm(Op, pos, ch, CurrentFont, DestForm) =
  let val (w, h, fontform, offset) = CurrentFont
  in
    BitBLT(Op, fontform, offset[Ord(ch)], (w, h), DestForm, pos, (w, h))
  ni
nuf
```

A *TextToForm* function could be defined in terms of successive calls to *CharToForm* for each character in the text string. These ideas are not meant to represent the most efficient means of displaying text, but are further illustrations of *BitBLT* (see Exercises 11.11 and 11.12 for a discussion of these functions).

A remaining question concerns how the font data is to be stored. A simple solution is to create files, one for each available font, consisting of the information stored in the *FontData* objects: the width, height, font form and offset sequence. There must also be a *ReadFontFile* function that takes as its argument the name of the font file to be read and returns a corresponding *FontData* value.

11.7 Filling and Clipping

In Section 4.7, a polygon fill algorithm was defined which produces a solid colour fill in the boundary determined by a polygon. Exercise 4.17 suggested that a hatch fill can be generated by a simple change to the algorithm.

Suppose horizontal hatch lines vertically spaced at k pixels apart are required. Then the main iteration of the algorithm would become:

> **for** $ymin \leqslant i \leqslant ymax$ **do**
> $AET := sort(Update(i, AET) \ @ \ ET[i])$;
>   **if** $i \ mod \ k = 0 \Rightarrow JoinLines(i, AET)$ **fi**
> **od**

and the hatch lines would only be drawn when $i \ mod \ k = 0$. For example, when $k = 2$ every alternate hatch line would be drawn. Vertical hatch lines can be generated by reversing the role of x and y in the algorithm.

However, *BitBLT* provides the opportunity for a general approach to hatch and pattern fills based on the polygon fill algorithm. Consider the problem of generating a polygon fill with hatch lines at angle a to the horizontal, as shown in Figure 11.5. One way to accomplish this without using *BitBLT* would be to rotate the polygon vertices by $(-a)$, scan convert the rotated polygon, and when applying the *JoinLines* function rotate the point pairs back through $+a$ prior to actually drawing the lines. There are two disadvantages to this approach. First, the floating-point calculations involved in the rotations decrease the speed and introduce possible floating-point errors. Second, although the polygon would usually be clipped prior (or during) scan conversion, so that the y values of its vertices would always lie within the range of valid indices of the edge table ET, the rotated polygon may not be wholly within the clip region. The dimension of ET would have to be extended to allow for this.

Producing a polygon fill with slanted hatch lines is only one possible extension. GKS, for example, allows for a pattern fill. A pattern is specified as a rectangular array of colours, in a way similar to a cell array. This pattern is then replicated throughout the inside of the polygon. Clearly, it would be quite difficult to generate such an interior style by conventional means.

Consider first the problem of generating a hatch fill with arbitrary sloped lines. This can be easily achieved. When making the edge table ET determine the minimum and maximum x and y vertex values. These values then provide the rectangular extent of the polygon. Suppose this has width w and height h. The next step is to obtain an offscreen form (*Background*) of size w by h and draw the solid polygon into *Background* using the original algorithm. Having done this, another offscreen form (*HatchForm*) of the same size is needed, in which the slanted hatch lines are drawn. Next,

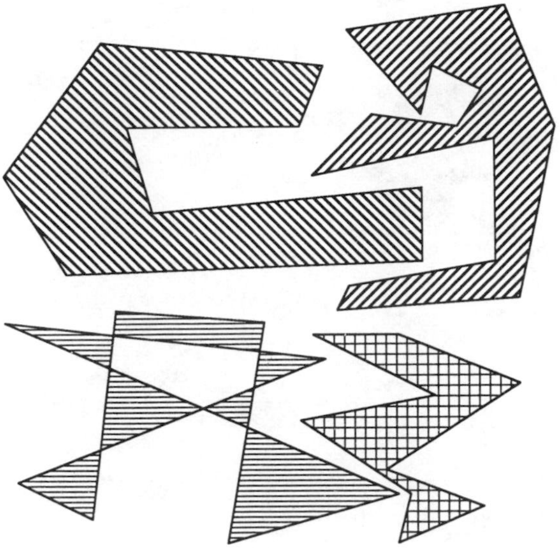

Figure 11.5
Examples of a hatch fill.

Background (destination) is combined with *HatchForm* (source) using the *CR_AND* combination rule. The *Background* will now contain the polygon fill, where the interior style is the slanted hatch lines. The final step is to copy the *Background* form to the screen, which involves a further *BitBLT* with *Background* as source and *DisplayForm* as destination. This is shown in Figure 11.6.

The combination rule would clearly be *CR_OR*, provided that the fill area colour is supposed to be black, and assuming as usual a black and white display (see Exercise 11.13). Suppose the fill area is to be in white (in GKS, the fill area colour index is 0). In such a case, the combination rule must be such that all black pixels in the source combine with the destination to form white, whereas all white pixels in the source combine with destination pixels so as to leave the destination pixels unchanged. The combination rule bit pattern is therefore 0100, which is the rule *CR_DNS* (destination and not source).

Pattern fill can be achieved in a similar manner. Suppose *PatternForm* is a form containing the appropriate bitmap representing the pattern. (In GKS, the pattern is defined using the function *SetPatternRepresentation*.) As before, a *Background* form is obtained and the solid polygon drawn into this. The *PatternForm* is then *BitBLT*ed into *Background* using the *CR_AND* combination rule ORed with the number 16, to obtain the required replication effect (or however replication is to be achieved on the system in use). The final step is to copy *Background* to *DisplayForm* (see Exercise 11.14).

There is a close relationship between area filling and clipping objects

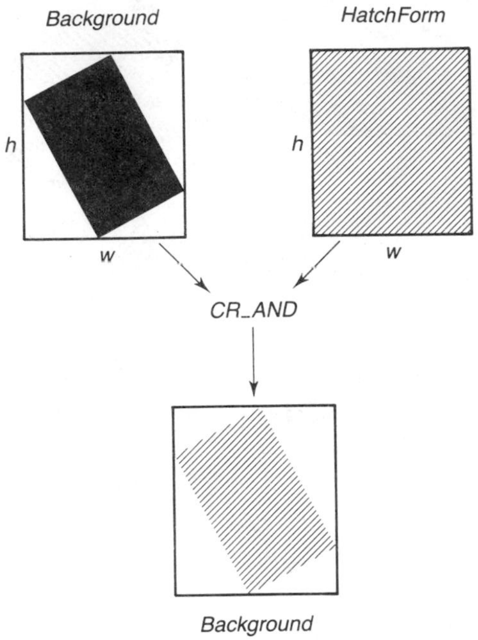

Figure 11.6
Hatch fill area generated using two forms.

to arbitrary polygons. Recall that the PostScript system allows graphical output to be clipped to any path (although the default inside test is different to that in GKS). There are algorithms for clipping objects against arbitrary polygons (Pavlidis, 1982, Chapter 15), but a discussion of these is beyond the scope of this book. The required effect can also be achieved by employing the ideas relating to polygon fills. Suppose graphical output is to be clipped to an arbitrary polygon. As before, the filled polygon is drawn into an offscreen form (*ClipForm*). However, before painting the graphical output on to the display, it is drawn into an offscreen form (*PaintForm*) of the same size as *ClipForm*. A *BitBLT* of *PaintForm* to *ClipForm* (using *CR_AND*) will then produce the required clipping effect. (Note that PostScript does *not* achieve its clipping by this method.)

11.8 Simple Interactive Curve Drawing

Consider the curves of Figure 11.7 generated by the listed PostScript program. PostScript includes the ability to describe curves based on the so-called **Bezier** form, discussed later in this section. PostScript provides the

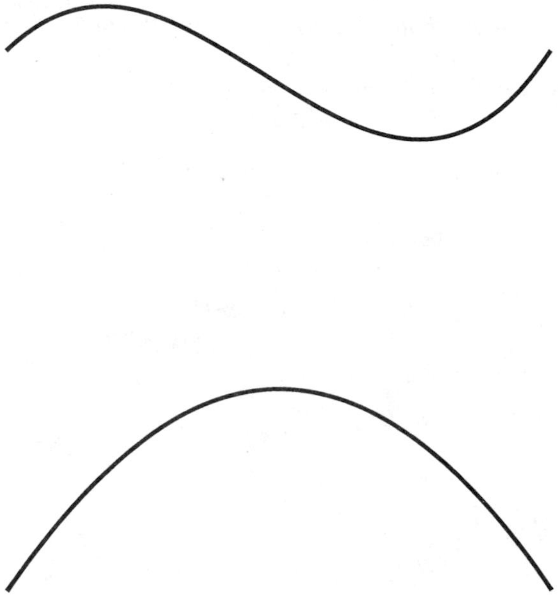

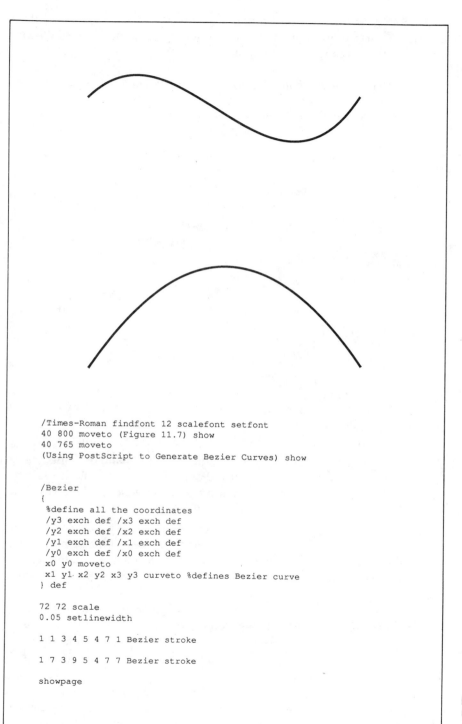

```
/Times-Roman findfont 12 scalefont setfont
40 800 moveto (Figure 11.7) show
40 765 moveto
(Using PostScript to Generate Bezier Curves) show


/Bezier
{
 %define all the coordinates
 /y3 exch def /x3 exch def
 /y2 exch def /x2 exch def
 /y1 exch def /x1 exch def
 /y0 exch def /x0 exch def
 x0 y0 moveto
 x1 y1 x2 y2 x3 y3 curveto %defines Bezier curve
} def

72 72 scale
0.05 setlinewidth

1 1 3 4 5 4 7 1 Bezier stroke

1 7 3 9 5 4 7 7 Bezier stroke

showpage
```

Figure 11.7
Using PostScript to generate Bezier curves.

means for static picture description, but Bezier curves are particularly suitable for curve drawing in an interactive setting. One method for allowing interactive curve drawing is illustrated in the following program:

```
FreeHandCurve: Position*(state → boolean) → Position;
fun FreeHandCurve(initpos, interrupt) =
  let val p0 = store initpos and p1 = store initpos
  in
    do
      ~interrupt(..) ⇒ p1 := SamplePos(..);
                        if ?p1 ≠ ?p0 ⇒
                          Line(CR_OR, ?p0, ?p1);
                          p0 := p1
                        fi
    od;
    ?p1
  ni
nuf
```

As the cursor is moved across the screen, the lines are joined between successively sampled points. This is equivalent to free-hand drawing with a pen on a piece of paper. For some purposes, this method might be satisfactory, however there are disadvantages:

(1) It is very difficult to produce a smooth-looking curve in this way because of the jerkiness of hand movements exaggerated by the use of the mouse. This could be overcome by embedding the free-hand drawing in an algorithm that smooths the sampled points.

(2) It is difficult to modify a curve produced by free-hand drawing, except by deleting parts and redrawing them. Since there is no underlying representation of the curve, modifying the curve as a whole (to make it slightly shorter or more curved) would not be possible.

(3) The problem of modification is highlighted bearing in mind that the curves may need to be stored in segments or files. If the sample rate is in the order of 60 sampled points per second, then 300 points will be returned in five seconds. This is clearly an unsatisfactory way of generating a curve – *too much* information is supplied – especially since better results can be achieved with very few points and an underlying mathematical representation.

A method often employed in CAD is to allow the operator of an interactive program to select a small number of **control points**, which determine the shape of the curve according to a mathematical formula. The advantage of this method is that there is a precise and predictable relationship between the control points and the shape of the curve. If the

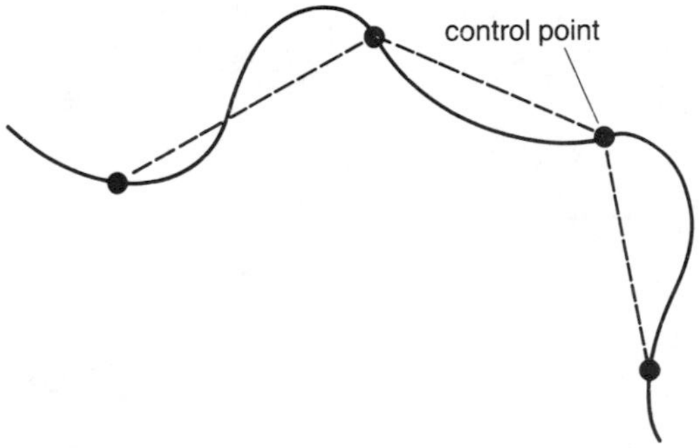

Figure 11.8
Variation increasing curves. The fitted curve has more turning points than the polyline joining the control points.

position of one of the control points is changed, then the curve is changed in a predictable way. Also, the generated curves are smooth (up to the display resolution).

Let $p_0, p_1, \ldots, p_m$ be a set of $m + 1$ control points. Furthermore, let $P(t)$ be a vector function of t where:

$$P(t) = (x(t), y(t)) = \sum_{i=0}^{m} p_i \, B_{k,i}(t) \qquad (0 \leq t \leq 1 \text{ and } k \leq m)$$

where $B_{k,i}(t)$ are polynomials in t of degree at most $m-1$. Hence, the $B_{k,i}$ are of the form:

$$B_{k,i}(t) = a_{i0} + a_{i1}t + a_{i2}t^2 + \ldots + a_{ik}t^k \qquad (k \leq m)$$

These $B_{k,i}$ polynomials are called **basis** functions, and it is the properties of these that determine the properties of $P(t)$.

Usually, it is required that:

$$B_{k,i}(t) \geq 0 \qquad (\text{all } 0 \leq t \leq 1)$$

$$\sum_{i=0}^{m} B_{k,i}(t) = 1 \qquad (\text{all } 0 \leq t \leq 1)$$

If the first property is violated, then the generated curve may be **variation increasing**, which means that the number of turning points in $P(t)$ could exceed the number of vertices in the polygon formed by the p_i (see Figure 11.8). The second property ensures axis independence (see Exercise 11.18). The second property in addition to the first ensures that the generated curve lies within the *convex hull* formed by the control points (see Figure 11.9). This property is desirable because it guarantees that the curve will always be closely controlled by the control points.

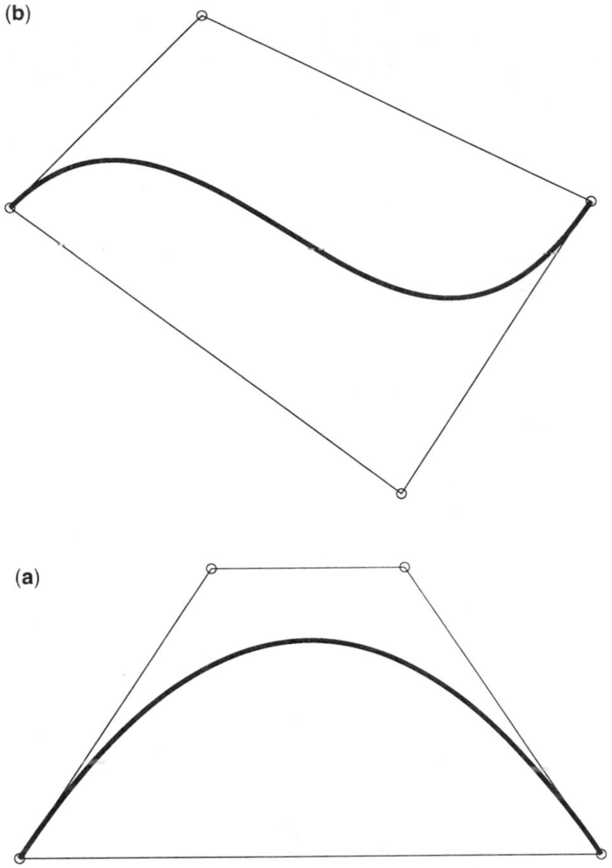

Figure 11.9
Bezier curves lie within the convex hull of the control points.

There are many different possible choices for $B_{k,i}$ satisfying both of these properties. A popular form is to choose these as **Bernstein polynomials**, resulting in $P(t)$ generating a Bezier curve. (A full mathematical treatment is given in Bezier, 1986.) The Bernstein polynomial is defined as:

$$B_{k,i}(t) = \binom{k}{i} t^i (1 - t)^{k-i}$$

where:

$$\binom{k}{i} = \frac{k!}{i!\,(k - i)!} = \frac{k(k - 1) \ldots (k - i + 1)}{i!} \qquad (k = m)$$

Using this definition for $B_{k,i}$, it is easy to show that:

$$P(0) = p_0 \quad \text{and} \quad P(1) = p_m$$

so that the curve starts at the first control point and ends at the last. In general, it will not actually pass through any other control point.

By differentiating $P(t)$ with respect to t:

$$P'(t) = (x'(t), y'(t))$$

and setting $t = 0$ and $t = 1$ it is easy to verify that the lines $[p_0, p_1]$ and $[p_{m-1}, p_m]$ (the line joining the first two control points and the line joining the last two control points) are tangents to the curve at the curve's start and end. Then, by the requirement $B_{k,i}(t) > 0$, everywhere else in the curve is within the convex hull of the control points (see Figure 11.9)

Consider the case $m = 3$, to give cubic Bezier curves. Here:

$$P(t) = p_0(1 - t)^3 + p_1 3t(1 - t)^2 + p_2 3t^2(1 - t) + p_3 t^3$$

This can be rearranged as:

$$\begin{aligned} P(t) = {} & t^3[-p_0 + 3p_1 - 3p_2 + p_3] \\ & + t^2[3p_0 - 6p_1 + 3p_2] \\ & + t\,[-3p_0 + 3p_1] \\ & + p_0 \end{aligned}$$

in a form suitable for implementation.

Horner's method for evaluating a polynomial can be defined as:

```
Poly: int*(real sequence), real → real;
fun Poly(m, a, t) =
  let val c = store a[m]
  in
    for 0 ≤ i ≤ m − 1 do
      let val j = m − 1 − i in c := c*t + a[j] ni
    od;
    ?c
  ni
nuf
```

For example, in the case of a cubic:

$$a_0 + a_1 t + a_2 t^2 + a_3 t^3 = ((a_3 t + a_2)t + a_1)t + a_0$$

To generate the curve, the coefficients a for the x and y components of the control points are evaluated. Then for increasing values of t:

$$0 = t_0 < t_1 < t_2 < \ldots < t_N = 1$$

$P(t)$ is evaluated and the straight lines $[P(t_{i-1}), P(t_i)]$ drawn. Although the number of values of t chosen will determine the smoothness of the curve's appearance, it is inversely related to the computation time needed. The limits are the display resolution and the speed needed for interactive modification. (See Exercise 11.19 for a more efficient method of evaluating a polynomial. Chapter 13 discusses an elegant and efficient method that does not require the actual evaluation of the formula.)

An interactive framework for the generation of such curves can be constructed from the following considerations. The operator selects control points and these are marked, for example, by small circles – the method of selection could be by a *RequestLocator* function. This sequence of point selections is ended by a suitable break action upon which the initial Bezier curve is displayed. This ends the initialisation phase.

The repetition phase consists of the operator 'picking up', moving and 'putting down' the control points. For example, the cursor is moved to a control point and a mouse button is depressed. While the button is held down, the control point follows the cursor movements and the Bezier curve is redrawn in accordance with the new position of the control point. This can be achieved by methods similar to the rubber banding technique discussed earlier. When the button is released (the control point is 'put down'), the point is released from the cursor. The operator is then free to select another control point or trigger the break action, which ends the repetition phase.

The termination phase requires deletion of the control point markers and, depending on the context, possibly painting in the Bezier curve using the *CR_OR* combination rule (to remove gaps resulting from intersections of the curve with itself or other graphics on the display). An alternative, more complex framework for interaction is discussed in Exercise 11.20.

It is possible to achieve the real-time interaction just described, certainly in the case of cubic Bezier curves, even on some home microcomputers. Higher order Bezier curves, of course, take longer to generate, and the same speed cannot be achieved. It should be noted that these curves do not possess a local control property – a change of *one* of the control points requires the *whole* curve to be recomputed and displayed. There are other basis functions (the Cubic B-Spline) that allow local modification, where a change of the position of one control point only requires a partial curve redraw (see Foley and Van Dam, 1982, pp. 514–523 for a more extensive, but still mathematically simple discussion of curves).

A kind of local control can be introduced even using Bezier curves. Suppose only cubic curves are catered for, but yet more complex shapes are required, more complex than is possible with single cubics (a cubic polynomial has at most two turning points). The more complex shapes can

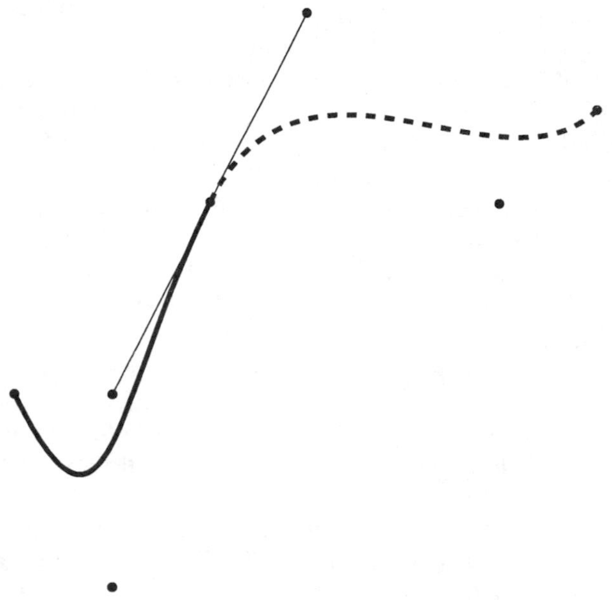

Figure 11.10 Joining Bezier curves with continuity of slope.

be formed by the piecewise joining of several cubic curves. Smoothness at the joins can be achieved, to a certain degree, by making use of the tangent property. Suppose *C*0 and *C*1 are two curves where the end of *C*0 is joined to the beginning of *C*1. In general, there will be a discontinuity of slope at the join. However, provided that the slope of the line joining the last two control points of *C*0 is the same as that of the line joining the first two control points of *C*1, there will be continuity of slope at the join (see Exercise 11.21). This is shown in Figure 11.10.

11.9 Raster Control Functions in the Computer Graphics Interface

The reader will have noticed that the techniques described in this chapter are not directly available within GKS. For example, there is no *BitBLT* function in GKS, nor can the primitives be drawn to offscreen forms. (This is discussed further in Chapter 12.) There is, however, another graphics standard at the stage of a working draft called the **Computer Graphics Interface** (**CGI**) (ISO, 1986a). This is concerned with "*Interfacing techniques for dialogues with graphical devices. . .*" and "*describes the interface between device-independent and device-dependent parts of a graphics system... .*" In other words, this proposed standard is for systems programmers rather than applications programmers, and is something that device manufacturers and systems implementors may use. In the most recent version of the working draft, Part 6 is devoted to bitmapped graphics, and the techniques described in this chapter can be easily implemented in terms of the CGI functions. A systems description of the CGI is given in Section 16.5.1.

The rest of this section is devoted to a description of the **raster control functions** in the proposed CGI. It should be noted that following the tradition of GKS, the CGI is very much state driven. For example, instead of the combination rule being a parameter of the CGI equivalent to *BitBLT*, it is set in a separate function, and the combination rule argument is then stored in a state list as an entry called **drawing mode**, which is used for subsequent graphical output. The functions listed here are represented as *functions*; that is, with a computed return value, whereas in line with GKS return values in the CGI working draft are represented as output parameters.

The CGI uses the notion of bitmaps, which are the same as forms as described earlier in this chapter, and the idea of special displayable bitmaps, which can be viewed by the user. There is one displayable bitmap corresponding directly to the memory from which the display is refreshed (the frame buffer). Bitmaps have names, and this displayable bitmap has name *bitmap* 0. The bitmaps named *bitmap* 1 through to *bitmap N*, where *N* is a fixed implementation-defined number (stored in the raster description table), are the displayable bitmaps, which may be of varying sizes. These might be very useful in the implementation of a window manager display, for example. Those with names higher than *bitmap N* are user-defined offscreen bitmaps and cannot be directly viewed (although their contents may be viewed by copying them to a displayable bitmap).

11.9.1 Creating an Offscreen Bitmap

An offscreen bitmap may be obtained by use of the *CreateBitmap* function:

CreateBitmap: VDCPoint∗VDCPoint∗BitmapType → BitmapName;

This requires two points in virtual device coordinates (VDC) space specifying the bitmap extent. VDC space is defined in the CGI as "*A two-dimensional, Cartesian coordinate space of infinite precision and extent. Only a subset of VDC space… is realizable in a CGI… .*" This subset of the space is known as the **VDC range**, which represents the coordinates actually representable in the particular instance of the CGI on a given graphics device. Note that unlike the manner in which bitmaps are addressed on most devices, CGI bitmaps have the normal coordinate axis representation, with the positive *y* axis pointing North.

The *BitmapType* is one of two values: MAPPED or FULL_DEPTH. MAPPED means that pixels in the bitmap are two valued, whereas FULL_DEPTH bitmaps have the same number of bits per pixel as the displayable bitmap (corresponding to the screen). This difference is only important for full-colour displays.

For example:

b := *CreateBitmap*((0, 0), (100, 100), MAPPED);

creates *b* as the name of a bitmap with the given extent and type.

11.9.2 Deleting a Bitmap

DeleteBitmap(*b*) frees the space occupied by the bitmap *b* allocated by *CreateBitmap*.

11.9.3 Displaying a Bitmap

The *DisplayBitmap* function allows the user to display one of the displayable bitmaps.

11.9.4 Selecting the Destination Bitmap

The function *SelectDrawingBitmap* selects the bitmap into which all future graphical output is diverted. This is the same as the destination form acting as arguments to *BitBLT* and, for example, *LineToForm*, defined earlier.

11.9.5 Choosing the Drawing Mode

The function *DrawingMode* takes as its argument one of the 16 combination rules of Table 11.1, represented as decimal integers corresponding to the bit patterns. For example:

SetDrawingMode(10)

corresponds to the combination rule *CR_ND* (not destination). This drawing mode is in force for subsequent output operations.

11.9.6 *BitBLT*

The CGI defines two versions of *BitBLT*, one called **two operand *BitBLT*** and the other tile **three operand *BitBLT***. Only the first of these is described here; the other is used to achieve the replication (tiling) effects discussed earlier in this chapter. The function is called here simply *CGI_BitBLT*. This function has type:

```
CGI_BitBLT: BitmapName*VDCPoint*VDCPoint*VDCCoord*VDCCoord
              → Void;
```

The execution of:

CGI_BitBLT(sourceBitmap, sourceOrigin, destinationOrigin, Xoffset, Yoffset)

results in the named source bitmap being copied to the destination (determined by *SelectDrawingBitmap*). The rectangular extents are determined by the origins and offset given. (The type *VDCCoord* is assumed to be in whatever units the VDC space is measured in.)

For example, a version of the *BitBLT* function given in Section 11.3 may be defined as follows (assuming suitable changes in types and that coordinate axes are oriented the same):

```
BitBLT: int*form*Position*(int*int)*form*Position*(int*int) → Void;
fun BitBLT(Op, SourceForm, SourcePos, SourceSize,
                 DestForm,   DestPos,   DestSize) =
  SelectDrawingBitmap(DestForm);
  SetDrawingMode(Op);
  let val (Xoffset, Yoffset) = SourceSize
  in
    CGI_BitBLT(SourceForm, SourcePos, DestPos, Xoffset, Yoffset)
  ni
nuf
```

Note that the original *BitBLT* is slightly more general, since it allows source and destination forms to be of different sizes to allow the destination to act as a clipping region (when, for example, the destination is smaller than the source), and to allow tiling replication (when the destination is larger than the source and the combination rule is ORed with the replication value).

Unfortunately, there do not appear to be any inquiry functions, so that the actions of selecting the drawing bitmap and drawing mode cannot be isolated within this definition; that is, the values selected remain in force once this version of *BitBLT* is executed – until changed elsewhere.

Summary

This chapter has been concerned with the kind of graphical operations typically available on bitmapped displays, usually found on modern personal workstations. These operations, based on *BitBLT*, provide for powerful, yet often simple, methods for achieving a variety of effects, especially in relation to dynamic (or real-time) modification of displays, as required in many input techniques. Of course, the methodology is ultimately limited by its rectangular nature, but in many applications this is not a drawback.

Exercises

11.1 Table 11.1 gives 16 Boolean combination rules for source and destination pixels. What is the minimum number of rules needed for all 16 to be derivable? (For example, the last eight rules can clearly be obtained as the negation of the first eight.)

11.2 Explain why the *CR_XOR* combination was used for redrawing the line in the repetition phase in the rubber band line program of Section 11.4. Why, for example, can the rule *CR_0* not be used to delete the last line and then *CR_1* to draw the new line?

11.3 In the rubber band line program, the line is only redrawn if the cursor is not moved. Why is this? Implement a version of the program where the line is redrawn irrespective of whether the cursor has moved. If the cursor is not moved and the line continually redrawn, the stationary line flickers. It could be argued that this is a good idea, as it constitutes feedback to the operator, showing that the line is transitory and not really part of the display. However, consider the rubber band echo in the context of sample mode input. There are disadvantages in redrawing a non-moving line. What are they? Consider the effects on the eyes of the operator.

11.4 For rubber band lines, the model discussed in the text involved picking up a line endpoint by pressing a mouse button and putting the line down by releasing the button. Find a suitable model for stroke input, where the rubber band echo is to be used on the lines joining successively chosen points.

11.5 Design algorithms for a rubber band rectangle and a spanning cross, as discussed in Chapter 5. Show how rubber banding can be used to drag a graphical object constructed out of lines, in real time.

11.6 In a pop-up interaction, suppose the position of the echo box in relation to the cursor is that the cursor is always attached to the top of the echo box; that is, the top edge of the echo box is initially aligned with the current cursor position. In a sequence of interactions involving a pop-up menu, what would the consequence of this arrangement be?

11.7 Fully design and implement a pop-up menu function and a valuator function. For the pop-up menu, the function might be as follows:

> *PopUpMenu*(*string*) where *string* is a sequence of character strings to be used as the menu prompts. The function returns an integer value corresponding to the index of the string chosen by the operator.

For the valuator, the parameters must include the minimum and maximum values on the scale. The number of divisions might also be included.

11.8 Suppose the same pop-up menu is to be used over and over again in a program. The arrangement discussed in the text is not efficient, because each time the menu is called its echo box has to be reconstructed (memory obtained, strings written into the form and so on). Design a system where a menu can be efficiently recalled without the need to reconstruct its echo on each occasion.

11.9 The string input echo requires the implementation of a simple line editor based on a string cursor. Use of the ERASE or backspace key must move the string cursor back one space, then forward again overwriting the last character with a blank space, then back again to be in the correct position. Design an algorithm for this, assuming the availability of a *TextToForm* function.

11.10 It was stated in the text that immediately after an interaction, such as a rubber band action or pop-up action, the display is in the same state as it was prior to the interaction. This follows as a consequence of the separation between graphical output and input. Does dragging a segment in real time follow this separation? Suppose a circular dial is displayed on the screen and as the operator moves the hand of the dial a segment rotates in real time. Can it be said that there is a clean division between output and input here? Design a program to implement the example of the dial.

11.11 The *CharToForm* procedure would position the character so that the top left-hand corner of its character box aligned with the *pos* parameter. This is far from satisfactory, since programmers would expect the bottom left-hand corner to correspond with *pos*. Adjust the function so as to meet this requirement.

11.12 In Section 11.6, a method for the representation of text was discussed. Show how a similar method might be used for the case of proportionally spaced fonts (where the character widths are not all the same).

11.13 If hatch or pattern fills are combined with the display using *CR_OR*, then they will be transparent. (GKS does not specify whether hatch fills can be seen through.) Modify the algorithm so that hatch fills are opaque.

11.14 Suppose that the *BitBLT* function does not support the tiling replication described in the text. Nevertheless, this technique could still be implemented. How?

11.15 How could animation effects be achieved by using *BitBLT*? Generate a cartoon sequence.

11.16 The lassooing technique allows an operator to interactively describe a path on the display (for example, by using a stroke interaction). One version of this would then allow the operator to move the inside of the area defined by the path around the display in real time. An alternative version would allow the operator to move all segments, wholly or partially, within the path around the display. Design an implementation of these techniques.

11.17 Show that the Bezier form of curve generation discussed in Section 11.8 meets the two requirements for the basis functions. Prove that the tangent property is true.

11.18 Consider the representation of a curve based on $m + 1$ control points:

$$p(t) = \sum_{i=0}^{m} p_i B_{k,i}(t)$$

Suppose the control points are transformed by a linear transformation:

$$x_i^* = \alpha + \beta x_i$$
$$y_i^* = \gamma + \delta y_i$$

Generally:

$$p_i^* = a + b p_i$$

If the corresponding transformed curve is denoted by:

$$p^*(t) = \sum p_i^* B_{k,i}(t)$$

under what condition would $p^*(t) = a + bp(t)$? Why is this important?

11.19 Let $y_0, y_1, y_2, \ldots$ be evaluations of an mth degree polynomial at equally spaced intervals; for example, $y_0 = y(x)$, $y_1 = y(x + dx)$, $y_2 = y(x + 2dx)$ and so on. Let $Dy_i = y_{i+1} - y_i$ be the first (forward) differences. These first differences will correspond to a polynomial of degree $(m - 1)$. Similarly, the first differences of this new sequence (Dy_i) will form an $(m - 2)$th degree polynomial and so on. Clearly, if $m = 3$, then the third differences D^3y_i will be constants. How can these results be used to construct an algorithm for the evaluation of a (cubic) polynomial at equally spaced intervals, using only addition?

11.20 The model for interactive Bezier curve generation discussed in the text allowed the operator to first select the control points, then see the generated curve, and then modify it. Consider an alternative model where as new control points are added so the currently defined curve is displayed. In other words, when two points are selected there is a line; when another point is added the line is replaced by a (quadratic) curve; when a further point is added the curve is redisplayed once again. The model devised should also allow modification of the position of any existing control point.

11.21 Design an interactive program that allows users to build complex shapes from the piecewise joining of cubic Bezier curves. The program must give users the option to allow joins that are not smooth, and the program must enforce smooth joins should the user desire this. In other words, a way must be found to enforce the tangent constraint.

11.22 Chapter 8 discussed a method where two full screen size forms are used as the alternate destinations of graphical output to achieve dynamic modifications. This method, known as double buffering, can be implemented using, for example, the raster functions of the CGI. Explain in detail how double buffering could be implemented using the CGI. (The remaining CGI functions are not too dissimilar from GKS; that is, it would not be a difficult undertaking to implement a GKS workstation using the CGI functions.)

CHAPTER 12

GKS: A CRITICAL ASSESSMENT

To fully understand a system it is also necessary to appreciate its shortcomings. The purpose of this chapter is to take a critical look at GKS, to help potential programmers make the best use of the system. Attention is first focused on the problem of GKS efficiency. This is followed by a discussion of the complexity of the programming environment provided by GKS. Next, the graphical output tools provided by GKS are discussed. Finally, suggestions are given for the potential role of the system in project development.

12.1 Introduction

GKS is a relatively straightforward system in terms of the time it takes to grasp its major concepts. A programmer with no prior experience of GKS or computer graphics systems, but with some knowledge of elementary geometry, can quickly learn how to use GKS.

Experience has shown that it is possible to relay the main ideas of the use of GKS to programmers with little or no prior graphics experience in about two hours of lecture time. Of course, it takes longer to learn a particular language binding, implementation characteristics, and the methods for compiling and loading programs. A morning's lecture and an afternoon's practical can achieve wonders.

To understand the 'innards' of GKS, however – to learn something about its implementation and limitations – is a more involved undertaking, and part of the motivation of this book.

12.2 GKS Efficiency

Although it is easy to learn to use, GKS in use is over complex in a number of ways. Consider the following program.

```
OpenGKS(_, _);
OpenWs(1, _, _);
ActivateWs(1);
Polyline [(0.0, 0.0), (1.0, 1.0)];
DeactivateWs(1);
CloseWs(1);
CloseGKS ()
```

At first glance, it does not appear to do very much – it draws a single line. But imagine this program loaded with a level 2*b* GKS library. The size of the executable object file is unlikely to be less than about 100 Kbytes. (This will vary from implementation to implementation.) Why would it be so large? There are two seemingly innocent function calls: open GKS (*OpenGKS*) and open workstation (*OpenWs*). *OpenGKS* loads the GKS global data structures (the GKS description table and state list). This has (according to the standard) about 60 basic entries, many of which are complex data types, such as arrays or sets. (For example, the list of normalization transformation numbers, the list of windows and so on.) *OpenWs* loads in the workstation description table and the workstation state list – about 240 basic entries in total, many of which are again arrays, lists or sets. Altogether, the data for one outin workstation included within GKS requires about 300 basic entries. But this is without the GKS code for the top-level functions right through to the device driver and code generator. Often, the latter constitute one large object, with entry points to the various individual instructions (draw lines, draw text, fill area, clear screen and so on). So the calls to *OpenGKS* and *OpenWs* load and initialise large amounts of data, and together with the *Polyline* call (this involves the normalization transformation, clipping, attribute gathering, device driver, code generator) load a significant proportion of the total GKS library code. It should now be clear to the reader that this small (innocent) applications program will generate a disproportionately large executable object.

When executed this program will be seen to carry out a number of visible actions: opening the workstation will involve the delay necessary for initialisation; on workstations with bitmapped displays, memory may have to be allocated for the graphics screen or window in which the application is to run; the screen is cleared; the line drawn; the screen cleared again; and the GKS workstation memory deallocated and the system shut down. As an exercise, execute this program a number of times and find the average execution time.

But with what should these figures (time and space) be compared? Unfortunately, many critics of GKS make inappropriate comparisons. Irrespective of the system in use it is clearly possible to bypass GKS and write a program that draws a line on the display (for example, by directly calling the code generator functions). The object code for such a program would be a few bytes in size, and the execution time could well be significantly less than that of the GKS program. The conclusion here is that GKS is too slow and too large; that is, GKS is inefficient.

Although often heard, this argument is spurious. It is essentially on the level of: "*I can draw lines and set windows on my four hundred dollar 32K home micro – why do I need GKS?*." GKS is a general device-independent system. It is precisely because of this generality that it is bound to be inefficient, large and slow, when compared to the low-level routines available on any particular graphics device or personal workstation. However, exactly the same program (up to changes in workstation connection and type names) would generate the line on any system running GKS. It is bound to be the case that a general system will perform at least as badly as any locally bound system. The problem is that *every* time GKS is used, it is on a *particular* system. So, GKS will always be large and inefficient compared to what might be achieved in a given computer graphics environment. This is an inevitable and obvious, but often overlooked consequence of any high-level programming system. (Why use Pascal when writing in assembler could be more efficient?)

The efficiency question is particularly important in graphics, and in the light of current developments in computing. Graphics is increasingly being used on personal workstations, which have limited memory (2 Mbytes, for example) and disk space (20 to 40 Mbytes) yet offer the advantage of very fast (usually bitmapped) graphics. GKS seems to negate the very advantages that personal workstations offer: it is large, takes up a lot of memory during execution and a lot of disk space, and it is relatively slow.

There is more to efficiency than can be measured in terms of speed and disk space. It is true that in graphics speed is often all important, and there is a threshold below which a program becomes unusable. However, 'human efficiency' is just as important, if not more so. People do not program everything in assembler code because programming in a high-level language is easier, more productive and more efficient in human terms. Crucial parts of code are often written in assembler (or included as firmware) but in program development even this code is first written and proved in a high-level language and then later optimized. It is almost certainly the case that in most circumstances it is easier, faster and safer to write applications software code in a high-level system such as GKS, rather than using device-specific functions. However, this does lead on to a genuine point of criticism.

12.3 GKS Complexity

> *"Men make their own history, but they do not make it just as they please; . . . but under circumstances directly encountered, given and transmitted from the past. The tradition of all the dead generations weighs like a nightmare on the brain of the living."*
>
> Karl Marx, *Marx and Engels: Selected Works in One Volume*, Lawrence & Whishart, 1968, p. 97.

As already stated, GKS is easy to learn to use, but it is not the best of systems for developing complex, provably correct, programs. It is a system where everything seems to depend on everything else: where a change in a single parameter in a GKS function call can have ripples of effects throughout the program execution. GKS is a highly *state-bound* system. To illustrate this, consider the following piece of GKS code, in isolation from the rest of the applications program in which it is embedded:

Polyline [(0.5, 0.5), (1.5, 1.5)]

Now try and predict the precise effect of the execution of this instruction. Think about this for a few minutes before reading on.

The possible effects might be as follows:

(1) GKS might be in the wrong state – it must be in the state of at least one workstation active or segment open. Hence, the outcome might

be that an error message is generated. (Count this as two possible states: one correct and the other not.)

(2) A line might or might not be displayed. There are many circumstances where no line would be displayed. Consider one for the moment: a normalization transformation other than 0 has been selected, the required line is outside of the clipping region and the clipping indicator is set to 'on'. There is also an infinite set of possible choices for windows. Ignoring this for the moment, suppose that there are only two normalization transformations (0 and 1). Then there are four further states the system might be in: there is a choice of two transformations and each with a choice of whether clipping is on or off.

(3) Even if the window or clipping indicator is such that the line could be displayed, it still might not be. The reason for this is that the deferral state might be set to *asti* (at some time), and this line has yet to overflow the workstation output buffer. This introduces a further two possible states.

(4) Suppose that the line is actually displayed – *what* would it look like? Suppose there are two possible line widths and two colours. There must always be at least four line types, but assume here that there are only 4. This introduces a further 16 possible states. (In fact, even here the line might not be visible, for half of the states correspond to the line being drawn in the background colour.)

(5) If the line is displayed – *where* will it appear and will it look right? Suppose that the zero normalization transformation is in force. Then the line should be on the diagonal from the middle of the effective display space to the upper right-hand corner (assuming the default workstation transformations). But it might not be there, even under these circumstances. A segment might be open, and this segment might have a non-identity transformation matrix; or the segment might be invisible; or if visible maybe it is highlighted; or maybe it has a priority lower than some other segment on the display that the line intersects. If two possible states are counted here for each of these (default workstation transformation, identity segment transformation, visible segment, not highlighted, high priority), then this introduces a further 32 possible states.

Counting very conservatively there are 2*4*2*16*32 = 8192 possible outcomes. This is, of course, unfair because if the system is in the wrong GKS state to start with, then half of these states are redundant. This leaves only 4096 outcomes. A similar argument holds for the case when there is no segment open. That leaves only 2048 outcomes. (The real number of outcomes is infinite because of the continuum of choices for windows, viewports and transformations.) This argument makes it seem to be a miracle that anything can ever be displayed at all.

The point of this (admittedly rather light hearted) analysis is that when designing an application based on GKS, it is not a trivial task to design pieces of program in isolation and be sure that the right thing is going to happen on execution. Everything interlocks to everything else: change one thing and who knows what the consequences might be. This tendency always exists with sequential programming languages, since to understand the effect of a single instruction, the entire history of the computation up to that instruction must be known. But GKS exaggerates the difficulties by having so many possible states at each stage in an execution. Generation of a single output primitive requires consideration of the states of six subsystems: the workstation states, the normalization transformations, the deferral states, the individual and workstation attributes in addition to the aspect source flags, the segments and the workstation transformations. There are defaults for some of these, and the applications program is free to inquire the state of every system variable before taking any action, but programming in an environment such as this is like playing snooker (or pool): before any good shot can be made the state of the whole table must be known.

Before the effect of any line of code can be predicted in GKS, the entire history of the program execution must be known, and with GKS this is a lot of history. But programming does not have to be like this.

As an example of how badly things can go wrong, consider the following realistic scenario. Using an interactive drawing program, the operator has painstakingly constructed the almost perfect picture. Almost perfect in the sense that the operator decides to experiment with a slightly different colour palette. After selecting the appropriate menu option, the colour palette is modified. But as a consequence the screen is cleared and the picture lost. The reason for this could only happen in a poorly designed program. But the fact is that GKS makes it easy to write poor programs.

The approach of the program given in Example 8.3(c) illustrates how the problems of interdependency can be diminished. This approach might be called **state invariant**: the programmer establishes a neutral state that GKS is always in prior to the execution of each procedure and when the procedure execution is complete. This can be achieved by use of the inquiry function.

But such an approach can only be used to a limited extent, with those GKS functions that effect state changes but do not have potentially immediate effects on what has already been displayed. For example, the normalization transformation number, or the current line width scale factor, could be treated in this way. However, functions such as *SetWorkstationWindow*, or *SetDeferralState*, cannot be part of the state invariance, if their state is to change within a procedure execution. If, say, a workstation window is changed, then this can have a dramatic and immediate effect on the display, which cannot be restored on resetting the window to its state on entry to the procedure. (Resetting the window would, of course, also have an effect.) As a more extreme example, consider the workstation state (closed, open or active).

GKS has grown up in a programming environment dominated in practice by imperative programming languages, especially FORTRAN. Every program executes a sequence of instructions, carrying out a recipe of how to reach the desired goal: do this, then that, and if this, then that, else the other... . It is well known from the theory of programming languages that programs written in the imperative style are hard to design and prove. GKS exaggerates the difficulty by having so many internal states of which the applications programmer must be aware for the program to be successful. This is in contrast to applicative (or functional) programming where programs are not recipes but definitions or specifications. For example, the *ClipLine* function of Section 4.2 does not provide a sequence of steps to execute to achieve the effect of clipping a line, but is rather a definition of what it means for a line to be clipped. The program was derived from a discussion of what clipping is, rather than from the steps necessary to achieve the effect of clipping.

Functional languages really need computer systems based on parallel architecture for efficient implementation – current projects leading to the 'Fifth Generation' of computers are heading in this direction (notably the Flagship project backed by the UK's Alvey initiative). It is not surprising that in the present circumstances GKS is defined in an imperative style. However, it cannot be argued that the vast number of states is inevitable in a general-purpose, device-independent graphics system. Here, the comparison should be made with PostScript. This does have a graphics state, but one that is far more economically defined than in GKS. (The comparison should be made with GKS level 0*a*.) And PostScript is a richer system than GKS after all. (For an introduction to the ideas of applicative programming see the August 1985 issue of *Byte*. For further reading see Henderson, 1980, or Glazer *et al.*, 1985).

12.4 The Paucity of GKS Graphical Output

12.4.1 Comparison with PostScript

GKS supports the five output primitives polyline, polymarker, text, fill area and cell array. These offer a very basic set of tools for graphical output, which is in contrast with PostScript which provides these with the addition of arcs and curves. PostScript, moreover, provides attributes that surpass those of GKS – in the manner in which lines are connected and rounded, and the choice of interior definition and colour models. GKS can clip to rectangular clipping regions, while PostScript clips to arbitrary regions.

There can be no argument against this – to the extent that the two systems are comparable (at level 0*a*), PostScript is the more compact, richer system for graphical output. It is also general and device independent. However, there is one area in which GKS is superior: it provides a viewing system that is particularly easy to use (via the window and viewport concepts). In PostScript, on the other hand, there is no separation between viewing and modelling – the modelling transformations must be used for both purposes.

GKS enthusiasts might argue that the feebleness of GKS output is compensated for by the *GeneralizedDrawingPrimitive* (GDP) discussed in Chapter 8. This allows for the possibility of new primitives being incorporated into a GKS implementation and offers a standard way of providing extensions to the GKS graphical output functionality. But the GDP has a different status to the other output primitives. Every GKS implementation must support the five primitives already mentioned, but GKS implementations are under no obligation to support even the registered GDPs (that is, those recognized as standard). Moreover, GDPs exist on workstations in the sense that an implementation might support several GDPs, but no GDP exists on more than one workstation. There is no portability of GDPs even within an implementation, let alone across implementations. Once an applications program is forced into using GDPs, it is no longer a portable program, which is a major benefit of using GKS in the first place.

It is difficult to favourably compare the GKS graphical output capabilities to those of PostScript. There is a crude but useful statistic for comparison of the two systems: GKS level 0*a* has approximately the same functional scope as PostScript, in the sense that it only deals with one workstation and has no input or segments. GKS level 0*a* has over 90 functions. PostScript has in total 80 functions dealing exclusively with graphics. Many of the PostScript operators are functionally equivalent; for example, *lineto* and *rlineto*, one of which could be deleted without having any affect on the functionality of the system. With GKS, the ultimate products are programs that can draw lines, markers, text, fill areas and cell arrays. The programmer using PostScript can, of course, do all of these easily and, in addition, has access to a number of more powerful primitives (such as curve drawing), which in GKS would have to be programmed by the applications programmer. Taking a wider view, GKS has a greater field of application than PostScript – GKS supports dynamic graphics in addition to the static picture description of PostScript – although PostScript has evolved into a fully fledged interactive graphics system (Gosling, 1985) in the Sun NeWs environment. At the level where the two systems are comparable, GKS is hardly a contender.

12.4.2 GKS Has no *BitBLT*

In comparison to PostScript, GKS can be said to be inferior with respect to higher level graphical output and the factors relating to this (clipping regions and attributes). In comparison to Smalltalk-80, GKS lacks the low-level functionality possible on raster-based devices. Graphical output cannot be displayed using the Boolean combination rules (or their possible generalizations for colour displays). There is no *BitBLT* function.

However, there is an argument contrary to this criticism. If GKS provides the right high-level primitives, then the low-level pixel-based graphics functionality is not necessary, and in fact at too low a level to be included in a standard for portable and device-independent graphics. For example, rubber band and pop-up prompts are directly available in GKS and therefore should not have to be implemented by an applications programmer using GKS. GKS supports segments for dynamic modifications, so that recourse to rubber banding or pop-up techniques for dynamic graphics should not be necessary. (The implementation of, for example, dynamic modification would have to use these techniques, but this is the concern of the systems implementor rather than the applications programmer.)

There is a suitable use for forms and *BitBLT* functions in the GKS implementation, even though these are not available at the applications level. On personal workstations with appropriate hardware and software support for raster operations, forms could be used as a way of implementing the display spaces for several GKS workstations. Each workstation would have a display space represented by a form, which may at any time be on or off screen. The total screen display might look very much like that of the Smalltalk-80 example shown earlier, where each window now corresponds to a different GKS workstation. This could be best implemented on a system supporting a window manager, or by using the idea of displayable bitmaps used in the CGI. There would have to be implementation-defined methods to allow the applications programmer to choose the display sizes, to choose the screen position of each of the logical displays, and to choose whether or not any particular workstation display is on screen at any time. These functions could, however, be easily embodied in the GKS *Escape* function.

It is sometimes thought that *CellArray* is the GKS answer to *RasterOp*. But this is not the case. *CellArray* is a painting operation, which is determined by a rectangle size and a 2D array of colours. *RasterOp*, on the other hand, may be thought of as a function of source and destination forms together with a combination rule to a (destination) form – with the notion of form generalized to 2D colour arrays – and a corresponding extension in the combination rules. *CellArray* is a special case where the source form is the colour array together with the rectangle size parameters, and the destination form is the display, the combination rule always being *CR_S*.

In spite of the foregoing arguments, the fundamental criticism remains: GKS does not allow the programmer access to the underlying raster operations so prevalent on modern workstations. Although it can be validly answered that these have no place in an applications level standard, this will not satisfy project managers and programmers who need access to these functions. Of course, intelligent GKS implementations will make the best possible use of the graphics capabilities provided on the underlying devices. (This in itself implies that the notion of easily portable *implementations* of GKS – that is, those that can be easily ported from one computer and set of devices to another – may well not be the best implementations.) But there will always be goals that projects need to realize which are straightforward using raster operations and difficult, if not impossible, to implement using pure GKS. An example is the interactive curve drawing discussed in Section 11.8. This is almost trivial to do on bitmapped displays using the *CR_XOR* combination rule to achieve the dynamic curve modifications. Theoretically, it is possible to implement this in GKS (at level 2*c*) using segments and sample input. But remembering the difficulties involved in allowing for dynamic modifications in GKS on raster displays (discussed extensively in Chapter 8), it is quite likely that the necessary real-time curve modification could not be achieved by relying on the GKS functions.

The solution? Well, there is only a problem if a project team decides that use of GKS is necessary, for example, for portability reasons. In this case, a sensible solution would be to use GKS as far as possible, but mix the use of GKS functions with the raster-based functions available wherever necessary. To cater for portability, the project would have to define a set of abstract raster functions which provide an interface to the raster capabilities on the underlying devices (a library of raster functions), or preferably use the CGI raster functions if these are available.

12.5 A Strategy for the Use of GKS

A team starting out on a new project involving computer graphics would nowadays inevitably evaluate GKS as a potential implementation tool. The major reasons for using GKS would be:

- It is easy to learn and it is likely that new people joining the project team would already be familiar with GKS, so that training time is saved.
- It already exists, which is time saving, as there is no need to write afresh a new applications library environment.
- It results in programs that are relatively portable.

- It is one of a number of standards and developing standards in the computer graphics and communications area. (This is not to say that all the standards are compatible.)

This chapter has considered some of the arguments against GKS. However, rather than adopt the negative view, which rules out further consideration of the standard because of these problems, some positive proposals can be derived from a consideration of the problem areas.

The modern approach to software development involves a rigorous mathematical specification of goals and programs, and proofs that the programs do precisely realize the required goals. (Such an approach is described, for example, by Jones, 1986, and by Bornat, 1986.) In an ideal world, the abstract programs would be directly executable on a real computer. However, given the relative inefficiencies of functional programming languages on sequential machines, it is usual for there to be a further, major step in the development of any system, where the abstract programming notation is transcribed into an executable and efficient target language, such as Pascal. Such transcription must, of course, also be based on exact and verifiable rules, otherwise the whole point of the rigorous approach is lost at this crucial stage of implementation.

In a project involving computer graphics, the same approach should obviously be adopted, and perhaps the functional approaches to graphics outlined in Chapter 10 might be useful here. However, in the case of computer graphics, there is an extra level of difficulty introduced at the implementation stage. Pascal, for example, is a very precisely defined target language (ISO 7185) and any Pascal compiler that meets the standard should work in the same way on any comparable machine. (Clearly, it would perform differently in terms of speed and numerical precision on a home micro compared to a powerful mainframe computer.) Now, with the introduction of GKS there is also the first major and internationally agreed specification of a target set of functions for computer graphics programs. However, unlike Pascal, which is relatively well established, GKS is in its early days, and it is likely that for some time to come there will be major differences in performance of different GKS implementations, and even of the same implementation on different machines. Moreover, the GKS levels concept ensures that this difficulty is compounded: it is not enough to know that GKS is available on a certain machine, one also has to know which of the *nine* varieties of GKS is supported.

The manner in which GKS became a standard is indeed quite unusual. First, it was decided that a standard was needed, and then (over a ten year period) one was defined. (Of course, the original FORTRAN GKS package served as a starting point.) In the case of Pascal, for example, Wirth invented Pascal (Wirth, 1971; Jensen and Wirth, 1974) and it was only many years later in the light of its great popularity that it became an international standard – and for all practical purposes without too much discrepancy from the original Wirth definition. In other words, by the time that Pascal became a standard it had already been in use for many years.

Another case closer to graphics is the manner in which PostScript is emerging as a *de facto* standard for communicating descriptions of pictures to graphical output devices. It is becoming a *de facto* standard because of its quality, and therefore because people wish to use it – it is emerging as a standard from the bottom up.

With GKS, and the whole suite of associated standards (PHIGS, CGI, CGM), it is very much a case of imposition 'from above'. Whereas other standards have often reached standardization after many years of experience, this is not the case with GKS. Consequently, implementations must, for some time to come, remain something of an unknown quantity.

To decide whether GKS is a suitable target for the graphics component in a project the following question must be considered: Can the concepts and functions embodied in the GKS specification be used to provide a satisfactory and relatively straightforward expression of the realization of the project goals? If the answer is *no*, then there is no point in considering GKS further – something else must be used in its place. If the answer is *yes*, then GKS can be used as the target for transcription of the abstract notation describing the graphics into something closer to the code of the real implementation.

Given that a particular GKS implementation is to be used by a project, there will be certain programs that can be expressed in terms of GKS functions but which cannot be achieved with the chosen implementation. For example, in the case of the interactive curve drawing problem mentioned earlier, it is certainly possible to write an abstract GKS program to meet the required goal. However, it is very unlikely that a GKS implementation will be available either at the right level or able to meet the speed demanded in such an application. A suitable approach to take here is to transform the abstract GKS program into a new program that uses GKS functions, where these are appropriate, and translates those components that cannot satisfactorily rely on GKS into a 'lower level' and probably device-dependent code.

The approach then is that GKS is used as a further specification tool at the stage in software development where implementation is being considered. Program transcription is then used to create executable and efficient programs from the GKS abstract functions. To ensure the correctness of the derived, more efficient program the project team must develop a rigorous set of transcription rules, which specify how each GKS function is to be transformed into lower level functions. This process can be taken to any required depth, until a completely satisfactory executing program is derived. The advantage of using GKS in this situation is that it will aid portability: the depth of transformations may well be different in implementations of the program on different machines. On a machine with a particularly superior GKS, the first-level implementation might actually be suitable as the final version. It is hoped that in years to come superior implementations will be the norm.

Finally, it must be stressed that the real importance of GKS is that it has dramatically opened up the floodgates of discussion in the computer graphics community, and interest in computer graphics generally. It is stimulating new research in software, in graphics systems and device architecture. The computer graphics world would be a poorer place without it.

Summary

GKS provides a portable and device-independent system. The cost of these advantages is its relative inefficiency and large size. Moreover, compared to more recent developments, such as PostScript and bitmapped graphics, it suffers from a lack of both high- and low-level graphics functions. Furthermore, although it is easy to learn, it suffers from the large number of system states it allows, thus making it hard to use in real applications. On the positive side, being an agreed standard it has a role to play in projects with a computer graphics component, as a target language into which abstract specifications are transcribed on the road towards implementation.

Possibly future revisions of GKS will overcome some of the problems mentioned in this chapter, although international committees are not famous for compactness. Future revisions are likely to be more powerful in the sense of the graphics primitives supported, but also slower, larger and more complex.

Exercises

12.1 In Section 12.3, an example was given of a GKS program that allowed an operator to lose all of a picture in response to an instruction to change a workstation colour representation. How could this happen?

12.2 Translate the programs of Chapter 10, describing plants and gardens, into GKS terms. Try to construct a set of transcription rules which, for any functional program using descriptors, descriptions and objects, translate into a GKS program to produce the equivalent effects.

12.3 Write a set of PostScript procedures that are (in so far as possible) equivalent to the GKS graphical output primitive functions and attributes.

12.4 Write a set of Pascal procedures that use GKS to implement the PostScript graphical output operators and their associated attributes.

12.5 List all the information that would be required to successfully include calls to underlying device raster-based functions (such as *BitBLT*) in a GKS applications program. As an example, suppose a viewport is defined using GKS (*SetWindow* and *SelectNormalization Transformation*) and it is required to make a copy of the corresponding part of the screen to another part of the screen or to an offscreen raster. How could this be done?

12.6 Implement the simple 'draw a line' program of Section 12.2, and examine the size of the executable file and the execution time. Write the equivalent program using the basic graphics functions available on your equipment, and again check the size and execution time.

12.7 In Exercise 12.2, it was suggested that the garden program be written in GKS. Expand this program so that it includes as many of the features of GKS as possible; for example, use different windows and viewports, use the primitive attributes to give style to the garden, use segments (if not already used), allow an operator to build a garden by interactively placing plants and so on. Once this program has been successfully implemented, check the size of the executable file, and compare the result with your program in Exercise 12.6. The result may be surprising!

12.8 Use the GKS functions to write a program that allows interactive manipulation of Bezier curves.

12.9 Although PostScript and PHIGS are both based on concepts of graphics modelling, there is a major difference between them: PHIGS allows dynamic graphics. Ideally, a change in a transformation would be effected immediately on a display. Write a PHIGS-based program that draws a simple 2D view of a table, on which there is resting a flower pot. The table itself is resting on the floor, which can be shown as a horizontal line. Now move the table across the display, ensuring that the flower pot moves with it. Write a program using GKS to simulate this action. Remember, it is important that the flower pot remains an object that can be transformed independently of the table top (for example, it can be lifted off of the table top). Can this be done using GKS segments?

12.10 Rethink the interactive drawing program of earlier chapters given the discussions of this chapter.

CHAPTER 13

BASIC IDEAS OF 3D GRAPHICS

The most visually stunning computer-generated images are often those which portray a 3D scene. The scene may be a realistic one, such as an image of a landscape as seen by an airplane pilot or, for example, other images as shown in the colour plates in this book. Alternatively, and of greater interest to some people, are the attempts to portray realistic images of places and events that are purely fictitious, as in many recent science fiction films – for example, the creation of the Genesis Planet in the movie *Star Trek II: The Wrath of Khan* (Smith, 1982).

It is quite beyond the scope of this book to describe the methodology of 3D animated graphics, or even the production of realistic static pictures. Much of the work in this field is very recent, and requires a mathematical background and general understanding of physics and optics, which a book such as this cannot pursue. Moreover, it would require a book of at least equal length to do justice to the full body of knowledge now available. This chapter has the more modest aim of introducing some of the basic ideas of 3D graphics and to point the interested reader towards the relevant material for further study.

13.1 Introduction

Realistic **image synthesis** is concerned with the concepts and algorithms used in the computer construction of a picture. This should be distinguished from **image processing** which is concerned with the *analysis* of images already available via some other means. Feature enhancement of frames captured on a video camera, such as those taken during space exploration, is a good example of the use of image processing. Computer graphics, however, is only concerned with image synthesis, although sometimes techniques adopted in the two disciplines are the same (Pavlidis, 1982; Gonzalez and Wintz, 1981).

There are three paramount components in computer graphics, and recognition of these becomes particularly important in image synthesis: these are geometry, shading and sampling (Whitted and Cook, 1984). The first component is concerned with the definition and description of the picture in geometric terms. This includes the 3D representation of the picture, the modelling necessary in the picture description and the projection of the 3D description on to the 2D display coordinates of the graphics device in use.

Shading is concerned with the methods for reproducing the effects of lighting on a scene. Principles from physics must be employed to simulate different lighting conditions and the reflection properties of the materials out of which the modelled objects are constructed. As an extreme example, the reflection properties of gold are rather different from those of a human face. Graphics image constructors must take this into account in the same way as photographers.

Finally, sampling is concerned with overcoming the problems caused by the fact that a computer graphics rendering of an image is a discrete sample (for example, 512 times 512 pixels) of a continuous object. In 2D graphics, this sampling shows up, for example, as jagged edge lines. Generally, the problem can show itself as jagged boundaries between objects, confused rendering of complex detail, and the incorrect (or complete lack of) rendering of small or thin objects. Such effects are particularly unfortunate in 3D graphics, where the aim is usually to render images that look realistic. The techniques adopted to overcome such problems are called **anti-aliasing**. When the images belong to a sequence of frames of an animation, then there is the additional problem of temporal sampling, which is overcome by temporal anti-aliasing techniques (Crow, 1981).

Geometry, shading and sampling are, of course, all present in 2D graphics. However, an additional problem of 3D graphics is concerned with **visibility**. This is often referred to as the problem of hidden line and hidden surface removal. Computer generation of 3D scenes must ensure that only those aspects of the scene normally visible to an observer are displayed. The

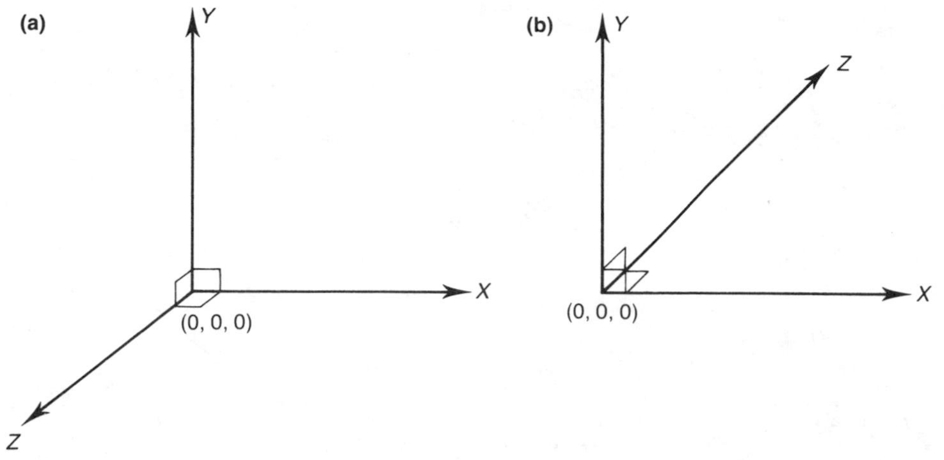

computations involved can be done at the geometric level, but more usually form part of the final stage of the rendering process. (Some aspects of visibility in 2D graphics are discussed in Section 8.2.)

Figure 13.1
(a) Right-handed and (b) left-handed coordinate systems.

13.2 Coordinate Systems

3D graphics is an order of magnitude more complex than 2D graphics. This becomes clear as soon as an attempt is made to describe even a simple 3D object. The first problem encountered is due to the fact that there are two choices of coordinate system. Figure 13.1 shows the so-called **right-handed** and **left-handed** coordinate systems. To understand these, imagine that the 2D *X–Y* system is inscribed on your desk top. Then, in the case of the right-handed system (RHS), the positive *Z* axis points upwards from the desk; in the left-handed system (LHS), it points into the desk top. (These names derive from an association between the thumb as the *X* axis, the first finger as the *Y* axis and the second finger as the *Z* axis.)

Computer graphics systems generally make use of both the LHS and the RHS. The RHS is the one normally employed in mathematics and, it is usually argued, is the system most applications programmers would be most comfortable with. Since applications programmers work with WC, these are therefore best described in a RHS. However, it is also argued that the viewing of a 3D scene is best described in a LHS. This is supposedly due to the natural association between the graphics screen and the *X–Y* coordinate system with the *Z* axis pointing into the screen, so that displayed objects are best thought of as being 'inside' (or behind) the graphics screen.

Whether these associations are natural or not is besides the point,

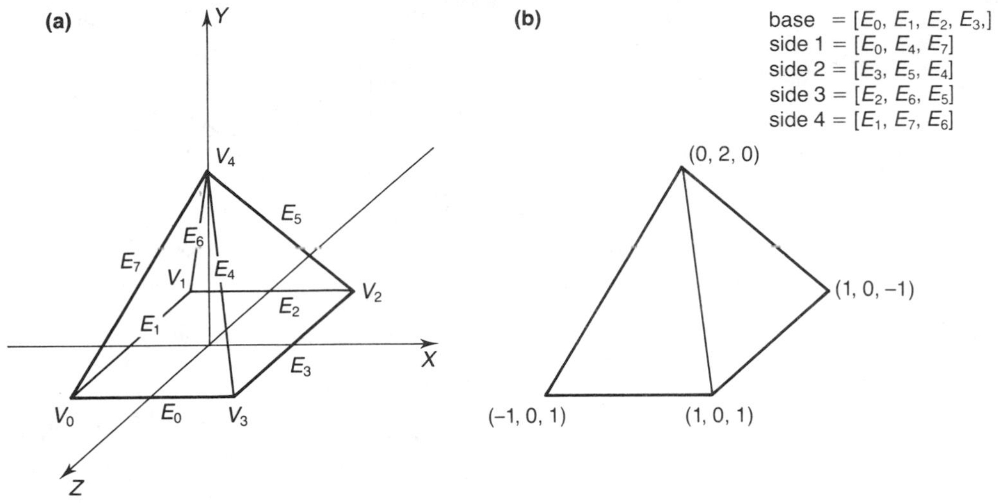

Figure 13.2
Pyramid in a RHS.
(a) All edges and vertices shown.
(b) With hidden faces removed.

since graphics packages supporting 3D have been heavily influenced by discussions of the Graphics Standards Planning Committee of the ACM SigGraph in the United States. In the late 1970s, these discussions led to the definition of the CORE standard for computer graphics (GSPC, 1979). CORE does adopt the view that WC are in a RHS and viewing coordinates are in a LHS. The proposed 3D extension to GKS, however, specifies all coordinates as RHS (ISO, 1986b).

In this chapter, both the LHS and RHS are used, and the system in use at any time should be clear from the context. Whatever the system used, coordinates are described as (x, y, z); that is, the last element in the 3-tuple is the measurement along the Z axis.

13.3 Basic Ideas of Object Representation

Consider the drawing of a pyramid, as shown in Figure 13.2(a). There are many different ways in which the pyramid may be mathematically described in a 3D coordinate system. For example, it may be specified as a set of eight line segments (or **edges**) – four forming the base and four the edges of the triangles. However, such a representation does not relay the fact that the pyramid is constructed from five sides or **faces**. This information could prove to be vital to the method used to display the pyramid, since if the pyramid is described *only* as individual lines, it would be impossible to discover which of the edges and faces of the pyramid are visible to an observer located in the coordinate system. Hence, the drawing shown in Figure 13.2(b) could not be computer generated.

Let each face of the pyramid be described by a (closed) polygon, then the object could be specified in a RHS as follows:

```
Simple polygon representation.
val pyramid =
  let val base = [(−1, 0, 1), (−1, 0, −1), (1, 0, −1), (1, 0, 1)]
      and side1 = [(−1, 0, 1), (1, 0, 1), (0, 2, 0)]
      and side2 = [(1, 0, 1), (1, 0, −1), (0, 2, 0)]
      and side3 = [(1, 0, −1), (−1, 0, −1), (0, 2, 0)]
      and side4 = [(−1, 0, −1), (−1, 0, 1), (0, 2, 0)]
  in
    [base, side1, side2, side3, side4]
  ni
```

Suppose there is a function that takes a polygon face as its argument and (somehow) draws the polygon edges on to the display. (How such a function might be implemented is the subject of later sections.) Let this function be called *Polygon3D*. Then the pyramid of Figure 13.2(a) could be rendered by the following program:

```
for 0 ≤ i < Length pyramid do
  Polygon3D(pyramid[i])
od
```

This is a simple but inelegant method for the representation and drawing of the pyramid, and the same conclusion would apply if the method was used for any polyhedral object (one described as a set of polygonal faces). It is obviously simple: each face is described as a sequence of vertices and the object consists of a set of such faces. The picture generation is achieved by drawing each polygon in turn.

A clear disadvantage is that each edge in this example is drawn twice, because each edge belongs to two faces. For example, edge E_1 belongs to faces *side*1 and *base*. The simple polygon representation is not a suitable data structure for discovering the common edges between polygons, and therefore should be rejected for all but the simplest applications.

13.3.1 Edge Polygon Representation

Consider now the following more extensive data structure, which is termed here the **edge polygon representation**:

```
Names for the faces.
val BASE = 0 and SIDE1 = 1 and SIDE2 = 2 and SIDE3 = 3 and
    SIDE4 = 4;
```

Vertex and edge lists.

```
val vertexList = [V0, V1, V2, V3, V4]
and edgeList  = [((0, 3), (BASE, SIDE1)),
                 ((1, 0), (BASE, SIDE4)),
                 ((2, 1), (BASE, SIDE3)),
                 ((3, 2), (BASE, SIDE2)),
                 ((4, 3), (SIDE1, SIDE2)),
                 ((4, 2), (SIDE2, SIDE3)),
                 ((4, 1), (SIDE3, SIDE4)),
                 ((4, 0), (SIDE4, SIDE1))]
```

Face table.

```
and pyramid  = [
                 [0, 1, 2, 3],
                 [0, 4, 7],
                 [3, 5, 4],
                 [2, 6, 5],
                 [1, 7, 6]
               ]
```

The **vertex list** consists of a sequence of all the vertices in the pyramid, whereas the **edge list** is a sequence of entries providing information about each of the edges in the pyramid. The first entry for each edge points back to the vertex list, defining the two vertices that make up the edge. The second entry points to the **face table**, showing the faces to which the edge belongs. (For simple polyhedra, the edge can belong to only one or two faces.) The pyramid is finally defined by the face table, which, for each face, is a sequence of pointers back to the edge list, showing the edges defining the face. For example, the *BASE* of the pyramid is defined by edges 0, 1, 2 and 3. Edge 0 is defined by entries 0 and 3 in the vertex table (V_0 and V_3). Also, edge 0 belongs to *SIDE*1 of the pyramid.

To actually draw the pyramid a 3D line drawing function is required (*Line3D*). Each of the edges in the edge list is given as argument to this function, resulting in:

```
for 0 ≤ i < Length edgeList do
  let val ((v0, v1), _) = edgeList[i]
  in
    Line3D(vertexList[v0], vertexList[v1])
  ni
od
```

This data structure is suitable for applications requiring any subset of the faces to be displayed, as the corresponding set of edges can be easily computed as the union of the sets referenced by each face. A simple example of this is given in Section 13.3.3 in relation to hidden surface removal.

The edge polygon representation is not the last word in relation to data structures for polyhedra. For example, in some applications it is necessary to know the set of faces meeting at a particular vertex. This could be catered for by extending the definition of the vertex list to reference the appropriate elements in the edge list. Clearly, for each new type of computation required an *ad hoc* addition to the basic data structure could be invented. The **winged edge** data structure, invented by Baumgart (Baumgart, 1975), is an attempt to provide a comprehensive structure capable of efficiently meeting the requirements of many different types of computation required in analyzing and rendering polyhedral objects. It consists of three interconnected doubly linked lists – of vertices, edges and faces, with both face and vertex elements pointing forwards and backwards to their predecessor and successor links, and to the edge list. The edge list elements themselves point to the vertices and faces, and to other edges on adjacent faces. An introductory description of this and other structures is given in an excellent review by Kilgour (Kilgour, 1986).

13.3.2 Plane Equation of a Polygon

Given a polygon, the equation of the plane on which it is inscribed may be computed given any three of the polygon's vertices (assuming that the three do not lie in a straight line). The equation of a plane is in general:

$$ax + by + cz = 1 \qquad \textbf{(13.1)}$$

where $1/a$, $1/b$ and $1/c$ are the respective intercepts of the plane with the X, Y and Z axes, respectively. (See Gasson, 1983, Chapter 3, for a discussion of this and other useful results.)

Given three polygon vertices (x_1, y_1, z_1), (x_2, y_2, z_2) and (x_3, y_3, z_3), substitution into Equation (13.1) results in three simultaneous equations, which can be easily solved for a, b and c. Generally:

$$\begin{aligned} aD &= y_1(z_2 - z_3) + y_2(z_3 - z_1) + y_3(z_1 - z_2) \\ bD &= x_1(z_3 - z_2) + x_2(z_1 - z_3) + x_3(z_2 - z_1) \\ cD &= x_1(y_2 - y_3) + x_2(y_3 - y_1) + x_3(y_1 - y_2) \end{aligned} \qquad \textbf{(13.2)}$$

where:

$$D = x_1 y_2 z_3 + x_2 y_3 z_1 + x_3 y_1 z_2 - x_1 y_3 z_2 - x_2 y_1 z_3 - x_3 y_2 z_1$$

Equation (13.1) may be multiplied throughout by any (non-zero) constant without altering its meaning – in particular, it can be multiplied throughout by D. Hence, the right-hand sides of Equation (13.2) may be used as the expressions for a, b and c, thus avoiding the necessity for division. The corresponding form of the plane equation is :

$$a x + b y + c z = D \tag{13.3}$$

13.3.3 Computing the Hidden Faces of Polyhedra

One important application of the plane equation for a polygon is to provide a quick way of computing hidden faces – for example, the faces *base*, *side*3 and *side*4 in the view of the pyramid shown in Figure 13.2(b).

The **normal** to a plane is a vector at right-angles to any line inscribed on the plane (see Figure 13.3); thus, it forms a right-angle with the plane itself. It is easy to show that the **normal vector** for the plane given by Equation (13.3) is (a, b, c); in other words, a straight line from the origin (0, 0, 0) through the point (a, b, c) is at right-angles to the plane, so that for any point (x, y, z) on the plane the line (x, y, z) to $(x + a, y + b, z + c)$ is normal to the plane.

A plane partitions 3D space into two regions: the region 'behind' and the region 'in front' of the plane. 'Behind' and 'in front' are relative terms, because such a classification is arbitrary without some other information as to what is meant by 'behind' and 'in front'. For example, when you are in a room, you stand in front of the walls, and adjoining rooms are behind the walls. However, when you enter an adjoining room, you are then in front of these walls and the original room is now behind.

The region of space that lies on the same side as the normal to a plane is termed the space *in front* of the plane, and the other region *behind* the plane. This still does not resolve the ambiguity, as the normal is determined by (a, b, c) from Equation (13.3) and multiplication of this equation throughout by -1 results in the normal pointing in the opposite direction $(-a, -b, -c)$ (and, of course, this new equation still describes the original plane).

Consider the expressions of Equation (13.2): these express a, b and c in terms of the three points $P_1(x_1, y_1, z_1)$, $P_2(x_2, y_2, z_2)$ and $P_3(x_3, y_3, z_3)$. If the formulae are evaluated with any two of the points interchanged (for example, use the coordinates at P_1 as the values of (x_2, y_2, z_2)), this reverses the signs of a, b and c. (Readers familiar with determinants will be able to prove this result easily. The overall result for the equation will be unchanged because the sign of D will also be reversed.) Hence, the *order* in which the three points are presented to Equation (13.2) is important in the evaluation of (a, b, c) and therefore determines the *direction* of the normal vector to the plane. It turns out that the appropriate order in which to present the three points is in an anti-clockwise direction around the polygon

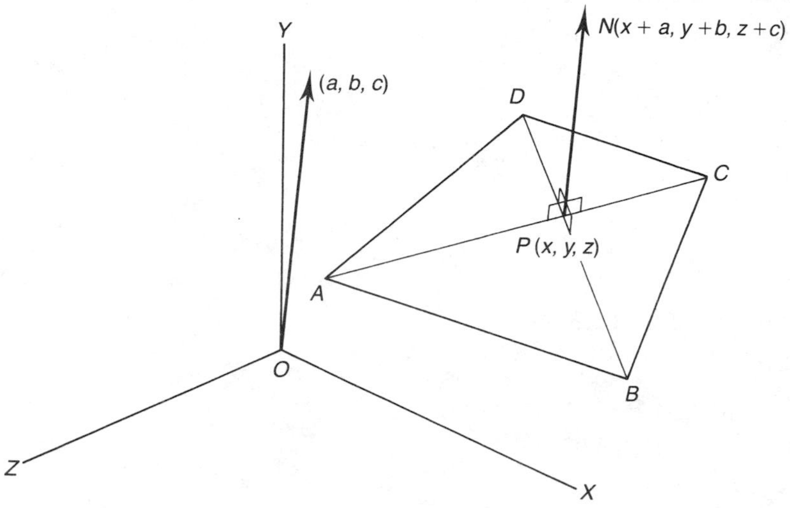

Figure 13.3
PN is normal to the plane $ax + by + cz = d$ (*ABCD*). It is at right-angles to any line in the plane.

when looked at from *in front* of the polygon. If this convention is adopted, then the normals to the faces of a polyhedra will always point to the outside (in front) of the polyhedra. Program 13.1, in Pascal, performs these calculations for the pyramid of Figure 13.2. The following results are obtained:

Face	**Normal Vector** (a, b, c)
base	(0, −4, 0)
*side*1	(0, 2, 4)
*side*2	(4, 2, 0)
*side*3	(0, 2, −4)
*side*4	(−4, 2, 0)

Suppose an observer is somewhere in the quadrant of 3D space bounded by the positive X, Y and Z axes (and below a certain height; see Exercise 13.7). Any normal vector not pointing into this quadrant corresponds to a face of the pyramid that cannot be seen by such an observer. Clearly, the observer would only see faces *side*1 and *side*2, as shown in Figure 13.2(b). Similarly, an observer located in the opposite quadrant (bounded by the positive Y axis and the negative X and Z axes) would only see faces *side*3 and *side*4. Sometimes in computer graphics the observer's eye position is placed along the (positive) Z axis. In this case, any face with a normal vector that has a negative or zero z component is termed

```
program normal(input, output);

const
  BASE  = 0;
  SIDE1 = 1;
  SIDE2 = 2;
  SIDE3 = 3;
  SIDE4 = 4;

type point = array[1..3] of integer;

procedure EvalCoeff(x, y, z : point; var a, b, c : integer);
{evaluates the coefficients for three points, assumed in anti-clockwise order}
begin
  a := y[1]*(z[2] - z[3]) + y[2]*(z[3] - z[1]) + y[3]*(z[1] - z[2]);
  b := x[1]*(z[3] - z[2]) + x[2]*(z[1] - z[3]) + x[3]*(z[2] - z[1]);
  c := x[1]*(y[2] - y[3]) + x[2]*(y[3] - y[1]) + x[3]*(y[1] - y[2])
end;

procedure Coefficients(side : integer);
var
  x, y, z : point;
  a, b, c : integer;
begin
  case side of
    BASE : begin
             writeln('BASE');
             x[1] := -1;  y[1] := 0; z[1] :=  1;
             x[2] := -1;  y[2] := 0; z[2] := -1;
             x[3] :=  1;  y[3] := 0; z[3] := -1;
           end;

    SIDE1 : begin
             writeln('SIDE1');
             x[1] := -1;  y[1] := 0;   z[1] := 1;
             x[2] :=  1;  y[2] := 0;   z[2] := 1;
             x[3] :=  0;  y[3] := 2;   z[3] := 0;
           end;
```

Program 13.1 Computing the normal vectors for the pyramid.

a **back face** and clearly cannot be seen by such an observer.

Assuming for the moment that the 3D scene consists of a single polyhedron, this back face elimination is sufficient to solve the visibility problem. The set of visible polygon faces corresponds to those that have normal vectors which do not point away from the position of the observer. This set of visible polygons is rendered by reference to the edge polygon

```
SIDE2 : begin
          writeln('SIDE2');
          x[1] := 1;  y[1] := 0;  z[1] :=  1;
          x[2] := 1;  y[2] := 0;  z[2] := -1;
          x[3] := 0;  y[3] := 2;  z[3] :=  0;
        end;

SIDE3 : begin
          writeln('SIDE3');
          x[1] :=  1;  y[1] := 0;  z[1] := -1;
          x[2] := -1;  y[2] := 0;  z[2] := -1;
          x[3] :=  0;  y[3] := 2;  z[3] :=  0;
        end;

SIDE4 : begin
          writeln('SIDE4');
          x[1] := -1;  y[1] := 0;  z[1] := -1;
          x[2] := -1;  y[2] := 0;  z[2] :=  1;
          x[3] :=  0;  y[3] := 2;  z[3] :=  0;
        end;
  end;
  EvalCoeff(x, y, z, a, b, c);
  writeln('(a, b c) = (', a:3, b:3, c:3, ')')
end;

procedure pyramid;
var i : integer;
begin
  for i := BASE to SIDE4 do Coefficients(i)
end;

{main}
begin
  pyramid
end.
```

Program 13.1 (cont.)

structure of Section 13.3.1. This structure should therefore be extended so that the plane equation coefficients (a, b, c, d) are stored in the face table. Each face is examined to see if the normal vector points towards the observer. The union of all the edges corresponding to such visible faces is therefore constructed and used to render the polyhedron.

In reality, the scene is likely to consist of many polyhedra. Back face elimination then becomes a useful pre-processing phase to the main visibility algorithm. The visibility problem is discussed in Section 13.8.

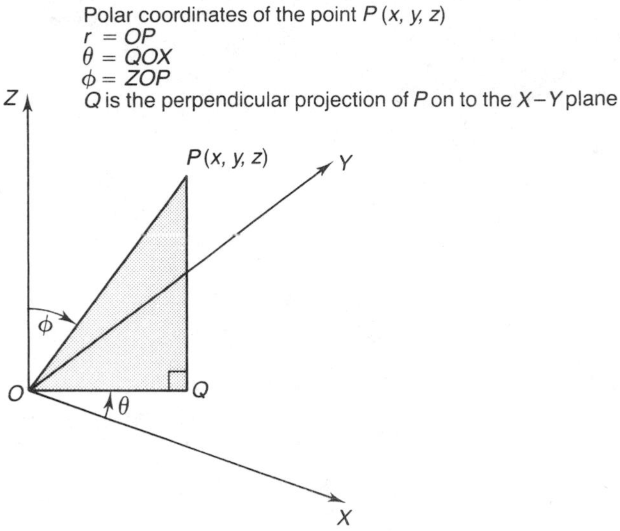

Figure 13.4
Polar coordinates.

13.4 3D Transformations

The viewing pipeline in 2D graphics involves transformations between various 2D coordinate systems: WC, NDC and DC. Moreover, at one of the stages the objects may be transformed by a matrix, usually representing some combination of translate, scale and rotate operations. In 3D graphics, the pipeline is more complex as there is a **projection** stage, where the 3D WC, in which the scene is described, are projected on to (ultimately) the 2D display space of the graphics device. Transformations may be applied explicitly by the application to 3D objects described in WC to achieve some desired effect, such as a rotation. Transformations are also effected implicitly to obtain a particular view of an object. This section discusses some of the basic mathematics involved in 3D transformations.

13.4.1 3D Polar Coordinates

The use of polar coordinates simplifies some of the mathematics of 3D transformations. (This insight is exploited by Ameraal, 1986, Chapter 4, and has influenced the following presentation.)

Consider Figure 13.4 which shows a point $P(x, y, z)$ in a RHS. Let Q be the perpendicular projection of P on to the X–Y plane. In **polar**

coordinates, P is specified by:

- the distance (r) OP;
- the angle (θ) between the positive X axis and Q;
- the angle (ϕ) between OP and the positive Z axis.

By construction, the angle OPQ is also ϕ. Therefore:

$$OQ = r \sin \phi$$

and hence:

$$\begin{aligned} x &= r \sin \phi \cos \theta \\ y &= r \sin \phi \sin \theta \\ z &= r \cos \phi \end{aligned} \qquad \textbf{(13.4)}$$

These expressions show how to find the cartesian coordinates given the polar coordinates (r, θ, ϕ). The inverse relationship is easily found to be:

$$\begin{aligned} r &= \sqrt{x^2 + y^2 + z^2} \\ \theta &= \arctan\left(\frac{y}{x}\right) \\ \phi &= \arccos\left(\frac{z}{r}\right) \end{aligned} \qquad \textbf{(13.5)}$$

(See Exercise 13.8.)

13.4.2 Homogeneous Coordinates

The homogeneous representation of a point (x, y, z) is (wx, wy, wz, w) (any $w \neq 0$). Equivalently, given the homogeneous coordinate (x, y, z, w), the cartesian equivalent is (x/w, y/w, z/w) ($w \neq 0$). Clearly, (x, y, z, 1) is equivalent to (x, y, z). (The importance of homogeneous coordinates in graphics is discussed by Reisenfeld, 1981.)

The homogeneous formulation allows the specification of 4 by 4 transformation matrices. Generally, given a point (x, y, z), and a 4 by 4 transformation matrix **T**, the transformed point is given by:

$$(x', y', z', w') = (x, y, z, 1)\,\mathbf{T}$$

and the resulting cartesian coordinate is therefore:

$$\left(\frac{x'}{w'}, \frac{y'}{w'}, \frac{z'}{w'}\right)$$

13.4.3 Translation

Given a point (x, y, z) and a translation vector (a, b, c), the translated point is clearly:

$$(x + a, y + b, z + c)$$

Hence, the following function definition:

type Point3D = real*real*real;

T: Point3D → (Point3D → Point3D);
fun *T*(*a*, *b*, *c*) (*x*, *y*, *z*) = (*x* + *a*, *y* + *b*, *z* + *c*) **nuf**

Equivalently, **T** may be expressed as an homogeneous transformation matrix:

$$\mathbf{T}(a, b, c) = \begin{pmatrix} 1 & 0 & 0 & 0 \\ 0 & 1 & 0 & 0 \\ 0 & 0 & 1 & 0 \\ a & b & c & 1 \end{pmatrix}$$

13.4.4 Scaling

Let (a, b, c) be scaling factors (relative to the origin). Then, for any point (x, y, z), the scaled point is (ax, by, cz). In functional terms:

S: Point3D → (Point3D → Point3D);
fun *S*(*a*, *b*, *c*) (*x*, *y*, *z*) = (*a***x*, *b***y*, *c***z*) **nuf**

In matrix terms:

$$\mathbf{S}(a, b, c) = \begin{pmatrix} a & 0 & 0 & 0 \\ 0 & b & 0 & 0 \\ 0 & 0 & c & 0 \\ 0 & 0 & 0 & 1 \end{pmatrix}$$

Note here that this transformation may be used for **reflection** – that is, to achieve the effect of changing the direction of an axis. For example, if $a = -1$, then positive values of x are converted to their equivalent negative values.

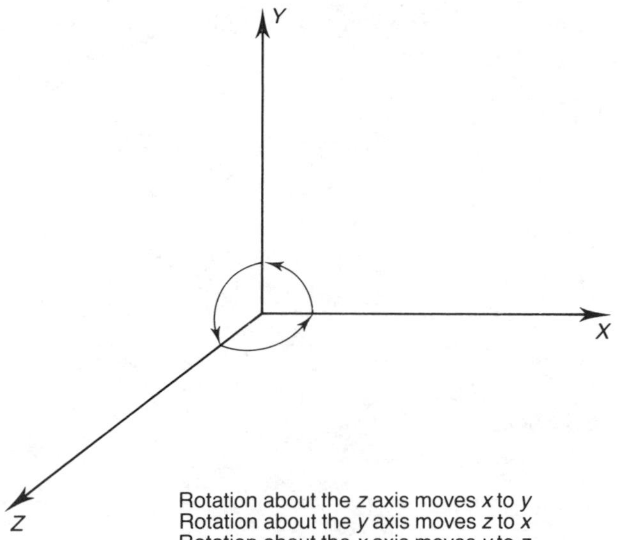
Y
X
Z
Rotation about the z axis moves x to y
Rotation about the y axis moves z to x
Rotation about the x axis moves y to z

Figure 13.5
The direction of positive rotation.

13.4.5 Rotation About the Principal Axes

While translation and scaling are simple generalizations of 2D translation and scaling, rotation is more complex, because rotations about the three axes have to be considered. It is therefore important in this context to specify the *direction* of the rotation. In a 2D system, rotating a point (x, y) by a positive angle moves the point in an anti-clockwise direction. However, when locating the X–Y plane in a 3D system, the equivalent rotation is about the Z axis. Hence, the convention adopted is that a positive rotation is anti-clockwise when looking down the axis of rotation towards the origin (see Figure 13.5).

ROTATION ABOUT THE *Z* AXIS

The rotation in the X–Y plane (about the z axis) by an angle θ results in (x, y) being transformed to (x', y') where:

$$x' = x \cos\theta - y \sin\theta \qquad \textbf{(13.6)}$$
$$y' = x \sin\theta + y \cos\theta$$

Since the distance of the point from the origin in the direction of z remains constant in a rotation about the Z axis, the required transformation function is:

R_z: real → (Point3D → Point3D);
fun $R_z\,\theta\,(x, y, z) = (x\,cos\,\theta - y\,sin\,\theta, x\,sin\,\theta + y\,cos\,\theta, z)$ **nuf**

In matrix terms:

$$\mathbf{R_z}(\theta) = \begin{pmatrix} \cos\theta & \sin\theta & 0 & 0 \\ -\sin\theta & \cos\theta & 0 & 0 \\ 0 & 0 & 1 & 0 \\ 0 & 0 & 0 & 1 \end{pmatrix}$$

ROTATION ABOUT THE *Y* AXIS

Argument by symmetry (that is, by replacing z by y, interchanging the corresponding elements, replacing x by z and y by x) shows that the rotation about the Y axis is:

R_y: real → (Point3D → Point3D);
fun $R_y\theta(x, y, z) = (z\,cos\,\theta - x\,sin\,\theta, y, z\,sin\,\theta + x\,cos\,\theta)$ **nuf**

$$\mathbf{R_y}(\theta) = \begin{pmatrix} -\sin\theta & 0 & \cos\theta & 0 \\ 0 & 1 & 0 & 0 \\ \cos\theta & 0 & \sin\theta & 0 \\ 0 & 0 & 0 & 1 \end{pmatrix}$$

ROTATION ABOUT THE *X* AXIS

Similarly, by replacing z by x, interchanging the elements, replacing y by z and x by y gives:

R_x: real → (Point3D → Point3D);
fun $R_x\,\theta\,(x, y, z) = (x, y\,cos\,\theta - z\,sin\,\theta, y\,sin\,\theta + z\,cos\,\theta)$ **nuf**

$$\mathbf{R_x}(\theta) = \begin{pmatrix} 1 & 0 & 0 & 0 \\ 0 & \cos\theta & \sin\theta & 0 \\ 0 & -\sin\theta & \cos\theta & 0 \\ 0 & 0 & 0 & 1 \end{pmatrix}$$

13.4.6 Composition and Inversion of Transformations

To scale a point, say, by (a, b, c) with respect to the fixed point (x_0, y_0, z_0), it is necessary to first translate the fixed point to the origin, then apply the scale and then apply the inverse translation to return to the original coordinate system. Such a transformation can be constructed by the **composition** of the transformation functions already defined or, equivalently, by multiplying the corresponding matrices.

Each of the transformations has obvious inverses:

$$\mathbf{T}^{-1}(a, b, c) = \mathbf{T}(-a, -b, -c) \qquad \text{(all } a, b, c\text{)}$$
$$\mathbf{S}^{-1}(a, b, c) = \mathbf{S}(1/a, 1/b, 1/c) \qquad \text{(all } a, b, c \neq 0\text{)}$$
$$\mathbf{R}^{-1}(\theta) = \mathbf{R}(-\theta) \qquad \text{(all } \theta\text{, for each of } x, y, z\text{)}$$

Hence (in matrix notation), to achieve the effect of scaling with respect to a fixed point:

$$\mathbf{M} = \mathbf{T}(-x_0, -y_0, -z_0) \quad \mathbf{S}(a, b, c) \quad \mathbf{T}(x_0, y_0, z_0)$$

Therefore, if (x, y, z) is the point to be transformed, then the result in homogeneous coordinates is:

$$\mathbf{pM} \qquad \text{where } \mathbf{p} = (x, y, z, 1)$$

Equivalently, in functional notation, composition of the three functions yields the *Point3D* → *Point3D* function:

$$\mathbf{M} = \mathbf{T}(x_0, y_0, z_0) \circ \mathbf{S}(a, b, c) \circ T(-x_0, -y_0, -z_0)$$

and therefore $\mathbf{M}(x, y, z)$ is the transformed point.

13.4.7 Rotation About an Arbitrary Axis

Rotations are particularly important in 3D graphics: an observer can be given a 'feel' for the shape of an object by viewing it from many different positions and directions. To achieve the required effect, rotation about one of the principal axes is not suitable. Rather, the rotation must be with respect to a line that passes through some point on or near the object: a sequence of such rotations will give the impression of an observer flying around the object or of the object spinning, as in the rotation of the Earth about its axis viewed from space. This requires the construction of a transformation that rotates an object about some given arbitrary line.

Let the line be $[(x1, y1), (x2, y2)]$. The idea is to generate a matrix **M** that transforms this line so that it coincides with one of the principal axes, say the Z axis. For the homogeneous point **p**, the resulting point would be **pM**. This new point is then rotated about the Z axis by the required amount, say α, yielding the point $\mathbf{p}\mathbf{M}\mathbf{R}_z(\alpha)$. Finally, the point is transformed back to the original coordinate system by applying the inverse transformation to **M**.

M may be constructed as follows:

(1) Perform a transformation so that one of the endpoints of the line is at the origin:

$$\mathbf{T}(-x1, -y1, -z1)$$

(2) Now let $(x, y, z) = (x2 - x1, y2 - y1, z2 - z1)$ be the other endpoint of the line, represented in polar coordinates as (r, θ, ϕ).

(3) Apply the rotation $-\theta$ about the Z axis (see Figure 13.4):

$$\mathbf{R}_z(-\theta)$$

This places the line in the X–Z plane.

(4) Apply the rotation $-\phi$ about the Y axis:

$$\mathbf{R}_y(-\phi)$$

This makes the line coincident with the positive Z axis.

Hence, the matrix **M** is defined by:

$$\mathbf{M} = \mathbf{T}(-x1, -y1, -z1)\,\mathbf{R}_z(-\theta)\,\mathbf{R}_y(-\phi)$$

and so the complete transformation is:

$$\mathbf{R} = \mathbf{M}\,\mathbf{R}_z(\alpha)\,\mathbf{M}^{-1}$$

where:

$$\mathbf{M}^{-1} = \mathbf{R}_y(\phi)\,\mathbf{R}_z(\theta)\,\mathbf{T}(x1, y1, z1)$$

(Remember that the inverse of a matrix multiplication is the product of the inverses in reverse order, and the same is true with respect to function composition.)

This is an expensive computation, but things are not quite as bad as they seem. For a sequence of incremental rotations about the same axis (to give the effect of a spinning object), **M** and its inverse need only be computed once. Moreover, it is easy to compute $\mathbf{R_z}(\alpha)$ in such a way that repeated computations of sines and cosines are avoided (see Exercises 13.9 and 13.10).

13.5 Viewing

Sections 13.1 to 13.4 concentrated on the description of objects in a 3D WC system. This section is concerned with the capture of a 3D scene on the 2D display space of a graphics device. For this to be accomplished, a viewing model must be established which specifies a number of parameters determining how the 3D scene will ultimately appear on the 2D display. These viewing parameters can be derived by analogy with a pseudo camera, sometimes called the **synthetic camera model**. (It is a pseudo camera because the model does not include a basic feature of the camera – the lens – although Potsemil and Chakravarty, 1982, have developed a system that properly reflects the true properties of a camera-generated image.) The model is, in fact, more like a pin-hole camera, where light rays enter a tiny hole in the side of a box and expose a film negative inside.

13.5.1 Specifying a View

The CORE system, and the recently proposed 3D extension to GKS (ISO, 1986b), adopt a similar viewing model. The parameters of the model include the viewing direction of the synthetic camera and the point in the scene on which the camera is focused, called the **view reference point** (**VRP**). The **view plane** (**VP**) is the plane on to which the scene is to be projected. This is specified by a normal, called the **view plane normal** (**VPN**), and the distance of the VRP to the VP along the VPN, the **view plane distance** (**VPD**). The VPN should be thought of as the direction in which the camera is pointing (see Figure 13.6).

Referring to the camera analogy, the box camera may be rested horizontally or tilted at an angle. This orientation is specified by another parameter called the **view-up vector** (**VUV**). Let the plane parallel to the VP and passing through the VRP be called the **view reference plane**. Now, project a ray from the VUV parallel to the VPN and find its intersection with the view reference plane. The line from the VRP to this intersection point determines the Y axis of a new coordinate system called the **view coordinate system**. The Z axis of this system is the VPN. In the CORE specification, the X axis of the view coordinate system is such that the new

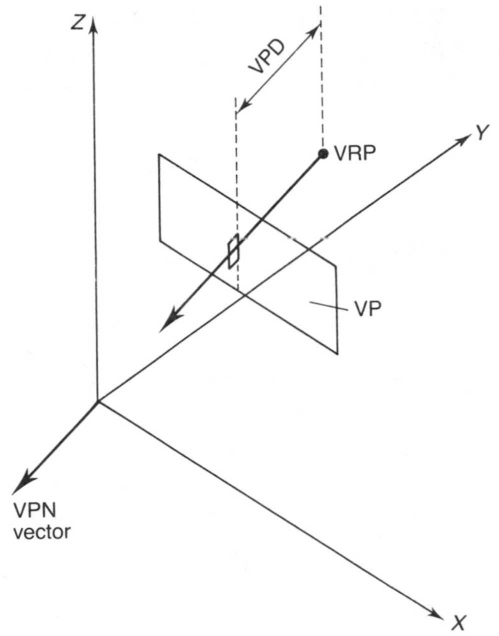

Figure 13.6
The VPN vector and the VPD specify the position of the VP relative to the VRP.

system is left-handed, the idea being that the *X* and *Y* axes are parallel to the sides of the screen, and the *Z* axis points to behind the screen. In GKS 3D, the view system is a RHS. In this book, however, the LHS is adopted. (Interchanging between the two is a trivial task.) These ideas are illustrated in Figure 13.7. The new coordinate system is also called the **UVN** system, with the *Z* axis denoted as *N*, the *Y* axis as *V* and the *X* axis as *U*.

The VRP, VPN and the VUV are specified relative to the WC system. Further parameters of the model are in the new view coordinates. It is important to note that the view system has the *same* metric as WC; in other words, all distances are preserved – the transformation from one system to another involves no scaling, only translation and rotation.

13.5.2 Types of Projection

The two major classes of projection are called **perspective** and **parallel**. Perspective projection requires a **centre of projection (COP)** as an additional parameter, whereas parallel projection requires a **direction of projection (DOP)**. In the case of perspective projection, the projected image is formed on the VP, by projecting rays back from the objects in the scene to the COP. For any point in WC, the intersection of the VP with the ray from the point to the COP is the projection of that point. Perspective projection aims at realism, in the sense that (for a constant VPD) the further away the

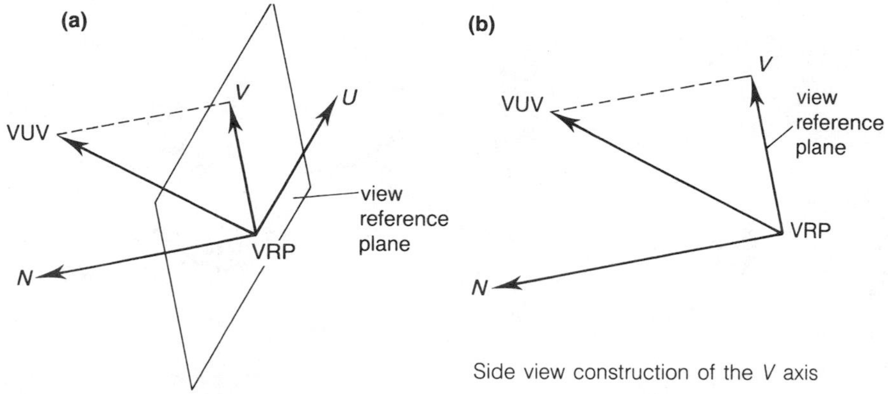

Figure 13.7
The view coordinate system.

object is from the VP, the smaller its projection, approximating the behaviour of a camera or normal eyesight (see Figure 13.8(a)).

A parallel projection of a point, on the other hand, is constructed by projecting a ray from the point that is parallel to the DOP. The intersection of the ray with the VP is the projected point (see Figure 13.9). An **orthographic** parallel projection is one in which the direction of the projection is parallel to the VPN. This is most suited for engineering draughting applications, since relative proportions of lines in the projection are the same as those in the original 3D space.

Within the two main classes of projection there are many different types, a study of which is beyond the scope of this book. (Readers should consult the paper by Carlbom and Paciorek, 1978, for further information.) In this book, the attention is mainly focused on perspective projections; it is left as an exercise for the reader to derive equivalent results for the case of general parallel projections.

The basic mathematics of projection is straightforward. Consider Figure 13.8(b), which shows a side view of a perspective projection, in the case where the COP is at the origin of a left-handed viewing coordinate system and the VP is at distance D from the origin. The y coordinate of the projection is clearly at point B. Since OCP and OAB are similar triangles:

$$\frac{AB}{OA} = \frac{CP}{OC}$$

so that:

$$AB = y\frac{D}{z}$$

By a similar construction, the projected x coordinate is $(x\,D/z)$ and the

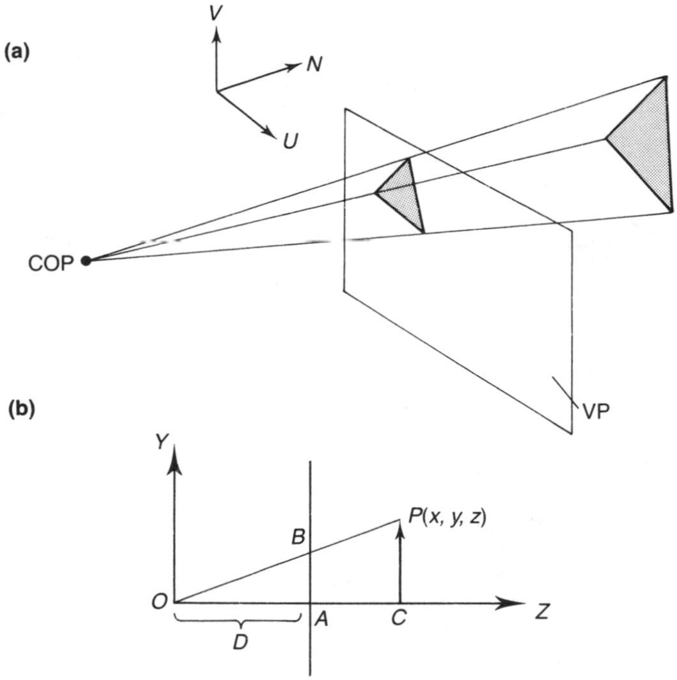

Figure 13.8
Perspective projection.

projected z coordinate is obviously D. Hence, the perspective projection may be summarized as:

$$(x', y', z') = \left(x\frac{D}{z}, y\frac{D}{z}, D\right)$$

where (x', y', z') is the projected point corresponding to (x, y, z).

In the case of an orthographic parallel projection, it can be seen from Figure 13.9(b) that the corresponding result is:

$$(x', y', z') = (x, y, D)$$

Clearly, in the case of orthographic parallel projection the projected x and y coordinates are the same as the original values (see Exercises 13.11 and 13.12).

13.5.3 Specifying the View Volume

The functions required to determine the view of the scene described in WC are as follows:

type Point3D = real*real*real;

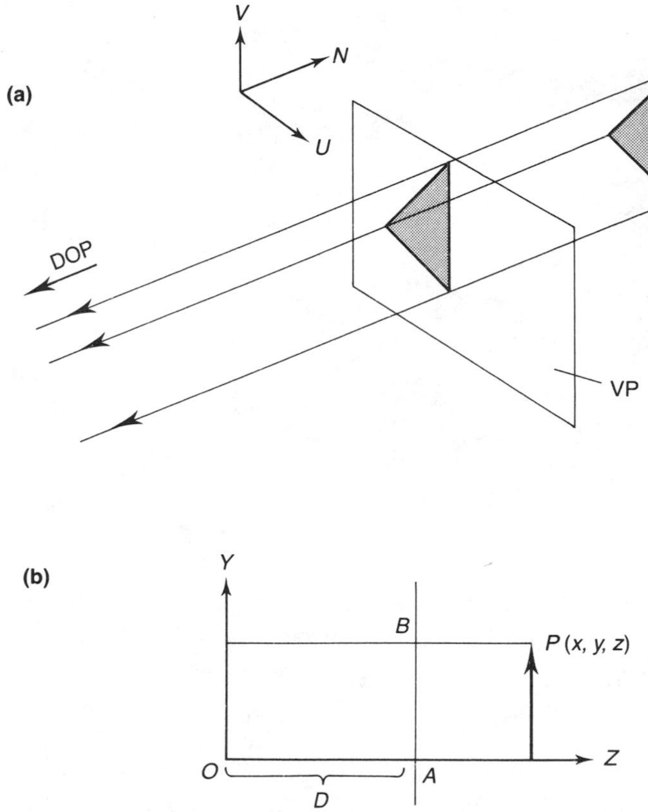

Figure 13.9
Orthographic parallel projection.

- *SetVRP*(*r* : *Point3D*) sets the VRP in WC.
- *SetVPN*(*n* : *Point3D*) sets the VPN as a vector relative to the origin of the WC system. The line parallel to this vector and through the VRP is the VPN and forms the *Z* (or *N*) axis of the view coordinate system. The plane passing through the VRP, normal to the VPN, is the view reference plane.
- *SetVUV*(*v* : *Point3D*) determines the VUV. A vector parallel to this relative to the VRP which is projected on to the view reference plane by a ray parallel to the VPN determines the *Y* (or *V*) axis of the view coordinate system. The *X* (or *U*) axis is specified so that *UVN* forms a LHS.
- *SetViewDistance*(*d*) is the distance of the VP from the VRP along the VPN. This is relative to view coordinates, so that a positive value of *d* means that the VP is in front of the VRP and a negative *d* that it is behind the VRP (on the negative *N* axis).
- *SetProjectionType*(*p*) where *p*, which is PARALLEL or PERSPECTIVE, determines the type of projection.

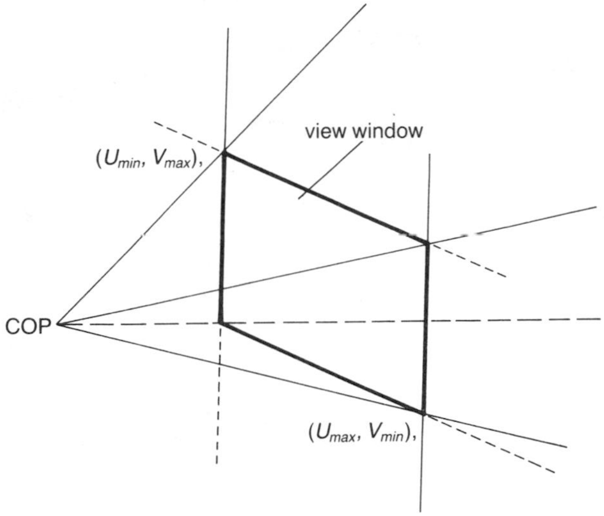

Figure 13.10 Representation of the view window.

- *SetCOP(p : Point3D)* specifies the COP in view coordinates (relative to VRP as origin) for the case of perspective projection.
- *SetDOP(d : Point3D)* specifies the DOP relative to view coordinates for the case of parallel projection.

Attention will now be limited to perspective projections. Following the camera analogy (or indeed normal eyesight), there is still a crucial aspect of viewing that is missing from the discussion so far. A camera captures only a relatively limited view of a scene; for example, the photographer looking through the viewfinder does not see objects in the scene behind, and in fact can only see a cone-shaped area of the scene in front. (The angle at the apex of the cone depends on the camera lens.) The area of the scene that can be seen by the observer is called the **view volume**. In the graphics case, this volume is specified by a 2D window on the VP in addition to two clipping planes parallel to the VP.

Let $(U_{min}, U_{max}, V_{min}, V_{max})$ be a window on the VP called the **view window**. The rays projecting forwards and backwards from the window corners to the COP determine the view volume to be an infinite pyramid, as shown in Figure 13.10. Note that the pyramid is typically irregular, as there is no restriction as to where the window must be located on the VP – only that the window sides are parallel to the U and V axes.

The idea behind the view volume is that objects (and parts of objects) outside of it are not projected; that is, the view volume acts as a 3D clipping region. In addition, to exclude objects that are far away or too close to the COP, two further planes may be specified called the **front clipping plane** and the **back clipping plane**, as shown in Figure 13.11. These may be used to

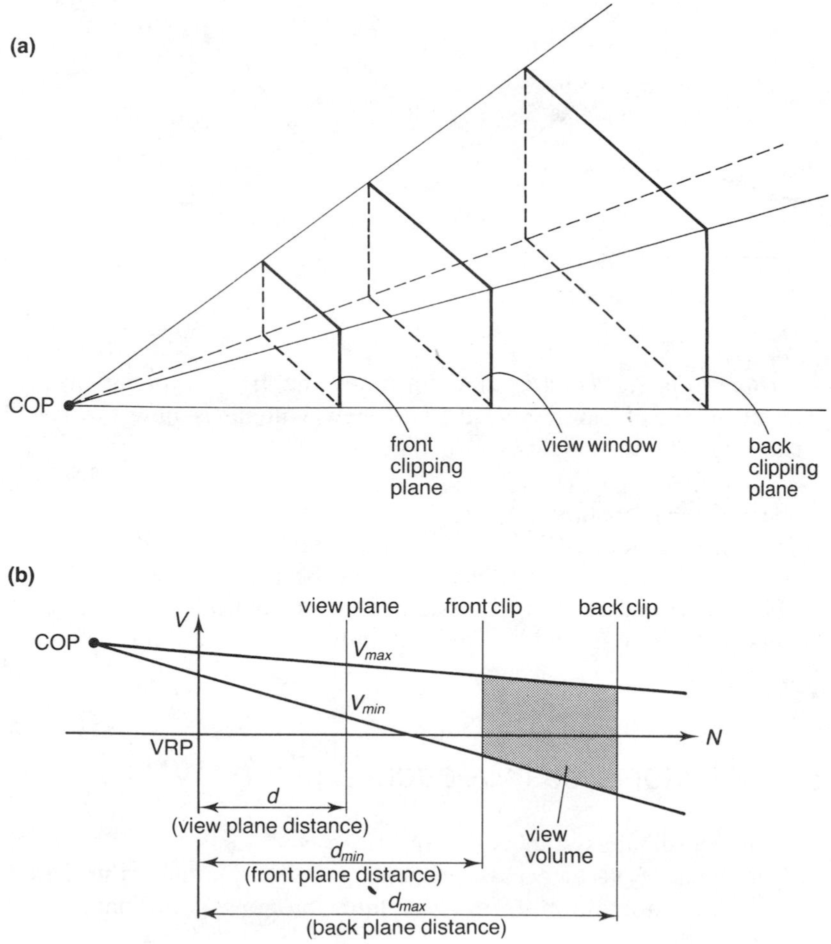

Figure 13.11
Representation of the view volume.

further restrict the view volume, which now becomes a doubly truncated pyramid, sometimes known as a **frustrum**.

The view volume can be determined therefore by three further functions:

- *SetViewWindow*(U_{min}, U_{max}, V_{min}, V_{max}) sets the window on the VP. The view volume now becomes the infinite pyramid with apex at the COP and with sides passing through the corners of the view window.
- *SetFrontClippingPlane*(d_{min}) determines the front clipping plane at distance d_{min} from the VRP along the VPN. The view volume is now the truncated infinite pyramid with apex at the COP and front at this plane.

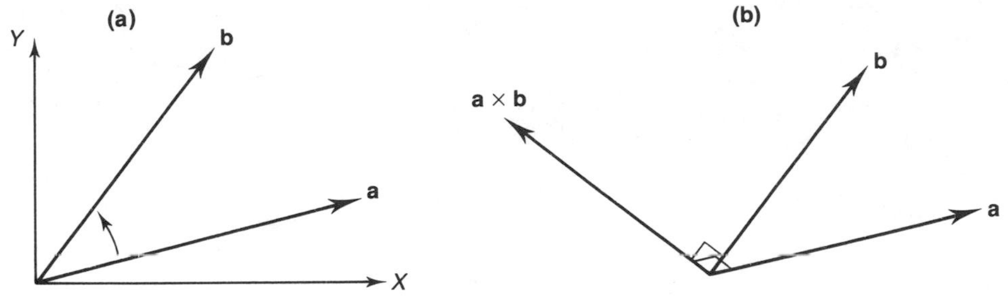

Figure 13.12
Defining the cross product of **a** and **b**.

- *SetBackClippingPlane*(d_{max}) determines the front clipping plane as distance d_{max} from the VRP. The view volume is now the doubly truncated pyramid as shown in Figure 13.11.

There are no special restrictions on these view volume parameters, except that $d_{min} < d_{max}$. Figure 13.11 shows these planes on either side of the VP, but there is no special reason why this should be the case.

This now completes the discussion on the specification of the viewing parameters (see Exercise 13.13). The remainder of this section is devoted to implementation.

13.5.4 Vector Cross Products and the UVN System

The viewing coordinate system is determined by the VRP, the VPN and the VUV. The idea of **vector cross products** greatly simplifies the task of deriving the transformation from WC into the new coordinate system determined by these three vectors.

Let **a** and **b** be any two vectors such that rotation of **a** by a positive angle less than 180° rotates it into **b**, as shown in Figure 13.12(a). Then the cross product of **a** and **b**, written **a** × **b**, is a vector perpendicular to both **a** and **b** such that the three vectors form a RHS. (For example, if **a** and **b** are inscribed on your desk top, then **a** × **b** points out of the desk.) (See Gasson, 1983, pp. 437–439.)

Recall that the length of a vector **a** is:

$$|\mathbf{a}| = \sqrt{a_1^2 + a_2^2 + a_3^2}$$

Then, the length of the cross product is given by:

$$|\mathbf{a} \times \mathbf{b}| = |\mathbf{a}|\,|\mathbf{b}| \sin\theta$$

where θ is the angle between **a** and **b**.

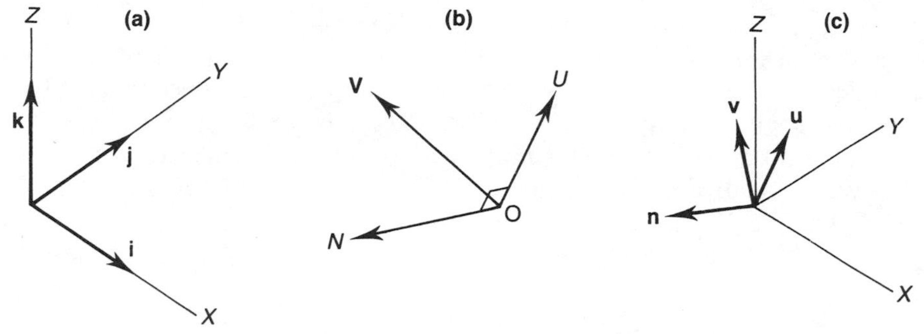

Figure 13.13 Defining the UVN system.

Let **i**, **j** and **k** be the unit base vectors in a RHS so that:

$$\mathbf{i} = (1, 0, 0)$$
$$\mathbf{j} = (0, 1, 0)$$
$$\mathbf{k} = (0, 0, 1)$$

as shown in Figure 13.13(a). Then, the following results follow from the definition:

$$\mathbf{i} \times \mathbf{i} = \mathbf{j} \times \mathbf{j} = \mathbf{k} \times \mathbf{k} = (0, 0, 0) \qquad \text{(since } \sin 0 = 0\text{)}$$

$$\begin{array}{lll} \mathbf{i} \times \mathbf{j} = \mathbf{k} & \mathbf{j} \times \mathbf{i} = -\mathbf{k} & \text{(by direction of angles)} \\ \mathbf{j} \times \mathbf{k} = \mathbf{i} & \mathbf{k} \times \mathbf{j} = -\mathbf{i} & \\ \mathbf{k} \times \mathbf{i} = \mathbf{j} & \mathbf{i} \times \mathbf{k} = -\mathbf{j} & \end{array}$$

Any vector can be written as a linear combination of the base vectors **i**, **j** and **k**. In the case of **a** and **b**:

$$\mathbf{a} = a_1\mathbf{i} + a_2\mathbf{j} + a_3\mathbf{k}$$
$$\mathbf{b} = b_1\mathbf{i} + b_2\mathbf{j} + b_3\mathbf{k}$$

and therefore:

$$\mathbf{a} \times \mathbf{b} = (a_1\mathbf{i} + a_2\mathbf{j} + a_3\mathbf{k}) \times (b_1\mathbf{i} + b_2\mathbf{j} + b_3\mathbf{k})$$

Evaluating this product yields:

$$\mathbf{i}(a_2b_3 - a_3b_2) - \mathbf{j}(a_1b_3 - a_3b_1) + \mathbf{k}(a_1b_2 - a_2b_1)$$

which, for the purposes of memorization only, can be written as the pseudo determinant:

$$\begin{vmatrix} \mathbf{i} & \mathbf{j} & \mathbf{k} \\ a_1 & a_2 & a_3 \\ b_1 & b_2 & b_3 \end{vmatrix}$$

A paper by Singleton (1986) suggests the following use of vector cross products for the determination of the UVN system. But, first, recall that the normalization of a vector **a** is one that points in the same direction as **a**, but has unit length. Clearly, the normalization of **a** is $\mathbf{a}/|\mathbf{a}|$.

Let **n** be the VPN vector normalized so that it has unit length and **V** the VUV (relative to the origin of WC). Then, the **u** vector, which is parallel to the *U* axis relative to the origin is:

$$\mathbf{u} = \frac{\mathbf{n} \times \mathbf{V}}{|\mathbf{n} \times \mathbf{V}|} \tag{13.6}$$

In this case, the objective is to form a LHS, but this result is correct only if the angle from **V** to **n** in an anti-clockwise direction is less than 180°. The VUV must clearly not lie on the VPN, excluding the possibility of the angle between them being exactly 180° (see Exercise 13.15). Division is therefore by the length of the cross product, to ensure that the resulting **u** vector has unit length.

Given the **n** and **u** vectors, the unit length **v** axis vector can be determined by:

$$\mathbf{v} = \mathbf{u} \times \mathbf{n} \tag{13.7}$$

The results are shown in Figures 13.13(b) and (c).

This section has shown how to construct the unit vectors **u**, **v** and **n** at the origin of the WC system, which are respectively parallel to the UVN system axes. This result is used in the next section to derive the viewing transformation.

13.5.5 The Viewing Transformation

The viewing transformation transforms objects described relative to the WC system into a description relative to the viewing system. This transformation can only involve rotation and translation, since the metrics of the two systems must be the same. For example, look at any right-hand corner of the room you are now in. Let the vertical corner be the *Z* axis of a RHS with origin on the floor in that corner. Imagine all the objects in the room described relative to that coordinate system. Now let the point between your eyes be the origin of a viewing coordinate system, with the *N* axis (the VPN) corresponding to the direction in which you are looking, the *V* axis pointing upwards and perpendicular to the viewing direction, and the *U* axis perpendicular to *N* and *V* and pointing to your right. The point between your eyes is the origin of a left-handed UVN system. Now imagine describing all of the objects in the room relative to your personal UVN system. Clearly, all of the measurements in the room (across and between objects, for example) are the same in this new system as in the original system. The new object descriptions can be formed from the old system by translation (from origin to origin) and a series of rotations.

Let the viewing transformation be represented by a 4 by 4 homogeneous matrix **M**. This can be represented in partitioned form as follows:

$$\mathbf{M} = \left(\begin{array}{c|c} \mathbf{M_0} & \mathbf{0} \\ \hline \mathbf{m_1} & 1 \end{array}\right)$$

In this representation, $\mathbf{M_0}$ is the purely rotational part of **M** (that is, it involves no translation effect). From Figure 13.3(c), it can be seen that application of $\mathbf{M_0}$ to the **u**, **v** and **n** vectors must rotate them into the corresponding unit vectors on the principal axes: **i**, **j** and **k**. (By construction, $\mathbf{M_0}$ will also contain a reflection element, since the two sets of axes are left-handed and right-handed, respectively.) Hence:

$$\mathbf{u\,M_0} = \mathbf{i}$$
$$\mathbf{v\,M_0} = \mathbf{j}$$
$$\mathbf{n\,M_0} = \mathbf{k}$$

This is equivalent to:

$$\mathbf{L\,M_0} = \mathbf{I}$$

where:

$$\mathbf{L} = \begin{pmatrix} u_1 & u_2 & u_3 \\ v_1 & v_2 & v_3 \\ n_1 & n_2 & n_3 \end{pmatrix}$$

and **I** is the 3 by 3 identity matrix.

Since **u**, **v** and **n** are orthogonal (at right-angles), the inner products $\mathbf{u}'.\mathbf{v} = \mathbf{u}'.\mathbf{n} = \mathbf{v}'.\mathbf{n} = 0$. Furthermore, since they are unit vectors it follows that:

$$\mathbf{L}'.\mathbf{L} = \mathbf{I}$$

(**L** is an orthogonal matrix with its inverse equal to its transpose.) Hence:

$$\mathbf{M_0} = \mathbf{L}' = \begin{pmatrix} u_1 & v_1 & n_1 \\ u_2 & v_2 & n_2 \\ u_3 & v_3 & n_3 \end{pmatrix}$$

It is an easy task to find the $\mathbf{m_1}$ component of $\mathbf{M}$, since the VRP must translate into the origin of the WC system. Hence, writing VRP as point $\mathbf{r}$:

$$(\mathbf{r}, 1)\begin{pmatrix} \mathbf{M_0} & \mathbf{0} \\ & \\ \mathbf{m_1} & 1 \end{pmatrix} = (0, 0, 0, 1)$$

and therefore:

$$\mathbf{r}\,\mathbf{M_0} + \mathbf{m_1} = (0, 0, 0)$$

and:

$$\begin{aligned} \mathbf{m_1} &= -\mathbf{r}\,\mathbf{M_0} \\ &= -(r_1 u_1 + r_2 u_2 + r_3 u_3, r_1 v_1 + r_2 v_2 + r_3 v_3, r_1 n_1 + r_2 n_2 + r_3 n_3) \end{aligned}$$

Complete specification of the **M** matrix is therefore:

$$\mathbf{M} = \begin{pmatrix} u_1 & v_1 & n_1 & 0 \\ u_2 & v_2 & n_2 & 0 \\ u_3 & v_3 & n_3 & 0 \\ -\mathbf{r}.\mathbf{u}' & -\mathbf{r}.\mathbf{v}' & -\mathbf{r}.\mathbf{n}' & 1 \end{pmatrix}$$

Thus, for any point **p** in WC, the corresponding homogeneous point in view coordinates is (**p**, 1)**M**.

13.5.6 Transforming the View Volume to Canonical Form

The previous sections have shown how to construct the transformation that maps WC objects into their equivalent viewing coordinate description. After this transformation has taken place, a possible picture of the situation is as shown in Figure 13.11(b).

The next stage of implementation of this 3D viewing pipeline is to clip the objects in the scene to the 3D view volume and then project this on to the VP. These actions can be carried out in view space, but the irregular shape of the view volume makes the clipping operation difficult. Instead, a further transformation is applied which has the effect of mapping the view volume into a box (technically known as a **rectangular parallelpiped**). This has three advantages:

(1) It makes the clipping operation very straightforward – in fact, hardly more complex than 2D clipping.

(2) It aids the operation of hidden surface removal.

(3) This transformation implicitly carries out the perspective projection.

This transformation is derived in the following three stages, of which the first is trivial.

COP AT THE ORIGIN

It is now convenient to have the COP as the origin of the viewing coordinate system. Since the COP is measured relative to the VRP as origin, this requires the translation $\mathbf{T}(-C_x, -C_y, -C_z)$, where C is the COP. This results in the situation shown in Figure 13.14(a). Clearly, the translation will affect the window boundaries and distances of the VP and clipping planes along the Z axis. The view window boundaries are now referred to as (x_1, x_2, y_1, y_2) and the plane distances as D, D_{min} and D_{max}.

TRANSFORMING THE VIEW VOLUME TO A (TRUNCATED) REGULAR PYRAMID

This step involves finding a transformation that maps the original view volume into a regular pyramid – that is, with sides sloping at 45°. Figure 13.14(b) shows a side view of such a view volume. In this transformation, distances along the Z axis are preserved, and the result can be achieved purely by rotation and scaling of the Y and X axes relative to the origin. (Such a transformation is known as a **shear**.) In the case of y and z, the transformation is of the form:

$$\begin{aligned} y' &= A\,y + B\,z \\ z' &= z \end{aligned} \qquad \textbf{(13.8)}$$

From Figure 13.14, it must be the case that:

$$\begin{aligned} D &= A\,y_2 + B\,D \\ -D &= A\,y_1 + B\,D \end{aligned}$$

which results in:

$$A = \frac{2D}{dy} \quad \text{where } dy = y_2 - y_1 \qquad \textbf{(13.9)}$$

$$B = -\frac{(y_1 + y_2)}{dy}$$

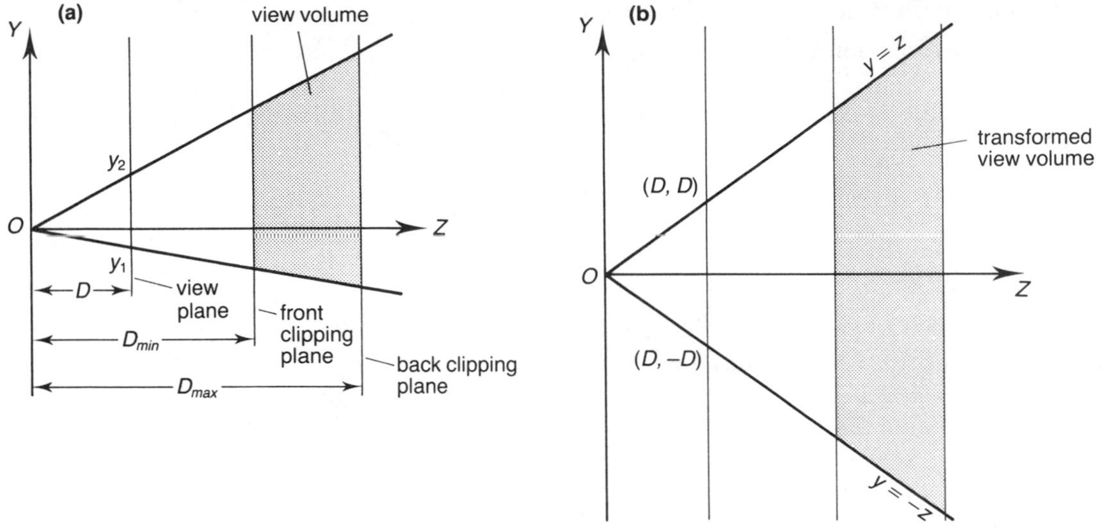

Figure 13.14
(a) View volume with origin at COP.
(b) Canonical view volume.

A similar result for x shows that the transformation matrix **R** (for regular) is:

$$\mathbf{R} = \begin{pmatrix} \frac{2D}{dx} & 0 & 0 & 0 \\ 0 & \frac{2D}{dy} & 0 & 0 \\ -\frac{px}{dx} & -\frac{py}{dy} & 1 & 0 \\ 0 & 0 & 0 & 1 \end{pmatrix}$$

where $px = x_1 + x_2$ and $py = y_1 + y_2$. Application of the transformation **R** maps points in the viewing space (with COP as the origin) into the regular canonical viewing space shown in Figure 13.14(b).

TRANSFORMING TO A RECTANGULAR PARALLELPIPED

The final transformation maps the truncated regular pyramid into a box, with x and y boundaries being from -1 to 1 and the z boundary from 0 to 1. (These choices are for convenience – any values would do.) The front clipping plane is mapped to the $z = 0$ plane in the new system and the back clipping plane to the $z = 1$ plane. The COP is in effect pushed back to minus infinity. The resulting coordinate system is called the **projection coordinate system** and is really the view volume transformed to correspond

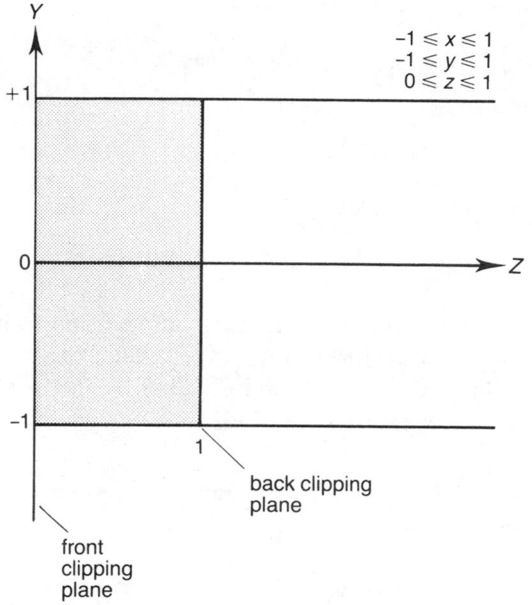

Figure 13.15
Canonical view volume as a box.

to an orthographic parallel projection. (It is also sometimes called here 'box space'.)

The corresponding transformation matrix (**B** for box) can be constructed by using the fact that the change from Figure 13.14(b) to Figure 13.15 can be achieved by scaling according to the value of z: the smaller the value of z, the greater y must be scaled (and similarly for x). Since, in addition, the old origin maps to minus infinity, this suggests the following transformations for y and z:

$$y' = A + B\frac{y}{z}$$

$$z' = E + \frac{F}{z} \qquad \textbf{(13.10)}$$

Substituting the corresponding values of y and z into this equation and solving for A, B, E and F results in:

$$y' = \frac{y}{z}$$

$$z' = \left(\frac{D_{max}}{D_{max} - D_{min}}\right)\left(\frac{z - D_{min}}{z}\right) \qquad \textbf{(13.11)}$$

with a similar result for x. This transformation can be written in homogeneous form as:

$$\mathbf{B} = \begin{pmatrix} 1 & 0 & 0 & 0 \\ 0 & 1 & 0 & 0 \\ 0 & 0 & \dfrac{D_{max}}{D_{max} - D_{min}} & 1 \\ 0 & 0 & \dfrac{-D_{max} D_{min}}{D_{max} - D_{min}} & 0 \end{pmatrix}$$

Note that this produces a genuinely homogeneous point (with z as the last element) when used to transform $(x, y, z, 1)$. This can be easily seen by evaluating the product $(x, y, z, 1)\mathbf{B}$ and dividing by the last element of the homogeneous point (see Exercise 13.21).

13.5.7 Projection

Multiplication of the matrices **R** and **B** derived in Section 13.5.6 results in the matrix **P** which transforms the objects from the viewing space (with origin at the COP, this will be assumed from now on) into the rectangular (box) space – the projection coordinate system. The form of **P** can be easily shown to be (see Exercise 13.22):

$$\mathbf{P} = \mathbf{R}\,\mathbf{B} = \begin{pmatrix} \dfrac{2D}{dx} & 0 & 0 & 0 \\ 0 & \dfrac{2D}{dy} & 0 & 0 \\ -\dfrac{px}{dx} & -\dfrac{py}{dy} & \dfrac{D_{max}}{D_{max} - D_{min}} & 1 \\ 0 & 0 & \dfrac{-D_{max} D_{min}}{D_{max} - D_{min}} & 0 \end{pmatrix}$$

Now the projection coordinate system represents the original objects in this new space, which is equivalent to an orthographic parallel projection space. Therefore, to compute the x and y projection values in this space is simply a matter of ignoring the z coordinate. In other words, for any point (x, y, z) in view space, the corresponding homogeneous point in projection space is $(x, y, z, 1)\mathbf{P}$, and the x and y projection coordinates of the equivalent 3D coordinate is the projected 2D point on the VP. The remainder of this section shows this result in detail.

Let (x, y, z) be a point in view space. Assume a view window of (x_1, x_2, y_1, y_2) and a viewport in NDC of $(V_{xmin}, V_{xmax}, V_{ymin}, V_{ymax})$. Then, in view space, the projection of the point to the VP is:

$$\left(\frac{xD}{z}, \frac{yD}{z}\right)$$

Therefore, using the results of Chapter 4, the corresponding screen coordinate point (x_s, y_s) is:

$$x_s = V_{xmin} + \left(\frac{dV_x}{dx}\right)\left(\frac{xD}{z} - x_1\right)$$
$$y_s = V_{ymin} + \left(\frac{dV_y}{dy}\right)\left(\frac{yD}{z} - y_1\right) \qquad \textbf{(13.12)}$$

where $dV_x = V_{xmax} - V_{xmin}$, $dx = x_2 - x_1$, and similarly for y.

Alternatively, the point (x, y, z) can be transformed into projection space by using the matrix **P**. The resulting homogeneous point in projection space is:

$$\left(\frac{(2Dx - zpx)}{dx}, \frac{(2Dy - zpy)}{dy}, \frac{D_{max}(z - D_{min})}{(D_{max} - D_{min})}, z\right)$$

where $px = x_1 + x_2$ and $py = y_1 + y_2$. Hence, transforming this to 3D space by dividing throughout by the last element, z, the corresponding point is:

$$\left(\frac{\frac{2Dx}{z} - px}{dx}, \frac{\frac{2Dy}{z} - py}{dy}, \frac{D_{max}\left(1 - \frac{D_{min}}{z}\right)}{D_{max} - D_{min}}\right) \qquad \textbf{(13.13)}$$

Since this is now in projection space, the projected 2D point has the same x and y coordinate values. However, the view window has now been transformed to the region $(-1, 1, -1, 1)$ (see Figure 13.15), and hence using the window to viewport transformation:

$$x_s = V_{xmin} + \left(\frac{dV_x}{2}\right)\left(\frac{\frac{2Dx}{z} - px}{dx} + 1\right)$$
$$y_s = V_{ymin} + \left(\frac{dV_y}{2}\right)\left(\frac{\frac{2Dy}{z} - py}{dy} + 1\right)$$

A rearrangement of these expressions gives the same result as shown in Equation (13.12).

13.5.8 3D Clipping

One of the advantages of transforming to projection space is that the view volume is box shaped, which makes the clipping process relatively straightforward. Recall the algorithm for clipping lines discussed in Section 4.4. Let the line be $[p1, p2]$. The set of edges of which $p1$ is outside (*out*1) is constructed, and similarly for $p2$. The intersection of *out*1 and *out*2 is not empty when the line is completely on one side of a clipping edge, in which case the clipping function returns no line. The union of *out*1 and *out*2 is empty when both endpoints are completely inside the clipping region, in which case the original line is returned. Otherwise, the line is intersected with one of the edges in the union and the resulting line is clipped.

Exactly the same approach can be adopted in the 3D case. Here, the clipping region is defined by six planes, $x = 1$, $x = -1$, $y = 1$, $y = -1$, $z = 1$ and $z = 0$, with the interior as $-1 \leqslant x \leqslant 1$, $-1 \leqslant y \leqslant 1$, $0 \leqslant z \leqslant 1$. Generally, the clipping region can be defined by:

$$\begin{aligned} left &\leqslant x \leqslant right \\ lower &\leqslant y \leqslant upper \\ front &\leqslant z \leqslant back \end{aligned}$$

The equivalent function to *EdgeSet* is as follows:

```
Returns the set of planes that a point is outside.
fun ClipPlaneSet(p, clipregion) =
  let val (x, y, z) = p
     and (left, right, lower, upper, front, back) = clipregion
  in
    let val isoutside = [x < left, x > right, y < lower, y > upper, z < front,
                         z > back]
    in
      {plane | isoutside[plane]}
    ni
  ni
nuf
```

The main function *ClipLine* reads the same as in Section 4.4, except that *EdgeSet* is replaced by *ClipPlaneSet*. The remaining consideration concerns the intersection calculations performed by the intersection function.

In the case of 3D, it is convenient to represent the line by a parametric equation for the purposes of computing the intersections. For the line segment joining (x_1, y_1, z_1) to (x_2, y_2, z_2):

$$\begin{aligned} x(t) &= x_1 + t\,dx \\ y(t) &= y_1 + t\,dy \\ z(t) &= z_1 + t\,dz \end{aligned} \tag{13.14}$$

and:

$$p(t) = (x(t), y(t), z(t))$$

where $dx = x_2 - x_1$, and similarly for dy and dz. The locus of $p(t)$ as t ranges between 0 and 1 is the required line.

To compute the intersection of the line with, for example, the plane $x = X$, the following equation:

$$x(t) = X$$

must be solved for t, which results in:

$$t = \left(\frac{X - x_1}{dx}\right) \qquad \textbf{(13.15)}$$

If the line segment actually intersects the plane, then $0 \leqslant t \leqslant 1$. The resulting t can then be substituted into Equation (13.14) to compute the corresponding y and z. When calculating the intersections in the context of the clipping function, it will always be the case that t is in the range $0 < t < 1$ (see Exercise 13.23). Hence, the intersection of the line with the plane $x = X$ is at the point:

$$\left(X, y_1 + \left(\frac{dy}{dx}\right)(X - x_1), z_1 + \left(\frac{dz}{dx}\right)(X - x_1)\right)$$

Similar results for the intersections with the y and z planes can easily be obtained (see Exercise 13.24).

Clipping a line to the truncated regular pyramid view volume derived in Section 13.5.6 is, in fact, no more difficult. The same strategy may be used, except in this case the clipping planes are expressed so that the elements of the *isoutside* sequence in *ClipPlaneSet* are different. In addition, the intersection calculations are different in detail, although they may be derived in the same way (see Exercise 13.25).

In 3D graphics, polygons are more important than lines, as should be clear from the fact that the basic way in which objects are represented is as polyhedra. Hence, efficient polygon clipping is essential. However, an inspection of the Sutherland–Hodgman algorithm of Section 4.9 shows that it is essentially based on the intersection and *EdgeSet* functions. Hence, a 3D version can be easily constructed based on the 3D intersection and *ClipPlaneSet* functions discussed earlier. The resulting changes to the Sutherland–Hodgman algortihm are obvious and trivial (see Exercise 13.26).

13.6 Basic Concepts of Shading

Sections 13.1 to 13.5 have presented sufficient information to allow rendering of wire-frame polyhedral objects. If there is one such object in a scene, then back face elimination may be used to solve the visibility problem. However, realistic image synthesis clearly requires rendering techniques that go beyond the wire-frame concept. Indeed, it would be a waste of modern-day computer graphics resources if the colour-generation techniques (see Chapter 15) and the knowledge of the human response to colour (Chapter 14) were not used to the full (Clark, 1981). A state-of-the-art example of what can be achieved is shown in Plate 27.

This section makes a first step in the direction of realism by introducing some basic ideas about shading in the context of 3D graphics. First, a simple shading model for grey scale is developed, assuming a single point light source and objects that can take various shades of grey: zero intensity light is black and intensity 1 is white. One simple generalization to colour is made in Section 13.6.6.

13.6.1 Lambert's Law for Diffuse Reflection

Lambert's law gives the intensity of light reflected by a perfectly diffuse surface – that is, one that reflects light equally in all directions (for example, chalk). For a given point on the surface, let **N** be the unit normal vector and **L** a unit vector in the direction of the light source. Then the amount of reflected light is proportional to the cosine of the angle between **N** and **L** (see Figure 13.16(a)). For example, if **L** is in the same direction as **N** (when $\theta = 0$), then the reflection would be at a maximum. Conversely, if **L** is at right-angles to **N**, then the reflection would be at a minimum. Lambert's law encapsulates these ideas since $\cos 0 = 1$ and $\cos (\pi/2) = 0$.

If I is the amount of light reflected at a point, then this simple model may be expressed as:

$$\begin{aligned} I &= I_p k_d \cos \theta \\ &= I_p k_d \, \mathbf{N}.\mathbf{L} \end{aligned} \qquad \textbf{(13.16)}$$

where I_p is the intensity of the point light source and k_d is the **coefficient of diffuse reflection**. This coefficient has a value between 0 and 1, and is determined by the proportion of light reflected by the surface. In the extremes, if $k_d = 0$, then the surface would be invisible, since all light would be absorbed; and if $k_d = 1$, then the surface would reflect all light back from the source. **N.L** may be used as the value for $\cos \theta$ since these are assumed to be unit vectors.

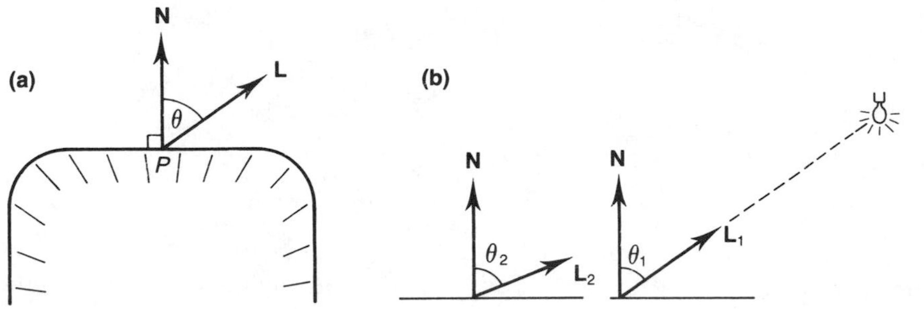

Figure 13.16
Lambert's law.

13.6.2 Ambient Light

In addition to the point light source, there would usually be **ambient light**, which is a background light at constant intensity throughout the scene. Thus, extending the model:

$$I = I_a k_a + I_p k_d \mathbf{N.L} \qquad \textbf{(13.17)}$$

where I_a is the intensity of ambient light and k_a is the proportion of this light reflected by the surface.

If the object is polyhedral, then all surfaces are planar polygons. Although the normal vector will be the same across a whole polygon, the **angle of incidence** (θ) will vary and so will the intensity (see Figure 13.16(b)). However, if the light source is at infinity (for example, the Sun), then a single intensity will apply across a whole polygon.

13.6.3 Specular Reflection

Equation (13.17) provides a simple and useful model for matt surfaces, but many real surfaces also reflect light specularly – that is, they are glossy, such as billiard balls, apples, china and, as an extreme, mirrors. However, a highlight seen on a glossy surface depends on the direction of the observer's eye position in relation to the direction of the light source.

Figure 13.17(a) shows that the direction of maximum highlight is at an angle θ to the normal in the opposite direction to the direction of the light source. Hence, if the observer's eye position is in this direction, the maximum highlight will be visible. Note that this situation occurs when the normal vector exactly bisects the angle between the light source vector and the direction of the observer (**E**). Therefore, the amount of highlight visible to an observer depends on the angle between a vector (**H**) that bisects the angle between **E** and **L**. If this angle (α) is 0, then the maximum highlight

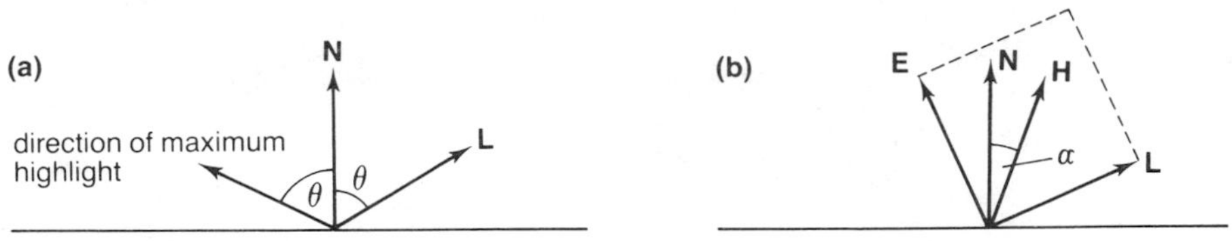

Figure 13.17
Specular reflection.

occurs. Due to the nature of highlighting, the greater the disparity between the eye direction and the direction of maximum highlight, the faster the highlighting effect falls away (see Figure 13.17(b)).

If **H** is the bisector unit vector, then:

$$\mathbf{H} = \frac{\mathbf{E} + \mathbf{L}}{|\mathbf{E} + \mathbf{L}|}$$

so that the cosine of the angle between **H** and **N** is **H**.**N**. Bui-Tuong, Phong (1975) proposed the following model for specular reflection, which has since come to be known as the model for **Phong shading**:

$$I = I_a k_a + I_p(k_d \mathbf{N}.\mathbf{L} + k_s(\mathbf{H}.\mathbf{N})^n) \quad \textbf{(13.18)}$$

Here, $n > 1$ is used to control the degree of highlighting. The larger the value of n, the sharper the highlighting, since small departures from $\mathbf{H}.\mathbf{N} = 1$ are exaggerated for larger powers of n. k_s is the **coefficient of specular reflection** and represents the proportion of light reflected specularly.

Equation (13.18) is not an exact physical model, but an approximate one producing good results empirically. A more detailed discussion of shading can be found, for example, in Rogers (1985, Chapter 5). A classic paper on the subject is by Cook and Torrance (1982), which is based more closely on true physical models of illumination.

13.6.4 The Effect of Distance

Equations (13.17) and (13.18) do not take into account the distance of the object from the light source: the intensity of the light is inversely proportional to the square of the distance of the light source. However, dividing the relevant portions of the equations by this value does not give good empirical effects, and is, anyway, not possible for light sources at infinity. The usual solution to this problem is to recast the models so that the light falls away in inverse proportion to the distance of the COP from the point of illumination. In this way, points nearer the eye position have the greatest intensity, and the intensity decreases in proportion to the distance from the COP. This is very important since surfaces at different distances that have the same colour but which overlap from the viewpoint of the COP would be otherwise indistinguishable. The models now become:

$$I = I_a k_a + \frac{I_p k_d \, \mathbf{N}.\mathbf{L}}{(d + K)} \tag{13.19}$$

for diffuse reflection and:

$$I = I_a k_a + \frac{I_p(k_d \mathbf{N}.\mathbf{L} + k_s(\mathbf{H}.\mathbf{N})^n)}{(d + K)} \tag{13.20}$$

for specular reflection, where d is the distance from the COP and $K > 0$ is an arbitrary constant.

13.6.5 Interpolation for Curved Surfaces

When planar polygons are used to approximate curved surfaces, greater realism can be achieved by an interpolation scheme introduced by Gouraud (1971), which has come to be known as **Gouraud smooth shading**. Assuming the diffuse reflection model of Equation (13.19), intensities reflected at the polygon vertices are computed: in other words, the normals of the underlying true curved surface at these vertices are computed and then Equation (13.19) is used to calculate the 'true' intensity values. These values are used to interpolate both along polygon edges and to the interior of the polygon. The idea is illustrated in Figure 13.18.

In the case of the specular reflection model, the same approach can be taken, but with the crucial difference that interpolation must be on the basis of the *normals*, rather than the intensities. For example, referring to Figure 13.18, the approximate normals $\mathbf{N}'$ and $\mathbf{N}''$ at P' and P'' must be found by interpolation between $\mathbf{N}_2$ and $\mathbf{N}_3$ and between $\mathbf{N}_5$ and $\mathbf{N}_6$, respectively. These interpolated normals must be normalized to unit length before they can be used to calculate the intensities at P' and P'' using Equation (13.20). Similarly, the approximate normal at P''' can be found by interpolating between $\mathbf{N}'$ and $\mathbf{N}''$, and the result must again be normalized before being used in the intensity computation (see Exercise 13.27).

A special advantage of these schemes is that they fit in well with the scan line algorithms for filling polygons, such as the one discussed in Section 4.8. For example, in the case of Gouraud shading, the *ETValue* (edge table value) data structure must be extended to include information about the intensities at the vertices of the corresponding polygon edge. These values are then used for interpolation during the processing of the edge table, as in the function *ProcessET*. In the case of Phong shading, on the other hand, the normal vectors, rather than intensities, must be stored. The details are left as an exercise for the reader (see Exercise 13.29).

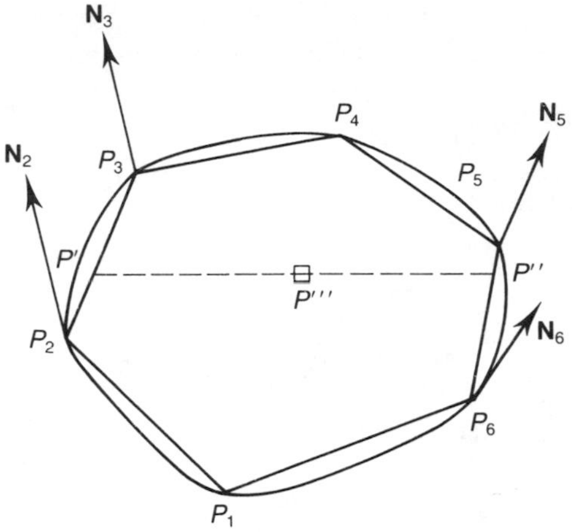

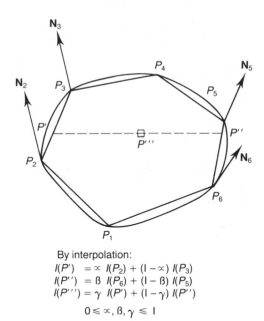

By interpolation:

$$I(P') = \alpha\, I(P_2) + (1 - \alpha)\, I(P_3)$$
$$I(P'') = \beta\, I(P_6) + (1 - \beta)\, I(P_5)$$
$$I(P''') = \gamma\, I(P') + (1 - \gamma)\, I(P'')$$
$$0 \leqslant \alpha, \beta, \gamma \leqslant 1$$

Figure 13.18
Gouraud smooth shading.

13.6.6 Colour

The methods just described are for grey scale shading. However, recalling that colour can be represented in the RGB model by a triple of red, green and blue intensity levels, these same methods must be employed independently for the three components, resulting in intensity levels for red, green and blue. The diffuse component of the model should be assigned colour values according to the colours of the object to be rendered. However, the colour of the specular component depends on the colour of the light source (highlights take on approximately the colour of the source). Again, these are crude approximations to the true situation, but suffice as a starting point for the investigation and experimentation of the reader.

13.7 Anti-Aliasing

The methods for shading discussed in Section 13.6 are, unfortunately, only one step towards greater realism in computer-generated graphics. No matter how sophisticated the basic shading model, this in itself cannot overcome the consequences of sampling a continuous scene with a finite (however large) number of elements. Such sampling is, of course, an inevitable outcome of the very raster graphics technology that has made shaded image generation possible.

An **alias** is a technical term used in signal theory to describe the signal produced when a high frequency signal is sampled at too low a rate. **Anti-aliasing** techniques are used in graphics in an attempt to overcome this problem. (See Pavlidis, 1982, Chapter 2, for further mathematical details from information theory.)

In graphics, aliasing can show itself in at least three ways. The first is the most familiar and can be seen in any application of graphics on raster displays – namely, the typical jagged edges of straight lines and polygon boundaries. The second arises when an object is smaller than pixel size or contains very thin regions, such as very thin lines or polygons. In such cases, either the object is not displayed at all or it is displayed in a patchy manner – for example, a thin line might be displayed as an irregular sequence of dots. Finally, the third occurs when a region of a scene is complex – for example, containing much fine detail such as a rendering of the patterns on a net curtain. Here, unless special measures are taken, the fine detail is either totally lost or distorted beyond recognition.

Aliasing is of crucial importance in animation sequences. Each of the three manifestations described would be enhanced and spoil the animation effect. Even a single line when, for example, rotated in real time would show a rippling effect as the jaggedness varied from one orientation of the line to the next. (Imagine your reactions when watching your favourite Star Trek movie if the boundary of the hull of the Enterprise looked as if it were made of a moving sawtooth.) The problem with small or thin objects is that they would pop in and out of existence during the progress of the animation sequence. Finally, the net curtain would appear to change its pattern as the camera moved into and across the scene.

Although a full discussion of anti-aliasing techniques is beyond the scope of this book, the following sections briefly describe three approaches. A general approach is discussed in Crow (1977) with experimental and follow-up results presented by Crow (1981). Some hardware-related aspects of anti-aliasing are given in Section 16.4.12.

13.7.1 Special Techniques for Anti-Aliasing Specific Objects

The fundamental idea of anti-aliasing is to treat each pixel as if it covers a finite area of the scene, instead of an infinitesimally small dot. Every object in the scene then makes some contribution to at least one pixel: the intensity of each pixel is based on an average of the intensities of the objects that pass through it.

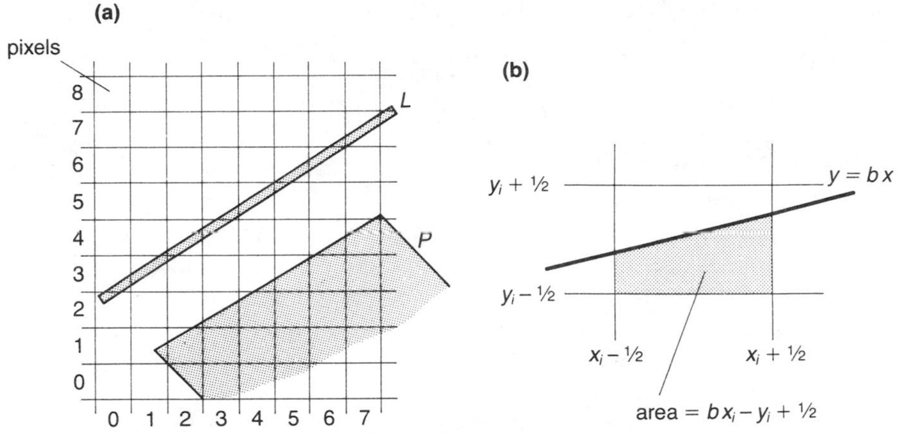

Figure 13.19
Basic ideas of anti-aliasing as applied to lines and polygon boundaries.

Consider Figure 13.19(a) which shows a thin line L on a pixel grid. It is clear that the line is actually thinner than the size of the pixels, and hence cannot be correctly rendered by, say, a straightforward application of Bresenham's algorithm. Rather, for each pixel impacted by the line, the fraction of the pixel's area occupied by the line must be computed. Then, the intensity of the pixel is set in such a way as to reflect the computed area. For example, suppose the line is crossing a black background area (intensity = 0) and the colour of the line is white (intensity = 1). Suppose also that for a particular pixel (say, (3, 4) in the figure) the line occupies 20% of the pixel area. The intensity of the pixel should then be set at 0.2. These ideas are developed in detail by Crow (1978), but generally result in methods that are too slow for, say, typical interactive work.

A special technique has been developed by Pitteway and Watkinson (1980) for anti-aliasing polygon boundaries, excluding corners and thin polygons (see Figure 13.19(b)). The method is a very simple generalization of Bresenham's line drawing algorithm, and is based on the observation that the discriminatory error term of the algorithm (variable e in the *LineToPixels* function of Section 4.7) is closely related to the area of the pixel to be set, which intersects the polygon (see Exercise 13.30).

13.7.2 Sampling at Higher Resolution

Perhaps the most obvious anti-aliasing technique is to sample the image at a higher resolution than the display and then average down to the true pixel level. For example, for a scene that is to be rendered at 512 × 512 resolution, the image is first computed at 1024 × 1024 and then each actual pixel intensity is computed as the mean of the four pseudo pixel cell intensities. Elementary statistical theory shows that the averaged values

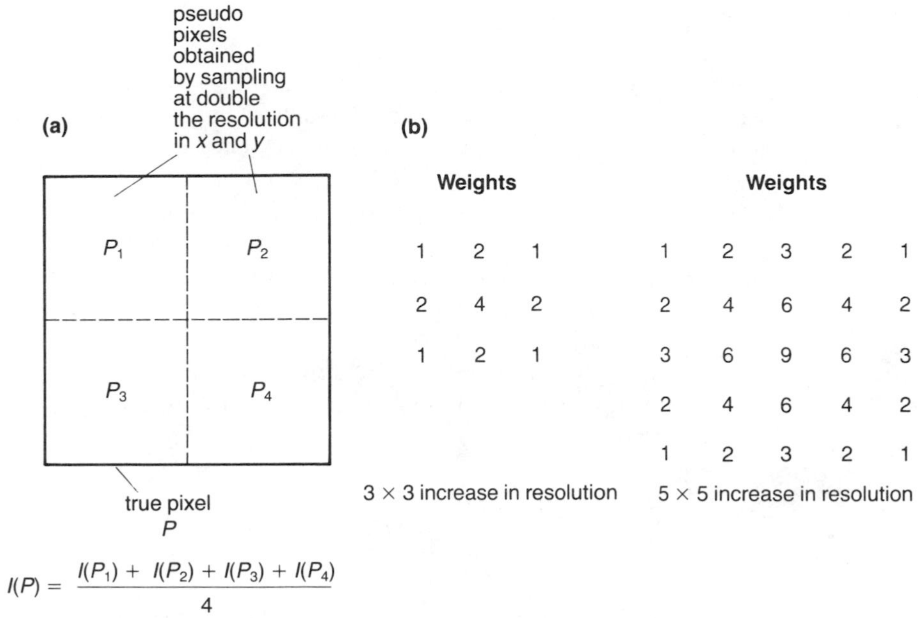

Figure 13.20
(a) Sampling at higher resolution.
(b) Crow's weighted average intensities.

contain more information about the true image than if the sampling had been performed at display resolution size. This idea is illustrated in Figure 13.20(a).

There are three drawbacks to this approach. First, computing the image at a higher resolution increases the computation involved more than linearly. Typically, a complex scene is rendered on a pixel-by-pixel basis. If the resolution is doubled, then each real pixel is divided into four, so that four times the amount of work is required. Usually, doubling of the resolution is insufficient.

The second problem is that objects smaller than even the pseudo pixel size will still not be sampled correctly, and thus the averaging process will not aid their representation in the image.

Finally, straightforward averaging is rather too crude – it does not take into account the fact that pseudo pixels nearer the centre of the true pixel should make a higher contribution to the pixel intensity than those at the boundary. Crow (1981) suggested a weighted averaging scheme based on statistical theory to give greater weight to the central pseudo pixels. This is illustrated in Figure 13.20(b). For example, given a 3×3 increase in resolution, suppose the intensities of the pseudo pixels are denoted by I_{ij}. Then, the pixel intensity would be computed as:

$$I = \frac{(I_{11} + I_{13} + I_{31} + I_{33}) + 2\,(I_{12} + I_{21} + I_{23} + I_{32}) + 4\,\mathrm{I}_{22}}{16}$$

13.7.3 Filtering

Aliasing occurs especially when the intensities in the scene change sharply within a region, for it is in precisely such regions that the sampling rate is not high enough to capture the changes. The idea of filtering, discussed extensively by Crow (1977), is directly based on the idea of a pixel covering a finite area (rather than a single point) of the scene. A filter applied to the scene definition has the effect of spreading, theoretically, the influence of the scene intensities to all pixels covering the scene. In this way, every part of every object makes some contribution to each of the final image pixel intensities.

Suppose the function $f(x, y)$ represents the scene intensity at point (x, y), and suppose h is a filter function; then the filtered image $g(x, y)$ may be expressed as:

$$g(x, y) = \sum_{i=-\infty}^{\infty} \sum_{j=-\infty}^{\infty} h(i, j) f(x + i, y + j)$$

In practice, h would be a non-zero function over a small rectangular region. For example, $h(i, j)$ might have the values shown in the following table – note that it is 0 for all i, j less than -1 and greater than 1.

Symmetric filter function: the values give $h(i, j) \times 16$

i \ j	-1	0	1
-1	1	2	1
0	2	4	2
1	1	2	1

This corresponds to one of the suggested weighting functions for the high resolution sampling method discussed earlier. The effect of this filter would be the same as that occurring if something like a Gaussian distribution were to blurr the intensity at each point in the scene over the set of pixels covering and near to the point.

For example, consider the 7×7 pixel grid shown in Figure 13.21. Suppose the image consists of the infinitesimally thin line $y = x$ in white on a black background. Then, the scene definition function is:

$$f(x, y) = \begin{cases} 1 & y = x \\ 0 & \text{otherwise} \end{cases}$$

Using the filter in the table above, the filtered image is:

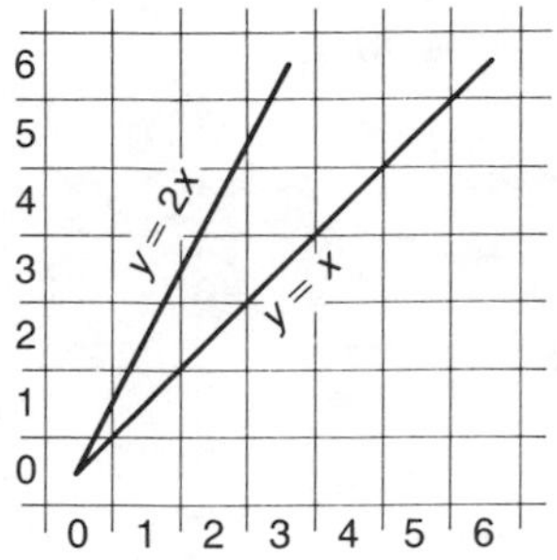

Filter function

i \ j	−1	0	1
−1	1/16	2/16	1/16
$h(i, j) =$ 0	2/16	4/16	2/16
1	1/16	2/16	1/16

$-1 < i, j < 1$

Filtered image intensities (x16)

0	0	2	4	3	4	6
0	1	3	4	5	6	4
0	2	5	6	6	4	1
1	4	7	7	4	1	0
3	8	8	4	1	0	0
5	8	5	1	0	0	0
6	4	1	0	0	0	0

Figure 13.21
Anti-aliasing by filtering.

Filtered image intensities ×16 for the line $y = x$

0	0	0	0	1	4	6
0	0	0	1	4	6	4
0	0	1	4	6	4	1
0	1	4	6	4	1	0
1	4	6	4	1	0	0
4	6	4	1	0	0	0
6	4	1	0	0	0	0

Note how the intensities are highest at the pixels within which the true line lies, but tail off smoothly in neighbouring pixels.

As another example, the corresponding table of intensities for the line $y = 2x$ are:

Filtered image intensities ×16 for the line $y = 2x$

0	0	2	4	2	0	0
0	1	3	3	1	0	0
0	2	4	2	0	0	0
1	3	3	1	0	0	0
2	4	2	0	0	0	0
3	3	1	0	0	0	0
4	2	0	0	0	0	0

It is remarkable that just looking at these figures gives a more pleasing (smooth) effect than the set of stark 0s and 1s that would be produced by a straightforward application of Bresenham's algorithm (see Exercise 13.31).

In his 1977 paper, Crow made special assumptions about the form of the filter function in an attempt to make the method tractable for the large amount of computation necessary in a graphics setting. In a later paper (1981), he showed that the filtering method performed better than other methods considered, at least over the range of scenes considered.

The amount of space given to the anti-aliasing problem in this book is disproportionate to its importance in computer graphics. No matter how clever and fast the algorithms, nor how realistic the shading models,

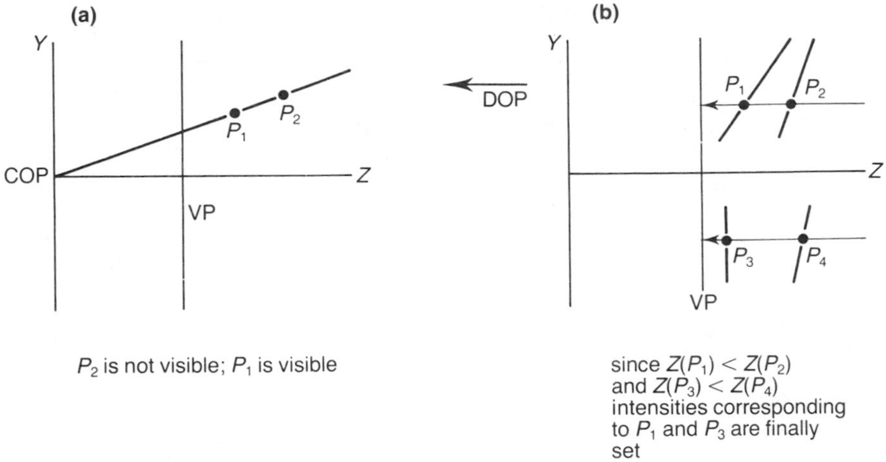

Figure 13.22
(a) Visibility and (b) the *z*-buffer algorithm.

computer-generated images cannot be produced satisfactorily unless anti-aliasing measures are taken. A brief discussion of possible hardware solutions to aliasing is given in Section 16.4.12.

13.8 Visibility

A point **P** in a scene is visible if there is no other scene point on the ray joining **P** to the eye position and which is nearer to the eye than **P** (see Figure 13.22(a)). Visibility algorithms, also called *hidden line* and *hidden surface elimination*, are concerned with the computation and rendering of the visible points in the scene. In a classic 1974 paper, Sutherland, Sproull and Schumacker (Sutherland *et al.*, 1974) investigated ten such algorithms. It was concluded that the visibililty problem could be characterized as a large-scale sorting problem, since a basic feature of such algorithms involves depth comparisons of intersection points between objects in the scene and projection rays or planes.

There are two basic approaches to the visibility problem, called **object space** and **image space** algorithms. Object space methods attempt to solve the problem geometrically in the 3D space of the scene definition. The back face elimination method for polyhedra, discussed in Section 13.3.3, is an example of an object space approach. Image space algorithms, on the other hand, solve the visibility problem during the process of rendering – deferring, in a sense, the visibility calculation until the last moment. Image space algorithms are specifically designed for modern raster graphics image generation, and are more popular and widely used than object space algorithms. In any case, the 1974 survey by Sutherland showed that image space algorithms tend to be faster (and the crudest method the fastest!) for scenes with large numbers of polygons (in the order of tens of thousands).

In this section, four image space algorithms are outlined. The simplest and, in the case of a complex scene, the fastest is known as the ***z*-buffer algorithm** (Catmull, 1974). Next, a modification of the polygon scan conversion algorithm discussed in Chapter 4 is considered. Third is a **divide and conquer** algorithm due to Warnock (1969), which is based on the idea of area coherence. Finally, recent techniques of **ray casting** and **ray tracing** are discussed. (These could also be considered to be object space methods.) An extensive discussion of the object space approach can be found in Rogers (1985, Chapter 4).

It is assumed here that the scene has been transformed into the projection coordinate system (box space) discussed in Section 13.5.

13.8.1 The *z*-Buffer Algorithm

The z-buffer is an array that stores the z depths corresponding to the pixels currently set. Clearly, it must have the same dimensions as the display frame buffer. Initially, the value of all elements in the z-buffer is set to 1 (the maximum z depth) while the corresponding display pixels are set to the required background colour. Then, for each point in the scene, the pixel position and intensity are computed. Next, the pixel is set to this intensity, only if the depth of the point (its z coordinate) is less than the value stored at the corresponding position in the z-buffer. By the time all of the objects in the scene have been processed in this way, the displayed pixel intensities will correspond to the points in the scene that have the minimum z depth along each projection ray. This is illustrated in Figure 13.22(b).

In outline, the algorithm is as follows:

```
Let I (x, y, z) be a function that returns the colour at point (x, y, z) in the scene.

Let Z be a 2D array with the same dimensions as the display resolution XMAX, YMAX.

for 0 ≤ x < XMAX do
  for 0 ≤ y < YMAX do
    Z[x, y] := 1.0
  od
od;

for each pixel (i, j) corresponding to point (x, y, z) in the scene do
  if
    z < Z[i, j] ⇒ Z[i, j] := z;
                  SetPixel(i, j, I(x, y, z))
  fi
od
```

If the scene consists of objects defined as polyhedra, then the algorithm is particularly simple. For now each polygon in the scene can be processed (in any order) – for example, by using the scan line method of Chapter 4. In the normal application of the polygon fill algorithm, during the processing of the edge table (*ProcessET*), the scan lines are rendered by joining up the successive pairs of (sorted) x values at height y (*JoinLines*). But the situation is different here, because the depth corresponding to each pixel along each scan line must be computed to decide whether the point is visible or not.

The plane equation of the polygon is:

$$ax + by + cz = d$$

Successive pixel positions on scan line y are x_i and x_{i+1}. The corresponding points on the polygon are (x_i, y, z_i) and (x_{i+1}, y, z_{i+1}), since in projection space the x and y coordinates on the VP are the same as on the object. (It is assumed that the VP is equivalent to the display space; however, this is not actually the case – see Exercise 13.33 for further discussion.) Substituting these points into the plane equation and solving for z_{i+1} results in:

$$z_{i+1} = z_i - \left(\frac{a}{c}\right) \tag{13.21}$$

So, for each scan line, once the initial z depth has been computed, successive values may be computed incrementally. This **depth coherence** property may be exploited vertically as well as horizontally (see Exercise 13.34).

The obvious advantage of this algorithm is that it is computationally simple and its performance is independent of the complexity of the scene in terms of visibility. Its running time is proportional to the number of polygons to be processed, and not the relationship between the polygons. A disadvantage of the method is that it does require a large amount of memory to maintain the z-buffer. For example, for a 512×512 display, the z-buffer size is a megabyte of memory if the z value precision is a 32-bit floating-point number. In practice, a z value precision of 16 to 20 bits would suffice. But in any case, the current relatively low cost of memory allows the realistic marketing of fast access z-buffer hardware memory boards, which is perhaps the ideal solution.

A more serious drawback to the method is that it makes anti-aliasing very difficult. The reason for this is that the image is built up in an essentially random order. The fundamental idea of anti-aliasing is that each pixel covers a finite area of the scene and that every object intersecting with that pixel makes some contribution to its colour. But if the image is constructed in random order, the set of objects contributing to any pixel cannot be known until all objects have been processed. Moreover, pixels adjacent at any moment during the running of the program may or may not be assigned colours belonging to the same surface, and may or may not form an edge that is going to be visible on termination of the program (Crow, 1977). There are ways around this problem, but generally the z-buffer approach discourages serious anti-aliasing.

Carpenter (1984) has greatly extended the idea of the z-buffer to what he called the **A-buffer**. This combines the idea of filtering, the z-buffer technique and the scan line method discussed in the next section.

13.8.2 Scan Line Polygon Filling

In the z-buffer algorithm, each polygon is individually processed by a scan line algorithm. However, it is possible to process all polygons simultaneously with only marginal changes to the polygon fill method (see Foley and Van Dam, 1982, Chapter 15). The general class of algorithm is called **plane sweep**, and this has been thoroughly investigated by researchers in computational geometry (Nievergelt and Preparata, 1982).

Consider Figure 13.23 which shows three polygons A, B and C as projected to image space. It is assumed for the purposes of the example that in the projection coordinate space A has z depths that are all smaller than B, which in turn has z depths all smaller than C; that is, the polygons do not intersect, although the algorithm works even if they do intersect.

The algorithm is the same as that presented in Section 4.8, except for three changes.

(1) The edges of *all* the polygons in the scene are processed into the edge table.

(2) Recall that the edge table is a sequence, where each element is in turn a sequence of 3-tuples of the form:

$$e = \left(y_{max}, x_{min}, \frac{dx}{dy} \right)$$

where e is a representation of a polygon edge that has y_{max} as its maximum y coordinate, x_{min} as the x coordinate of the other end of the edge and dx/dy is the reciprocal of the slope. For the new application of the algorithm, the basic edge table entries have the same first three elements, but the final element is a pointer to information about the polygon of which the edge is a part (see Exercise 13.36). This information must be sufficient to allow depth calculations for any (x, y) on the polygon and computation of the colour at any point. It is assumed that the pointer references the plane equation of the polygon and an intensity function which computes the colour $I(x, y, z)$ at point (x, y, z) on the polygon. Hence, the edge table entries are of the form:

$$e_{new} = \left(y_{max}, x_{min}, \frac{dx}{dy}, polygon\_pointer \right)$$

(3) The edge table is constructed and processed in the same way as before, except that the interpretation of the *JoinLines* function changes. This function has as arguments the height of the current scan line i and a list of 4-tuples (of form e_{new}) sorted on x order. In addition, a new variable called, say, *PolygonSet* is introduced which is a set of polygon pointers, initialised at the start of each invocation of *JoinLines* to be empty.

Consider scan line $y = i$ in Figure 13.23. Let the active edge table (AET) at this scan line consist of [$e0$, $e1$, $e2$, $e3$, $e4$, $e5$]. This is processed as follows:

```
let val PolygonSet = store ∅
   and colour      = store 0
in
  for 0 ≤ j < 5 do
    let val (_, x0, _, pt0) = e[i]
       and (_, x1, _, _) = e[i + 1]
    in
      if
              pt0 ∈ PolygonSet  ⇒ PolygonSet := PolygonSet – {pt0};
        □ ~(pt0 ∈ PolygonSet) ⇒ PolygonSet := PolygonSet ∪ {pt0}
      fi;
      if PolygonSet ≠ ∅ ⇒
        colour := MinZColour(PolygonSet, x0, i);
        DrawLine((x0, i), (x1, i), colour)
      fi
    ni
  od
ni
```

The algorithm maintains the invariant that *PolygonSet* always contains the pointers to the polygons that are covered at each intersection of the scan line with the active edges.

First, the *PolygonSet* is initialised to be empty and the colour is initialised to some arbitrary value (assume that the colour is an entry to the colour table, so that it is an integer). Then, running through the elements of the active edge sequence, pick up the next two each time (this can obviously be made more efficient, but for the purposes of explanation it is satisfactory). From these elements, the x value and the polygon pointer are

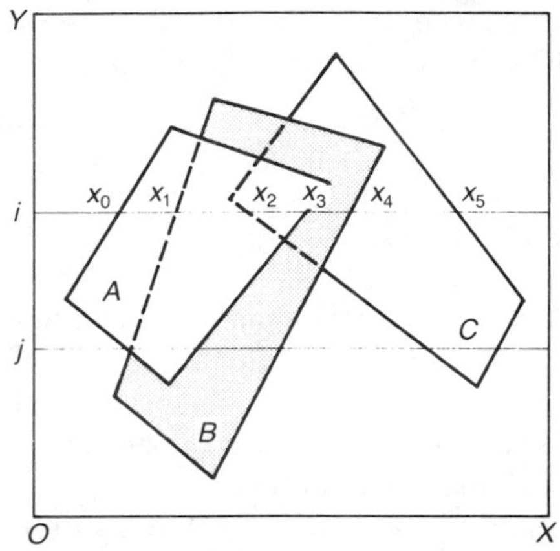

Figure 13.23
The scan line algorithm.

obtained. Now, if the polygon pointer is already in the *PolygonSet*, then the corresponding edge must be a right-hand edge of the polygon. Hence, this pointer is removed from the *PolygonSet*. Alternatively, if *pt*0 is not in the set, then put it in. Now the current *PolygonSet* contains the set of pointers to polygons that are intersected by a ray parallel to the z axis through the point (x0, i). Here x0 is the x value corresponding to the first of the elements being considered and i is the height of the scan line.

The function *MinZColour* computes the z intersections of this ray (at (x0, i)) for each polygon referred to by the set. This calculation is straightforward, being accomplished by substituting (x0, i) into the polygon plane equations and solving for z. The minimum z so found will be the polygon closest to the VP, and hence the colour of this polygon should be used to draw the current segment of the scan line. *MinZColour* returns this colour.

In terms of Figure 13.23 and scan line i, the first two entries in the AET are x_0 and x_1. Hence, the pointer to polygon A enters the polygon set and the colour of A is used to draw the line segment x_0 to x_1. Next, the segment x_1 to x_2 is considered. The pointer to B joins the polygon set and the smallest z coordinate will correspond to the plane equation for A. The segment x_1 to x_2 is coloured according to A. When the segment x_3 to x_4 is encountered, it is found that A is already in the polygon set, so it is deleted. Then only B and C remain in the set, and evaluation of the z values at (x_3, i) reveals B to be the nearest polygon, so that x_3 to x_4 takes its colour from B. Finally, at x_4, B leaves the polygon set, so that the colour of the segment from x_4 to x_5 is that of C (see Exercise 13.37).

The foregoing algorithm is suitable for scan converting scenes described in terms of polyhedra. Lane, Carpenter and Whitted (1980) showed how the method could be used for the display of parametrically defined surfaces (such as bicubic patches based on the Bezier form of curve discussed earlier). Schweitzer and Cobb (1982) have extended these ideas, which are discussed in Section 13.9.

13.8.3 Divide and Conquer

The z-buffer and polygon fill methods succeed by reducing the dimensionality of the sorting problem. In the z-buffer case, the sort becomes a simple minimization in one dimension – that is, the z depth at each pixel position encountered. In the scan line method, the dimensionality is first reduced to two – the intersection of the plane through the scan line parallel to the z axis intersects the scene – and then to one dimension by only considering the line segments on the plane with minimum z. The z-buffer based on polyhedra also makes use of depth coherence to improve the speed of computation, whereas the scan line method is based on the edge and scan line coherence.

Warnock's algorithm (Warnock, 1969) is based on area coherence and solves the general sorting problem by attempting to avoid it altogether. This algorithm can be stated as follows. The view window is a rectangle. If the scene in this rectangle is simple enough to render, then render it. Otherwise, divide the rectangle into four, and apply the same principle to each of the four subrectangles. And so the algorithm proceeds recursively. The only 'detail' is the exact meaning of *simple* in this context. Area coherence means that pixels close together are likely to correspond to the same object and have a similar colour, which is the underlying assumption of the algorithm. Obviously, if the principle of area coherence is false, then subdividing into smaller regions would not help. Unless a scene is one of total chaos, area coherence seems to be a sound idea.

Consider Figure 13.24 which shows four cases that must be considered in the decision about whether to render the scene in a window or subdivide. In case (a), the polygon completely surrounds the window; in case (b) there are no polygons intersecting the window; case (c) is where a polygon intersects a window and (d) is where the window contains a polygon.

Thus, first set the entire display to the required background colour. Then:

- If (case a) the window is surrounded by a polygon, and there are no other polygons in the window closer to the VP than the surrounding one, then set the window to the colour(s) determined by the surrounding polygon.
- If (case b) there are no polygons intersecting the window, then do nothing.
- If (case c) a single polygon intersects the window, then set the colour of the intersecting region to the colour(s) determined by the polygon.

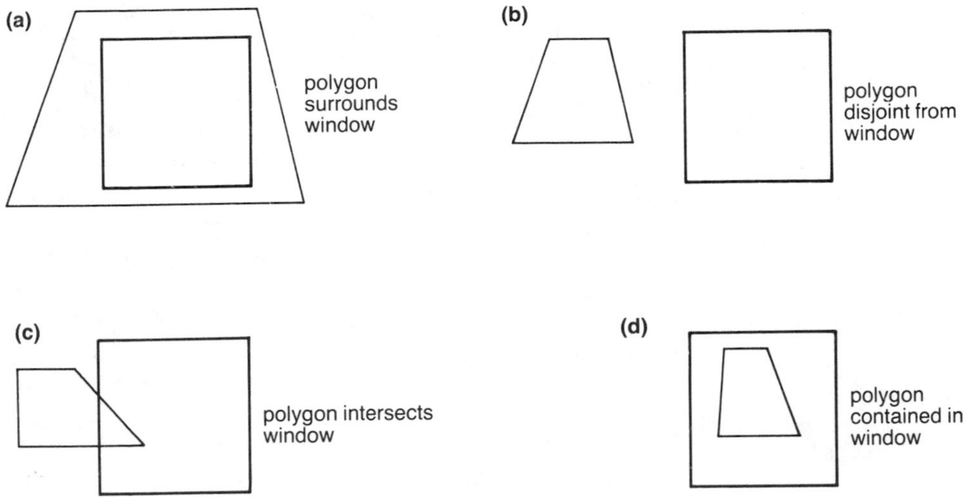

Figure 13.24
Examples of divide and conquer.

The intersected region can be displayed by using the usual polygon fill method, but with the window as a clipping region; for example, the scan lines are clipped at the window boundaries.

- If (case d) the window contains a single polygon, then scan convert the polygon.

Otherwise, if none of the four cases apply, then subdivide the window into four and apply the same procedure to each. Eventually, of course, one of the tests will succeed when a window of pixel size is attained.

The computations involved in the detection of these cases are simple, bearing in mind that the algorithm is applied in projection coordinate space. To test cases (b), (c) and (d), polygon extents in the x and y directions can be used. To test (a) when there is more than one polygon impacting the window, the z depths of the polygons at the four window corners can be used for the comparisons. The details are left as an exercise for the reader (see Exercise 13.38).

Performance of the Warnock algorithm is generally worse than the scan line method of the previous section. The reason for this is clear: when projections of polygons overlap, the algorithm certainly involves more work to sort things out. According to the data collected by Sutherland *et al.* (1974), the scan line method is about three times faster than the divide and conquer method.

The divide and conquer algorithm is particularly suited to anti-aliasing based on increasing the resolution to smaller than pixel size. The method will automatically detect those regions where anti-aliasing is most important; that is, where there is greater variability in the scene (for example, at a vertex common to several polygons). Here, it would be desirable to split to subpixel level and then set the final pixel value as the average colour intensities of the pseudo pixels.

For an interesting recent development, closely related to Warnock's algorithm, the reader should consult the literature on **quad tree** representations of an image (Pavlidis, 1982, pp. 383–387; Carlbom *et al.*, 1985; Hunter and Steiglitz, 1979a, 1979b). Here, the root of the tree is the entire image. If the image is of one colour, then the root is the tree; otherwise, the image is split into four equal subwindows and the same principle is applied to each. The terminating nodes of the tree are either windows of constant colour or pixel-sized windows (of constant colour). The parallel with Warnock's algorithm should be obvious.

13.8.4 Ray Casting and Ray Tracing

These are direct and somewhat brute force methods for solving the visibility problem; nevertheless, ray tracing algorithms have produced some of the most spectacular results in computer-generated images. A superb example of a ray-traced image is shown in Plate 30.

The idea of ray casting is a very simple one: for each pixel, trace a ray from the eye position (in image space) through the pixel and find the intersections with all the objects in the scene. The intersection that has the smallest z value determines the colour of the pixel. For example, in Figure 13.25 the intensity at pixel (x, y) would be determined by surface A.

Ray tracing is more complex, since once the first intersection is found the ray is reflected off the object surface and traced back further – and so on recursively – until it passes out of the scene or is traced to one of the original light sources. Similarly, if the surface is transparent, then an additional ray is *refracted* through the surface and traced. In this way, a number of features can be easily introduced into the rendering which are extremely difficult with other methods: not only is the visibility problem obviously solved, but also shadows, the reflection of objects in the scene on each other and transparency.

In the case of ray casting, the calculations involved are not difficult. Suppose that the eye position is at the origin and the VP is at distance D from the eye position along the Z axis. Hence, the coordinate of a pixel (x_p, y_p) in 3D space is (x_p, y_p, D). The parametric equation of a ray passing through a pixel is therefore:

$$(x(t), y(t), z(t)) = (tx_p, ty_p, tD) \qquad \textbf{(13.22)}$$

Substituting this result into the plane equation of a polygon and solving for t gives the value of t at the intersection of the ray and the polygon, and this

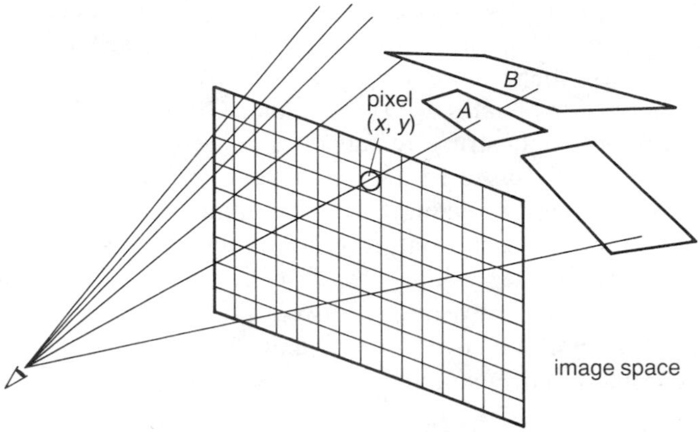

Figure 13.25
Basic idea of ray casting.

value can be used to find the 3D point. Further calculations are necessary to then see if the point is actually inside the polygon (see Exercise 13.39). Bearing in mind that there may be many thousands of polygons, and that this operation must be done for *each* pixel (for example, 512 × 512 times), this is a lot of computation.

Roth (1982) estimated that about 50% of the time in a ray casting algorithm is spent doing the intersection calculations. He suggested the use of 3D extents around objects to avoid doing unnecessary intersections. An alternative and perhaps better approach would be to use the tiling methods for picture segments discussed in Chapter 8. In this method, each primitive object in the scene would be labelled and the entire scene traversed once without reference to visibility, to compute the tile sets – that is, the set of labels of primitive objects intersecting each tile. (The image should not be displayed during this process.) Then the ray casting method could be used, but the intersection calculations would be dramatically reduced, since only the set of objects referenced by the tile to which each pixel belonged would need to be searched for intersections. Furthermore, the smaller the tiles, the smaller the set of intersection tests that would have to be made, but the larger the initial overhead of computing the tile sets. However, this overhead is likely to be small in comparison to the major computation.

Once into the realm of ray casting and ray tracing it becomes nonsensical to represent objects polyhedrally. Roth discussed ray casting with quadric surfaces, which is a particularly tractable case since the intersection calculations involve the solution of quadratic equations. This is discussed in Section 13.9. See also Williams, Buxton and Buxton (1985) who discuss an algorithm for ray tracing quadrics suitable for parallel implementation.

The fundamental reference for ray tracing is Whitted (1980). Further references are Cook, Porter and Carpenter (1984), Kajiya (1983) and Toth (1985).

Ray tracing is a slow process, and in Whitted's original 1980 paper he estimated that about 90% of the time in a ray trace is spent in intersection calculations. Since then, there have been many attempts to reduce the number of calculations required. For example, Glassner (1984) represented the entire scene in a data structure called an **oc tree** (a 3D equivalent of the quad tree structure discussed earlier; Meagher, 1982). At each node of the tree, a list of objects intersecting the corresponding region of 3D space is stored. Hence, the ray need only consider these lists as it traverses the scene. This is similar to the tiling idea just discussed. A recent attempt at speeding up ray tracing by using convex hulls as bounding extents is discussed by Kay *et al.* (1986). Methods akin to 3D tiling are presented by Wyvill *et al.* (1986) and Fuyimoto *et al.* (1986).

13.9 The World Is Not Made of Polygons

Almost all discussions in this chapter have assumed that scenes are represented as polyhedra. Although this is often the simplest method of representation, it is far from the most satisfactory in terms of realism. The first problem arises because to represent curved surfaces a large number of polygons need to be used to obtain a satisfactory approximation. If curved surfaces could be used directly, then this would clearly be an advantage. Second, when polygons are used it is extremely difficult to avoid a faceted appearance: human perception is especially good at edge detection (even when edges are not really there – this is called **mach banding**). Again, direct representation by curved surfaces would help to overcome this problem. Finally, there are aspects of the natural world that just cannot be represented in any satisfactory manner by polyhedra or even by mathematically perfect surfaces – for example, clouds, trees, forests, fire. Stochastic based **fractal** and **particle cloud** methods are used in such cases. This section briefly reviews some non-polygonal techniques.

13.9.1 Quadrics

A quadric surface is specified by the implicit equation:

$$ax^2 + ey^2 + hz^2 + 2bxy + 2cxz + 2fyz + 2dx + 2gy + 2iz + j = 0$$

and in matrix notation as:

$$(x, y, z, 1)\begin{pmatrix} a & b & c & d \\ b & e & f & g \\ c & f & h & i \\ d & g & i & j \end{pmatrix}\begin{pmatrix} x \\ y \\ z \\ 1 \end{pmatrix} = 0$$

or:

$$\mathbf{p}\mathbf{Q}\mathbf{p}' = 0 \qquad \textbf{(13.23)}$$

Choice of values for the constants a to j gives rise to different surfaces; for example, $b = c = f = d = g = i = 0$ (a, e, $h > 0$, $j < 0$) results in the equation for an ellipsoid (a sphere if $a = e = h$). Similarly, equations for a cylinder, cone and plane are special cases.

A useful result in relation to quadrics is that their transformation by homogeneous transformation matrices results in a new quadric; that is, the class of quadric surfaces is closed under the operation of linear transformation. Suppose $\mathbf{p}$ is a point on a quadric surface that is transformed by matrix $\mathbf{M}$. Then, the equivalent point on the transformed surface is $\mathbf{q} = \mathbf{p}\mathbf{M}$, so that $\mathbf{p} = \mathbf{q}\mathbf{M}^{-1}$. Substitution into Equation (13.23) gives:

$$\mathbf{q}\mathbf{M}^{-1}\mathbf{Q}\mathbf{M}'^{-1}\mathbf{q}' = 0$$

and therefore:

$$\mathbf{q}\mathbf{R}\mathbf{q}' = 0 \qquad \textbf{(13.24)}$$

where:

$$\mathbf{R} = \mathbf{M}^{-1}\mathbf{Q}\mathbf{M}'^{-1}$$

Equation (13.24) is, of course, the equation of a quadric surface.

Given a scene described in terms of quadric surfaces a straightforward z-buffer algorithm may be used to render the scene. First, it is assumed that the scene is transformed to projection space. Since this is accomplished by homogeneous transformation matrices, the resulting scene is still one consisting of quadric surfaces. Then, for each quadric surface, the (projected) x, y extent box is computed and, for each pixel (x_s, y_s) in the box, this is substituted into Equation (13.23), and the resulting quadratic equation solved in z. If both roots are imaginary, then the pixel is not covered by the quadric surface; otherwise there will be two real roots – the smallest of which is the one nearest the VP. This is then used to determine whether the pixel should be set according to the colour of this point on the surface by comparison with the current value in the z-buffer at this pixel position.

As mentioned in Section 13.8.4, quadrics are particularly popular in ray tracing, because ray intersection calculations are straightforward. Equation (13.22) gives the parametric equation for the ray emanating from the origin and passing through (x_p, y_p, D). Substituting $(x(t), y(t), z(t))$ into Equation (13.23) results in a quadratic equation in t. This has either two imaginary roots, meaning that the ray does not intersect the surface, or two real roots. The smaller of the two roots allows calculation of the point of intersection nearest to the VP.

13.9.2 Bicubic Bezier Patches

A more general method for surface representation can be obtained by generalizing the curve representations outlined in Chapter 11. Recall the equation for a Bezier curve based on the $m + 1$ control points $p_0, \ldots, p_m$:

$$P(t) = \sum_{i=0}^{m} B_{m,i}(t)\, p_i \qquad (0 \leqslant t \leqslant 1) \tag{13.25}$$

where $B_{m,i}$ are the Bernstein basis functions:

$$B_{m,i}(t) = \binom{m}{i} t^i (1 - t)^{m-i} \tag{13.26}$$

Consider the cubic case when $m = 3$. Then, by expressing Equation (13.26) directly as cubic polynomials, it is easy to show that Equation (13.25) can be written in matrix form as:

$$\begin{aligned} P(t) &= (t^3, t^2 t, 1) \begin{pmatrix} -1 & 3 & -3 & 1 \\ 3 & -6 & 3 & 0 \\ -3 & 3 & 0 & 0 \\ 1 & 0 & 0 & 0 \end{pmatrix} \begin{pmatrix} p_0 \\ p_1 \\ p_2 \\ p_3 \end{pmatrix} \\ &= \mathbf{t\,B\,p}' \end{aligned} \tag{13.27}$$

(A similar matrix form can be derived for any order of Bezier curve, of which cubic curves are just one – often used – example.) Remember here that $P(t)$ is a vector function of the form $(x(t), y(t))$, where Equation (13.25) is evaluated separately for the x and y components of the p_i.

Now let p_{ij} be the control points (x_{ij}, y_{ij}, z_{ij}) $(i = 1, \ldots, m;$ $j = 1, \ldots, n)$ in 3D, where the points form a matrix as shown in Figure 13.26. Then the 3D Bezier surface formed by this **control graph** has equation:

$$P(t, u) = \sum_{i=0}^{m} \sum_{j=0}^{n} B_{m,i}(t)\, p_{ij}\, B_{n,j}(u) \tag{13.28}$$

As t and u vary (independently) between 0 and 1 so the surface is mapped out (see Figure 13.27).

Using Equation (13.27) a matrix representation for Equation (13.28) can easily be seen to be:

$$P(t, u) = \mathbf{t\,B\,P\,B'\,u'}$$

where **P** is the matrix of control points.

It is not difficult to generate a wire-frame drawing of a Bezier surface – this is left as an exercise for the reader (see Exercise 13.45). For further details on curve and surface representations see Barksy (1984).

More interesting are methods for rendering such bicubic surface patches with a shading. These employ an approach akin to the polygon fill hidden surface scan line algorithm discussed earlier. The very elegant Lane–Carpenter algorithm is discussed in full by Lane, Carpenter, Whitted and Blinn (1980) and is based on earlier work by Catmull (1975). See also Lane and Reisenfeld (1980) for the theoretical basis of curve and surface subdivision on which the algorithm is based.

The Lane–Carpenter algorithm is a divide and conquer approach to the display of parametrically defined cubic (Bezier) surfaces. The idea is that if a bicubic patch is easy to render, then render it; otherwise split it into four bicubic patches and apply the same algorithm recursively to each. 'Easy to render' in this context means that the surface may be approximated within some tolerance to a planar polygon. This polygon can then be rendered by a scan line method.

In the terminology of the paradigm, a surface is *conquered* when it can be approximated by a polygon. The *divide* step is what makes such approximation possible – by treating smaller and smaller subpatches of the original surface. The scan line method works by first sorting all patches with respect to a minimum bounding y value (which can be computed on the basis of the convex hull of the control points). Then, as the scan conversion proceeds, the set of candidate patches are found that might be intersected by the current scan line. These are (ultimately) treated as planar – in fact, four-sided polygons.

The idea of dividing a Bezier surface is best illustrated with respect to curves. Since a surface is simply a **tensor product** of two curves (as shown in Equation (13.28)), the result for curves can be easily generalized to surfaces.

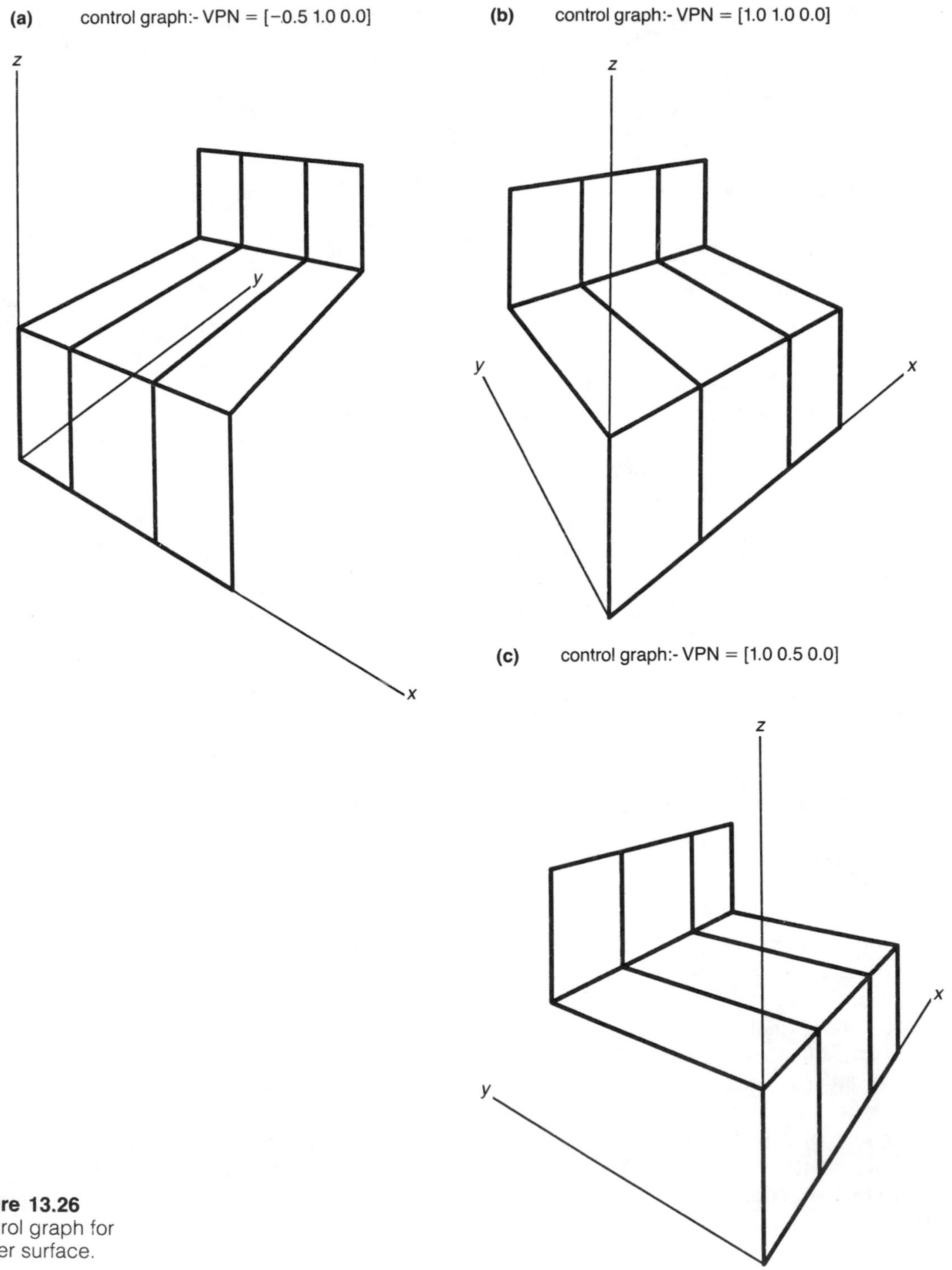

Figure 13.26
Control graph for
Bezier surface.

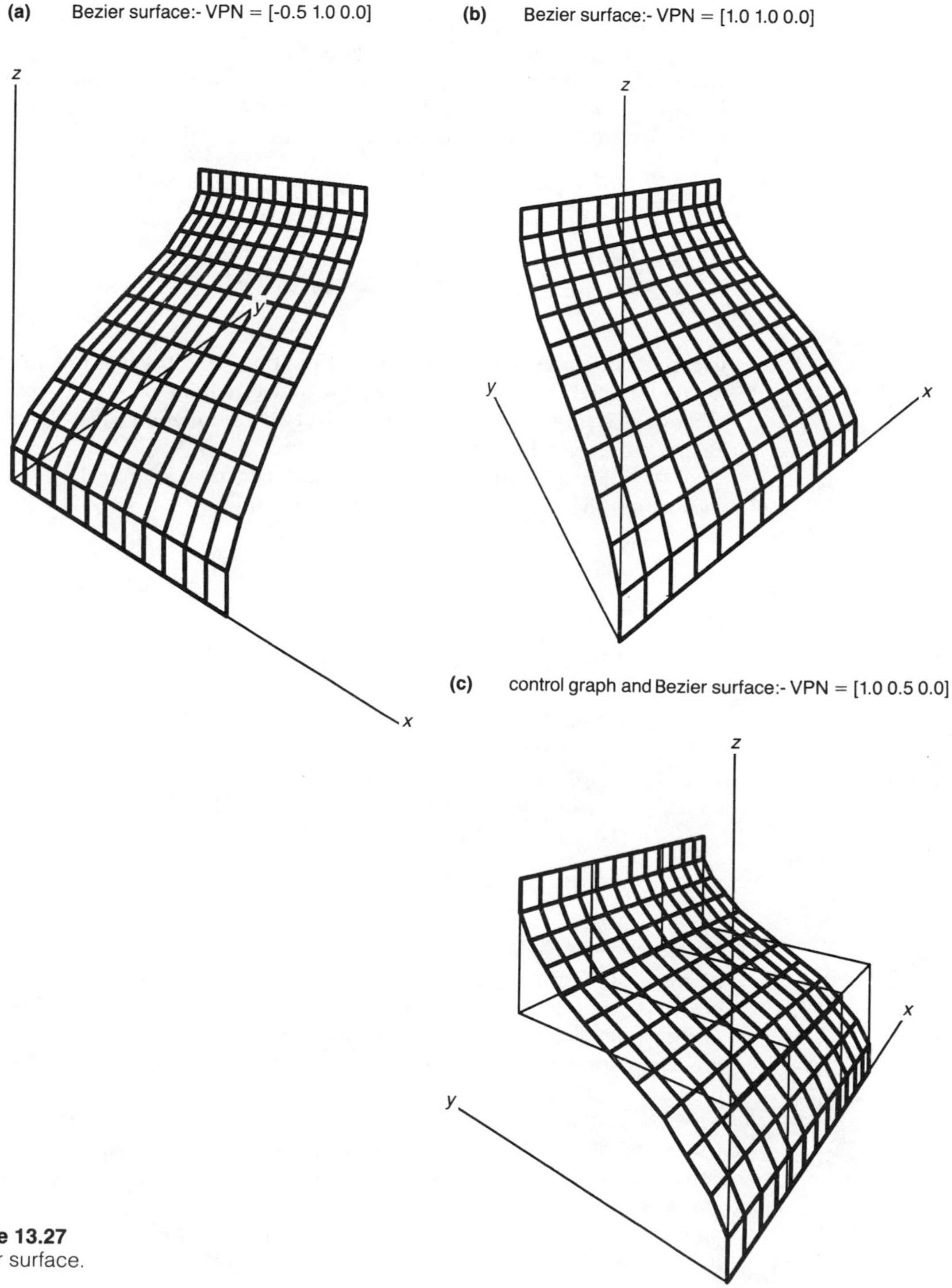

Figure 13.27
Bezier surface.

Consider Equation (13.25) which defines a Bezier curve for the case $m = 3$. To split the curve at α requires finding points q_0, q_1, q_2, q_3, and r_0, r_1, r_2, and r_3 for any α in the range 0 to 1 such that **q** and **r** are vectors of control points for two Bezier curves, which together are equivalent to the original single curve. Hence, **q** and **r** are required so that:

$$P(\alpha t) = \sum_{i=0}^{3} B_i(t)\, q_i \qquad (0 \leqslant t \leqslant 1) \tag{13.29}$$

$$P((1-\alpha)t + \alpha) = \sum_{i=0}^{3} B_i(t)\, r_i \qquad (0 \leqslant t \leqslant 1) \tag{13.30}$$

Clearly, as t varies between 0 and 1, Equation (13.29) generates the points on the original curve between 0 and α and Equation (13.30) the points on the original curve between α and 1. But these equations also define valid Bezier curves for the control points q_i and r_i.

Of particular interest, is the case when $\alpha = \frac{1}{2}$, for then it can be shown that the required new control points are:

$$\begin{aligned}
q_0 &= p_0 \\
q_1 &= \frac{(p_0 + p_1)}{2} \\
q_2 &= \frac{q_1}{2} + \frac{(p_1 + p_2)}{4} \\
q_3 &= \frac{(q_2 + r_1)}{2} \\
r_0 &= q_3 \\
r_1 &= \frac{(p_1 + p_2)}{4} + \frac{r_2}{2} \\
r_2 &= \frac{(p_2 + p_3)}{2} \\
r_3 &= p_3
\end{aligned} \tag{13.31}$$

A graphical interpretation is shown in Figure 13.28, from which it should be clear that the values **q** and **r** are found by a process of midpoint subdivision of the original control points. Lane and Reisenfeld further proved that if the process is continued, then the successive sets of new control points converge to the true Bezier curve.

Note that this splitting process is based only on additions and shifts (divisions by 2 and 4), and can therefore be computed quickly. As a consequence, it can form the basis of an algorithm for generating the Bezier curve without actually ever evaluating it. For, if the original curve approximates a straight line, then it is drawn; otherwise, the curve is split into two, in the manner shown, and the same principle applied to each half.

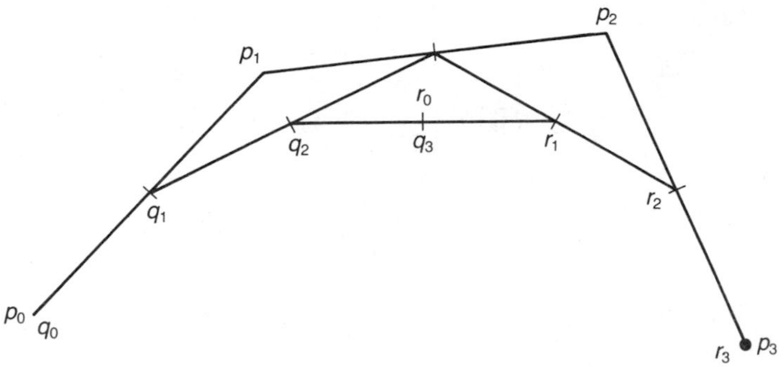

p_0, p_1, p_2, p_3 are control points of Bezier curve

r_0, r_1, r_2, r_3 are Bezier curves that split the original
q_0 q_1, q_2, q_3 into two

If this process is repeated, then in the limit the true Bezier curve is obtained

Figure 13.28
Splitting a Bezier curve.

To test whether the curve approximates a line is easy, for (as explained in Chapter 11) the curve is always inside the convex hull of the control points. If the curve is a straight line, then the four control points must also be colinear. Hence, a linearity test can be based on a suitable comparison of the inner control points with the two endpoints (see Exercise 13.46). The simplicity of this method is shown in the following program fragment:

```
fun Bezier(p) =
  if Colinear(p) then Line(p)
  else
    let val (q, r) = Split(p)
    in
      Bezier(q);
      Bezier(r)
    ni
  fi
nuf
```

Here, p is an array of four control points and *Colinear* returns true if the control points are approximately on a straight line. If this is the case, then the line connecting $p[0]$ to $p[3]$ is drawn, otherwise p is split into two sets of control points and the function called recursively.

The generalization to surfaces is relatively straightforward, and is accomplished by splitting each row and each column of the control graph. Hence, four new control graphs **q**, **r**, **s** and **t** are required, so that for α

and β between 0 and 1:

$$P(\alpha\, t, \beta\, u) = \sum_{i=0}^{3} \sum_{j=0}^{3} B_{m,i}(t)\, q_{ij}\, B_{n,j}(u)$$

$$P(\alpha\, t, \beta(1 - u) + \beta) = \sum_{i=0}^{3} \sum_{j=0}^{3} B_{m,i}(t)\, r_{ij}\, B_{n,j}(u)$$

$$P(\alpha(1 - t) + \alpha, \beta\, t) = \sum_{i=0}^{3} \sum_{j=0}^{3} B_{m,i}(t)\, s_{ij}\, B_{n,j}(u)$$

$$P(\alpha(1 - t) + \alpha, \beta(1 - t) + \beta) = \sum_{i=0}^{3} \sum_{j=0}^{3} B_{m,i}(t)\, t_{ij}\, B_{n,j}(u)$$

Choosing $\alpha = \beta = ½$ divides the original patch into four corresponding to:

$0 \leqslant t \leqslant ½;\quad 0 \leqslant u \leqslant ½$
$0 \leqslant t \leqslant ½;\quad ½ \leqslant u \leqslant 1$
$½ \leqslant t \leqslant 1;\quad 0 \leqslant u \leqslant ½$
$½ \leqslant t \leqslant 1;\quad ½ \leqslant t \leqslant 1$

It is left to the reader to compute the required values for **q**, **r**, **s** and **t** (see Exercise 13.47).

Appendix B gives the complete PostScript program used to generate Figures 13.26 and 13.27, which employs these ideas.

13.9.3 Fractals

Natural scenes often cannot be described using traditional techniques based on continuous mathematics. A fundamental property of nature is statistical self-similarity. The usual example of this is a coastline that has the same sort of irregularity when viewed from outer space, 30 000 feet, 10 000 feet or indeed from ground level. The interesting mathematical observation is that at any level of magnification the coastline could be drawn by joining together lots of small straight-line segments. But at each greater level of magnification, what was previously approximated by a single line segment, must now be rendered by a sequence of line segments, and so on *ad infinitum*. It follows that at any stage in this process, the dimensionality of the coastline is unity, but in the limit the dimension (or so-called **fractal dimension**) is some number between 1 and 2.

Curves that exhibit such self-similarity at any level of detail have long been studied by mathematicians. The most famous perhaps is the Hilbert curve (see Figure 13.29). (For an interesting application of Hilbert curves in computer graphics see Witten and Neal, 1982. An algorithm for generating a Hilbert curve is given by Goldschlager, 1981.)

```
%Hilbert curve program
%based on Goldschlager, 1981

/H 0.125 def
/-H 0.125 neg def

/North 0 def /South 1 def /East  2 def /West  3 def

/MoveDict 1 dict def

/Move
{
  MoveDict begin
    /direction exch def
    North direction eq {0  H rlineto} if
    South direction eq {0 -H rlineto} if
    East  direction eq {H  0 rlineto} if
    West  direction eq {-H 0 rlineto} if
  end
} def

/Hilbert
{
  6 dict begin
     /i exch def
     /U exch def /L exch def /D exch def /R exch def
     /j i 1 sub def
     i 0 gt %if i > 0 then
        {
         D R U L j Hilbert   R Move
         R D L U j Hilbert   D Move
         R D L U j Hilbert   L Move
         U L D R j Hilbert
        }
     if
  end
} def

/main
{
 72 72 scale
 1 1 translate
 /Times-Roman findfont 0.25 scalefont setfont
 0.05 setlinewidth
 newpath
   1 4 moveto
   East South West North 4 Hilbert
 stroke
 1 6 moveto (Figure 13.29 - Hilbert Curve) show
 showpage
} def

main
```

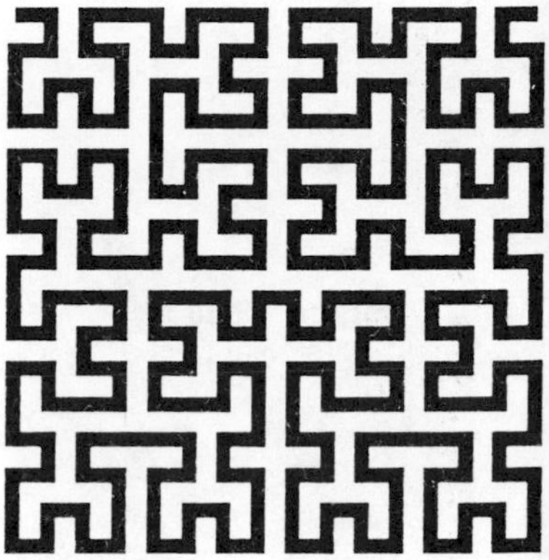

Figure 13.29
Hilbert curves.

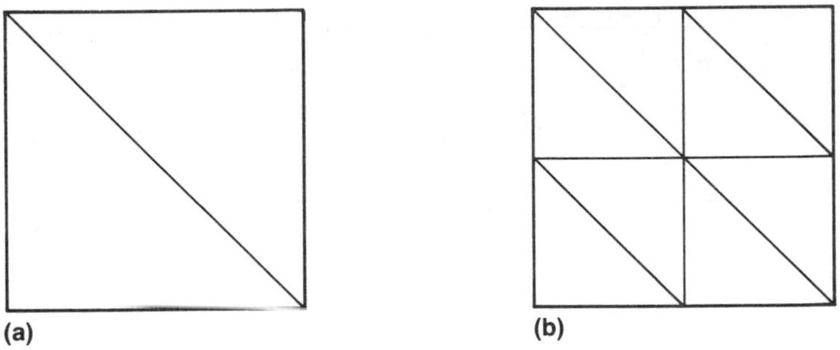

Figure 13.30 Self-similarity of a triangle scene.

It is the work of Mandelbrot (1977 and 1982) which has inspired the recent interest in such curves and surfaces in the computer graphics community. Fournier, Fussel and Carpenter (1982) have defined a number of 'fractal primitives' (for example, fractal polygons) for direct use in graphics. The basic idea is illustrated in Figure 13.30 (Miller, 1986). Here, a scene consists of two triangles. At the next stage of magnification, each triangle in turn is found to consist of four triangles, and so on. This is accomplished by midpoint subdivision. A stochastically self-similar scene can be obtained by adding a random value to each midpoint in the process.

Further discussion of these techniques is beyond the scope of this book. However, Plate 30 shows an application of this method and another recent method called **particle systems** (Reeves, 1983) originally used in the creation of the Genesis Planet in the Star Trek film mentioned earlier in this chapter and shown here in the rendering of Halley's comet.

13.10 Standards

The Computer Graphics Working Group of ISO is currently discussing a 3D extension to GKS and the PHIGS system (the modelling aspects of which were discussed in Chapter 10). Although PHIGS and GKS-3D share a similar viewing model, they do differ in certain respects, and there are strong pressures to bring about a greater convergence between them. So it is likely that by the time they are each standards, they will have an identical viewing model.

In fact, that model is not too dissimilar from the one discussed in this chapter (all originally derived from CORE). However, it is more complex, perhaps because of the need to make GKS-3D a genuine extension of GKS. There are, for example, five coordinate systems of which the applications programmer has to be aware: 3D WC are mapped to 3D NDC (in a manner similar to the equivalent 2D transformation); 3D NDC space is transformed to the UVN system (as discussed in this chapter, except that in GKS, UVN and all systems are right-handed); the UVN system (called view reference coordinates) is mapped to normalized projection coordinates (NPC); and 3D versions of *SetWorkstationWindow* and *SetWorkstationViewport* map a region of NPC to 3D device coordinates. Interestingly, the standard does not say anything about what should happen if device display space is two dimensional. But the answer should be obvious (see Exercise 13.48).

The output primitives are essentially straightforward generalizations of 2D GKS with, for example, *Polyline3* drawing the lines connecting a sequence of points in 3D. The ordinary *Polyline* function is just a special case of this for the $z = 0$ plane. The only new primitive is *FillAreaSet*, which allows the specification and rendering of a set of 3D planar polygons. Attributes for the output primitives are controlled in a manner identical to the standard GKS.

It is early days yet to speculate on the possible impact of GKS-3D on the computer graphics community. Unlike the original GKS, it is very complicated, and probably beyond the reach of all but computer graphics experts. Moreover, it is limited: planar polygon sets are the richest output primitive. Nevertheless, just the very discussion of the standard and its ultimate publication will stimulate interest in 3D graphics, which can only be a good thing.

Summary

This chapter has considered the basic ideas of 3D graphics: representing a 3D scene by polyhedra and associated data structures; specifying a view in 3D following the synthetic camera model; the use of homogeneous transformations to transform the scene into a tractable viewing space from the point of view of projection, visibility and shading; problems involved in rendering – shading models and the under-sampling corrected by anti-aliasing methods; and finally, methods for rendering scenes for non-polyhedrally defined objects.

Exercises

13.1 Describe the pyramid of Section 13.2 in a LHS.

13.2 Describe a unit cube (that is, with all edges of length 1) in a RHS using the simple polygon representation.

13.3 Let P be a polyhedra consisting of N polygons, where the ith polygon consists of n_i edges. If the simple polygon representation is used for the object, how many lines would be generated in a display (assuming no hidden surface removals)?

13.4 Define the *Polygon3D* function in terms of the *Line3D* function.

13.5 Provide an edge polygon representation of a unit cube.

13.6 Prove the results given in Equation (13.2).

13.7 At what height must an observer be to see the four upper sides of the pyramid from the positive quadrant of 3D space?

13.8 The expressions of Equation (13.5), showing how to translate cartesian coordinates to polar form, are not quite complete. For example, what is the result if x, y or z are 0? Give the full relationships, allowing for all of these special cases.

13.9 Suppose Equation (13.4) needs to be computed for a sequence of values θ, $\theta + d\theta$, $\theta + 2d\theta$, ... Construct an incremental formula that does not involve more than one evaluation of a sine or cosine for the entire iteration.

13.10 For a small θ, it is known that $\sin\theta \approx 0$ and $\cos\theta \approx 1$. How could this result be used to effect a sequence of rotations with a constant (small) angle of rotation? What is the danger involved in using the scheme you have invented?

13.11 Consider the pyramid shown in Figure 13.2. Find the vertices of the pyramid when rotated through an angle of 45° about the Y axis. Describe the resulting pyramid in a LHS and translated by ten units along the (left-handed) positive Z axis. Assuming that the COP is at the origin and the VP is five units along the Z axis, derive the perspective projection of the pyramid. Choose a window on the VP and derive the transformation from this window to device coordinates (for example, assuming a 512×512 display). Hence, draw the resulting image of the pyramid projected on the screen. Repeat the exercise for a VP at 7.5 and 2.5 units along the Z axis.

13.12 Repeat Exercise 13.11 for the case of an orthographic parallel projection. Does the VPD have any affect on the projected image in this case?

13.13 Extend the ideas presented about view volumes in Section 13.5.3 to the case of general parallel projections.

13.14 For the pyramid of Figure 13.2, describe a complete set of viewing parameters so that the pyramid can be viewed from the point (10, 10, 10) using perspective projection, assuming the VRP to be at the origin.

13.15 Justify Equation (13.6) for the formation of the **u** vector from the VPN vector and the VUV. How could the angle between the **n** and **v** vectors be determined?

13.16 Simplify the expression for $|\mathbf{n} \times \mathbf{v}|$ in Equation (13.6).

13.17 Why is there no division by $|\mathbf{u} \times \mathbf{n}|$ in Equation (13.7), and yet it is claimed that **v** is a unit vector?

13.18 Find the viewing transformation matrix **M** corresponding to your view specification of Exercise 13.14. Hence, find the view coordinates of the pyramid.

13.19 Derive the formula for perspective projection corresponding to the diagram showing the viewing coordinate system, as in Figure 13.11(b).

13.20 What is the relationship between the view plane distance d, the front plane distance d_{min} and the back plane distance d_{max}, as shown in Figure 13.11(b), and the corresponding distances D, D_{min} and D_{max}, as shown in Figure 13.14(a)?

13.21 Check that the transformation matrix **B** of Section 13.5.6 is equivalent to the transformation given by Equation (13.11).

13.22 Derive the matrix expression for transformation **P** of Section 13.5.7.

13.23 Justify the statement in Section 13.5.8 that in the context of its use in the clipping algorithm, the value of t computed by Equation (13.15) will always be in the range $0 < t < 1$.

13.24 Obtain results for the intersection of a line segment [$p1$, $p2$] with the planes $y = Y$ and $z = Z$. Hence, construct the complete definition of the intersection function for 3D line clipping.

13.25 Use the method of Section 13.5.8 to construct a clipping algorithm suitable for the truncated pyramid view volume of Section 13.5.6.

13.26 Construct a 3D version of the Sutherland–Hodgman algorithm for clipping polygons.

13.27 Calculate the number of arithmetic operations involved in the interpolation shading methods discussed in Section 13.6.5. How many adds, multiplies, divides and square roots are needed for the computation of each pixel intensity?

13.28 The equation of a unit sphere is $x^2 + y^2 + z^2 = 1$. Suppose points p_0, p_1, ..., p_{n-1} are chosen on the surface of the sphere, and the planar polygon with these points as vertices is used to approximate the corresponding surface patch. Show in detail how the linear interpolation methods of Section 13.6.5 could be used in this case. Note that for a surface with implicit equation $f(x, y, z)=0$, the normal at any point is the vector of partial derivatives $(\partial f/\partial x, \partial f/\partial y, \partial f/\partial z)$. (Of course, this is unlikely to be a unit normal.) Do the interpolation schemes offer any real advantage in this example?

13.29 Show in detail how the polygon fill algorithm of Section 4.8 must be extended to cater for the shading interpolation methods of Section 13.6.5.

13.30 Given a line with equation $y = bx$ with $0 < b < 1$, and a square with corners $(x_i - 0.5, y_i - 0.5)$, $(x_i + 0.5, y_i + 0.5)$ such that the line intersects the square and $b(x_i + 0.5) < y_i + 0.5$, show that the area of the square *underneath* the line is $bx_i - y_i + 0.5$ (see Figure 13.19(b)). Compare this quantity with the discriminatory error term in Bresenham's line drawing algorithm. Hence, show how the algorithm can be trivially modified to anti-alias polygon boundaries.

13.31 Compute the pixels that would be set by a straightforward application of Bresenham's algorithm for the two lines shown in Figure 13.21. Compare these with the corresponding tables of intensity values for the filtered image of Section 13.7.3. The Bresenham lines would look jagged and, of course, misrepresent their true thickness. What can be said in this regard about the filtered image lines?

13.32 Compute the filtered image for the 7×7 pixel grid of Figure 13.21, where the scene consists of the circle centred at (3, 3) with radius 3 (of infinitesimal thickness).

13.33 Equation (13.21) showing the incremental formula for z depths on a polygon is not strictly correct in the context of the viewing pipeline. Usually, the scan conversion process is carried out in display coordinates, whereas Equation (13.21) is based on the x and y coordinates on the VP in projection space. A further linear transformation is carried out to display the coordinates before processing the polygons. Derive the correct updating formula equivalent to Equation (13.21) for this situation.

13.34 Section 13.8.1 shows how to incrementally compute z depth values for successive pixel positions on a scan line. Derive the corresponding formula for successive vertical pixels and explain how this result may be used in the z-buffer algorithm.

13.35 Explain why, for example, the method of Pitteway and Watkinson for anti-aliasing polygon boundaries does not work for corners or thin polygons.

13.36 The polygon fill method of Section 13.8.2 requires each entry in the edge table to contain a pointer to information about the polygon, of which the edge is a part. Yet, typically, each edge is a common boundary between two polygons. How can this ambiguity be resolved?

13.37 Explain in detail what happens at scan line j in Figure 13.23 illustrating the polygon fill method of hidden surface removal.

13.38 What is the maximum recursive depth of the Warnock algorithm discussed in Section 13.8.3 in the case of a 512×512 display? Provide a detailed description of how to test the four cases of this algorithm. Hence, provide a complete implementation.

13.39 Section 13.8.4 discusses a method for calculating the intersection of a ray from the origin through a pixel for the ray casting method. Suppose that prior to the intersection calculations the scene is transformed into perspective (box) space. Now the rays would all be parallel to the Z axis. How could this be used to simplify the intersection calculations?

13.40 Show that the equations for a cone, cylinder and plane are special cases of the equation for a general quadric surface.

13.41 How could the x, y extent of the projection of a quadric surface be computed?

13.42 To shade a quadric surface, the normal vector at any point on the surface must be computed (for example, for Phong shading). How can the normal be found?

13.43 If the intersection of a ray and a quadric surface results in two real, equal roots, what does this indicate about the surface? What is the geometric interpretation of the fact that the intersection calculation must *always* yield either two imaginary or two real roots?

13.44 Derive an expression for a transformation of a Bezier curve by a homogeneous transformation matrix. Repeat the same exercise for a

Bezier surface. Is the class of Bezier curves (surfaces) closed under the operation of homogeneous transformation (as quadrics are)?

13.45 Using Equation (13.28), construct an algorithm to render a Bezier surface in wire-frame form, as shown in Figure 13.27.

13.46 Develop a test for (approximate) linearity of a Bezier curve.

13.47 On the basis of the splitting of a Bezier curve, derive the splitting control graphs for a Bezier surface.

13.48 What is the 'obvious' answer as to what should happen in GKS-3D if the system is used on a device with a 2D display space (as would normally be the case)?

13.49 GKS-3D incorporates no shading models. How, for example, might a Phong or Gouraud shading model be standardized into a set of applications level callable procedures?

13.50 How might hidden line and surface methods be incorporated into a computer graphics library? Consider the following: polygon fill areas in GKS may be solid or hollow. Suppose a hollow polygon obscures part of the scene. How should this be handled by a visibility procedure? (*Note*: This problem occupied many hours of heated discussion in the standards committees.)

PART TWO

GRAPHICS SYSTEMS AND INTERFACE

CHAPTER 14

SOME ASPECTS OF THE HUMAN–COMPUTER INTERFACE

This chapter looks at some general considerations important in designing a good human–computer interface in addition to the basic ideas in the more specific area of user interface design. It also considers aspects of the user–display interface, especially regarding the importance of colour.

14.1 Introduction

Whenever someone uses a machine, of any type, an **interface** is set up between that person and the machine. It may be a simple machine, like an electric drill, or it may be a complex one like an aircraft or a nuclear power station. Whatever the type of machine it is, the person using it needs to be able to observe its performance and control it: what is the drill's speed, for example, and how can the drill be made to go faster or slower. It is this communication with the machine that can make it very easy or very difficult to use.

This communication is known as the **man–machine interface (MMI)** – which is the general term used in the study of the use of any type of machine by a human operator – and is a major branch of **ergonomics**. When the machine is a computer and the user communicates via an interactive device, such as a VDU or voice input, then the interface is known as the **human–computer interface (HCI)**. (HCI also stands for human–computer interaction.) However, the term **user–machine interface (UMI)** is often used, as it may not always be recognized that the interface is to a computer. For example, if the design in question was for the display of aircraft flight status information in a cockpit, as shown in Plates 20 and 21, then the presence of the display and control computers would not necessarily be obvious to the users, in this case the pilot and co-pilot.

One of the most striking changes in computing in recent years has been the spread of the use of computers to many aspects of people's everyday and working life. This has been made possible by conscious attempts on the part of computer specialists to make their products accessible to people who are not computer professionals. Some examples of this include the use of spreadsheets systems for business accounting and statistics, word processors for textual document preparation and the recent introduction of desk top publishing systems.

It is an understatement to say that the study of HCI principles is a large area, and it is still in its infancy in spite of an already very extensive literature. It has brought into computer science, experts in applied ergonomics and psychology, who now play a major role in advancing the understanding of what constitutes good design.

What characterizes serious HCI research is the recognition that interfaces are more likely to succeed if they rest on a sound model of the behaviour of users. In other words, principles that supposedly govern user interface design should be empirically verified in the context of a predictive psychological model, otherwise there are no grounds for elevating them to the status of principles (why should anyone believe them?). For example, consider the following statement: 'A good user interface is one that uses pop-up menus rather than textual commands'. If 'good user interface' means, say, one that users can learn quickly, and perform their tasks with a minimum of errors, then this statement is a hypothesis about human behaviour. There are no grounds for believing it to be a useful rule without a properly organized psychological study.

Any deep analysis of the material covered by the heading 'human–computer interaction' is beyond the scope of this book. Readers are ultimately introduced to this area, already touched on to some extent in Part One, by means of examples from systems that are generally agreed by users to provide good user interfaces. These examples have their history in the research carried out at Xerox PARC during the 1970s, mentioned earlier in Chapter 11. The fundamental ideas are discussed in a classic paper written by some of the Xerox team, which reviews the design decisions underlying the Xerox Star user interface (Smith *et al.*, 1982).

At first sight, much of the material in this chapter has little to do with computer graphics. Yet the most successful and striking user interfaces are those that are pictorially based, and therefore have required substantial input from computer graphics specialists in their design and implementation. Given this necessary relationship between user interface design and computer graphics, there is a widely held view that a substantial part of the training of students of computer graphics should be in the area of user interface design. For example, at a recent Teaching Workshop organized by the UK Chapter of Eurographics in conjunction with Manchester University, a core syllabus for computer graphics for all computer science students was constructed. In the 45 teaching hours suggested on such a course, nearly one-quarter (11 hours) is recommended for user interfaces (second only to graphics concepts and algorithms, which is allocated 14 hours). A report on this workshop can be found in Duce (1986).

Whole books have been written on even single aspects of the HCI and it is impossible to do the subject justice in a single chapter. This chapter aims to provide the reader with an introduction to the issues involved in the design of the user–computer interaction and the display interface. An excellent recent text where the reader can follow up this subject in more detail is Shneiderman (1987).

14.2 General Considerations for a Good HCI

HCI includes anything that affects the use of the system by the user. This can include all aspects of the system from the design of the messages that are issued to the user by the system right down to the height and contour of the chair on which the user sits while operating the system. These are all important to the overall performance of the total system – the machine *and* the user.

14.2.1 Why Good HCI?

Why is a good HCI necessary? Why not let the user adapt to the system? Isn't the human being supposed to be highly adaptable? These questions are worth considering to see what a good HCI is trying to achieve.

An example that goes a long way towards illustrating the importance of these questions is in the field of computer-based education and training. Computer graphics is widely used in this field, but its use is of no benefit if the user is forced to spend a lot of time learning the purely computer-specific aspects of the system. Therefore, the HCI must be simple to use and self-explanatory in concept so as not to distract the student from the main learning task. Another example is offered by command and control systems. Here, the user must be able to make quick decisions on the basis of any graphical images provided by the system. Again, if the user has to spend time grappling with the burden of a complex interface, he or she will not be able to respond effectively in the command situation.

People are highly adaptable and flexible elements of the system but this may have to be paid for in other ways. If users are forced to behave in a manner that is unfamiliar or in circumstances that are uncomfortable, this will undoubtedly affect their ability to perform their tasks. This in turn may impair their speed of reaction or their rational decision-making capability or both, and overall system performance will suffer as a consequence. In some circumstances, such as in the control of a nuclear power station, the consequences may be disastrous.

Good or bad HCI affects both simple and complex systems. A programmer may develop a very useful and desirable program but, because it is difficult or confusing to use, nobody else will want to use it. Many very good systems, notably those in the area of CAD, have suffered from a poor HCI. It should be a design aim for all systems, whether they are large and complex or small and simple, that they should be easy to use by an average user. All systems should be designed with other users in mind, and not just for use by the designer who, after all, is rarely the ultimate end user.

14.2.2 The User Population

For each interactive system, there will be a set of users performing a set of tasks. The intended purpose of the system – word processor, CAD and so on – will define the set of users. This set may be clearly and concisely defined, as in the case of an air traffic control system where the users will always be trained controllers, or the user set may be broader, as in the case of a word processor where it may be used by both experienced typists and complete novices.

Users are always the starting point for a good HCI. It is necessary to carefully consider all that is known about the set of users defined for the system. Firstly, the users are very rarely a single person, but many different people who use the system from time to time. The more useful and popular the system, the larger the assortment of users. Therefore, the HCI must cater for the whole range of users that will use the system. Some users will be experts on the system and some beginners. Some users may even be complete beginners to the whole subject. For example, in the case of a computer-aided draughting system, the user may be a highly trained draughtsman new to CAD systems or a trainee draughtsman.

14.2.3 The Role of Users

When constructing a system, Pew (1983) suggests that designers should distinguish between what *people* are generally good at and what *computers* are good at. It is argued that people are good at the following:

- They have the ability to function very effectively as monitors. That is, they can be used to monitor the behaviour of a system, looking for abnormal situations as well as the normal progress of a system in operation.
- They have the ability to locate and recognize patterns either in terms of display images or in terms of behaviour. They are also capable of doing several of these tasks in parallel.
- They have great versatility in handling many different input and output symbols. They are, however, relatively slow information processors.
- They have the ability to adapt to a situation that involves risk and uncertainty and can effectively guide a computer-based system where decisions have to be made quickly and intuitively on data that itself may be subject to error.

14.2.4 The Role of Computers

Computers tend to excell in the following tasks:

- Computers are good at tasks requiring large amounts of memory capacity. It is better to rely on the computer's memory and its ability to quickly and accurately display its memory contents. Users can then concentrate on the things that they are good at, like making decisions.
- Computers are good and fast at making deductions where the information and rules are complete. However, they are usually at a

loss when either there is data missing or some of the rules for deduction are incomplete. People, on the other hand, have great ingenuity and can exercise judgement in situations of missing data or rules.

- Computers are very good at high-speed and repetitive monitoring of data and can filter this data to display it in summary form. People are less efficient at both of these, but good at monitoring and acting as adaptive controllers based on this type of data.

As stated earlier, the obvious conclusion is to let the computer do what it is good at and let the users do what they are better at. This may seem a rather trite statement, but it is not always applied. The human user is an integral part of the overall system and should be considered as such.

14.3 Task Analysis

14.3.1 Levels of an Interface

A user interface may be regarded as having an *abstract* level, which embodies the high-level functionality and concepts of the system, including a representation of the concepts, skills and knowledge that users bring to the system. These abstract entities are mapped to a *communications* level, which determines how they are represented on the display and the interactive command language that the user needs to learn to manipulate the objects of the system. Finally, there is an *applications* level which embodies the specific methods that implement the algorithms and procedures needed to supply the semantics of the user and system operations. (This discussion is taken up in detail in the next section, in the context of the command language grammar.)

These three levels may be considered independently, but are related by means of the mappings between them. As a very simple example, consider a system whose only function is to allow users to draw a single straight line on the display. At the abstract level, users require an understanding of what it means to draw a straight line. The abstract objects of such a system might be points and lines. At the communications level, given the notions of points and lines, there are many different ways that these might be represented on a display. Moreover, there are alternative command styles that allow input of point information – by textual commands or by pointing, or even by voice input. Moreover, within any one of these classes of input, there are again different methods; for example, the pointing might be done with a light pen, a touch-sensitive screen or a mouse. Finally, given the command to draw a line, the computer system has to employ a method to do this, based, for example, on Bresenham's algorithm considered in Chapter 4.

The user interface is the *total* impact of all of these levels. Every choice made by the designer can have a crucial, be it beneficial or damaging, impact on how the user perceives and comes to terms with the system. Even a seemingly unimportant physical choice between a mouse, tablet or touch-sensitive screen may determine whether the system is usable at all. For example, if the purpose of the interface is to allow drawings, where accuracy of positioning is of vital importance, then the crudity of a mouse or touch-sensitive screen as the physical method for input would be inappropriate, no matter how well designed the higher levels of the system (see Chapter 17).

(Before going any further, it is important to realize that none of the foregoing statements, or in fact any of those in most of this chapter, should be *believed* by readers. They are not assertions that can be proven in the same sense that the clipping algorithm discussed in Chapter 4 can be guaranteed to clip lines. They are hypotheses that require empirical validation. The HCI area is full of pitfalls for uncritical students, and teachers, and everyone should be aware of this fact.)

Although simple, the last example leads to a major point. Why choose a tablet as an input device rather than a touch-sensitive screen? This question cannot be answered in the abstract, for it depends on the tasks for which the system is being designed. For CAD, a touch-sensitive screen is usually inappropriate. However, in the main undercover shopping mall in Toronto, members of the public can quickly and easily access a large amount of information about the different shops in the mall using a system based on touch-sensitive screens. For this set of tasks, such a screen seems not only adequate but ideal. A task analysis to discover the detailed knowledge and methods of working of the potential user population for a new system is therefore essential to help in making choices through all the levels of the interface.

14.3.2 An Example of File Management

When confronted with using a computer system, say, for the purposes of word processing or program development, a user has at the very least to know how to manage files; that is, how to create, copy, delete, edit and rename a file. Files are ultimately stored in coded form on a magnetic medium such as a disk. The extent to which ordinary users have to understand the physical or logical organization of files on the disk, to perform these basic operations, is one measure of the success or otherwise of those aspects of the user interface to the computer operating system dealing with file handling.

The filing system is usually organized as a tree structure. Some files,

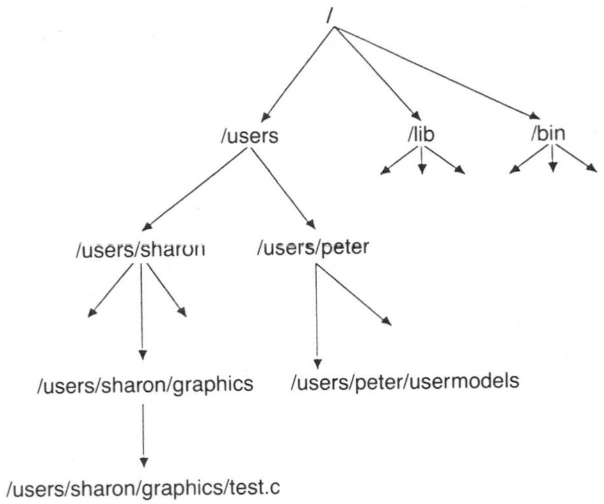

Figure 14.1.
UNIX file system.

usually called **directories**, are special in that they contain other files, some or all of which may be directories. Navigation through such an hierarchical filing system is obviously a prerequisite to successful use of the computer.

The UNIX system has in recent years established itself as something of a standard operating system. It is worth briefly considering some of the ways in which a user performs basic file management on the UNIX system. Files are organized hierarchically, as shown for example in Figure 14.1. Some basic commands are *cp* for copy, *rm* for remove and *cd* to change directories.

Novice users are immediately faced with a bewildering variety and number of commands to learn, to be able to do the most basic things. They have to understand the rather abstract idea of the hierarchical structure of files and that operations are relative to the current directory. Most commands have special flags that make the commands perform variations on their normal operation. Moreover, the user must to some extent understand aspects of the implementation of the system. An example of this is that when the *-r* flag is used in *cp* it stands for *recursive*. This is a technical term understood by computer scientists, but this cannot be expected of someone using a system for document preparation in an ordinary office working environment.

Historically, operating systems were designed and implemented for the convenience of the designers, implementors and the computers themselves, rather than the population of ultimate users. The same has traditionally been true of general computer applications programs, even those that are nominally interactive, such as CAD systems: the user has to adapt to the concepts and methods imposed by the computer system or fail to use the system to achieve the required goals. Such adaptation is almost always possible, especially when unavoidable and necessary, although it is often costly in terms of training time and work performance.

People invented files to efficiently store related chunks of information. Typically, there are pieces of paper containing information in the form of text and graphics. Pieces of paper logically related according to a classification dependent on the relevant information are grouped together in a higher order entity, perhaps called a folder. Groups of folders, again related or sorted according to some criterion, are themselves 'filed' away into still higher order groupings (such as filing cabinets). Filing cabinets exist in different rooms, rooms on different floors or departments of a building, buildings in different locations and so on. The essential feature here is that units of information are grouped according to some organizing criteria into higher order units. The depth and height of the hierarchy depends on context: in one context (that of printing) the individual marks on the piece of paper form the lowest level of the hierarchy; in another context (school records) the individual pieces of paper containing annual reports for a given student are at the lowest level.

14.3.3 Objects and Operations

It was a fundamental insight of the Xerox PARC researchers to see that analysis of the tasks carried out by users must be undertaken before work can begin on the design and implementation of the interactive computer system intended to meet these task requirements. The analysis of the tasks must be independent of and prior to design of the interactive computer system. A fundamental procedure in task analysis is the identification of the conceptual objects and the operations that users perform with them.

Suppose that for a particular filing environment, the lowest unit of information is called a *document* and that higher levels are called *folders*, which in turn may contain documents or folders. In addition, there must be at least one further object, which is the World in which all of these documents and folders exist. What actions are performed on these objects (relative to the particular task domain under investigation)? Such actions might, for example, be as follows. Objects can be *moved* into and out of folders. Objects can be *deleted* altogether. A folder can be *opened* to allow *inspection* of its contents, or *closed*. In addition, the objects will have various *properties* which can be *inquired*; for example, the date of object creation, a measure of size, the type of object (whether it is a folder or a document) and what kind of information it stores, if a document. Objects may also be duplicated or *copied*.

The foregoing discussion on objects–actions–properties is an attempt to illuminate the basic techniques of (what is here) a very primitive example of **task analysis**. Note that the analysis is quite abstract: it does not require assumptions about the actual form of documents or folders, nor what is contained in documents. The same analysis might apply if the information were represented by hieroglyphics carved on stone. The essential feature is a set of objects, relations between those objects, object properties, and actions over the collection of objects and properties.

14.3.4 The Role of Task Analysis

The task analysis just outlined is very simple, partly because it is an artificial example unrelated to any particular concrete group of people carrying out definite file management tasks. More importantly, task analysis is best carried out in the context of a psychological model of users, so that the results discovered by the analysis are endowed with meaning determined by the parameters of the model. For example, if a particular user always errupts into laughter when filing away documents, this may be because of some personal predilection and may remain unnoticed by the analysis. Alternatively, if the analysis is undertaken in the context of a model that predicts a high degree of mirth in certain situations in the process of handling certain sorts of files (for example, written scripts of a comedian), then the laughter will be significant. If the laughter affects the ability of the operator to successfully carry out the task, then it is even more significant. Card, Moran and Newell (1983, pp. 121–138) carried out a detailed task analysis of a problem concerning typing, and in the context of a psychological model. Johnson (1985) shows, in an analysis of messaging, how Task Analysis for Knowledge Descriptions (TAKD) can be used in the construction of an abstract description of the interactive computer system, this description being a staging post on the road to the full system design and implementation.

Ideally, a task analysis should result in a formal model of the actions (including concepts held) by a user population to achieve specified goals in a task framework. The greater the degree of model specificity, the greater the extent to which it can be used to derive predictions about user performance when the parameters of the model are varied. In the HCI context, the parameters *are* to be varied considerably, for the task analysis is but one step on the road to providing an interactive computer system with which the user population would be expected to perform at least the same set of tasks as before. This would almost certainly require users to become familiar with a completely novel environment and set of physical actions and yet still achieve the same goals as before, at an improved performance rate (otherwise what would be the point of the introduction of computer technology?).

Task analysis is not only vital to find out what users are doing and how they are doing it (to build a model of their mental model of the task and task activities), but for two other important reasons. First, it provides a conceptual framework within which the new interactive system can be set. It was asserted that users would be in a different physical environment than before, performing different physical actions, which is unavoidable. However, the transition would be less traumatic if users could bring their familiar conceptual model over from the old environment and find that it is still valid in the new. Second, task analysis is fundamentally predictive: on the basis of the task analysis, hypotheses can be formed about user performance in the new situation. These hypotheses can then be rigorously tested after system implementation or prototyping. This *evaluation* stage is the last in the iterative cycle: task analysis → user conceptual model → system design → prototyping → evaluation →... . A discussion of system evaluation is outside the scope of this book, but interested readers should see Totterdell and Cooper (1986) for an example.

It should be clear that task analysis plays a very major role in interactive system design, even though this section has only introduced the very basic ideas of this subject area.

14.4 User Conceptual Models

The basic idea of **user conceptual models** (UCMs) was introduced in Chapter 6: the user model consists of the set of concepts that the user invents, acquires and infers to explain how to use the system. It is part metaphore: for example, a task might be described as 'moving a file from a folder to the desk top' although in reality no such event actually happens, and the actions of performing such a task may consist of mouse moves and button clicks. Yet the metaphore is useful in explaining to the user the meaning of those actions – better than, say, talking about moving bytes stored on a disk from one physical location to another.

Recognition of the fact that users form a model of how to operate the system is a crucial aid to the designer, for the designer would hope to determine to a large extent the model formed by the user, to improve the usability of the system in a number of ways. This is so important that, for example, Moran (1981) has gone so far to say that "*to design the user interface of a system is to design the user's model.*"

14.4.1 Reasons for a UCM

A fundamental reason for the necessity of an explicit UCM determined by the designer was hinted at in the last section. Users already have a model about how they perform their tasks. If the essence of this model can be captured as the real UCM underpinning the interactive computer system, then there are grounds for believing that the system will become easier to learn to use than if it requires totally new concepts, unrelated to those previously held. It should be noted that this is a hypothesis about user behaviour which must be proven (or otherwise) by experience and study rather than an assertion. Nevertheless, it is a hypothesis that provides designers with a basic design principle.

In addition, introduction of an explicit UCM allows the designer to clearly separate those parts of the system that are concerned with the semantics of the application and those that relate to the abstract user model. Another way of saying this is that there are many different possible implementations consistent with any given abstract description of the functionality and conceptual objects and actions of the system. It therefore follows that each object and action in the UCM can be represented in quite different ways (in different implementations). This is important for the designer because it clearly indicates that the abstract description of the system, styles of representation and interaction, and implementation are logically separate in the design process; that is, each can be treated as a modular activity in its own right. Such a breakdown of a complex process into smaller logical units is a basic principle of computer science.

This separation is important because it also allows a degree of objective evaluation of different interactive styles and representations, especially in a computational environment that allows rapid prototyping of alternatives. For example, suppose that an abstract UCM is propounded by designers for the file management problem discussed earlier. Some designers might argue that a text-driven command interface is most appropriate for a given user population, something like the UNIX system provides. Others may argue, for the same user model, that an interface using pop-up menus would be most appropriate. Since both implementations would be built on the same underlying abstract model, they are comparable from the point of view of evaluation. Hence, an experiment could be designed to test the two alternative hypotheses; that is, the question can be settled empirically. Reisner (1981) gives an example of how two interfaces to a drawing program can be represented using an abstract notation, and then rigorously compares the interfaces on the basis of this analysis.

Some readers will no doubt be throwing up their hands in despair, at the cost involved in implementing alternative interactive styles. However, there are two answers to this objection. First, if user interface design is taken seriously by a design team, then there is no excuse for not carrying out these sorts of evaluations. In a commercial context, if your competitors are doing this, then for you not to do so would be risky. (The designers of the Star interface report that 30 person-years were spent on the design of the system.) Second, it is very likely that the cost of prototyping different alternatives will reduce dramatically in the near future. There are systems already on the market that allow designers to *interactively* generate user interface styles. Such systems permit a designer to use an interactive drawing and painting program to design screen layouts, using interactive command sequences. These systems *generate* the implementation code for the human–computer interaction leaving the programmer the task of hooking in that layer of the overall system purely concerned with the particular application semantics. These systems allow such a fast generation of prototypes that it is possible for the designer to design, implement and evaluate the interface in conjunction with users (Myers and Buxton, 1986). Another approach is given by Alexander (1986).

Clearly, for this sort of system to work, the highest levels of the user model must be defined in an abstract manner independent of the interface, and in turn the interactive interface and pure applications program must be treated as independent modules, otherwise each change of the interface would require corresponding changes in the applications layer. This relationship is summarized in Figure 14.2.

14.4.2 The Command Language Grammar

In his paper, Moran provides a systematic and structured approach to user interface design using the **command language grammar** (**CLG**). The major dimension of this approach is that the user interface is seen as a layered set of components ranging from the abstract task and user model, through syntactic and interactive communications, to the physical level of screen layout and input devices. The main components of a user interface in the CLG are now outlined.

CONCEPTUAL

This component consists of the **task level** and the **semantic level**.

The Task Level This is concerned with an analysis of user goals and needs, and a detailed breakdown of tasks the users are supposed to be able to perform. The results of such an analysis would normally include the basic task *entities* (conceptual objects) and relationships between them, the task goals, the *procedures* used to accomplish those tasks and the *methods* associating procedures with tasks. For example, the task objects in the file management example might be the pieces of paper (documents) and cardboard wallets (folders). A specific goal might be to file pieces of paper together that are related according to some external criterion. The procedure (or the means) for doing this might involve the tasks of *locating* all such documents, *creating* a new folder and *moving* all of the documents into the folder. Clearly, these tasks can themselves be broken down into subtasks; for example, creating a new folder involves many other tasks, including perhaps the final one of writing the name of the folder on its outside. The *method* is what links this procedure to the specific goal of filing related documents together. This may be summarized schematically as:

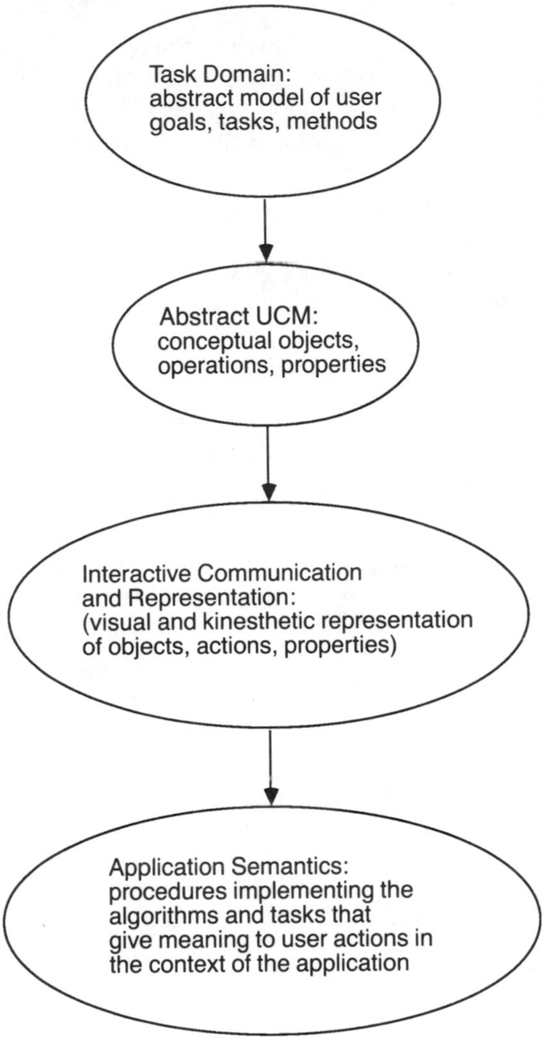

Figure 14.2
Levels of a user interface design.

Task entities: paper, wallets, ...

Task goal: filing related documents together

Task procedure FileTogether(type of information *I*, name of folder *N*) =
begin
  CreateNewFolder(*N*);
  for each (*document* with information of given type *I*) **do**
    move (*document* into new folder *N*)
  od
end

Task method: to achieve the goal of filing related documents together, use the procedure *FileTogether*.

In a real analysis, there might be dozens of such objects, goals, procedures and methods.

The Semantic Level The task level describes what the users already do and know. The semantic level describes how these are embodied in the interactive system in an abstract sense. The system *entities* are the system representations of the task entities – these are the conceptual objects of the system. The system and user *operations* are the operations defined over the entities, which can be performed by the system and user respectively. The *semantic procedures* are sequences of user and system operations. Again, *methods* are the links between these procedures and system tasks. Continuing the filing example:

System entities: These are the abstract objects called documents and folders, their properties and the relations between them.

System operations: The system can report information about its objects (information about the properties of documents and folders), in particular that information in a document is, in some sense, of a certain type; it can represent the fact that a particular document is or is not inside a particular folder; it is capable of responding to and representing commands such as creation of a new object, deletion of an object and so on.

User operations: Users can inspect information in objects and can move objects into or out of folders, delete and create objects, and so on.

Semantic procedures: An example of such a procedure might be as follows. The user creates a new folder; the system represents the fact that a new folder has been created; for every document represented by the system the user inspects the document for its type, and the system responds by reporting the type of document; if the document is of a certain type, then the user issues the command to move the document into the folder; the system responds by echoing the fact that the document has been moved into the folder. Schematically, this can be summarized as:

Semantic procedure FileTogether(type of information *I*, name of folder *N*) =
begin
  User: *CreateNewFolder*(*N*);
  System: show creation of new folder with name *N*;
          for each *document* represented by the system **do**
    user: *inspect* document type;
    system: *report* document type;
    if user: *observes* that document type has information of type *I* **then**

```
        begin
          user: move (document to folder N);
          system: represent the document moving into N
        end
            od
    end
```

Semantic method: The task of moving the documents of a related type into a new folder can be accomplished by the semantic procedure *FileTogether*.

Note that this remains highly abstract and says nothing at all about the interactive style or implementation. However, at this level, the system functionality is completely described in an abstract way.

COMMUNICATIONS

This component forms the second layer of the CLG and consists of a **syntactic level** and an **interaction level**.

The Syntactic Level The semantic procedure *FileTogether* provides a method for filing related documents into a common folder: this is how the corresponding filing task is coded at the highest level of the system. However, in a real system, there must be a command language with a syntax that can be described and learned, to actually allow users to communicate commands to the system and accomplish such a task. The semantic procedure *FileTogether* must be transcribed to a sequence of such commands. Typically, such a command language will have a few syntactic building blocks out of which a rich variety of grammatically correct and meaningful 'sentences' can be formed. (The use of the term 'command language' should not invoke the idea that this language is necessarily textual.)

The Interaction Level Ultimately, user commands are expressed as mouse moves, button clicks, key strokes, voice inputs or whatever combination of actual physical actions users must take, together with the responses of the system that cause changes on the physical screen or perhaps in the form of generated sounds. These actions and reactions describe the terminal nodes of the interactive system.

14.4.3 UNIX Commands for the Filing Example

Returning to the filing example, consider two alternative forms of communication, and the task of filing related information. In the UNIX system, the semantic procedure *FileTogether* might be accomplished as follows (comments are shown in italics, and assume that the name chosen by the user for the new folder is 'financial'):

create a new folder = make a new directory
% mkdir financial

In UNIX, the system does not automatically show that such a new folder has been created. The system response to the above command, if successful, is simply to output another prompt on the next line.

Now list the names of all files in the current directory.
% ls

The system would respond by displaying the names in alphabetical order. One of the names would, of course, be 'financial'.

Now the user must inspect these names, and assuming that the names have been chosen to convey the type of information stored in the corresponding file, the user must move each file required into the new directory. For example:

% mv banking financial
% ls financial
% mv insurance financial
% ls financial

Here, the user is moving one file at a time into the financial directory and then listing all the files in this new directory as a check that the move has taken place. Typically, experienced users would not make this check, or perhaps only after all the required moves had been accomplished. More advanced users would create another file representing a script of commands to be executed by the UNIX interpreter to carry out the complete task of file manipulation, especially if this task were repeated many times on different occasions.

The syntactic level here is the command structure of the UNIX system. The interaction consists entirely of key strokes to form the commands, with the system responding by returning a prompt, displaying certain specifically requested information, carrying out some (invisible) action, or reporting an error – for example, if the directory financial already exists.

14.4.4 A Graphical Interface for the Filing Example

Another completely different syntax and interaction style can form the communications component for the same set of tasks. Consider here, briefly, the interface provided by the Apple Macintosh, perhaps the most popular and successful realization of the approach to user interfaces originally pioneered by Xerox and exemplified in the Star user interface. The style of interface is illustrated in Figure 14.3(a). Figure 14.3(b) shows an example of the SunView display.

In the Macintosh interface, the abstract entities documents and folders are represented pictorially as icons on the screen, which look, respectively, like pieces of paper with text on or as folders (document wallets). These are displayed in a window on to part of the world created by the user (and the system designer). Windows reside on a 'desk top' which is represented as a grey (halftone) colour, contrasted with the white windows.

User commands are typically by direct manipulation of objects displayed on the screen. For example, to move a document into a folder the user first 'picks up' the document by moving the mouse so that its cursor is over the folder's icon. When the user presses the mouse button, the icon is highlighted, indicating that the folder is now attached to the cursor. The user can then move the icon to any arbitrary place on the screen; for example, if it is moved over the icon representing the folder and then the mouse button released, the document (really its iconic representation!) disappears into the folder.

A folder can be opened, displaying its contents, by moving the mouse cursor to its icon and then double clicking the mouse. The icon then unfolds into a window, displaying iconic representations of all of the objects (documents or folders) inside it.

In this system the higher, abstract levels of the user interface are represented as animations of pictures of system objects and user actions. At the abstract level the user is performing very similar tasks to users of the UNIX-like system, but typically the two systems are experienced in a substantially different manner (this statement is based on personal experience and anecdotal evidence). However, it cannot be claimed that one system is *better* than another, since the real question is 'better under what circumstances?'. If the prime consideration is, say, one of the speed at which users can learn to do useful things, then undoubtedly the Macintosh style is superior. (Some experimental evidence relevant to this discussion can be found in Rogers, 1986.)

14.4.5 A Top-Down Methodology

The command language grammar – the expressive power of which has only been hinted at in this section – provides a useful design methodology, a framework for thinking about the issues in user interface design. It forces the designer to adopt a **top-down** approach which starts from an analysis of the goals and activities of users. There is then a direct mapping between the objects and actions elucidated at this level to the system level – the

(a)

(b)

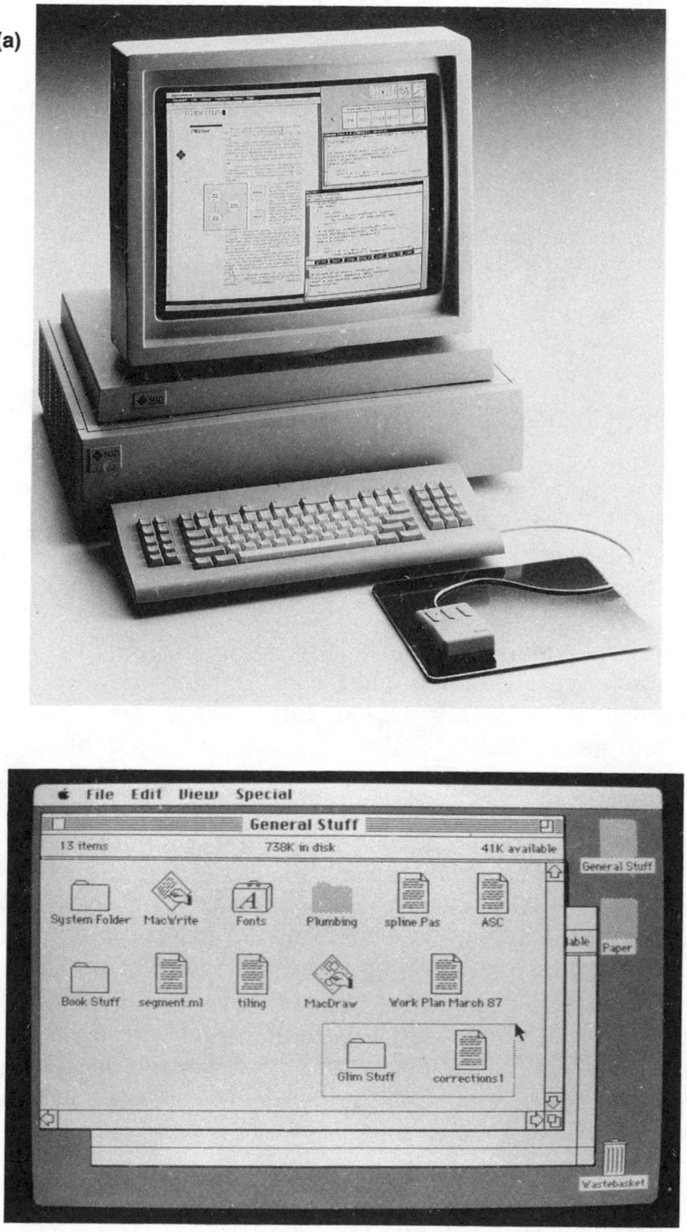

Figure 14.3

conceptual objects and operations in the system. This must then be mapped to the communications level: the syntax of the users' command language, and the form of interactive dialogue between users and the system. Finally, these are mapped to the physical level of screen layout and representations, and basic user actions denoting command sequences.

This methodology does not tell the designer what the realized user interface should actually look like, but it does provide steps on the road to getting there. Moreover, since it separates different logical components of the overall user interface, it also provides an organizing paradigm, and one that can be used as the basis for evaluation of interfaces in the sense of testing hypotheses concerning various aspects of the system. For example, given the definition of the conceptual level of the system (which itself must be validated), hypotheses about different styles of communication (interaction) can be formed and tested. Issues concerning interactive style are considered in the next section.

14.5 Styles of Interaction

The communications layer is clearly a vital aspect of the user interface: it includes what the user sees, the actions he or she takes and the responses of the system. No matter how well accomplished is the task analysis and conceptual model, if this abstract level is mapped to an unworkable interaction style, then the analysis would have been in vain. The user interface must be understood as a totality: of the model in the mind of the user, the system representations and the real interaction.

Although these layers are logically independent, the mappings between them are crucial in determining the usability of the system. An extreme but simple example is as follows. If the task of moving a document into a folder required the user to remember and issue 20 different commands (whether these are textual or graphical is not relevant), then such an interface would fail. (It would probably fail if the user had to execute even three commands.)

It is at this level that computer graphics plays a major role in user interface design, for interfaces that work are typically graphically based. This section considers a number of principles that have been suggested and used in the Star and other interfaces, most notably the Macintosh, which characterize what might be called a 'modern' graphical user interface. *Principles* is too strong a term to use here as in fact they are hypotheses, with a large degree of popular and anecdotal support.

14.5.1 Pointing Instead of Typing

In the case of a command-driven textual interface, users have to remember commands and the entities on which commands are to be executed. In such a system, deleting a file, for example, requires the user to first see if that file can be referenced in the current context – in UNIX to see if the file is in the current directory. This requires a command to list the files in the current directory. Second, the user must give the command to delete the file. After having given this command, there is no way of retrieving the file, except through often very tedious means, requiring the help of system programmers. This simple operation requires a lot of memorizing and basic typing skills.

In a graphical interface, objects can be selected by pointing, by using the mouse to point at a graphical representation of the object on the screen. On the Apple Macintosh, for example, deletion of a document requires the user to move the corresponding icon to an icon representing a waste bin. No typing is required, nor any memorization of command names. The pointing and moving operation mimicks what a user does with real pieces of paper and waste bins. Moreover, the interface to the waste bin is similar to any other folder on the desk top. A double click will open it as a window, and its contents can be seen. Therefore, if the user has a change of heart about deleting the item, it can be moved back out of the waste bin on to the desk top, or into another folder. In such a system, the user is continually interacting with direct representations of the underlying system objects defined at the higher levels of the user model. Smith *et al.* (1982, p. 260) noted that:

> "*A subtle thing happens when everything is visible:* the display becomes a reality. *The user model becomes identical with what is on the screen. Objects can be understood purely in terms of their visible characteristics. Actions can be understood in terms of their effects on the screen. This lets users* conduct experiments *to test, verify, and expand their understanding – the essence of experimental science.*"

The last point here is particularly telling: as soon as a user learns, for example, that windows into folders can be opened by double clicking on their icons, this knowledge transfers to other similar operations. Now the idea of 'opening' a folder is a familiar one from everyday life. What should happen if the icon representing a plain document (not a folder) is double clicked? That document 'opens' to reveal its contents, typically by calling for the execution of the text editor or drawing program used in the creation of the document. Similarly, if a document representing an application (a drawing program) is double clicked, then that program is 'opened' and starts to execute. There becomes a sense in which pointing and double clicking are applied to many different instances of the same underlying operation: point at an object and get it to do its stuff – whatever that may be for the particular object.

14.5.2 WYSIWYG

WYSIWYG stands for *what you see is what you get*. This means that what the user sees on the screen at any moment is a direct and true representation of the state of the application. For example, a page layout editor should show on the screen at any time an exact likeness, within the constraints imposed by resolution, of what would be printed. The principle is violated if, say, the system cannot show a good likeness of the fonts and images in use, or their true spatial layout and relationships. A more mundane example, the authors are familiar with, is an operating system, which after the command to delete a file had been given, would still display the name of that file in response to a list files command. The reason for this was subtle: the file deleted had been made 'temporary', and would disappear altogether at some further convenient (for the computer) moment. The confusion this could cause to novice, as well as experienced, users is obvious. Finally, in Chapter 8 an example was given relating to GKS segments. In the interactive drawing program based on GKS, when a segment was deleted or transformed this would not be reflected by a change on the screen – the modified segment would appear unchanged, until the next execution of *UpdateWorkstation*.

If what is on the screen does not reflect the true state of the application, then users are unable to make rational decisions about their next course of action, and can never be sure whether previous commands have been correctly interpreted. It is akin to driving a car and not being sure that what you see through the windscreen accurately reflects the state of the road ahead.

14.5.3 Command Economy

The Star-like interfaces provide a small number of operations that are applicable to a large number of objects. One example of this in the Macintosh interface is the double click, which can be applied to a large number of different types of objects, and which can be interpreted as a message to the object on the lines of 'you are selected, now do whatever you are supposed to do in response'. Other such fundamental commands are, for example, move, copy, delete, again, undo, cut and paste. A folder can be moved (to somewhere else on the desk top), a document can be moved within or to another folder, a piece of text can be moved within and across documents, a character can be moved within a piece of text and so on.

This idea is similar to the object-oriented programming paradigm, as exemplified in Smalltalk-80, the basic graphics model of which was discussed in Chapter 11. In an object-oriented system, objects respond to a set of messages. When an object receives a message, it executes a corresponding method. For example, when a folder receives the message represented by 'double click', it executes a method that results in the screen representation of the folder opening up into a window. In Smalltalk-80, objects are organized into classes (themselves objects), and every object belonging to a certain class can respond to all of the messages defined for that class. Classes are organized hierarchically and any object that belongs to a subclass of a given class (called its super-class) can respond to all of the messages in its super-class, and an additional set of messages that are defined only for the subclass (and all of its subclasses). Hence, the object–message structure can be used to arrange the command system so that there are a few general messages that apply to all objects in the system (for example, 'delete yourself' might be such a message), but where there are specialized messages that apply only to objects at and below certain depths in the class hierarchy. For example, it may be the case that in a certain system, windows themselves and all objects within windows can be translated, but only geometrically defined graphical objects can be arbitrarily rotated.

Designers generally have two choices regarding the means by which users can apply operations to objects: **pre-fix** or **tool based** as against **post-fix** or **object based**. In tool-based systems, the user first selects the operation and then the argument to which it is to be applied. The object-based interactive style requires the user to first select the object and then the operation to be applied to it. For example, suppose in a drawing program the user is provided with polyline, fill area and markers as the basic drawing tools. In a tool-based system, the user would first choose the operation required, say by selecting from a menu with the choices 'Lines', 'Fill Area', 'Markers'. Having made the selection, a stroke input tool might be used to select the points on the screen. Alternatively, in an object-based approach, the user would first use the stroke tool to select the points on the screen and then go to the menu to select the operation to be performed on the selected points. As a further example, consider a set of graphics objects represented on a display, for which there are several possible operations: translate, scale, rotate, delete, copy and so on. In the tool-based approach, the user would first select the operation and then the object to which the operation is to be applied. The object-based approach, on the other hand, would require the user to select the object and then the operation to be performed on that object.

There are several arguments in favour of the object-based approach:

(1) It obviates the need for a RETURN key or BREAK operation. In the drawing tools example, the user can continue selecting points and no special action is required to indicate the final point, for when the final point has been chosen the next action is to choose the operation. With the tool-based paradigm, the user must have some special way of indicating the final point (for example, with a reserved mouse button or a BREAK key). In the second example, the various operations

should be capable of operating on several objects simultaneously. The object-based approach allows several objects to be selected (for example, by enclosing them all in a rubber band rectangle or lassoo) and then the operation selected. The tool-based approach requires first the operation and then the set of objects, again necessitating a BREAK action to signify completion of the list.

(2) Once an object has been selected, users can change their mind about what to do with it: it might have been selected with the idea of deletion, but in fact the user might decide to file or copy it. Generally, the choice of an action is more crucial than choice of object. Changing one's mind about the object selected is normally an easy operation, accomplished by simply pointing at another object and selecting it instead. However, in the tool-based approach, once an operation is selected, it is often a more cumbersome task to change one's mind.

(3) The object-based approach reduces the need for error messages. In the drawing example in the context of a system built on top of GKS, the user might run into trouble with the tool-based paradigm, if the fill area operation had been chosen, but then only one or two points selected. The object-based approach provides sufficient information to allow the menu to indicate which operations are valid for the object selected: if the object consisted of only two points, then the fill area option in the command menu could be made unselectable (with, of course, an appropriate appearance to indicate this temporary unavailability). If the user genuinely wanted to generate a filled area, then rather than being forced to select the inappropriate line or marker option, he or she could add more points.

(4) The previous argument relates to an issue first discussed in Chapter 7 in the context of the interactive drawing program – namely, modeless interaction, or without hidden states. The object-based paradigm is more supportive of this desirable feature of interactive systems. Once the *Polyline* operation has been selected in the tool-based approach, the system is then in a mode where the next selections will try to interpret as points in the making of a polyline. To get out of the mode, the user has to take action to put the system into another mode. A more drastic example discussed in Chapter 7 concerns the idea of allowing the user to create picture segments. A straightforward application of the tool-based method would be messy: requiring a *CreateSegment* and *CloseSegment* command, with the system sometimes being in the 'segment open' mode, with all of the difficulties this can cause. In the object-based approach, there is a simple solution: the user can simultaneously select a number of on screen objects and choose a 'group into segment' operation. This generalizes simply into hierarchically organized segments, which would be a nightmare to do in tool-based systems.

In spite of these arguments, it must not be concluded that in all circumstances for all applications that the object-based approach is preferable to the tool-based one. However, the evidence and psychological arguments suggest that it generally provides interfaces that work better for their users (Smith, 1982, p. 276) than the tool-based approach.

14.6 Some Specific Interaction Methods and Techniques

Section 14.5 discussed some general issues relating to the communication level of a user interface. This section considers some basic interactive techniques.

14.6.1 Windowing

Windows are views on to the state of an application or an object, and allow interaction with the objects and processes whose representations are displayed within them. Users of a system generally require access to several related objects or applications when performing a task. For example, when designing a page layout the designer may wish to see examples of similar layouts previously constructed, a palette of fonts that might be employed, use of an interactive drawing program, a word processor and maybe a library of photo images. It would be tedious, to say the least, if the designer could only access these objects and applications sequentially. Ideally, all of these objects and applications should be simultaneously available and selectable on the 'desk top'.

14.6.2 Cut and Paste

If several windows are simultaneously available this is (obviously) because the user needs access to all of them to complete the current task. However, the different windows represent a group of related interactions, each of which plays a role in fulfilling the task. It must therefore be possible to extract things from one window and put them into another. This may be accomplished by the **cut and paste** paradigm, which is a computer emulation of what has to be done if a designer is working with real pieces of paper. For example, having found an image from the photo library, the designer has to paste it on to the page at the appropriate position (and to the right scale).

The cut and paste operation usually requires that the user selects an object, and then chooses a cut or copy operation. The cut operation actually removes the representation of the object from its window, but places a copy of it into a buffer area. Ideally, the buffer area should be visible and viewable. On the Apple Macintosh, for example, the buffer area is represented as a **clipboard** (which is extant across applications), which is itself another window. The copy operation copies the object into this buffer area, and nothing else. The paste operation copies the items in the current buffer into a selected position in another (or maybe the same) window. The total effect is like the real physical cut and paste with which typists are familiar.

14.6.3 Undo

Cutting, and generally deleting, are rather drastic operations. Graphical operations that are sometimes less drastic are shifting, scaling and rotation: they can be drastic if the prior state of affairs is either irretrievable or only by very painstaking work. The undo facility is crucial in allowing a user to feel safe in carrying out operations that would otherwise permanently change the state of the application. This command simply means reverse the previous operation: if an item has been deleted, then restore it as if the deletion had never taken place; if something has been rotated, then rotate it back again. Undo is somewhat fraught with philosophical problems (can an 'undo' be undone?). Also, undo has to be built into the original design of the program: it is not something that can be tacked on at an arbitrary stage in implementation.

14.6.4 Browsing

Sometimes finding things on real desk tops as well as computer ones is easier said than done. 'Having found the image from the photo library' may itself be a short phrase representing a major task. **Browsing** is a technique exemplified in the Smalltalk-80 interface. This system provides a vast amount of information: class names, class and object methods, protocols, documentation. The Smalltalk-80 programmer generally has to search for particular classes and descriptions of the messages understood by objects belonging to those classes. Smalltalk-80 provides a system browser, which displays a hierarchical categorization of the overall system, as shown in Figure 14.4. The system browser is a rectangular window partitioned into five regions. The four regions at the top are reserved for fixed position menus, while the larger region at the bottom is a text editor region. (See, for example, Kaehler and Patterson, 1986, pp. 14–25). The left-hand menu contains a categorization of the highest level classes. The next menu shows

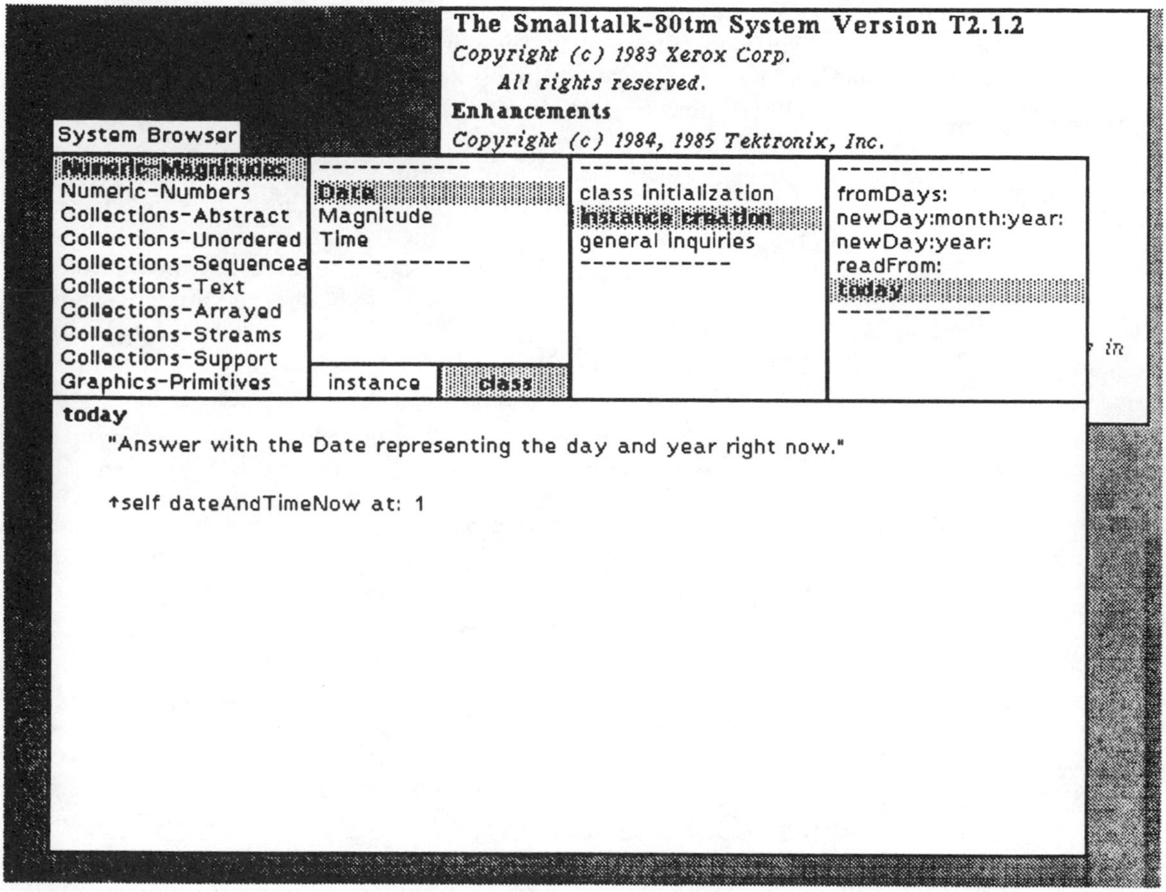

Figure 14.4
Smalltalk-80 system browser.

class names. The third menu provides classification of sets of messages applicable to the class or objects of that class, and the final menu the message selectors. For example, the user might first select the 'Numeric–Magnitudes' category, which is done in the usual way by pointing. The classes under that category then display in the next column. The user may choose, for example, the subclass 'Date' from the second menu. The third menu would then display a list including, for example, 'instance creation' (messages that create an object of class date) and 'arithmetic' (messages that allow arithmetic on dates). Suppose that the 'instance creation' category is now chosen, then the fourth menu would then contain a list of messages that can be used to create an instance of 'Date'; for example, 'today', a message that when sent to the class 'Date' returns a date that represents the current day's date. Finally, if 'today' in the fourth column is selected, then the text of the method implementing 'today' would display in the edit region below.

It should be noted that the browser is easy to use, easier than perhaps has been explained. Its simplicity lies in the fact that a rather vast system is relatively painlessly made available to users.

Other interesting features of the browser are:

(1) Typically, there are more items in any menu than can be displayed within the space provided by the menu. Hence, it is possible to use the **scroll bar**, which appears on the left-hand side of each menu whenever the cursor passes into a sensitive region on the left-hand border of the menu. The scroll bar can be dragged up or down by use of the mouse, and as the bar moves so the text in the menu scrolls accordingly. Of course, the scroll bar technique has a wider use than just looking at text in menus.

(2) Each fixed-position menu as well as the edit area have a pop-up menu providing access to operations appropriate to that point in the browser. Obviously, the menu obtainable from the edit area contains commands useful for editing, such as cut, paste and copy. The menu containing the class names gives access to commands that are useful for exploring the meaning and structure of the class hierarchy, and for manipulation such as allowing removal of a class, for example. There is also a menu applicable to the browser window as a whole, which is obtained by selecting on the title bar: this menu allows resizing of the browser window, collapsing it into an icon, repositioning and so on.

14.6.5 Command Hierarchy

A browser is a convenient way of organizing hierarchical information and the same idea might be used to organize a hierarchical series of commands, such as discussed in relation to the drawing program of Chapters 6 and 7. Alternatively, a tree of pop-up menus can be used, as was discussed and dismissed in Section 6.7. In that chapter, the idea of a fixed set of pull-down menus was explored and illustrated.

Stacked menus provide an attractive alternative. In this scheme, a related class of hierarchically organized operations are essentially made simultaneously available. In the drawing program example, suppose the drawing operations are 'Line', 'Fill' and 'Text'. In Chapter 6, these were separated into different menus. A stacked menu example might be as follows (see Figure 14.4). The highest level commands are displayed as usual and obtained with a pop-up interaction. Suppose the user has selected some text and wishes to change its style. The menu item 'Text' would be selected by holding down the (required) mouse button while the cursor is over the text item in the menu. Now, as the cursor is moved horizontally across to the right, a second level menu appears containing items, say, 'Size'

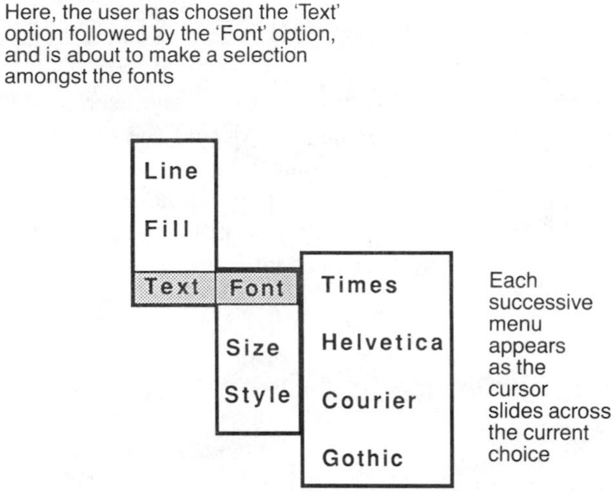
Here, the user has chosen the 'Text' option followed by the 'Font' option, and is about to make a selection amongst the fonts
Line
Fill
Text
Font
Size
Style
Times
Helvetica
Courier
Gothic
Each successive menu appears as the cursor slides across the current choice

Figure 14.5
Example of a stacked menu.

and 'Font'. While the user is holding down the mouse button, if the cursor is made to slide over, say, the font item, then a further level of menu appears showing the set of fonts available, and selection can now be made at this level.

Again, this idea is much easier to use than to explain. It is the style of menu made available as part of the interface released with an early version of the Sun NeWS system (see Plate 28). Personal experience suggests that it is a well thought out method for presenting hierarchy without clumsiness or confusion. The earlier SunView window manager employed essentially the same strategy.

REMARKS

A word of caution: although the human–computer interface has greatly improved in recent years, there is still a long way to go. In an interview in 1984, Andreas Van Dam (Van Dam, 1984) made the following comments when discussing these issues:

> *"Right now, I believe the Macintosh has the best user interface of any personal computer in its price range. When viewed from the perspective of what the interface will probably be in a few decades from now, however, the Macintosh is like a three-month old baby. . . . The ideal situation, of course, would be to interact with the computer as if it were a helpful human being, perhaps chatting in a natural language. The computer interface may eventually metamorphose into a total sensory environment. For example, could the walls of your room be the display medium, complete with sound and other sensory channels?"*

Perhaps, as long as the system doesn't crash.

14.7 The User–Display Interface

Interest is now focused on the interface between the user's eye/brain system and the image on the display. Before considering the images that are to be displayed, it is necessary to know something about the human eye/brain system that detects the images on the display. In addition, there are certain aspects of the display, other than the design of the image, that are important for the creation of a good user–display interface.

14.7.1 The Structure and Operation of the Human Eye

The process of vision in humans is carried out by the eyes and specialized areas of the brain. The basic structure of the human eye is shown in Figure 14.6. A normal person has two eyes each connected to the brain by the **optic nerve**.

The human eye is essentially a globe that sits in the eye socket or **orbit** of the skull. The outer coat of the eyeball consists of the tough **sclera**, protecting the eye itself and helping to maintain the globe shape. The **cornea** is contiguous with the sclera and forms the transparent and protective window of the eye. It is almost circular in shape, but its degree of curvature varies between individuals and with age, flattening in later life. An aperture at the rear of the sclera serves as an access to the eyeball for the optic nerve as well as providing a channel for arterial blood carrying oxygen and other nutrients to the eye. Attached to the sclera are the set of **rectus** and **oblique** (not shown) muscles which allow the eyeball to move in the orbit to achieve rotary movement in all axes.

Inside the sclera, the **iris**, **ciliary body** and **choriod** form the next layer. The iris consists of a set of circular and radial muscle fibres forming a diaphragm with a circular opening known as the **pupil**. Contraction of the circular muscles makes the pupil smaller, reducing the amount of light admitted into the eye, whereas contraction of the radial muscles makes the pupil larger (dilate), increasing the amount of light admitted. (The pupil also dilates under conditions of fear or pain.) The choriod, which covers about 80% of the inside of the sclera, is a coating carrying the capillary ducting for blood supply and return. Between the iris and the cornea there is the **aqueous humour**, a very weak saline solution.

Also attached to the ciliary body is the **lens**, which focuses the light rays entering through the pupil, inverted on to the **retina**. For this to happen under all geometric conditions, the lens must be able to alter its curvature. This is done by the **ciliary muscle**. When this muscle contracts, the **suspensory ligament** is slackened and the tension on the lens capsule is

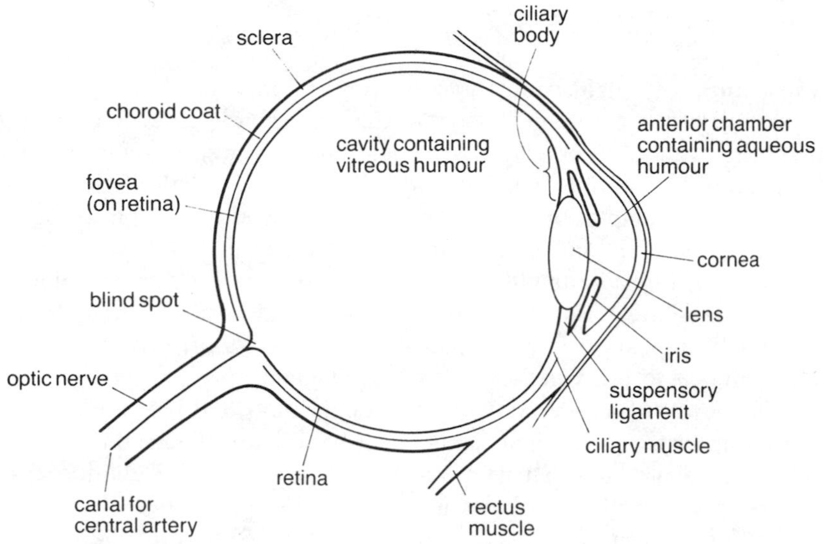

Figure 14.6 Section through the eyeball.

relaxed. This, combined with pressure from the **vitreous humour**, causes the anterior surface of the lens to bulge forward and the lens itself to become more convex. A decrease in focal length of the lens brings close objects into focus. This focusing action is an automatic or reflex action and is known as **accommodation**. Inverse actions occur to focus distant, greater than six metres (20 feet), objects.

The retina is the inner or nervous coat of the eye and is very complex, being made up of ten layers. The first, outermost layer is a pigmentation layer, while the second contains the **cones** and **rods** that are the photochemical receptors of vision. The remaining layers, through which the light rays must pass on their way to the rods and cones, consist of junctions or integrating neurones **(nerve cells)** that combine the nerve impulses from the six million cones and 120 million rods in the retina into a more manageable number for transmission to the brain.

The cones and rods are not distributed evenly over the retina. The cones are concentrated mostly into a small area, approximately 0.25 mm (0.01″) in diameter, known as the **yellow spot** or **fovea**. They are stimulated by bright light and colour, and when an object is to be viewed in detail the eyes are directed so that the image falls on the fovea of each eye. The rods, and a remaining small percentage of the cones, are spread over the peripheral areas of the retina and are sensitive mainly to the intensity of the light, sensing brightness and movement. The retina also has a **blind spot** where the nerve fibres from all parts of the eye converge into the optic nerve bundle. It has no cones or rods and is insensitive to light.

14.7.2 Brightness and Luminance

The **brightness** of a light source is not a physical measure but a measure of the response of the eye/brain system to the light energy it receives from the source. The eye is able to adapt to the amount of light entering it by varying the diameter of the pupil, thus allowing a large range of lighting levels to be detected. This adaptation also appears to include the photochemical response of the rods and cones, and possibly trigger levels in the brain. Unfortunately, this adaptability reduces the eye/brain system's capability to distinguish absolute levels of illumination. For example, the light from an electric torch appears bright at night or in a dark room, but in daylight it may be difficult to see whether it is even switched on.

The **power** of a light source, be it a light bulb, CRT or flame, can be measured in terms of the light energy that it radiates. The radiation of the torch could be measured in watts, a unit of power. The radiation that is *perceived* by the eye/brain system is known as the **luminance** of the source and takes into account the reaction of the eye/brain system to the radiation. Psycho-physiological measurements of luminance are made by comparison with standard light sources and the values are given in **lumens**, their detailed definition not being necessary here.

14.7.3 Colour

For many people, colour is what computer graphics is all about but this is by no means true. Technically, the use of colour in a picture is a minor part of its definition, but the effect and the information that it can convey is a major element of the image.

Colour has a tremendous effect on all walks of life. All nationalities and cultures use colour in their daily lives whether to please or entertain, or to inform or command. In addition, the human race cannot claim a monopoly of the use of colour as the animal and plant worlds probably use colour to a greater extent than people do.

Colour is a very powerful medium for information exchange. It can affect our mental state and, indirectly, our physical state. It can generate feelings of warmth and well being or feelings of cold and insecurity. Artists are, of course, the great technicians of colour using it to create mood and atmosphere as well as merely reproducing and interpreting what they see around them. Colour is used by interior designers to create a mood in a room and similarly by architects to create the atmosphere of a building as a whole. The designers of advertisements use colour to create the right atmosphere for selling their product. Individuals use colour in their dress and appearance and in their homes to please, impress, comfort or sometimes, unintentionally, to amuse others.

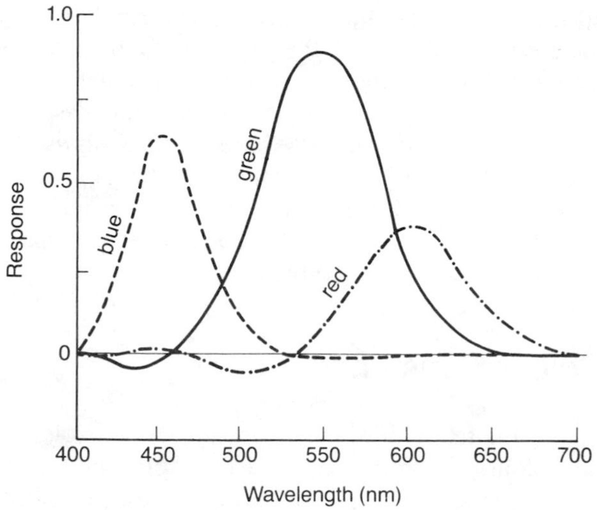

Figure 14.7
Response of the eye to a spectrum of light of equal energies in every narrow waveband.

Colour is a rather strange thing. It cannot be *touched*, *smelt* or *made*. An individual can dip a brush into a pot of paint and apply it to a wall or door, thereby *transferring* the colour from the paint pot to the wall. Paints of various colours can be mixed together to create a paint of a *different* colour. However, all of these tasks are with the paint and not with the colour itself. The colour is a *property* of the paint in the same way as its consistency or temperature.

14.7.4 Colour Vision

The human eye responds to electromagnetic radiation within what is known as the **visible spectrum**; namely, in the range 400 to 700 nanometres (nm, 10^{-9} metres). The cones and rods in the eye only respond to this range of wavelengths – radiation outside of this range cannot be detected by the human eye. Recent research has indicated that there are three types, or variants, of cone, each responding to a range of wavelengths within the visible spectrum. One type responds to the longer wavelengths or to **red light**, one type to the middle wavelengths or **green light** and one type to the shorter wavelengths or to **blue light**. Red, green and blue are merely labels that are given to light within these different bands. The responses of the three types of cones are not mutually exclusive, but overlap each other as shown in Figure 14.7 (Weale, 1978, p. 66). Therefore, light of a particular wavelength or small waveband falling on the retina may excite more than one type of cone, but by a different amount.

Light of a particular colour is rarely of one single wavelength, but a *mixture* of wavebands and excites the cone types that respond to those bands. The degree to which the cones are excited depends on the total amount of the radiation within the band. The eye/brain system registers the amount by which each cone type is excited and *computes* the resultant colour. For example, if the light consists of wavelengths from the red and green bands, then the eye/brain system *perceives* it as yellow light. If the light consists of wavelengths from all three bands in equal amounts, then the eye/brain system perceives white light.

14.7.5 Colour Constancy

The foregoing explanation does not completely explain the human perception of colour. One particular aspect of colour vision puzzled scientists for many years. This is the response of the eye/brain system under different lighting conditions. In the late eighteenth century, the Frenchman Gaspard Monge demonstrated a rather curious phenomenon to the Royal Academy in Paris. The experiment consisted of viewing a sheet of red paper illuminated by daylight through a piece of red glass. To their surprise the piece of paper appeared white. The red glass allows only light in the red frequency band to pass through and therefore the red paper should have appeared red to the viewers. However, when the piece of red glass was placed at the end of a tube and the red paper viewed through the tube so that all external light was obscured, the paper indeed appeared red. Somehow, the eye/brain system was *computing* a different colour, namely white, instead of red when the red light was part of a larger scene.

When inside a room under artificial light, objects appear the same colour as if they were outside under sunlight. However, colour photographs taken under the same two differing conditions appear quite different unless a correcting filter or special film is used. Under such lighting conditions, the eye/brain system is displaying **colour constancy**; that is, it automatically compensates for the change in ambient lighting conditions.

Edwin Land, the inventor of the Polaroid Instant Camera, has recently suggested a theory to explain this behaviour by the eye/brain system. It suggests that each cone in the retina passes a signal to the brain that, instead of being directly proportional to the light that is triggering it, is *weighted* against the sum of the signals from neighbouring cones of the same type; this process happening for all three types of cone. Therefore, the eye/brain system *sees* a colour at a point that is a function of the colours and the level of illumination in the whole image. This theory does appear to explain colour constancy and it also helps to explain why a large number of people can be colour blind without apparently knowing it – any deficiency in the cones of one type being partially made up by the input from the other types of cones.

Table 14.1 Additive primary colours.

	Primary Colours (%)		
	Red	Green	Blue
Red	100	0	0
Green	0	100	0
Blue	0	0	100
Yellow	100	100	0
Magenta	100	0	100
Cyan	0	100	100
White	100	100	100

The consequences of this for colour image generation are quite startling. In particular, the perceived colour of any image element will be a function of all of the other image elements and their colour on the display, as well as elements from the area surrounding the display.

14.7.6 Colour Specification and Colour Models

Red, green and blue are known as the **additive primary** or, simply, the **primary colours** because of the property that when they are *added* together in varying quantities any colour can be produced. The simple addition of equal amounts of red, green and blue light is illustrated in Plate 25(a) and the colours that are produced are given in Table 14.1. Note that the colours are *not* the same as the colours of the rainbow, nor those obtained when white light is split by a prism. (This table is essentially the same as that shown in Section 6.1.)

This description of colour, models the psycho-physical human response in terms of the additive primary colours and is known as the **RGB model** of colour (see Section 6.1). This three-dimensional model presents a very convenient system and it is analogous to many of the manifestations of colour mixing in the physical world. The effect of colour mixing can be observed by mixing red, green and blue light from a projector and seeing the colours that can be achieved. For example, if maximum intensity cyan is required, then 100% green and 100% blue is specified. If a dull cyan is required, then reduced intensity green and blue would be specified. Note, however, that if a small amount of red is added to the dull cyan, then the effect is of adding a low intensity of white, or grey, to the cyan and **desaturating** it. Figure 14.8 illustrates a 3D diagram of the RGB colour model.

This model closely approximates models for the operation of the human eye and, most importantly, models the methods used in colour

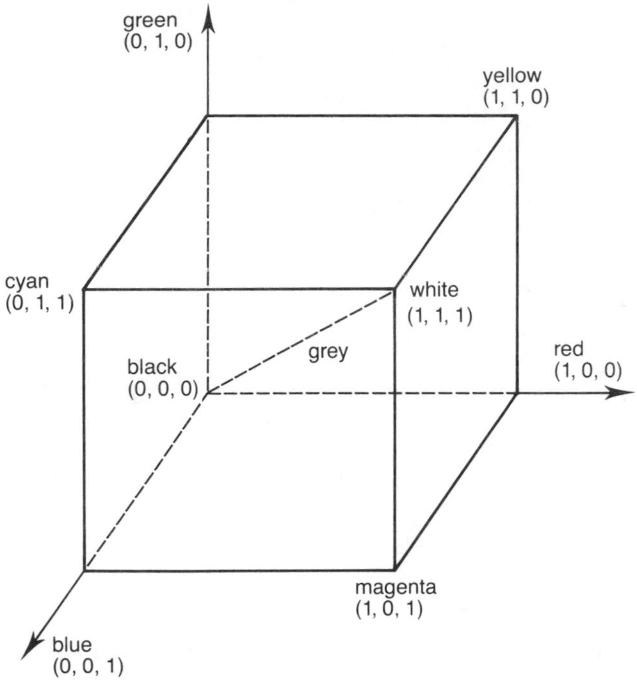

Figure 14.8
The RGB colour model.

emitter display devices to generate their colour effects. The RGB colour model is used by GKS for its colour definition where colours are defined using their red, green and blue constituents in the function *SetColour Representation* (see Section 6.2).

A second colour model uses the **complementary colours** of the RGB model. Any *two* colours that, when added together, produce white light are complementary colours. For example, yellow and blue are complementary colours. Humans perceive the colour of an object by the light that is reflected from its surface, and in everyday life most objects are illuminated by white light or sunlight. An object that is of the colour yellow in daylight, is absorbing its complementary colour blue. This gives rise to what are known as the **subtractive primaries** of cyan, magenta and yellow, and the **CMY model** of colour. These are illustrated in Plate 25(b).

Each CMY colour is essentially a filter for its complementary primary and this relation can be represented by:

$$\begin{pmatrix} C \\ M \\ Y \end{pmatrix} = \begin{pmatrix} 1 \\ 1 \\ 1 \end{pmatrix} - \begin{pmatrix} R \\ G \\ B \end{pmatrix} \qquad \textbf{(14.1)}$$

The analytical inverse of this represents the conversion from RGB to CMY, while the unit column vector represents white and black in the RGB and CMY representations, respectively.

The CMY model is used on all colour hardcopy devices where the required colours are achieved by mixing the three CMY primaries. Computation of the colours from the RGB model is usually necessary as the CMY model is rarely used by graphics library systems. This computation will normally be carried out in the device driver for the particular device using a linear relation of the form of Equation (14.1). It should be noted, however, that this linear relation is only a theoretical relation as it is rare, if not impossible, to achieve an exact match between the RGB and CMY primaries of any two display devices. It is normal, therefore, to modify this relationship in a real system to achieve an acceptable match.

A further hardware-oriented colour model is that used for the transmission of domestic colour TV signals. Any model used for this purpose must be efficient in addition to compatible with black and white TV receivers. The system was developed in the USA by the National Television System Committee (**NTSC**) and was employed in the world's first colour TV service in 1953. In Europe, its variants are the **PAL** (Phase Alteration Line) system, developed in the UK and Germany and used throughout most of Europe, and the **SECAM** (Sequential Couleur a Memoire) system, developed in France and used in France and the USSR, amongst others. The basic requirement is to deliver the RGB data to the TV receiver, although it is not transmitted in this form. Instead, a signal is constructed that consists of a luminance subsignal of the form:

$$Y = 0.30R + 0.59G + 0.11B \tag{14.2}$$

and two colour-difference signals of the form:

$$(B - Y) \quad \text{and} \quad (R - Y) \tag{14.3}$$

where R, G and B are the three colour signals. The luminance Y signal gives all the information required to produce a tonally balanced monochrome picture for black and white TV receivers. When combined with the two colour-difference signals it allows the full RGB information to be reconstructed. In practice, the NTSC system uses a more complex encoding where the red and blue difference signals are combined to form what are known as the I and Q (and thus the **YIQ** model) signals, to increase the amount of colour information transmitted. Readers are referred to Pritchard (1977) for more information on this system.

The RGB, CMY and YIQ models are all hardware related, but none of them really describe how colour is actually perceived. People use descriptions such as 'dark brown' and 'bluey green', but these of course do not represent any reliable model. A model that better approximates to the psycho-physiological characteristics of colour is the **HIS** model, which

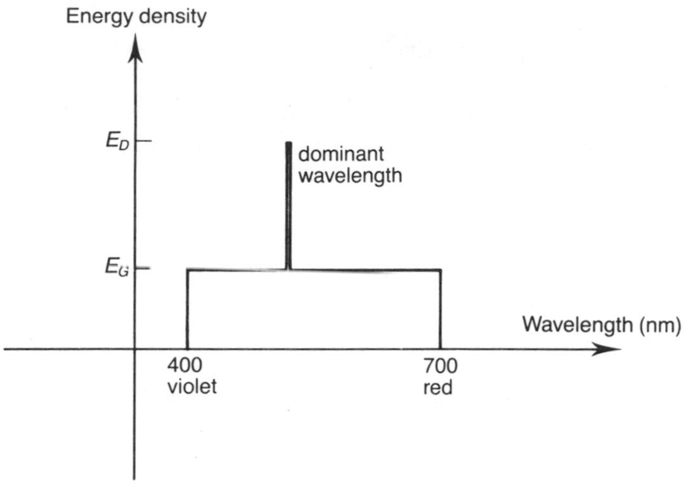

Figure 14.9
The DLP colour model.

defines a colour in terms of its **hue**, **intensity** and **saturation**:

- Hue is literally the *colour* of the colour, such as red or blue, and is analogous to its wavelength. It should be noted that hue is a psychological variable while wavelength is a physical one. The perception and recognition of any particular hue may vary between individuals.
- Intensity is the *brightness* of the colour.
- Saturation is the *purity* of the colour or the inverse of the amount by which the colour is *polluted* by its complementary colour. It is therefore the inverse of the amount of grey in the colour. A colour that contains no grey is said to be **fully saturated**, while one that has **zero saturation** will be black, grey or white.

A person perceives the light from a source or reflective object as having a colour, which can be defined or labelled, a relative brightness and a *quality*, where terms such as pastel or pale can be used to describe it. The HIS colour model is used in some graphics systems, in particular the CORE system (ACM, 1978), where it is used in addition to the usual RGB model. Similarly, PostScript allows a choice between the RGB and HIS models, where HIS is alternatively called **Hue, Saturation and Brightness (HSB)**.

A psycho-physical version of this model is the **DLP model** which uses **dominant wavelength**, **luminance** and **purity**. Dominant wavelength corresponds to the hue of the colour, the luminance to the amount of light and the purity to the saturation. This model is illustrated in Figure 14.9 (Foley and Van Dam, 1982). The dominant wavelength is the spike with an energy of E_D. The grey light that is present in the colour is represented by the uniform

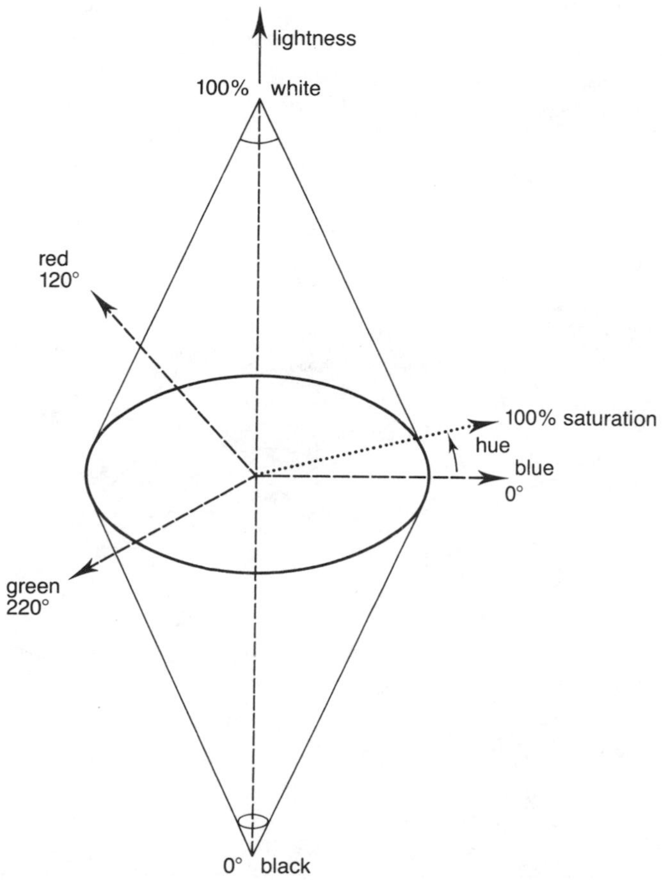

Figure 14.10
The HLS colour model.

band of energy over the visible spectrum at level E_G. Purity depends on the relative values of E_D and E_G. When $E_G = 0$ and $E_D \neq 0$, then the colour is completely pure, and when $E_G = E_D$, purity is zero. Luminance is represented by the total area under the curve.

A model developed specifically for use with colour display systems is the **HLS model** – Hue, Lightness and Saturation – introduced by Tektronix Inc. (Ostwald, 1931). The model defines hue to lie on a circle centred on and at right-angles to the 50% point of the lightness scale, as illustrated in Figure 14.10. Blue is at 0°, red at 120° and green at 220°, and each hue is arranged so that it has its complementary colour diametrically opposite on the circle. Saturation increases from 0% at the circle centre to 100% on the circle itself. The complete model resembles a double cone with black – 0% lightness – at the lower apex and white – 100% lightness – at the upper apex. Using this model, any colour can be specified in terms of an angle and two percentage values for hue, lightness and saturation, respectively.

(a)

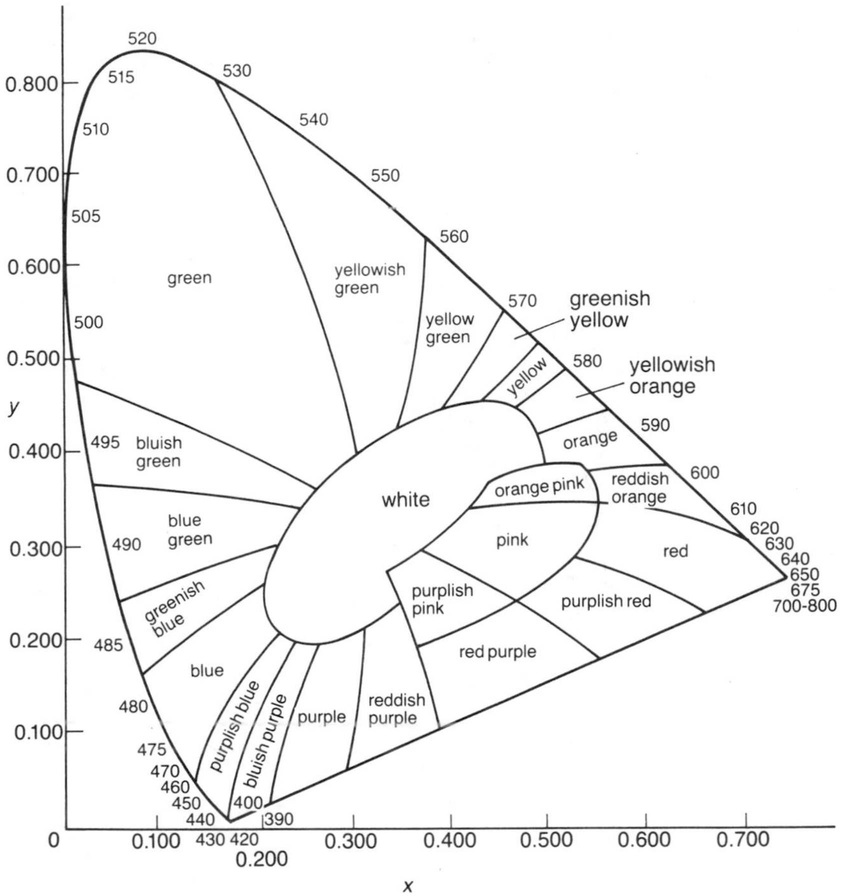

Figure 14.11
(a) The CIE chromacity diagram.
(b) Definitions of colours on the 1931 CIE diagram.

None of the models described here can be described as analytic definitions or tools for colour, but it is obvious that such a model would be very useful. This need was satisfied in 1931 (long before colour TV and computer graphics became practical) when the Commission Internationale L'Eclairage (CIE) met in England to define a 2D diagram on which any set of primary colours could be plotted and aligned against a reference colour white. The CIE defined three hypothetical primary colours, none of which are visible to the human eye/brain system: red X, green Y and blue Z. These form a triangle that completely encloses all visible colours, and the Y colour was defined to have an energy distribution that exactly matches the luminosity response of the eye. The standard 1931 CIE chromacity diagram

(b)

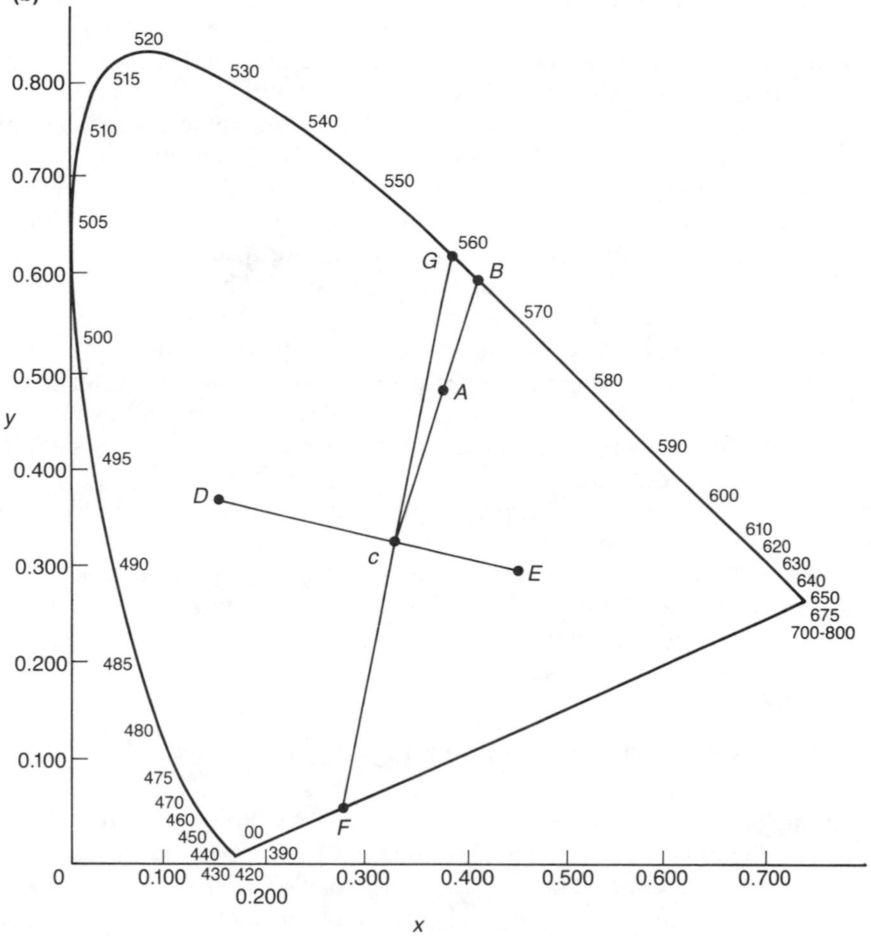

is shown in Figure 14.11(a) (Murch, 1986). Figure 14.11(b) shows the definition of a set of colours on the diagram. Colour *A* is defined in terms of standard white (illuminant *c*) and its dominant wavelength *B* which, along with all other such pure colours, lie on the chromacity curve. The complementary colours *D* and *E* are shown, suitably weighted either side of illuminant *c*. Some colours, like that at *F*, in the lower portion of the diagram cannot be defined directly by a dominant wavelength and therefore the complement of that at *G* is said to be the dominant wavelength. In 1976, a transformation of the 1931 CIE diagram was defined to produce a more uniform colour space and is known as the 1976 CIE Uniform Colour Space (Murch, 1986).

14.7.7 Colour Discrimination

The ability of the eye/brain system to discriminate one coloured object from another requires that the edge between the two objects must be sharply focused. This edge can be created by a difference in colour, brightness or both. The lack of colour correction in the eye's lens means that if the colours differ in hue and are both relatively saturated, then the eye will not be able to focus on both sides of the edge simultaneously. A simple difference in colour is insufficient to allow accurate focusing and therefore objects should differ in both colour and brightness for good discrimination.

Generally, it is wise to avoid fully saturated colours on the display at the same time. The presence of two or more such colours means that the eye will be continuously having to refocus over the image and will suffer strain and fatigue. Saturated blue characters on a red background would be particularly fatiguing. If these colours must be used, then simply desaturating them may do the trick.

Certain colour combinations are particularly garish and difficult for the eye/brain system to discriminate between, while others are easier to distinguish. Pace (1984) showed that magenta on green and green on white had high error rates, while black on blue and blue on white had low rates in a series of tests on character reading.

14.7.8 Human Response to Colour

From the foregoing, it can be seen that a person's response to colour is very much a combination of psychological and physiological processes. The response depends not only on the eye/brain reaction to the colour, but also on the cultural and emotional background of the observer. Colour and combinations of colours can generate different responses in different individuals. For example, in many cultures the colour red signifies danger or stop, while the colour green means clear or go. This colour coding is widely used on traffic lights. However, during the Cultural Revolution in The Peoples Republic of China, the traffic light colour coding, for ideological reasons, in some areas of the country, was reversed with red meaning go and green meaning stop, thereby reversing the peoples' response to the two colours. Moreover, in some countries, the colour of mourning is black and in others it is white. Because of the non-physiological aspects of a person's response to colour, care must be exercised when choosing colours for a display.

There are some *emotional* or *reflex* human responses to colour. For example, some people regard some colours, such as red and orange, as being *warm* colours whereas others, such as blue, are cool colours. Low intensity red light tends to impose a warm and comforting atmosphere and blue light, a cool and *airy* feeling. However, brighter reds tend to generate a feeling of stress or alarm, while green tends to impose a calm and relaxed atmosphere. These emotional responses to colour should also be considered during display design.

14.7.9 Uses of Colour

After all this discussion about colour, how can it be used to best effect within the world of computer graphics? Unfortunately, given a free hand, a lot of programmers new to graphics will use most of the available colours whenever possible. The brighter, the better too! However, as with most system features, unless they are used carefully and as part of the overall system interface design, then they can be a disaster. Therefore, this section first considers where colour can be used and then suggests some guidelines of how it could best be used.

There are three categories for the use of colour in computer graphics systems.

(1) *Colour for artistic effect or realism* This simply means applying the colours in an effective manner. In this context, the image will have been generated for its effect as fine art, a simulated scene or a picture. The skills required here are those of the training, experience and intuition of the artist (see Section 1.3.6). However, most computer graphics systems will severely limit the number of colours that can be used on the display at the same time and will therefore limit the subtlety of shading, especially in 3D scenes, that can be achieved. Many different artists' skills, previously used on signs and posters, magazines and in the television arts, are now being redeployed to the new computer graphics medium as well as other new ones developed.

The other two uses are relevant to data or information displays using colour text or graphics, and are essentially the main subject of this section.

(2) *Colour for coding* By applying colour, either as a foreground or as a background, the data or information will tend to be categorized by the user according to the colour grouping. A simple example is where a system displays all error messages as orange text. The user will soon begin to associate any item that appears in orange as an error message and, hopefully, will be attracted to it. The system must not, of course, display any non-error messages in orange as the coding would then be inconsistent across the system.

Colour coding can take advantage of common or cultural expectations of colour, as discussed earlier. The example using orange as the coding for error messages follows the general experience of the western populations where orange is used for warning lights on service vehicles, indicators on automobiles, caution on traffic lights and so on. It would, of course, be possible to use any available colour on the display system for the error messages, but it would probably require a much longer learning curve for the user and involve the risk of the user reverting to traditional coding and possibly ignoring the error.

Similarly, any data items that are displayed in the same colour will be grouped together by users according to the colour coding. They will associate any item in green, for example, as belonging to the same set. Should most of the displayed data be in green, then no particular grouping will be assumed but smaller groups will be associated together. Again, it is important that any coding, explicit or implicit, is consistent across the system and across to other systems where they are being used together in the same environment. One particular system feature that can be employed is to parameterize the colour coding that a system under design will employ. This will allow the installer of the system to match colour codings with systems that have been previously installed within the same organization. This can also be useful where systems are to be employed outside the cultural background of the developer.

(3) *Colour for weighting* Colour can be used to give weight to particular display items. For example, maximum weight is required for emergency situations and traditionally, in the West, highly saturated red is used where the user's attention is required quickly. However, more subtle use can be made of colour weighting, these uses being generally similar to those described under the heading of contrast weighting in Section 14.8.4. Colour weighting can be used to lead the user around the display and in this case the weighting can be dynamic, according to the user's requirements of the display and the data.

No simple set of rules can be safely defined for the use of colour within the display environment. The reaction of individuals to colour, as described previously, may well be a function of their cultural and educational background, and any set of hard and fast rules would be complex and undoubtedly controversial. Therefore, a set of guidelines are offered here, based on those suggested by Shneiderman (1987). These can be followed by display designers so that they will avoid some of the more obvious pitfalls and take advantage of the colour facilities that their displays offer.

(1) *Use colour conservatively* It is very tempting for programmers to use all of the colours at their disposal, especially saturated colours.

Colour is a very useful additional dimension to the display but excessive use can be fatiguing and make the image difficult to read. For example, at first thought it may seem like a good idea to colour each item in a long menu with a different colour coding for each selection, but the effect would probably be quite overwhelming to the user. It would be better to simply apply different colours to the menu title, any instructions and the set of menu items with a dynamic weighting applied to the currently selected item.

(2) *Limit the number of colours used on a display* Design guides suggest that the number of colours used on a single alphanumeric display page should be limited to four. The number of colours used across the system should be no more than seven.

(3) *Use colour coding to support the task* Colour coding of data should result from the task analysis. This will reduce the possibility of colour coding becoming inconsistent. It should be a natural part of the interface and should not require the user to initiate it. It may, however, be convenient for the user to have the ability to switch off any colour coding when they are not working with the data groupings to which it has been applied.

(4) *Use colour for formatting* When the data or the system design forces the designer to locate items close together on the display, dissimilar colours can be used to differentiate between the closely spaced but logically distinct data fields. A good example of this is the use of different colours to distinguish between the nesting levels on the display of a computer program written in a block-structured programming language.

(5) *Be consistent* This cannot be overstressed. If consistency of colour coding within the display cannot be achieved, then avoid using it altogether.

(6) *Be aware of cultural expectations of colour codings*

(7) *Use dynamic colour codings to indicate a change of status of a data item* For example, in an air traffic control system the different positional or height level status of the aircraft in controllers sector can be assigned different colours as they move around the airspace. Saturated colours could be limited to abnormal or dangerous aircraft positions.

(8) *Beware of colour pairings that the eye/brain system will find difficult to handle* In particular, highly saturated colours will force the user's eye to use excessive focusing movements.

Finally, Shneiderman makes the following very interesting suggestion: whether the display actually uses colour or not, it should initially be designed as if it were a monochrome display system. Colour coding or weighting cannot compensate for poor logical or positional layout. The display should be enhanced by the use of colour and not dependent upon it for clarity and understanding. In addition, the system may be used in situations where colour displays are not available and, more significantly, where colour coding is of little relevance – for example, the 9% of the male population of the US and the European continents who are to some extent colour blind.

14.8 The Display Image and the Eye

The previous sections have described the psycho-physiological process of vision. It is now possible to combine this knowledge with the parameters of the hardware to see how display systems can be used.

14.8.1 Display Viewing Distance

At distances of less than six metres (20 feet) the eyes must accommodate to see objects clearly. They must *converge* by turning inwards under the actions of the rectus and oblique muscles and they must focus the lens so as to form a sharp image on the retina. Objects that are further away than six metres do not need accommodation, the sight lines and light rays being virtually parallel. The limit to which the eyes can accommodate an object is known as the **near point**, which varies with age and the shape and performance of the various elements of the eye. Correcting lenses, or spectacles, are used to correct the vision if the near point or the **far point** – normally about six metres – are not within acceptable limits.

A graphics display device must be outside the near point distance for comfortable viewing and this dictates a minimum distance of 25 to 30 cm (10″ to 12″). If the device is part of an interactive system, then the display must also be within the user's comfortable reaching distance. This makes the most suitable distance to be about 40 to 45 cm (16″ to 18″).

14.8.2 Visual Resolution

The eye's visual resolution is its ability to distinguish between objects and is a function of the performance of a number of different features of the eye. In particular, it depends on the eye's ability to focus and the distance between the cones in the fovea, both of which will vary between individuals.

However, the limits of resolution cause image elements below the eye's visual resolution to be merged. In this way, colour images become acceptable when generated using a shadow mask CRT (see Section 15.2.4) or similar dot matrix systems. Similarly, lines or objects drawn on raster type systems are merged into continuous image elements. The normal limit of visual resolution of the human eye is about 1 minute of arc.

The density of rods and cones on the retina decreases with the distance from the fovea and therefore the objects that the eye can resolve must be larger the further they are from the visual axis. The edge of the eye's cone of vision is known as **peripheral vision** and because of the reduced resolution acts as a *warning zone*, reacting more to image change or movement than to content.

In fact, the eye/brain system is quite sensitive to movement in the peripheral vision and must be considered when designing display systems. Because of the eye's peripheral sensitivity to movement it can be disturbing if additional displays, not related to the immediate task of the user, are placed within the peripheral vision. Any image movement on the display, because of either a change in image content or because of display *flicker*, may cause distraction or hindrance. However, movement can also be used to notify the user of changing situations, such as warnings, on the display. The flashing of a warning signal, away from the main image data content, is a common method of attracting the user's attention.

The limit of the eye's high resolution vision also places a limit on the useful size of the display with respect to the viewing distance. With raster display systems, the larger the display size, the larger the display area of each pixel (for a particular frame buffer), with the result that the eye may no longer merge the individual pixels into the intended image elements. The converse is true in that with smaller displays, the visual resolution is higher.

14.8.3 Display Flicker

The reasons why displays flicker are discussed in Chapter 15. However, the critical frequency at which the user notices the onset of flicker is also a function of the performance of the eye/brain system. The time required for the photochemical activity in the rods and cones to achieve a detectable level and for the nerve impulses to traverse the nerve cell network to the brain sets a limit to the system's ability to detect a change of image and to its time of image retention.

The critical frequency for flicker detection by the eye/brain system can only be obtained empirically and, to make matters even more difficult, it also depends upon image content. Because of the eye's ability to integrate aspects of the image, as well as limits to its resolving power, flicker is more discernible in image elements of small area than larger ones. This is particularly true on raster displays where horizontal lines that occupy single

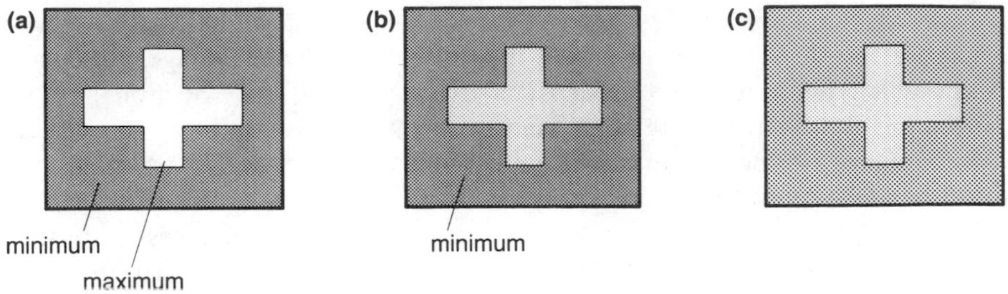

Figure 14.12
Contrast and contrast ratios.

raster lines will be seen to flicker, while lines of two or more raster lines in width will not flicker so obviously. Non-interlaced raster scanned display systems (see Section 15.3.4) usually refresh the whole image above the critical frequency, even for single raster line widths. Therefore, the display of horizontal lines of single raster line width on interlaced display systems should be avoided. CRTs with small display sizes also have a lower flicker threshold because the exposure time of each phosphor particle to the electron beam is longer.

14.8.4 Contrast, Reflection and Filters

The eye/brain system reacts more to the ratio between two light sources, or more commonly, their **contrast**, than to their absolute values. The contrast or **contrast ratio** of two light sources is defined as:

$$\text{contrast ratio} = \frac{\text{luminance source 1}}{\text{luminance source 2}}$$

In the case of the contrast of a display device, this becomes (CONRAC, 1980):

$$\text{device contrast} = \frac{\text{maximum display luminance}}{\text{minimum display luminance}}$$

and the ratio is between the maximum and minimum luminances that are perceived from the display. The higher the contrast ratio for a device, the better the **legibility** of the image. For a monochrome device, the minimum display luminance is the luminance of the display background. Figure 14.12(a) shows the effect of high contrast between a maximum luminance object and a minimum luminance background. If the luminance of the object is reduced, then the result in Figure 14.12(b) is obtained with an overall reduced contrast ratio. If the luminance of both the background and the object is increased, then the effect is as in Figure 14.12(c), again with a reduced contrast ratio.

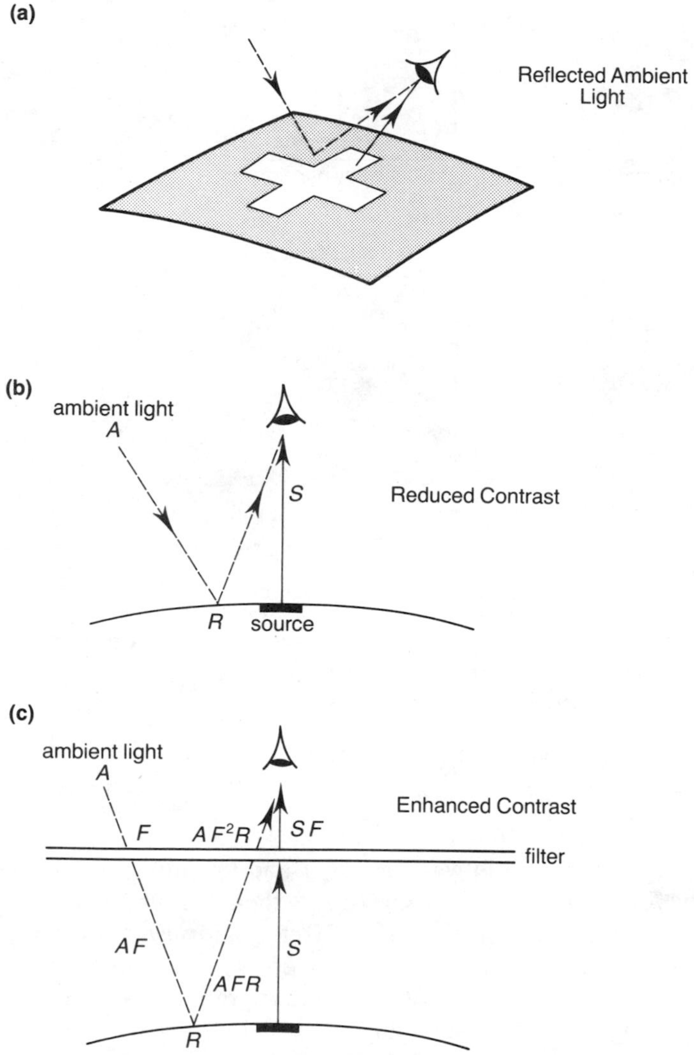

Figure 14.13
Use of a filter in front of a display screen.

The last case considered can occur when there is high ambient lighting and reflected light is added to both luminances. For example, consider the case when the maximum contrast ratio is S:1, where S is greater than 1. If an ambient light source of value A is diffusely reflected from the surface of the display with reflectivity factor R (the amount reflected by the surface), then:

$$\text{contrast ratio} = \frac{(S + AR)}{(1 + AR)}$$

as shown in Figures 14.13(a) and (b), which will result in a reduced contrast

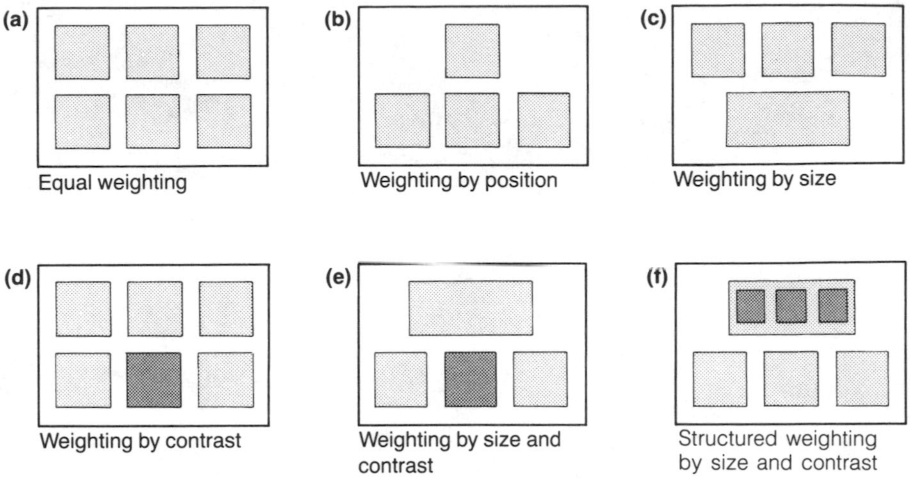

Figure 14.14
Image weighting.

ratio. The contrast ratio can be increased if an absorbing filter is introduced. If the filter, which absorbs light equally at all frequencies, with an absorption factor F (the amount of light that passes through) is placed in front of the display screen, then:

$$\text{contrast ratio} = \frac{(S + AFR)}{(1 + AFR)}$$

If the original contrast ratio was, say, 10:1 and the ambient light A and the reflectivity R are 5 and 0.5, respectively, then the new contrast ratio is reduced to 3.57:1. However, if a filter of factor 0.5 is used, the contrast ratio is increased to 5:1. If a filter of factor 0.25 is used, the contrast ratio is 6.54:1. Thus, it can be seen that the contrast ratio, in conditions of high ambient lighting, can be considerably increased if a filter is placed between the user and the display screen (see Figure 14.13(a)).

It must be emphasized that the formulae and computations used here are only approximate, as the total light entering the eye is a function of the light from the whole of the display area, although, as discussed previously, the eye is considerably more sensitive along the axis between the lens and the fovea.

There also exists a contrast ratio between the display and the scene behind or surrounding it. If the surroundings are very bright or very dark compared to the display, then this ratio may cause fatigue, as the user may be required to regularly look away from the display (to some note papers perhaps) and the eye/brain system has to adjust between the two lighting levels.

14.8.5 Viewing Angles

The angle at which the user views a CRT display also affects the contrast ratio. A maximum contrast ratio is obtained by viewing the display directly and not from an angle to one side or above or below. This is because maximum light radiation occurs normal to the display surface and reduces, sinusoidally, to 0 when parallel to the surface. Therefore, only under special circumstances should the display be tilted away from the user's direct view. This applies to most kinds of display and in the case of some display types, like the liquid crystal display (see Section 15.5.1), the effect is considerably more pronounced.

14.9 Display Image Composition

The eye/brain system is essentially a *parallel* input device and when the eye/brain system views a scene, it processes information at a very high rate. The other main sensory and communication organs, the ear and the mouth, are essentially *serial* devices. By presenting the user with a graphics display image, as opposed to a character display, the eye/brain system is being used in its most efficient manner; that is, the data are presented by the computer as parallel rather than serial data. There is little point in generating graphics displays where the user is forced to scan the data in a serial form as with a pure text display.

The careful design of display images can help users extract the information they require from the display. Badly designed images can be tiring, irritating, confusing and possibly dangerous if they are to be used in situations where the safety of people or equipment are concerned.

14.9.1 Partitioning the Image and Leading the User

The design of an image affects the manner in which a user will scan that image. Advertisement designers use techniques to attract the attention of newspaper or magazine readers to their advertisements and to particular aspects of the advertisement. Such techniques involve the use of shape and colour to lead the reader's attention around the image.

Presented with a display consisting entirely of text, or large blocks of text, someone with a traditional western education will read it, starting from the top left, in a left to right, top to bottom scan. People with other cultural backgrounds may adopt a different text scanning process. Again, it is wise to know something about the user. If the user is presented with several blocks of similar information of the same size, as in Figure 14.14(a), then again they might be expected to adopt their traditional page scanning strategy.

The user's common scanning process can be influenced by attracting their attention first to one image element and then to another by visually **weighting** elements of the display. This can be done in several different ways (Van Deusen, 1981):

(1) *Position* Image elements that are separated from the other image elements tend to stand out, as in Figure 14.14(b).

(2) *Size* The user's eye/brain system tends to examine larger elements of the image first, all other weightings being equal. Therefore, placing information in a larger block or using larger text all tend to have the same effect. Figure 14.14(c) shows the use of size to attract the eye away from its normal scan.

(3) *Colour* As discussed earlier, the user will be attracted by related and distinguishing colours. For example, colour may be used to highlight important text strings.

(4) *Contrast* The user will notice elements that have a high luminance or colour contrast with other elements. Figure 14.14(d) shows the use of contrast to divert the user's attention from the normal scan pattern.

(5) *Dynamics* The user will be attracted towards dynamics or movement in the display. For example, making an element *flash* or *blink*. Care must be exercised when using dynamics in an image as it can be easily overused.

Weightings can also be mixed on an image. Weighting by size may be used to draw the user's attention first to one element and then brightness used to apply weight to other display elements of similar size, as in Figure 14.14(e). Weightings may also be structured so that the user, having been attracted to one element by size, is then attracted to a smaller subelement within the first by contrast, as in Figure 14.14(f). Weightings such as contrast and colour are best used dynamically in situations where the weighting of image elements changes with time or occurrence. There is no point in using weighting as in Figure 14.14(d) if each appearance of the image is to be the same. It would be better to use the user's common scan strategy.

14.9.2 Image Content, Density and Crowding

Generating images with the correct information content can be a very difficult task. The correct content depends on the application, the user, the display type and resolution. It is therefore possible only to provide a few general rules for image content.

Any tendency to crowd information on to the image should be

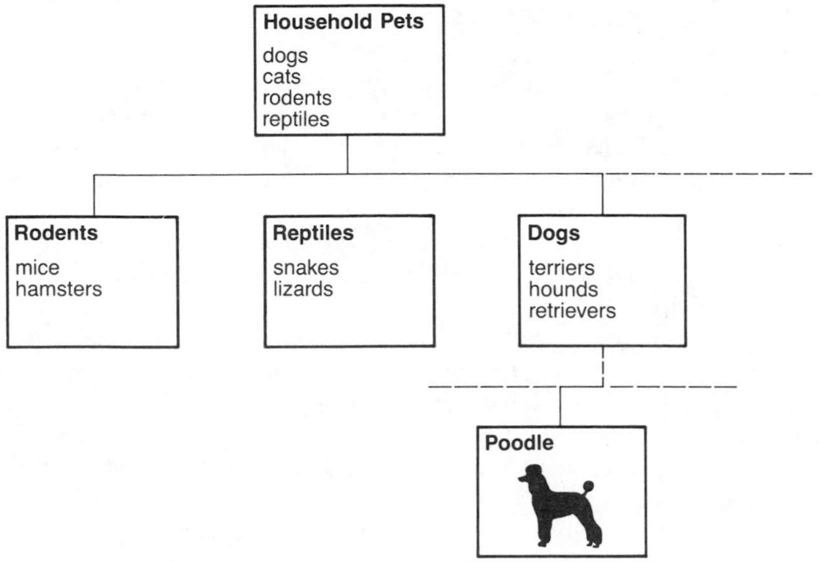

Figure 14.15 Hierarchical image structure.

avoided. The user should not have to search too hard for the information that is required. It always helps to structure the information into logical units, keeping information of equal importance to the same level of weighting. Information that suddenly gains a higher level of importance, such as a warning signal, can be dynamically assigned a higher weighting, such as a change of colour.

If, when designing an image, the content appears to be too high for relaxed, stress-free examination by the user, it should be divided into smaller elements on additional display images, usually known as **pages**. It is common to create a hierarchy of pages with each level of the hierarchy displaying a more detailed level of information. For example, Figure 14.15 shows how part of a hierarchy of information for a list of household pets might be constructed. It may be possible, on a very high-resolution image display, to list all of the common household pets, but it would probably be very difficult to read and would take some time to locate the information on the pet of interest. However, if a hierarchical list system is generated, then the first image would list only the general groups of pets – dogs, cats, rodents, etc. The user would then be able to quickly select the group of interest and progress to additional pages with information at the next level where, for example, the types of dogs are listed. Further progress down the hierarchy of pages may eventually result in a graphic image of the type of dog of interest with information on its size, diet, temperament and so on. In this way, the user can quickly access the information and need never have any information displayed that is more detailed than required for the current task. This relates back to the discussion in Section 14.6.4.

14.9.3 Graphics and Text

Mixing graphics and text on the same image needs to be carefully planned. If an image contains any form of graphics, especially any areas of solid colour, then the image is basically a graphics image. The user's eye will gravitate to the graphics on the image and the text will be supplemental. Trying to *illustrate* text with graphics tends to have quite the opposite effect.

Text itself needs to be carefully arranged for ease of reading. Character height and spacing is important and interline spacing must be in proportion to the text itself. If the text is too closely spaced, then the eye will be dominated by the *block* of the text, and if it is too widely spaced, then it will be tiring to read as well as taking up too much space on the display. High-resolution display systems allow a large number of characters to be displayed on an image line. The temptation to take advantage of this capability should be avoided and a maximum of 60 to 80 characters per line maintained.

Some fonts and styles of text are more *legible* and more *pleasing* to read than others. Plain text, as displayed on most computer terminals and graphics displays, is not particularly easy to read, whereas the text styles found in magazines are much better. However, this quality of text is rarely found on graphics displays because it is very expensive in terms of storage space, each character requiring additional coordinate data points to describe it. However, the use of PostScript in the NeWS window manager system is beginning to change this situation for the better.

Summary

This chapter has attempted to give an indication of what the careful design of the human–computer interface can achieve and its importance to the overall use of the system. The HCI should be a major part of the system design and its design should be understood before construction of the system is started.

The chapter has emphasized that good HCI starts with an analysis of the needs and goals of users (task analysis). The careful separation of the different levels of a user interface was discussed in the context of the command language grammar. Specific examples of interaction techniques based on systems with popular user interfaces were considered. Finally, the 'human hardware' of the visual system and the human response to colour was discussed. Guidelines for the use of colour were given based on this analysis.

Exercises

14.1 Completely redesign and re-implement the interactive drawing program discussed in Part One, in the light of the ideas presented in this chapter.

14.2 Allot colours, including highlights, to the meny system shown in Figure 14.4. Give reasons for your choice.

14.3 Design a hierarchical display structure for a shoe catalogue for implementation on a colour graphics display system. The top of the structure should allow the user to make global choices, such as between winter and summer shoes. The bottom of the structure should, of course, display a graphics image of each possible shoe that can be purchased, as shown in Plate 10.

CHAPTER 15

ELECTRONIC DISPLAYS

The discussion of hardware and systems starts with that of the display equipment available to the modern system designer. The electronic display is the fundamental device for use in interactive computer graphics systems and this chapter examines the different types, and compares and contrasts their characteristics.

15.1 Introduction

Electronic displays generate their images by electronic means. They can be classified into two types: those that generate their own light energy and those that rely on the reflection or transmission of a separate light source, such as a light bulb or daylight. The first type are known as **emitter displays** and the latter as **non-emitter displays**.

Of the emitter dislays, there is one that has dominated the field; namely, the **cathode ray tube** (**CRT**). This is also by far the oldest of the electronic displays and has many years of sophisticated development behind it, and probably in front of it too! No other display type can approach the CRT in its flexibility, ease of use and low cost. However, it is not without its drawbacks, especially taking into account the high voltages required to drive it.

An emitter display that has become very popular recently, especially when combined with touch-sensitive overlay panels for interaction with the displayed images, is the **gas discharge panel** or **plasma panel**. However, its limited colour display capability and very high voltage requirements have discouraged its use.

At one time, scientists thought that they had discovered the answer to the CRT in the form of the **electroluminescent display**, a flat screen display, but technical difficulties have delayed its acceptance. However, its day may still come.

Cathodoluminescent displays have also found use in small pixel matrix displays, especially where character-only display is required. These are also known as **vacuum fluorescent displays**.

Finally, there are the **light-emitting diode** (**LED**) displays. This type of display initially became popular for use in hand-held and desk top portable calculators, but now the diodes can be formed into matrices where they form a very compact and rugged 2D display.

15.2 Cathode Ray Tubes

Towards the end of the nineteenth century scientists began to investigate the effects of passing an electric current through various gases. One of the discoveries made as a consequence of this work was that when electrons impacted with the glass wall of an evacuated container, the wall was seen to emit light or **fluoresce**. This discovery led to the development of the cathode ray oscilloscope, which has found many uses in displaying the transient behaviour of electronic equipment. As early computers were equipped with oscilloscopes to display the state of their computations, they became the first

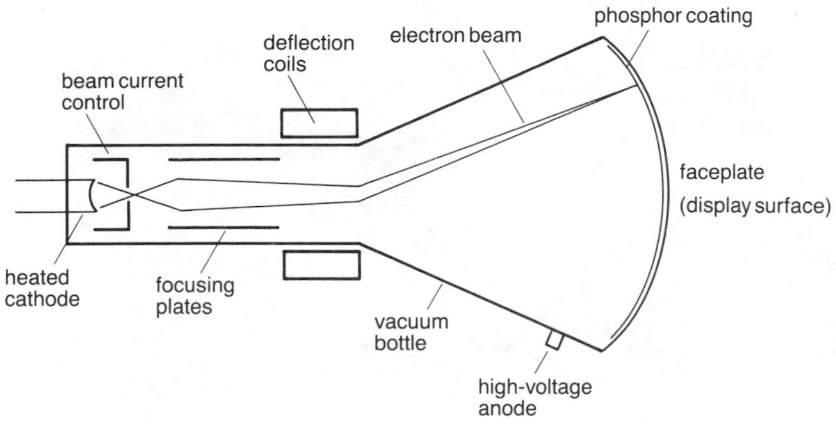

Figure 15.1
Schematic diagram of a cathode ray tube.

visual display devices connected to a computer. However, to say that they were also the first graphics display devices may be stretching the point. The modern CRT is, however, merely a modified oscilloscope.

15.2.1 Principles of Operation

Figure 15.1 shows a schematic of a basic CRT. The heated cathode produces a generous stream of electrons, which are formed into a beam by a controlling grid surrounding the cathode. The grid also controls the number of electrons allowed through and thus the strength of the beam. This beam is focused to form a fine point on the display surface or **faceplate** by an electronic lens consisting of a number of electrostatic plates or electromagnetic coils. The focused beam is attracted to the display surface by a high positive potential on the conductive (inside) surface of the faceplate. The position of the beam's impact point on the display surface is controlled by deflection plates or coils which attract or repel the beam about the neutral straight line path. The cathode, beam control grid and high voltage anode are all contained within a vacuum bottle, three examples of which are shown in Figure 15.2. The three CRTs shown are of sizes 35, 38 and 17.5 cm, (14″, 15″ and 7″), from left to right. The tube on the far left is fitted with a deflection assembly. The focusing and deflection plates or coils can be placed inside or outside the bottle, depending on the type, quality and manufacturer of the tube.

The schematic in Figure 15.1 shows a cross-section through a CRT and as such would allow the beam to be moved vertically. In reality, however, there is another set of deflection plates at right-angles to those shown which controls the horizontal deflection of the beam. By varying the deflection currents in both the horizontal and vertical axes, the beam can be

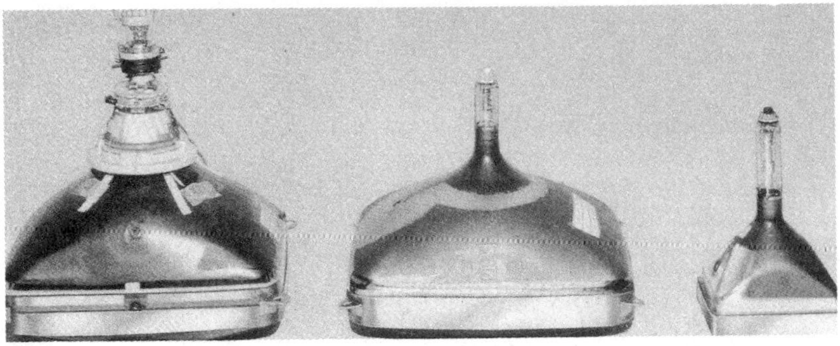

Figure 15.2
Three CRT vacuum bottles.

positioned at random anywhere on the display surface. By continuously and simultaneously varying the horizontal and vertical deflections, lines and curves can be traced out on the display surface. This is illustrated in Figure 15.3 where the application of a uniformally increasing current to each of the horizontal and vertical deflection plates causes a straight line, or vector, to be traced out. More complex lines and curves would require non-linear current changes in the plates.

The inside surface of the CRT faceplate is coated with a thin layer of particles to enhance the **fluorescence** when the faceplate is *excited* by the striking electron beam. These particles are usually a form of zinc sulphide and are known as **phosphor** particles. Once the electron beam has stopped striking phosphor particles at a particular point, either by switching the beam off or by moving it, the light output from the phosphor, now known as its **phosphorescence**, decays. The amount of time that the phosphor phosphoresces depends on the **persistence** of the phosphor used. The persistence of a phosphor is defined as the time, in microseconds, that it takes for the light given off by the phosphor to decay to 10% of its excited value. Therefore, the higher the persistence of the phosphor, the longer it glows. Phosphors are given names consisting of the letter P followed by a number. The higher the number, the higher the persistence. Table 15.1 lists a few of the phosphors that are of interest.

The use of a cathode to generate the stream of electrons places the CRT in the overall class of cathodoluminescent displays. However, this term is usually reserved for flat panel displays using this type of electron source.

By coating the inside display surface of the CRT with a particular phosphor, the colour of the light produced and the length of time it persists can be controlled. The brightness of the light point is controlled by the current applied to the beam control grid. However, only a single colour,

Table 15.1 CRT phosphors – colours and applications.

Phosphor	Colour	Application
P1	yellow/green	oscilloscopes; radar
P4	white	monochrome TV
P22-B	blue	colour TV
P22-G	yellow/green	colour TV
P22-R	red	colour TV
P22-G_{LP}	yellow/green	colour graphics
P39	green	low update rate displays
P45	white	visual display units

that emitted by the phosphor coating, can be shown. Therefore, it is a **monochrome** CRT. If more than one colour is required for display purposes, then additional phosphors must be applied to the display surface.

15.2.2 Colour CRTs

Before the operation of a colour CRT can be understood, it is necessary to understand how light of various colours is generated or, more accurately, *perceived* by the human eye. A detailed description of this phenomenon is given in Section 14.7. Those readers who are unclear on the subject of colour physics and human perception of colour are recommended to read this section before continuing here.

A CRT can produce an image of a specific colour by using a phosphor with the required characteristics (see Table 15.1). However, for a CRT to produce a range of colours, it is necessary for the light from two or three phosphors to be *added* together. For example, if the light emitted from a red phosphor and a green phosphor is combined, then yellow light is perceived. Modulation of the amounts of red or green light produced allows additional *hues* to be produced. It is by this means that a CRT can generate a *range* of colours.

The problem of creating a colour CRT is two-fold. Firstly, because an individual phosphor only emits light of one single colour, it is necessary to place on to the faceplate quantities of each of the phosphors required to generate the desired colours by additive colour mixing. The second problem is to accurately strike the phosphors with the electron beam. Naturally, the solution adopted to the first problem affects the solution of the second: the

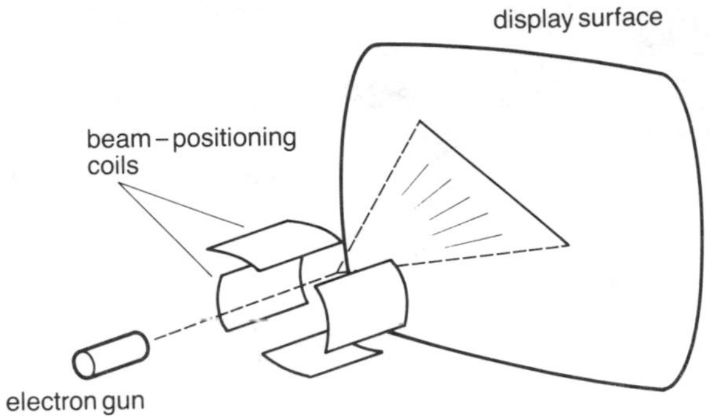

Figure 15.3
Tracing a straight line on the display surface of a CRT.

phosphors must be made to share the available space on the CRT faceplate. There are two ways in which this can be done and each gives rise to a different type of colour CRT.

15.2.3 Beam Penetration Tubes

The first solution is to cover the inside of the CRT display surface with a layer of each of the phosphors necessary to generate the required colours (see Figure 15.4). This is accomplished in the following way. The CRT faceplate is internally coated with a layer of phosphor that emits green light when excited by the electron beam, a thin barrier layer and then a layer that emits red light when similarly excited. This layering is rather like the layers of an onion. The two phosphors are switched 'on' and 'off' by changing the energy of the electron beam. If the phosphor layers are struck by a beam of low power, then the red phosphor is excited, absorbing all the electrons. The red light is visible through the green phosphor and the CRT faceplate. By raising the energy of the electron beam to such a level that some of the electrons are able to penetrate through the red phosphor to the green phosphor, then that layer is also excited and the combined output is yellow light. Raising the energy of the beam still further excites the green phosphor to a level such that its light output, as perceived by the eye/brain system, dominates the red output. Using this particular arrangement of phosphors, three colours – red, green and yellow – can be generated.

Realistically speaking, the maximum number of phosphors that can be used in this way is two, because if there were three layers of phosphor, the light emitted by the innermost layer would be unable to penetrate the two outer layers. The red and green phosphor combination is the most typical and the most common on this type of CRT.

As the size of the electron beam spot can be adjusted to give very precise images, these types of tubes have found wide use in radar displays

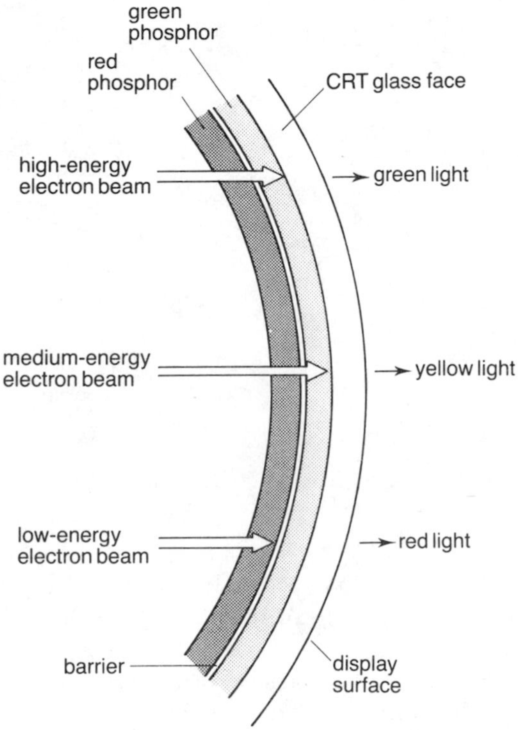

Figure 15.4
Section through a beam penetration tube faceplate and phosphor layers.

and in displays requiring the drawing of very fine lines, such as those needed for CAD systems. Such CRTs were also very common in high-quality colour graphics displays, and for a long time they were the only type of tube that was available. However, due to the disadvantages of this type of CRT – the limited number of colours that can be generated, its relatively short useful lifetime and high cost – it is not suitable for use in domestic television receivers, and it was this shortcoming that led to the development of the second type of colour CRT, the **shadow mask CRT**.

15.2.4 Shadow Mask CRTs

The shadow mask CRT uses a different method of arranging the phosphor particles on the CRT faceplate. Instead of placing them, as in the beam penetration tube, as a series of layers, they are arranged as a pattern of dots in a single layer. In this way, any number of different phosphor types can be arranged on the faceplate. Furthermore, all of the colours of the visible spectrum can be obtained by combining the light from phosphors that produce the three additive primary colours, red, green and blue. Only

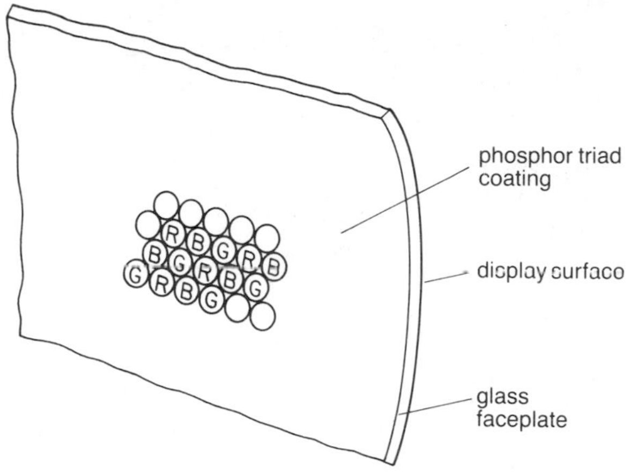

Figure 15.5.
Phosphor triads on the faceplate of a shadow mask CRT.

phosphors that emit these colours need to be placed on the faceplate, and to obtain even mixing of the light from the three phosphors they need to be placed as close together as possible. This is done by placing them in triangular or delta patterns, as illustrated in Figure 15.5.

By exciting the three different phosphors, either singly or in combination, all of the required colours can be generated. The amount of light that is required from each of the phosphors is controlled by modulating the strength of the electron beam current applied to each phosphor. The higher the beam current, the brighter the light emitted from the phosphor. The problem now is how to excite a particular phosphor dot without, necessarily, exciting its neighbours.

The shadow mask CRT accomplishes this by having three electron guns with each gun set to excite the phosphor particles of only one particular colour. These are known as the red, green and blue guns. To stop each gun from exciting phosphors of the other two colours, a mask is placed between the guns and the phosphors so that, for example, the red gun can only *see* the red phosphor dots. This mask is known as a **shadow** or, **aperture**, **mask**, hence the name shadow mask CRT. The mask is, in fact, placed directly behind the phosphor layer, as shown in Figure 15.6. This arrangement of the phosphors into delta patterns also requires that the electron guns be placed into either a corresponding delta pattern, as in Figure 15.6, or into an in-line arrangement, as shown in Figure 15.7. The former type of tube is known as a **delta-delta CRT**, or simply a **delta CRT**, and the latter as a **precision in-line** or **PIL-delta CRT**.

For each delta of phosphors to be evenly illuminated by their respective electron gun, the three beams must be made to *converge* on to the shadow mask hole; that is, they *cross over* at the hole. To do this, each

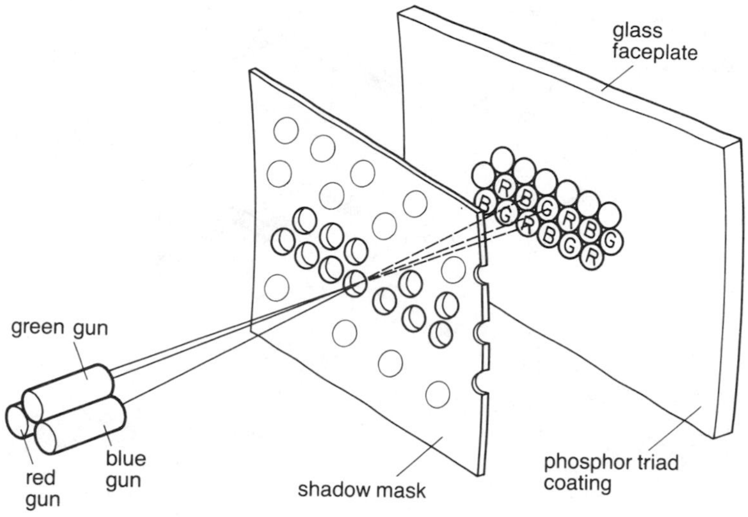

Figure 15.6
Delta gun arrangement for a shadow mask CRT.

gun must be precisely focused and aimed at the hole. This convergence is so delicate that, with very high performance CRTs, the slightest vibration can change this adjustment. In addition, even if the three guns are set so that they converge at the holes in the centre of the screen, they may not do so at the edges. Therefore, it is usual to control the convergence of the beams electronically.

The problems presented by the precise adjustment of the beam convergence of colour CRTs led to the development of tubes that did not require such fine adjustment. In these tubes, the guns were arranged in an in-line configuration with the phosphors in strips on the faceplate (see Figure 15.8). Such a tube is known as a **precision in-line** or **PIL gun CRT**. The mask shown in Figure 15.8 has vertical in-line slots, but some tubes of this type have no cross pieces at all and the mask is merely a set of vertical metal strips. In the PIL gun CRT, the faceplate is cylindrical, rather than spherical, as is the case for the delta gun layout. The dot pattern formed on the display surface is no longer triangular but appears as an oval.

Recently, several CRT manufacturers have developed **self-converging CRTs**. This is accomplished by building small calibration devices on the inner surface of the faceplate that can be illuminated by the three electron beams. Sensitive detectors register the position of the beams on each of the devices and automatically adjust the convergence circuitry by means of a microprocessor. Tube convergence can be accurately adjusted in less than 20 seconds. A cutaway diagram of one of these tubes is illustrated in Figure 15.9. (A more detailed description of their operation is given by Denham, 1986.)

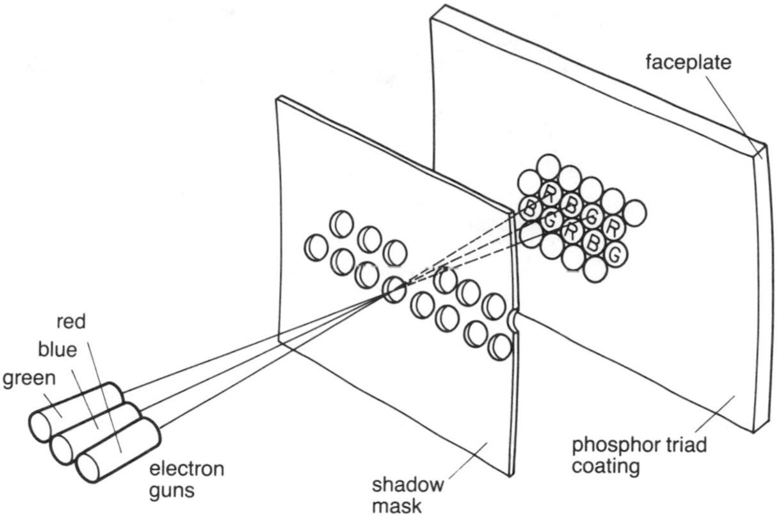

Figure 15.7
PIL-delta gun arrangement for a shadow mask CRT.

15.2.5 Shadow Mask CRT Resolution

The size of the holes or slots in the shadow mask and the diameter of the electron beam dictate the smallest light spot that can be illuminated on the display surface. Therefore, the **resolution** of the tube is a function of the distance between the hole centres, or the **pitch**, of the shadow mask and the electron beam spot size. In a standard resolution CRT, the pitch is about 0.6 mm (0.024″) for a 0.5 metre (19″) tube and the gap between columns is about 0.4 mm (0.16″). A high-resolution CRT has a pitch of 0.31 mm and a gap of 0.22 mm (0.012″ and 0.009″). With PIL gun CRTs, the structural supports between the slots are thin enough to make the vertical resolution effectively infinite and the column-to-column distance is about 0.8 mm. Therefore, although the PIL gun CRT has considerable advantages in terms of ruggedness and simplicity of use, the delta gun CRT offers better overall resolution.

The spot size must be at least twice the dot trio spacing on a delta shadow mask to generate uniform colour. Therefore, the resolution is restricted to twice the dot pitch, approximately 0.6 mm (0.024″) on a high-resolution colour tube. These, of course, are the best possible figures as they assume perfect performance from all aspects of the display.

Higher resolution CRTs are currently under development by several manufacturers and shadow masks of 0.2 mm pitch are possible. The possibility of even higher resolutions will depend on the CRT engineer's ability to produce shadow masks of even smaller pitch.

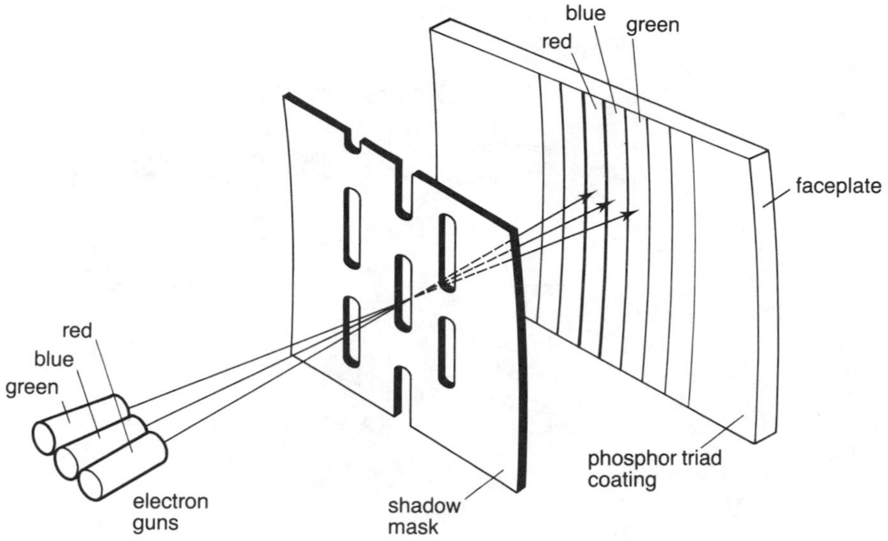

Figure 15.8
PIL gun arrangement with a slotted shadow mask.

15.2.6 Flat CRTs

For obvious reasons, the bottle shape of the conventional CRT requires a large enclosure to contain and support it. Most CRT cabinet enclosures must be at least 0.3 to 0.45 metre (12″ to 18″) deep. There have been many research and development projects throughout the world aimed at producing what has become known as a **flat CRT**. Such a device would not only enable the size of monochrome and colour televisions and graphics display devices to be reduced considerably, but would also bring the long desired pocket TV to reality. Several companies have produced small, battery powered, monochrome television sets based on such CRT devices. However, to describe them as pocket TVs is stretching a point – as well as pockets. One of these TVs, with its front cover removed to show the flat CRT, is illustrated in Figure 15.10. The schematic in Figure 15.11 shows the principles of operation.

The basic operation of this type of flat CRT is the same as with the conventional CRT, but instead of the electron beam cathode and focusing and deflection plates being at the back of the tube, they have been *folded* to one side and are parallel to the tube faceplate. The electrons leave the cathode, are focused and deflected as in the conventional tube, but are then deflected towards the phosphor coating on the rear surface of the tube, and the image is viewed through a viewing port in the front of the tube. As can be seen from Figure 15.11, the electrons strike the phosphor at a narrow

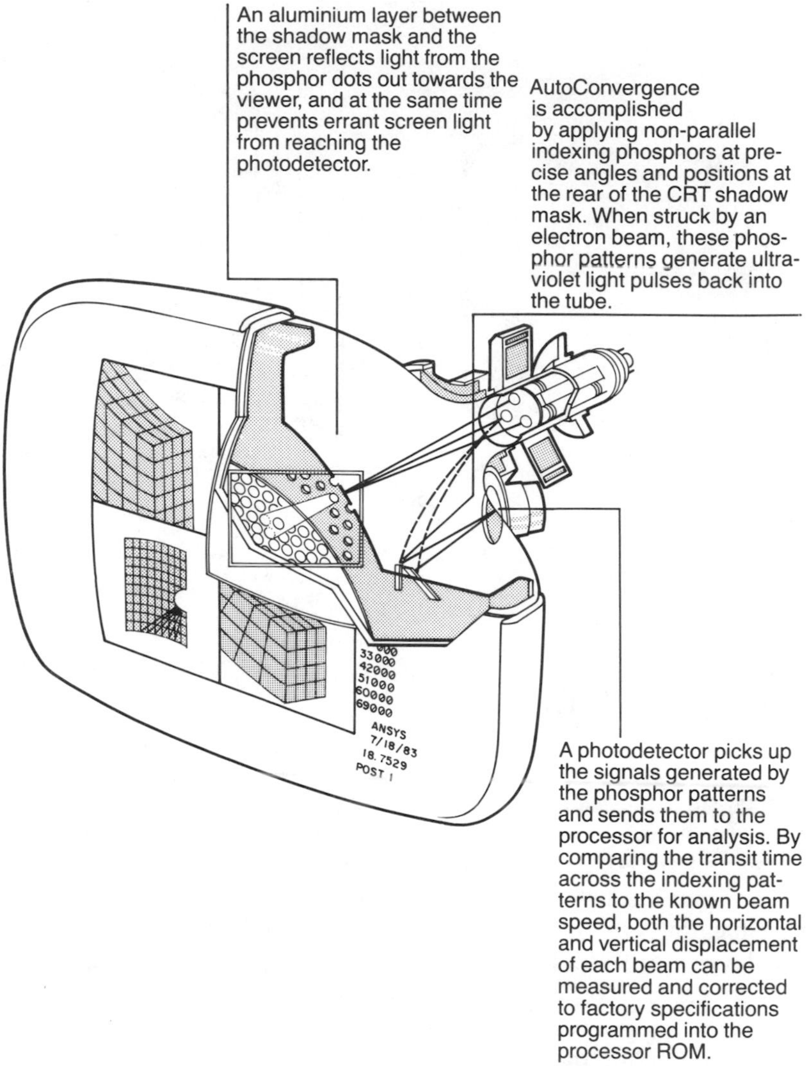
An aluminium layer between the shadow mask and the screen reflects light from the phosphor dots out towards the viewer, and at the same time prevents errant screen light from reaching the photodetector.
AutoConvergence is accomplished by applying non-parallel indexing phosphors at precise angles and positions at the rear of the CRT shadow mask. When struck by an electron beam, these phosphor patterns generate ultraviolet light pulses back into the tube.
33000
42000
51000
60000
69000
ANSYS
7/18/83
18.7529
POST 1
A photodetector picks up the signals generated by the phosphor patterns and sends them to the processor for analysis. By comparing the transit time across the indexing patterns to the known beam speed, both the horizontal and vertical displacement of each beam can be measured and corrected to factory specifications programmed into the processor ROM.

Figure 15.9
Cutaway diagram of a self-converging CRT.

grazing angle and unless corrected the image will appear distorted. This distortion is removed either by electronically *predistorting* the image or by building a special lens into the viewing port, or a combination of both.

15.2.7 Electron Multiplier CRTs

The phosphor layer on the inner surface of the faceplate of a CRT is excited by an electron beam of relatively high energy, several kilovolts in fact. This requirement for a high energy beam means that the beam can be only

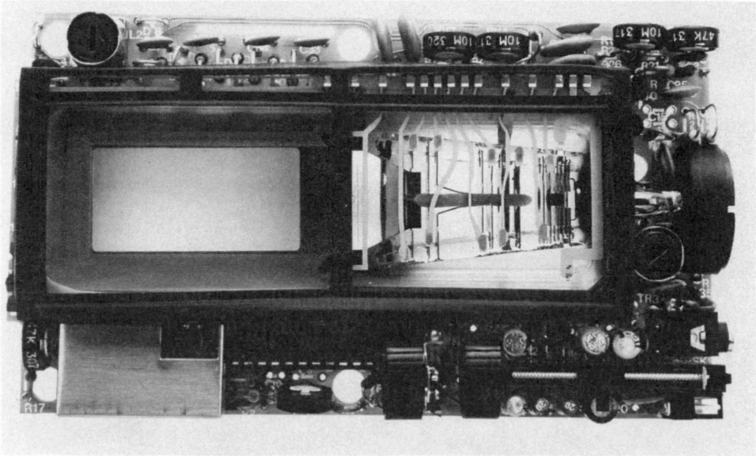

Figure 15.10
Flat CRT with a side-located gun mounted in a hand-held portable TV set.

steered through relatively small deflection angles, resulting in a CRT that is either bulky or has a very small screen. To reduce the volume and weight of a CRT, the electron beam voltage needs to be reduced considerably so that the beam can be steered through larger angles. However, the beam then has to be amplified so that it possesses enough energy to generate a useful amount of light at the display surface.

This amplification can be performed by an **electron multiplier**. The multiplier consists of a series of perforated, rectangular metal plates separated by insulators and placed directly in front of the screen phosphor layers. The plates are electrically charged such that there is an electric potential between each of them. The perforations form a channel so that when the electron beam strikes the rear of the multiplier it starts a cascade of electrons from one plate to the next, with each plate amplifying the number of electrons in the stream. The electron stream exits the multiplier and strikes the phosphor screen. Use of an electron multiplier in a conventional type CRT is illustrated in Figure 15.12(a) and a section through the multiplier is shown in Figure 15.12(b).

An electron multiplier has been incorporated into a recent development of a flat CRT. Because only a low-power electron beam is required to excite the electron multiplier, the beam can be *folded* through very large angles. The proposed CRT layout is illustrated in Figure 15.13. The beam is generated by the gun at the bottom of the tube and travels up to the top, where it is turned through 180° by an electronic reversing lens. It then travels back down the tube and is turned towards the required point on the multiplier by electrodes on the centre plate. These electrodes control the height of the spot on the screen. Deflectors near the electron gun control the horizontal position of the beam. A representation of what such a CRT will

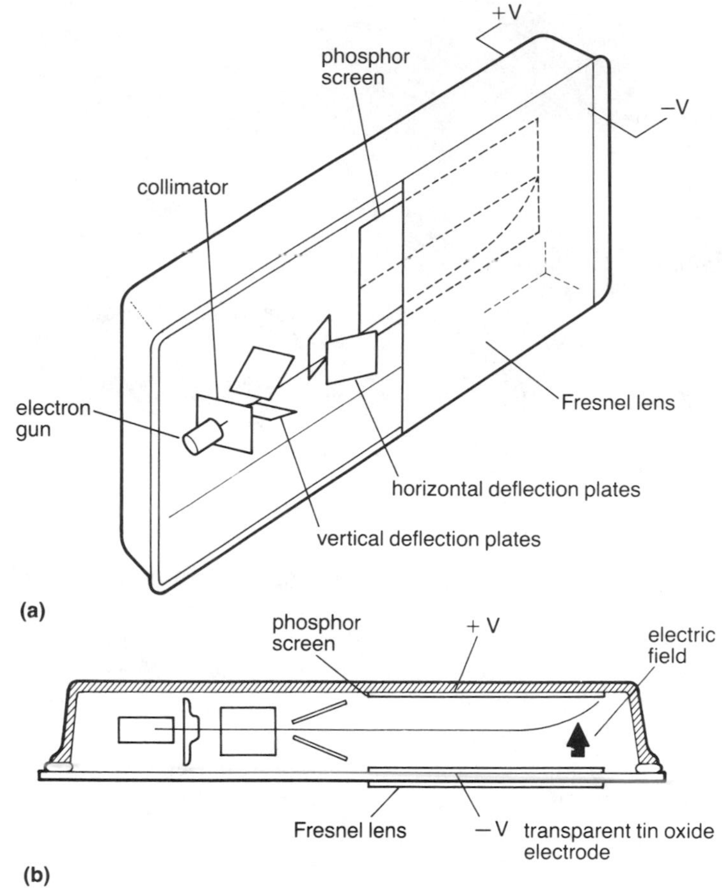

Figure 15.11
Principles of operation of a flat CRT.

look like is shown in Figure 15.14. CRTs of this type are still in the development stage but show promise of being able to provide bright monochrome and colour images on screen sizes up to 50 cm (20″) diagonal.

15.2.8 Storage CRTs

CRT devices that can retain or store the image that has been *written* on to the phosphor layer are known as **storage CRTs**. The construction of such a device is shown in Figure 15.15.

In a storage CRT, there is an anode coating on the faceplate that is kept at a potential of about 200 V and a set of **flood guns** that emit electrons on to the phosphor layer surface to keep it at a potential of about 0 V. The electron beam has a large negative potential of several thousand volts and

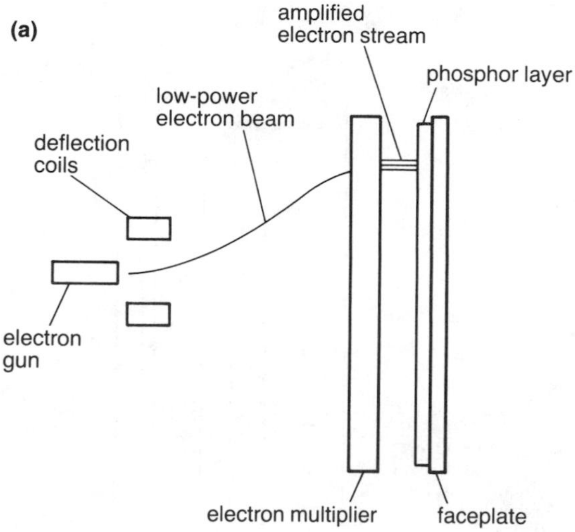

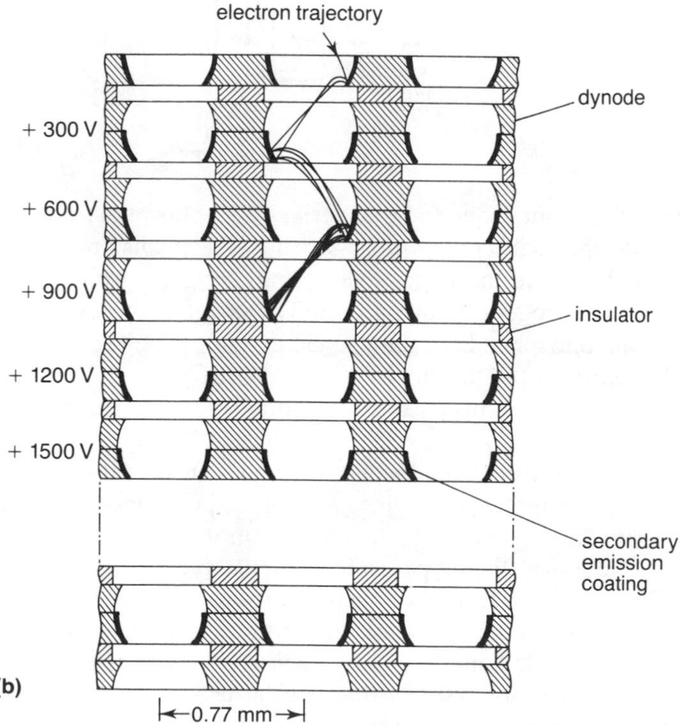

Figure 15.12
(a) Use of an electron multiplier in a conventional CRT.
(b) Section through an electron beam multiplier.

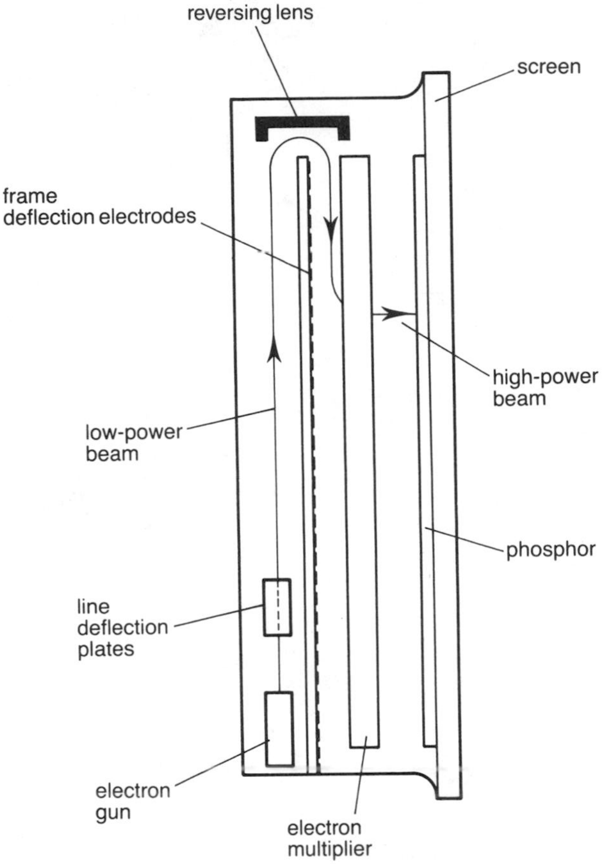

Figure 15.13
Layout of a flat CRT using an electron multiplier.

when the beam from the gun strikes the phosphor, electrons are emitted from the particles in the near vicinity. Electrons from the flood guns are attracted to the now positively charged area which in turn sets up a continuously regenerating pattern. The image is therefore written and stored on to the phosphor layer in a single action of the electron beam. The image is cleared from the display by increasing the potential of the faceplate anode voltage, which in turn causes the flood guns to flash the phosphors with electrons.

Variations on this method of storing images inside the tube have been developed using a very fine wire grid positioned on the inside of the phosphor layer, the image being regeneratively stored on its surface.

Tubes of this type were initially very popular for high-resolution display systems because of their ability to store the drawn image, thereby reducing the requirement for supporting electronics. However, the storage tube is a complex and expensive device and with the development of cheap electronic memory systems that can be used to store the image these tube types have decreased in popularity.

Figure 15.14
Representation of a flat CRT using an electron beam multiplier.

15.3 Video Monitors

To generate an image using a CRT a considerable amount of supporting electronics is required, which in turn require chassis structures and a casing to protect them in what is known as a **video monitor**. There are two different types of video monitor, each using two fundamentally different methods of constructing the graphics image on the CRT. These are the **vector refreshed monitor** and the **raster scanned monitor**. However, to confuse matters, there are now **mixed mode monitors** that combine the image display techniques of both of the other two.

15.3.1 Vector Refreshed Monitors

Images are drawn on to the display of a vector refreshed monitor by steering the beam along the vectors that make up the image. This is also known as **stroke drawn** or **calligraphic** image construction and the corresponding monitors are known as stroke or calligraphic monitors.

Consider the drawing of a triangle, as shown in Figure 15.16. The beam starts at the bottom left-hand corner, point P_1, is steered in a straight line, as seen on the display surface, up to point P_2, then point P_3 and finally back to point P_1, where it is switched off so that no further points are illuminated on the phosphor. The process is of course directly analogous to

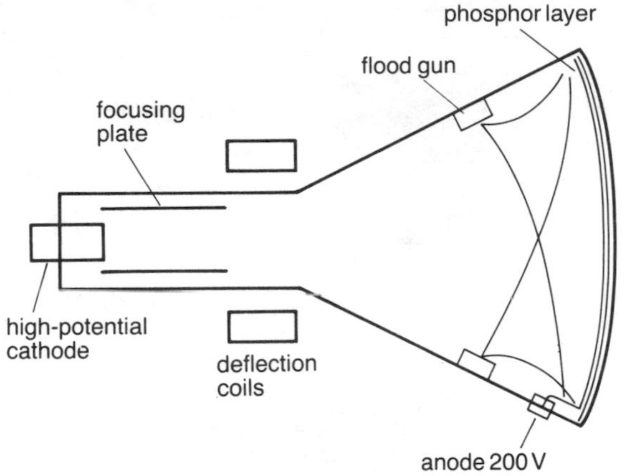

Figure 15.15
Construction of a storage CRT.

the *Polyline* function. The steering of the beam around the triangle is carried out by deflection of the beam using appropriate voltages on the CRT's deflection plates. In real systems, this is not as simple as it sounds. The beam, for example, cannot be turned through acute angles, such as those that occur at the corners of a triangle. Therefore, the beam must be switched off for a brief period, at each vertex, while it is repositioned for the next vector. Random geometric shapes and characters can be drawn in this way with each character being drawn using the vectors that define its shape.

Once a vector has been drawn on to the phosphor, it begins to fade, with the time taken for it to disappear depending on the persistence of the phosphor. Therefore, it is necessary for the image to be completely refreshed before this fading becomes apparent to the viewer. If the phosphor is allowed to fade too much between refresh cycles, then the display will be seen to **flicker**. Refresh rates for an image are usually about 30 times per second (30 Hz), and this requirement places an upper limit on the number and length of vectors that can be drawn without flicker occurring. These parameters vary from device to device depending on the quality and sophistication of the monitor.

Vector refreshed monitors invariabily use monochrome or beam penetration types of CRT, not the shadow mask tube. Increasing or decreasing the energy of the electron beam allows the brightness of the shape to be changed on monochrome CRTs, and the colour to be changed on the beam penetration tube.

For the electron beam to be steered accurately around the display surface, the monitor must contain electronics to control the position of the beam. Signals are required to steer the beam in the horizontal and the vertical directions as well as for controlling the energy of the beam for brightness or colour selection. The electronic logic that contains and interprets the data for the shapes to be drawn may be contained in the

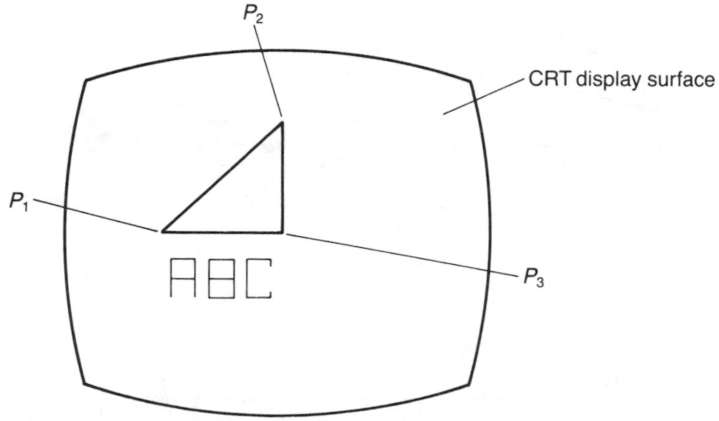

Figure 15.16 Vector-generated shape and characters.

monitor or it may be separate. These aspects of vector refreshed displays are discussed in more detail in Section 16.3.1 on vector refreshed generators.

The vector refreshed monitor is capable of displaying very high quality images of high resolution. It has found application in the computer-aided design/engineering (CAD/CAE) fields as well as in radar and command and control displays, where it is still common to find them in use.

15.3.2 Raster Scanned Monitors

A raster scanned monitor regularly and systematically scans the whole display surface from top to bottom and from left to right, modulating the electron beam according to the image that is to be displayed (see Figure 15.17). The horizontal lines are known as the raster lines and the spacing between them is equal. When the beam reaches the end of a horizontal scan, it returns to the (left-hand) start of the next line. This is known as the **horizontal retrace**. Similarly, when the beam reaches the bottom of the screen, it must return to the top. This is known as the **vertical retrace**. During both the horizontal and vertical retrace periods, the beam must be switched off so as not to leave a trace on the screen. A raster monitor always employs either a monochrome CRT or a shadow mask CRT, if a colour display is required.

The display of a shape, again a triangle, using a raster technique is shown in Figure 15.18. Figure 15.18(a) shows the shape to be displayed. Because the raster scan lines are equally spaced, only the elements of the shape that coincide with the raster lines are displayed. If the display can switch the beam at any point on the horizontal scan, the triangle appears as shown in Figure 15.18(b). Notice that the shape's outline only appears at the intersections of the shape and the raster lines, but the horizontal line

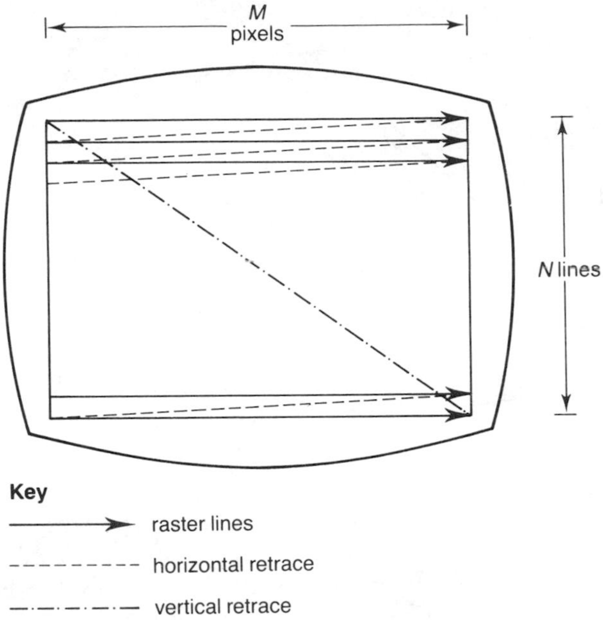

Figure 15.17
Raster scanning a CRT monitor.

appears as a continuous line. This produces a very uneven display, as it shows the shape divided into discrete elements in the vertical direction and continuous in the horizontal. To avoid this, the horizontal scan is also divided into discrete points in a similar way and with similar separation to the vertical raster. The shape is only displayed at the nearest discrete points (or pixels) in the horizontal direction and this results in a display as shown in Figure 15.18(c). Now the shape has the same form in both the horizontal and vertical directions, but it can be seen that the angled line now appears as a series of straight-line segments. These segments are the nearest approximations to the required line that can be drawn with the discrete resolution now available and are known as the **aliases** of the line. All graphical raster scan systems suffer from this aliasing phenomenon. Its effect can be reduced by increasing the horizontal and vertical resolution of the display system or by using special anti-aliasing hardware and software (see Section 13.7). Note that vector refreshed monitor displays do not suffer from aliasing problems since the vectors are drawn as continuous straight lines between the vertices of the shape.

Note here how easy it is to display the triangle as a *solid* shape, merely by switching the beam on at the left-hand edge and off at the right-hand edge. This feature of raster scanned systems is the one separating them from the vector refreshed systems; namely, the ability to display solid fill areas without heavily loading the display electronics.

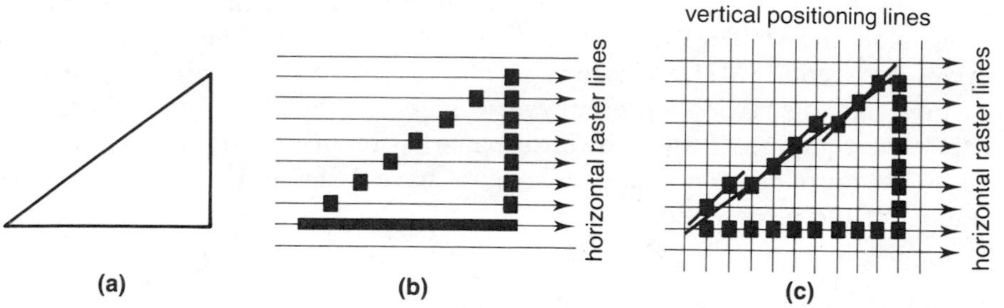

Figure 15.18
Display of a shape on a raster scanned device.

15.3.3 Raster Display Resolution

The number of raster lines that a monitor is capable of displaying depends on the speed at which the electron beam can be moved across the screen and on the quality of the electronics that control the beam. Similarly, the number of horizontal points that can be plotted depends on the speed at which the beam can be switched on and off. The more raster lines and horizontal points that can be drawn, the greater the total number of points that can be displayed, and hence the greater the resolution of the display.

Consider again Figure 15.17 where the display is shown to have N raster lines and M pixels on each line. If the time required to draw one pixel is p_t and the time for the horizontal retrace is h_t, then the total time required to display one raster line is:

$$l_t = Mp_t + h_t \tag{15.1}$$

and if the time for the vertical retrace is vt, then the total time to draw one complete image is:

$$\begin{aligned} t &= Nl_t + v_t \\ &= N(Mp_t + h_t) + v_t \end{aligned} \tag{15.2}$$

If there are to be r raster frames per second, then, rearranging the above for pt, the time to draw one pixel is:

$$pt = \frac{1}{MNr} - \frac{v_t}{MN} - \frac{h_t}{M} \tag{15.3}$$

This value, usually expressed as a frequency, represents a measure of the display resolution capability of the monitor and defines the performance of the monitor electronics required to achieve a particular display resolution. It is generally known as the monitor **bandwidth**.

Typical bandwidth figures for a monitor refreshing the whole image 60 times a second (60 Hz) are, for a display of 512 by 768 pixels, 28 million cycles per second (MHz) and for a display of 1024 by 1024 pixels, 88 MHz. Figures of this type represent very high performance and therefore expensive equipment. Methods of display that reduce these figures, yet still allow the display of acceptable images, have been devised and are the subject of the next section.

15.3.4 Raster Interlacing

A line refresh rate of at least 30 Hz is required to avoid the onset of significant display flicker. At any lower rate of refresh, the top of the screen begins to fade at the end of the vertical scan by an amount that is noticeable to the human eye/brain system, and a very disturbing display flicker rate is perceived. However, it is not necessary to refresh all of the lines on the screen on each scan as displayed shapes, more often than not, cover more than one raster line. Therefore, a display technique exists in which only the odd-numbered raster lines are refreshed on one top-to-bottom scan and the even-numbered raster lines on the next scan. Therefore, the whole image is refreshed every two display cycles. This technique is known as **raster interlacing** and means that the overall refresh rate of the display is now typically 25 to 30 Hz. For an interlaced display, the line rates and the beam switching rates are roughly halved in relation to a **non-interlaced** display with the consequence that the electronics supporting the CRT can be reduced in specification and therefore cost.

The perceivable flicker can also be reduced by using longer persistence phosphors; in fact, these are often used where the display is in use for long, continuous periods. Non-interlaced displays are still required where very high resolution data is to be displayed and where any display flicker would be a serious problem.

15.3.5 Broadcast Television Raster Displays

All modern television (TV) broadcasting systems use interlaced raster scanned display techniques. The picture frames are broadcast such that complete images are transmitted at 25 Hz in European countries and at 30 Hz in the USA with each interlace transmitted at 50 Hz and 60 Hz, respectively. The European PAL and SECAM image-encoding techniques use 625 raster scan lines while the American NTSC system uses 525 raster scan lines.

Details of TV image-encoding techniques are not important here, but the fact that different systems exist is of note because TV broadcast receivers are commonly used as displays for home or personal computers which must in turn be capable of generating the required signal standard. Video recorders also use these broadcast standards to record the video signal on to magnetic tape and this is important when recording or replaying display images.

15.3.6 CRT Monitor Adjustments and Controls

The controls found on a CRT monitor are usually an on/off switch, a brightness control for setting the overall radiation levels of the display and a contrast control for adjusting the relative brightness of the displayed image with respect to the background or non-illuminated areas of the display.

Colour delta CRT monitors also have controls for adjusting the convergence of the electron guns on to the shadow mask. These normally consist of a set of potentiometers that control the exact positioning of the beam from each electron gun at different positions on the display surface. As these controls are generally used only by a qualified engineer, they are usually placed inside the monitor enclosure itself.

A commercial raster scan, high-resolution colour monitor is illustrated, showing in particular the controls of the front panel, in Figure 15.19.

15.3.7 CRT Monitor Input Signals

Beam penetration CRT equipped monitors rarely exist in their own right; rather, they are usually combined with image creation electronics and then they are known as a **vector graphics generator**. The input requirements for these devices are described in Section 16.3.

Raster scan monitors require different input signals depending on their type. All raster monitors need to receive synchronization signals for the horizontal and vertical scans in phase with the display signals. Within the monitor, there is no synchronization between the horizontal and vertical scans and therefore the monitor requires timing pulses for both of these to independently trigger the internal timing circuits. These two timing pulses are usually combined into a single signal known as **composite sync** and fed to the monitor on a single coaxial line.

A monochrome monitor requires a display signal containing the beam control information; that is, it modulates the beam according to the image that is to be displayed, as well as turning the beam on and off during the horizontal and vertical retrace periods. Naturally, the display and composite sync signals themselves have to be synchronized. These two signals can be combined into a single signal and input into the monitor on a single coaxial line. This is known simply as a **composite signal**.

Figure 15.19
A commercial raster scan monitor.

For a colour raster monitor, three display signals are required, one each for red, green and blue. These are usually fed into the monitor as display signals on three separate coaxial lines, resulting in a total of four lines including the composite sync signal. In the same way that the display and composite sync signals can be combined on a monochrome monitor, the sync signal for a colour monitor can be combined with one of the colours, normally green. Some colour monitors also accept an **encoded** colour signal with all of the colour and sync signals coded on to a single line. The coding techniques used are those used on TV broadcast systems; namely, the PAL, SECAM and NTSC systems. As well as allowing the colour signal to be supplied on a single line, these techniques have the advantage that they can be fed into monochrome monitors for the display of the colour image in black and white. This type of combined signal is known as **composite video**.

When using a TV broadcast receiver as a computer terminal, the TV set normally requires the signal to be fed into it via the aerial socket. The signal expected by the TV set is one of the standard composite video signals PAL, SECAM or NTSC, modulated on to a TV broadcast signal. Sound may also be present in the signal. This type of connection is common on home computer systems. However, some personal and home computers generate a composite video signal, while some generate a full RGB plus sync signal.

15.3.8 Mixed Mode Monitors

Monitors have been developed that are capable of combining the vector refresh and raster scan display techniques into a single monitor, thus gaining some of the advantages of both systems. These developments have been prompted by the requirement to display solid coloured fill areas plus high-resolution, non-aliased lines and characters. The monitors are used for the display of computer-generated images (see Section 1.3.8) and in real-time aircraft instrumentation displays (see Section 1.3.10). Such monitors have to be capable of moving the electron beam around the screen at random, as well as carrying out a raster scan of the whole screen. Shadow mask CRTs are used and the raster scan is usually carried out after the vector drawn image has been displayed. This type of display is not currently used on general-purpose graphics systems because of the relatively high cost.

15.3.9 CRT Video Projectors

An extension of the use of the CRT for the display of video and graphics images is the CRT video projector. The basic principles of operation of the CRT projector are the same as conventional CRT video monitors except that CRTs of exceptionally high brightness are used to generate the images. The light generated by the electron beam exciting the phosphor is bright enough for it to be projected over a distance of several yards to produce a displayed image of up to 3 m (10′) in width. The CRTs used are usually about 13 cm (5″) in diameter and are fitted with optical lens systems for focusing the image on to the projector screen. Generally, for colour projectors, three monochrome projection CRTs are used, one for each of the additive primary colours. The three coloured light beams are then converged on to the projection screen where the light combines to produce the required colours. Although this process requires very careful adjustment of the projector and screen, it removes the requirement for the CRT to be equipped with a shadow mask which would, with such a large displayed image, be obvious and disturbing to the viewers.

CRT video projectors can be mounted on a stand, as with a conventional slide or movie projector, or they can be attached, inverted, to the ceiling. Usually, video projectors are used to display raster scan images, but they can also be used to display vector refresh images. The usual input signals of RGB plus sync can be used as well as PAL/SECAM/NTSC composite video signals.

Video projectors are now finding use in many aspects of video and graphics display. Broadcast TV and recorded video can be displayed and these systems are often found onboard commercial aircraft providing inflight entertainment. They are also used for displaying graphics where a large

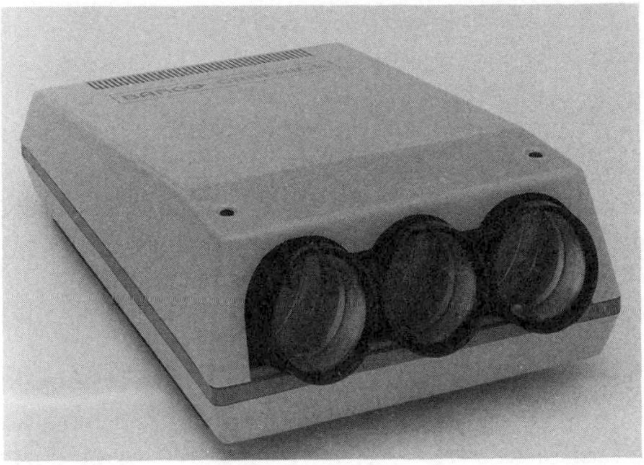

Figure 15.20
A triple CRT video projector.

viewing audience must be catered for. This includes education and training situations, business meetings, conferences and command and control environments. Very high quality systems are also employed displaying images for out-of-the-window views on flight simulators. A commercial triple CRT video projector is shown in Figure 15.20.

15.4 Flat Panel Displays

So far, only one display type has been discussed, that using the CRT. Although some developments have produced the so-called *flat* CRT, none can be described as a flat panel display. Considerable work has been carried out in trying to develop a *true* flat panel display but none, so far, has emerged as the future flat display screen. In the following sections, some of the technology is reviewed and the various techniques discussed. Those displays discussed in Section 15.4 are emitter type devices, while Section 15.5 introduces non-emitter flat panel displays.

15.4.1 Gas Discharge (Plasma) Panel

The gas discharge panel or plasma panel generates its light output from the interaction between an electric current and an ionized inert gas such as neon. In fact, the plasma panel can be regarded as a set of very small neon bulbs.

The gas is ionized by a high potential electric field set up between a cathode and an anode. Once the gas is ionized, an electric current flows

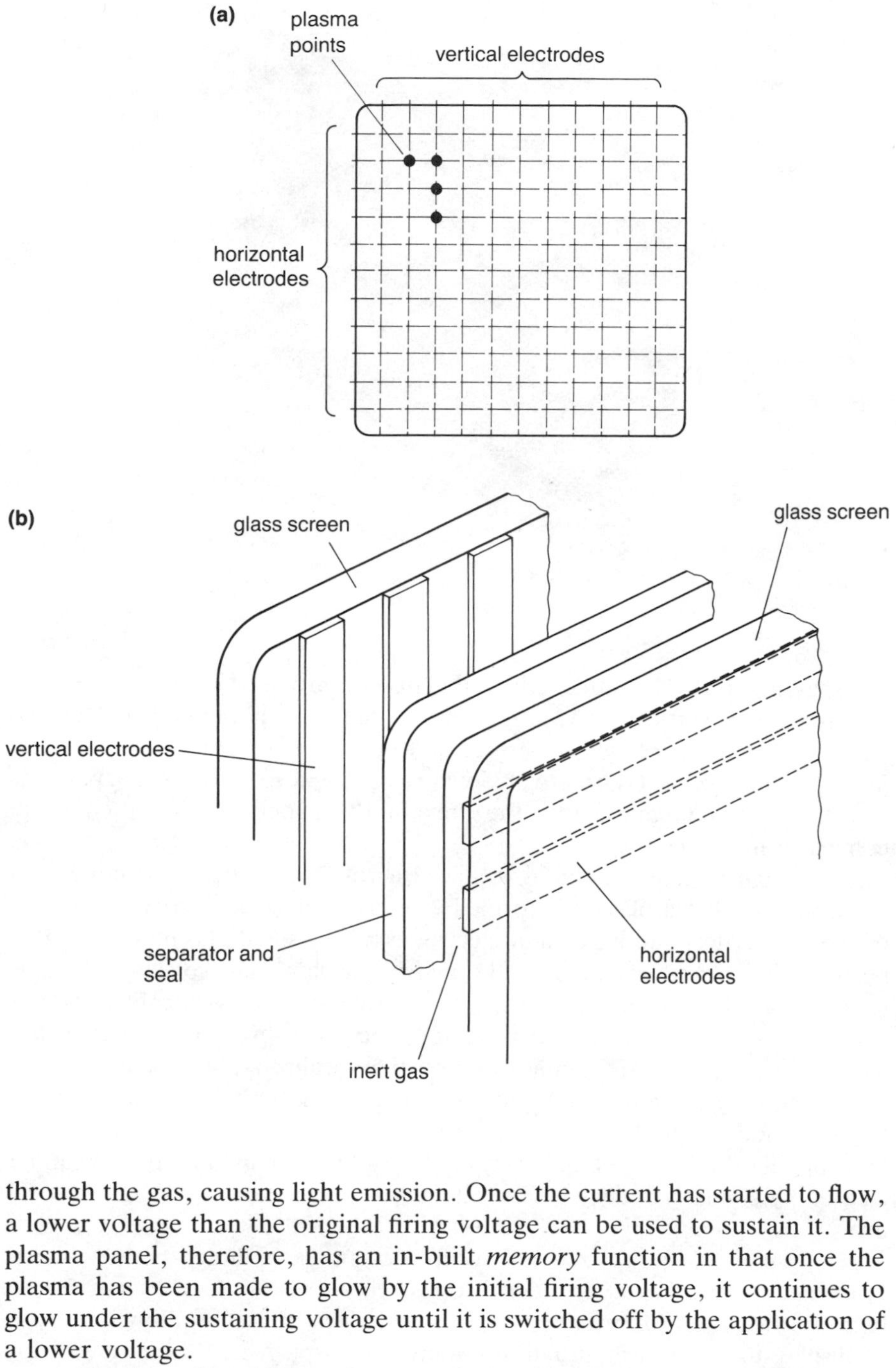

Figure 15.21
(a) Schematic of the display surface of a plasma panel.
(b) Schematic configuration of a typical plasma panel.

through the gas, causing light emission. Once the current has started to flow, a lower voltage than the original firing voltage can be used to sustain it. The plasma panel, therefore, has an in-built *memory* function in that once the plasma has been made to glow by the initial firing voltage, it continues to glow under the sustaining voltage until it is switched off by the application of a lower voltage.

The configuration of a typical plasma panel is shown in Figures 15.21(a) and (b). The device consists of two glass panels with thin

Figure 15.22
AC plasma panel display.

transparent electrodes attached to the inside surface. On one panel, the electrodes run vertically and on the other they run horizontally. The two panels are kept apart by a separator and seal, which form a cavity for the inert gas. The gas is at a relatively low pressure and so additional separators are placed at intervals across the area of the panels to stop them from collapsing in on themselves.

A high ionizing potential is placed across the vertical and horizontal electrodes so that a plasma is formed where the electrodes cross. Selection of specific vertical and horizontal electrodes allows small plasma glows to be positioned at random on the 2D matrix display. The plasma remains localized at the crossing points of the horizontal and vertical electrodes selected and with synchronized switching, vectors of pixels can be activated to generate the required image. Once the localized plasmas have been produced, they are retained by holding the potential difference across all of the electrodes at the lower sustaining voltage. The whole display is cleared by dropping this voltage below the sustaining level; individual points can be cleared by similarly reducing the voltage on specific horizontal and vertical lines.

Displays with up to 1024 electrodes in each direction have been fabricated. These have very fast response times as well as flicker-free and high-contrast ratio (up to 30:1) displays. The lack of flicker allows this type of display to be used in situations where the display has to be viewed for long periods of time, such as in computer-based training systems. The fact that the whole display can be transparent means that other types of display can be viewed through them. For example, maps can be placed behind the panel and the plasma display used to annotate new or dynamic information on top. The displays are also very rugged and compact with a complete display system being no more than 12.5 to 15 cm (5 or 6″) deep. Their main disadvantage is the lack of colour display capability, the image being pure monochrome. A photograph of an AC type plasma panel is shown in Figure 15.22.

15.4.2 Electroluminescent Displays

An electroluminescent display uses the property that a phosphor will emit photons when placed in an electric field. It consists of a sandwich of a set of horizontal electrodes, an insulating layer, a layer of phosphor, a second insulating layer and a set of vertical electrodes. One set of electrodes and its neighbouring insulating layer must be transparent so the image can be viewed through them. The sandwich is completed by a glass face panel. Points in the horizontal and vertical dimensions are activated in the same manner as with the plasma panel. Electroluminescent displays can be of AC, as described above, or DC types, the latter being a newer technology that is beginning to show promise.

The electroluminescent display is very compact, rugged and is not subject to catastrophic failure, and for some time has shown promise as a serious competitor to the CRT. Research is currently under way to develop colour electroluminescent displays using thin film construction techniques. However, current examples of the display show only medium levels of brightness and low contrast because the phosphor layer has relatively high reflectivity. A small portable battery-powered computer equipped with an electroluminescent monochrome (orange) display panel is shown in Figure 15.23.

15.4.3 Cathodoluminescent Displays

Cathodoluminescent displays use the same basic properties as the CRT to generate photons of light; that is, they use electrons generated by a heated cathode to bombard a surface coated with phosphor particles. In a CRT, the cathode is a single source that is steered around the phosphor-coated screen while, for cathodoluminescent displays, the cathode is distributed over the area of the display screen. The device consists of a set of cathode array elements separated from the phosphor-coated anode elements by a wire mesh. Switching of the anode and cathode selection lines allows the image to be formed with the result being viewed through the transparent cathode grid.

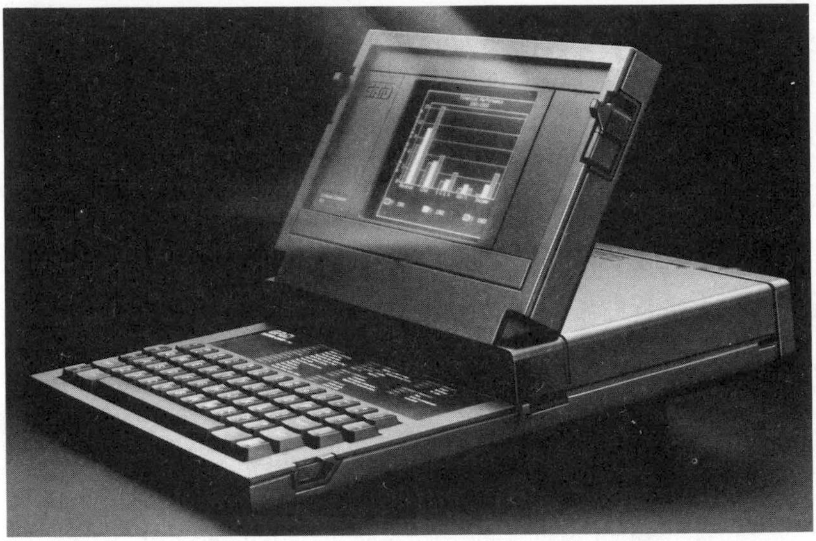

Figure 15.23
Portable computer equipped with an electroluminescent graphical display panel.

Cathodoluminescent displays have several advantages including their small compact structure and low operating voltages. Uses have been restricted to character type displays, but recent work has seen the development of matrix element displays with colour capability.

15.4.4 Light-Emitting Diode Displays

A light-emitting diode (LED) is constructed from a P–N semiconductor junction and will emit light, of a colour that depends on the type of semiconductor material used, when a current of the correct polarity is passed through it. Low voltages, in the order of 6 V, are required to operate the diodes. LED displays have been used in calculators and similar display situations for many years where the diodes, as point light sources, have been arranged to form the segments of character shapes. For the construction of general-purpose graphics or alphanumeric displays, they are arranged as large arrays of dots, and complex circuitry is required to drive the individual LEDs. This circuitry must be able to select and maintain any number of LED junctions at a time.

LEDs are capable of being switched at very high rates and have response times of less than one microsecond, allowing update rates of up to 250 Hz for a large matrix display. They have average life expectancies of over 100 000 hours and the advantage that, when arranged in large arrays, the loss of individual LEDs has a negligible effect on the performance of the whole display. In fact, up to 20% of the LEDs in an array can be lost before the image content becomes seriously degraded. High brightness levels can be generated, making the displays readable in high ambient lighting conditions. This high light output does, however, generate relatively large amounts of heat, which must be removed from the display by large heat sinks attached to the rear of the display. The displays also have high viewing angles, of up to 85° on either side.

Each LED junction emits light of a single colour and for multi-coloured displays LEDs constructed of different semiconductor material are placed adjacent on the display. To date, displays of two LED colour types, red and green, have been constructed, but research continues into the development of an efficient blue LED.

Plate 26 shows a LED array display that has been developed for use as an aircraft flight instrument display. The display is made up of 2.54 cm (1″) square blocks each containing 4096 LEDs and is about 3.8 cm (1.5″) deep. Because of its modularity, displays of various sizes can be constructed using the square modules and displays of up to 1.2 m (48″) square are planned.

15.5 Non-Emitter Displays

Non-emitter displays are display types that do not themselves generate light energy but rely on light from an external source that they modulate in some way. To do this, they change their physical properties and so alter the amount of light that they absorb. This can then be used to modulate either reflected light, where the light source is in front of the display, or transmitted light, where the light source is behind the display surface. These effects can result from absorption, transmission, scattering or polarization of the light or a combination of these properties. The light source can be ambient, such as sun light or artificial background light, or it can be built into the display itself.

Of the various types of non-emitter displays available, the **liquid crystal display (LCD)** is by far the most common. It is simple, compact and cheap, and has many years of development behind it. Other non-emitter displays are available, although they are rarely encountered. These include **electrochromic**, **electrophoretic** and **ferroelectric displays**.

15.5.1 Liquid Crystal Displays

Liquid crystal displays use the property that certain common organic compounds, within specific temperature limits, adopt a state where their crystal structure allows them to flow like a liquid. While in this state, the orientation of the crystals can be controlled by an applied electric field. With the crystals in any parallel orientation, the compounds are relatively transparent, but if the crystals are allowed to adopt any other form of non-parallel lattice structure, the light is scattered and the material becomes opaque.

A typical liquid crystal display consists of a very thin layer of liquid crystal compound sandwiched between two transparent insulating layers. The insulating layers are chemically treated to determine the initial orientation of the crystals; that is, whether the crystals, without the application of an electric field, lie perpendicular or horizontal to the surface of the insulating layers. In a typical display, the treated surfaces are arranged so that the crystals at one surface lie at right-angles to the crystals at the second surface. The crystals in between adopt a spiral or **twisted lattice**, as their orientation changes through the 90° rotation imposed by the insulating layers. On either side of this sandwich are polarizing layers which orientate the light passing through them to the same polarization as their neighbouring insulating layers. Light entering the device is then oriented in the same direction as the surface crystals and as it passes through the liquid crystal layer is twisted around by its interaction with the spiral lattice. By the time it reaches the surface in contact with the second insulating layer, its orientation is the same as the second layer of polarizing material. Now if the twisted lattice of the crystal layer is disturbed by an electric field, the light is no longer in the correct orientation to pass through the polarizing material and the sandwich becomes opaque, producing a dark image on a light, usually grey, background. Other arrangements of polarizers and crystal lattice can be used to obtain light on dark or dark on light for either transmissive or reflective displays.

The construction of such a device is illustrated in Figure 15.24 where the layers can be clearly seen. The two insulating layers have transparent electrodes attached, one set horizontal and one vertical. The application of an electric potential on electrodes in each direction generates an electric field at their intersections and the twist of the crystal lattice is broken between the two. The light leaving the crystal layer is then incorrectly aligned to pass through the upper polarizing layer. Instead of the light source being at the bottom of the sandwich, it is common to use a reflecting layer at the bottom and the light source at the top of the sandwich. With this arrangement, the light travels through the sandwich twice, thereby increasing the overall absorption and the maximum display contrast. The electrode array can be replaced by character segment arrays, as in the case of hand-held calculator displays.

Relatively low voltages, of about 6 V, are used to operate LCD displays and the whole display structure can be compact and rugged. The switching time of liquid crystals has often been criticized for being too slow, resulting in smeared images, but recent developments have produced compounds with image response times in the 100 ms range. Various optical

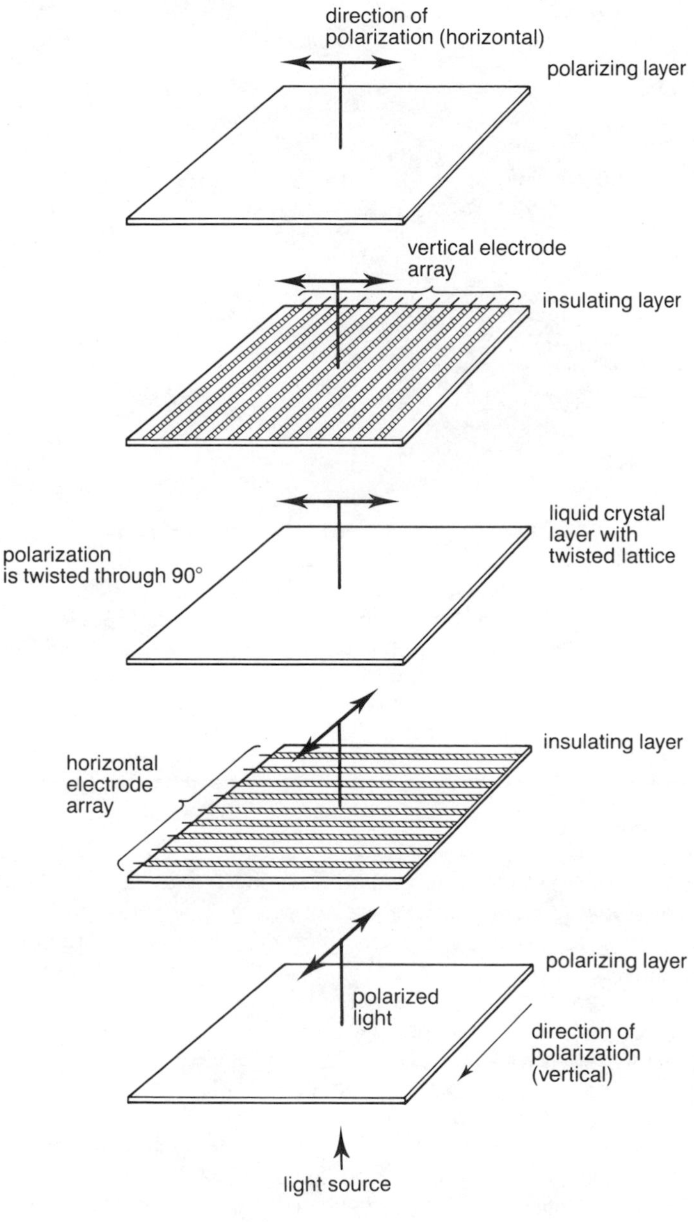

Figure 15.24
Construction of a typical LCD panel display.

dyes have also led to the development of coloured LCD displays, but a full colour matrix display has still not been commercially realized. Since liquid crystal compounds are temperature dependent, the behaviour of the displays themselves alters with the local temperature, often restricting the application of LCDs.

Figure 15.25
Portable computer with a large LCD dot matrix display.

Figure 15.25 shows a portable battery-powered personal computer which uses an LCD matrix display. The matrix display consists of 200 rows and 640 columns.

Summary

The CRT monitor is still the best general-purpose display device available and it will probably remain so for some considerable time to come. Its relatively low cost and ability to display high-resolution monochrome and full colour images remains unchallenged by any of the other technologies. There is, however, great commercial pressure on the display manufacturers to produce economically and technically viable flat screen displays for use with broadcast TV receivers. This may result in the flat CRT being the best solution, but their high-drive voltage requirements and relatively high weight are significant disadvantages.

Some of the currently available small flat devices do show promise for the future, but at the moment promise is all that it is. The CRT monitor manufacturers continue to squeeze yet higher performance out of their products, but the CRT appears to be coming close to the limit of its development. The near future will probably see the various display technologies being put to specialized uses, each suited to its individual capabilities yet in combination with each other. For example, LCDs being used for character display and interaction in conjunction with a CRT for graphics display.

Exercises

15.1 Which display devices would you use for the following applications:

(a) a desk-top publishing system (for writing books, articles, etc.);

(b) a CAD system;

(c) a moving map display for an automobile;

(d) an artist's worksation;

(e) a computerized cartography system.

Give reasons for your choice.

15.2 Would you use a vector refresh or raster display system as part of a command and control system of a nuclear power station? Explain your answer.

15.3 Describe three ways of reducing display flicker.

CHAPTER 16

GRAPHICS IMAGE GENERATORS

Chapter 15 considered the hardware that displays and supports the image itself. However, none of this hardware is capable of creating the image by itself. A **graphics generator** is required for this task. This is the subject of this chapter.

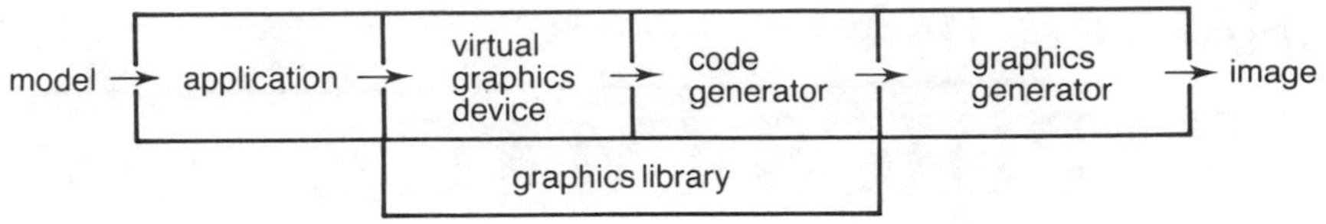

Figure 16.1
The graphics pipeline for a single graphics device.

16.1 Introduction

Part One of this book introduced and discussed in great detail the graphics processing pipeline, along which all graphical output must travel in order to be displayed (see Figure 16.1). The start of the pipeline is the model or application, followed by the graphics library, which continues the process in terms of the virtual graphics device (VGD) and the code generator. It is this latter process that produces the functional commands required by any given graphics device, and in particular its graphics generator.

Usually, the application and graphics library reside in the system's CPU, while the graphics generator and its image display system are in a separate unit known as a **graphics display system** or combined with interactive input devices such as keyboards or data tablets to form a **graphics display terminal** or simply **display terminal**. A typical graphics terminal is shown in Figure 16.2. The graphics generator may also be implemented in the CPU, sharing its computational power and resources with the application and graphics library.

In specialized systems that have a very powerful graphics generation capability, the graphics generator and display represent a sizeable system in their own right. Such systems are typically required for real-time image generation in, for example, the computer-generated image systems, as described in Section 1.3.8. As graphics generation and display systems are now being used in many diverse applications and situations, it is difficult to describe such systems in general terms. However, their logical and functional operations are the same, which is the subject of the rest of this chapter.

16.2 Graphics Image Generation

The previous section discussed how the graphics generators and display systems continue and complete the image pipeline through to the final image. This pipeline, because of the physical constraints of the display system, will have a known destination in terms of the type of display that is to be created. In Chapter 15, it was seen that there are two basic techniques

Figure 16.2
A typical graphics terminal.

for displaying the final image – namely, those of vector- and pixel-based systems. Of the latter systems, the most common are raster display systems using monochrome or shadow mask CRT displays.

16.2.1 Graphics Generator Model

The basic functions required of both display types are, however, the same and are illustrated in Figure 16.3. In order of execution they are:

(1) *Command interpretation* The graphics generator function commands are accepted from the CPU, decoded and executed (these are discussed further in the next section). Commands that actually affect the image in some way are applied to or entered into the image memory.

(2) *Image memory* The image memory stores the image in a form suitable for the image display system in use and from which the display system can refresh the image as required. There are three different types of image memory:

- *The display list*, which is used by vector refresh systems and, lately, some pixel-based systems.
- *The frame buffer*, which is required by pixel-based raster display systems.

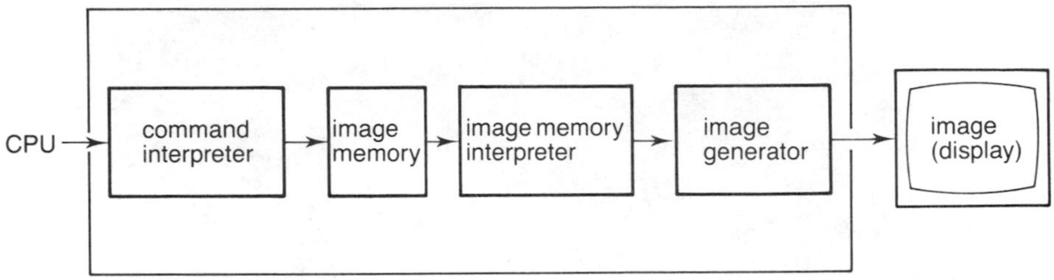

Figure 16.3
Functional model of a graphics generator.

- *The bitmap memory*, which is logically the same as a frame buffer but, by definition, only stores bilevel images.

Each of these image memories will be discussed in the sections covering the specific image-generation systems. It should be noted, however, that recent developments in raster displays have employed both a display list and a frame buffer in the same system; hence, two versions of the same image exist in the system at the same time (these are discussed in Section 16.4.13).

Certain display technologies, principally the storage tube CRT (see Section 15.2.8) and the plasma panel (see Section 15.4.1), have an inherent image storage capability in their own right, which may obviate the requirement for a specific image memory in the system.

(3) *Image generation* The image memory is scanned and the image extracted, decoded as required and sent to the display system. Where the display has no inherent storage capability or where the image fades over a relatively short period of time, this will have to be a repetitive process. At the end of each scan of the image memory, the cycle is repeated.

16.2.2 Graphics Generator Functions

The commands that can be obeyed by graphics image generators vary considerably from system to system. Some of the cheapest and simplest systems can only obey the most basic commands, while other systems are able to obey commands that are similar to the higher level logical graphical functions such as *Polyline* and *FillArea*. To describe all of the commands for all devices is not possible, and anyway it would repeat a lot of the work in Part One. It is more constructive here to consider the basic groups of commands that can be obeyed and the operations that they will instigate on the devices. These can then be related to the descriptions of Part One, if required.

16.2.3 Control and Configuration Functions

Control and configuration functions are used to exercise basic control and configure the device for use. For example, functions such as *initialise the image* and *redraw the image* are in this category. In addition, there may be general housekeeping functions that, for example, allow the display surface or the device coordinate space to be redefined, or reset the speed at which the device communicates with the CPU and so on.

16.2.4 Primitive Functions

Primitive functions are used for graphical output. The most basic being those that define a single pixel to be set to a particular value or vector to be drawn, such as the *WritePixel* (see Section 3.2) and *DisplayLine* functions (see Section 3.4). As all possible graphics shapes can be constructed from these two commands, they will always be the fundamental functions of any graphics generator.

Primitive functions to be obeyed by the graphics generator usually consist of at least two sets of data. The first is the function code, which informs the generator which primitive is to be drawn, and the second comprises the parameters that define the coordinate points, which depends on the geometry of the primitive. Most primitives can make use of a variable number of points for each function, so there is usually an additional data item (the number of coordinate points) that is sent with each function command.

Most real devices have many more primitive functions available, the versions of the GKS primitives polymarker, polyline, fill area, cell array and text, or their equivalents, being the most common. Some devices also have geometric functions such as circle, ellipse and general curves based on spline or Bezier (see Section 11.8) functions.

16.2.5 Attribute Functions

All devices have functions, some explicit and some implicit, that define the *appearance* or *style* of the primitive function images displayed on the device. For example, there may be functions for setting the colour and width of a polyline. Most devices use explicit global functions that define the *current* attribute value for a primitive or group of primitives. For example, it may be possible to issue a command to set the current global colour attribute of polylines to red. Thereafter, all polylines drawn will appear in red, until a further colour attribute for polylines is received by the generator.

There are many variations of an attribute setting. Some very simple devices allow only one current global value for each attribute. For example, if only one global colour can be set, all primitives appear in the same colour, until the attribute is reset. At the other extreme, there are systems that allow quite subtle primitive attribute settings, with colours, line types and widths, shading styles, text styles and so on, each of which is set individually very much along the lines of the GKS attribute model, as described in Chapter 6.

As with the primitive functions, the function code and parameters are required by the graphics generator. For example, when setting the polyline colour attribute, the relevant function code is required in addition to data to specify the colour itself.

16.2.6 Display Lists

Graphics generators, as described in Section 16.2.1, require a mechanism by which the image can be stored for display. One of these mechanisms is the display list, and as this is used extensively nowadays on both vector refresh and pixel-based raster displays, it will be useful to examine its features in more detail.

A display list stores all of the attribute and primitive functions required to reproduce a display image. The functions are stored in the list in a form that preserves their original structure in the CPU in terms of function code and required parameters. Functions may be added to or subtracted from the display list, thereby allowing modification of the displayed image with the addition or removal of primitives or modification to their style. Some graphics generators also allow the coordinate points within the stored primitive functions to be modified, to change the geometry of the displayed image. When the functions in the display list are next scanned and executed to produce the display image, the modified image appears. Functions that operate on the contents of the display list are known as **display list functions**.

A simple display list is analogous to a simple linear (unstructured and with no jump instructions) computer program. Each time it is scanned, the first function is executed and the resulting image elements displayed. Then the second function is similarly executed and so on until the list is exhausted. This process is then repeated to refresh the displayed image with modifications to the list occurring between scans.

Most display lists allow some form of structuring, thereby greatly enhancing the power and intelligence of the device. Most commonly, the primitive and attribute functions can be grouped into segments, these being logically the same as those described in Chapter 7. The analogy to a simple computer program can now be extended to that of a structured program with functions or procedures. Complex shapes constructed from any of the available primitives can be created and formed into segments within the display list. As a segment, they can then be used as if they were a new primitive.

Such lists are known as **segmented display lists** or **structured display lists**. The segments, like primitives, can themselves have attributes, in that they may be made visible or invisible and have priorities assigned to them that specify the order in which they are drawn on to the display. Individual segments may also undergo transformation, as described in Section 7.2, in relative size (independently in x and y), rotation and translation to anywhere on, or for that matter off, the display surface. Each segment has a unique name and a set of display list functions that can be extended to include functions to manipulate the segments themselves. These include functions to create a segment, delete it, rename it and copy it.

Segments within a display list may also refer to each other, in that one segment may use or *call* another. In this case, it is said that the segment list is a **hierarchical display list**. When a segment calls another segment, it applies a transformation before the act of displaying, but the original segment is not affected in any way. A segment may call another segment any number of times and many different segments can call the same segment, thus allowing the use of the same group of primitives many times without having to duplicate their specification. A called segment may also call other segments, thus allowing complex structured images to be built up. Recursion, where a segment either directly or indirectly calls itself, is not possible. These are the same ideas as used in the PHIGS system described in Chapter 10.

There are several advantages in using such structured display lists compared to simple linear lists. The first and most obvious is that it saves space and allows more economic use of the display list. A set of primitive and attribute functions that are to be used many times need only be stored once in the display list. Each time they appear on the display, they can simply be referred to as a single unit. For example, the display of a closed triangle requires a total of ten entries into the display list (ignoring for now any references to attributes), these being the function code, the number of coordinate points (4) and the four pairs of coordinates themselves. To form this into a segment, three more entries are required, those of the segment name, the jump to the next segment and the segments total length, making 13 in all. To call this segment, a total of six entries is required, these being the name of the segment, the x and y coordinates of its new position, its x and y scaling, and its rotation (again ignoring segment attributes). Therefore, each time that (same) triangle is to be displayed, three display list entries are saved. The overhead in creating a segment is constant in that the same number of entries is required to call a simple segment as would be required for a more complex one. In addition, modifications to the displayed image can be carried out much quicker, with less computation in and communication with the CPU.

In GKS, an alternative mechanism to hierarchical structuring is employed, known as *InsertSegment*, and this is fully described in Section 7.5.3. In terms of the display list, this function requires a copy of the segment to be inserted into the display list where the call would have been made after transformation. Once this process has been completed, the display list is executed as an unstructured display list, but at the expense of inefficient use of the display list.

16.2.7 Windows and Viewports

One of the most important concepts discussed in this book is that of windows and viewports. The ideas behind these are fundamental to the geometry of graphics and are used extensively within the functionality of GKS. Section 2.2 introduced the concepts and the reader is referred to that section for full details. However, the concepts of windows and viewports is used here to continue the discussion on graphics generators. Unfortunately, the term window is now used for several slightly different, albeit related, display concepts and therefore a reiteration of some of the basics will be useful before continuing. It should be emphasized, however, that the discussion here is a generalization on the window and viewport relationships used by GKS.

A window can be defined as a (normally) rectangular area that specifies the part of the scene to be displayed. Here, *scene* is used to mean any information, be it graphical or textual, that is to be displayed. In graphical terms, the windows could be defined by means of the coordinates of their lower right-hand and upper left-hand corners. However, a window may also be a page of text or graphics or possibly the dynamic output from a computer process or program, whatever its form. An example set of windows, containing several different types of image, is shown in Figure 16.14.

However, a window only defines *what* is to be displayed and not where. Each window therefore requires a corresponding viewport, which defines the space into which it is to be displayed. Referring again to Figure 16.14, each window appears in a clearly defined area – a viewport – on the display. Some windows appear whole, while some are obscured by other windows. A viewport obscures another viewport when it has a higher priority than the obscured viewport. Viewports may be moved around the display area without affecting their information content, except when they are moved relative to an obscuring viewport.

Describing a viewport as being *displayed* is a generalization. Viewports may also be virtual and simply logically contain an area of the image. This is so in the case of the GKS viewport. Another window is required to define the subarea of the viewport that is to be displayed as a real image. In GKS, this is the workstation window that is displayed in the workstation viewport (see Section 4.5). There is no reason why the chain of window/viewport pairs could not go on *ad infinitum*.

Windows and viewports do not, conceptually, have to be rectangular – any shape would do. However, usually the sides of the windows and viewports are defined to be parallel to the horizontal and vertical axes of the coordinate system in use, although rotated viewports may be encountered. For example, this restriction is not adhered to in Sun NeWS.

The movement of a window about the scene gives the effect of moving the observer's view of the picture. Making the window smaller, but keeping the viewport the same size, produces the effect of **zooming in** on the picture, while making the window larger gives the effect of **zooming out** (see Exercise 4.9). Moving the window laterally produces the effect known as **panning**, and moving it vertically the effect known as **scrolling**.

16.2.8 Device Coordinates and Units

When a picture is being drawn on to a display device, it is necessary to instruct the device in measures or coordinate units that it understands. The coordinates may be in units employed in everyday life, such as inches or metres, or they may be in non-dimensional units, such as a count of the number of pixels from a known origin or datum. The distance between pixels may vary from device to device and may not be the same in the horizontal and vertical axes. Another way of looking at this is to say that the display system does not have square pixels. Whichever type of unit is used, they are said to be **device units** and they are specified in device coordinates.

16.3 Vector Refresh Graphics Display Systems

Having discussed the basic instructions and functions that can be used to control a graphics generator, the requirements of real display systems can now be examined. The first of such systems is the vector refresh graphics display system.

16.3.1 Vector Refresh Generators

A vector refreshed display creates its image by continuously redrawing the contents of a display list on to the CRT display surface at a high repetition rate. Rates as high as 30 Hz are required to avoid the onset of display

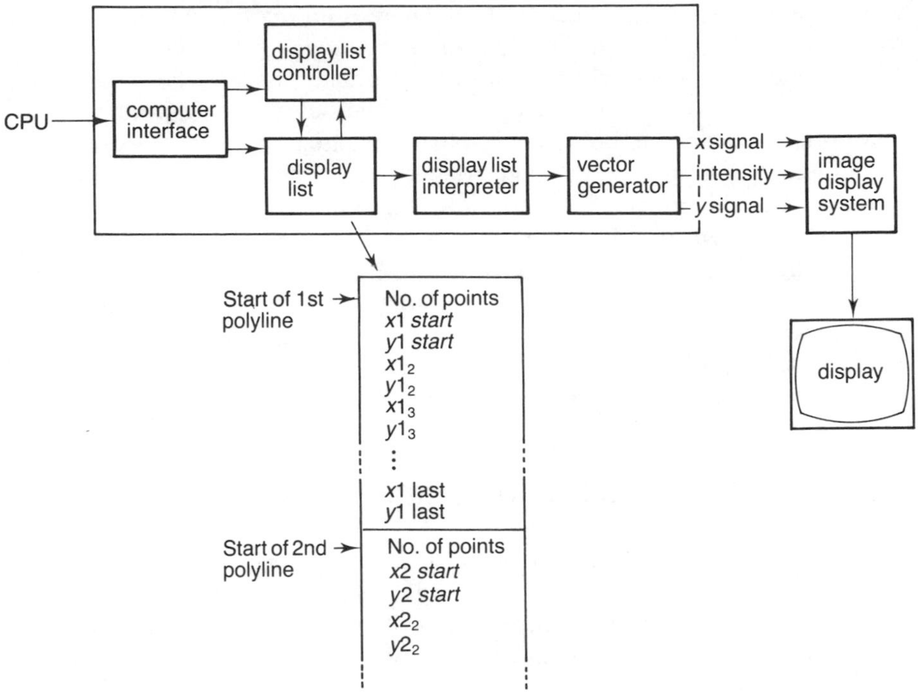

Figure 16.4
Functional diagram of a vector refreshed graphics display with a simple display list.

flicker, making the task of a vector generator very demanding. It must be able to:

- Move the electron beam between any two points on the display screen.
- Switch the beam on and off at the ends of the vector strokes.
- Maintain constant brightness along the length of the vector and independent of the length of the vector.

and if it is a beam penetration colour display:

- Modulate the beam power to generate the required colour.

Figure 16.4 represents the functional layout of a vector generator: it does not necessarily represent the modular layout. The functional flow is from left to right. Instructions received from the CPU are interpreted by the **display list controller** and entered into the display list. The contents of the display list are processed by a **display list interpreter**, which translates and scales the data to values that can be passed on to the **vector generator**. The vector generator then derives, from these values, the beam position signals that will create the visual image, and switch the beam on and off between

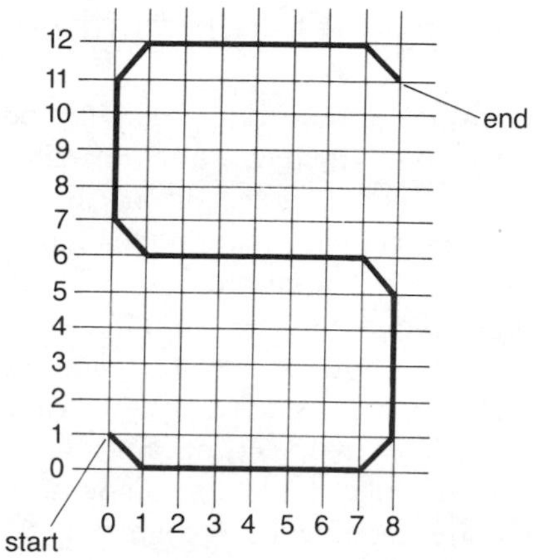

Figure 16.5
A stroke character font shape.

individual vectors. When the display list interpreter has processed all of the data in the display list, it returns to the beginning of the list and repeats the process.

16.3.2 Vector Refresh Primitives

The vector generator interprets the primitive commands in the display list to construct the display image and is optimized to generate polyline-type primitives. The value range in which the primitive coordinates are held in the display list is the device coordinate range of the device.

Vector generators are not at all efficient at generating display primitives requiring solid area fills. For this type of primitive, the generator has to complete the infill by drawing a set of closely spaced parallel lines (see Section 4.7), which rapidly consume the display's allotted refresh period. This means that solid area fill style is not practical and is best simulated using hatch patterns.

16.3.3 Vector Refresh Text Primitives

In the case of text, the shape or font of each character is stored in the memory of the display list interpreter, which draws the characters as required by the display list. These fonts consist of a list of coordinates that specify the shape of the character to be drawn. An example is shown in Figure 16.5, where a font shape for the letter 'S' is illustrated as consisting of a polyline of 12 points. The display list processor positions the character at the start coordinates and draws the character shape around the relative points of the font shape. These are the so-called stroke drawn characters.

16.3.4 Vector Refresh Colour Attribute

If the vector graphics display system has a beam penetration colour CRT, then references to the colour attribute function can be processed by the vector generator from instructions in the display list. When the display list interpreter encounters this function, it commands the vector generator to set the beam power to generate the required colour.

It is possible to include intelligence to improve the quality of the final image in the display list interpreter and vector generator. For example, one feature of vector refresh graphics systems is that *bright spots* are formed at points in the image where lines intersect, because the phosphor at that point has had a double dose of the electron beam. Some of the more sophisticated vector refresh systems are capable of recognizing this and modulate the beam to reduce the illumination at that point.

An image generated on what is probably one of the most powerful and sophisticated vector generators is shown in Plate 1. The image shown is that of a line drawing of an F-15 fighter aircraft. The graphics system is capable of 3D real-time animation. This requires a display list processor and vector generator of exceptionally high speed.

16.3.5 Vector Refresh Windows and Viewports

Vector graphics windowing is achieved by setting a window on to the display list. Manipulating the parameters of this window allows the normal zoom, pan and scroll functions to be performed. Viewports are declared by specifying the area of the CRT display surface on to which the output from the vector generator is to be drawn. Multiple viewports are constructed by dynamically changing the viewport specification as the interpreter progresses down the list.

16.4 Raster Graphics Display Systems

16.4.1 Raster Generators

A raster graphics display system constructs the image on the display surface as a series of horizontal lines, each line being made up of an equal number of pixels which are stored in a frame buffer. The operation of a raster scan display is described, in detail, in Section 15.3. The raster generator must supply the signals to the display system to generate this image type and must

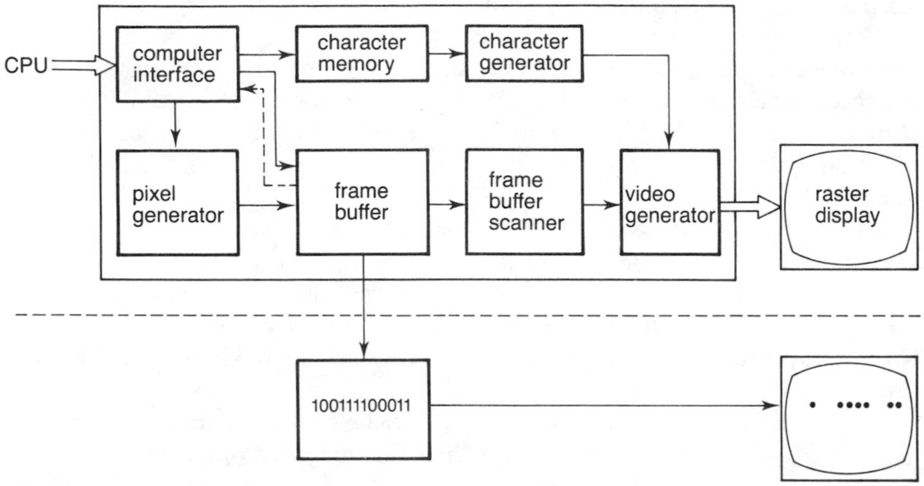

Figure 16.6
Functional diagram of a raster graphics display terminal.

therefore be capable of:

- Interpreting the commands from the main processor to construct the pixel image in the frame buffer.
- Scan the frame buffer in a left-to-right, top-to-bottom manner and interpret its contents.
- Generate the left-to-right, top-to-bottom beam control signals, modulate the beam energy using data from the frame buffer and switch the beam off during the horizontal and vertical blanking periods.

and if it is a colour system:

- Generate the three separate control signals for the three CRT electron beam guns.

16.4.2 Raster Frame Buffer Memory

The key element of a raster generator is the frame buffer and its position can be seen in the functional diagram in Figure 16.6. The frame buffer stores the image in a pixel-by-pixel manner and is arranged so that it represents the 2D display surface with the pixel locations in rows and columns. Each location in the frame buffer represents a single pixel of the image in terms of its intensity or colour at that point.

Instructions from the CPU are interpreted by the **pixel generator**. For example, when the command to draw a straight line between two points is received, the pixel generator calculates the coordinates of the pixels that lie on, or are the nearest to, the required line and set the frame buffer locations of those pixels to the prescribed value. This is the same as the function *LineToPixels* described in Section 3.6. The pixel generator only writes into the frame buffer when instructed to do so, either directly or implicitly by the CPU.

Frame buffers are usually sized, in the horizontal and vertical directions, as a power of 2, in particular 256 by 256 (2^8), 512 by 512 (2^9) or 1024 by 1024 (2^{10}) pixels. Sizes that take into consideration the aspect ratio of the screen – for example, 768 by 512 or 1536 by 1024 – are also common. In this way, the dimensions of the frame buffer are the device coordinates of the raster scan display system.

The frame buffer is scanned by the **frame buffer scanner** in a left-to-right, top-to-bottom sequence. (Note that this may not reflect the physical organization of the random access memory (RAM).) It modulates the CRT beam signal in proportion to the values in the frame buffer. These signals are fed to the **video generator**, which produces the video signal for the display system. The scanner and video generator run autonomously from the rest of the generator, because they are required to service the requirements of the raster display system.

16.4.3 Organization of the Frame Buffer Memory

The previous section has described how the frame buffer memory is scanned to generate the control signals for the raster scan image generation. Each frame buffer location (pixel) contains a value that controls the strength of the electron beam current at the corresponding point in the image. The higher the value, the *brighter* the illumination on the display. The number of different brightness levels that each pixel can represent is dictated by the range of values that can be stored in each frame buffer location and, in particular, the number of binary bits allocated to each location.

The simplest case is that when each pixel location consists of just one binary bit, which can represent the value 0 or 1; that is, the pixel can only have two values – off or on, black or white – and the display can only generate pure monochrome images. This configuration is a special case known as a **bitmap display** and is described more fully in Section 16.4.17. If each pixel location consists of two bits, then a total of four different brightness or grey levels can be generated; if three bits, eight grey levels, and so on. The frame buffer, therefore, can be looked upon as consisting of a number of **pixel planes**, each one bit deep. A frame buffer where each pixel location consists of three bits will have three memory planes. The greater the number of pixel planes in the frame buffer, the greater the number of grey levels and the more subtle the image.

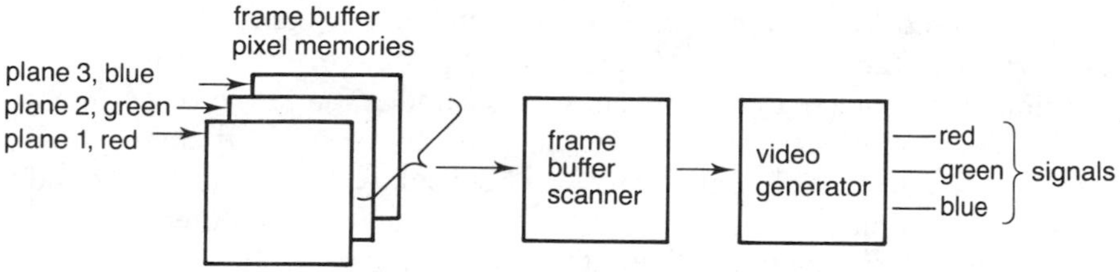

pixel memory plane			value	colour
1 (red)	2 (green)	3 (blue)		
0	0	0	0	black
0	0	1	1	blue
0	1	0	2	green
0	1	1	3	cyan
1	0	0	4	red
1	0	1	5	magenta
1	1	0	6	yellow
1	1	1	7	white

Figure 16.7
Multiple pixel memory planes for colour representation.

16.4.4 Colour Raster Display Generation

To be able to generate and display colour raster graphics images, two or more frame buffer planes are required. If three frame buffer planes are used, then each plane can store the pure monochrome value of one of the primary colours. Frame buffer plane 1 can hold the red values, plane 2 the green and plane 3 the blue. The range of colours that such a system can generate is shown in Figure 16.7. This arrangement is a very simple but inflexible method of storing and generating a colour image.

A system for producing more colours is obtained by using a two-stage colour generation system utilizing a **colour lookup table**, as shown in Figure 16.8. Now, instead of the value from the frame buffer generating the colour directly, it is used to point to a colour value in the lookup table. Each position in the colour lookup table contains three values, one for each of the primary colours. The value for each primary colour can have a much greater range than the limited values of the frame buffer. Typical ranges are 0 to 255 ($2^8 - 1$) or 0 to 4095 ($2^{12} - 1$). For example, a value of 3 in the frame buffer points to the fourth (numbering from 0) location in the colour lookup table. This contains a value for each of the primary colours and the video processor extracts the three values, one for each electron gun in the CRT. It is usual for the computer to be able to set the values of the colour table dynamically, using an attribute command allowing almost any combination of colours to be available.

It should be remembered that the number of planes of frame buffer memory gives the number of *different* colours that can be displayed at any one time, whereas the range of values for each location in the colour lookup table gives the *colour resolution* available on the system. If there are five planes, then 32 (2^5) different colours can be displayed simultaneously; and if each primary colour in the colour lookup table is represented by values between 0 and 15, then a total of 4096 (16^3) colours can be displayed. It is common for the raster generator to be able, under functional command from the CPU, to set the values in the lookup table. Colour lookup tables also save memory in systems where subtle colour resolution is required.

16.4.5 Pixel Generator Primitives

The pixel generator interprets the graphics primitive commands to construct the image in the frame buffer. Polyline, polymarker, text and fill area primitives are usually available. Commands to clear the frame buffer, change the colour lookup table and so on are available in addition to special-purpose functions, which depend on the particular terminal type. Polylines are drawn into the frame buffer using such functions as *LineToPixel*. Polymarkers can be drawn using predefined polyline shapes or using font shapes similar to those used for drawing text characters.

16.4.6 Raster Text Generation

The text function uses a different font type to the vector graphics system where the fonts are made up of polylines to describe the individual characters. With a raster system, the character fonts consist of the pixel patterns that make up the character shape. The font of the letter 'S' is again used as an example in Figure 16.9. Here, the character is formed in a 9 by 7 font space but an 11 by 9 total character space is used to give automatic character and line spacing. Other font sizes can be used to give higher definition characters. The pixel generator, when commanded to copy a given character into the frame buffer, copies the whole of the font pixel matrix from its own memory. Fonts are usually pre-programmed into the pixel generator, but some systems allow the CPU to load new fonts into the character font memory. For details of the specialized bitmap functions such as *BitBLT* that are used for this type of form manipulation see Chapter 11.

The storage of fonts in the form of pixel patterns is more economical and their display in the frame buffer more efficient than with the stroke type fonts. Characters defined in this way only maintain their true shape if they are displayed along the same path as the frame buffer axes – that is, horizontally or vertically. Character size can be increased in multiples of the font size by **pixel replication**. Each pixel in the font is transferred to square

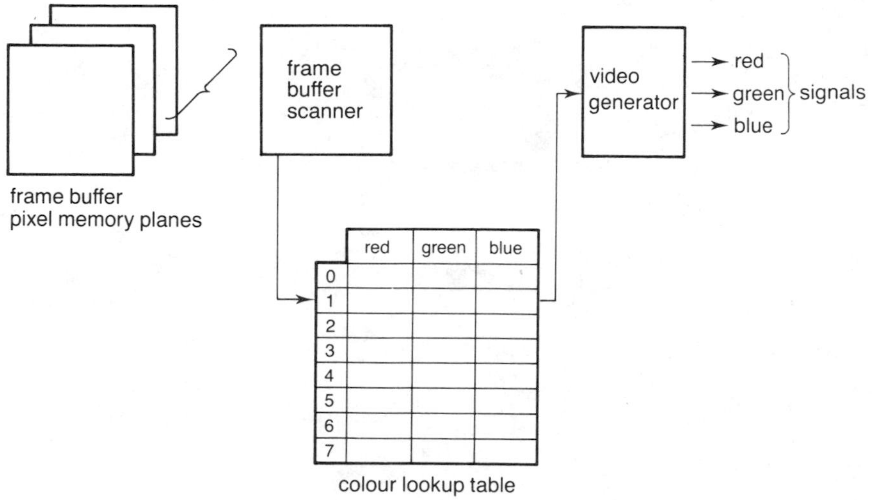

Figure 16.8
The colour lookup table.

arrays of pixels in the frame buffer to magnify the character's size. Characters cannot be reduced in size, as the defining font space is the minimum into which the character shape can fit.

16.4.7 Raster Area Fill

A feature of raster graphics display systems is their ability to efficiently display areas of solid colour for fill area functions. This is because the whole of the frame buffer space is displayed on each scan, irrespective of what is stored in the planes. Once a shape has been written into the frame buffer planes, it places no further computational or display load on the raster graphics display. This is not the case for vector graphics display systems, because a solid fill area function requires the specified area to be shaded line by line on each refresh cycle.

There are two methods for constructing fill area primitives in the frame buffers. In the first, the outline of the polygon is drawn into the memory planes and then a *seed* is placed within the border. The pixel generator then scans outwards horizontally and line by line vertically from the seed until it meets the border, filling in the shape as it goes. This is known as **seed fill**. If, by an oversight, the border is not completely closed, then the seed fill algorithm bursts out and starts to fill in the outer area with, invariably, unwanted results (see Exercises 4.14 and 4.15).

The second method of fill area is to scan convert the polygon. The polygon border is presented to the pixel generator which calculates the start and endpoints of the shape for each line. The parameters for each line are then passed to the pixel generator for writing into the frame buffer. For a detailed explanation of this algorithm refer to Section 4.8.

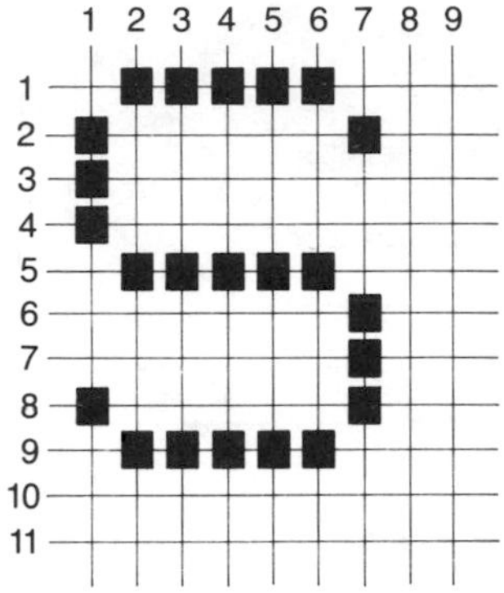

Figure 16.9
Raster character font in an 11 by 9 matrix.

16.4.8 Frame Buffer Operations

To carry out the pixel-generation functions efficiently, a set of special functions has been developed to operate directly on the frame buffers. These functions are collectively known as *RasterOp* or *BitBLT* functions and they were first described formally by Newman and Sproull (1973, pp. 263–265). All *RasterOp* functions logically operate on a pixel-by-pixel basis, working from a source form to a destination form. Chapter 11 describes these functions in detail, but to summarize they include operations to:

- Read a rectangular array of pixels from the memory. For example, from a special pixel storage memory such as a character font.
- Write a rectangle of pixels into a destination rectangle in the memory.
- Copy a rectangular region from one area of memory to another, possibly via a temporary buffer area of memory.

16.4.9 Frame Buffer Windows

Use of frame buffer windows provides zoom, pan and scroll facilities. This can be done by commanding the scanner to restrict its scan to a window on to the frame buffer while still using the same viewport on to the display area. Each pixel in the buffer is then magnified on to the display by the **zoom factor**. Factors are usually restricted to multiples of 2, with 2, 4, 8 and 16 being the typical range. If a zoom factor of 4 is used, then each pixel in the window is displayed at four adjacent points along the scan line and on four consecutive scan lines. Only one-quarter of the area of the frame buffer

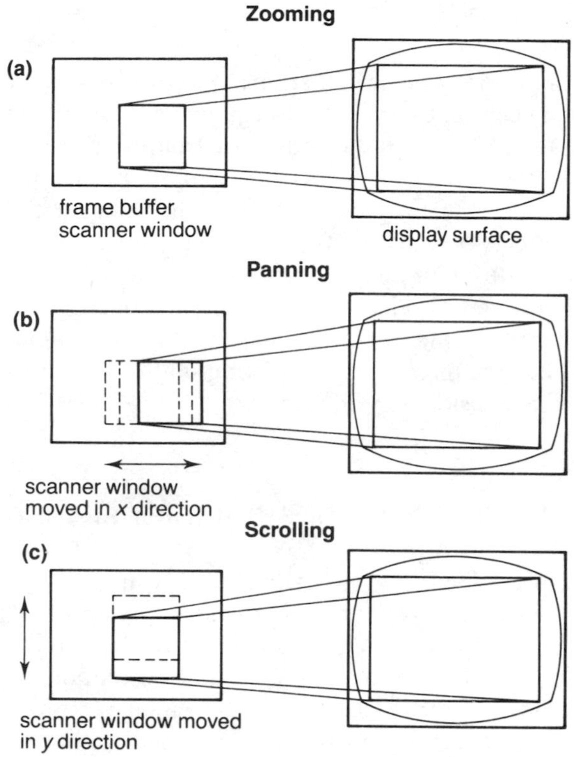

Figure 16.10
Raster zoom, pan and scroll.

can be viewed at this zoom factor. This type of zoom is known as **hardware zoom** or pixel replication because it is carried out by the display hardware of the system. Once a zoom factor has been selected, the window can be moved laterally for panning and vertically for scrolling the frame buffer. These concepts are illustrated in Figure 16.10.

16.4.10 Frame Buffer Viewports

On occasions, it is useful to be able to address a rectangular subarea or viewport of the frame buffer; that is, the *RasterOp* functions are not allowed to write any pixels into the frame buffer outside the viewport, but the scanner still constructs the video output from the same window on to the frame buffer. Such viewports are useful when data written into the frame buffers must not be changed, no matter what subsequent commands are to do.

16.4.11 Frame Buffer Memory Switching

Frame buffer planes may be switched or masked in two ways. Firstly, they may be switched such that a frame buffer plane can be made unalterable by the pixel generator. This stops the generator from writing into that memory plane and changing the image already stored there. Planes may also be switched so that the scanner does not extract the data for the pixels in that plane. Using these two switching functions, individual or groups of planes can be set to store different images, which can be switched on to the display as required. Planes may also be set up to contain a background image that is to remain unchanged, while the other planes contain elements of the image that regularly change. In this way, the computational load of constructing dynamic images is considerably reduced.

16.4.12 Aliasing and Constant Intensity Lines

Section 15.3.2 described the zig-zag effects generated by the limited resolution of pixel-based systems, known as aliasing. The lower the resolution of the display system, the more the aliasing effect will be apparent to the viewer. Even on relatively high-resolution systems, aliasing can detract considerably from the effect of an image.

The aliasing effect is most apparent along high-contrast diagonal edges. Scan-converted edges that are parallel to either of the principal axes do not suffer from aliasing, as their image representations model the required line exactly. There are occasions where any aliasing within the image is undesirable and techniques, known as anti-aliasing, have been developed to reduce its effect (see Section 13.7).

The fundamental idea behind the display of alias-free edges is to create, within the limitations presented by the pixel matrix of the frame buffer, an illumination pattern on the display surface that is closer to that of a vector edge model. Consider the diagonal line shown superimposed on a pixel grid in Figure 16.11(a). Although the line shown is of approximately one pixel in width, this discussion holds for any diagonal edge on lines or fill areas that are greater than one pixel in width. It can be seen that the line never actually occupies 100% of the area of any particular pixel.

A further example of the aliasing problem is the representation of the line generated by a Bresenham (1965) type algorithm, as shown in Figure 16.11(b), where the illuminated pixels are modulated at 100% of the required line intensity level. A better representation would be for the intensity of each pixel traversed by the required line to be set proportional to the area of overlap. This is illustrated in Figure 16.11(c). The line image will now be smooth and closer to the ideal.

In reality, each pixel in the frame buffer can only represent a limited

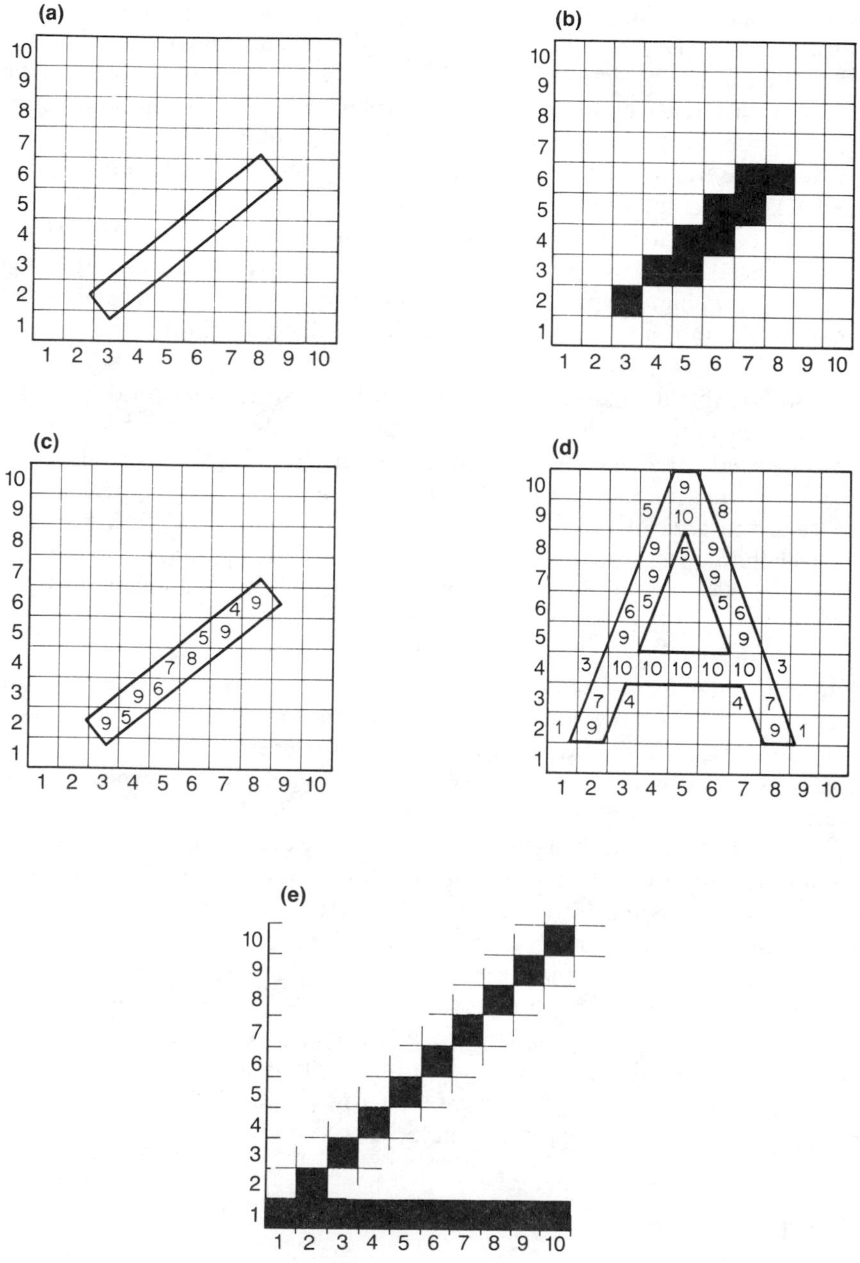

Figure 16.11
Anti-aliasing.
(a) Idealized line superimposed on a pixel matrix.
(b) Line representation from a Bresenham-type algorithm.
(c) Anti-aliased pixel levels for a vector.
(d) Anti-aliased pixel levels for a character.
(e) Unequal intensity of horizontal and vertical lines.

number of intensity levels and therefore the area can only be translated to a level quantized to a usually small set within the total intensity range. In addition, these intensity levels may not be those represented by the preset range set for general display of the images. Therefore, additional planes, known as **anti-aliasing planes**, may be required to provide the required intensity range. These additional planes will definitely be required if the anti-aliasing is to be implemented on a colour raster system where the number of different colours that can be displayed at a time is limited. Even so, on colour systems, the range of anti-aliasing colours that can be used may itself be limited and the anti-aliasing functions limited to certain edge/background colour combinations.

The computation required to calculate the area and the pixel intensity of anti-aliased lines is considerable, and to provide this function on interactive graphics display systems special hardware, often employing parallel computation techniques, will be required – and will have to be paid for!

So far, this discussion has centred on the scan conversion of polyline or fill area primitives. However, anti-aliasing may also be applied to raster scan converted character display. This is illustrated in Figure 16.11(d), from which it can be seen that the same ideas of proportional representation with respect to the area of each pixel overlapped are used. Now, however, not only will there be a requirement for additional pixel planes in the frame buffer, but also the proportional intensity values of each pixel must be stored in the character memory.

An alternative to the use of additional planes is to use the memory required to increase the overall frame buffer resolution. This will have the effect of improving the whole image, not just those elements of it that have been anti-aliased. It should be remembered, however, that this increase in display resolution may require increases in performance in the whole image-generation process from pixel generation to CRT itself.

It should be noted that diagonal lines, assuming square pixels, will have a lower intensity per unit length than horizontal or vertical lines of the same width. This is illustrated in Figure 16.11(e). The diagonal line shown has the same number of pixels illuminated as the horizontal line but the line itself is longer by a factor proportional to the angle. The relative intensities will differ most when the line is at 45°. Anti-aliasing the lines would automatically correct this problem, as additional pixels along the diagonal line would be illuminated. An analytic account of anti-aliasing has been given in Section 13.7 and the papers of Crow (1977, 1981 and 1982) will provide readers with further study material.

16.4.13 Pixel Dump

Some pixel-based display systems allow for the direct transfer of pixel data from the CPU to the frame buffer via the computer interface, the pixel data being stored on high capacity storage devices available to the CPU. This capability allows complete images to be transferred from the CPU to the frame buffer and, on some systems, back to the CPU again. These images may have been previously created in a frame buffer and transferred to the CPU or, more usually, they are the digitized version of real-life images, such as photographic or video images. This gives the display system what is known as an **image display capability**. If the device also has built-in functions to manipulate the frame buffer, then the device is said to have an **image processing capability**. These functions may include the ability to add and subtract pixel values, average them over an area as well as many specialized pixel-processing algorithms.

16.4.14 Character Display Memories

Some raster graphics displays, especially those forming part of a terminal, have an additional display memory that can only store characters for display. The characters are not stored in pixel form but are stored as character codes, and a character display generator accesses the codes and constructs the character shapes. The character memory is independent of the frame buffer and usually only allows the display of characters in a single colour, the video signals being mixed in with the graphics signals just before output to the display system, as shown in Figure 16.6. This memory is normally used for direct, non-graphical communication with the CPU.

16.4.15 Raster Display Lists

The display terminal system shown in Figure 16.6 has no display list. The function commands that are sent from the CPU are obeyed by the pixel generator and then lost. The only storage on the terminal is that of the frame buffer. This implies that a version, at least, of the display list must be kept in the CPU. If a significant change is to be made to the displayed image, then it is necessary for the frame buffer to be initialised and then all the primitive and attribute functions sent from the CPU to the graphics generator. This is a very time-consuming process, especially if the image is complex.

To speed up the generation of modified images, the primitive and attribute functions can be stored in a display list in the graphics generator. A graphics generator with such a display list will then be able to draw the image into the frame buffers in a similar manner to a vector refresh system. Only modifications to the image then need to be sent to the device as required and the image can be redrawn into the frame buffers at high speed. Redraw time is limited only by the speed of the display list processor and the pixel generator. A functional diagram of a generator with a local display list is shown in Figure 16.12.

The addition of a display list or segment list to a pixel-based display system brings with it all of the advantages of a vector refresh display system and creates, with a few reservations, a graphics display system with the capabilities of both systems. Such systems do not currently have the true image update speed of vector refresh display systems, where any changes to the images appear at the next refresh of the display – generally, 1/30 of a second. However, this type of device has the capability of showing solid filled areas and a wide range of colours. This does not, however, solve the problem of the frame buffer dynamic modification problem as discussed in Section 8.2. A solution to this is satisfied by double-buffered pixel memories, as discussed in the next section.

16.4.16 Double-Buffered Pixel Memory Systems

The frame buffer of a raster graphics display is always on display to the viewer. This means that the viewer sees all of the display changes as they are constructed by the pixel generator. But this can be annoying as well as time consuming because the pixel generator can only write pixel data into the memory planes when the scanner does not need access to them; that is, during the horizontal and vertical retraces. These problems can be removed by having two independent sets of frame buffer planes as shown in Figure 16.12. One set is accessed by the scanner for display and the second set is only available to the pixel generator. When the pixel generator has completed building the modified image, the roles of the frame buffer memory sets are swapped over. This type of frame buffer switching is known as **double buffering** and the main effect, as far as the viewer is concerned, is the apparent instantaneous image update as the scanner switches between the two memory sets.

16.4.17 Bitmap Displays

In the raster graphics display devices described so far, the frame buffers have been part of the display terminal itelf with the terminal connected to the CPU. Recently, however, computer systems have appeared that have the frame buffers situated either close to or actually inside the CPU. Usually, these frame buffers have only one bit plane and, until recently, this has been the norm for this type of display, resulting in the name bitmap display becoming synonymous with closely coupled display systems. There is no reason, however, why there cannot be several pixel planes so that grey level and colour images can be displayed. As the cost of random access memory continues to fall, multi-planed closely coupled systems are becoming common.

The functional layout of such a display system and its relationship to the processing and memory units of the CPU is shown in Figure 16.13. The frame buffers may be part of the CPU memory or they may form a separate

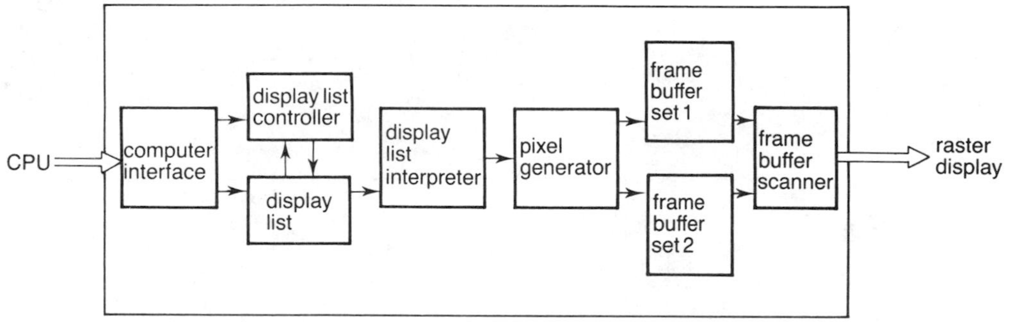

Figure 16.12
Functional diagram of a raster graphics generator that uses a local display list and double-buffered memories.

memory that is directly accessible by the CPU via the computer's main data highway or data bus, as in Figure 16.13. There is a scanner and video generator in the normal way. Much use is made of *RasterOp* functions in such displays with the images being constructed by form manipulation.

With the frame buffers closely coupled to the CPU, the image can be updated quickly, keeping pace with rapid changes to the image data inside the computer. Therefore, images can be used to represent the state of the computer and its internal processes, such as text editors, computer language compilations, applications programs, etc., and user interaction is directly with these processes. In computers where several of the tasks are active at the same time, the output generated by a task can be assembled in a window and displayed in a separate viewport, which can be manipulated in the normal way (see Section 16.2.7). An example is shown in Figure 16.14 where three different processes are occupying windows on the display. These displays are becoming increasingly popular as they allow very close monitoring and efficient use of the computer.

16.4.18 Window-Managed Raster Displays

The use of a frame buffer scanner that reads the memories in the left-to-right, top-to-bottom raster scan sequence dictates that the frame buffers must contain a pixel-by-pixel map of the whole image. This is not always the most efficient or convenient manner in which to store raster images, especially if the display is to consist of several independently managed windows and their viewports.

A different approach to raster scan image generation has been developed in which each window is stored in a separate area of the frame buffer (Wilkes *et al.*, 1984). The windows may then be modified and viewports manipulated as distinct image units. The functional diagram of such a window-managed display system is shown in Figure 16.15.

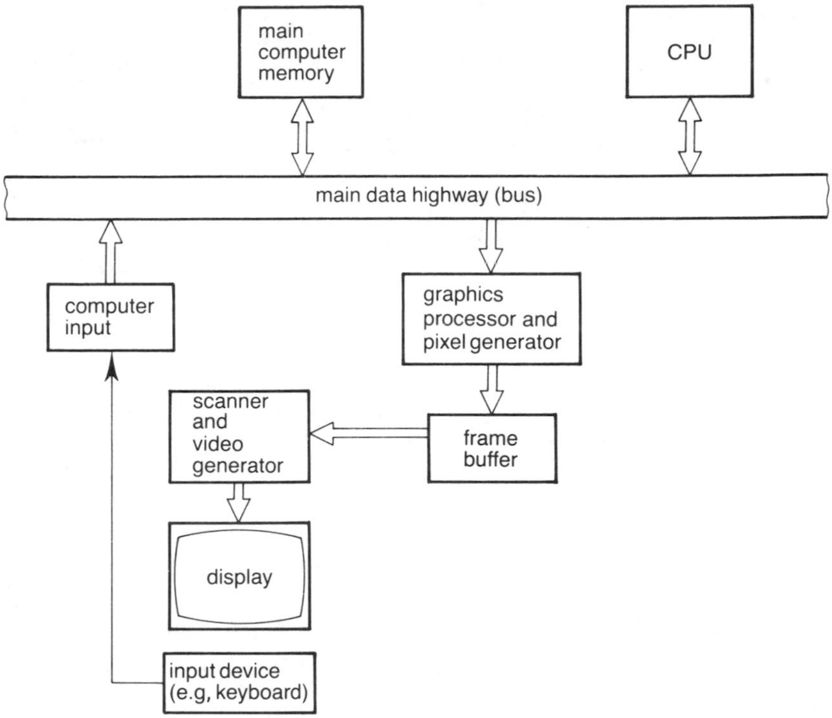

Figure 16.13
A bitmap display system with its CPU and memory units.

The pixel image data for each window is generated in the normal way by a pixel generator, but each window is stored in a separate and contiguous area of frame buffer memory. For each window, there is an entry in an **image description table**, which contains data on where the pixel data starts and ends in the memory, the position of each window's viewport on the display, the size of the window in the frame buffer and the dimensions of the viewport on the display surface. The image is constructed in the usual raster scan left-to-right, top-to-bottom manner by a **pixel memory controller**, which replaces the frame buffer scanner of the standard raster generator. The pixel memory controller, as it progresses down and across the display, monitors the contents of the image description table looking for the start of viewports (at the top left-hand corner) within the raster scan sequence.

To see how the image is constructed, consider the single raster line in Figure 16.16. As the controller scans across the marked raster line, it encounters the start of viewport 1, and from the window data in the image description table calculates where in the memory to find that line of the window's image. The pixel data for that line is then sent to the video generator. As the controller continues along the raster line, it next

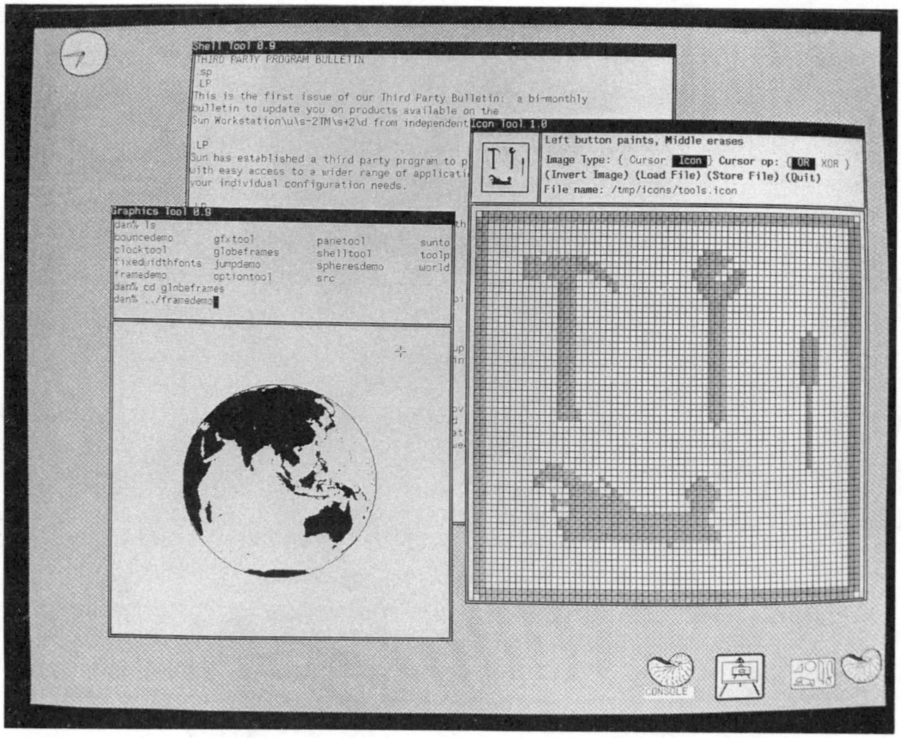

Figure 16.14
A bitmap display system showing three computer processes occupying separate windows.

encounters the start of viewport 2 and starts to collect data for that window from the memory for inclusion in the image. The output from both windows is now required to be displayed simultaneously. However, one window's data will normally be given priority over the rest. The end of viewport 1 is then encountered and the data for that window is terminated. Finally, the end of viewport 2 is encountered and the data for that window is terminated. Windows are only considered for inclusion in the display if the current raster line is between the top and bottom of its viewport.

Windows can be moved rapidly around the display surface by changing their viewport position data in the image description table. The table will also contain data on the relative priority of each window to determine which of two, or more, overlapping windows has display priority. The pixel generator updates the windows in the memories following commands from the CPU.

This type of display generation is new and requires a large amount of computational power in the graphics generator, especially the pixel memory controller. The cost of including this level of power is dropping and these display types will undoubtedly become cost effective and common.

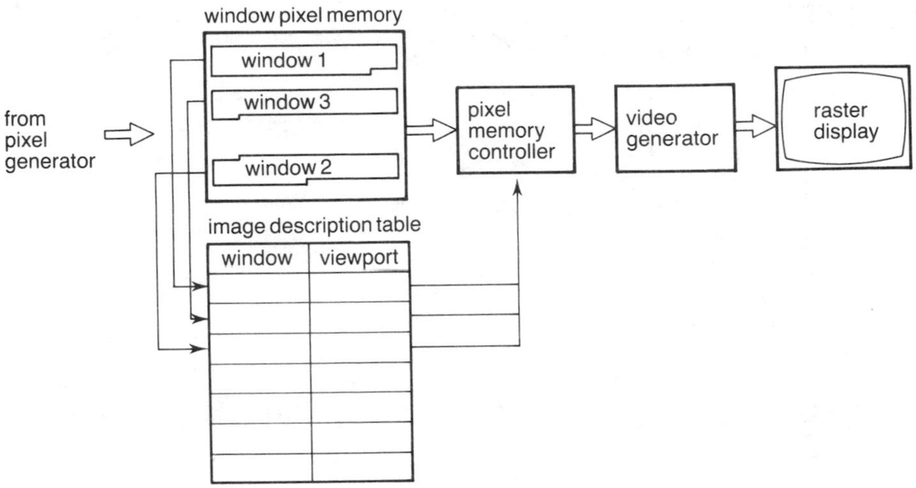

Figure 16.15
Schematic of a window-managed display system.

16.5 Communicating with a Graphics Generator

Previous sections have described how the graphics generator interprets the primitive, attribute and control commands from the CPU. These commands are sent from the computer to the graphics generator by way of the CPU interface with the generator. The commands that are sent have to be coded by the CPU into a form that the generator can accept and understand. For example, to clear the display's screen, a command in a form that the generator can understand needs to be sent. Sometimes, these commands are coded as numbers represented in character form. So, continuing the example, assume that the code for the clear screen command is the value 10. However, the value 10 may need to be sent to signify many other items of data for the display of images, like the width of a line, the position of a point on the x axis of the display and so on. Therefore, the generator needs to know exactly what *type* of data the item is. Is it a primitive command, a line width, a coordinate value?

The system used to code these commands is known as the generator's **interface protocol**, and it defines exactly what action is to be taken by the generator when data arrives from the CPU. Consider the data required for the polyline primitive. The first data item the generator receives, however, is not the coded polyline primitive command, but a special command to inform the generator that the next data item will be a graphics command.

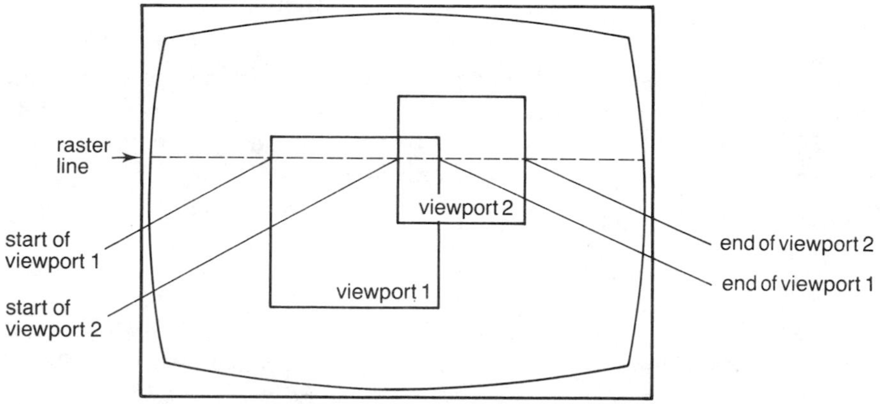

Figure 16.16
Raster line construction in a window-managed display system.

This is because most generators are capable of displaying a great many characters and obeying a great many commands. The number of possible commands is greater than the range of values that can be sent to the generator as a single item. Thus, the special command sets the generator into a state where it *expects* a graphics command to follow. This is often known as the generator's **graphical state**. The generator then interprets the next data item as a graphics command. In the case of a polyline primitive command, the generator then expects the next data item to be the number of points in the polyline, and then expects the coordinate data to follow. It can be seen that the generator is always in a state where it is expecting a particular data item type. If it does not receive the correct data type, then an error occurs, which may have disastrous results and the generator may or may not be able to recover. Return from the graphical state to the normal state of the generator may be commanded by a second special command or it may happen by default at the end of a graphics command.

The generation of the command data in the correct protocol is carried out in the CPU, the generator relying on the data it receives to be correct in format and content. The CPU requires very careful programming to ensure that the commands sent to the generator are logically sensible and correctly coded in the protocol. Data travelling in the opposite direction – from the generator to the CPU for the purposes of inputting data – must similarly be coded in the generator's protocol.

Most commercial graphics generators have their own communications protocols and the protocol generated by a CPU to command one type of generator will be, more likely than not, incorrect for other generators. For some time now, simple alphanumeric generators have had a standardized communications protocol, allowing them to be interchanged without changes to the command protocol generator in the CPU. This is the American Standard Code for Information Interchange, or the ASCII code.

16.5.1 The Computer Graphics Interface

A proposed computer graphics standard that is as significant as GKS is the Computer Graphics Interface (CGI). The CGI has been introduced to establish a standard for the interface between CPU-based graphics software and the graphics output and input hardware. Any hardware devices that adhere to this standard will appear to be the *same* device to the graphics library.

In the words of the draft standard (ISO, 1986a):

> *"The Computer Graphics Interface (CGI) is a standard functional and syntactical specification of the control and data exchange between device-independent graphics software and one or more device-dependent graphics device drivers."*

As such, the CGI uses a model of graphics similar to that of GKS and draws extensively on the model of a graphics picture of the Computer Graphics Metafile (CGM) (ISO 8632). GKS uses its workstation models to communicate with the devices connected to it and the CGI must be able to support this communication irrespective of the level of functionality available on each device. In addition, it should be straightforward to generate and interpret a CGM through the CGI. The CGI is, however, not limited to working only with GKS or CGM systems.

The CGI employs the concept of a virtual device so that each available device presents a set of idealized graphics device capabilities to the graphics software or system. The virtual device has a standardized coordinate system and command set for use by the CPU graphics software.

The CGI can represent an interchange between two software modules or between software and hardware. In the latter case, the hardware itself would implement the interpretation of the control and display commands, and the generation of the input responses of the CGI and the requirement for driver software in the CPU would be reduced to virtually nothing.

To do all this, the CGI provides the syntax and the semantics of a set of functions for use by the graphics applications programmer or library implementor. This set of functions consists of:

- Control functions, which specify the modes of operation of the device and the device coordinate space to be used, select the protocol parameters for the exchange of data and provide for device behaviour at session initialisation and termination.
- Attribute functions.
- An ESCAPE function, which describes functions that are system or device dependent (for example, issue a *tone* to the operator).
- External functions, which communicate data or control not directly

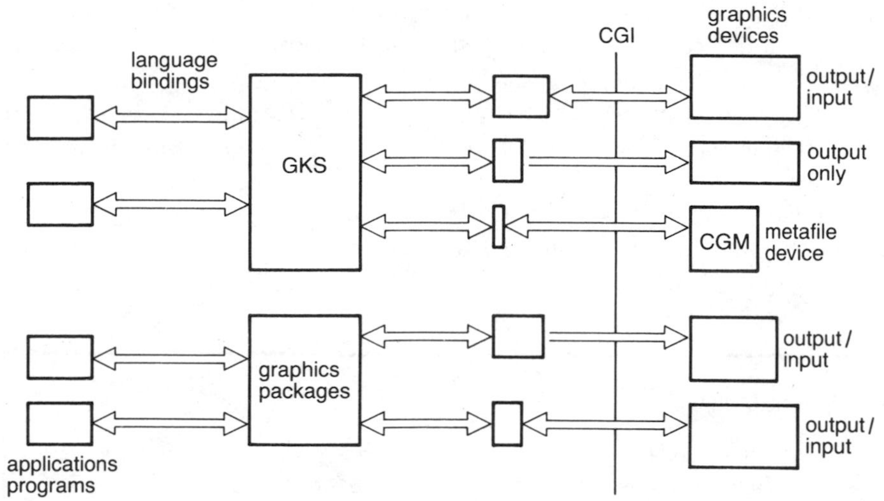

Figure 16.17
The CGI in a graphics system.

related to the generation of the graphics image.

- Segmentation functions.
- Input functions.
- Inquiry and interrogation functions, which return information on the CGI state lists and the virtual devices' characteristics and capabilities, respectively.
- Raster control functions (see Section 11.9).

The inclusion of the latter group of functions reflects the importance given to raster scan systems and pixel-based images. They describe an optional set of functions that can be used to generate and manipulate images on raster, or more correctly, pixel-based devices. (The reader should refer to Chapter 11 for details of this type of function.)

The implementation of the CGI on any CPU will, in a similar manner to GKS implementations, use specific computer language bindings and these will eventually be available for most of the standardized languages. In addition, there will be a set of standardized protocols or encodings for communication with the real graphics software or hardware. The CGM employs a similar, but not functionally identical, set of encodings (see Section 8.5). The standardized encodings are of three types:

- Character encoding, where the protocol appears as strings of standardized characters (conforming to ISO 646 and ISO 2022). This is likely to be the most common encoding, as it offers a compressed form of encoding and is suitable for transmission over the commonly available interfaces and networks.

- Binary encoding, which offers a protocol that is easily interpreted by each device and is especially suitable for closely coupled devices.
- Clear text encoding, which provides a verbose protocol that can be created, displayed and edited by most text editors. It is the most flexible, although the most inefficient in communications terms.

The relationship between the CGI and the other parts of a computer graphics system are shown in Figure 16.17.

Summary

There are two significant graphics image technologies, vector refresh systems and pixel-based systems. Although the former systems have limitations for general-purpose graphics display, they currently retain a significant position in their use with specialized display systems, such as radar and command and control systems. Pixel-based display systems have achieved considerable advances in their technologies and use, and there is still much potential growth left in both these areas. Resolution will continue to increase as memory devices are developed with still higher densities, and the support electronics will become more powerful and smaller until even the most compact devices will have most of the high-level graphics functions and features implemented directly. High-performance graphics, probably in the form of window-managed display functionality, will be a basic feature of any terminal, workstation or personal computer.

Exercises

16.1 Construct an instruction set for a colour, pixel-based generator system that does not possess a display list of any type. Assume that it has the basic GKS set of primitives and that all attributes are global and unbundled.

16.2 Add the instructions necessary for a structured display list to those in Exercise 16.1.

16.3 What are the advantages of double-buffered pixel memories. For which applications are they particularly useful and/or necessary?

CHAPTER 17

GRAPHICS INPUT DEVICES

The hardware devices that are used for the input of data by a graphics system and its subsequent modification can often be used in many different ways. This chapter considers what input hardware is available, what it is capable of doing and how each type can be used.

17.1 Introduction

Graphics data input hardware can be classified into three types: those that allow data to be input directly by the graphics system, those that employ user interaction with the currently displayed graphics image and those having special display control devices. The direct input devices do not necessarily require a displayed image to be available, but when one is, it may only reflect the input process. These devices include the typewriter-type **keyboard** (often known as the QWERTY keyboard after the first six characters on the top left-hand of the keyboard) and the graphics data **digitizer**. Interactive devices allow the user to work with the displayed image by driving a cursor to indicate items or positions on the display. These devices are described as **cursor drivers** and include the **joystick**, the **data tablet** and the **touch-sensitive screen**, amongst others. Finally, use can be made of special input devices such as special function keys and control knobs.

17.2 Direct Input Devices

17.2.1 Keyboards

The typewriter class of keyboard has always been one of the principal sources of input to computer systems. In its minimal form, the keyboard has a key for each of the alphabetic characters, the decimal digits 0 to 9, punctuation, special characters such as ! and #, and keyboard control keys such as SHIFT and CONTROL. Most character keys have at least two meanings, the second meaning usually selected by use of the shift key. Data formatting keys, such as DELETE, BACK SPACE and RETURN, are usually also available. Computer keyboards often include additional decimal digit keys in a separate but integrated **keypad** to speed up numeric data entry.

The CONTROL key is often used with computer systems to extend the use of each key to further values and these are used to exercise specific functions from the keyboard. Special cursor control keys and function keys may also be integrated into the keyboard.

Upon the depression of any key, either on its own or in conjunction with a SHIFT or CONTROL key, the keyboard electronics generate a specific digital code, which can be sent to the CPU via the interface. The CPU, which also *knows* the code used for each character, interprets the meaning of the transmitted characters in the current context. Most keyboards generate the standard ASCII code for transmission to the CPU.

Figure 17.1
A detachable, low-profile graphics terminal keyboard with cursor control keys.

The use of this code allows different makes and types of terminals to interpret the codes from the keyboard without requiring modification.

The keyboard, although not always the most efficient device for the input of data to a computer, is the most flexible and useful, and most systems assume that there is one available. They can be used to input command words as strings of characters, descriptive character strings for inclusion in the graphics image, and numeric data for primitives and attributes. An example of a keyboard that is used with a graphics display terminal is shown in Figure 17.1.

17.2.2 Digitizers

The digitizer is a device that is used for the direct input of two-dimensional x and y coordinate data. The user indicates the desired point on the flat table using a transmitting or sensing device. The table itself contains corresponding sensor or transmitter elements that divide the area into a fine matrix array. Different types of digitizer are available that use various types of transmitters and sensors including electromagnetic, electrostatic, infra-red and ultrasonic systems.

The logical operation of each type of digitizer is similar so, as an example, the technique used in the electromagnetic type of table will be considered. This type of digitizer uses a matrix of wires embedded in the table top, as shown in Figure 17.2. Continuous signals are transmitted down each wire with the signals coded to identify each line. A **probe**, which contains a small receiving element, senses the transmitted signals and sends them to a set of electronic decoding logic. Using the relative strength of the

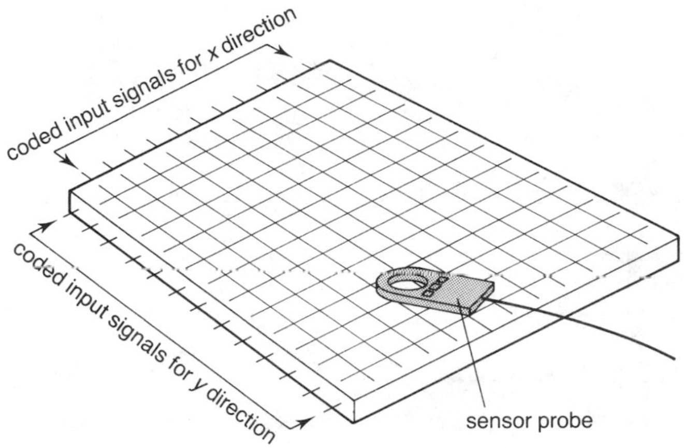

Figure 17.2
Electromagnetic digitizing tablet.

coded information, the logic calculates the position of the probe relative to the table surface. Accuracies of up to 25 microns (0.001″) can be obtained with this technique and the electronic logic can be programmed to carry out scaling, calibration, rotations and other calculations if required. A digitizer that uses this technique is shown in Figure 17.3. This digitizer has a large surface area with a probe that is a hand-held **puck** with a round window. The window has a cross-hair **sight** at its centre that the user places over the positions to be digitized. The puck also has several small buttons that the user can click to indicate that its current position on the table is to be digitized and transmitted to the computer.

In the case of the digitizer just described, the table is *active* and the probe is *passive*. Other types of electromagnetic digitizing table use an active probe and passive table with the probe transmitting the coded signal and the wire mesh detecting the position. Digitizers also exist where a current is applied to each wire in the x and y directions in turn and the position of the probe is calculated by sensing the time at which the peak magnetic field is detected. Other types of tablet use transmitters along the edge of the tablet and the probe detects the signals transmitted from these. These edge transmitters are usually either acoustic or infra-red in nature.

The positional data generated by the digitizer is then coded, often using the same ASCII data codes used by the keyboards, and transmitted to the CPU. This positional data is in the form of scaled x and y values and can be sent with the button number that was clicked to activate the digitizing.

This type of large digitizing tablet is normally used for the input of maps or drawings into the CPU. Smaller versions, using the same digitizing techniques, can be used directly with graphics terminals as cursor drivers. These are known as data tablets and are discussed in detail in the following section.

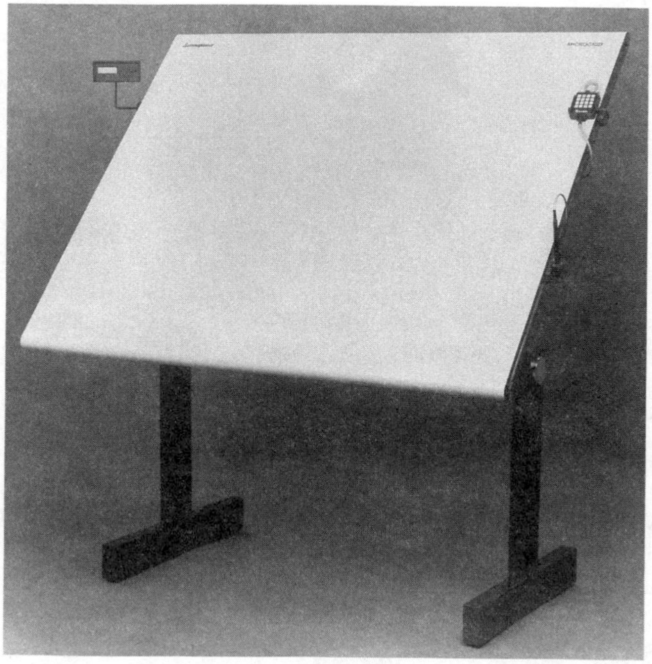

Figure 17.3
Large, high-resolution electromagnetic digitizer equipped with a multi-key puck, stylus and digital display.

17.3 Cursor Drivers

Once graphics data has been entered into the computer, and possibly, into the graphics generator, the user may want to modify it. Such modifications could be carried out by directly changing the graphics data in the CPU but, more commonly, the user would want to modify the data, and thereby the image, by working interactively with the displayed image. Operations for such interaction require the user to be able to either select positions on the display for coordinate input, or point to parts of, or *pick*, the current image. To do either of these, the user requires a moveable marker, or cursor, on the display that can be positioned at the required point or image element. Cursors are produced by the graphics generator and can appear as one of many different shapes. A selection of typical cursor shapes is shown in Figure 17.4. Each cursor has a point that is the true cursor position. In the case of the arrow shape, this would be the tip of the arrow. Cursors of this type are usually generated by special circuitry in the electronic displays and are not part of the defined display image. Their image is mixed in with the main display image such that the cursor can always be seen no matter what the background colour. Some display generators allow the applications program in the CPU to redefine the shape of the cursor.

Figure 17.4
Typical cursor shapes.

The user may drive the cursor around the display using a range of different devices or cursor drivers that are normally connected to the graphics display system, thereby controlling the position of the cursor directly. When the user has placed the cursor in the desired position on the display, a key is clicked. The terminal then calculates the position of the cursor in terms of device coordinates. These coordinates are then either passed back to the CPU or processed further by the terminal. In addition, the device may allow the CPU to regularly sample the cursor position without the interaction of the user. This enables the CPU to carry out actions dependent on cursor position only. This is particularly useful when, for example, the cursor is being used to pick items on the display, as they can be highlighted when the cursor contacts them (see Section 17.6.8).

17.3.1 Cursor Control Keys

Cursor control keys can be included on the terminal keyboard. There will be at least five keys involved: one key for cursor directional movement in the four horizontal and vertical coordinate directions, and a *hit* key to indicate that the current cursor position is to be sent to the terminal. Pressing one of the cursor movement keys causes the cursor to move one device coordinate unit in the selected direction. If the device is a raster display, then the cursor moves one pixel. If the device is a vector graphics display, then the cursor is moved a distance equivalent to one display list coordinate unit. The keyboard SHIFT and CONTROL keys are often used to multiply up the number of units moved for each cursor key depression. The cursor control keys can be seen on the keyboard illustrated in Figure 17.1.

17.3.2 Joysticks

The joystick is a vertical control stick that is used for moving the cursor around the display surface. It is so called because of its similarity to the control column or joystick used to control the elevators and ailerons of an aircraft. A typical graphics system joystick is shown in Figure 17.5. Although the joystick operates as a cursor driver, its control of the cursor position is different to that of the cursor control keys. In this case, the joystick *pushes* the cursor about the display surface. When the joystick is

Figure 17.5
A joystick.

moved in a given direction, it causes the cursor to move in the equivalent direction on the display surface, and the cursor continues to move in that direction so long as the stick is held in position. The further the joystick is moved from its centre or neutral position, the faster the cursor moves. Placing the joystick back at its neutral position causes the cursor to stop moving. Most joysticks are spring loaded and self-neutralizing when released.

A joystick will have at least one associated hit key, which is used to signal the return of the current cursor coordinates to the CPU. If the joystick is built into the terminal's main keyboard, then one of its control keys, such as the RETURN or cursor control hit key, can be used.

17.3.3 Data Tablets

The data tablet or, as it is sometimes known, the **bit pad** is a physically smaller version of the digitizer and is used primarily as a cursor driver. The display cursor is constantly driven by the data tablet such that when the puck or stylus is moved the cursor moves correspondingly. It is usual for the whole of the data tablet to be mapped to the whole of the display surface so that when the puck is at the bottom left of the pad the cursor is at the bottom left of the display surface, and similarly for the top right corner. It is often possible to map a subarea of a pad to the whole of the display surface, leaving the remainder of the working pad area free. This free area can then be used for command or item selection by means of an offscreen or **virtual cursor**.

It should be noted here that the interactive movement between the pad's puck and the display cursor is quite different from that of the keyboard control keys and the joystick. Instead of being *driven* around the display surface, the cursor is now *placed* at the absolute point required by the user. Every small movement by the user of the puck results in a movement of the cursor, which corresponds precisely in both direction and

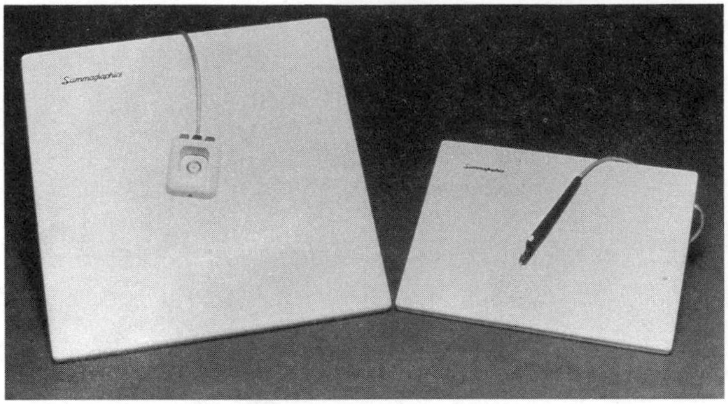

Figure 17.6
Two data tablets with puck and stylus probes.

length. This type of cursor control has been found to offer a type of user-cursor interaction that is particularly natural and simple to use.

The only difference between a data tablet and a digitizer is that of scale, the operation of the two devices being identical. Data tablets are often described in the literature as digitizers and it is only in their logical use that they are separated as data tablets or bit pads. A data tablet can always be used to digitize small drawings or maps. Figure 17.6 illustrates two data tablets or small digitizers. The one on the left is equipped with a cross-hair puck and the one on the right with a stylus for indicating the points to be digitized. The puck has three hit keys and the stylus one.

17.3.4 The Mouse

The mouse is a simple, low-resolution, low-cost cursor driver that operates in terms of relative cursor movement, not absolute cursor position as with the data tablet. To move the cursor, the mouse is moved in the required direction: the distance moved by the cursor is proportional to the distance the mouse is moved. If, at any time, the mouse is raised from its running surface and moved, there will be no change in the position of the cursor. The mouse only generates *movement* data when it is actually on the running surface. Large cursor movements are produced with a *shuffling* motion of the mouse, similar to a child running a toy car. The movement-generating electronics are contained entirely inside the mouse. Resolution is typically 0.25 mm (0.01″) and, because it can only sense movement, the mouse cannot be used as a digitizer.

There are two types of operation that are employed to generate the x and y coordinate values. The first is to build in a small rolling ball, which runs along on the flat surface and senses the bidirectional movement. Any flat surface can be used to run this type of mouse. In contrast, the second

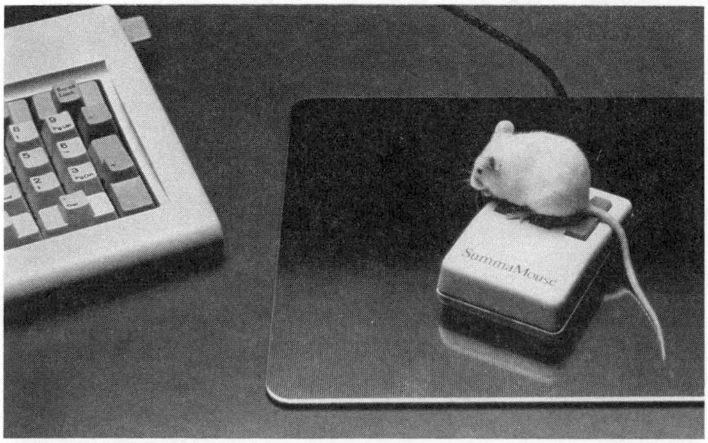

Figure 17.7
An electro-optical mouse, with a biomechanical relation.

type of mouse uses a small patterned plate. The movement of the mouse on the plate is sensed by photocells that can see the pattern through holes in the bottom of the puck. An example of this latter type of electro-optical mouse is shown in Figure 17.7. It can be seen that the patterned plate on which the mouse runs is small when compared to the data tablets in Figure 17.6. The mouse input device has become particularly popular with desk top and home computers due to its very low cost and the fact that it only requires a small flat area to work on.

17.3.5 Tracker Balls

The tracker ball, or **roller ball**, is a cursor driver that controls the relative movement of the cursor in the same way as the mouse. The device consists of a large metal or plastic ball protruding through the top of a box. The user rolls the ball with his or her hand and the relative movement is used to drive the display cursor. The movement is to a higher resolution than that of the mouse, and so roller balls are often used as cursor drivers on high-resolution raster and vector refresh graphics display systems. A typical example is shown is Figure 17.8 where the device's hit keys can be clearly seen.

17.4 Direct Screen Interaction

The interactive cursor drivers just discussed all use input devices remote from the display screen itself. In some cases, however, the user may wish to interact directly with the display surface. There are several reasons for this.

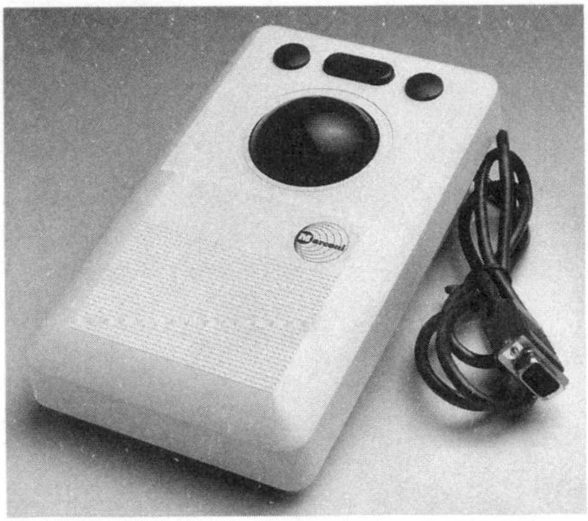

Figure 17.8
A tracker ball.

For example, there may be no room for a data tablet in the work area, or the user may want to have a more intimate contact with the displayed image. To achieve this form of interaction, two different types of device can be used. The first, the **light pen**, uses light energy radiated from the display surface and a light-sensitive probe. The second, the touch-sensitive screen, uses various techniques to detect the position of a passive probe placed on to or near to the display surface. The resolution depends on the size of the probe, but in any case will be less than half the display resolution.

17.4.1 Light-Sensitive Pens

The light-sensitive pen or light pen is a pen-like probe that is activated by light energy radiated from the displayed image. Figure 17.9 shows the functional operation of a light pen system. The pen itself contains a photoelectric cell that *looks out* of the end of the pen through a focusing lens. The pen is placed close to the surface of the display and the activating hit key initiates the detecting process. The output from the photocell is amplified and compared to a threshold value, which is set so that ambient light will not trigger the device. The device generates an output pulse when it sees the light from the display increase as the electron beam passes the end of the pen. This pulse, along with the timing signals from the scanner, or in the case of the vector refresh display, the vector generator, are combined to give the exact point of the pen on the display surface. The coordinates are then calculated in device units.

The light pen can only detect pixels or graphics elements that are part of the currently displayed image. The pen cannot sense positions on the dark area of the display and therefore cannot be used for random coordinate input. One solution to this problem is to systematically illuminate all

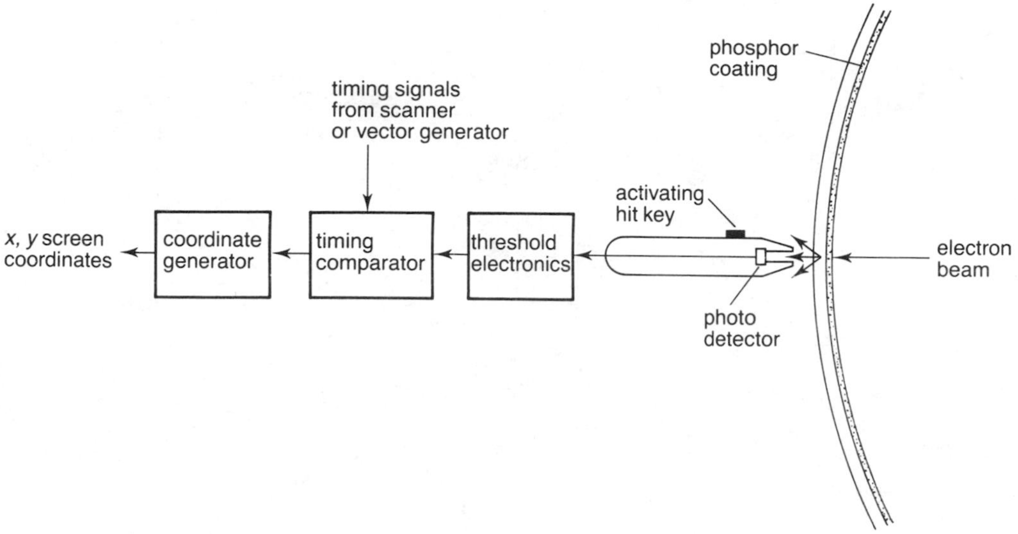

Figure 17.9
Functional diagram of the operation of a light-sensitive pen.

positions on the display surface. However, this requires special hardware on both raster and vector refresh displays and also generates a visible flash on the display which is invariably unpleasant and distracting for the user.

An alternative solution to this problem is to use the light pen for *dragging* the cursor around the display. This is done by placing the light pen on to the cursor at its current position on the display surface. The movement of the light pen is then *tracked*, such that when the light pen loses the image of the cursor, the area immediately surrounding the cursor point is illuminated. The new position of the light pen relative to the position of the cursor is then obtained and the cursor moved to *follow* it. If the light pen is moved too fast by the user, then contact with the cursor can be lost altogether. This is a system that is often used on vector refresh display systems.

17.4.2 Touch-Sensitive Screens

The light pen is an active probe that detects the light emitted from the display. Under certain circumstances, it may be more convenient to use a passive probe such as a stylus or even the user's own finger. This requires that the screen, or at least a screen overlay, is the sensor element of the system. This overlay can be a sensing *field*, such as infra-red, or it can be a *film*, such as a transparent plastic sheet with embedded sensing elements.

In the case of an infra-red touch-sensitive device, the sensing system consists of a frame with infra-red transmitters along two adjacent sides and infra-red receivers along the other two opposite sides, as shown in

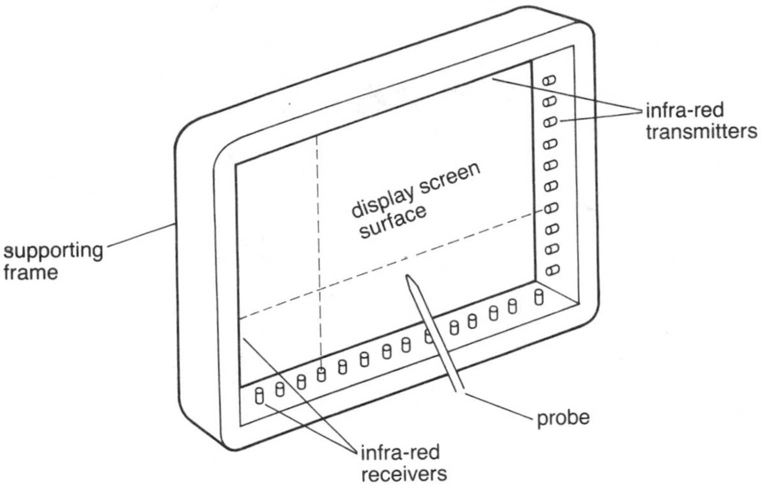

Figure 17.10
Infra-red touch screen overlay system.

Figure 17.10. This arrangement creates a 2D sensing area and any probe placed into this field will interrupt at least two – one horizontal and one vertical – transmitter/receiver paths. Electronic logic senses these interruptions and calculates the device coordinates of the probe on the display surface. This type of touch-sensitive device is often used where the user's finger is the probe and the required resolution of the selected point is usually no more than 1.2 cm (0.5″).

Higher resolution touch-sensitive devices can be constructed using transparent plastic sheet placed on a frame in front of the display screen. A fine stylus is used to activate the device by pressing it on to the plastic sheet which contains embedded electrodes. The position of the probe is calculated by measuring the change in resistance of the electrodes due to the probes pressure. Again, the position is generated in device coordinates for further processing by the graphics device or CPU. Touch-sensitive screen overlays can also be constructed using acoustic and capacitive sensing technologies amongst others.

17.5 Special Input Devices

All the input devices discussed so far, with the exception of the keyboard, generate 2D coordinate data. However, it is often useful to be able to input simple values controlled by a pointer, control dials or almost any type of

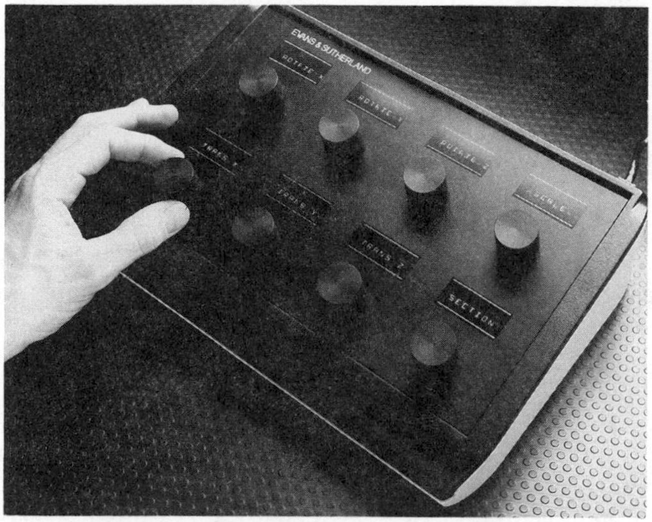

Figure 17.11
Special input device with eight control dials.

analogue positional device. Many types of such devices have been devised and it would not be realistic to try to describe them all in detail here. An example of a typical device that has eight continuous dials is shown in Figure 17.11. Each dial has an LED character readout above it and generates scaled digital values dependent on its position. The use that is made of this input data depends on the application, but control of window or viewport size and position is typical.

17.6 Logical Input Functions

Most of the devices described can be used for the input of several different types of data. For example, the data tablet can be used for the input of 2D coordinate data as well as for selecting items that are already part of the displayed image.

As discussed in Section 5.3, to describe the input of graphics data to a system, a set of logical input functions is used for different types of data. In the following sections, each of these logical input functions, or input classes, is related to the input device hardware described in the previous sections. In reality, these logical input devices are rarely found fully implemented on a single piece of graphics input hardware and so it is often necessary to complete the full set of features of the logical device by implementing them in the supporting hardware and software.

17.6.1 Locator

Nearly all of the input hardware types can be used for the input of locator data (see Section 5.5.1). The hardware devices that are most readily used are the cursor drivers, which generate 2D coordinate values. These are the digitizer and the cursor driver devices such as the data tablet, joystick, tracker ball, mouse, light pen and touch-sensitive display. The digitizer generates the coordinates without any necessary reference to a display, while the others require a display of the current image and the cursor. The keyboard can also be used by simply typing in two coordinate values, within a predefined range, as character strings.

17.6.2 Stroke

Stroke input is used for the input of a set of coordinate points and is effectively a multiple locator (see Section 5.5.2). Because of its similiarity to locator input, the stroke logical device can be implemented using the same devices.

17.6.3 Valuator

The valuator is used for the input of numeric values (see Section 5.5.3). These values can be simple integers or true decimal values and there are many ways in which they can be input. The simplest is by means of the character strings representing the value. For example, the character string 0.5 conveys the value of one-half. Therefore, any of the string input devices, the keyboard being the most common, can be used for valuator input. The same value could, however, also be conveyed by placing a cursor exactly at the midpoint of a straight line which is part of the displayed image. Therefore, any of the cursor driver devices could be used. Special input devices especially those with rotary dials, such as that shown in Figure 17.11, are frequently used for valuator input.

17.6.4 String

String input is used for the input of sequences of alphanumeric characters (see Section 5.5.4). The obvious hardware input device for use here is the keyboard where the characters can be input directly from the character and numeric keys. However, cursor drivers can also be used where the cursor is used to point to the required characters forming part of the display image. If the characters are not part of the display image, then devices like the data tablet can be used for character selection where only part of the tablet area is mapped on to the display surface area. The tablet's puck is used to point to the required characters, which are represented by positions on the tablet. These are indicated to the user by an overlay placed on to the data tablet. An overlay of this type is shown in Figure 17.12, where the positions on the tablet for the alphanumeric characters as well as many additional special menu items can be seen. This type of character input is similar to the graphics item selection carried out by the pick logical input device, which is discussed in a following section.

17.6.5 Choice

Choice input is used for the selection of an item from a list of alternatives (see Section 5.5.4). This type of input requires that the user be aware of the list of alternatives currently available, and this is usually done by displaying them as part of the current display image. However, the list may, for example, be permanently displayed as on a data tablet overlay used by pick type input, which is discussed in the next section. The user must then respond by choosing one of the alternatives. This may be done in several ways: a number or letter may be typed on a keyboard, the item may be *picked* or a special function key may be used. The actual method used should be tailored to suit the particular application.

17.6.6 Pick

The pick device is used to select items that are part of a display (see Section 7.4). Because of the very nature of pick input, the cursor and therefore cursor drivers are the usual hardware devices used for picking. However, if different elements of the picture on the display have been allocated references or names that are known to the operator, then they can be picked by typing in that reference as a character string, for example. This is common in command and control systems where direct screen interaction may not be possible or may be dangerous. The graphics element picked does not necessarily have to be part of the current display image. In this case, a cursor driver is used, such as the data tablet, where a subarea of the device has been mapped on to the display surface. If the puck is used outside this subarea, as a virtual cursor, then elements can be selected by absolute positional selection on the input device. This is a generalization of the input of characters using a data tablet for string input, as described earlier, and a data tablet overlay is required to show the user the positions of the items that can be picked. This type of display picking is often used for the selection of applications system commands. The menu overlay in Figure 17.12 shows the types of commands that are used.

Figure 17.12
Data tablet overlay.

Pick input can also be used with a digitizer in a manner similar to that of the data tablet just described. A subarea of the digitizer is used for the locator input and the remainder, with an overlay showing the pick input positions, is used for applications system commands. Under these circumstances, there need be no generated image for pick input at all.

17.6.7 Input Device Prompt and Echo

A good interactive dialogue usually requires the input device to *prompt* the user when the next input is required. These prompts can come in many different forms and are discussed in detail in Section 5.4. They are not usually a function of the input device except in the case where the device has been fitted with a specific prompt, such as a bell, tone or indicator lights.

In addition, when operating the device, the user may wish to see its current value displayed or *echoed* in some way. Keyboard echoes would usually take the form of the characters that have been input appearing as part of the image. Cursor driver echoes normally appear on the graphics display device unless they are virtual cursors. Pick and choice are very much device and application dependent.

17.6.8 Device Input Mode

When a logical input function is issued by the applications system, it may wait for the user to complete the input action or it may carry out some additional required computation or input/output requests and then return to collect the input data. Three input modes have been devised so that these actions can be specified.

The request mode is used if the applications system is to wait for the input to be completed by the user. In such circumstances, the system will suspend its execution of the applications program until the user takes the required action. Thus, the necessity of input prompts here is very apparent.

The sample mode is used when the applications system simply wishes to obtain the current value of the input device, with no action required by the user. Hence, the system samples or *polls* the data that it requires from the input and continues with execution of the program.

The event input mode is used when input is triggered by specific actions by the user, as in the case of request. Under this type of input mode, the user inputs data on the device asynchronously. The data is stored and is not returned to the application until it is specifically asked for. This type of input mode has, until recently, rarely been found in the input devices themselves, the queuing of input values normally being carried out in the CPU. Modern intelligent devices are now capable of storing this input locally so that it can be sent to the CPU when later requested. GKS event mode input is described in detail in Chapter 10.

17.7 Three-Dimensional Input

The direct input of coordinate data into a system implies that some form of representation of the object to be digitized must already exist. In the case of 2D data input, the representation might be an engineering drawing and original input would use one of the digitizer devices already described. However, 3D data digitization requires a *solid* 3D object, which implies that (at least) a *model* of the object already exists. If, in this latter case, it is a subscale model, then inaccuracies due to scaling will always be introduced, and so it is rarely used. Therefore, 3D digitization usually involves the capture of dimensional data from the real subject.

The requirement for 3D digitization also suggests that the data does not already exist in a computer or in any suitable printed form from which it could be entered into the computer system in character form. Therefore, most 3D input is of natural objects; that is, such things as the topographical measurement of the surface of the earth for map making, human or animal bone structures or unrecorded objects such as old buildings. Occasionally, it is used to measure man-made objects where there has been either inherent errors in the manufacturing process or there has been some use of free-hand work and this must be recorded. This latter example is often found in the design of car body shapes where the prototype shape is hand finished as a full size clay model and the 3D coordinates must be taken from the model for later manufacture.

17.7.1 3D Locator Input

3D coordinate input can be achieved through a sequence of 2D data inputs, and 2D locator systems are often used in this way. However, 3D data can be input using 3D locator devices, these being a logical extension of 2D locator systems with x, y and height, or z, coordinates input as related triads. These devices are rarely seen and still tend to be experimental. Sonic, electronic and mechanical systems have all been implemented, although they are all limited in resolution and size and only relatively small volumes can be enclosed by any practical system (Foley and van Dam, 1982, pp. 190–192).

17.7.2 Photogrammetric Systems

One of the most practical and most used methods of 3D locator measurement is that of photogrammetry. This technique has been developed mainly for the measurement of geographic topology data for mapping and involves the use of stereoscopic photographic images. Aerial surveys using two cameras mounted in an aircraft collect the twin photographs and these are later analyzed to generate the 3D data.

The method has been adapted for the measurement of 3D data in a technique known as **close range photogrammetry**. The twin cameras used in this technique must be capable of generating very accurate images, which means using very high quality lenses, with low distortion and calibrated characteristics. To further reduce any errors on the images, flat glass plates coated with photographic emulsions, or roll film flattened against a glass plate, are used to record the images.

The twin cameras are rigidly mounted on to a base bar which in turn is attached to a substantial tripod. Such a camera set up is illustrated in Figure 17.13(a). It is usual to set marks on the object or to collect some easily recognizable linear measures within the camera's view for calibration of the final data.

The two photographs collected are then set into a high-precision stereoscopic viewer, an example of which is shown in Figure 17.13(b), where the images from the two cameras are presented simultaneously to an operator. The operator mechanically scans the images observing and marking the points required for digitization. The operator has a set of controls that allow cursor marks to be moved in the horizontal and vertical directions relative to the plane of the photographs. The depth value, at right-angles to the plane of the photographs, is generated by adjusting the optical separation so that two precise points coincide optically.

This process generates coordinates relative to the plane of the photographs, which may or not be what is required. 3D transformations may therefore be required to set the digitized points into the required frame, as

(a)

(b)

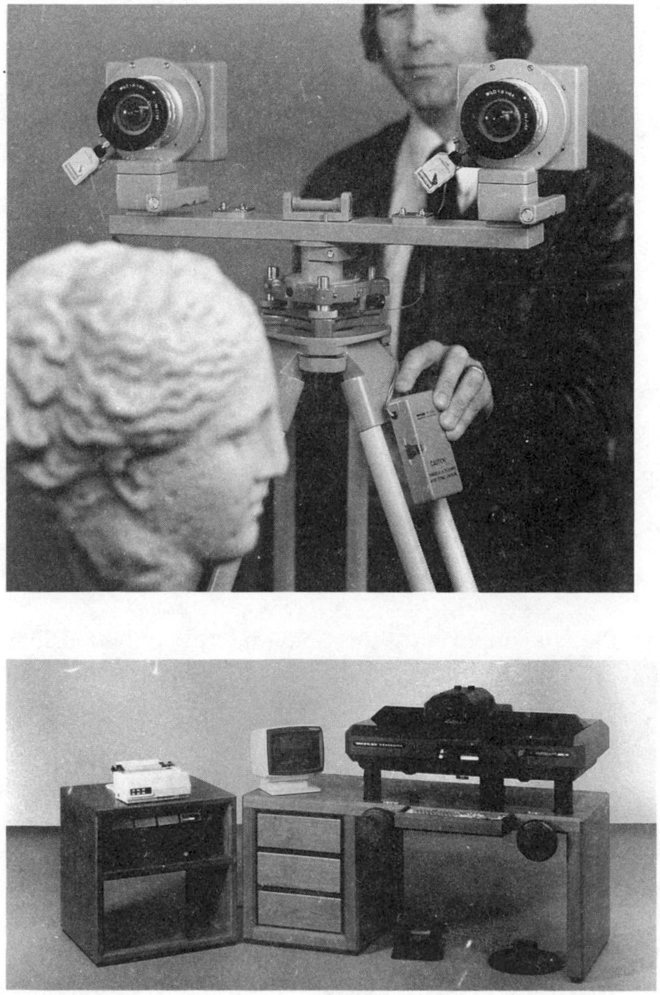

Figure 17.13
(a) A terrestrial stereoscopic camera.
(b) A photogrammetric measurement system.

well as to include any calibration marks that have been set on the images to produce the correct dimensional scaling. This requires a considerable amount of computation using sophisticated numerical techniques and the whole process can take several hours or even days.

The data that can be generated from such systems can be of very high resolution, up to 1 part in 10 000, but the cost of acquiring the data is high. It was emphasized earlier that the stereoscopic camera must be of the highest quality and the same goes for the photograph measurement systems. In addition, the whole process is very time consuming; but in many instances

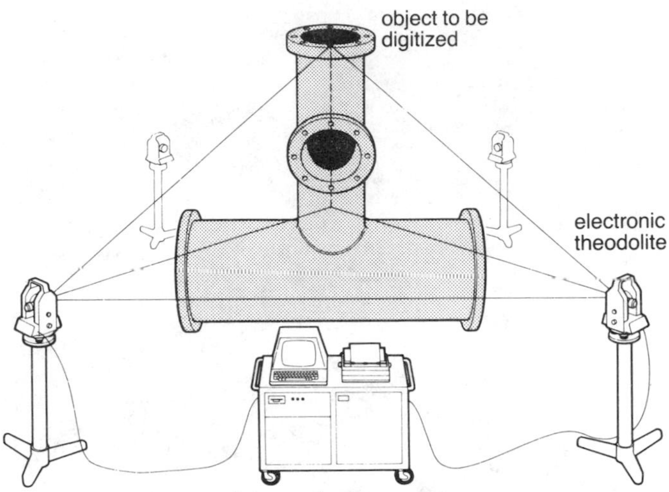

Figure 17.14
Theodolite system for remote sensing of 3D locator input.

where the data is important, this may be the only feasible method of acquiring it. A study of the application of photogrammetric methods to 3D coordinate data collection is described in Cooper (1979).

17.7.3 Theodolite Systems

Computerized theodolite systems can also be used for 3D locator measurement. Modern systems use two or more electronic theodolites linked online to a portable computerized data collection and storage system. The nature of 3D coordinate acquisition means that it would be unlikely that the system could be directly coupled to a computer graphics system.

These systems use the basic principles of triangulation. The theodolites are set up in a well-defined spatial relationship by being pointed at each other and at a calibrated reference scale. The general arrangement is shown in Figure 17.14. The computer then determines the precise spatial relationship of the two instruments and calculates a base upon which the measurements of the object can be taken. The theodolites are then aimed at the object to be measured and the computer generates the 3D coordinate data from the triangulations.

The resolution from these systems can be very high with precisions of 1 part in 100 000 being achieved. They are also cost effective and relatively straightforward to use.

Summary

The basic QWERTY style keyboard remains the most common and flexible input device, even on specialized graphics workstations, and as such represents the standard input device. The mouse is now relatively common for both input and interaction, but the tracker ball has a higher resolution and often a better ergonomic interface. Direct interaction with the display by means of touch devices has significant but limited uses. Perhaps the only significant new input device, but not one discussed in this book, will be that of the human voice, which may eventually become a standard input for any suitable computer-based system. 3D coordinate data input remains a specialized and relatively expensive technology but has important uses in the fields of general engineering as well as graphics.

Exercises

17.1 Describe how a QWERTY keyboard that does not have cursor control keys can be used to implement each of the GKS logical input classes.

17.2 Repeat Exercise 17.1 but consider a light pen instead of a keyboard. No other input device can be used to supplement the functionality of the light pen.

17.3 Select a set of input devices for use on an artist's workstation. Give the reasons for your choice.

CHAPTER 18

HARDCOPY DEVICES

The display devices discussed so far have had an electronically generated image that disappears when the device is switched off. These devices are undoubtedly the workhorses of computer graphics and the types most often encountered. However, it is also necessary for images to be generated on media that can be stored and displayed separately from the computer graphics generating system. Devices that allow the generation of permanent copies of the displays are known collectively as **hardcopy devices**.

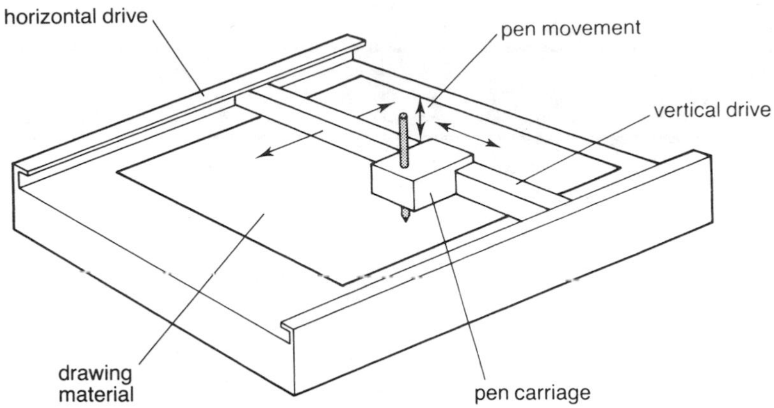

Figure 18.1
Flatbed plotter.

18.1 Introduction

Hardcopy devices can be classified in a similar way to CRT display terminals; namely, those that create the image by drawing a series of vectors – vector-based devices – and those that display a raster type image consisting of a 2D matrix of pixels – pixel-based devices. The first type of device can take graphics primitive and attribute commands and obey them by drawing the required vectors. The pixel-based devices, on the other hand, require the image to be first produced as a pixel image before it can be transferred to the hardcopy medium. This pixel generation can be carried out by the CPU or special-purpose hardware. Commonly, this special hardware is a pixel-based electronic display device with the pixel image being extracted directly from the frame buffer for transfer to the hardcopy device. However, there are also devices that copy the displayed image off the electronic display, especially CRT displays. These normally use a photographic technique to produce the hardcopy image.

18.2 Pen Plotters

The pen plotter is a vector hardcopy device that can draw lines between coordinate points directly on to the hardcopy medium. With one type of pen plotter, the paper is held down on a flat surface by a vacuum, electrostatic charge or sticking tape; this type of pen plotter has the appropriate name **flatbed plotter**. The pen is held in a mount, in which it can be raised or lowered on command, on to the paper. The pen mount rides along a carriage which itself can move longitudinally across the plotter table.

Figure 18.2
Table top flatbed pen plotter with automatic paper feed and multiple pen pack.

Movement of the carriage and pen mount is accomplished by electric stepper motors and gears that can move and hold position to a very high precision. Using the movement of the carriage and the mount, the pen can be positioned over any point on the table. Device coordinates for this type of device are expressed in terms of a linear measurement, such as centimetres or inches. The diagram in Figure 18.1 illustrates these movements.

Pen plotters can only draw with a single pen and therefore can only produce a single colour at a time. To produce images of several colours, the pen in the mount needs to be changed. In early models, this had to be done by hand, but modern plotters have the ability to replace and collect a new one from a pack containing pens of various colours and widths. Paper is not the only hardcopy medium that can be used with pen plotters. Clear plastic film and tracing paper are amongst the others that may also be used.

The graphics primitives and attribute functions that the pen plotter can obey are sent to the device from the CPU. Early pen plotters could only accept simple movement commands, such as 'pen up', 'pen down', 'move one unit left' (or right) and 'move one unit up' (or down), but modern devices can accept most of the common primitives and communication with them uses similar protocols to the electronic displays. Flatbed plotters vary considerably in size from huge tables of 2 by 3 m (6 by 10′) to small desk top

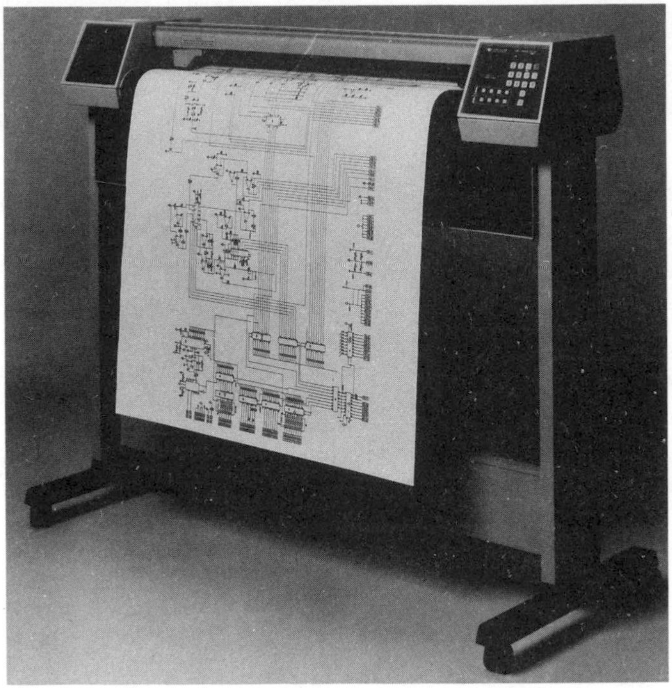

Figure 18.3
A drum-type pen plotter.

devices that use standard A4 paper. An example of this type of intelligent pen plotter is shown in Figure 18.2. This device has an automatic paper feed system and a multiple pen pack giving it the ability to work for long periods without human intervention.

As large flatbed plotters can occupy a considerable amount of floor space, the **drum plotter** was developed to allow large plots to be generated more conveniently. In these plotters, the paper is wrapped over a drum. Horizontal motion of the paper is achieved by moving the paper around the drum and vertical motion is achieved by moving the pen mount across the width of the drum. An example of a drum-type plotter with a paper width of over a metre is shown in Figure 18.3. The paper can be fed in as single sheets or it can be fed from a roll. Again, multiple pen packs may be used.

18.3 Character and Line Printers

Although not strictly designed or intended for graphics printing or plotting, **character** and **line printers** are occasionally found being used for graphics production. Both are serial printers that, in the case of the character printer, print a character at a time and the line printer, a line at a time. The print data is sent from the CPU, also usually in a serial manner, and stored or *buffered* in a small memory. The character printer then takes one character at a time and prints it, using a typewriter-type print head, on to the paper. Print speeds of about 60 characters per second can be achieved on economically priced devices and print quality varies depending on the type of print head and the speed of printing.

Line printers take all of the characters from the buffer and, using a print head for each print position on a line, produce the whole line in one print cycle. Current line printers use a metal band with the character fonts engraved on to it, rotating at high speed, and a set of print hammers, one for each print position, to strike the character on to the paper as it passes. These printers are capable of very high print speeds (of up to 3000 lines per minute) with high quality, consistent print definition.

Both character and line printers can also use matrix print heads. In this case, the character font is constructed from a rectangular pattern or matrix of dots identical to those used for font shapes by pixel-based electronic graphics display devices. The print head consists of a set of impact needles arranged in a rectangle, each needle being operated by an electromagnetic solenoid. A matrix character printer has one such head whereas a matrix line printer has a set for the number of characters to be printed on any line. Matrix character printers can achieve speeds of 500 characters per second and matrix line printers up to 1000 lines per minute.

There are two methods that can be used with these printers to generate graphics hardcopy. The first produces crude graphics images by using the different alphanumeric and punctuation character font shapes to simulate the required pixel grey levels. This, of course, implies that the image must first be constructed in a frame buffer, probably in the CPU. Software in the CPU then decides which characters to use to simulate the pixel grey levels. Overprinting (that is, printing two or more characters at a print position) can be used to improve the simulation, but this will make the print process very slow. This method of image hardcopy is rarely used nowadays.

Matrix character and line printers lend themselves better to graphics hardcopy. These printers use their ability to generate random dot patterns within the character font shape to produce more subtle pixel grey levels. The resulting image appears smoother and clearer with, in some cases, virtually no demarcation between pixels. Again, the image must be transferred a pixel line at a time from a frame buffer resident either in the CPU or in another graphics device. For example, the image may already exist in the frame buffer of a raster scan display system. A matrix printer can then be connected directly to the raster device and the pixel data transferred to the printer under the control of the software in the raster generator. This type of graphics image production is very slow, five minutes a page being typical, but does not require the image to be regenerated, if it is merely a copy of an existing image.

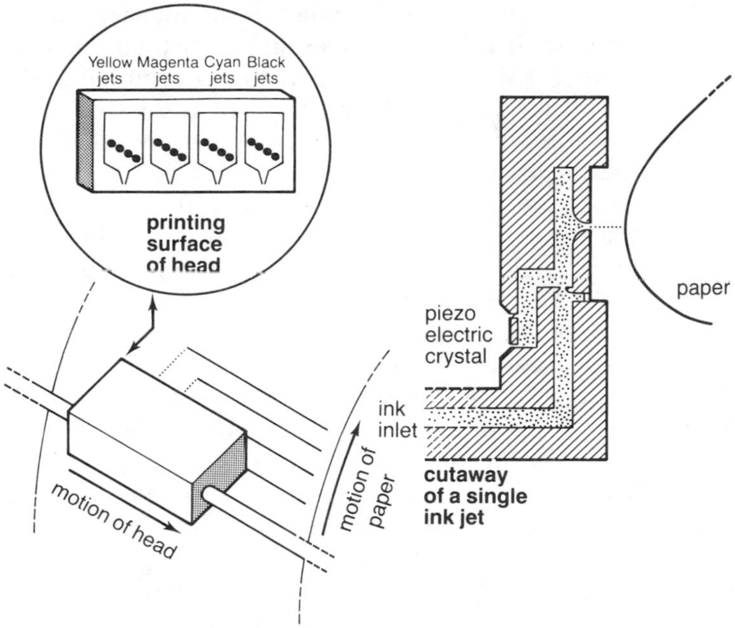

Figure 18.4
Operation of an ink jet printer head.

Dot matrix line printers can be equipped with a set of coloured printing ribbons to enable colour images to be produced. Four different coloured ribbons are available, usually with colours of magenta, yellow, cyan and black. These colours are the subtractive primary colours (see Section 14.6.4) and by mixing them in varying quantities all the required colours can be generated. Black is included for efficiency of printing. To produce a full-colour pixel image using this type of printer, the image must be printed three or four times, once for each of the ribbon colours, with the second and third image overprinted on the first. The image is printed line by line, pixel by pixel using the first colour; the paper is then moved back to its starting position so that the next colour can be printed over the first, and the process is repeated again for the third and fourth colours. On each pass, only pixels containing the current colour are printed. Very acceptable graphics hardcopy can be produced in this way, but the process is very slow, with 10 to 15 minutes required for a full-colour image.

18.4 Ink Jet Printers

A more recent development has been the **ink jet printer**. Its mode of operation is the same as the colour matrix printer but jets of coloured ink are *shot* on to the paper, replacing the single print head and multiple coloured print ribbons. For full-colour image printing, the four constituent colours are deposited in a single pass, making the whole process considerably quicker than with the dot matrix printer. The principles of operation of the ink jet printing head are illustrated in Figure 18.4, where the piezo electric crystal pump for shooting the ink jets can be seen. Hardcopy images produced using this method of printing have crisp and clear colour production and the printers operate with very little noise.

18.5 Electrophotographic Printers

The name **electrophotographic printers** is used to encompass several different types of printer, all of which use the same fundamental print process. The process is that developed by the Xerox Corporation for photocopying documents and is known as the xerographic process. Electrophotographic printers are also known as **page printers** because, not surprisingly, they print a page at a time.

The most common of these printers is the **laser printer** and it is its operation that is used here to describe the basic print process. The electrophotographic print process uses an electrostatically charged rotating photosensitive drum. The drum, which is usually made of aluminium with an outer layer of organic photoconductor, is initially given a uniform electrostatic (normally negative) charge. As the drum rotates, the beam from a single semiconductor or gas laser is mechanically scanned across it at right-angles to the direction of rotation, resulting in an overall scanning effect similar to that of a raster scan display system. The overall resolution, however, in both the horizontal and vertical scanning directions is very much higher (up to 300 lines per inch). As the laser beam scans the drum, its intensity is modulated on and off such that it strikes the drum and neutralizes the charge where the image is to be *light*. The drum then has a charge pattern that consists of remaining negative charge in areas where the image is to be *dark* and an approximately zero charge in the light areas where the beam has exposed the drum. (Some systems generate the opposite charge pattern; that is, the beam discharges the dark areas of the image.)

After the latent electrostatic image has been created on the drum, a (normally) black powder, known as **toner** (and consisting of pigment, magnetite and resin), is applied to the surface of the drum. The toner is first applied to a rotating, magnetic developing cylinder and transported on the surface of the cylinder to the drum. The toner particles are charged to a negative potential by friction with the rotating cylinder and when close to the drum attracted to the potentially neutral areas of the latent image, converting it into a visible toner image. An alternating bias voltage applied to the developing cylinder prevents any fogging of the image by excess

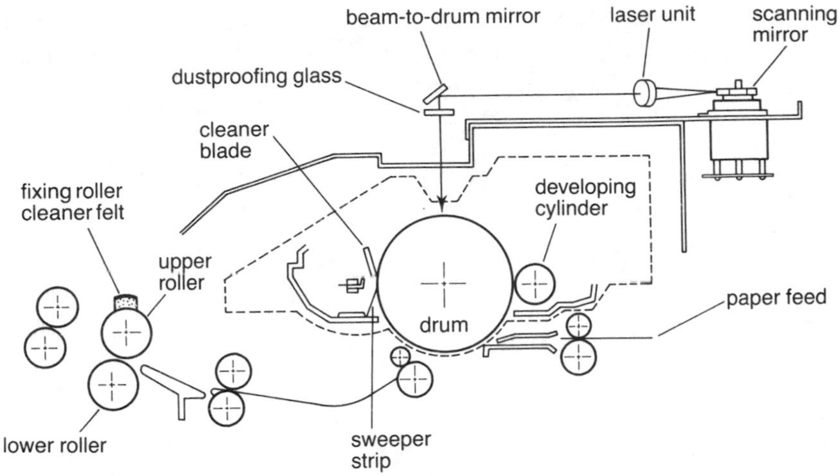

Figure 18.5
Schematic of the operation of a laser printer.

toner. The toner image is then transferred on to paper by inducing a positive charge on to the paper as it is passed close to the drum, so that the toner particles are attracted away from the drum and on to the paper's surface. The paper carrying the toner image is then passed between heated rollers to fuse the toner and fix the image to the paper. A schematic of the operation of a laser printer is shown in Figure 18.5.

Very high resolutions can be achieved using this print process, with between 200 and 300 dots per inch being typical. Higher resolution can be achieved if liquid or semi-liquid toner is used, but these require special paper and tend to lose the advantage of powder systems as being **plain paper printers**. Print speeds of 10 to 12 pages per minute are typical.

Page printers use both character and frame buffer methods of defining the image to be printed. The printer can be treated as a character or line printer where the individual character and page formatting codes are transmitted to the printer from the CPU. The printer may have internally stored character font shapes or may use font cassettes that are manually loaded into the printer. This allows virtually any character font to be used, including that for the non-greek alphabets, without any change to the printer mechanism. Page printers may also have local RAM storage for font shapes down-loaded as pixel patterns from the CPU. The page image will only be printed when an end-of-page control character is received from the CPU.

The printers may also have a local frame buffer memory so that pixel images can be down-loaded from the CPU. Normally, a page printer does not have its own graphics generator and the pixel images must be created in a frame buffer in the CPU and sent to the printer as pixel images. A single pixel is created by printing an array of dots with the density of the dots in a

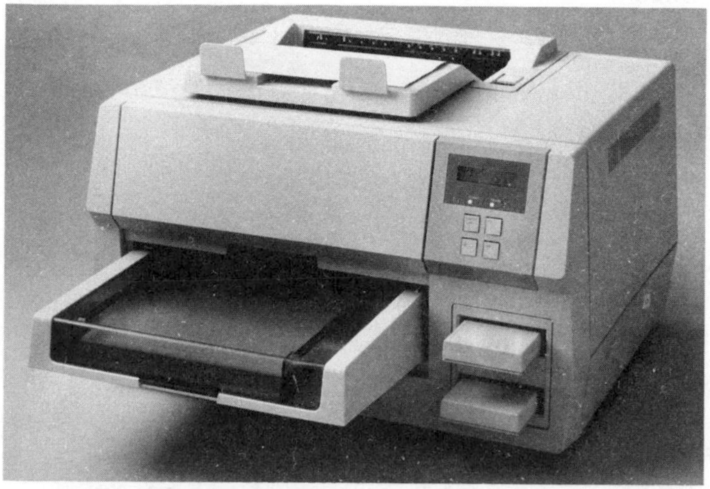

Figure 18.6
Laser printer.

unit area controlled to modulate the intensity of the pixel image created. It is to be expected that in the future page printers will be equipped with their own graphics generators, allowing them to be treated as graphics devices and not merely pixel dump systems. There are no electrophotographic page printers currently available that are capable of generating colour images.

The first laser page printers were developed in the mid 1970s but at a very high cost. The cost has fallen dramatically and is now in the region of 5000 to 10 000 dollars. Most laser page printers, such as that shown in Figure 18.6, can be accommodated on an office table top.

Another type of page printer using the electrophotographic print process is the **LED printer**. Instead of a mechanically scanned laser beam being used to photo etch the charge pattern on to the drum, the light from an array of light-emitting diodes (LEDs), guided to the photosensitive surface by a set of rod lenses, is used. The resolution of LED printers (300 dots per inch) is the same as a laser printer, but there are fewer moving parts and therefore higher reliability. The print speed of 12 pages per minute is also about the same as for the laser printer, but the cost of an LED printer is about two-thirds that of a laser printer.

A further variation on the electrophotographic print process is that of the **ion deposition printer**. With this printer, the imaging drum is made of steel offering a far more robust surface for the print process. A plasma is created in a charging chamber and accelerated towards the drum by a second electric field. The jet of ions is modulated as it passes across the drum, imparting the required virtual image as a negative charge. The remainder of the process is similar to the basic electrophotographic system except that the toner is cold pressure fused to the paper after transfer from the drum. Ion page printers are faster than other electrophotographic

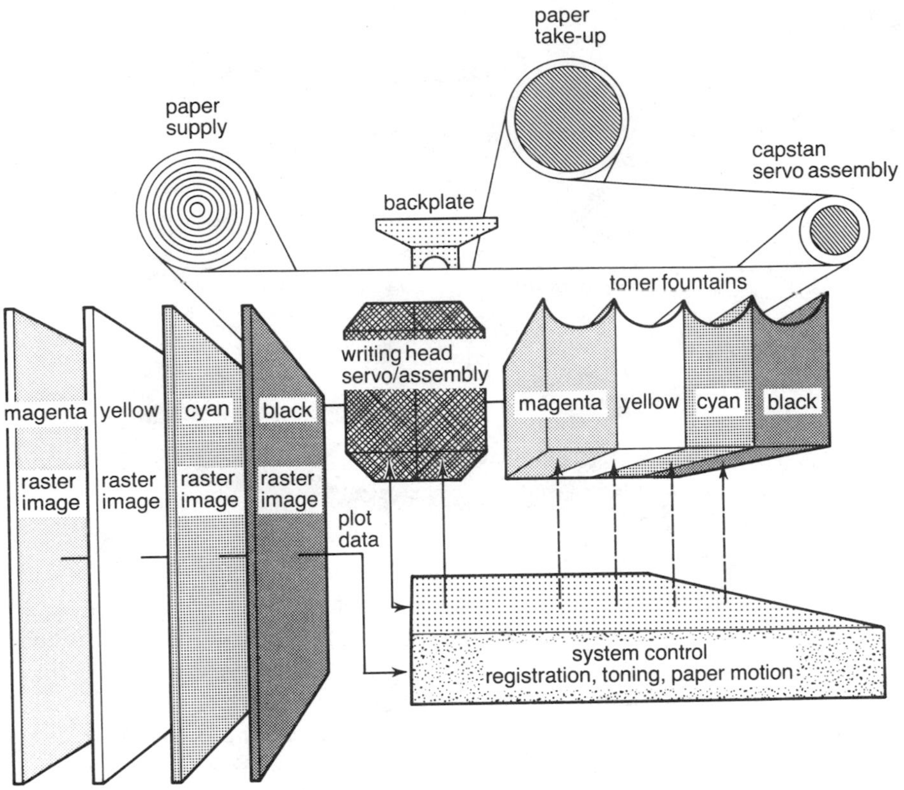

Figure 18.7
Principles of operation of an electrostatic colour plotter.

systems, with print rates of up to 100 pages per minute, but their costs are ten times that of a laser printer. They have the additional advantage that they can accept a larger range of hardcopy media than laser printers.

Finally, there is the **electrostatic printer/plotter**. The basic electrophotographic process remains, but this time there is no drum for the virtual image. The virtual image charge pattern is created directly on to the paper and the charged toner powder is sprayed on to the surface where it is then fused to the surface. This process, illustrated in Figure 18.7, has the advantage, however, that colour images can be created by using the usual three or four pass process, one for each of the subtractive primary colours plus black. High-quality, high-resolution colour images can be produced, but print time is relatively slow.

18.6 Laser Displays

Lasers are used in several other ways to produce graphics images. The simplest is to use the laser to draw the image on to a photographic plate in the same way as the pen plotter draws on to paper. The plate is then

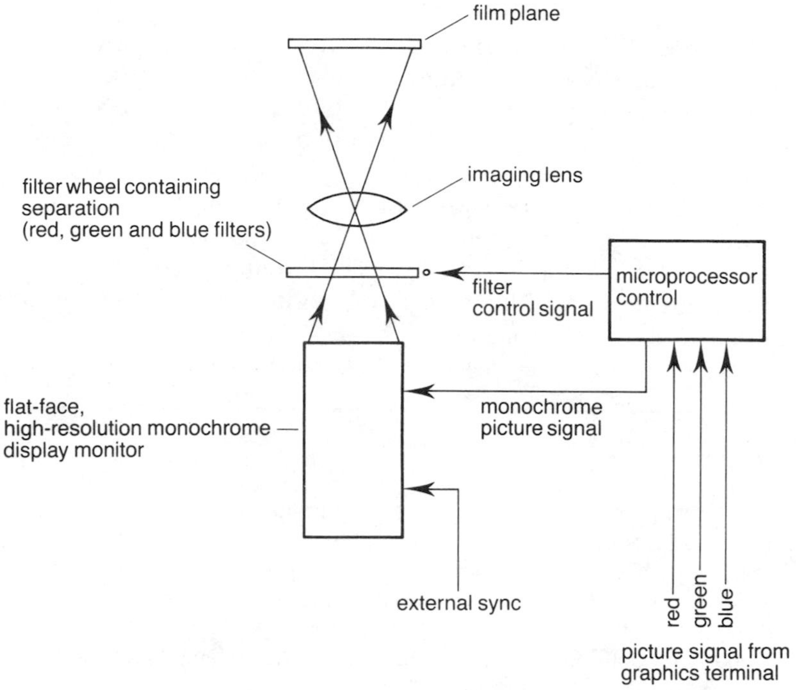

Figure 18.8
Layout of a colour camera system.

developed as a positive image and used as a slide transparency in a projector. Very large projected imags of high resolution can be produced in this manner, but the time to create the image is of course slow due to the developing process. Recent work has seen the photographic plate replaced with a liquid crystal cell and the laser *burns* the image on to the cell. The LCD cell is then used as the projection slide.

18.7 Photographic Systems

Perhaps the simplest method of reproducing the image on a vector or raster scan display is to take a photograph of the screen. Usually, a black hood is placed over the screen and the camera to keep out unwanted light. Long exposure times are used with a very small lens aperture. This often gives more than adequate results although the developing process means that image production is slow.

The method just outlined suffers from distortion of the image due to curvature of the CRT display surface as well as, if a colour raster system is used, from the reduction in resolution due to the shadow mask. To improve this type of image production, special colour camera systems have been developed, which include flat-faced CRT displays. These displays are monochrome and the photograph needs to be exposed three times, once for each of the additive primary colours of red, green and blue. Colour filters are placed in the path between the CRT and the photographic plate to impart the required colour to the image. The layout of such a camera system is shown in Figure 18.8. Colour negative, positive (for slides) and instant film can be used in these cameras.

Summary

Most of the hardcopy device types that are currently available are far from perfect. The laser printer does, however, come closest to the ideal, although it is currently limited to monochrome image production. This device offers very high resolution (higher than the equivalent electronic displays) at relatively low cost. Image-generation times are short and the image itself is of high quality for both pure text and graphics. The basic features of the device make it compatible with the latest and most popular electronic displays – namely, the window-managed pixel-based systems.

Exercises

18.1 Which is the most versatile hardcopy device? Give reasons for your choice.

18.2 Producing colour hardcopy is a relatively slow (and expensive) process. List the devices that can produce it and discuss the advantages and disadvantages of each.

18.3 The financial director of your company says that you cannot buy a colour hardcopy device for your system. What could you do as an alternative?

18.4 What are the possible applications of a device that produces genuine 3D output. Is such a device feasible?

CHAPTER 19

BUILDING A COMPUTER GRAPHICS SYSTEM

In Chapters 15 to 18, the specialized graphics display and interaction hardware were described. Electronic displays, graphics generators, input devices and hardcopy devices have all been examined in detail. Chapters 2 to 9 have derived some of the software algorithms that are used to create and manipulate the shapes and their appearance. Now, in this chapter, it is time to put all this information together and construct a computer graphics system.

The discussion here is based on practical experience of building computer systems in industrial applications, rather than on an abstract analysis. Hence, this chapter does not constitute a precis of any of the formal system design methodologies; rather, it offers a few pragmatic hints of what to look for when beginning a new development.

A still from the BFI film *The Draughtsman's Contract.*

19.1 Introduction

Before proceeding to construct a computer graphics system, it is necessary to consider the questions: Why build a system? What is it going to do? Is it going to help the user design automobiles, bridges or shoes maybe? Or is it going to be an education system displaying and instructing the user on the operation of the organs of the human body? Perhaps it is just going to be used to display pretty pictures! It is its use, however, that is going to dictate its design and the specification of the graphics equipment and computer that are to be used. This, of course, appears obvious, but it is essential to work out exactly what tasks a system is required to perform and, equally important, what tasks it does *not* have to perform.

As an example, this chapter considers the development of a draughting system – The Draughtsman's Contract. But first consider the elements of a system that must be included in the design, including the main processor and, in particular, the parameters that specify each element.

19.2 The Elements of a System

Consider the following elements of a graphics display system. Some of the elements are actual hardware but some are system parameters that must also be considered to formulate a useful design.

19.2.1 The Applications Host Computer

The applications host computer is the hub of the system on to which all of the display, input and storage devices are attached. It also includes the CPU for the application, graphics package and device driver software. This computer can take many different forms. It can be closely coupled to the graphics system or loosely coupled. It can be a microprocessor or a mainframe computer or, less common, a mini computer. Closely coupled systems have been discussed in detail in Chapter 16. A loosely coupled system is one in which the various elements of the total system communicate over relatively slow serial channels, such as networks.

When considering which computer to use, it is necessary to estimate the computational power required to support the application, graphics package and any drivers; how many graphics devices are to be connected; and what external storage devices are required. The software tools that are available on the computer are extremely important. Before any decision is made on the computer to be used, it is essential to verify that the required tools exist and that they operate according to the requirements of the task's

Figure 19.1
Personal workstation.

construction. These tools will probably consist of text editors for use on the applications programs, language compilers for the programming languages selected for writing the application software, suitable software debugging aids and software management tools, such as program library handlers. Naturally, it is also important to verify that the graphics library, device drivers and code generators all work correctly in conjunction with the selected display and input hardware. All of this should be done *before* a decision is made regarding the applications computer. It is, however, a rare luxury for this to be the case, with the choice of the applications computer often being a *fait accompli*.

19.2.2 Workstations

The term *workstation* has recently become a little overused. In the past, it was used to describe a set of display and input devices which were connected to a computer and which provided the user with all the peripheral facilities required to carry out the task. All of the applications and most of the graphics software was in the main processor. A typical modern workstation is shown in Figure 19.1.

Recently, the development of powerful microprocessors has allowed

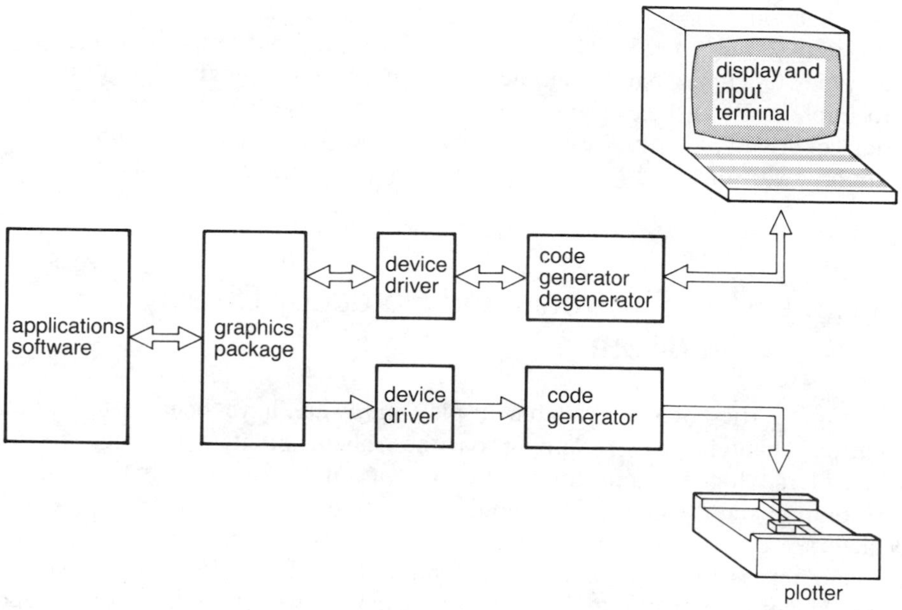

Figure 19.2
Structure of a typical graphics software system.

the computational capabilities of large computers to be incorporated in units having the same physical size as that of the workstation alone. The graphics generation and display system are closely coupled to the microprocessor CPU (see Section 16.4.16). The configuration may also include devices for storing and transporting programs, data and graphics, such as floppy disks or cassette tapes. Connection to a larger mainframe computer may be completely unnecessary although possible. The accepted term **personal workstation** is used to describe these systems. It is common to use personal workstations in conjunction with a network system, as described in Section 19.2.7.

19.2.3 Applications Software

Figure 19.2 shows the basic structure of the software for a computer graphics system. The applications software implements the logic and algorithms of the specialized tasks that the system is to perform. It also provides the specialized user interface in terms of instructions, prompts and echoes, as well as accepting and verifying any user input or interaction. It is the applications software that gives the system its personality and intelligence. The applications software communicates directly with the graphics packages by means of the logical display and input functions, which are defined by the virtual graphics device (VGD) appropriate to the library (see Section 3.3). It may also use additional specialized software packages for non-graphics tasks. The library package interprets and manages the graphics functions that the application requires and uses the device drivers to implement the logical graphics functions used for the real devices. The device drivers, in turn, use the device code generators to communicate directly with the hardware, using the device's interface protocol.

19.2.4 The Electronic and Hardcopy Display Hardware

The properties of the available display hardware have been discussed in earlier chapters, but recapping on the salient points that need to be considered for the application, it is important to know both the display resolution and the number of colours required by the application. These two factors are not always as easy to determine as it would seem. One way round this is to simply say that the highest resolution and the maximum number of colours obtainable are to be used. However, as the cost of such devices is very high and usually places an upper limit on the hardware that can be used, the choice is often a cost/performance compromise.

It is also important to consider the interconnection of the devices with the computer, the availability and suitability of input devices and, significantly, the intelligence of the device. This is important because the more computational and graphics functions that are programmed into the graphics generator hardware, the less that has to be included in the applications CPU. This has two significant effects. The first is that for a given overall performance a less powerful and, therefore cheaper, applications CPU can be used. The second is that the effort required to implement the application is considerably reduced. In addition, if the device has its own display list, then the amount of communications with the device to achieve a given effect is reduced considerably. This reduces both the communications loading on the device/CPU interconnections and the time required by the system to change the displayed image.

19.2.5 Interaction

An important aspect of the design of a computer graphics system is the type of interaction required and the type of devices to be used to supply the interaction. It may be that no interaction with the system is required, because once the processing has started no further data needs to be supplied by the user (for example, image processing). However, this is unlikely in the case of a graphics system, since some form of interaction with a running applications system is invariably required.

What type of interaction does the application need? Does the user need to be able to pick graphics image elements or can all the interaction be achieved through a keyboard? Is any digitizing required? When making a decision concerning the type of interaction needed, it is necessary to consider the typical users. Do they prefer to use a data tablet and puck or do they like to point to the actual image on the display? These questions are all vital to the development of a successful system.

19.2.6 Data and Image Storage

The system may be required to store the data, from which the images have been created for later use. Additionally, it may be a requirement to store the *commands* that created the images or a *recording* of the image creation and editing session in metafiles. Metafiles store the images in the form of a special protocol, a standardized version of which is the Computer Graphics Metafile (CGM). All of these require some type of backing storage, on to which the data can be recorded. Most computers have a backing store medium, usually in the form of a fixed or removable magnetic disk system. A fixed disk enables the data to be stored on the computer for later use, whereas removable disks can be taken to other computer systems for subsequent use, assuming that the second system is able to read the type of disk and knows the data codes that have been used. The most common type of removable disk is the **floppy** disk, which is available in sizes from 3 to 8 inches in diameter. Magnetic tape, either on large reels or in sealed cassettes, can also be used for data storage and transfer. Data, and programs, can now also be stored on laser disks, with a data capacity being measured in terms of gigabytes (10^{10} bytes). The equipment to write these disks will not normally be available on small or medium systems. The laser disk offers the capability of being able to access vast databases that have been assembled on large, high-capacity computer systems, on small, microprocessor-based computer systems.

19.2.7 Networks

Data and images, in various forms, can be directly transferred from system to system on **networks**. Networking consists of connecting parts of a system together on a common electronic link. These links are relatively slow (compared with the internal communications within a CPU say) serial links between systems or devices – known as **nodes** – on the network. Data can be

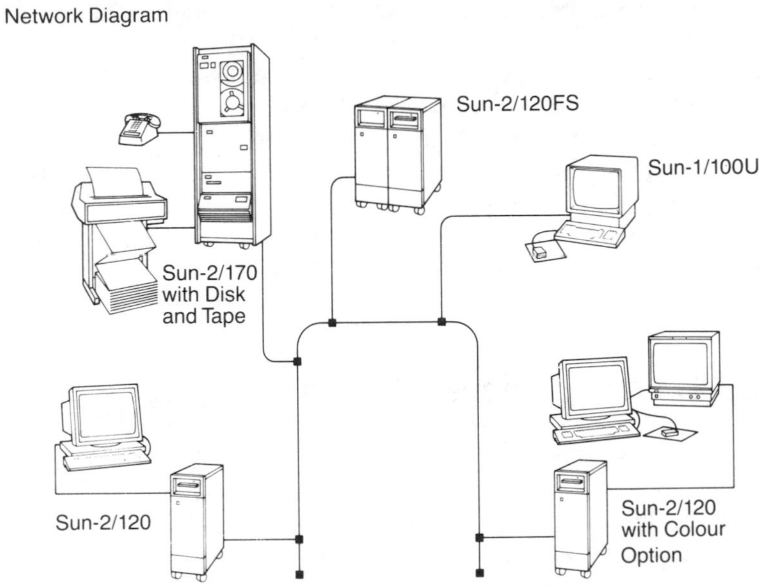

Figure 19.3
Network diagram.

dispatched from one device to any other device on the network using destination address codes for each device. Not only is it possible to share data and programs between computers on networks, but it is also possible to share their *resources*. For example, a hardcopy may need to be generated of an image that has been created on a system that only has an electronic display. If the system is resident on a network that has another system with a hardcopy device, then the image can be transferred across the network to this other system and a hardcopy generated.

It is also possible to share processing power across networks. In this case, one or more graphics display terminals can communicate with a single CPU on the network. It is common nowadays for workstations to be connected to a network, enabling their processing power and peripheral resources to be shared between users. In addition, in the situation where several applications programmers are working on the same project, the network will allow them to communicate, sharing developed software and problems. Figure 19.3 shows the way that resources can be shared over a network consisting of a large computer system with magnetic tape and disk units and a printer, but no display devices. There is also a smaller computer system without a display device, which together with the other system provides computational power to the rest of the devices on the network. There are two other computer systems on the network that each have a display terminal, one with an additional display subsystem and monitor.

Finally, there is a small, low-power system that has a limited computational capability and this relies on the other systems on the network for high computation power, backing storage and so on.

19.3 The Draughtsman's Contract

This section outlines the steps that must be taken when confronted with the task of building a particular graphics system – in this case a draughting system. The design and construction of the computer draughting system is not considered in detail, but is merely a muse about which the discussion of graphics system development in general can take place. The details of a particular computer graphics system development may well focus attention on particular features unique to that system, thereby diverting discussion from the general principles.

Before any steps are taken in the design of a system, there are many important pieces of information that have to be collected, some of which may seem surprising.

19.3.1 Why a New System?

Why has the contract been placed? Why is a computer graphics system seen to be necessary? What has it got to do with the designer why the customer wants a new system? These might seem odd questions. Surely the designer should get on and develop the system and leave the reason why to the customer. However, this information may be the most important, because the answer will influence many of the detailed system parameters that are to be decided later on. Assuming that there is a current system in use, which may or may not be computerized, then consider some of the reasons why a computer graphics system might be an advantage and what the consequences to the design will be.

(1) *Speed and productivity* One of the most common reasons for wanting to introduce computerized systems is to reduce the time taken to complete a task, and computers are well endowed with features that fulfil this demand, such as speed of calculation, speed of recall of work from previous work sessions, reduced operating time due to automated repetitive processes and so on. If this is one of the reasons why a computer system is required, then the design must ensure that the required time savings are achieved. An obvious example of this is as follows: if there is no way of manipulating shapes (by segmentation) in the system, then all parts of the drawing will

have to be drawn from scratch, the draughting process being slow, laborious and error prone.

(2) *Accuracy* The draughtsman may not be able to work to or maintain the required accuracy with the current system. Although computer graphics systems may not be able to draw any more accurately than a skilled draughtsman, the data that they can store can be to very high precision.

(3) *Errors* Thc draughtsman may find that the type of draughting being carried out is prone to error. Computerized systems can carry out automatic checking and verification of the drawings. The design must ensure that hidden errors cannot be generated and that any mistakes made are trapped and the operator alerted.

(4) *Versatility* The draughtsman may need a more versatile system so that different types of drawings can be carried out on the same system. Therefore, the designer must ensure that the system will not be limited in its use, allowing only a restricted range of work to be carried out.

(5) *Easier to use* The current system may be difficult to use, requiring highly trained or experienced operators. Chapter 14 discussed the HCI in relation to computer graphics systems and the consequences of a system that is difficult to use are far ranging and may be disastrous. A system that is difficult to operate will always be expensive in use.

(6) *Everybody else has got one!* This may be the real reason and it is not as silly as it sounds. For example, because there are many systems around, there is a pool of ready-trained operators; thus, it may be possible to transmit work from one system to another sharing work between systems.

(7) *Cost* Last, but not least, there is the question of cost. Most of the foregoing, if achieved, should result in savings in time, effort, skills and therefore cost. The system may increase cost in the short term, but save it in the long term.

There may be many reasons why a computerized system has been asked for by, in this case, the draughtsman, and it is important to identify what they are. Determine why the new system is needed and, in addition, look carefully at the systems currently in use and identify why they are not satisfying the users or their owners.

Once all the reasons for requiring a system have been identified, then they should be written down in a formalized manner. This document should be entitled the **system requirement** and should be written in the terms of the customer's environment and not those of the computer's (graphics) environment. It is very important that the draughtsman should carefully check the requirement document at this stage and it is very probable that several stages of modification will be required before everyone is satisfied.

19.3.2 The Draughtsman's Task

The requirement specification states what the draughtsman wants and why it is wanted. Now it is necessary to find out exactly what a draughtsman does; that is, to analyze his task. A considerable amount of research has been carried out into the subject of task analysis (see Chapter 14) and some aspects of this will be contained in the requirement specification. It is, however, necessary for the designer to take an independent view of the task and, if possible, specify it formally. Naturally, it will only be possible to analyze the current version of the task if one exists. In other words, analyze what the draughtsman does by watching him do it and asking him about it. If the task is a completely new one, then the task will have to be simulated.

If the task, like that of the draughtsman, already exists, then it may be necessary to extend it to achieve the requirement specification. Again, it will be necessary to simulate the new subtasks, but at least there will be more data on which to base this than if the task was completely new.

To analyze the task, it is necessary to divide the overall task into subtasks and analyze each in detail. Observe the actions made, the information used and the object of each task. Interdependencies between subtasks should be very carefully noted. For example, is it necessary to complete one subtask before another? If so, the new system may be required to trap any tasks performed out of order. It may also be necessary to go as far as timing each of the subtasks. Having completed the task analysis, it should be discussed with the draughtsman, who may be quite surprised to see exactly what the job involves, and will undoubtedly notice errors very quickly.

19.3.3 The Draughtsman's System

The next stage is to specify exactly what features the system requires to enable it to satisfy the draughtsman's requirements. These should be specified down to the fine detail of, for example, what parameters the draughtsman will have to specify for each command. There will be four sources for this information.

(1) *The system requirement* The list of features that the draughtsman requires to see in the system will be largely subsequent to the answers to the question why.

(2) *The task analysis.*

(3) *The customer* Does the draughtsman really know what is wanted? Yes, probably, but may have great difficulty in describing it. Customers often take some elements of the system for granted and it is therefore important to make sure that all aspects of the system have

been considered and described by the customer. As an example, in any draughting system, a command for drawing circles will certainly be required, but it is highly unlikely that a simple function that requires the user to supply only the centre and the radius will suffice. The draughtsman may want to pick a number of points that lie on the circle or the angle of the arc of the circle to be constructed. Therefore, if circle drawing is required, it is necessary to specify exactly how it will be used. If there are undue restrictions on the use of such commands, because they were not fully specified at this stage, the system may not be of use to the customer.

(4) *Extensibility* It is unlikely that there has ever been a system specified that has not required to be extended in some way. The customer will always think of a new feature that is *essential* to the system, shortly after it is finished. Therefore, one of the most important aspects of any system specification, whether the customer requires it or not, is that it should be flexible and capable of being easily extended or modified. Try to predict what the draughtsman is going to ask for next.

19.3.4 Specifying the System

It should now be possible to choose all of the system parameters of both the software and the hardware. There will be many such parameters for even a simple system, so it is valuable to have a check list. The first part of the list for a graphics system should be based on the human–computer interface (HCI), and will cover such items as the displays and interaction. Its importance cannot be overstressed. A poor interface will ruin an otherwise good system.

(1) *Displays* It is necessary to identify how many displays will be required and their performance. Most early draughting systems used a single display with both the drawing display and user prompts and echoes displayed on the same device. Recently, systems have appeared that use two displays, with the drawing and user commands on a separate display. The advantages of this are that all of the display space can be assigned to the drawing and a more stable display system used. Prompts and interaction echoes that do not use the displayed image itself do not require such high-quality displays.

(2) *Type of display* Does the system require simple vector or stroke drawn images or are functions unique to pixel-based displays required (for example, solid modelling).

(3) *Resolution* The resolution of the displays should be considered

carefully. The higher the resolution, the better; but the cost will also rise rapidly with higher resolution. Therefore, there will be a compromise. It should also be remembered that the resolution of the displays, as well as being dictated by the tasks required of them, is also a function of colour, and possibly the functional capability of the displays.

(4) *Size* Display size is an important parameter. Briefly, there will be an optimum size for the comfort of the user and the other parameters of the display.

(5) *Colour* The colour capability of the display is a complex problem involving cost as well as HCI issues. If colour is deemed necessary or desirable, then great care should be taken in deciding at this stage what colours are to be used for which display elements.

(6) *Flicker* Another aspect of the displays that must be considered here is how long a typical user is likely to spend interacting with the display. If these periods are likely to be lengthy, it may be necessary to use flicker-free displays to reduce user fatigue.

(7) *Interaction* The final aspect of the HCI to be considered is that of the interaction with the display and the devices that should be used to achieve it. This could be a complex problem, as it will depend on the functions that the system must provide as well as display type and again cost.

It will soon be realized that the display and interaction parameters selected may be nothing more than a series of compromises, one parameter against another. After defining the HCI, the system parameters that must be decided are slightly more mundane but no less important.

(1) *Graphics hardcopy* It is unusual for there not to be a requirement for graphics hardcopy on a system. The parameters for hardcopy will include most of those for the displays, such as type (vector or pixel) size, colour, resolution and cost, in addition to the medium (paper, transparency, etc.).

(2) *Main processor* The size and power of the main processor is, of course, important and it should always be remembered that the system is more likely than not to grow. Therefore, avoid selecting a computer that only just meets the capabilities (speed, memory, etc.) to handle the task. Try to estimate the computational and local communications requirements and add at least 50% for system growth.

It is also worth considering at this point the use of the 'computer' that is supplied with every interactive system; that is, of course, the human operator. There is, currently, no man-made computer that has the capability of average human beings and any system that does not allow the operator to use his or her full potential is wasting a valuable resource.

(3) *Communication with other systems* Most systems, at some time in their working lives, will be required to communicate with other systems. As this may be on a regular basis (several times a day), a high-speed electronic communications link will be required. If it is a very rare occurrence, then a slower manual (floppy diskettes) interface would suffice. Consider the requirements and include provision for at least that level of communication.

(4) *Backing storage* Only rarely will a system not be required to provide a method of storing or saving the work that has been carried out on it. It may also be necessary to save the intermediate results from an interrupted work session. Backing storage systems can vary from simple hardcopy through to networked mass storage systems. Study the requirement and make sure that it is catered for. Facilities for backing storage may be combined with those required for inter-system communication.

(5) *Standards* Early in the development of the system, the use of, or the adherence to, any standards should be decided. Much of the work in this book is based on the ISO computer graphics standard GKS and the use of this standard in the development of a new draughting system might be sensible. Other standards could also be considered, especially in the areas of data communication. Trying to introduce them at a later date will be very difficult.

Now, most of the important system parameters and performance issues have been derived and the system can be fully specified. The resulting formal specification should result in a document known as the **system specification**, which should define every aspect of the operation of the system, including all responses to user interaction, data exchange, error conditions and system failures. The implications of this document should be discussed, in detail, with the customer as it will define exactly what the required system will do. Any detail that the customer does not like must be modified now, because including such changes at a later date may be difficult and expensive.

It is at this point that the tests through which the final system will be put should be defined. The system is now fully defined and its response to any data or situation known. Tests should be defined for each aspect of the system, so that when they are applied to the system itself it will exercise all of its operations. These tests should be collected in a document known as the **test specification** and its development will often show, at this stage, shortcomings in the system itself. If the system specification has been defined formally, then the test specification itself can be a formalized scheme.

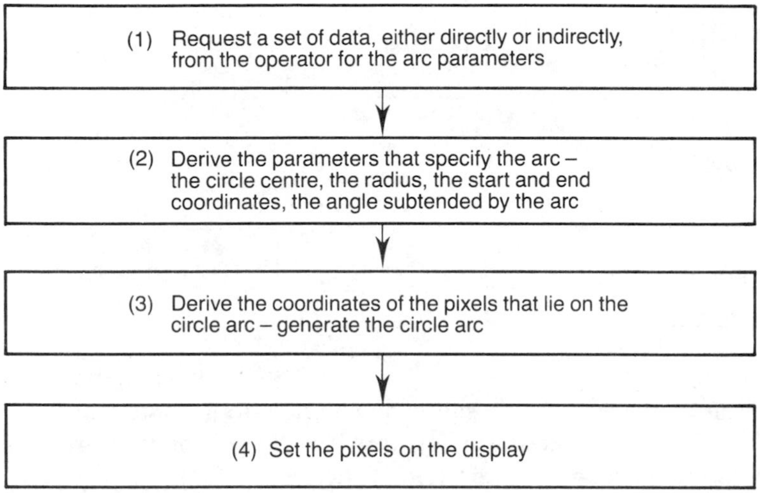
(1) Request a set of data, either directly or indirectly, from the operator for the arc parameters
(2) Derive the parameters that specify the arc – the circle centre, the radius, the start and end coordinates, the angle subtended by the arc
(3) Derive the coordinates of the pixels that lie on the circle arc – generate the circle arc
(4) Set the pixels on the display

Figure 19.4
Function path for the circle arc command.

19.3.5 How Is It Going to Work?

Once the system specification has been agreed, and not before, work can begin on deciding how to achieve this specification. How are the circles to be drawn and how is the interactive display going to be driven, for example? Each item in the system specification must be examined and the functions that are to be used identified.

Using the example of the draughtsman who requires the system to draw the arcs of circles, it is necessary to identify what functions the system must perform to achieve this facility. For a display that possesses its own frame buffers, the functions would be as shown in Figure 19.4. The implementation of some of these functions, such as (3) and (4), will be, for most graphics systems, hidden from the applications programmer in that they are inside other hardware or software. These functions would probably be available for use in a library. The system specification will have described the operation of (1) because it will specify how the draughtsman wishes to request circle arcs. (There may have been more than one method requested.)

The specification of the functions also requires that any mathematical or logical processes used are defined and, where necessary, researched. It is important that at the end of this design stage, no functions have been left for later development, because it is at this stage that the feasibility of implementing the system specification will be realized. Any aspects of the system specification that cannot be defined in terms of the functions required for implementation must be examined carefully – it may be that the system, as specified, cannot be built!

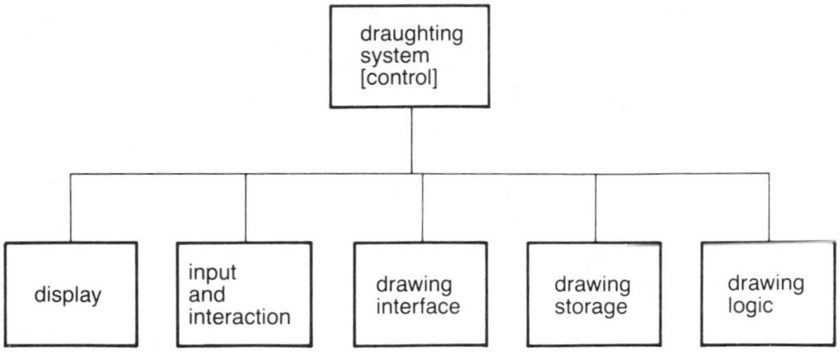

Figure 19.5
Logical functions of a draughting system.

This design stage will result in a definition of the system in terms of its operating functions. The document in which these functions are defined is known as the **functional specification** of the system. This document does not need to concern the customer, since it is describing the system in terms of computer and computer graphics science, and it is unlikely that the customer will understand it anyway. However, if any aspects of the system specification are discovered to be infeasible at this stage, then they will have to be conveyed to the customer, so that the system specification, and possibly the system requirement, can be modified.

19.3.6 Designing the Basic System

The system can now be designed using the data from the function specification. Design should start at the top of the system – in this case, the draughting system – and progress down through the different layers of the design until the *machine level* (the computer program) is reached. Figure 19.5 shows the first two layers of such a design. The top layer simply signifies that it is a draughting system and contains the control for selecting the functions on the next layer down. This layer shows the very basic operating components of the system. At this stage, it can be seen that the design does not necessarily represent a computer graphics system. It could still be a manual system; this generalization may, in fact, still apply until relatively deep in the design.

It may be possible to use a formal system design language. This allows the system design to be specified in a rigorous and formalized manner based on logic. This has three advantages:

(1) The design can be readily and unambiguously understood by anyone familiar with the system design language.
(2) It forces completeness of design.
(3) It often lays itself open to formalized design evaluation.

For a comprehensive design and specification language, the reader is referred to Jones (1986). For an example of a formal specification in an interactive system see Sufrin (1986a).

At various stages of the design, a *walk through* should be carried out; that is, the designer, and preferably additional people who can be persuaded to help, *simulate* the hardware and the software so the system is operated as it will be in actual use. Although this may seem a slow and laborious method of checking the design, the human computers that are taking the place of the system hardware and software are far more intelligent than any computer, and will therefore be far more likely to spot errors.

The walk through process is, in fact, very simple: it is a bit like rehearsing a play. Each function that the system will perform is selected in turn and the operational path of the system followed through. Each person could possibly act out the part of a piece, or pieces, of hardware or software. For each path, a range of parameters should be selected and followed through. Considering the example of the draughtsman again, a range of circle arc radii and subtended angles should be used. It is, of course, not possible to follow through all such values – *that* would make the task laborious! Furthermore, some errors will undoubtedly slip through, but if the examples are chosen carefully, many errors will be trapped.

At the end of this stage in the design process, a complete design should exist for the system and this is collected into a document called the **system design specification**. It is from this that the system will be built.

19.3.7 Building a Prototype

Most computer-based systems are built as if they were going to be perfect first time. This particular feature appears to be unique to those developments that include software engineering. It is, of course, not good practice. When an aeronautical engineer is tasked to build a new passenger-carrying airplane, he or she does not design the concept, build it and immediately start charging the public to fly in it. Instead, the engineer will design and build a prototype and thoroughly evaluate it for safety and performance. The design is then refined as required and the production models built, possibly preceded by a production prototype.

Therefore, building a prototype of the system is very important. (It may be necessary to call it Version 1.0 to avoid the 'no prototype' ideas just described. The production version would then, of course, be Version 2.0.) That is not to say that many elements of the prototype will not be used later in the production system. If the design is good, then much of the software and hardware can be transferred to the production system.

When constructing the prototype, make it flexible so that it can be easily modified if any of the ideas built into the design do not work as planned. For example, if it proves difficult to create circle arcs with the prototype system, then it should be designed so that other schemes can be easily implemented and evaluated.

When the applications programmers and engineers have carried out a full evaluation of the prototype, the draughtsman should be given the opportunity to use and evaluate it – not just play with it, but use it to carry out a reasonable draughting task. Do not forget that the customer is part of the design team and now is the time for any faults to be found. Do not be afraid to have the design and the system criticized – constructive criticism leads to a much better design. The evaluation must be rigorous and thorough and should be carried out against the system test specification, and therefore against the system specification.

Following this evaluation, the design should be completely reviewed and any necessary changes integrated into the system specification – Version 2.0 – of the production system. Review the design thoroughly. Have all the decisions about the system parameters been proved correct? Have the right colours been selected for the different elements of the display, for example? Now is the time to change them where necessary.

The production system can now be constructed. As already described it will, unless the original design was completely wrong, use much of the software and hardware that was used to construct the prototype. Some parts may need replacing or modifying following the review of the prototype's performance. It will often be better to replace than modify, especially in the case of software. The temptation to compromise the design if parts from the prototype are modified is often too great to resist and therefore rewriting a module will usually give superior results.

19.3.8 The End of the Contract

The last stage is to deliver the system to the draughtsman. If the customer has been, as suggested, involved in all the stages of the design and development, then there should not be too many surprises. There are some aspects of the contract that will follow delivery such as training the customer and staff to use the system, maintenance and support. The production of documentation (user or operator manuals) has not been discussed here, but they are a vital part of any system and should be produced in parallel with the system.

At the end of the contract, it may be worthwhile asking some pertinent questions about the final system designed:

- Has the draughtsman got exactly what was wanted?
- Has the question of why the system was required been satisfied in full?
- Will the draughtsman buy a further system from you?
- Was the draughtsman's contract your last?

Summary

This final chapter has provided a high-level discussion on computer graphics systems and how to set about building one. Detailed descriptions of design methodologies would fill a similar-sized book to this one and therefore only a basic approach and concepts have been described here.

The computer-generated graphics image is rapidly becoming the fundamental interface of many computer-based systems, whether the ultimate purpose of the system is graphics related or not. The reasons are two-fold: first, the technology is available and becoming very cost effective; and secondly, the human being accepts and interacts well with pictorial representations of the task at hand. Therefore, a growing percentage of computer systems include a graphics display subsystem, the design and implementation of which are important factors in its acceptability by the user.

Exercise

19.1 Design a system that can be used to design greeting cards, such as birthday cards, Christmas cards, get well cards and so on. This exercise may best be done in a group, each member playing the role of the customer or one of the design and development team. Write each of the system documents in turn. First, the system requirements document and the task analysis, then the system specification and the test specification, the functional specification and then the system design specification. Those students with suitable computer graphics equipment available can then proceed to implement a prototype system.

APPENDIX A

PROGRAMMING NOTATION

A.1 Introduction

This appendix provides an informal and intuitive introduction to the main ideas of the abstract programming notation used in the text to present programming ideas and algorithms. Although the abstract notation relies heavily for its inspiration on the programming language ML (Milner, 1985; Harper, 1986), the ML language is not adhered to exactly, and other sources are also used (Gries, 1981; Bornat, 1986). The reader is advised to read quickly through this appendix and then refer back when necessary while reading the rest of the book.

A.2 Basic Types

The abstract language supports operations on the basic types, which are **literal**, **character**, **integer**, **real** and **boolean**.

Literals are denoted by Roman font in the program texts. They are literally *literal* names and have no meaning other than that conferred on them by their usage. For example, in GKS there are types that have values such as OK, NONE, CLIP, NOCLIP and so on. In Pascal, these are represented as enumerated types; but this confers on them an ordering property that is not implied by GKS. (Note that literals in ML can be represented as data type constructors.)

Examples of integers are: 1, 2, −56, 10101, −98. Reals must always be shown with a decimal point: 8.9, 1.0, −1.234, 0.999, 987.998. Characters are enclosed in single quotation marks: '*a*', '9', '&', '?'. Boolean values are *true* or *false*.

The usual operations are assumed for both numbers and booleans. For example, the following expressions are valid:

4 + 5	
34.0 − 78.9	
234*89	(* used for multiplication)
12.4*67.0	
98.4/12.2	(/ used for division)
~true = false	(~ used for not)
true $\vee$ true = true	($\vee$ used for logical OR)

$\text{true} \vee \text{false} = \text{true}$
$\text{true} \wedge \text{true} = \text{true}$ ($\wedge$ used for logical AND)
$\text{true} \wedge \text{false} = \text{false}$

More complex types may be constructed using **sets**, **tuples**, **sequences** and **function definitions**.

A.3 Sets

A **set** is a collection of objects such that any object is unambiguously either a member of the set or not. The members of a set are also referred to as its **elements**. For example the set consisting of the integers 1,2,3,4 is denoted as:

$$\{1, 2, 3, 4\}$$

and writing, for example:

$$E = \{1, 2, 3, 4\}$$

means that whenever the name E is used (in the appropriate context), it may be validly substituted for by $\{1, 2, 3, 4\}$, and conversely, whenever $\{1, 2, 3, 4\}$ appears, E can be used instead. (The name E is said to be *bound* to $\{1, 2, 3, 4\}$).

The set with no members is said to be the **empty set** and is denoted by the Greek letter $\varnothing$.

Set membership is denoted by the $\in$ symbol. Hence:

$1 \in \{1, 2, 3, 4\}$ or $1 \in \mathrm{E}$
$3 \in \{1, 2, 3, 4\}$ or $3 \in \mathrm{E}$
$5 \notin \{1, 2, 3, 4\}$ or $5 \notin \mathrm{E}$

(This last example means that 5 is *not* a member of the set E.) The empty set has no members and so it is always true that for any object x, $x \notin \varnothing$.

It is possible to construct a set without writing down all of its elements by employing the notation:

$$\{x \mid S\}$$

which is read as 'the set of all x's satisfying S', and denotes the set of all objects x such that the statement S is true. Interesting sets are usually infinite, and this notation is the *only* formally correct way of specifying such sets, since obviously it is not possible to write down all the members of an infinite set. For example, the finite set:

$$LC = \{x \mid x \text{ is a lower-case character of the alphabet}\}$$

means that LC is the set of characters {'*a*', '*b*', ..., '*z*'}

$$Z = \{x \mid x \text{ is an integer}\}$$

means that Z is the set of all integer numbers, or informally $\{\ldots, -3, -2, -1, 0, 1, 2, 3, \ldots\}$.

$$N = \{y \mid y \in Z \wedge y \geqslant 1\}$$

means that N is the set of all natural numbers, or informally $\{1, 2, 3, \ldots\}$.

If R is the set of all real numbers, then the set, F, of numbers between 0.0 and 1.0 (inclusive) is denoted by:

$$F = \{z \mid z \in R \wedge 0.0 \leq z \leq 1.0\}$$

A.4 Operations on Sets

Some basic operations on sets are **union**, **intersection** and **difference**.

The union of two sets A and B is the set of objects that are members of A or of B or both and is denoted by $A \cup B$. More formally:

$$A \cup B = \{x \mid x \in A \vee x \in B\}$$

For example:

$$\{1, 2, 3\} \cup \{2, 3, 4\} = \{1, 2, 3, 4\}$$
$$\{(1, 2), (2, 3), (4, 5)\} \cup \{(5, 6), (7, 8), (9, 9)\}$$
$$= \{(1, 2), (2, 3), (4, 5), (5, 6), (7, 8), (9, 9)\}$$
$$\{\text{"}abc\text{"}, \text{"}def\text{"}\} \cup \varnothing = \{\text{"}abc\text{"}, \text{"}def\text{"}\}$$

The intersection of two sets A and B is the set of elements that are in both A and B, denoted by $A \cap B$. Hence:

$$A \cap B = \{x \mid x \in A \wedge x \in B\}$$

For example:

$$\{1, 2, 3\} \cap \{2, 3, 4\} = \{2, 3\}$$
$$\{(1, 2), (2, 3), (4, 5)\} \cap \{(5, 6), (7, 8), (9,9)\} = \phi$$
$$\{\text{"}abc\text{"}, \text{"}def\text{"}\} \cap \varnothing = \varnothing$$

The difference of two sets A and B, denoted $A - B$, is the set consisting of elements that are in A but not in B. Hence:

$$A - B = \{x \mid x \in A \wedge x \notin B\}$$

For example:

$$\{1, 2, 3\} - \{2, 3, 4\} = \{1, 4\}$$
$$\{(1, 2), (2, 3), (4, 5)\} - \{(5, 6), (7, 8), (9, 9)\}$$
$$= \{(1, 2), (2, 3), (4, 5)\}$$
$$\{\text{"}abc\text{"}, \text{"}def\text{"}\} - \varnothing = \{\text{"}abc\text{"}, \text{"}def\text{"}\}$$

A.5 Tuples

Let $A_1, A_2, \ldots, A_n$ be n sets. An n-tuple is an object $(x_1, x_2, \ldots, x_n)$ where:

$$x_1 \in A_1 \wedge x_2 \in A_2 \wedge \ldots \wedge x_n \in A_n$$

For example, with the two sets $E = \{1, 2, 3, 4\}$ and $LC = \{\text{'}a\text{'}, \ldots, \text{'}z\text{'}\}$ defined earlier, some 2-tuples are:

$$(1, \text{'}z\text{'}), (3, \text{'}a\text{'}), (4, \text{'}x\text{'}), \ldots$$

From this example, it should be clear that there are 26×4 (= 104) possible 2-tuples based on these two sets. In fact, these 2-tuples are simply the members of the **product set** constructed from the two sets E and LC. This product set is denoted $E*LC$ and may be defined by:

$$E*LC = \{(a, b) \mid a \in E \wedge b \in LC\}$$

Generally:

$$A_1*A_2* \ldots *A_n = \{(x_1, x_2, \ldots, x_n) \mid x_1 \in A_1 \wedge x_2 \in A_2 \wedge \ldots \wedge x_n \in A_n)\}$$

Tuples are clearly useful for representing objects that have a number of components. An obvious example in computer graphics is the representation of a point in a coordinate system. Any point is a 2-tuple consisting of the x and y components or (x, y, z) in 3D graphics, where x, y and z are numbers. A further example is tuples of the form:

$$((x_1, y_1), (x_2, y_2))$$

which is a 2-tuple, with components that are 2-tuples of numbers. Such a type of object could usefully be used to represent the line joining the two points.

A.6 Sequences

Let X be any set. A sequence is constructed by choosing members of X. Let x_0 be the first element chosen, x_1 the second element, and so on to the nth element x_{n-1}. The resulting sequence is denoted:

$$x = [x_0, x_1, x_2, \ldots, x_{n-1}]$$

If no choices are made, then an empty sequence is constructed, which may be denoted by [] or by the word **nil**.

There are a number of further points to note about sequences:

(1) All members of a sequence must be of the same type.

(2) There is no stipulation that all the elements be different members of x – they might even all be the same.

(3) The ordering is crucial; for example, the sequence [3, 2, 1] is not the same sequence as [1, 2, 3].

(4) A sequence has a length, corresponding to the number of times choices were made from the basic set, corresponding to the number of elements in the sequence. For example, *Length*[2, 3, 4, 5] = 4. It also follows that all sequences of a given length constitute a set – the set of sequences of characters of length 5, for example. The length of the empty sequence is 0.

Examples of sequences are:

[1, 2, 3, 4, 5, 6]	a sequence of numbers
['*a*', '*b*', '*c*', '*z*']	a sequence of characters
[(1, 2), (2, 3), (3, 4), (3, 4)]	a sequence of 2-tuples of numbers
[[1, 2, 3], [3, 4, 5], [5, 6, 7], [4, 5, 6]]	a sequence of sequences of numbers of length 3 (the length of this sequence is 4)

Sequences of characters are called **strings** and are enclosed in double quotes. Thus:

$['h', 'a', 'l', 'l', 'o'] = ''hallo''$

A.7 Operations on Sequences

If a sequence is not empty, then it has a **head** and a **tail**. The head of a sequence S is the first element of S, S_0, and denoted *head S*. The new sequence obtained by deleting the head of S is called its **tail**. Hence, the tail of S, denoted *tail S*, is the sequence consisting of all but the first element. For example:

$head[4, 5, 6, 7] = 4$
$head[(1, 2), (2, 3), (3, 4)] = (1, 2)$
$head[[1, 2, 3], [4, 5, 6], [7, 8, 9]] = [1, 2, 3]$
$head\ ''abc'' = 'a'$
$head[(1, 4)] = (1, 4)$
head nil – undefined

$tail[4, 5, 6, 7] = [5, 6, 7]$
$tail[(1, 2), (2, 3), (3, 4)] = [(2, 3), (3, 4)]$
$tail[[1, 2, 3], [4, 5, 6], [7, 8, 9]] = [[4, 5, 6], [7, 8, 9]]$
$tail\ ''abc'' = ''bc''$
$tail[(1, 4)] = nil$
tail nil – undefined

If T is a sequence and H an object of the same type as the elements of T, then a new sequence can be **constructed** which has head H and tail T. This new sequence is denoted:

$H :: T$

(:: is often called the *cons* operator, since it constructs a new sequence.)

From the definition and examples, it should be clear that for any sequence S which is not empty:

$S = head\ S :: tail\ S$ and $head(H :: T) = H$
$tail(H :: T) = T$

For example:

$4 :: [5, 6, 7] = [4, 5, 6, 7]$
$'h' :: ''allo'' = ''hallo''$
$7 :: nil = [7]$

The **append** operation is a way of joining two sequences together. Let S and T be two sequences with elements of the same type. Then, S @ T is the sequence obtained by concatenating T to the end of S. For example:

[1, 2, 3] @ [4, 5, 6] = [1, 2, 3, 4, 5, 6]
''hallo '' @ *''how are you?''* = *''hallo how are you?''*
[(1, 2), (3, 4)] @ [(3, 4), (1, 2)] = [(1, 2), (3, 4), (3, 4), (1, 2)]

A number of other useful operations on sequences may be defined by using the basic operations of construct :: and append @.

The **subscripting** operation allows any element of a sequence to be specified according to its position in the sequence. Let S be a non-empty sequence, then $sub(S, i)$, is the ith element of S (where $i = 0$ would give the first element). The *sub* operator satisfies the following equations:

$$sub(S, 0) = head\ S$$
$$sub(S, i) = sub(tail\ S, i - 1)$$

For these equations to be valid, S must not be empty and $0 \leqslant i < Length\ S$.

A more precise way of writing these equations is:

$$\begin{array}{lll} sub(nil, \_) & = \text{undefined} & \\ sub(H :: T, 0) & = H & \\ sub(H :: T, i) & = sub(T, i - 1) & \text{if } 0 \leqslant i < Length\ H :: T \\ sub(S, i) & = \text{undefined} & \text{if } i < 0 \text{ or } i \geqslant Length\ S \end{array}$$

The underscore symbol _ here stands for a 'don't care' value; whatever value is substituted for _ in $sub(nil, \_)$, this subscripting operation is still undefined.

The *sub* operator is used so often that the notation $S[i]$ will be employed. In other words, $sub(S, i)$ can be denoted by $S[i]$. For example, if:

$$S = [(1, 2), (3, 4), (5, 6), (7, 8), (9, 10)]$$

then the following would all be true:

$$S[4] = (9, 10)$$
$$S[2] = (5, 6)$$
$$S[0] = (1, 2)$$

but $S[-1]$ and $S[5]$ are each undefined. Further examples are:

$$[5.9, 4.5, 1.0, 4.9][1] = 4.5$$
$$''computer\ graphics''[4] = 'u'$$

If S is a non-empty sequence, then $update(S, i, x)$ is a new sequence that has the same elements as S except that $S[i]$ is replaced by x. For example:

$$\begin{array}{l} S = [(3, 4, 5), (5, 6, 7), (7, 8, 9), (10, 11, 12)] \\ update(S, 0, (9, 9, 9)) = [(9, 9, 9), (5, 6, 7), (7, 8, 9), (10, 11, 12)] \\ update(S, 1, (9, 9, 9)) = [(3, 4, 5), (9, 9, 9), (7, 8, 9), (10, 11, 12)] \\ update(S, 3, (9, 9, 9)) = [(3, 4, 5), (5, 6, 7), (7, 8, 9), (9, 9, 9)] \end{array}$$

The *update* operator satisfies the following equations:

$$\begin{array}{lll} update(nil, \_, \_) & = \text{undefined} & \\ update(H :: T, 0, x) & = x :: T & \\ update(H :: T, i, x) & = H :: update(T, i - 1, x) & 0 \leqslant i < Length\ H :: T \\ update(S, i, \_) & = \text{undefined} & \text{if } i < 0 \text{ or } i \geqslant Length\ S \\ update(S, \_, x) & = \text{undefined} & \text{if the type of } x \text{ is not the same as the elements of } S \end{array}$$

It should be clear that:

$$update(S, i, x)\ [i] = x$$
$$update(S, i, x)\ [j] = S[j] \qquad \text{if } j \neq i$$

The notation $(S[i] = x)$ is used for $update(S, i, x)$. It is important to note that $(S[i] = x)$ is a *new* sequence, which has every element the same as S, except possibly the ith element, which will be different if $x \neq S[i]$.

Initialisation of sequences can be achieved by using the *reshape* operator ~ (the idea borrowed from the language APL). For example, suppose a sequence of length 10 is required, with elements all equal to one, then:

$$1\tilde{}10 = [1, 1, 1, 1, 1, 1, 1, 1, 1, 1]$$

Hence:

$$x = 1\tilde{}10 \quad \text{and} \quad x = [1, 1, 1, 1, 1, 1, 1, 1, 1, 1]$$

result in the same value for x. A two-dimensional sequence can be obtained in this way. For example:

$$x = 5\tilde{}(4, 4)$$

makes x a 4 by 4 matrix of values, with every element equal to 5.

The infinity symbol ∞ is used to denote the length of a sequence of arbitrary size; thus:

$$x = 1\tilde{}\infty$$

means that for any $i \geqslant 0$, $x[i]$ has the value 1. (These are used in the main text as a way of saying that x is a sequence, and its length is as large as it needs to be in the application.)

A.8 Types

The word *type* has already been used, but was not defined. An informal discussion follows. The basic types are integer, real, boolean and character where the abbreviation **int** is used for integer, **bool** for boolean and **char** for character. (Literals are added in this book for convenience.) There is clearly a close relationship between types and sets because, for example, objects of type *int* are always members of the set of integers (Z), and every element of Z is an object of type *int*. Hence, *int*, *char* and *real* also denote the corresponding sets.

The type of a tuple corresponds to the product set of its elements. For example:

(1, 2)	is of type	int*int
(1, 2, 3)	is of type	int*int*int
(4, '*a*', '*b*')	is of type	int*char*char

Thus, a new type may be formed from the product set of the basic types. However, a new type may also be formed from the product sets corresponding to any types. For example:

((1, 1), (2, 2))	is of type	(int*int)*(int*int)
('a', '!', (4, 5))	is of type	char*char*(int*int)

These expressions are often cumbersome, so **type synonyms** are defined. For example, defining:

> **type** Point = real*real

then:

(4.5, 7.8)	is of type	Point
((4.5, 7.8), (3.4, 6.7))	is of type	Point*Point

Similarly, if:

> **type** Line = Point*Point

then:

((10.2, 0.0), (4.0, 6.0))	is of type	Line

Note that defined in this way, *Point* and *real*real* are the *same* type. *Point* is just another way of referring to the type *real*real*. In Chapter 10, the ideas of **data type** and **abstract data type** are used, which allow the construction of completely new types.

When sequences are used to create a type, the following notation is used:

[1, 2, 3]	is of type	int sequence
[3.4, 5.6, 7.8]	is of type	real sequence
([3.4, 6.8), (5.6, 7.8), (2.3, 4.5), (4.5, 5.4)]	is of type	Point sequence

This discussion of types will be resumed when functions are considered in Section A.14.

Usually, types are inferred from context; for example, in the expression $(x + 4)$, x must be of type *int*. Sometimes there may be some ambiguity; for example, in $(x*x)$, it is not clear if x is an *int* or a *real*, unless there is some other information available. To avoid ambiguity, it is possible to explicitly type an object: $x : T$ means that x is of type T.

A.9 Value Bindings

A **value binding** is created by expressions of the form:

> **val** variable = expression

For example:

> **val** *x* = 4.5
> **val** *y* = "*hallo*"
> **val** *p*1 = (4.5, 6.8)
> **val** *line* = [(0.0, 0.0), (1.0, 1.0)]

The meaning is that wherever, in the appropriate context, the variable appears, it may be substituted for by the expression (and vice versa) without changing the meaning of anything. For example:

> **val** *ps* = [(0.0, 0.0), (1.0, 1.0), (2.0, 2.0)];
> **val** *x* = *ps*[2];
> **val** *q* = *x* :: [(8.8, 8.8), (9.9, 9.9)];

This is equivalent to:

val *ps* = [(0.0, 0.0), (1.0, 1.0), (2.0, 2.0)];
val *x* = [(0.0, 0.0), (1.0, 1.0), (2.0, 2.0)][2];
val *q* = *x* :: [(8.8, 8.8), (9.9, 9.9)];

which is equivalent to:

val *ps* = [(0.0, 0.0), (1.0, 1.0), (2.0, 2.0)];
val *x* = [(0.0, 0.0), (1.0, 1.0), (2.0, 2.0)][2];
val *q* = [(0.0, 0.0), (1.0, 1.0), (2.0, 2.0)][2] :: [(8.8, 8.8), (9.9, 9.9)]

which is equivalent to:

val *ps* = [(0.0, 0.0), (1.0, 1.0), (2.0, 2.0)];
val *x* = (2.0, 2.0);
val *q* = [(2.0, 2.0), (8.8, 8.8), (9.9, 9.9)]

If *q* is referred to subsequently, then the expression [(2.0, 2.0), (8.8, 8.8), (9.9, 9.9)] may be validly used in its place.

Now, the above was qualified by the phrase 'in the appropriate context'. Writing, for example:

val *x* = *e*

binds *x* to *e*. Consider the following sequence of equations:

val *x* = 5;
val *y* = *x* + 5;
val *x* = 100;

The first binds *x* to the value 5. The second binds *y* to 10, since *y* is equal to *x* + 5 and *x* is bound to 5 and therefore may be substituted for 5 in the evaluation of the expression for *y*. Finally, *x* is bound to 100; but this does not undo the earlier binding for *x*, as *y* remains 10. However, it establishes a new binding so that subsequent occurrences of *x* can be substituted by the value of 100.

There is also a notation for specifying the **scope** of application of a value binding. Consider:

```
val x = 20;
val y = let val x = 5
        in
          x + 5
        ni;
val z = x + 30;
val x = 40;
```

Here, the first equation binds *x* to the value 20. Next, a new identifier *x* is introduced (**let val** *x* = 5), which is bound to the value 5, but only within the scope bracketed by **in**...**ni**. Hence, *y* is bound to 10. Next, *z* is bound to 50 and then *x* bound to 40 (with *y* and *z*, of course, retaining the values 10 and 50, respectively). Such **let**...**in**...**ni** clauses may be arbitrarily nested, as in the following:

```
val z = let val x1 = 1 and y1 = 2
        in
```

```
        let val x2 = x1 + 1 and y2 = y1 + 2
        in
          [(x1, y1), (x2, y2)]
        ni
      ni
```

In this example, *z* would be bound to [(1, 2), (2, 3)], which is of type int*int sequence.

A.10 Parallel and Sequential Equations

The last example introduced the idea of **parallel bindings**. For example:

val *x*1 = 1 **and** *x*2 = 2 **and** *x*3 = 3 **and** *x*4 = 4

simultaneously binds *x*1 to 1, *x*2 to 2 and so on. Such an expression is only legal if the individual equations are independent. For example, it would not be possible to write:

val *x* = 1 **and** *y* = *x* + 1 **and** *z* = *x* + *y*

These must be written in sequence:

val *x* = 1; **val** *y* = *x* + 1; **val** *z* = *x* + *y*

The semicolon denotes a sequence of equations – that is, the equations are to be evaluated in the order presented.

A.11 Patterns

Consider the equation:

type Point = real*real;
val *square* = [(0.0, 0.0), (1.0, 0.0), (1.0, 1.0), (0.0, 1.0), (0.0, 0.0)];

square is an object of type *Point sequence*. It gives the coordinates of the corners of a unit square. Now, a later equation may wish to refer to *square*, and in particular to distinguish its head and tail. It is then possible to write, for example:

val *h* :: *t* = *square*

which binds *h* to the value of the head of *square* and *t* to the value of the tail. Continuing:

val *h* :: *t* = *square*;
val (*x*1, *y*1) = *h*;
val (*x*2, *y*2) :: *t*2 = *t*;

The bindings established by this sequence of equations are:

h = (0.0, 0.0)
t = [(1.0, 0.0), (1.0, 1.0), (0.0, 1.0), (0.0, 0.0)]
*x*1 = 0.0
*y*1 = 0.0

$x2 = 1.0$
$y2 = 0.0$
$t2 = [(1.0, 1.0), (0.0, 1.0), (0.0, 0.0)]$

A.12 Stores

Consider the binding:

val *x* = **store** 5

This means that *x* is bound to a 'place' that stores the value 5 (in computer terms, such a place is usually called an **address**). The type of *x* is *int store* – it is a variable that acts as a storage place for integers. Some more examples are as follows:

Binding	**Type**
val *x* = **store** "*abc*"	string store
val *z* = **store** (1, 2)	int*int store
val *x* = **store** [2, 3, 4, 5, 6]	int sequence store
val *x* = **store** [(1, 2), (3, 4)]	int*int sequence store

If *x* is a *store* variable, then *content x* is the value stored in *x*. For example:

val *x* = **store** 5;
val *z* = *x*;
val *y*1 = *content z* **and** *y*2 = *content x* + 1;

would bind *z* to be the same store as *x*, *y*1 to the value 5 and *y*2 to the value 6. The notation ?*x* is used as an equivalent to *content x*. Hence:

val *x* = **store** 100;
val *y* = **store** (*content x* + 1);
val *z* = **store** (?*x* + 1)

binds *y* and *z* to be *int stores* containing the value 101.

Once a variable has been initialised as a store, then values of the appropriate type can be **assigned** to the variable. This means that the content of the store is updated to a (possibly) new value. The assignment operation is denoted by the familiar := symbol:

x := *e*

If *x* is of type *T store* and *e* is of type *T*, then the effect of this operation is to replace the previous value of ?*x* by *e*. For example:

val *x* = **store** 5;
x := 2

initialises *x* to be an *int store* variable, with content 5, and then the 5 is replaced by the value 2.

Another example is:

val *x* = **store** 100;
x := ?*x* + 1

Here, the value of ?x is 101. Whenever the assignment symbol := is employed, any store variables on the right-hand side of the assignment are automatically **dereferenced**, as a notational convenience. The ? symbol is assumed, and does not have to be present: the content of the store variable is used. Hence, the above example could also validly be written as:

val x = **store** 100;
x := x + 1;

Parallel assignments to store variables are denoted as follows:

val x = **store** 100 **and** y = **store** (1.0, 2.0);
x, y := 101, (2.0, 3.0);

Here, x and y are *int store* and *real***real store* variables, respectively. The second line assigns new values to the contents of x and y.

In the case of *sequence store* variables, it is assumed that every element of the sequence is itself a store variable (to allow easy updating of the sequence elements). Hence:

val x = **store** 1~5;
$x[3]$:= 2;

This is allowed because x is a *sequence store*, and hence each $x[i]$ is a store, and in particular $x[3]$ is a store, which can therefore be assigned a new value.

A.13 Guarded Commands: Conditional Equations and Iteration

Conditional Equations

Ordinary mathematical notation allows the expression of conditional equations; that is, where a variable is defined in such a way that its value depends on which of a number of conditions is true. For example:

$$x = \begin{cases} 1.0 & \text{if } y \geqslant 100.0 \\ -1.0 & \text{if } y < 100.0 \end{cases}$$

The notation used here for similar equations is:

val x = **if**
  $y \geqslant 100.0 \Rightarrow 1.0$
  $\square\ y < 100.0 \Rightarrow -1.0$
fi

Consider the **guarded** expression of the form:

if
  $g_1 \Rightarrow v_1$
  $\square\ g_2 \Rightarrow v_2$
  .
  .
  .

$\square\ g_n \Rightarrow v_n$

fi

The boolean expressions $g_1, g_2, \ldots, g_n$ are called **guards** and the values $v_1, v_2, \ldots, v_n$ are the corresponding **arms**. The value of the guarded command is found by choosing any one of the true guards and evaluating the corresponding arm. Usually, one and only one of the guards is true. If more than one guard is true, then an arbitrary choice may be made between them. The result is undefined if all are false. For example:

val x = **if**

$y = [1, 2, 3] \Rightarrow (0.0, 0.0)$

$\square\ y = [4, 5, 6] \Rightarrow (1.0, 1.0)$

$\square\ y \neq [1, 2, 3] \wedge y \neq [4, 5, 6] \Rightarrow (99.9, 99.9)$

fi

Hence, x is bound to the value (0.0, 0.0) if y is the sequence [1, 2, 3] or else x is bound to (1.0, 1.0) if y is the sequence [4, 5, 6], otherwise x is bound to (99.9, 99.9).

Iteration

Iteration is a fundamental operation in mathematics and computing. It involves a repetition of similar operations while certain specified conditions are satisfied. Consider the following example. Most computer languages have a built-in function for finding the square root of a number. The symbol most often used is *sqrt*, so that *sqrt*(2) evaluates to $\sqrt{2} = 1.414214\ldots$. The accuracy to which the answer is computed depends on the language compiler, implementation and computer. Suppose, however, that such a function is not provided – how could square roots be computed? There is a need particularly in computational geometry for using square roots, since the formula for the length of the line joining two points in 2D space is:

$$\sqrt{(x_1 - x_2)^2 + (y_1 - y_2)^2}$$

for points (x_1, y_1), (x_2, y_2).

It can be shown using Newton's method for the iterative solution of equations that an algorithm for computing the square root of any positive number a is:

$$z_i = 0.5*\left(z_{i-1} + \frac{a}{z_{i-1}}\right)$$

where z_0 is an initial guess at $\sqrt{a}$, and $z_1, z_2, \ldots$ are closer and closer approximations. For example, in the case $a = 2$ and the initial guess $z_0 = 1$, the following answers would be obtained by an application of the algorithm:

$z_0 = 1.0$ (initial guess)
$z_1 = 1.5$
$z_2 = 1.4166667$
$z_3 = 1.4142157$
$z_4 = 1.4142136$

The iteration to compute $\sqrt{a}$ to, say, four decimal places, can be expressed in programming notation as follows:

```
let val EPS = 0.00001 and MAX = 20
in
  let val z = store a/2.0 and oldz = store a and i = store 0
  in
    do
      abs(?z − ?oldz) > EPS ∧ (?i < MAX) ⇒
        oldz, z, i := z, 0.5*(z + a/z), i+1
    od
  ni
ni
```

Here, *EPS* is a value used to test for convergence. If at any stage the absolute difference (*abs*) between the newly calculated *z* and the last value of *z* (*oldz*) is less than *EPS*, then the iteration terminates. The variable *i* is used to count the number of cycles of the iteration. Newton's method is not foolproof; for example, if an inappropriate initial guess is chosen, then the iteration may not converge. Hence, *i* is used to count the number of cycles, and if this becomes equal to an upper bound (*MAX*) before convergence, then, again, the iteration terminates. It should be clear that at the end of the iteration the following condition is true:

$$abs(?z - ?oldz) \leqslant EPS \vee ?i \geqslant MAX$$

If $?i < MAX$, then z is an approximation to $\sqrt{a}$.

The meaning of the **do**...**od** iteration is as follows. Consider:

```
do
    g1 ⇒ v1
  □ g2 ⇒ v2
       .
       .
       .
  □ gn ⇒ vn
od
```

Choose any true guard g_i and evaluate the corresponding arm v_i. Repeat this instruction until all the guards are false. If more than one guard is true, then choose a true one arbitrarily. Usually, only one will be true.

As another example, consider the following, which constructs a sequence of points (*pseq* of type *real**real*) that could be used to plot a graph of the function $y = x^2$ between the range $x = -3.0$ to $x = 3.0$ in increments of $dx = 0.05$:

```
let val xlower = −3.0 and xupper = 3.0 and dx = 0.05
in
  let val pseq = store [(xlower, xlower*xlower)] and x = store (xlower + dx)
  in
    do
      ?x ≤ xupper ⇒ pseq, x := (x, x*x) :: pseq, x + dx
    od
  ni
ni
```

Sequential Iteration

Let P stand for any sequence of instructions and a, b integers with $a \leqslant b$, then the notation:

```
for a ≤ i ≤ b do
  P
od
```

is equivalent to:

```
let val i = a      in P ni;
let val i = a + 1  in P ni;
      .
      .
      .
let val i = b      in P ni
```

In other words, the index variable i takes each value $i = a, a + 1, a + 2, \ldots, b$ and for each value of i, P is evaluated. For example:

```
val s = store 0;
for 0 ≤ i < Length(iseq) do
  s := s + iseq[i]
od
```

accumulates the sum of the int sequence *iseq* in the store variable s. If, say, $iseq = [3, 5, 6, 7]$, then $?s = 21$ at the end of the iteration.

Parallel Iteration

Another kind of instruction is also used which allows the index variable to take each value in a set. Although the notation is similar, the meaning is quite different. Let A be any set, then:

```
forall i ∈ A do
  P
od
```

means that P is evaluated in parallel for each member of A (which had better be finite!).

A.14 Functions

Let A and B be two sets. A **function** is a rule that associates every member of A with a unique member of B. In this context, A is called the **domain** of the function and B the **range**. The notation:

$$f : A \rightarrow B$$

is used to express the fact that the function f is from A (domain) to B (range). Considering A and B as types, then $A \rightarrow B$ is the **type of the function** f.

If $a \in A$, then $fa \in B. fa$ is sometimes called the **image** of a in B. Also, the **value** of the function at a is fa. Brackets may be used to avoid ambiguities: for example, $f(a)$ is the same as fa which is the same as (fa).

Suppose B is the set of integers {0, 1, ..., 9} and A is the set of digit characters {'0', '1', ..., '9'}. Further suppose that for each $x \in A$, *Ord* x is the value of the digit, in the obvious sense, so that:

Ord '0' = 0
Ord '1' = 1
Ord '9' = 9

The type of this function is *char* → *int*, it takes a character into an integer. Let *IsDigit* be another function which, given any character, has the value 1 if the character is a digit and the value 0 otherwise. Hence:

IsDigit '0' = 1
IsDigit 'a' = 0
IsDigit 'Z' = 0
IsDigit 'x' = 0
IsDigit '8' = 1
IsDigit '&' = 0
IsDigit '?' = 0

The type of this function is also *char* → *int*. What distinguishes it from *Ord* is that it has a different **rule**. The rule of a function can be defined as in the following examples:

```
fun Ord x = if
                 x = '0' ⇒ 0
               □ x = '1' ⇒ 1
               □ x = '2' ⇒ 2
               □ x = '3' ⇒ 3
               □ x = '4' ⇒ 4
               □ x = '5' ⇒ 5
               □ x = '6' ⇒ 6
               □ x = '7' ⇒ 7
               □ x = '8' ⇒ 8
               □ x = '9' ⇒ 9
            fi
nuf

fun IsDigit x = let val D = {'0', '1', '2', '3', '4', '5', '6', '7', '8', '9'}
                in
                  if
                       x ∈ D ⇒ 1
                     □ x ∉ D ⇒ 0
                  fi
                ni
    nuf
```

A function definition is established by an expression of the form:

fun fp = *rule* **nuf**

where f is the **name** of the function and p is the parameter of the function. The rule is a value-delivering expression showing how the image value is computed for any x of the same type as p. The whole definition is bracketed between **fun**...**nuf**.

The function definition establishes a binding in much the same way as the value bindings discussed earlier. When the function is applied (for example, *IsDigit* '%') so the actual parameter (in this case '%') replaces the formal parameter (x) in the rule, then the evaluation can proceed. (This raises all sorts of questions about bound and free variables, which are beyond the scope of this book – see Glaser *et al*., 1984; Bornat, 1986).

Some further examples are as follows.

(a) Evaluating the sum of a sequence of integers

Suppose *sum* is a function that delivers the sum of a sequence of numbers. The type of *sum*: $int \rightarrow int$. This function may be defined as follows:

```
fun sum s = if
                  s = nil ⇒ 0
                □ s ≠ nil ⇒ head s + sum(tail s)
            fi
nuf
```

This says that the sum of a sequence is 0 if the sequence is empty, or else is the first element in the sequence plus the sum of the remainder of the sequence. For example:

$$sum\ [1, 2, 3] = 1 + sum\ [2, 3]$$

since:

$$1 + 2 + 3 = 1 + (2 + 3)$$

The function can be defined more concisely using a **case analysis** approach:

```
fun sum nil    = 0 |
    sum h :: t = h + sum t
nuf
```

This notation is sometimes more elegant and uses the idea of patterns discussed earlier. The cases correspond to the guards in the guarded command in the first definition of sum. The different cases are distinguished by the | symbol.

The *sum* function could, of course, also be defined using stores:

```
fun sum s = let val seqsum = store 0
            in
              for 0 ≤ i < Length s do
                seqsum := seqsum + s[i]
              od;
              ?seqsum
            ni
nuf
```

However, the earlier definition of *sum* (the recursive definition) is preferable from the point of view of clarity. This functional definition of *sum* can be *derived* from the meaning of sum: the sum of a sequence can be defined as the first element plus the sum of the remainder of the sequence. The second definition, using stores, gives a computational recipe ('how should a sum be calculated?') which has a relationship to the meaning of the *sum* function far more difficult to elucidate, even in this relatively simple example. The approach using recursive equations to define functions is usually called **functional** or **applicative** programming. The approach using stores (which is usually bound up with iteration) is called **imperative programming** – the program is a sequence of instructions: do this and then do that. . . to achieve the required result. Often, given the subject matter, use of the imperative style is unavoidable in this book.

(b) Rotating a point by an angle

The following function definition describes the rotation of a point *p* by angle *a*:

```
type Point = real*real;
Rotate: Point*real → Point;
fun Rotate(p, a) = let val (x, y) = p
                   in
                     (x*cos(a) − y*sin(a), x*sin(a) + y*cos(a))
                   ni

nuf
```

The function has a tuple as its parameter, consisting of the point *p* and the angle *a*. Pattern matching is used to unravel the individual *x*, *y* coordinate values from *p*. Then a tuple is computed which is the rotated point. The definition type of this function is *Point*real → Point.*

(c) The *map* function – applying a function to every element of a sequence

A frequent requirement in programming is to apply a function to every element of a sequence. For example, given a sequence of numbers, a new sequence is to be constructed with every element squared:

```
fun sqr x = x*x nuf;

fun squares nil    = nil |
    squares h :: t = sqr h :: squares t
nuf
```

A seemingly more complex example is to define a function to find the distance of each of a sequence of points from the origin:

```
fun D (x, y) = sqrt(x*x + y*y) nuf

fun Distances nil    = nil |
    Distances h :: t = D(h) :: Distances t
nuf
```

Let *map* be a function such that if *f* is a function and *s* is a sequence, then *map fs* is the sequence with *f* applied to each element of *s*. This function can be defined as:

```
fun map f nil      = nil |
    map f (h :: t) = f(h) :: map ft
nuf
```

Hence:

squares s = map sqr s and *Distances s = map D s*

(This has surreptitiously introduced the idea of functions as arguments – see Section 2.16.)

A.15 Procedures: Functions with a Void Result

Sometimes the *effect* produced by a function is of more interest than the value computed by the function. This is especially the case in computer graphics. For example, a line drawing function is of importance for its side effect of drawing a line on the display screen. Suppose *Line*(*p*1, *p*2) is to draw a line between the two points *p*1 and *p*2, the *effect* of drawing the line being the purpose of the function. Such functions, of interest for their side effects rather than their computed value, are usually called **procedures**. More formally, let *Void* be the name of a type, which contains a single value (nothing) denoted by empty brackets (). Then, a procedure is a function of type $T \rightarrow Void$ (where T is the type of the parameter).

As another example, let *print* be a function that prints its (character string) argument. For example:

print "hallo"

has the effect of printing the characters in the string *"hallo"* on the computer terminal. *print* is a function of type $string \rightarrow Void$.

Another class of functions of interest are those that have no parameter. Here, the parameter is of type *Void* and the type of such functions is $Void \rightarrow T$ (where T is the type of result). In the following trivial example:

fun *One* () = 1 **nuf**

is a function that always delivers the value 1 (of type $Void \rightarrow int$). Another example of a $Void \rightarrow Void$ function is:

fun *ErrorMessage* () = *print "An error has occurred"* **nuf**

and a function that says where an error has occurred ($string \rightarrow Void$) is:

```
fun ErrorInProc proc = print "An error has occurred in procedure";
                       print proc
nuf
```

A.16 Functions as Arguments

Consider the function *Scale* which scales a point *p* by *x* and *y* scaling factors:

```
Scale: Point*Point → Point;
fun Scale(s, p) = let val (sx, sy) = s and (x, y) = p
                  in
                     (sx*x, sy*y)
                  ni
nuf
```

This is of type *Point***Point* → *Point*. Suppose, however, that the function definition were written as follows:

fun *Scale s p* = **let val** (*sx*, *sy*) = *s* **and** (*x*, *y*) = *p*
in
(*sx***x*, *sy***y*)
ni
nuf

This function rule is identical to the first definition. However, the declaration of name and parameters violates the stipulation that functions have a single parameter. The first definition of *Scale* had a single parameter which was a 2-tuple with *Points* as components. The second definition appears to have two separate parameters, both *Points*.

This second function is nevertheless valid. Its meaning can be understood as the definition of *Scale s* as a function which takes a point *p* and delivers a point as the result; that is, the type of *Scale s* is *Point* → *Point*. For example, *Scale*(2.0, 2.0) is a function that when applied to any point computes a new point scaled up by two. It is perfectly valid to write:

val *ScaleByTwo* = *Scale*(2.0, 2.0)

to define a new function that scales by two. The value of *ScaleByTwo*(5.0, 10.0) is (10.0, 20.0), as is the value of:

Scale(2.0, 2.0) (10.0, 20.0)

The type of the function *ScaleByTwo* is *Point* → *Point* and *Scale* is *Point* → (*Point* → *Point*). Given a point *s*, *Scale s* is a function that maps a point to a point.

Another, perhaps, simpler example, might make these ideas clear. Consider:

fun *add x y* = *x* + *y* **nuf**

add x is a function that adds the value *x* to its parameter *y*. For example, *add* 1 applied to 100 delivers 101. If:

val *add*10 = *add* 10

then the value of *add*10#7 is 17. The type of *add*10 is *number* → *number* and the type of *add* is *number* → (*number* → *number*).

A.17 Composition of Functions

Let $f : A \rightarrow B$ and $g : C \rightarrow A$, then $f \circ g$ is the **composition** of the two functions, with $f \circ g : C \rightarrow B$. In other words, *g* is applied first and then *f* is applied to the result. For example, suppose:

fun *g x* = 5 + *x* **nuf**;
fun *f x* = 10**x* **nuf**

then $g\,100 = 105$ and $f\,105 = 1050$ so that $f \circ g\,100 = 1050$. Since the types of *f* and *g* in this example are each *int* → *int*, the type of the composition $f \circ g$ is also *int* → *int*.

The three functions used for point transformations (translate, scale, rotate) are defined as follows:

```
Translate: Point → (Point → Point);
fun Translate tp = let val (tx, ty) = t and (x, y) = p
                   in
                     (x + tx, y + ty)
                   ni
nuf

Scale: Point → (Point → Point);
fun Scale sp = let val (sx, sy) = s and (x, y) = p
               in
                 (sx*x, sy*y)
               ni
nuf

Rotate: real → (Point → Point);
fun Rotate ap = let val (x, y) = p
                in
                  (x*cos(a) − y*sin(a), x*sin(a) + y*sin(a))
                ni
nuf
```

Transformations can be constructed as concatenations of matrices representing the translate, scale and rotate operations. Here, it can be seen that once these basic transformations are represented as functions, then the more complex transformations can be achieved by function composition. For example, scale by a factor of two for both x and y, rotate by 45° ($\pi/4$), shift by ten units in the x direction, relative to the origin, is equivalent to applying the function:

$$Translate(10.0,\ 0.0) \circ Rotate(\pi/4) \circ Scale(2.0,\ 2.0)$$

If this operation is to be used several times, then it might be bound as:

val *Transformation* = $Translate(10.0,\ 0.0) \circ Rotate(\pi/4) \circ Scale(2.0,\ 2.0)$

which has type *Point* → *Point*. Now suppose this transformation is to be applied relative to the fixed point (4.0, 10.0) (instead of relative to the origin), then the application of:

$$Translate(4.0,\ 10.0) \circ Transformation \circ Translate(-4.0,\ -10.0)$$

will achieve the required result.

A.18 Lambda Notation

Sometimes it is useful to be able to refer to function values anonymously – that is, without giving the function an explicit name. For example:

$$\lambda x.\,(x*x)$$

is a way of denoting the function that squares a number. x is the argument to the function and $x*x$ is the rule. Hence:

$$(\lambda x.(x*x))(4) = 16$$

is an application of this anonymous function to the argument value 4. The notation employed here (following ML) is:

$$fn\, x \Rightarrow x*x$$

For example, the following two bindings are equivalent:

$$\textbf{val}\ f = fn\, x \Rightarrow x*x \qquad \textbf{fun}\ f x = x*x\ \textbf{nuf}$$

A.19 System State

A function always delivers the same result for the same argument; for example, in the foregoing example, $f4$ is always 16, and can never be anything else. However, as a notational convenience, this book sometimes stretches the idea of functions to situations where this is not the case. As an example, suppose *read* is a function that delivers as its value the next character that a user types on the computer keyboard. Obviously, the value of *read* () will depend entirely on the behaviour of the user and the state of the overall system. A similar situation in graphics is where an input device, such as a mouse, is used to select a point on the display. In this case, a function such as *Locate* is used, which returns a point, according to where the screen cursor was when the operator pressed a certain button on the mouse. Again, *Locate* is clearly not a function, since the point returned depends on the actions of the operator and the state of the system.

To overcome this problem, a new type is introduced called **state**, which has one value denoted by two dots ..; hence, *read* is a function that has type *state* → *char* and *Locate* has type *state* → *Point*. For example:

$$\textbf{val}\ (x, y) = Locate(..);$$

means that *Locate* computes the value of the return point taking into account all the relevant aspects of the system state (including the actions of the user as translated into mouse movements and button clicks), and the returned x and y coordinates are bound to x and y.

A.20 Relationship to ML and Pascal

The programming notation and semantics introduced here are similar to the programming language ML. However, there are some differences in notation; for example, in ML **end** is used instead of **ni**, conditional expressions and iteration are different in ML – the ideas used here for these are taken from David Gries' book *The Science of Programming* (Gries, 1983). ML does not treat sequences as described in this appendix (for a discussion of the relationship between lists and arrays, see Henderson, 1980, Section 10.3). There is no *state* type in ML, nor are there sets. ML includes the notion of modules, and also polymorphic types, which are hardly used in this book. Abstract data types are discussed where they are used in Chapter 10.

The notation used here has been made slightly different from ML to warn the reader that it is *not* ML. However, readers familiar with ML will easily understand the notation used, and those who understand the notation will have no difficulty in quickly learning ML.

Pascal is totally different. It is beyond the scope of this book to develop a set of transcription rules from the ML style of notation to Pascal. Richard Bornat's book *Programming from First Principles* (Bornat, 1986) does develop transcription rules from an abstract language (not ML) to Pascal, and this should be consulted. Some transcriptions are fairly obvious: tuples can be represented as Pascal records, sequences by Pascal lists or arrays. The conditional and iteration commands translate fairly easily into Pascal **while**, **if**, **case** and **for** statements. Much of the rest of the language can be translated, although usually clumsily, and this is the whole point of avoiding such clumsiness when discussing the concepts of computer graphics. As a final example in this section, consider the following program for rotating the points of a triangle through an angle of 45° (π/4 radians):

```
type Point = real*real;

Rotate: real → (Point → Point);
fun Rotate a p = let val (x, y) = p
                 in
                   (x*cos(a) − x*sin(a), x*sin(a) + y*sin(a))
                 ni
nuf

val triangle = [(0.0, 0.0), (2.0, 0.0), (1.0, 2.0), (0.0, 0.0)];
val RotatedTriangle = map (Rotate π/4) triangle;

program rotation(input, output);
const MAX = 3;

type Point = record
               x, y : real
             end;
     PointArray = array[0..MAX] of Point;

procedure Rotate(a : real; p : Point; var rp : Point);
begin
  with p do
  begin
    rp.x = x*cos(a) − y*sin(a);
    rp.y = x*sin(a) + y*cos(a)
  end;
end;

procedure RotatePoints(a : real; n : integer; p : PointArray;
                       var rp : PointArray);

var i : integer;
begin
  for i := 0 to n do Rotate(a, p[i], rp[i])
end;
```

```
procedure triangle;
var p, rp : PointArray;
    piby4: real;
begin
  pilby4 := arctan(1.0);
  with p[0] do begin x := 0.0; y := 0.0 end;
  with p[1] do begin x := 2.0; y := 0.0 end;
  with p[2] do begin x := 1.0; y := 2.0 end;
  p[3] := p[0];
  RotatePoints(piby4, 3, p, rp)
end;
begin triangle end.
```

One further word of explanation, the value π can be computed by *arctan*(1.0)/4.0, since *tan*(π/4) is 1.0.

APPENDIX B

A POSTSCRIPT PROGRAM FOR 3D VIEWING

This appendix provides a complete PostScript program for 3D viewing and drawing wire-frame Bezier surfaces. It is the program used to generate Figures 13.26 and 13.27. The program presented here was initially developed using the Sun NeWS system, and then, with minor alterations, made to work on the Apple Laserwriter. The program certainly needs further work, which is left as a major exercise for the reader. For example, there is no error checking, so if invalid viewing arguments are specified, then the program will fail. Also, 3D clipping and hidden surface removal would be useful additions.

To fully understand this program, the reader must consult the PostScript books (Adobe, 1985a, 1985b). As the program makes great use of arrays and iteration, some brief comments are provided here on the relevant operators. Note that arrays are indexed with element 0 as the first position, and an array is obtained by declaring `n array` to make an array of size `n`.

- `put` is used to put an element into an array. For example, if `A` is an array, `i` an index into the array and `x` a value, then `A i x put` overwrites element `i` with `x`.
- `get` is used to place an element of an array on to the operand stack. For example, `A i get` leaves the element `i` of `A` on the operand stack.
- `aload` loads the elements of an array and the array itself on to the stack. For example, `A aload` leaves each successive element and finally `A` on the stack. Conversely, `astore` expects a sequence of values followed by an array, and leaves an array with those values on the stack.
- The `for` operator allows iteration in the sense of **for...do**. For example, `a b n proc for` repeatedly executes `proc`, each time pushing a control variable on to the operand stack, which has initial value `a`, final value `n` and increment `b`.
- `forall` runs through the elements of an array (dictionary or string) and executes a procedure for each element (somewhat like the ML *map* function). For example, `A proc forall` successively pushes each element of `A` on to the stack and executes the procedure `proc`.

In the following program, the convention is adopted that what each procedure expects on the operand stack, and what it leaves on the stack, is denoted by `b procname` ⇒ `a`. Here, `b` is what should be on the stack, and after the execution of `procname`, `a` is left on the stack. For example, the `add` operator would be commented by `a b add` ⇒ `a + b`. The 'nothing' symbol is '-'.

```
%PostScript program for 3D viewing, and wire frame Bezier Surfaces

%------------------------------------------------------------------
%The Prologue
%------------------------------------------------------------------
%Matrix handling package
%Here a matrix is a 4*4 matrix represented as a flattened array

/MatrixWithValueDict 2 dict def

%delivers a matrix with every element equal to value
%value MatrixWithValue => [value value ... value]
/MatrixWithValue
{
  MatrixWithValueDict begin
    /value exch def /matrix 16 array def
    0 1 15 {matrix exch value put} for
    matrix
  end
} def


/IdentityMatrixDict 1 dict def

%delivers an identity matrix
% - IdentityMatrix => 4*4 identity matrix
/IdentityMatrix
{
  IdentityMatrixDict begin
    /matrix 0 MatrixWithValue def
    0 5 15 {matrix exch 1 put} for
    matrix
  end
} def


/IndexDict 2 dict def

%delivers the index into the flattened array corresponding to (i,j)
%i j Index => i*4+j
/Index
{
  IndexDict begin
    /j exch def
    /i exch def
    i 4 mul j add
  end
} def


/MatMultiplyDict 9 dict def

%matrix multiplication
%MatrixA MatrixB MatMultiply => MatrixA*MatrixB
/MatMultiply
{
  MatMultiplyDict  begin
    /B exch def
    /A exch def
    /sum 0 def  /matrix 16 array def

      0 1 3
      {/i exch def
```

```
         0 1 3
         {/j exch def
            /sum 0 def
            0 1 3
            {/k exch def
             /sum A i k Index get B k j Index get mul sum add def
            } for
            matrix i j Index sum put
         } for
      } for
      matrix
  end
} def


/CrossProductDict 3 dict def

%vector cross product
%a b CrossProduct => a * b  (cross product)
/CrossProduct
{
  CrossProductDict begin
    /b exch def
    /a exch def
    /c 3 array def
    c 0 a 1 get b 2 get mul a 2 get b 1 get mul sub put
    c 1 a 2 get b 0 get mul a 0 get b 2 get mul sub put
    c 2 a 0 get b 1 get mul a 1 get b 0 get mul sub put
    c
  end
} def


/NormDict 3 dict def

%vector normalization
%a Norm => b (normalization)
/Norm
{
  NormDict begin
    /a exch def
    /b 3 array def
    a b copy pop
    /n 0 b {dup mul add} forall def %sum of squares
    /n n sqrt def
    b {n div} forall b astore
  end
} def


/DotProductDict 5 dict def

%vector dot product
%a b DotProduct  => a.b (dot product)
/DotProduct
{
  DotProductDict begin
    /b exch def /a exch def
    /n 0 def
    0 1 2
    {/i exch def
     /n a i get b i get mul n add def
    } for
    n
```

```
  end
} def


/VectorSumDict 4 dict def

%vector sum
%a b VectorSum => a+b
/VectorSum
{
  VectorSumDict begin
    /b exch def /a exch def
    /c 0 0 0 3 array astore def
    0 1 2
    {/i exch def
     c i a i get b i get add put
    } for
    c
  end
} def


/VectorDiffDict 4 dict def

%vector difference
%a b VectorDiff => a-b
/VectorDiff
{
  VectorDiffDict begin
    /b exch def /a exch def
    /c 0 0 0 3 array astore def
    0 1 2
    {/i exch def
     c i a i get b i get sub put
    } for
    c
  end
} def


/PointByMatrixDict 6 dict def

%delivers non-homogeneous point resulting from the multiplication
%point Matrix PointByMatrix => point(3D)
/PointByMatrix
{
  PointByMatrixDict begin
    /m exch def /p exch def
    /hp 4 array def
    /q 3 array def
    0 1 3
    {
      /j exch def
      %hp[j] = m[3,j]
      hp j m 3 j Index get put
      0 1 2
      {
        /i exch def
        %hp[j] = hp[j] + p[i]*m[i,j]
        hp j  hp j get p i get m i j Index get mul add put
      } for
    } for
    %for i = 0 to 2 do q[i] = hp[i]
    hp aload pop pop q astore
```

```
    %for i = 0 to 2 do q[i] = q[i]/hp[3]
    q {hp 3 get div} forall q astore
  end
} def


/PointByMatrixToCoordsDict 6 dict def

%delivers x and y coordinates of the point resulting
%from the multiplication of the point by the matrix
%point matrix PointByMatrixToCoords => x y
/PointByMatrixToCoords
{
  PointByMatrixToCoordsDict begin
    /m exch def /p exch def
    /hp 4 array def
    0 1 3
    {
      /j exch def
      %hp[j] = m[3,j]
      hp j m 3 j Index get put
      0 1 2
      {
        /i exch def
        %hp[j] = hp[j] + p[i]*m[i,j]
        hp j  hp j get p i get m i j Index get mul add put
      } for
    } for
    /w hp 3 get def
    hp 0 get w div hp 1 get w div
  end
} def

%Data Structures and Procedures for specifying a 3D view

%dictionary to hold the internal representation of the current view
/ViewRepresentation 2 dict def
ViewRepresentation  begin
   %view matrix
  /ViewMatrix IdentityMatrix def
   %matrix for transformation to display
  /displaymatrix matrix def
end

%-----------------------------------------------------------------
%3D viewing package

%dictionary to hold the current view specification
/ViewSpecification 8 dict def
ViewSpecification  begin
   /vpn 0 0 -1 3 array astore      def %view plane normal
   /vuv 0 1  0 3 array astore      def %view up vector
   /vrp 0 0 0 3 array  astore      def %view reference point
   /cop 0 0 0 3 array  astore      def %centre of projection
   /vd  0                          def %view distance
   /dmin -1                        def %front clipping plane
   /dmax  1                        def %back clipping plane
   /vwin 0 1 0 1 4 array astore    def %view window
end


/SetViewportDict 10 dict def

%computes factor values assuming the given viewport.
```

```
%The 2D window is x and y between -1 and +1.
%The results saved in ViewRepresentation
%xmin xmax ymin ymax SetViewport => -
/SetViewport
{
  SetViewportDict begin
      /ymax exch def /ymin exch def
      /xmax exch def /xmin exch def
      /dx xmax xmin sub 2 div def
      /dy ymax ymin sub 2 div def

      /f0 xmin dx add def
      /f1 dx          def
      /f2 ymin dy add def
      /f3 dy          def

      ViewRepresentation begin
         /displaymatrix f1 0 0 f3 f0 f2 displaymatrix astore
      end
  end
} def


/SetViewDict 16 dict def

%computes the current view and saves in ViewRepresentation
%according to the data in ViewSpecification
%- SetView => -
/SetView
{
    ViewSpecification begin
      ViewRepresentation begin
        SetViewDict begin
          /n vpn Norm def
          /u n vuv CrossProduct Norm def
          /v u n CrossProduct def
            /VM IdentityMatrix def
            0 1 2
            { /i exch def
              %VM[i,0] = u[i]
              VM i 0 Index u i get put

              %VM[i,1] = v[i]
              VM i 1 Index v i get put

              %VM[i,2] = n[i]
              VM i 2 Index n i get put

              %VM[3,0] = VM[3,0] - vrp[i]*u[i]
              VM 3 0 Index
                 VM 3 0 Index get vrp i get u i get mul sub
              put

              %VM[3,1] = VM[3,1] - vrp[i]*v[i]
              VM 3 1 Index
                VM 3 1 Index get vrp i get v i get mul sub
              put

              %VM[3,2] = VM[3,2] - vrp[i]*n[i]
              VM 3 2 Index
                 VM 3 2 Index get vrp i get n i get mul sub
              put
            } for
```

```
            %transform cop to the origin
            0 1 2
            { /i exch def
              %VM[3,i] = VM[3,i] - (cop[i]+vrp[i])
              VM 3 i Index
                 VM 3 i Index get cop i get vrp i get add sub
              put
            } for

            %and redefine the view distances
            %VD = vd - cop[2]
            /VD vd cop 2 get sub def

            %DMIN = dmin - cop[2]
            /DMIN dmin cop 2 get sub def

            %DMAX = dmax - cop[]
            /DMAX dmax cop 2 get sub def

            %set the projection matrix
            %dx = xmax - xmin etc
            /dx vwin 1 get vwin 0 get sub def
            /dy vwin 3 get vwin 2 get sub def
            /px vwin 1 get vwin 0 get add def
            /py vwin 3 get vwin 2 get add def
            /dD DMAX DMIN sub def

            /P 0 MatrixWithValue def
            P 0 0 Index 2 VD dx div mul put

            P 1 1 Index 2 VD dy div mul put

            P 2 0 Index px dx div neg put

            P 2 1 Index py dy div neg put

            P 2 2 Index DMAX dD div put

            P 2 3 Index 1 put

            P 3 2 Index DMIN DMAX dD div mul neg put

            /ViewMatrix VM P MatMultiply store

      end
    end
  end
}def


/SetVPNDict 3 dict def

%sets the View Plane Normal in ViewSpecification
%x y z SetVPN => -
/SetVPN
{
  ViewSpecification begin
    SetVPNDict begin
       /z exch def /y exch def /x exch def
       /vpn x y z vpn astore store
    end
  end
} def
```

```
/SetVUVDict 3 dict def

%sets the View Up Vector in ViewSpecification
%x y z SetVUV => -
/SetVUV
{
  ViewSpecification begin
    SetVUVDict begin
        /z exch def /y exch def /x exch def
        /vuv x y z vuv astore store
    end
  end
} def


/SetVRPDict 3 dict def

%sets the View Reference Point in ViewSpecification
%x y z SetVRP => -
/SetVRP
{
  ViewSpecification begin
    SetVRPDict begin
        /z exch def /y exch def /x exch def
        /vrp x y z vrp astore store
    end
  end
} def


/SetCOPDict 3 dict def

%sets the Centre of Projection in ViewSpecification
%x y z SetCOP => -
/SetCOP
{
  ViewSpecification begin
    SetCOPDict begin
        /z exch def /y exch def /x exch def
        /cop x y z cop astore store
    end
  end
} def


%sets the View Distance, and planes in ViewSpecification
%viewDistance backPlane frontPlane SetViewDistance => -
/SetViewDistance
{
  ViewSpecification begin
    /dmax exch store
    /dmin exch store
    /vd   exch store
  end
} def


/SetViewWindowDict 4 dict def

%sets the View Window in ViewSpecification
%xmin xmax ymin ymax SetViewWindow => -
/SetViewWindow
{
```

```
  ViewSpecification begin
    SetViewWindowDict begin
       /ymax exch def /ymin exch def
       /xmax exch def /xmin exch def
       /vwin xmin xmax ymin ymax vwin astore store
    end
  end
} def


%-------------------------------------------------------------------
%Basic function for 3D drawing

/path3DDict 3 dict def

%a path is produced from an array of 3D points
%assumes an array of 3D points on stack, delivers path
%pointArray path3D => x0 y0 moveto x1 y1 lineto ... xn-1 yn-1 lineto
/path3D
{
  ViewRepresentation begin
    path3DDict begin
       /parray exch def
       /qarray parray length 1 sub array def

       %firstPoint moveto
       parray 0 get ViewMatrix PointByMatrixToCoords
       displaymatrix transform
       moveto

       /qarray parray aload length -1 roll pop qarray astore def
       qarray {ViewMatrix PointByMatrixToCoords
               displaymatrix transform
               lineto
              } forall
    end
  end
} def


%-------------------------------------------------------------------
%Bezier cubic patches
%Control point array represented by [[x0 y0 z0] [x1 y1 z1] ... [x3 y3 z3]]

/sumPointsDivDict 5 dict def

%sums elements of two points and divides by d
%p q d sumPointsDiv => (p+q)/d
/sumPointsDiv
{
   sumPointsDivDict begin
      /d exch def /q exch def /p exch def
      /s 3 array def
      0 1 2
      {
        /i exch def
        s i
           p i get q i get add d div
        put
      } for
      s
   end
} def
```

```
/sumPointsDict 4 dict def

%sums elements of two points
%p q sumPoints => p+q
/sumPoints
{
   sumPointsDict begin
      /q exch def /p exch def
      /s 3 array def
      0 1 2
      {
        /i exch def
        s i
           p i get q i get add
        put
      } for
      s
    end
} def


/pointDivDict 4 dict def

%divides elements of a point
%p d pointDiv => p/d
/pointDiv
{
   pointDivDict begin
      /d exch def /p exch def
      /q 3 array def
      0 1 2
      {
        /i exch def
        q i
           p i get d div
        put
      } for
      q
    end
} def

/splitDict 4 dict def

%splits control point sequence (p) into sequences q and r
%p split => q r
/split
{
  splitDict begin
     /p exch def
     /q 4 array def /r 4 array def       %initialise return arrays

     %q[0] = p[0]
     q 0
        p 0 get
     put

     %q[1] = (p[0]+p[1])/2
     q 1
         p 0 get p 1 get 2 sumPointsDiv
     put

     %t = (p[1] + p[2])/4
     /t p 1 get p 2 get 4 sumPointsDiv 3 array copy def
```

```
      %q[2] = q[1]/2 + (p[1] + p[2])/4
      q 2
         q 1 get 2 pointDiv
         t
         sumPoints
      put

      %r[3] = p[3]
      r 3  p 3 get put

      %r[2] = (p[2] + p[3])/2
      r 2
         p 2 get p 3 get 2 sumPointsDiv
      put

      %r[1] = (p[1]+p[2])/4 + r[2]/2
      r 1
         t
         r 2 get 2 pointDiv
         sumPoints
      put

      %q[3] = (q[2] + r[1])/2
      q 3
         q 2 get r 1 get 2 sumPointsDiv
      put

      %r[0] = q[3]
      r 0 q 3 get put

      q r
   end
} def

/splitControlGraphDict 9 dict def
/decomposeDict 5 dict def

%given a 4*4 array of control points p delivers q,r,s,t
%each of p,q,r,s,t are organized as [cp0 cp1 cp2 cp3]
%where cpi is an array of control points
%p splitControlGraph => q r s t
/splitControlGraph
{
   splitControlGraphDict begin
      /p exch def
      /q 4 array def /r 4 array def /s 4 array def /t 4 array def
      /u 4 array def /v 4 array def

      0 1 3
      {
       /i exch def
        p i get split %leaves two arrays of control points on stack
        %assign second to v[i] and first to u[i]
        v exch i exch put u exch i exch put
      } for

      /decompose
      {
       %runs through u in column order, and splits it for each
       %column, leaving the results in q and r
       decomposeDict begin
          /r exch def /q exch def /u exch def
          0 1 3
```

```
          {
            /j exch def
            0 1 3
            {
              /i exch def
              u i get j get
            } for
            4 array astore split
            r  exch j exch put q exch j exch put
          } for
       end
      } def

      u q r decompose
      v s t decompose

      q r s t
  end
} def


/pathControlGraphDict 3 dict def

%given a control graph, produces a path
%p pathControlGraph => -
/pathControlGraph
{
  pathControlGraphDict begin
       /p exch def
       0 1 3
       {
         /j exch def
         p j get path3D
         0 1 3
         {
          /i exch def
          p i get j get
         } for
         4 array astore path3D
       } for
  end
} def



%given a control graph(p) and a non-negative integer(n), recursively
%splits and draws the control graph
%the recursion is to a depth of n
%p n => -
/simpleBezier
{
  4 dict begin
    /n exch def /p exch def
    0 n eq
                                   %if n=0 then
       {p pathControlGraph stroke}
                                   %else
       {
        /nm1 n 1 sub def
        /g  p splitControlGraph 4 array astore def
        g {nm1 simpleBezier} forall
       }
     ifelse
  end
```

```
} def


%-------------------------------------------------------------------
%The Script
%-------------------------------------------------------------------
%Example of a Control Graph
%defines a control graph, looking like a step
%together with appropriate viewing parameters
/Step
{
  /G
  [
    [ [0.0 1.0 1.0] [0.3 1.0 1.0] [0.7 1.0 1.0] [1.0 1.0 1.0] ]
    [ [0.0 1.0 0.5] [0.3 1.0 0.5] [0.7 1.0 0.5] [1.0 1.0 0.5] ]
    [ [0.0 0.0 0.5] [0.3 0.0 0.5] [0.7 0.0 0.5] [1.0 0.0 0.5] ]
    [ [0.0 0.0 0.0] [0.3 0.0 0.0] [0.7 0.0 0.0] [1.0 0.0 0.0] ]
  ]
  def
  0.5 0.5 1.0 SetVRP
  1.0 0.5 0.0 SetVPN
  0.0 0.0 1.0 SetVUV
  -4 1 -4 1 SetViewWindow
  0 -4 4 SetViewDistance
  0 0 -3 SetCOP
  SetView
}
def


%draws 3D axes
/axes
{
 /Xaxis {[[0 0 0] [1.5 0 0]] path3D} def
 /Yaxis {[[0 0 0] [0 1.5 0]] path3D} def
 /Zaxis {[[0 0 0] [0 0 1.5]] path3D} def
 gsave
   1 setlinewidth
   Xaxis stroke Xaxis (X) show
   Yaxis stroke Yaxis (Y) show
   Zaxis stroke Zaxis (Z) show
 grestore
} def

/main
{
  0 72 translate
  /Times-Roman findfont 10 scalefont setfont
  0 500 0 500 SetViewport
  Step
  2.5 setlinewidth
  1 setlinecap
  1 setlinejoin
  G 2 simpleBezier
  1 setlinewidth
  G pathControlGraph stroke
  axes
  showpage
}
def

main
```

REFERENCES

Adobe Systems Incorporated (1985a), *PostScript Language Reference Manual*, Addison-Wesley.

Adobe Systems Incorporated (1985b), *PostScript Language Tutorial and Cookbook*, Addison-Wesley.

Alessi, S. M. and Trollip, S. R. (1985), *Computer Based Instruction, Methods and Development*, Prentice-Hall.

Alexander, H. (1986), 'A Technique for the Formal Specification and Rapid Prototyping of Human–Computer Interaction', in *People and Computers: Designing for Usability* (M. D. Harrison and A. F. Monk, eds.), Proceedings of the Second Conference of the BCS HCI Specialist Group, University of York, 23–26 September.

Ammeraal, L. (1986), *Programming Principles in Computer Graphics*, John Wiley & Sons Ltd.

Arya, K. (1984), 'A Functional Approach to Picture Manipulation', *Computer Graphics Forum* **3**, pp. 35–46, North-Holland.

Arya, K. (1986), 'A Functional Approach to Animation', *Computer Graphics Forum* **5**(4), pp. 297–312.

Assoc. for Comp. Mach. (1978), 'Special Issue: Graphics Standards', *ACM Computing Surveys* **10**(4).

Barsky, B. (1984), 'A Description and Evaluation of Various 3-D Models', *IEEE Computer Graphics and Applications* **4**(1), pp. 38–52.

Baumgart, B. G. (1975), 'A Polyhedral Representation for Computer Vision', *Proc. Nat. Comp. Conference, AFIPS*, pp. 589–596.

Baeker, R. (1979), 'Digital Video Display Systems and Dynamic Graphics', *Computer Graphics* **13**, pp. 48–56.

Bennett, J. (1985), 'Raster Operations', *BYTE The Small Systems Journal* **10**(12), pp. 187–296.

Bezier, P. (1986), *The Mathematical Basis of the UNISURF CAD System*, Butterworths.

Bramer, B. and Sutcliffe, D. C. (1981), 'Application of Gino-F to Use Display File Techniques on Raster Scan Displays', *Eurographics '81 Proceedings* (J. L. Encarnacao, ed.).

Bresenham, J. E. (1965), 'An Algorithm for Computer Control of a Digital Plotter', *IBM Syst. J.* **4**(1), pp. 25–30.

Bornat, R. (1986), *Programming from First Principles*, Prentice-Hall.

Bui-Tong, Phong (1975), 'Illumination for Computer-Generated Pictures', *Communications of the ACM* **18**(6), pp. 311–317.

BYTE: The Small Systems Journal (1985), August issue on Declarative Languages.

Card, S. K., Moran, T.P. and Newell, A. (1983), *The Psychology of Human–Computer Interaction*, LEA.

Carlbom, I. and Paciorek, J. (1978), 'Planar Geometric Projections and Viewing Transformations', *Computing Surveys* **10**(4), pp. 465–502.

Carlbom, I., Chakravarty, I. and Vanderschel, D. (1985). 'A Hierarchical Data Structure for Representing the Spatial Decomposition of 3-D Objects', *IEEE Computer Graphics and Applications* **5**(4), pp. 24–31.

Carpenter, L. (1984), 'The A-Buffer: An Antialiased Hidden Surface Method', *Computer Graphics* **18**(3), pp. 103–108.

Catmull, E. E. (1975), 'Computer Display of Curved Surfaces', *Proc. IEEE Conference on Computer Graphics, Pattern Recognition and Data Structures*, Los Angeles, May 1975, p. 11.

Clark, D. (1981), *Computers for Image-Making*, Pergamon Press.

Clowse, I., Cole, I., Ashad, F., Hopkins, C. and Hockley, A. (1985), 'User Modelling Techniques for Interactive Systems', in *People and Computers: Designing the Interface* (P. Johnson and S. Cook, eds.), Proceedings of the BCS HCI Specialist Group, September 1985.

CONRAC (1980), *Raster Graphics Handbook*, Conrac Division, Conrac Corporation, USA.

Cook, R. L. and Torrance, K. E. (1982), 'A Reflectance Model for Computer Graphics', *ACM Transactions on Graphics* **1**(1), pp. 7–24.

Cook, S. (1983), 'Playing Cards on the Perq: An Algorithm for Overlapping Rectangles, *Software-Practice and Experience* **13**, pp. 1043–1053.

Cook, R. L., Porter, T. and Carpenter, L. (1984), 'Distributed Ray Tracing', *Computer Graphics* **18**(3), pp. 137–145.

Cook, S. (1986), 'Modelling Generic User-Interfaces with Functional Programs', in *People and Computers: Designing for Usability* (M. D. Harrison and A. F. Monk, eds.), Proceedings of the Second Conference of the BCS HCI Specialist Group, University of York, 23–26 September.

Cooper, M. R. A. (1979), 'Analytical Photogrammetry in Engineering: Three Feasibility Studies', *The Photogrammetric Record* **9**(53).

Crow, F. C. (1977), 'The Aliasing Problem in Computer Generated Images', *Graphics and Image Processing* **20**(11), pp. 799–805.

Crow, F. C. (1978), 'The Use of Greyscale for Improved Raster Display of Vectors and Characters', *Computer Graphics* **12**(3), pp. 1–5.

Crow, F. C. (1981), 'A Comparison of Antialiasing Techniques', *IEEE Computer Graphics and Applications* **1**(1), pp. 40–48.

Deken, J. (1983), *Computer Images: State of the Art*, Thames & Hudson.

Denham, D. (1986), 'High Performance Colour Displays for Computer Graphics', *Computer Graphics Forum* **5**(1), pp. 57–63.

Duce, D. (1986), 'Teaching Workshop – December 1985', *Computer Graphics Forum* **5**(4), pp. 349–352.

Duce, D. A. and Fielding, E. V. C. (1986), 'Towards a Formal Specification of the GKS Output Primitives', in *Eurographics '86 Proceedings* (A. A. G. Requicha, ed.), North-Holland, pp. 307–324.

Foley, J. D. and Van Dam, A. (1982), *Fundamentals of Interactive Computer Graphics*, Addison-Wesley.

Fournier, A., Fussel, D. and Carpenter, L. (1982), 'Computer Rendering of Stochastic Models', *Communications of the ACM* **25**(6), pp. 371–384.

Fujimoto, A., Tanaka, T. and Iwata, K. (1986), 'ARTS: Accelerated Ray Tracing System', *IEEE Computer Graphics and Applications*, April.

Gasson, P. C. (1983), *Geometry of Spacial Forms*, Ellis Horwood Ltd.

Glaser, H., Hankin, C. and Till, D. (1984), *Principles of Functional Programming*, Prentice-Hall International.

Glassner, A. S. (1984), 'Space Subdivision for Fast Ray Tracing', *IEEE Computer Graphics and Applications* **4**(10), pp. 15–22.

Goldberg, A. and Robson, D. (1983), *Smalltalk-80: The Language and its Implementation*, Addison-Wesley.

Goldschlager, L. M. (1981), 'Short Algorithms for Space-Filling Curves', *Software-Practice and Experience* **11**, pp. 99–100.

Gonzalez, R. C. and Wintz, P. (1981), *Digital Image Processing*, Addison-Wesley, 3rd printing.

Gosling, J. (1985), 'SunDew – A Distributed and Extensible Window System', *Methodology of Window Management* (F. R. A. Hopgood, D. A. Duce, E. V. C. Fielding, K. Robinson and A. S. Williams, eds.), Springer-Verlag.

Gouraud, H. (1971), 'Continuous Shading of Curved Surfaces', *IEEE Transactions on Computers* **C20**(6), pp. 623–628.

Gries, D. (1981), *The Science of Programming*, Springer-Verlag.

GSPC (1979), 'Status Report of the Graphics Standards Planning Committee', *Computer Graphics* **13**(3).

Harper, R. (1986), *Introduction to Standard ML*, University of Edinburgh, LFCS Report Series, ECS-LFCS-86-14.

Hayward, S. (1984), *Computers in Animation*, Focal Press, London.

Henderson, P. (1980), *Functional Programming: Application and Implementation* (C. A. R. Hoare, ed.), Prentice-Hall International.

Henderson, P. (1982), 'Functional Geometry', *Conference of the 1982 ACM Symposium on Lisp and Functional Programming*, pp. 179–187.

Henderson, P. (1984), *Communicating Functional Programs*, Dept. of Computer Science, University of Stirling, September 1984.

Hopgood, F. R. A., Duce, D.A., Fielding, E. V. C., Robinson, K. and Williams, A. S. (1985), *Methodology of Window Management*, Springer-Verlag.

Hunter, G. M. and Steiglitz, K. (1979a), 'Operations on Images Using Quad Trees', *IEEE Transactions on Pattern Analysis and Machine Intelligence*, PAMI-1, 2, pp. 145–153.

Hunter, G. M. and Steiglitz, K. (1979b), 'Linear Transformation of Pictures Represented by Quad Trees', *Computer Graphics and Image Processing* **10**, p. 289–296.

ISO (1985), *Information Processing Systems – Computer Graphics – Graphical Kernel System (GKS) Functional Description*, ISO 7942 (also published as BS 6390:1985).

ISO (1986a), *Computer Graphics Interface (CGI) – Working Draft*, TC97/SC21 N1179 (May 1986).

ISO (1986b), *Computer Graphics: Graphical Kernel System for Three Dimensions (GKS-3D) Functional Description* (ISO/DP 8805).

ISO (1986c), *Information Processing Systems – Computer Graphics – Graphical Kernel System (GKS) Language Bindings – Part 2: Pascal* (ISO/DIS 8651/2).

ISO (1986d), *Information Processing – Computer Graphics – Programmer's Hierarchical Interactive Graphics System (PHIGS)*, TC97 SC21/N819 (June).

ISO (1986e), *Information Processing Systems – Computer Graphics – Metafile for the Storage and Transfer of Picture Description Information* (CGM), ISO/DP 8632.

Jacob, R. J. K. (1986), 'Using Formal Specifications in the Design of a Human–Computer Interface', in *Software Specification Techniques* (N. Gehani and A. D. McGettrick, eds.), pp. 209–222, Addison-Wesley.

Jensen, K. and Wirth, N. (1974), *Pascal User Manual and Report*, Springer-Verlag.

Johnson, P. (1985), 'Towards a Task Model of Messaging, in *People and Computers: Designing the Interface* (P. Johnson and S. Cook, eds.), Proceedings of the BCS HCI Specialist Group, Cambridge University Press.

Jones, C. B. (1986), *Systematic Software Development Using VDM*, Prentice-Hall International.

Kaehler, T. and Patterson, D. (1986), *A Taste of Smalltalk*, W. W. Norton and Company.

Kajiya, J. T. (1983), 'New Techniques in Ray Tracing Procedurally Defined Objects', *ACM Transactions on Graphics* **2**(3), pp. 161–181.

Kay, T. L. and Kajiya, J. T. (1986), 'Ray Tracing Complex Scenes', *Computer Graphics* **20**(4), pp. 269–278.

Kilgour, A. C. (1986), 'Techniques for Modelling and Displaying 3D Scenes', in *Advances in Computer Graphics II* (F. R. A. Hopgood, R. J. Hubbold, and D. A. Duce, eds.), Springer-Verlag.

Lane, J. M., Carpenter, L. C., Whitted, T. and Blinn, J. F. (1980), 'Scan Line Methods for Displaying Parametrically Defined Surfaces', *Communications of the ACM* **23**(1).

Lane, J. M. and Riesenfeld, R. F. (1980), 'A Theoretical Development for the Computer Generation and Display of Piecewise Polynomial Surfaces', *IEEE Trans. on Pattern Analysis and Machine Intelligence*, PAMI-2, no. 1, pp. 35–46.

Machover, C. and Blauth, R. E. (1980), *The CAD/CAM Handbook*, Computervision Corporation, Bedford, Massachusetts.

Magnenat–Thalmann, N. and Thalmann, D. (1985), *Computer Animation Theory and Practice*, (Tosiyasu L. Kunii, ed.), Springer-Verlag, Computer Science Workbench.

Mallgren, W. R. (1982), *Formal Specification of Interactive Graphics Programming Languages*, The MIT Press.

Mandelbrot, B. B. (1977), *Fractals: Form, Chance, and Dimension*, San Francisco: Freeman Press.

Mandelbrot, B. B. (1982), *The Fractal Geometry of Nature*, New York: Freeman Press.

Meagher, D. (1982), 'Geometric Modeling Using Octree Encoding', *Computer Graphics and Image Processing* **19**, pp. 129–147.

Mehlhorn, K. (1984), *Multi-dimensional Searching and Computational Geometry (Data Structures and Algorithms 3)* (W. Brauer, G. Rozenberg and A. Salomaa, eds.), Springer-Verlag EATCS Monographs on Theoretical Computer Science.

Miller, G. S. P. (1986), 'The Definition and Rendering of Terrain Maps', *Computer Graphics* **20**(4), pp. 39–48.

Milner, R. (1985), 'The Standard ML Core Language', *Polymorphism* II.2.

Moran, T. P. (1981), 'The Command Language Grammar: A Representation for the User Interface of Interactive Computer Systems', *Int. J. Man-Machine Studies* **15**, pp. 3–50.

Murch, G. M. (1986), 'Human Factors of Colour Displays', in *Advances in Computer Graphics II* (F. R. A. Hopgood, R. J. Hubbold and D. A. Duce, eds.), Springer-Verlag.

Myers, B. A. and Buxton, W. (1986), 'Creating Highly-Interactive and Graphical User Interfaces by Demonstration', *Computer Graphics, SIGGRAPH* **86**, pp. 249–258.

Newman, W. M. and Sproull, R. F. (1979), *Principles of Interactive Computer Graphics*, Second Edition, McGraw-Hill.

Nievergelt, J. and Preparata, F. (1982), 'Plane-Sweep Algorithms for Intersecting Geometric Figures', *Communications of the ACM* **25**(10), pp. 739–747.

Ostwald, W. (1931), *Colour Science*, Winsor and Winsor, London.

Pace, B. J. (1984), 'Color Conversions and Contrast Reversals on Visual Display Units', *Proceedings of the Human Factors Society*, 28th Annual Meeting, Human Factors Society, Santa Monica, CA, pp. 326–330.

Pavlidis, T. (1982), *Algorithms for Graphics and Image Processing*, Springer-Verlag.

Pew, R. W. (1983), *Human Skills and their Utilization*, Lecture Notes, Man/Machine Interface Symposium, CEI Europe, June 1983.

Pitteway, M. and Watkinson, D. (1980), 'Bresenham's Algorithm with Grey Scale', *Communications of the ACM* **23**(11), pp. 625–626.

Potsemil, M. and Chakravarty, I. (1982), 'Synthetic Image Generation with a Lens and Aperture Camera Model', *ACM Transactions on Graphics* **1**(2), pp. 85–108.

Preparata, F. P. and Shamos, M. I. (1985), *Computational Geometry: An Introduction*, Springer-Verlag.

Pritchard, D. H. (1977), 'US Colour Television Fundamentals – A Review', *IEEE Transactions on Consumer Electronics* **4**, pp. 467–478.

Reeves, W. T. (1983), 'Particle Systems – A Technique for Modeling a Class of Fuzzy Objects', *ACM Transactions on Graphics* **2**(2), pp. 91–109.

Reisenfeld, R. F. (1981), 'Homogeneous Coordinates and Projective Planes in Computer Graphics', *IEEE Computer Graphics and Applications* **1**(1), pp. 50–56.

Reisner, P. (1981), 'Formal Grammar and Human Factors Design of an Interactive Graphics System', *IEEE Transactions on Software Engineering* SE-7, 2, pp. 229–240.

Rogers, D. F. (1985), *Procedural Elements for Computer Graphics*, McGraw-Hill.

Rogers, Y. (1986), 'Evaluating the Meaningfullness of Icon Sets to Represent Command Operations, in *People and Computers: Designing for Usability* (M. D. Harrison and A. F. Monk, eds.), Proceedings of the Second Conference of the BSC HCI Specialist Group, University of York, 23–26 September.

Rosenthal, D. S. H., Michener, J. C., Pfaff, G., Kessener, R. and Sabin, M. (1982), 'Detailed Semantics of Graphics Input Devices', *Computer Graphics* **13**(3), pp. 33–38.

Roth, S. D. (1982), 'Ray Casting for Modelling Solids', *Computer Graphics and Image Processing* **18**, pp. 109–144.

Schweitzer, D. and Cobb, E. S. (1982), 'Scanline Rendering of Parametric Surfaces', *Computer Graphics* **16**(3), pp. 265–270.

Shamos, M. I. (1978), *Computational Geometry*, Ph.D thesis, Dept. of Computer Science, Yale Univ.

Shneiderman, B. (1987), *Designing the User Interface: Strategies for Effective Human-Computer Interaction*, Addison-Wesley.

Singleton, K. (1986), 'An Implementation of the GKS-3D/PHIGS Viewing Pipeline', *Eurographics '86 Proceedings* (A. A. G. Requicha, ed.), North-Holland.

Slater, M. (1984), 'GKS in Pascal', *Computer Graphics Forum* **3**, pp. 259–268.

Slater, M. (1986), 'Segments on Bit-Mapped Graphics Displays', *Software-Practice and Experience* **16**(11), pp. 965–980.

Smith, A. R., Carpenter, L., Cole, P., Duff, D., Evans, C., Porter, T. and Reeves, W. (1982), 'Genesis Demo' in *Star Trek II: The Wrath of Khan*, Paramount. Created by Lucasfilm Computer Graphics Project for Industrial Light and Magic.

Smith, D. C., Irby, C., Kimball, R. and Verplank, B. (1982), 'Designing the Star User Interface', *BYTE*, April, pp. 242–282.

Sufrin, B. (1986a), 'Formal Specification of a Display-Oriented Text Editor', in *Software Specification Techniques* (N. Gehani and A. D. McGettrick, eds.), Addison-Wesley, pp. 223–268.

Sufrin, B. (1986b), 'Formal Methods and the Design of Effective User Interfaces', in *People and Computers: Designing for Usability* (M. D. Harrison and A. F. Monk, eds.), Proceedings of the Second Conference of the BCS HCI Specialist Group, University of York, 23–26 September.

Sun Microsystems, Inc. (1987a), *NeWS Technical Overview*, October 1986.

Sun Microsystems, Inc. (1987b), *NeWS Manual.*

Sutherland, I. E. (1963), 'Sketchpad: A Man-Machine Graphical Communication System', *AFIPS* **23**, pp. 329–346.

Sutherland, I. E. and Hodgman, G. W. (1974), 'Reentrant Polygon Clipping', *Communications of the ACM* **17**(1), pp. 32–42.

Sutherland, I. E., Sproull, R. F. and Schumacker, R. A. (1974), 'A Characterization of Ten Hidden-Surface Algorithms', *Computing Surveys* **6**(1), pp. 1–55.

Toth, D. L. (1985), 'On Ray Tracing Parametrically Defined Surfaces', *Computer Graphics* **19**(3), pp. 171–179.

Totterdell, P. and Cooper, P. (1986), 'Design and Evaluation of the AID Adaptive Front-End to Telecom Gold', in *People and Computers: Designing for Usability* (M. D. Harrison and A. F. Monk, eds.), Proceedings of the Second Conference of the BCS HCI Specialist Group, Cambridge University Press.

Van Dam, A. (1984), 'Computer Graphics Comes of Age: An Interview with Andries Van Dam, *Communications of the ACM* **27**(7), pp. 638–648.

Van Deusen, E. (1981), *Computer Videographics: Color, Composition, Typography*, CC Exchange, PO Box 125, Laguna Beach, CA, USA.

Warner, J. and Keifhaber, N. (1979), 'The DIGRAF Implementation of the Proposed GSPC Standard, *Eurographics '79 Proceedings*.

Warnock, J. E. (1969), *A Hidden-Surface Algorithm for Computer Generated Half-Tone Pictures*, University of Utah Computer Science Dept., TR 4–15, NTIS AD–753 671.

Warnock, J. and Wyatt, D. (1982), 'A Device Independent Graphics Imaging Model for Use with Raster Devices', *Computer Graphics* **16**(3), pp. 313–320.

Weale, R. A. (1978), *From Sight to Light*, Oliver & Boyd.

Weiler, K. and Atherton, P. (1977), 'Hidden Surface Removal Using Polygon Area Sorting', *Computer Graphics* **11**(2), pp. 214–222.

Whitted, T. (1980), 'An Improved Illumination Model for Shaded Display', *Communications of the ACM* **23**(6), pp. 343–349.

Whitted, T. and Cook, R. (1984), 'Shading for Computer Image Synthesis', Advanced Course on 3D Graphics, University of Glasgow, Science and Engineering Research Council.

Wilkes, A. J., Singer, D. W., Gibbons, J. J., King, T. R., Robinson, P. and Wiseman, N. E. (1984), 'The Rainbow Workstation', *The Computer Journal* **27**(2), pp. 112–120.

Williams, N. S., Buxton, B. F. and Buxton, H. (1985), *Simultaneous Ray Tracing Computer Graphics*, GEC Research Labs, Long Range Research Report No. 16, 887A.

Wirth, N. (1971), 'The Programming Language Pascal', *Acta Informatica* **1**(1), pp. 35–63.

Witten, I. H. and Neal, R. M. (1982), 'Using Peano Curves for Bilevel Display of Continuous-Tone Images', *IEEE Computer Graphics and Applications*, May.

Woodwark, J. R. (1986), *Computing Shape*, Butterworths.

Wulf, W. A., Shaw, M., Holfinger, P. N. and Flon, L. (1981), *Fundamental Structures of Computer Science*, Addison-Wesley.

Wyvill, G., Kunii, T. L. and Shirai, Y. (1986), 'Space Division for Ray Tracing in CSG', *IEEE Computer Graphics and Applications*, April.

INDEX

Dubro Doekje Four frames from a 60 second TV commercial for a kitchen cleaning cloth. The animation images were created using 3D solid modelling with multiple light sources and both reflection and texture mapping. The kitchen cloth and water splashes were produced by cell animation and the whole sequence digitally composited. Other special effects were added using the Quantel Paintbox system. (Computer animation: Electric Image; Cell animation: Gingerbread; Paintbox work: The Framestore; Agency: SCC & B Lintas Worldwide; Art director: Edwin van der Meer; Illustrator: Ronald Slabbers; © SSC & B Lintas Worldwide)

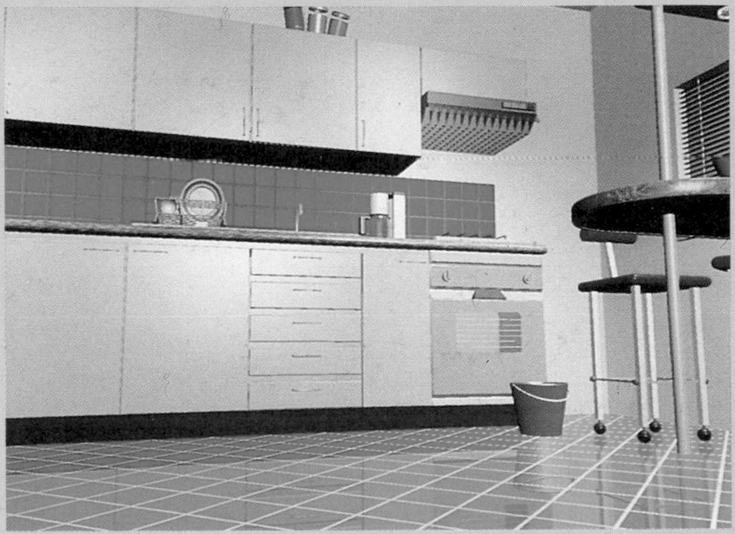

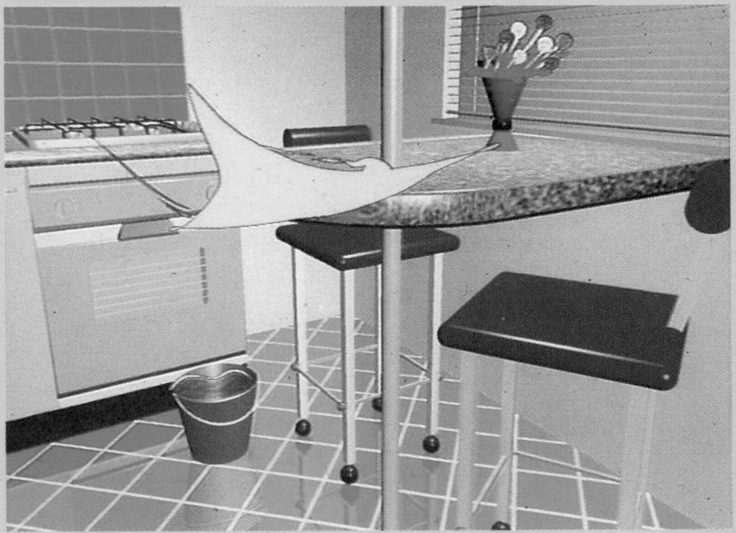